How to Use This Book

This book spans a three-week self-training period that converts a non-OOP C programmer to an OOP Visual C++ programmer in 21 days. OOP (object-oriented programming) is the new programming phenomenon that, with the help of Visual C++, is changing the way programmers across the country approach programming. You'll learn as early as Day 1 why so many programmers are switching to Visual C++ and OOP.

You'll learn that OOP is more of a philosophy than anything else. Object-oriented programming requires a different approach to writing programs. To support that approach, the programming language has to be revised a bit to support OOP, and C++ is the OOP language of choice. The leader in C++, Microsoft, has continually broken sales records since the first release of Visual C++.

In case you need some review, Appendix E highlights some of the features of the C language. Visual C++ was strongly based on C, and Visual C++ supports, compiles, and runs C programs. However, after you take this three-week, easy-to-learn course on Visual C++, you'll probably never write another C program. As a matter of fact, you'll wonder how you ever finished any program without OOP and Visual C++!

As an added bonus, you can find an Extra Credit Bonus section with a workweek's (five days') worth of material. This part of the book describes the ins and outs of the Visual add-on tools and the Visual C++ MFC classes, and even provides an introduction to Windows programming using Visual C++. In addition, the bonus section shows you how to use the MFC classes to add sizzling graphics to your Windows application.

Special Features of This Book

This book contains some special features unique to the "Teach Yourself in 21 Days" series. Syntax boxes show you how to write some of the new Visual C++ language features. Each syntax box provides an example and a full explanation of the syntax and use of the language element. For example, here's a syntax box found in Day 4's chapter (don't worry about the details now):

Defining References

dataType & *refName expression*

dataType is any intrinsic data type such as `int` or `float`, or a user-defined data type created with `struct`, `union`, `enum`, or `class`. *refName* is any valid variable name, and *expression* is the variable or expression you want to reference.

Example

```
// Filename: REFSYN.CPP
// Illustrates a reference to a variable and an expression
#include <iostream.h>
#include <iomanip.h>
main()
{
  float value = 123.45;      // Regular floating-point
  float value2 = 87.12;      // 2nd regular float
  float & ref1 = value;      // Reference to value
  cout << setprecision(2);
  cout << setiosflags(ios::showpoint);
  cout << "value is " << value << "\n";
  cout << "ref1 is also " << ref1 << "\n";
  ref1 = value2;
  cout << "Both value and ref1 now refer to " << value << "\n";
  return 0;
}
```

Throughout the book, you'll also find numerous DO/DON'T boxes that provide lots of tips and shortcuts as well as some warnings about what to avoid.

DO	**DON'T**

DO have fun as you learn Visual C++. This book will help!

DON'T take the material too fast. Twenty-one days is plenty of time to let the new OOP concepts sink in, but you'll want to practice along the way and write as much code as you can.

This book contains approximately 200 complete programs, with full explanations, to help you learn Visual C++. To help you review, you'll find a Q&A section containing pertinent questions and their answers. These Q&A questions are usually "thought" questions whose answers require some detailed answers, and the book includes those detailed answers below each question.

There is also a Workshop (you'll think you're in school!) after each Q&A section that contains lots of questions and programming exercises. You'll find the answers to the questions and exercises in Appendix D.

Conventions Used in This Book

The following typographic conventions are used in this book:

- ☐ Command and function names are in monospace. In addition to code lines, variable names and any text you would see on-screen are also in monospace.

- ☐ Placeholders, text that you'll replace with other values when you use a command, within code syntax appear in *italic* `monospace`.

- ☐ User input is shown in **`bold monospace`**.

- ☐ New terms, which can be found in the Glossary, are in *italic*.

Teach Yourself Object-Oriented Programming with Visual C++ 1.5 in 21 Days

Teach Yourself Object-Oriented Programming with Visual C++ 1.5 in 21 Days

Greg Perry

SAMS PUBLISHING

A Division of Prentice Hall Computer Publishing
201 W. 103rd Street, Indianapolis, Indiana 46290-1097 USA

I haven't seen two dear friends, Sharon Arms and Ken Woodhead, for a while, but their impact on my life still shines. Ken, thanks for the motivational encouragement that you never knew you gave me. Sharon, thanks for being a pal when I really needed it. This book is for both of you.

Copyright © 1994 by Sams Publishing
FIRST EDITION

All rights reserved. No part of this book shall be reproduced, stored in a retrieval system, or transmitted by any means, electronic, mechanical, photocopying, recording, or otherwise, without written permission from the publisher. No patent liability is assumed with respect to the use of the information contained herein. Although every precaution has been taken in the preparation of this book, the publisher and author assume no responsibility for errors or omissions. Neither is any liability assumed for damages resulting from the use of the information contained herein. For information, address SAMS Publishing, a division of Prentice Hall Computer Publishing, 201 W. 103rd Street, Indianapolis, IN 46290.

International Standard Book Number: 0-672-30487-2

Library of Congress Catalog Card Number: 93-87649

97 96 95 94   4 3 2 1

Interpretation of the printing code: the rightmost double-digit number is the year of the book's printing; the rightmost single-digit, the number of the book's printing. For example, a printing code of 94-1 shows that the first printing of the book occurred in 1994.

Composed in AGaramond and MCPdigital by Prentice Hall Computer Publishing

Printed in the United States of America

Trademarks

All terms mentioned in this book that are known to be trademarks or service marks have been appropriately capitalized. Sams Publishing cannot attest to the accuracy of this information. Use of a term in this book should not be regarded as affecting the validity of any trademark or service mark.

Publisher
Richard K. Swadley

Associate Publisher
Jordan Gold

Acquisitions Manager
Stacy Hiquet

Managing Editor
Cindy Morrow

Development Editor
Rosemarie Graham

Production Editor
Cheri Clark

Copy Editor
Joe Williams

Editorial Coordinator
Bill Whitmer

Editorial Assistants
Carol Ackerman
Sharon Cox
Lynette Quinn

Technical Reviewer
Gary Farrar

Marketing Manager
Greg Wiegand

Cover Designer
Dan Armstrong

Book Designer
Michele Laseau

Director of Production and Manufacturing
Jeff Valler

Imprint Manager
Kelli Widdifield

Manufacturing Coordinator
Paul Gilchrist

Production Analyst
Mary Beth Wakefield

Graphics Image Specialists
Tim Montgomery
Dennis Sheehan
Susan Van DeWalle

Production
Ayrika Bryant
Lisa Daugherty
Karen Dodson
Rich Evers
Kim Hannel
Stephanie J. McComb
Jamie Milazzo
Jan Noller
Rochelle Palma
Ryan Rader
Kim Scott
Michelle Self
Tonya R. Simpson
SA Springer
Elaine Webb
Dennis Wesner
Alyssa Yesh

Indexers
Jennifer Eberhardt
John Sleeva

Overview

How to Use This Book i

Week 1 at a Glance   **1**

  1 The C++ Phenomenon 5
  2 C++ Is Superior! 27
  3 Simple I/O 61
  4 Powerful Pointers 91
  5 Memory Allocation: There When You Need It 115
  6 Communicating with Functions 145
  7 Overloaded Functions Lessen Your Load 177

Week 1 in Review   **201**

Week 2 at a Glance   **207**

  8 Add Some *class* to Your Data 209
  9 Member Functions Activate *class* Variables 239
 10 Friends When You Need Them 277
 11 Introduction to Overloading Operators 297
 12 Extending Operator Overloads 341
 13 Constructing and Deconstructing 369
 14 Loose Ends: *static* and Larger Programs 405

Week 2 in Review   **441**

Week 3 at a Glance   **447**

 15 It's Hereditary: Inheriting Data 449
 16 Inherited Limits and Extensions 475
 17 Data Composition 501
 18 Virtual Functions: Are They Real? 531
 19 Introduction to Throwing and Catching Exceptions 555
 20 Easy File I/O 577
 21 The Visual C++ Tools 603

Week 3 in Review   **637**

Extra Credit Bonus

Bonus 1	Introduction to Windows Programming and MFC	641
Bonus 2	The MFC Classes: Power You Will Gain	675
Bonus 3	Files and More MFC	711
Bonus 4	Graphics and Visual C++	743
Bonus 5	What's Next?	771

Appendixes

A	ASCII Character Chart	787
B	Visual C++ Keywords	797
C	Operator Precedence	799
D	Answers	803
E	Review of C Concepts	877

Glossary   899

Index   907

Contents

Week 1 at a Glance 1

1 The C++ Phenomenon 5
    Welcome to OOP's C++ World 6
        The History of C++ 6
        The Way You Program Without OOP 7
        OOP Programming Advantages 9
        Relax and Enjoy 11
    What Is an Object Anyway? 12
    OOP, C++, and C 13
    Visual C++ and This Book 14
    Entering and Compiling C++ Programs 16
        Preparing for C++ Programs 18
        Running the Program 19
    What You Should Already Know 23
    What's Ahead for You 24
    Summary 24
    Q&A 25
    Workshop 26
        Quiz 26
        Exercises 26

2 C++ Is Superior! 27
    Commenting on Your Work 28
    Less Is More with Visual C++ 30
    C++ Prototypes 32
    Empty Prototype Argument Implies *void* 35
    C++ and Data 36
        char Consumes One Byte 36
        The Location of Variable Definitions 37
        Typecasting Isn't Just for Hollywood 40
        The Scope Resolution Operator, :: 40
        Scoping of Global Constants 42

Teach Yourself OOP with Visual C++ 1.5 in 21 Days

Throw Out *#define*	45
const Replaces Simple *#define* Constants	45
inline Functions Improve on *#define* Macros	48
Some Useful Visual C++ Identifiers	53
Summary	56
Q&A	57
Workshop	58
Quiz	58
Exercises	58
3 Simple I/O	**61**
Output Your Data with *cout* and <<	62
Input Is Just as Easy with *cin* and >>	66
How to Display Error Messages	68
What's Down the Road?	70
Manipulating the Output	72
Looking at Input	82
Summary	87
Q&A	88
Workshop	89
Quiz	89
Exercises	90
4 Powerful Pointers	**91**
Working with *void* Pointers	92
References Refer to Data	97
Constants Stay *const*	101
const Used with Pointers and References	103
Pointers to Constants	104
Constant Pointers	105
Constant Pointers to Constants	107
Read-Only Aliases	108
Summary	110
Q&A	110
Workshop	112
Quiz	112
Exercises	113
5 Memory Allocation: There When You Need It	**115**
new to Allocate, *delete* to Eliminate	116
The Concept of Memory Allocation	118

      Specifying *new* for a Heap of Memory 121
      Initializing While Allocating 124
      Deallocating with *delete* 126
      Multidimensional Arrays 135
      If the Heap Has a Problem 138
      Summary 141
      Q&A 141
      Workshop 142
          Quiz 142
          Exercises 143

6 Communicating with Functions 145
      Passing by Reference 146
      Pass by Address Cleanly by Passing
        Reference Variables 151
      Returning a Reference 154
      Default Arguments Speed Program Development 156
      Using Multiple Default Arguments 159
      Visual C++ and Command-Line Arguments 163
      Using Variable-Length Argument Lists 167
      Summary 171
      Q&A 172
      Workshop 174
          Quiz 174
          Exercises 175

7 Overloaded Functions Lessen Your Load 177
      Overloading Functions 178
      Calling Your C Functions 184
      Simple Operator Overloading 186
          Improving the Situation with Overloading 189
          The *operator...()* Functions 189
          Expanding the Power of Operator Overloading 191
          Some Final Warnings 193
      Summary 195
      Q&A 196
      Workshop 199
          Quiz 199
          Exercises 200

Week 1 in Review 201

Teach Yourself OOP with Visual C++ 1.5 in 21 Days

	Week 2 at a Glance	**207**
8	**Add Some *class* to Your Data**	**209**
	Abstract Data Types	210
	Building an Abstract Data Type	211
	From the Abstract to the Abstract	214
	Out with *struct*—In with *class*	217
	Getting into Objects—Finally!	219
	The Only Difference Between *class* and *struct*	222
	Overriding Public and Private Access	226
	Mix and Match Access Specifiers	229
	Summary	234
	Q&A	234
	Workshop	236
	Quiz	236
	Exercise	238
9	**Member Functions Activate *class* Variables**	**239**
	Member Functions Combined with Data Members	241
	Using Public Member Functions	242
	That's What Objects Are All About	246
	You Now Have Controlled Access	248
	main() Can Pass Data to an Object	250
	Returning from Member Functions	254
	Cleaning Up the Class	257
	Use *inline* for Efficiency	260
	Make Classes Self-Protecting	262
	A More Useful Example	267
	Here's a Tongue-Twister: Encapsulation	271
	The Hidden **this* Pointer	271
	Summary	273
	Q&A	274
	Workshop	275
	Quiz	276
	Exercises	276

10	**Friends When You Need Them**	**277**
	Why Use Friends?	278
	Friend Functions	279
	Use *friend* to Specify Friend Functions	280
	A Friend of Two Classes	283
	Friend Classes	290
	Summary	293
	Q&A	294
	Workshop	295
	Quiz	295
	Exercise	295
11	**Introduction to Overloading Operators**	**297**
	A Quick Review	299
	OOPing the Operator Overloads	301
	The Remaining Simple Math Operators	310
	Overloading Relational and Logical Operators	315
	Now, the Compound Operators Are a Snap!	321
	Mixing Class and Built-In Data Types	328
	Overloading ++ and --	330
	More Hints of Extensibility	334
	Summary	337
	Q&A	338
	Workshop	340
	Quiz	340
	Exercises	340
12	**Extending Operator Overloads**	**341**
	Overloading Input and Output Operators	342
	The Details of Overloading << for Output	345
	The Details of Overloading >> for Input	353
	Creating Your Own I/O Manipulators	358
	Subscript Overloading	361
	Summary	366
	Q&A	366
	Workshop	367
	Quiz	367
	Exercises	368

13	**Constructing and Destructing** **369**
	Defining Constructors 371
	Defining Destructors 372
	Why Constructors and Destructors Are Needed 373
	Timing Is the Key 376
	Constructing with Arguments 381
	You Can Now Overload Typecasts! 386
	When to Call Constructors Explicitly 388
	Default Constructor Function Considerations 390
	Constructing Arrays of Objects 391
	operator=() and the Copy Constructor 394
	Summary 401
	Q&A 402
	Workshop 403
	Quiz 403
	Exercises 404
14	**Loose Ends: *static* and Larger Programs** **405**
	All About *static* 407
	static Maintains Values 407
	There's One Slight Variation with *static* Globals 410
	Functions Can Be *static* Too! 411
	Objects Are No Exception 413
	Special Use of *static* Inside Classes 416
	Multifile Processing 422
	A Compile/Link Review Might Help 424
	Project Files Make Multifiles a Snap 428
	Summary 437
	Q&A 438
	Workshop 439
	Quiz 439
	Exercises 440

Week 2 in Review **441**

Week 3 at a Glance **447**

15	**It's Hereditary: Inheriting Data** **449**
	The Structure of Inheritance 451
	Diving into Visual C++ Inheritance 458
	Getting Around *private* with *protected* Access 460
	How Derived Classes View Inherited Members 462
	Where You're Headed 469
	Summary 470
	Q&A 471
	Workshop 472
	Quiz 473
	Exercise 474
16	**Inherited Limits and Extensions** **475**
	The Need for Initialization Lists 476
	Constructor Initialization Style 479
	Construct Base Classes First 482
	What About Destructors? 495
	Summary 496
	Q&A 497
	Workshop 498
	Quiz 498
	Exercises 499
17	**Data Composition** **501**
	Composition vs. Inheritance 502
	Composing with Code 506
	Shortening the Composition 519
	Assigning Composed Objects to One Another 521
	Summary 527
	Q&A 528
	Workshop 529
	Quiz 529
	Exercises 530
18	**Virtual Functions: Are They Real?** **531**
	For Ease of Discussion: This Is a Class Family 533
	When to Execute? Early and Late Binding 534
	Virtual Functions 541
	Specifying Virtual Functions 545

Polymorphism: "Many Forms" 546
Summary 550
Q&A 550
Workshop 552
    Quiz 552
    Exercises 553

19 Introduction to Throwing and Catching Exceptions ... 555
The Need for Exception Handling 557
    The Genesis of Exception Handling 557
    Kinds of Errors 559
The World Without Exception Handling 560
Some Terminology 568
Coding an Exception 570
Summary 573
Q&A 574
Workshop 575
    Quiz 575
    Exercise 575

20 Easy File I/O 577
Sequential I/O: Read, Write, and Append 579
Getting Ready 580
Writing Character Data to a Sequential File 581
Reading Character Data from a Sequential File 585
What If There Are Problems? 587
Appending Data to Sequential Files 589
Class Data and Disk Files 591
Random-Access Files 596
Summary 600
Q&A 601
Workshop 601
    Quiz 602
    Exercises 602

21 The Visual C++ Tools 603
The Evolution of Today's Programmer 604
Exploring the Rest of Visual C++ 608
    The Visual Workbench Editor 608
    A Look at Visual C++'s Debuggers 617
    The Remaining Tools Contain the True Power 624

Summary 633
Q&A 634
Workshop 635
    Quiz 635
    Exercise 635

Week 3 in Review 637

Bonus 1: Introduction to Windows Programming and MFC 641
An Overview of a Windows Program 643
Prepare Your Environment 645
It All Starts with AppWizard 646
Building the Project 650
Running the Program 650
What Just Happened 651
    The Application's Files 651
    The Application's Classes 653
Describing the Classes 668
Summary 671
Q&A 672
Workshop 673
    Quiz 673
    Exercise 673

Bonus 2: The MFC Classes: Power You Will Gain 675
Adding Some Details 676
    Start Easy: The About Box 677
    Adding Specifics with MFC 689
    The MFC String Class 698
    Getting Keyboard Input 701
Summary 706
Q&A 707
Workshop 708
    Quiz 708
    Exercise 708

21 Teach Yourself OOP with Visual C++ 1.5 in 21 Days

Bonus 3: Files and More MFC 711
   Adding Printing and Print Preview 712
   Working with Files 715
      Generating a New Application 716
      Adding Code for File Save, Open, and New 724
      Writing Other Data 730
   Introduction to MFC Exceptions 731
   Summary 739
   Q&A 740
   Workshop 741
      Quiz 741
      Exercise 741

Bonus 4: Graphics and Visual C++ 743
   Getting Started with Some Graphics 744
   Turning On and Off Points 745
      Getting Smarter with Coordinates 749
      Far Out 751
   Improving Your Graphics 754
   Drawing Squares 759
   Filling In the Rectangle 762
   Smooth the Path with Ellipses 766
   Summary 768
   Q&A 768
   Workshop 769
      Quiz 769
      Exercise 770

Bonus 5: What's Next? 771
   So, Do I Still Need to Learn Windows
     Programming in C? 773
   Other Environments 775
   Visual C++ and Windows NT 776
   Borrow from Visual Basic 781
   Stay Consistent 782
   Improve Your Resources 782
   Summary 784
   Q&A 784
   Workshop 785
      Quiz 785
      Exercises 786

A	ASCII Character Chart	787
B	Visual C++ Keywords	797
C	Operator Precedence	799
D	Answers	803

    Answers for Day 1, "The C++ Phenomenon" 804
        Quiz 804
        Exercises 804
    Answers for Day 2, "C++ Is Superior!" 805
        Quiz 805
        Exercises 805
    Answers for Day 3, "Simple I/O" 806
        Quiz 806
        Exercises 807
    Answers for Day 4, "Powerful Pointers" 807
        Quiz 807
        Exercises 808
    Answers for Day 5, "Memory Allocation: There When You Need It" 809
        Quiz 809
        Exercises 810
    Answers for Day 6, "Communicating with Functions" 811
        Quiz 811
        Exercises 812
    Answers for Day 7, "Overloaded Functions Lessen Your Load" 813
        Quiz 813
        Exercises 814
    Answers for Day 8, "Add Some *class* to Your Data" 817
        Quiz 817
        Exercise 818
    Answers for Day 9, "Member Functions Activate *class* Variables" 819
        Quiz 819
        Exercises 820
    Answers for Day 10, "Friends When You Need Them" 824
        Quiz 824
        Exercise 825

Teach Yourself OOP with Visual C++ 1.5 in 21 Days

Answers for Day 11, "Introduction to
  Overloading Operators" 827
    Quiz 827
    Exercises 827
Answers for Day 12, "Extending Operator
  Overloads" 831
    Quiz 831
    Exercises 832
Answers for Day 13, "Constructing and Destructing" .. 834
    Quiz 834
    Exercises 835
Answers for Day 14, "Loose Ends: *static*
  and Larger Programs" 838
    Quiz 838
    Exercises 839
Answers for Day 15, "It's Hereditary:
  Inheriting Data" 840
    Quiz 840
    Exercise 840
Answers for Day 16, "Inherited Limits
  and Extensions" 842
    Quiz 842
    Exercises 842
Answers for Day 17, "Data Composition" 848
    Quiz 848
    Exercises 848
Answers for Day 18, "Virtual Functions:
  Are They Real?" 849
    Quiz 849
    Exercises 850
Answers for Day 19, "Introduction to
  Throwing and Catching Exceptions" 854
    Quiz 854
    Exercise 854
Answers for Day 20, "Easy File I/O" 856
    Quiz 856
    Exercises 856
Answers for Day 21, "The Visual C++ Tools" 861
    Quiz 861
    Exercises 862

       Answers for Bonus Chapter 1, "Introduction to
           Windows Programming and MFC" 862
               Quiz 862
               Exercise 862
       Answers for Bonus Chapter 2, "The MFC Classes:
           Power You Will Gain" 863
               Quiz 863
               Exercise 863
       Answers for Bonus Chapter 3, "Files
           and More MFC" 866
               Quiz 866
               Exercise 867
       Answers for Bonus Chapter 4, "Graphics
           and Visual C++" 871
               Quiz 871
               Exercise 871
       Answers for Bonus Chapter 5, "What's Next?" 876
               Quiz 876
               Exercises 876

E Review of C Concepts **877**
       The C Difference 878
       The Format of C Programs 878
       C Comments 879
       Preprocessor Directives 880
       C Data 882
       Put Variables First! 884
       Input/Output 885
       Operators 889
       Additional Math Operators 890
       The Relational and Logical Operators 892
       Testing Data 893
       Pointers 896
       For Further Reading 897
               Absolute Beginner's Guide to C 897
               Teach Yourself C in 21 Days 897
               Advanced C 898

Glossary **899**

Index **907**

Acknowledgments

This book is the result of the caring editors at Sams who were patient where others wouldn't be. So many of the Sams editorial staff are becoming my friends. I want the reader to know that Sams Publishers want to produce the books you want, and they strive above and beyond the call of duty to produce these books.

I especially want to thank Stacy Hiquet for her devotion to this book and to every other book that she works on. Stacy leaves me alone while I write and supplies what I need when I request software, materials, books, or more time. I'd also like to thank Rosemarie Graham and Joe Williams.

Cheri Clark is solely responsible for putting wisdom to many of my words. Cheri's editing often rescues me from wordy predicaments that I get myself into. Often, after reading a correction that Cheri made, I question my ability to speak English fluently! Thanks, Cheri, for your patience with my problems.

My technical editor, Gary Farrar, takes his job more seriously than anyone I've ever known. Gary, I appreciate your keen eye more than you know.

My family is my backbone. My beautiful bride, Jayne, and my parents, Glen and Bettye Perry, encourage all that I do. I thank all three of you for being with me and for me in every way.

Greg Perry

About the Author

Greg Perry is a speaker and writer in both the programming and the applications sides of computing. He is known for bringing programming topics down to the beginner's level. Perry has been a programmer and trainer for the past 16 years. He received his first degree in computer science, and then a master's degree in corporate finance. Besides writing, he consults and lectures across the country, including at the acclaimed Software Development programming conferences. Perry is the author of more than 25 computer books, including *Absolute Beginner's Guide to Access, Absolute Beginner's Guide to C, Absolute Beginner's Guide to QBasic, Absolute Beginner's Guide to Programming, C++ Programming 101, Moving from C to C++, QBasic Programming 101,* and *Visual C++ Programming 101.* He also has a book on rental-property management. In addition, he has published articles in several publications, such as *Software Development, PC World, Data Training,* and *Access Advisor.*

Week 1 at a Glance

Get ready to begin a tour of the Visual C++ language! This first week launches your three-week training regimen that will teach you OOP (object-oriented programming) using Visual C++ in 21 days. If you don't have *any* idea what OOP is all about, the veil of mystery will be completely lifted in 21 days. This book was designed to offer a perfect combination of text, exercises, descriptions, review questions, and review exercises (with all answers listed in Appendix D) that work together to teach you OOP concepts and, more important, to teach you how to use Visual C++ to write OOP programs.

Each day's lesson ends with reviews and quizzes that hone your OOP skills learned that day. At the end of each day's chapter, you should be able to answer all the questions and write

working programs that fulfill the exercise requirements. (As you work through the exercises, please remember that there are several ways to write the same program. The exercise programs that you write, therefore, might not match the book's answer exactly, but that's OK.)

Welcome to the First Week

The first seven days walk you through Visual C++'s non-OOP concepts. You bought this book to learn OOP, and this book teaches you OOP. However, there are three distinct OOP-learning divisions that fit into a course on object-oriented programming, and this book's three weekly sections fit those three divisions perfectly. The first week, you'll learn non-OOP elements of the Visual C++ language so that you'll understand the foundation of OOP. (It turns out that the seemingly non-OOP language improvements offered by Visual C++ were really put there to support OOP logic.)

When you first learn OOP, you'll see that Visual C++ offers a better programming solution than its C predecessor language. If you never learn OOP, but only learn the first week's material, you would still think that C++ is better than C (and you would be right).

Note: This book assumes that you have some C background. If you want a quick refresher, read Appendix E for a review of the primary C language elements.

The creators of C++ did not set out just to make a better C. They designed the language so that the language supported OOP. As a result, C++ is better than C, but those improvements work to support OOP features as well as non-OOP programming.

In this first week, you'll learn a little about how to use the Visual C++ editing workbench to enter and compile C++ programs. You almost immediately see how C++ improves the way you input and output data to and from programs. You'll see why C++ programmers don't use `printf()` and `scanf()` anymore (just when you thought you had mastered them!).

The first week also shows you how to improve the way you design and write functions. C++ adds so many shortcuts and time-saving features that you'll begin using some in the first two days. From a simple change in the comment syntax to rewriting the built-in functions so that they work the way you need them to work, this first week provides a hands-on tutorial of the language's non-OOP commands and improvements over the C language that C++ was based on.

By the way, the nice thing about programming in Visual C++ is that all your C knowledge doesn't go to waste. Visual C++ supports almost every C feature, command, and idiom, and all the header files and functions you know and love (well, know and accept) work in Visual C++ programs. Usually, when you learn a new language, you have to start all over again learning about data types and assignment statements, but with Visual C++ you'll be writing long programs from the start.

After you master the first week's material, you'll be ready to use that information to dive into object-oriented programming with Visual C++.

DAY 1

The C++ Phenomenon

The C++ Phenomenon

Welcome to *Teach Yourself OOP in 21 Days with Visual C++*! This chapter begins whetting your appetite for C++. Today, you learn about the following topics:

- ☐ How C++ came to be
- ☐ What object-oriented programming (OOP) can do
- ☐ The advantages that C++ provides for the OOP programmer

Welcome to OOP's C++ World

C++ is here to stay! Although some people consider C++ to be an extension of C, C++ is much more than that—it's a stand-alone language. C++ greatly improves upon C. Nevertheless, C++ programmers would be fooling themselves if they didn't recognize that C is the firm foundation of the C++ language. One of the reasons so many people are moving to C++ is that so many people already know C. Whereas C blossomed in the 1980s, C++ is blossoming in the 1990s.

People make the switch from C to C++, and from other languages to C++, because of C++'s *object-oriented* features. Object-oriented programming, or *OOP* as it is affectionately known, takes the traditional programming approach a step beyond the procedural programming that got the industry to the 1980s.

Object-oriented programming provides a better vehicle to help programmers reach their goals (finished and debugged applications) faster than the straight procedural approach they are used to. In a nutshell, object-oriented programming makes your data active; instead of waiting around for code to manipulate variables, the program's variables know how to take care of themselves. When it comes time to print the contents of a variable, you don't print the variable; you tell the variable to print itself! This magical programming method is actually an extremely natural way of programming.

The History of C++

The man credited with creating C++ is Bjarne Stroustrup. He developed C++ to help program event simulations that he was modeling overseas a few years ago. Stroustrup found that regular non-OOP programming languages couldn't handle the task of simulating real-world events as well as an object-oriented language.

Stroustrup worked closely with AT&T's Bell Laboratories to develop and improve C++ over the years. The American National Standards Institute (ANSI), the group

that standardizes most computer-related languages, has yet to agree on a C++ standard, although the group is working diligently on one now. It is because ANSI has not yet standardized C++ that a *de facto* standard, the AT&T standard, is considered to be the C++ language to emulate.

Microsoft Corporation is the maker of Visual C++. Being AT&T–compatible is the benchmark that determines whether a compiler is modern enough to be used for a serious C++ compiler. Microsoft's C++ compiler closely follows the AT&T standard except for templates. Templates are hotly debated; some C++ programmers insist on having templates, and others have never programmed with templates. Some Visual C++ programmers, whether former template fans or not, write some of the most powerful programs available for PCs and never miss the template feature available in some other C++ compilers. Perhaps the rich set of tools supplied by Visual C++ makes templates useless, or maybe templates have been overrated.

Note: Over the years, AT&T approved many non-OOP features of C++ that made C++ better than C. So many improved features were added to C++ that the ANSI committee has borrowed several C++ elements for their approved C language. For example, function prototypes did not begin with C, although they've been part of the C language for several years now. Function prototypes first began with C++, and because they made for better programs, ANSI stuck the feature into the C language.

The Way You Program Without OOP

When you program without using OOP, you are programming procedurally. A *procedural* program is a step-by-step program that guides the application though a sequence of instructions. A procedural program executes each statement in the literal order of its commands, even if those commands cause the program to branch into all directions. C, Pascal, QBasic, and COBOL are all examples of procedural programming languages.

Today's computing world does not lend itself well to procedural programs. For instance, *graphical user interfaces* (*GUIs*) such as Windows can be programmed in procedural languages, but it makes more sense to write GUI programs with object-oriented languages.

The C++ Phenomenon

The icons, dialog boxes, and selection boxes on a GUI's screen become active when an event takes place, such as a mouse click or a keystroke. When writing GUI applications with a procedural language, you have to test continually for these events using programming constructs such as gigantic C `switch` statements. As mentioned in a previous section (and explained throughout the rest of this book), an object-oriented programming language allows for active data. All the GUI elements on-screen become active data items in the program.

> **Real-World Programming**
>
> As you progress through this book, you will see that OOP much more closely mirrors the real world than non-OOP procedural languages do. The pundits of OOP say that OOP "eliminates a layer of abstraction" from programs.
>
> Eliminating a layer of abstraction simply means that your programs more closely act like the applications they are modeling. The closer your programs model the applications, the faster you can write the programs and the easier it will be to debug them. For instance, if you were writing a CD-ROM controller in C++ to play your favorite audio CDs on your computer's CD-ROM drive, you could create variables for the play, rewind, fast forward, and eject buttons. When the user clicked the Play button on-screen, the play variable would actively take over for a while and start the music.

In procedural languages, variables have properties. A `Sales` variable might be single-precision and hold a number. A `FirstName` variable might be a string variable or character array that holds a person's first name. In OOP languages, variables have both properties and *behaviors*. The behaviors are the active triggers for the data. When you give a variable behavior, you teach the variable (by writing code) how to initialize itself, display itself, calculate its own values, and so forth.

When your variables take on behaviors as well as properties, the rest of your programming job becomes easier. You no longer have to write code that manipulates the variables every time you use them.

To activate variables, C++ approaches user-defined data much more thoroughly than C. When you define your own data type with `struct`, you are in many ways adding a new data type to the C++ language. In C, when you declare a structure, you must repeat the `struct` keyword when you define variables for that structure. In C++, when you declare a structure with `struct`, you don't have to repeat the `struct` keyword.

Although the use of user-defined data items goes much further than saving your typing of the `struct` keyword, it is important to note early that your own data types are almost as important to C++ as integers and characters.

Note: Incidentally, C++ programmers use the `class` keyword more often than `struct` to define their own data types.

OOP Programming Advantages

If you have been programming for a while using procedural non-OOP methods, there is nothing wrong with the way you now program. A well-written structured procedural program is always better than a poorly written OOP program. Today, companies use millions of lines of non-OOP code every day successfully. There is little reason to rewrite the code that now works well, no matter what method or language that code was written in.

Today's computing world, however, offers a few more challenges than yesterday's. Not only are people moving toward graphical user environments (which are inherently much more difficult to program and maintain), but the world is becoming a global economy, businesses must interact with all kinds of unforeseen data, the amount of data that must be processed is unthinkable, and backlogs in data processing departments continue to grow every day.

Something has to be done to lessen the programming load in today's world. New approaches to programming must be used to overcome the programming bottlenecks that everyone faces. Not a data processing department in existence has programmers sitting around idly because all the programs that need to be written are in place and the computer is on autopilot.

Object-oriented programming is not an answer to all of today's programming problems. Nevertheless, OOP does help solve many programming bottlenecks. There are many C++ industry leaders who say that C++ will more than double programmer productivity—they say that a veteran C++ programmer can produce faster, more accurate, and better-written applications by a factor of *ten* or *twenty* times compared with a procedural programmer! Also, you can reuse the code you wrote in C++ more easily than code written in other programming languages. After you write a C++ program, that program or a section of it can easily form the basis for other programs.

The C++ Phenomenon

Given the promised productivity increases in OOP, and given the bottlenecks of the procedural data processing industry, OOP is a natural progression and evolution for today's programmers. OOP is not a panacea that will solve the bottlenecks and produce blissful data processing managers, but proper OOP practices will help overcome the burdens of programming.

OOP is a natural way to program. There is a debate around the programming industry that goes something like this: OOP is such a better and more natural programming method that all beginning programmers should be taught to program using OOP. The opposing view is that OOP is better learned second, after a procedural programming language such as C is learned.

Both sides of the argument have good points, but the argument ignores this current problem: Whether or not OOP is best for beginners, we have an abundant supply of programmers today who don't know OOP but need to learn it. Whether they should have been taught OOP from the beginning is moot because many learned to program before OOP was ever dreamed of. The rest are well-founded in non-OOP programming today but must make the shift to OOP for tomorrow. This book helps you make that shift.

Almost everyone agrees that well-documented, well-structured programming techniques are better than unstructured techniques. Despite that agreement, how many of us find ourselves writing "quick and dirty" programs that are unstructured and undocumented, just to see what happens, just to scratch out a design, and just to get started? Too many of those quick-and-dirty programs later move straight into production. We never get around to rewriting them, and the nightmares flare when maintenance has to be done later.

OOP programmers find that it is difficult *not* to write OOP programs! One of the premiere advantages of OOP is its natural way of coding. You'll find yourself using OOP principles on even the smallest and most trivial programs. OOP is a technique that programmers practice; OOP becomes a good habit. On the other hand, as good as structured programming is, people find that it is all too easy to ignore structured principles "just for this one program."

DO	DON'T

DO approach OOP with the idea of easier, faster, and more productive programming.

DO expect to find OOP a natural way of programming.

DON'T expect results overnight; it takes a while to become acclimated to the OOP environment.

DON'T discount the learning curve to move from procedural programming to OOP. It takes time to make the mental switch.

Relax and Enjoy

All this talk about variable behaviors, properties, and OOP might seem to imply that you have a lot of learning ahead of you. You do, but the move from C to C++, or from any procedural language to an OOP language, is not as rigorous as it might first seem.

If you have read articles about C++, you might have heard terms such as *encapsulation, polymorphism,* and *inheritance.* These terms do nothing but frighten the newcomer to OOP. Any time you learn a new subject, you'll have to learn the new terms that go with that subject because there are new features and procedures that must be named something. However, the newcomer to C++ and OOP doesn't have to master these kinds of terms before learning the language. It is this author's opinion that the concepts underlying encapsulation and polymorphism are easier to learn than the terms themselves. Many times, this book will teach you new concepts before mentioning the names for those concepts.

Don't rush C++. Although OOP is a more natural way of programming, many people find that their productivity *decreases* at first when they are switching to OOP from C. The new syntax that is sometimes required and the new OOP concepts that come your way will slow you down at first. Often, you'll write new C++ programs by looking at existing C++ programs, such as the many examples from this book. It takes a while to write C++ programs from scratch, so be ready to follow examples and get ready to try a few things that won't work the way you first expect.

The C++ Phenomenon

What Is an Object Anyway?

You now know that OOP data becomes active, and you might have guessed that this active data composes the *object* in the term *object-oriented*. Technically, an object is nothing more than the variables you are already used to using. However, an OOP language such as C++ takes the concept of data to the next higher level, giving that data behavior as discussed previously in this chapter.

In C++, the term *object* is usually reserved for user-defined data types, such as those defined with `struct` and `class`. It is inside these user-defined data types that you specify the object's behavior by adding functions to the data itself. Whereas you used to write functions to work on objects, you will now write functions so that objects know how to behave. At this point, the distinction might be hazy; that's fine because you've got 20 more daily chapters to finish before the haze lifts completely!

Are All Variables Objects?

As previously explained, an object is data with behavior, and C++ objects are usually user-defined variables such as the structures you have worked with in the past.

A simple integer variable is technically an object, but OOP programmers generally reserve the actual term *object* for user-defined data types.

Any time that you have lots of occurrences of something, such as employee records, controls on the screen, and inventory items, those occurrences generally make good object candidates.

Knowing what to make as an object and what to leave as an ordinary variable sometimes takes practice and trial and error. A simple counter that keeps track of customers as they make purchases in your store might make a good candidate for an object rather than a stand-alone integer variable. You could have the counter increment itself as customers make purchases and display itself when you want a customer count. Requesting behavior from data almost always makes that data a good candidate for an object.

OOP, C++, and C

The nice thing about C++ is that it's an OOP language based on C, a language many people already know. C++ is called a *hybrid* OOP language because it is a procedural language with hooks that turn it into an OOP language. C++ was not designed completely from scratch to be an object-oriented language because so much of C++ was based on the non-OOP C. C++ was designed to take features found in C and make them available to OOP programmers who wanted to use them.

Most of a C++ program looks just like a C program. That's the beauty of C++ and why it is only natural that C fosters C++ programmers. Listing 1.1 shows an example C++ program. The program is neither the easiest nor the hardest C++ program you'll see in this book. Don't try to figure out the program at this time; instead, study how most of the statements look just like the C programming statements you are already familiar with.

Note: The only initial C++ difference worth noting at this time is that C++ comments begin with two slashes, //, instead of being enclosed in /* and */. You'll read more about C++ comments in the next chapter.

Listing 1.1. C++ programs look a lot like C programs.

```
 1:  // Filename: FIRST.CPP
 2:  // A first look at a C++ program
 3:  #include <iostream.h>
 4:  #include <ctype.h>
 5:
 6:  class animalType
 7:  {
 8:     char breed[40];        // Array of characters
 9:  public:
10:     void getBreed(void)    // Get the animal's breed name
11:       { cout << "What is the breed? ";
12:         cin >> breed;      // User types the name
13:       }
14:     void prBreed(void)
15:       { cout << "\nThe animal's breed is " << breed;
16:       }
17: };
18:
19: // Actual program starts here
20: void main(void)
```

continues

The C++ Phenomenon

Listing 1.1. continued

```
21:    {
22:      animalType *animals[25];    // C++ doesn't need class keyword
23:      int num = 0;
24:      char ans;
25:
26:      do
27:        { animals[num] = new animalType;    // Allocate space
28:          animals[num++]->getBreed();
29:          cout << "Do you want to enter another animal (Y/N)? ";
30:          cin >> ans;
31:        }
32:      while (toupper(ans) != 'N');
33:
34:      // Now, print each of the breeds
35:      for (int ctr=0; ctr<num; ctr++)
36:        { animals[ctr]->prBreed(); }
37:    }
```

One of the nice things about C++ is that you don't have to implement *any* of the object-oriented features to prefer C++ over C. The next six daily chapters of this book teach the non-OOP features of C++. It turns out that the designers of C++ had to add most of these features to implement object-orientation, but even if you don't use these features to their fullest OOP extent, your regular non-OOP programs will be easier to write.

The fact that C++ offers non-OOP advantages over C is another reason that C++ is a separate stand-alone language and should be considered on its own merits, not just because it is C-like.

C++ is a stronger type-checking language than C. Actually, C++ is a stronger *everything*-checking language. The C++ compiler is stricter than C. Many C programmers who want to write accurate and well-written C programs find that they can run their C programs through the Visual C++ compiler and find bugs and potential problem areas that their C compiler could not catch. It says a lot for the C++ language that it accepts both C (albeit well-written C programs) and C++ code and compiles both equally well.

Visual C++ and This Book

Every example in this book is written to the Visual C++ compiler specifications. Nevertheless, if you have another C++ compiler that conforms well to the AT&T C++ standard (3.0 or later), you should have little or no trouble making these programs work as written. If a Visual C++–specific command or function is used, the book will make it clear that the example might not work with some compilers.

This book is aimed at those who have programmed before, specifically in C. No time is taken to explain what a loop is, for instance, but if a C++ loop behaves differently from what you might expect in your previous programming work, you'll read why the difference appears.

Visual C++ Was Designed for Windows Programs

The first step in learning how to use Visual C++ to its fullest advantage is to learn C++. As you might already know, Visual C++'s primary strength lies in its Microsoft Windows programming tools. Microsoft Windows (and its offshoots, such as Windows NT) requires extensive programming tools and talents. Although writing Windows programs is easier using Visual C++ than almost any other programming tool, a Windows program is still very difficult for newcomers to Windows programming.

Here are the typical learning steps a programmer goes through from novice to advanced Visual C++ programmer:

1. Learn to program in an introductory language such as BASIC, QBasic, or Pascal.
2. Learn to improve coding efficiency and effectiveness by moving to C.
3. Learn C++.
4. Learn to program a GUI (graphical user interface) using C or C++.

Right now, you are beginning step 3. This book was written to cover step 3. While learning C++ using Visual C++, you'll probably be aware of the power beneath the language. That power comes in Visual C++'s capability to help advanced programmers write Windows programs. Although Windows programming using Visual C++ is beyond the scope of this book, the Extra Credit section at the end of the book introduces you to Visual C++ Windows programming and the Microsoft Foundation Classes that put Visual C++ at the top of the language charts.

The C++ Phenomenon

Entering and Compiling C++ Programs

This book does not walk you through each Visual C++ editor feature. The Visual C++ integrated Windows editor is one of the most powerful editors available, yet at this point you should concentrate on the C++ language features and should not get caught up in the editor's details. There are a few things, however, that you should know about the Visual C++ editor before you begin to learn C++.

Visual C++ is a Windows-based programming language; you must start Windows before using Visual C++. It is impossible to use this language without learning the programmer interface called the Visual C++ workbench. If you've used a former Microsoft workbench for compiling and running C programs, forget nearly all you know about using that editing workbench! With Visual C++, Microsoft redesigned the workbench, making it Windows-aware and adding a toolbar that you'll use frequently to save and compile programs.

As mentioned in the preceding section, Visual C++'s support for C++ programs is a small part of the entire Visual C++ compiler. If you've programmed in C, Pascal, or QBasic, you might think that Visual C++ is overkill when you want to write simple text-based C++ programs. However, if you have Visual C++, you bought the package because you know its capabilities. The odds are that as soon as you learn C++ with Visual C++, you'll want to move into the Windows programming it provides. As a matter of fact, all C++ programs that you learn about, enter, and compile in this book will look like Windows programs. Instead of learning to write them for the DOS environment, you'll see how to compile and run C++ programs within Windows using Microsoft's QuickWin feature. QuickWin enables you to compile and run text-based programs that a DOS-based C++ compiler would run, except QuickWin programs execute in a window and have some characteristics of a Windows program.

DO	DON'T

DO note that Visual C++ includes many programming tools, most of them powerful Windows application-development tools, that you'll be ready for only after learning C++.

DON'T be discouraged that compiling simple C++ programs under Visual C++ takes more steps than using a DOS-based C or Pascal compiler. With the added responsibility comes greatly added power that you'll be able to tap into when you learn C++.

> **DON'T** expect to be a Windows programmer soon just because QuickWin makes your C++ look Windows-like. Writing end-user true Windows-based programs involves much more than writing with QuickWin. Nevertheless, after you master C++ with QuickWin, you'll be able to move into Windows programming using Visual C++ much faster. (The Extra Credit section at the end of this book gives you lots of insight into true Windows-based programming with Visual C++.)

After starting Windows and loading Visual C++ (by clicking the Visual C++ icon within the Program Manager), you'll see the menu and toolbar shown in Figure 1.1.

Many of Visual C++'s buttons on the toolbar are related to project files that you'll learn more about in Day 14's chapter, "Loose Ends: *static* and Larger Programs." Also, all the buttons are available from the pull-down menus. Most have shortcut keys. For example, instead of clicking the Rebuild All button, you can select **P**roject **R**ebuild All from the menu or press the Alt+F8 shortcut key.

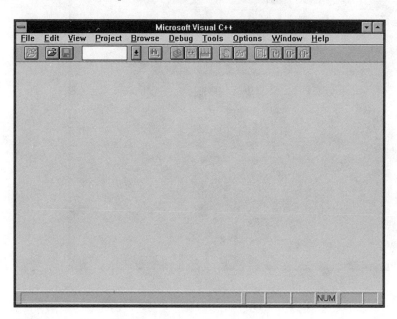

Figure 1.1. Visual C++'s menu and toolbar.

The C++ Phenomenon

Preparing for C++ Programs

Before diving into a C++ program, take a moment to change some options in your Visual C++ environment. Changing options helps streamline your C++ compiles by eliminating a lot of the overhead needed to compile Windows-based programs (Visual C++'s default setup). Here are the steps you should take before learning C++:

1. Select **O**ptions **P**roject. Click the down arrow in the **P**roject Type dialog box, and select `QuickWin application (.EXE)`. Doing so informs Visual C++ that you don't want to generate complete (and huge) Windows applications at this time.

2. Click the **U**se Microsoft Foundation Classes box to remove the X from that option's selection.

3. Click the **R**elease button to move the selection from the **D**ebug option. At this point, the dialog box should look like the one in Figure 1.2.

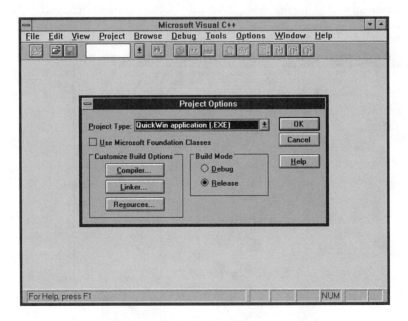

Figure 1.2. After setting up Visual C++ for C++ programs.

4. Press Enter or click **OK** to return to the Visual C++ environment.

You have now set up your Visual C++ to accept non-Windows C++ programs. The QuickWin option will run your non-Windows C++ programs inside a window for you, so you don't have to open a DOS window to see your results.

Running the Program

Throughout much of this book, you will follow these next steps to enter, compile, and run a C++ program in Visual C++. If you haven't started Visual C++, you should do so now and follow this example to practice compiling under Visual C++.

1. Select **F**ile **N**ew. (Ctrl+N is the shortcut keystroke to select **N**ew from the **F**ile menu.) Visual C++ opens an empty window on the screen titled UNTITLED.1.

2. Type `Listing 1.2` into the Visual C++ editor. As you do, you'll see that the usual editing keys such as Backspace, the arrows, Insert, and Delete work the way you're used to. If you want to increase the size of the program editing window, you can enlarge the editor window by double-clicking the window's title bar or by dragging an edge of the window to a new, expanded location.

Listing 1.2. A sample C++ program to try.

```
1:  // Filename: SAMPLE.CPP
2:  #include <iostream.h>
3:  main()
4:  {
5:      cout << "Learning Visual C++ in 21 Days!\n";
6:      return 0;
7:  }
```

3. Save the program by selecting **F**ile **S**ave and typing the filename. As with all of Windows file-saving dialog boxes, you can select an appropriate drive and path to hold the file before clicking **OK** to save the file. (The suggested filenames for all program listings in this book appear on the first line of each program. All C++ programs should end in the .CPP filename extension.)

4. You now must compile, link, and run the program. Be ready for a little more delay than you're probably used to. Visual C++ takes a while to complete the process. To compile, link, and execute a Visual C++ program (assuming that

The C++ Phenomenon

there are no errors), press Ctrl+F5, the shortcut key for **P**roject **Ex**ecute SAMPLE.EXE.

When you press Ctrl+F5, Visual C++ displays the dialog box shown in Figure 1.3. Visual C++ is asking whether you want to create SAMPLE.EXE, the compiled version of the source code that you typed earlier. Of course you want to create the compiled program—that's why you pressed Ctrl+F5! Therefore, select **Y**es.

Visual C++ works closely with project files, which you'll learn a lot about in Day 14's chapter, "Loose Ends: *static* and Larger Programs." Project files are needed when you're developing full-blown Windows programs, but they aren't critical when you're writing stand-alone programs such as this book's introductory C++ programs.

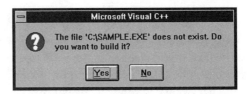

Figure 1.3. Tell Visual C++ that you want to create the .EXE file.

5. During the compilation, you'll see several compiler and linker messages. If there is an error, place the cursor on the error message and press Enter (or double-click with the mouse). Visual C++ will place you at the source code line that produced the error. If you are following along in this book, you shouldn't get errors except for a few typing errors that might slip in while you're entering the code. After you fix the error and recompile, you'll eventually see the following message on-screen:

```
SAMPLE.EXE - 0 error(s), 0 warning(s)
```

The program is now compiled and ready to run. You must press Ctrl+F5 again to run the program now that Visual C++ has compiled the program. The Ctrl+F5 does one of two things: runs your program if there is an up-to-date .EXE file on the disk with the same name, or creates a new .EXE file if one does not exist or if you've made changes to the source code since the last compile.

When you press Ctrl+F5 to run the program, you'll see the output appear in the output window shown in Figure 1.4. All text-based input and output appear in such a window because you're using the QuickWin compilation option. The window offers a tremendous advantage over the DOS-based output screens you've perhaps worked with in the past, because you can click the window's scroll bars to scroll through long output displays. As with any window, you also can double-click the window's title bar to expand the window to full screen. The QuickWin compiler also creates a familiar-looking menu above your output window so that you can get help or close the output screen when you are through with it.

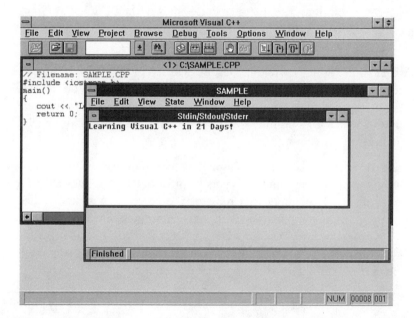

Figure 1.4. Looking at the output of the program.

Note: To move back and forth between the source code listing and the message screen, press Alt+1 (for the source code) or Alt+2 (for the message screen). Visual C++ displays a number in angled brackets (that is, <1> or <2>) to tell you what window number you're looking at. You can also move back and forth between windows by selecting from the **W**indow pull-down menu.

21

The C++ Phenomenon

QuickWin enables beginning Visual C++ programmers to compile and run text-based MS-DOS programs as simple Windows programs. All QuickWin programshave the following features:

- ☐ Standard Windows menu bar
- ☐ QuickWin on-line help
- ☐ A window for `stdin`, `stdout`, and `stderr` streams
- ☐ Limited Windows clipboard support

Some text-based programs won't work perfectly under QuickWin. For example, you cannot use the `\a` character to ring the PC's bell in QuickWin `printf()` function calls, but you can use most escape characters such as `\n` and `\t`.

6. When you're done viewing the output, select **W**indow Close **A**ll to close all the windows and return to a clean Visual C++ slate so that you can enter your next program. If you've made changes to the source code since you last saved it, Visual C++ prompts you to save your work before closing all the windows on the screen.

More steps are needed to compile a simple C++ program in Visual C++ than when you're using the C languages and tools you are probably used to, such as Turbo C or Microsoft QuickC. Remember that most of the power in Visual C++ lies in its Windows programming capabilities. Although a lot of steps are needed to compile a simple C++ program, no additional steps are needed to compile and run complete Windows Visual C++ programs. For now, concentrate on the C++ language so that when you're ready for Windows programming, you'll be able to slide right into it.

DO	**DON'T**

DO note that C++ relies a lot on your knowledge of C. Many features of C++ will quickly become second nature to you, not only because C++ is a natural way of programming but also because C++ is so C-like.

DO change the Visual C++ options to ease your transition to Visual C++.

DON'T attempt to compile a C++ program unless you've saved the program under the .CPP extension.

What You Should Already Know

There is no way this book could accomplish its mission, teaching you C++ in 21 days, unless a few assumptions can be made. The book assumes that you know C. "Knowing C," however, means different things to different people. Many know C but would never consider themselves masters at C. You don't have to be a master at C to learn C++. As a matter of fact, if you feel you are still learning C's finer points but are fairly comfortable in the language, it is probably time to move on to C++. Some of the things you do now in C will have to be "unlearned," so it might be a good time to change gears before you do consider yourself a "master" of C.

The following list describes a few C concepts and features that you should have used before or should feel that you have a basic understanding of. This list is intended only as a guide. For example, if you've never totally understood C's `malloc()` and `free()` functions, you might be fine with C++ because C++ allocates memory in a much cleaner way than those two C functions. Nevertheless, you should probably know something about most of the items on this list before tackling C++ in 21 days.

- [ ] The fundamental C data types such as `int`, `float`, and `char`.
- [ ] The concept of local and global variables.
- [ ] C arrays: how to initialize and work with array elements.
- [ ] Programming language commands such as `if`, `switch`, and `for`.
- [ ] `#include` and `#define`.
- [ ] `printf()`, `scanf()`, `getch()`, `putch()`, and related I/O functions.
- [ ] Passing and receiving arguments among functions.
- [ ] User-defined data types with `struct`.
- [ ] Dynamic memory allocation using `malloc()` and `free()`.

Appendix E provides a quick review of introductory C concepts.

The C++ Phenomenon

What's Ahead for You

Now that this chapter has prepared you with the advantages that OOP has to offer, get ready to purge all that from your mind and learn C++! C++ is a language that should creep up on you. Don't expect miracles, because C++ takes time to master. Learning the language syntax and object-oriented methods is not extremely difficult, but learning when and how to best use the new OOP mechanisms takes time, patience, and practice. Read and learn each day's chapter without worrying about improving your productivity, because you'll be disappointed if you keep score.

For about the first half of this book, you'll be learning additions to C that make C++ a better language, both a better procedural language and a better object-oriented language. Sometimes, you'll read about the way you now program in C and then you'll see how to accomplish the same result, with a completely different method, in C++.

The last half of the book is not as much involved with learning new C++ language elements as it is with learning philosophies and uses of C++ and OOP.

Summary

After reading this chapter, you should have more questions than answers! This chapter only whets your OOP appetite and tries to give you an overview of what to look for, as well as a brief feel for objects and OOP. The rest of this book explains in greater detail what OOP is and how to implement OOP using Visual C++.

In this chapter, you saw that writing a Visual C++ program involves a few steps, but Ctrl+F5 is the most important shortcut key to remember. With Ctrl+F5, you can compile, link, and run your program. All C++ source programs should end in the .CPP filename extension.

As long as you have a fair grasp of C, you are ready to learn OOP with Visual C++ in 21 days. This book presents OOP in a way that you have not yet seen—you'll learn why an OOP concept is important, and you'll see how to implement that concept before getting a long definition or a new term. Too many people teach OOP from a theorist viewpoint, but that style hinders the student. C++ is better than C, and OOP is better than the procedural way you now program. To convince you of that, however, will take lots of examples and explanation, so how about getting started on Day 2's chapter?

Q&A

Q. Why should I switch from C to C++?

A. To use the words of Bjarne Stroustrup, "C++ is a better C." Even if you never use the object-oriented concepts of C++, you'll like C++ more than C because the language is improved over C.

If you continue with C++ and master the OOP techniques that the language offers, you'll find your productivity increasing, your debugging time decreasing, and your programming throughput getting better and better. C++ also enables you to reuse code more easily than most other languages.

Q. How can Visual C++ help with learning C++ programs?

A. The Visual C++ compiler is a Windows-based editor, compiler, and linker, as well as the host for several other integrated tools that you'll learn about as your programming skills progress.

Q. What makes an OOP program stand apart from a non-OOP program?

A. OOP data, composing the *object* in *object-orientation,* becomes active. Instead of waiting around for other parts of a program to process them, OOP variables take active roles in their own behaviors. After you give behavior to an object, you don't have to worry about that object throughout the rest of the code, because the object will take care of itself. It sounds magical at this point, but before 21 days are up, the mystery will be unveiled to you.

Q. Why do OOP programmers tend to use OOP for all their programs?

A. OOP is a natural way of programming. Although structured programming is considered better than unstructured programming, too many programmers write unstructured code using the excuse of time. In the long run, programmers spend more time maintaining unstructured code than they would if they had structured the code in the first place.

OOP programmers find themselves using OOP without thinking about the process. Therefore, after you master OOP, the OOP side of your brain will go into autopilot mode, and you'll be writing OOP programs each time you start Visual C++.

Q. True or False: Only expert C programmers should attempt C++ programming.

The C++ Phenomenon

A. False. Knowing C helps you learn C++ much faster; however, you don't have to be an expert in C to move to C++. An average C programmer might make the best candidate for C++ for two reasons: he or she is already grounded in the primary C-like language elements, and he or she is not so firmly rooted in C's procedural way of programming that making the switch to OOP would be difficult.

Workshop

The Workshop offers quiz questions and exercises to hone your skills and give you feedback on today's lesson. You'll find some proposed answers in Appendix D.

Quiz

1. What does OOP stand for?
2. How much of a programming improvement can a skillful C++ programmer expect over that of a non-C++ programmer?
3. The ANSI committee has yet to approve a C++ standard. Does that mean there is no way to judge a good C++ compiler from a bad one? If not, why?
4. What is the term for non-OOP languages?
5. What is the keyword that C++ programmers use more often than struct when defining new object data types?
6. What filename extension should you use for C++ programs?

Exercises

1. Enter, compile, and run the program listed in Listing 1.1.
2. Change the comments in Listing 1.1 to the old-style /* and */ C comments, and rerun the program. You'll see that Visual C++ enables you to use C's style of comments as well as C++'s. Now that you've proven to yourself that the C++ compiler works with C code, turn the page to move to C++ code—you'll never go back to regular C again!

DAY 2

C++ Is Superior!

C++ Is Superior!

Change all your C program filename extensions to .CPP right now! Even if you wait to tackle object-oriented Visual C++, there are lots of non-OOP features of Visual C++ that will improve your programming accuracy, power, and enjoyment. You will find that several Visual C++ features make Visual C++ an easy language to write procedural programs in. Later, you will find out why these important features were really added to Visual C++; without many of them, object orientation would be impossible.

Many of the things you do in C++ require a shift in the way you already do things in C. All of C's functions, as well as C's commands, are available to Visual C++. Nevertheless, using the Visual C++–specific commands and style almost always makes your C programs more effective. Today, you learn about the following topics:

- [ ] C++ program comments
- [ ] How Visual C++ treats user-defined data
- [ ] Prototyping in Visual C++
- [ ] Specifying `void` argument lists
- [ ] Visual C++ data concerns: `char` sizes, variable definitions, constants, and scope
- [ ] Typecasting improvements
- [ ] A better alternative to `#define`

Commenting on Your Work

One of the first things a newcomer to Visual C++ notices is the new kind of comment specifier. The C-style comments are simply too cumbersome to use; every time you open a comment with `/*`, you must remember to close the comment with `*/`. Forgetting to close a comment is easy to do and is frustrating because it usually costs you time for an extra compile.

Another drawback to the C style of commenting is that you cannot nest C comments. The following lines from a C program will *not* compile error-free:

```
for (i=0; i<10; i++)     /* Start of the loop */
  { printf("%d\n", i);   /* Print a number    */
    /* i = i + 1;        /* Increment i an extra time */
      if (i == 5)
        { printf("Halfway\n"); } */
  }
```

It appears that the lines i = i + 1; through the `printf()` are commented out. Sometimes programmers will comment out one or more C statements by enclosing the statements within comment symbols. The problem here occurs because the first line already has a comment. When the programmer mistakenly tries to comment out the three lines, thinking that the lines would not then execute, Visual C++ complains because you cannot nest comments. Visual C++ thinks that the comment ends at the first `*/`. When the compiler then encounters the `printf()`'s `*/`, seemingly without an opening `/*`, an error results.

In your Visual C++ programs, you can begin any and all comments with two forward slashes, `//`. That's it. Everything after `//` is ignored. The following two statements are equivalent in every way:

```
if (x == y)     /* Test the coordinates */
```

and

```
if (x == y)     // Test the coordinates
```

The C++ Comment: //

[*C++ code*] // *Your comment text*

C++ code is optional, as the brackets indicate. The *C++ code* is any C++ statement or group of statements, whether you write a C++ command or function call. If you don't put *C++ code* before the `//`, the entire line is a comment. Notice that there is no ending comment symbol. Everything following `//` to the end of the line is a comment.

If you want to comment out a section of code, just insert two slashes at the beginning of the code. Even if another comment appears to the right of the code you are commenting out, Visual C++ will not complain but will consider the entire line a comment.

Example

```
// Filename: NEWCOMM.CPP
// This entire line is a comment
#include <stdio.h>
main()
{
  int age;
  printf("How old are you? ");        // Ask a question
  scanf(" %d", &age);
  // Test the age for a message
  if (age > 18)
    { printf("You are an adult.\n");  // Voting age
```

29

```
    }
    return 0;     // Go back to DOS
}
```

> **DO** switch to // C++ comments. These comments are easier to type. Visual C++ even enables you to use // comments in your regular C programs with the .C filename extension.
>
> **DON'T** try to end a // comment with any symbol, and don't put executable statements anywhere to the right of // unless you want to comment out the code. The end of the line ends a comment begun with //.

Less Is More with Visual C++

These are three ways you have probably used in the past for defining your own data types in C:

- ☐ struct
- ☐ enum
- ☐ union

These are sometimes collectively called *aggregate data types*. The most common, struct, enables you to define exactly how your data looks in a record format called a *structure*. The enum keyword enables you to create enumerated named constants, and the union keyword enables you to create structures whose members overlap the same memory location. Before you can define structure variables, enumerated constants, or union variables, you must first declare the "look" of the data.

Everything that you learned in C still applies in Visual C++, but Visual C++ respects your own data types more than C. For example, after you've defined a structure, you don't have to repeat the struct keyword because Visual C++ remembers your structure's definition.

Listing 2.1 shows a program that declares a structure, an enumerated constant, and a union. Probably, some readers have worked very little with enum or union, and that's fine. The struct keyword (and its improved class keyword, which you'll read about in the upcoming chapters) is much more common in both C and C++.

Listing 2.1. Declaring a struct, an enum, and a union the Visual C++ way.

```
 1: // Filename: USERDEFS.CPP
 2: // Demonstrates struct, enum, and union.
 3: #include <stdio.h>
 4: // First, declare the format of each aggregate data type.
 5: struct aStruct {
 6:   int i;
 7:   float x;
 8: };
 9: enum colors {
10:   Red, Blue, Green
11: };
12: union bitFields {
13:   int first;
14:   float second;
15:   double third;
16: };
17:
18: main()
19: {
20:   // Define variables for each aggregate data type
21:   int number1;
22:   float number2;
23:   aStruct myStructVar;
24:   colors myEnumVar;
25:   bitFields myUnionVar;
26:   // Store values in the new variables to show they are defined
27:   number1 = 10;
28:   number2 = 20;
29:   myStructVar.i = 100;
30:   myStructVar.x = 75.5;
31:   myEnumVar = Red;
32:   myUnionVar.second = 123.45;
33:   return 0;
34: }
```

This program produces no output, but study the code to see how Visual C++ handles aggregate data types. Visual C++ might issue a warning because the defined variables are not used for anything after you assign values to them, but that's OK. The important lines to consider here are lines 23 through 25. You don't have to place the `struct`, `enum`, and `union` keywords before each of the variable definitions. If this were a C program, `struct`, `enum`, and `union` would have to appear at the beginning of each line.

C++ Is Superior!

When you declare your own data type, Visual C++ remembers the name (called the *tag*) and adds that name to its list of internal data types. For the rest of the program, you can treat your data type *almost* as if it were part of the Visual C++ language.

DO	DON'T
DO declare your aggregate Visual C++ data types just as you do in C. **DON'T** repeat the `struct`, `enum`, or `union` keywords when you define variables for those aggregate data types.	

C++ Prototypes

C *recommends* that you prototype every function in your program—C++ *requires* that you prototype every function. The word *prototype* means model, and a prototype is just a declaration or a model for a function that follows somewhere in the program. By prototyping all your functions before calling those functions, you tell the C++ compiler what the upcoming function's *signature* will look like.

The signature of a function is the look of its return value (if any) and argument list (if any). The signature of a function whose first line is

```
void myfun(int a)
```

would be a void return type and one integer argument. The signature of the function

```
people * getName(long int empNumber, float salesTot)
```

would be a returned pointer to `people` and two arguments, one integer and the other single-precision floating-point. A prototype completely defines a function's signature.

If you haven't prototyped diligently, you might not understand the importance of prototypes, especially because C doesn't require them. A prototype tells the compiler what to expect when you call a function. If the first line of a function is

```
void myfun(int a)
```

but you try to call the function with the statement

```
myfun(39.6543)
```

the compiler does not complain if you haven't prototyped. It quietly converts 39.6543 to the integer 39 and uses the integer, even if the converted integer produces an incorrect answer later.

Prototypes end with a semicolon. Most programmers make their prototypes look just like the function's first line. The prototype for the previous statement looks like this:

```
void myfun(int a);
```

This prototype tells the compiler that you will never pass the `myfun()` any argument other than an integer. If you pass a floating-point, a character, or any other kind of non-integer argument, the compiler will catch the error and complain. The prototype helps keep errors from slipping into your output. If you don't prototype in C programs, some of the resulting errors are hard to find. If you don't prototype in C++, the compiler refuses to compile the program until you do prototype. (Options that ease Visual C++'s prototype restriction are available, but you should not use them.)

Note: You prototype built-in functions in Visual C++ (just as you do with any C compiler) by including the function's header file.

Put all prototypes before the `main()` function. Some programmers use `#include` to include a text file with nothing more than several lines of prototypes and header file inclusions.

DO / DON'T

DO always prototype every function in your C++ program, or Visual C++ will complain when you compile the program.

DON'T forget to prototype the built-in functions by including their header files.

DON'T confuse the terms *function declaration* and *function definition*. A function declaration is a prototype, and the function definition begins at the actual first line of the function.

It is easy for C programmers to get slack and forget to prototype. When you make the change to C++, the compiler will teach you right away to prototype. Even if you use a built-in function such as `printf()`, Visual C++ will refuse to compile the program

C++ Is Superior!

until you include STDIO.H. You never have to prototype `main()` because it is known as a *self-prototyping* function. `main()` is the first function to execute, and no other function calls `main()`.

A function that is prototyped with no return value should always return an integer. As in C, no return type in the function prototype or function definition tells Visual C++ to assume that you are returning an integer. The following prototypes are the same in Visual C++:

```
calcAmt(float a, int c);      // Assumes an integer return
```

and

```
int calcAmt(float a, int c);  // Explicit integer return
```

The program in Listing 2.2 includes a function named `compArea()` that returns the area of a room as an integer value.

Listing 2.2. Using prototypes.

```
1:  // Filename: AREACOMP.CPP
2:  // Program that includes a function to compute a room's area
3:  #include <stdio.h>
4:  int compArea(int length, int width);    // Prototype
5:  main()
6:  {
7:     int length, width, area;
8:     printf("What is the room's length in feet? ");
9:     scanf(" %d", &length);
10:    printf("What is the width? ");
11:    scanf(" %d", &width);
12:    // Calculate the area
13:    area = compArea(length, width);
14:    printf("\nThe room's area is %d.\n", area);
15:    return 0;
16: }
17: compArea(int length, int width)
18: {
19:    return (length * width);
20: }
```

```
What is the room's length in feet? 10
What is the width? 12

The room's area is 120.
```

34

Note: You don't have to specify variable names when prototyping. The fourth line in Listing 2.2 could have read like this and still have worked the same:

```
int compArea(int, int)     // Prototype
```

The 15th line in Listing 2.2 is optional in C, and even `return;` without the returned integer value is OK with C. However, C++ *requires* that Listing 2.2's `main()` and `compArea()` functions both return some kind of integer value. If you left the `return 0;` statement out of the program, Visual C++ would complain with a warning.

Prototypes are your contract with Visual C++ that you will follow the prototype exactly. If you specify a certain signature (even if you use the default `int` return type by not specifying a return type), you should follow that signature in the function's definition.

One last prototyping point is important to know about Visual C++: You can place `void` in front of `main()` to eliminate `return 0;` when you have nothing to return from `main()`. The true ANSI C standard will not enable you to specify a `void main()` function.

Empty Prototype Argument Implies *void*

If you leave argument parentheses empty in your Visual C++ prototype, Visual C++ assumes a `void` argument list. This differs from C. C assumes that you are passing an unspecified number of arguments if you don't specify any arguments in the prototype.

The following prototypes are exactly the same in Visual C++:

```
prBanner();        // No arguments will be passed
```

and

```
prBanner(void);    // No arguments will be passed
```

C++ Is Superior!

Note: You can use unspecified argument lists by typing ... for a prototype's argument list. Day 6's chapter, "Communicating with Functions," explains more about unspecified argument lists as well as variable argument lists.

C++ and Data

Visual C++ treats data differently from regular C in several ways. The next few sections explain how Visual C++ handles data differently from what you are used to.

char Consumes One Byte

All char data consumes one byte of memory. In regular Visual C programs, char data happens to consume one byte of memory as well, but the ANSI C committee does not require that chars take one byte of memory. It makes sense that a character is a single byte when you understand that ASCII characters each consume one byte.

Even though it seems that all characters *should* take a byte, you could never count on that with a regular C compiler. The C compiler that used to come with older C compilers (as opposed to Visual C++ since version 1.0) acted as though char data took two bytes, and sizeof verifies this. Many C compilers have traditionally stored characters as integers. There are times, however, when OOP requires that characters and integers remain separate, and the designers of C++ were much stricter in their definition of character data.

Note: The other data types, such as int and double, are always open to change in future versions of Visual C++, but the char will always consume a single byte.

The program in Listing 2.3 shows that Visual C++ stores character data as a single byte of memory.

Listing 2.3. Looking at the size of chars.

```
1:  // Filename: CHARSIZE.CPP
2:  // Program that prints the size of character data.
3:  #include <stdio.h>
4:  void main()              // No return necessary now
5:  {
6:     // Type cast the sizeof() operator to int for printing
7:     printf("\nThe size of char is %d\n", (int) sizeof(char));
8:  }
```

The size of char is 1

The Location of Variable Definitions

You can define variables anywhere within a Visual C++ program as long as you define the variables before you use them. Consider the program in Listing 2.4.

Listing 2.4. Four variables defined throughout main().

```
1:  // Filename: VARDEF.CPP
2:  // Program that defines four variables in 4 different places
3:  #include <stdio.h>
4:  void main()
5:  {
6:     int n1;     // Define the first variable
7:     n1 = 20;
8:     int n2;     // Define the second variable
9:     n2 = 30;
10:    int n3;     // Define the third variable
11:    n3 = 40;
12:    int avg = (n1 + n2 + n3) / 3;   // Define the last variable
13:    printf("\nThe average is %d\n", avg);
14: }
```

The average is 30

C++ Is Superior!

In most block-structured languages, including C, you can define variables only at the beginning of a block. As you know, a block begins with an opening brace, {, in C, and the same holds true for C++. The program in Listing 2.4 contains variable definitions on lines 6, 8, 10, and 12, with other executable statements in-between.

C++ enables you to define variables throughout a program, but Listing 2.4 is an extreme. For such a simple program, it would probably be clearer and therefore easier to maintain if you defined all four variables at the top of the block. Listing 2.4 is an extreme case to show you what is possible.

> **Where Oh Where?**
>
> There is disagreement among some C++ programmers as to the value of arbitrary variable definitions. Many staunchly hold the view that all variables should be defined together, at the top of every block. In this way, when you maintain the program later, you can easily go back to the variable definition section and find the data type for any variable in the block.
>
> Other C++ programmers feel that a variable should be defined only right before its use. When maintaining a program, you don't have to search back to the beginning of a block to find a variable's data type.
>
> (Still others argue that if you write well-structured OOP programs, with short function listings and well-documented variable names, the location of variable definitions doesn't matter because the definitions will always appear close to their use.)
>
> Being able to define variables close to their initial use does have some OOP advantages as well as the advantages mentioned in the next few paragraphs. The important thing to remember is that there is never one *correct* way to write any program—if you use what is most comfortable and most maintainable for you and other programmers who work with you, that way is usually the best way.

You will most commonly find the defining of variables right before their use in `for` loops (at least until you learn a few OOP concepts later). Consider the following loop:

```
for (int ctr=0; ctr<10; ctr++)
  { printf("Happy Birthday!"); }
```

The ctr variable is defined *inside* the for statement. There is no way to accomplish this in C because no executable statements can appear (or even begin as done here) until all variables in the block are defined. Almost all C++ programmers agree on this usage of variable definition because the ctr variable is a trivial variable, used for the loop's control, so there is no reason to define ctr a long way from the loop itself.

Being able to define variables anywhere before they are used introduces an interesting scope consideration, as Listing 2.5 demonstrates.

Listing 2.5. Considering the scope of free variable definition.

```
 1:    // Filename: SCOPFREE.CPP
 2:    // Illustrates the placement of local variable scope
 3:    #include <stdio.h>
 4:    main()
 5:    {
 6:       int i=10;
 7:       printf("i is %d\n", i);
 8:       // Loop with defined variable follows
 9:       for (int ctr=1; ctr<=5; ctr++)
10:         { printf("ctr is currently %d\n", ctr);
11:           if (ctr != 5)     // Don't print next message if last time
12:             { printf("(and getting larger...)\n"); }
13:         }
14:       // i and ctr are still known here
15:       printf("By the way -- i is still %d, ", i);
16:       printf("and ctr is at %d.\n", ctr);
17:       return 0;
18:    }
```

```
i is 10
ctr is currently 1
(and getting larger...)
ctr is currently 2
(and getting larger...)
ctr is currently 3
(and getting larger...)
ctr is currently 4
(and getting larger...)
ctr is currently 5
By the way -- i is still 10, and ctr is at 6.
```

Both variables, i and ctr, go out of scope at the end of the program, line 18, because that line closes the block to which both variables are local. All local variables, whether defined at the top or in the middle of a block, lose their scope at the end of the block. Some beginning C++ programmers mistakenly believe that `ctr` goes out of scope at line 13 because line 13 ends the `for` loop's block. However, `ctr` is defined before the `for` loop's block even begins, so it remains visible after the loop ends.

> **DO** **DON'T**
>
> **DO** define `for` loop variables within the `for` loop when you don't need those same variables before the `for` loop for something else.
>
> **DON'T** overdo the freedom of variable definition; until you decide which method is best for you, and until you learn a little more about OOP, continue defining variables at the top of code blocks (except minor loop variables) until you are comfortable with moving the placement of variable definitions.

Typecasting Isn't Just for Hollywood

C++ provides for a new typecasting syntax. The syntax for typecasting C data was rather confusing because you had to put the new data type inside parentheses before the value being typecast. In other words, to convert an `int` to a `float`, C required this:

```
x = (float)i;
```

C++ still supports that syntax, but C++ also supports a more convenient function-call syntax that makes typecasts look just like function calls. The previous statement can be written like this in C++:

```
x = float(i);
```

You know that `float` is not a function name, despite the look of this statement. In Day 12's chapter, "Extending Operator Overloads," you will learn how to write your own typecasting functions using some OOP components of C++. To support writing your own typecasting, the designers of C++ had to change the syntax of typecasting to make typecasting look more like the function calls you are already used to.

The Scope Resolution Operator, ::

Just when you thought you had learned all the operators a language (C) could possibly offer, C++ walks in with several additional operators. One of them, the *scope resolution operator,* provides a way for you to resolve the scope of different variable combinations.

The scope resolution operator is made up of back-to-back colons, ::. As with most features of C++, the scope resolution operator has many OOP uses, but non-OOP programmers can use the operator also.

Usually, if you have two variables with the same name, one global and one local, the local variable takes priority over the global variable. Listing 2.6 shows what happens without the scope resolution operator.

Listing 2.6. The most local variable takes priority.

```
1:  // Filename: MOSTLOC.CPP
2:  // The most local variable has priority.
3:  #include <stdio.h>
4:  // Define a global variable
5:  int aVar = 10;
6:  main()
7:  {
8:     int aVar = 25;    // Local variable
9:     // Print aVar to see which one is used
10:    printf("aVar is %d\n", aVar);
11:    return 0;
12: }
```

aVar is 25

Line 8 defines a second aVar variable, local to main(). The global variable holds a 10 while the local variable holds a 25. Because the most local variable always takes priority over a global variable with the same name, the value of the local variable prints in line 10.

The scope resolution operator tells C++ to use the global variable whenever a local and a global variable have the same name. (There are more important OOP uses of :: that you'll read about later.) Therefore, if you want the value of a global variable to take precedence over the local variable, precede the variable with :: as done in Listing 2.7.

Listing 2.7. Using :: to override the scope.

```
1:  // Filename: GLOBSCOP.CPP
2:  // Using the scope resolution operator to override local scope
3:  #include <stdio.h>
4:  // Define a global variable
```

continues

Day 2: C++ Is Superior!

Listing 2.7. continued

```
5:    int aVar = 10;
6:    main()
7:    {
8:      int aVar = 25;    // Local variable
9:      // Print aVar to see which one is used
10:     printf("aVar is %d\n", ::aVar);  // Notice before aVar!
11:     return 0;
12:   }
```

```
aVar is 10
```

You can see from the output that the global variable's value overrides that of the local variable due to the scope resolution operator before aVar's name in line 10.

Note: When you compile the program in Listing 2.7, Visual C++ might display a warning telling you that you've defined a variable, aVar, but never used it. Visual C++ is referring to the *local* variable aVar, and the compiler is correct. The scope resolution operator causes the global aVar to print, and the local aVar is completely ignored after its definition on line 8.

Scoping of Global Constants

The const keyword was introduced in an early version of C++. By using const, you can define variables whose values cannot change in the program; in other words, const values can never appear on the left side of an equals sign (known as an *lvalue*) or any other position in a program that might change (such as the object of an increment or decrement operator).

Note: const was not originally available in C. After const's use in C++, the ANSI C committee decided to add it to C.

When you define a global const value, the const value has *internal linkage.* Internal linkage is a fancy name that means the value has *file scope,* or is known for the rest of the file in which it is defined. Consider Listing 2.8, which defines a global const value and uses that same value in fun() without passing or defining the value again inside fun().

Type Listing 2.8. const values have file scope.

```
1:  // Filename: CONST1.CPP
2:  // Both main() and fun() share the same const value
3:  #include <stdio.h>
4:
5:  float fun(float a, float b);    // Prototype
6:
7:  const float cFact = .45;
8:  main()
9:  {
10:    float mainA = 10, mainB = 20;
11:    float factAns;
12:    // Call a function that uses global constant
13:    factAns = fun(mainA, mainB);
14:    printf("The resulting factor is %.2f.\n", factAns);
15:
16:    return 0;
17: }
18:
19: float fun(float a, float b)
20: {
21:    float temp;
22:    temp = (a + b) * cFact;
23:    return temp;
24: }
```

The resulting factor is 13.50.

Listing 2.8 might seem trivial if you understand the difference between global and local data (and you should, as Day 1's chapter, "The C++ Phenomenon," pointed out). The const value in line 7, cFact, can be used *only* in this source file, not in any other file that you link this code to. In other words, if you were to put fun() into its own file, compile the two modules separately, then link them together, the linker would complain because fun() could not use main()'s cFact.

C++ Is Superior!

The reason the file scope of const is worth pointing out is that C programmers who use const are used to const values having *external linkage,* meaning that the const values can be used inside other code linked to the program without being redefined or passed. In C++, if you want to share const values among several different compile modules that you will eventually link together, you must declare each of the const values in the linked modules as external variables (with the extern keyword).

> **Note:** By giving global const values internal linkage, Visual C++ keeps name clashes from occurring. If you are writing a large program with a team of programmers as is often the case in data processing departments, you can safely define global const values in your code without fearing that another programmer's global const value of the same name will interfere.

Listing 2.9 shows a stand-alone function that is separately compiled and linked to other code. The value of cAmt is defined elsewhere in one of the other modules that will eventually be linked to saFun().

Listing 2.9. A function that relies on another function to initialize cAmt.

```
1:  // Filename: CONST2.CPP
2:  // A stand-alone function that uses another
3:  // function's global const value
4:  #include <stdio.h>
5:
6:  extern int cAmt;
7:  int saFun(int i, float x)
8:  {
9:     if (float(i) > x)
10:       { return cAmt; }
11:    else
12:       { return i; }
13: }
```

> **Note:** Day 14's chapter, "Loose Ends: *static* and Larger Programs," describes how to go about compiling, linking, and running separate code modules using Visual C++'s project manager.

Throw Out #*define*

Now that you are used to using #define, forget about ever using #define again! C++ provides two much better alternatives to #define: const and *inline functions*.

const Replaces Simple #*define* Constants

The preceding section discussed const, the first replacement of the #define directive. Instead of defining constants with #define like

```
#define LIMIT 100
```

you can use const to define constants (also known as *naming constants*) like this:

```
const int LIMIT = 100;
```

If you are defining integer constants, you don't have to specify the int keyword. Therefore, this statement is equivalent to the preceding const statement:

```
const LIMIT = 100;
```

> **Be *con*stantly Clear!**
>
> Although you don't have to specify int if your const value is an integer, go ahead and explicitly state that the constant will be integer.
>
> Today's better programmers know that clear code produces more readable and maintainable code. If you explicitly define a constant as int even when you do not have to, you let the next person who maintains your code know that you intended for the constant to be an integer and you didn't leave out the data type accidentally (thereby creating possible data type errors later).

You can define any kind of variable as a constant. The following statement defines a constant array that holds a string:

```
const char myName[] = "Heath Barkley";
```

Visual C++ requires that you give the constant an initial value. After all, after the constant is created, nothing you do in the rest of the program can change it. If you didn't specify an initial value, the constant would *never* have another chance at initialization.

C++ Is Superior!

Unlike #define constants, the const constants have specific data types, so the C++ compiler can perform more stringent type-checking. Whereas #define directives blindly search and *replace* code, defining const variables (a seemingly contradictory statement!) creates better compile-time checking. More important, the const variables all have regular local or global scope depending on where you define them. #define values are always globally changed from the point of #define down in the source file.

Perhaps the most important reason to avoid #define is that it changes your source code after the code leaves your editor and heads for the compiler. What you saw is *not* what the compiler sees with #define. Listing 2.10 demonstrates a potential maintenance problem with #define.

Listing 2.10. Be careful when using #define.

```
 1:  // Filename: DEFPROB1.CPP
 2:  // Demonstrates a potential problem with #define
 3:  #include <stdio.h>
 4:
 5:  main()
 6:  {
 7:    int a = 1;
 8:    #define TOT1 a + a
 9:    #define TOT2 TOT1 - TOT1
10:    printf("TOT2 is %d\n", TOT2);   // Probably not what you expect!
11:
12:    return 0;
13: }
```

Before you're told the output of this seemingly simple program, what do you think is printed at line 10? Be careful, and look again.

It would first appear that this is printed:

TOT2 is 0

That's not the case, however. If you thought that a 0 would print for the value of TOT2, you are treating TOT2 as if it were a variable, but it is not. #define causes even the best programmers to get confused in such situations. Here is the output from the program:

TOT2 is 2

Here is what Visual C++ sees in place of your line 10:

printf("TOT2 is %d\n", a + a - a + a);

The precedence of addition and subtraction operators is the same for each. a plus a equals 2, then a is subtracted from the 2 giving 1, then one last a is added to result in the printed value of 2.

Listing 2.11 is just like Listing 2.10, except `const` replaces the two `#defines`.

Listing 2.11. const does not lend itself to ambiguity as does #define.

```
1:  // Filename: DEFCOR1.CPP
2:  // Correcting the potential problem with const
3:  #include <stdio.h>
4:
5:  main()
6:  {
7:     int a = 1;
8:     const TOT1 = a + a;
9:     const TOT2 = TOT1 - TOT1;
10:    printf("TOT2 is %d\n", TOT2);    // That's better!
11:
12:    return 0;
13: }
```

TOT2 is 0

The reason Listing 2.11 produces correct results is that `const` defines two variables that behave like variables, and the compiler sees exactly what you see on line 10. No preprocessor came in behind your back and changed the source code.

`const` values are great to use for array subscripts when defining arrays. Consider the following code:

```
#include <stdio.h>
main()
{
  const employees = 230;
  char * empNames[employees];    // Reserve the names
  float salaries[employees];     // Reserve the salaries
// and so on...
```

Whenever the rest of the program needs to step through the array values, you can now use `employees` for the boundary, such as

```
for (ctr=0; ctr<employees; ctr++)
```

C++ Is Superior!

instead of repeating the numeric literal 230 throughout the program. If the number of employees changes, you only have to change the const statement instead of searching through the program for all references to 230.

> **Note:** Many Visual C++ programmers spell const variable names with all uppercase letters, just as they learned with C #define constants. The uppercase letters warn you that you cannot assign values to the const variables later.

inline Functions Improve on *#define* Macros

The danger of #define constants can be seen even further when you use #define to define parameterized macros. Listing 2.12 shows a program with a parameterized macro that doubles whatever value is sent to the macro.

Listing 2.12. Program that uses a parameterized #define to double values.

```
 1:  // Filename: DOUBI.CPP
 2:  // Includes a macro to double values
 3:  #include <stdio.h>
 4:
 5:  #define doub(x) x * 2
 6:
 7:  main()
 8:  {
 9:    for (int i=1; i<=5; i++)
10:      { printf("%d doubled is %d.\n", i, doub(i)); }
11:
12:    return 0;
13:  }
```

```
1 doubled is 2.
2 doubled is 4.
3 doubled is 6.
4 doubled is 8.
5 doubled is 10.
```

48

Analysis The simple #define macro used in this program seems innocent enough. Whatever value is sent to doub's parameter x is doubled by the macro. These types of macros are often used to save the programming time and overhead of calling a separate function to perform a simple routine.

It is important to realize that all macros expand *inline* inside the program. In other words, the printf() statement does not look to the compiler the way you type it in line 10. Rather than

doub(i)

being sent to the compiler at the end of the printf(),

i * 2

is sent, because #define ensures that the occurrence of doub() is turned into the macro code.

Given this background, what do you think will print in the following printf()?

printf("1 + 2 doubled is %d.". doub(1 + 2));

Be very careful! It looks as though a 6 will print because 1 + 2 doubled is 6. Not so, according to the doub() macro! You must always keep in mind that a #define's code expands inline, and what you type is not what the compiler sees. Here is what the compiler sees after #define does its macro expansion:

printf("1 + 2 doubled is %d.". 1 + 2 * 2);

And here is what would print from this statement:

1 + 2 doubled is 5.

The precedence of operators forces the multiplication to calculate before the addition. Therefore, the 2 * 2 first produces 4, then a 1 is added to produce the 5.

Note: If you have never used parameterized #define directives before, consider yourself lucky because you have less to unlearn!

Despite the drawbacks of parameterized macros, many programmers use them for efficiency. When a program must call a function, lots of overhead is spent setting up return values and passing arguments. Instead of writing a separate routine for simple

C++ Is Superior!

functions, programmers can save function overhead by writing parameterized `#define` macros. The code within the macros will be expanded, as shown here, and no function will be called.

What do you do? Give up efficiency and use function calls, or live with the dangerous side effects that defined macros provide? With C++, you don't have to do either. By writing functions where you would have written parameterized macros before, and by using the `inline` keyword that tells Visual C++ to inline the function if possible, you get efficiency and safety at the same time.

To use `inline`, insert it before any function definition that you want to be expanded inline. Listing 2.13 shows an improved doubling routine specified as an inline function rather than as a macro. The inlined function offers all the advantages of macros without the side effects. The listing shows that the `inline` function works for single values as well as for expressions such as 1 + 2.

Listing 2.13. Using `inline` functions for efficiency.

```
 1: // Filename: DOUBINLN.CPP
 2: // Includes a macro to double values
 3: #include <stdio.h>
 4:
 5: inline doub(int x)
 6: {
 7:    return x * 2;
 8: }
 9:
10: main()
11: {
12:    for (int i=1; i<=5; i++)
13:       { printf("%d doubled is %d.\n", i, doub(i)); }
14:    printf("1 + 2 doubled is %d.\n", doub(1 + 2));
15:
16:    return 0;
17: }
```

```
1 doubled is 2.
2 doubled is 4.
3 doubled is 6.
4 doubled is 8.
5 doubled is 10.
1 + 2 doubled is 6.
```

Analysis: Listing 2.13 might not look right to you if you are used to seeing the `main()` function first in a C or C++ program. `main()` is usually placed first in a program. Although `main()`'s placement is not mandatory, `main()` is always the first function that executes, and consistent programmers like to list `main()` first in programs. A program with `inline` functions, however, cannot have `main()` listed first. An `inline` function must be completely defined before it can be called.

Most Visual C++ programmers put their `inline` functions in a header file and `#include` the header before `main()`. By including the header file, `main()` can still *look* as though it comes first in the program although the `inline` functions will actually be defined first.

Note: The placement of `main()` at the beginning of the program will become less and less important as you progress throughout this book. When you make data active with OOP, the data's code (yes, data can have code in Visual C++!) is almost as important, and many times more important, than the code in `main()`.

Perhaps the only *disadvantage* to using `inline` is that it is a request to Visual C++ but not an order. Visual C++ is free to ignore your inline request and treat the function as if it were a regular function with function call overhead. Therefore, if you use `inline` to gain efficiency (so that no real function calls take place, but the function's code is expanded inline where the function is called), Visual C++ might ignore the request, and you will not gain the efficiency.

When Visual C++ will ignore an `inline` request is difficult to determine. If your `inline` function is eight or more lines long, Visual C++ usually decides to ignore the `inline` request. If the function has any kind of looping statement, Visual C++ will probably refuse to inline the function. Visual C++ never inlines recursive functions either.

If Visual C++ did inline all of your inline requests, your code could grow to a tremendous size. All inline function calls would expand to the size of the entire function being called. If your Visual C++ program calls an inline function 20 times throughout the code, Visual C++ has to place 20 occurrences of the function throughout the code.

C++ Is Superior!

Syntax

The *inline* Function

`inline functionName(optionalArguments)`

To make a function inline, you only have to precede the function's regular definition with `inline`. The function can still receive arguments and return values. All `inline` functions must appear in full before the code that calls them.

Example

```
// Here is an inline function
inline int GetProd(int n1, int n2, int n3, int n4)
{
  int tot;
  tot = n1 * n2 * n3 * n4;
  return tot;
}
```

DO / DON'T

DO use `const` when naming constants in your program.

DO use `const` values for array subscripts when defining arrays.

DO remember to use the equals sign after a `const` variable's definition. `#define` does not enable you to put an equals sign because no assignment is made with `#define`.

DO always specify an initial value for `const` variables. If you don't, Visual C++ assumes an initial value of zero, and you can never change the value later (because it's a constant).

DO use inline functions when you want short functions to execute quickly and efficiently.

DON'T use `#define` because it changes your source code and too many problems can develop, especially when defining parameterized macros.

DON'T use inline functions if memory and disk space are at a premium. However, adding more memory and disk space to your PC never hurts either. Generally, you can and should use inline functions wherever you would use parameterized `#define` macros.

DON'T expect Visual C++ to respect all of your `inline` requests; however, if Visual C++ does not decide to inline a function or two, it generally has good reason to leave the function alone.

You might think that as long as you are aware of #define's potential problems, you can take the needed steps to avoid those problems. It's true that if you were extremely careful, you could use #define the proper way, but why bother with #define when using const and inline functions takes care of everything? You might as well use the C++-preferred way and get used to const and inlines; you don't have time to waste on bugs because there are too many programs waiting to be written!

Note: There is another advantage that inline functions offer over parameterized macros. In Day 7's chapter, "Overloaded Functions Lessen Your Load," you'll learn how to write *overloaded functions*. Overloaded functions save you programming time by enabling you to reuse function code for different types of arguments. You cannot overload parameterized #define macros.

Some Useful Visual C++ Identifiers

Visual C++ comes supplied with several identifiers that you can often use in your programs. These predefined identifiers are sometimes called *symbolic constants*. Table 2.1 lists some of the more useful identifiers. (The identifiers are just like global variables that you can use—but not change—in your programs.)

Table 2.1. Some useful predefined Visual C++ identifiers.

Identifier Name	Type	Description
__DATE__	String	Date when the source file is processed.
__FILE__	String	Name of the current source file (including disk name). __FILE__ changes whenever another #include runs.
__LINE__	Decimal	The number (beginning with 1) of the current source file that contains __LINE__.
__TIME__	String	Time when the preprocessor began processing this source file.

C++ Is Superior!

Note: There are many intrinsic Visual C++ time and date functions (such as `time()`) that return the date and time that a program runs; the `__DATE__` and `__TIME__` identifiers, however, use only compile-time values. Check your Visual C++ language reference manuals for more details on internal time and date functions.

Listing 2.14 uses the `__TIME__` and `__DATE__` identifiers to print the time and date of compilation, and functions to print the run time and run date.

Listing 2.14. Determining the date and time of compilation.

```
 1: // Filename: DATETIME.CPP
 2: // Program that uses __DATE__ and __TIME__ identifiers
 3: #include <stdio.h>      // For printf()
 4: #include <time.h>       // For date and time functions
 5: main()
 6: {
 7:   char cDate[] = __DATE__;  // Define and initialize both the
 8:   char cTime[] = __TIME__;  // date and time arrays
 9:   printf("This code was compiled at %s on %s.\n", cTime, cDate);
10:
11:   // Find the current run time and date
12:   time_t t;  // Required to store internal date
13:   time(&t);  // Must pass by address to fill time structure
14:   printf("This program was run at %s.\n", ctime(&t));
15:
16:   return 0;
17: }
```

This code was compiled at 09:02:40 on Jan 12 1994.
This program was run at Fri Oct 6 16:13:45 1994.

Notice that the `__DATE__` and `__TIME__` identifiers return strings that you store in arrays and that you treat just like any other string literals in your programs. This program initializes and stores the date and time in two arrays at lines 7 and 8.

The majority of the program is setting up C-like statements. The program demonstrates that all the usual C functions work as-is inside your Visual C++ programs. Two

header files included in lines 3 and 4 support the functions used in the program. (Be careful when using // C++ comments to the right of #include statements if you ever use a compiler other than Visual C++; not all C++ preprocessors recognize C++ comments to the right of the C-like directives.)

Lines 5 through 17 do nothing that you can't do with regular C. As you might or might not know from previous Microsoft C programming, you must define a special time_t structure variable before calling the functions that fill that structure with date and time values. Of course, thanks to Visual C++, line 12 doesn't need the struct keyword. The declarations for the time structures appear in the TIME.H header file.

Listing 2.15 uses the two identifiers __LINE__ and __FILE__. Often, Visual C++ programmers use these identifiers for debugging programs. If you are producing several lines of output throughout a program, you might want to print the __LINE__ value every once in a while so that you can tell from the program's output which source code lines produced the output. The __FILE__ can help find lost source files. Although most Visual C++ programmers give their compiled programs the same name as the source code (such as PROG.EXE and PROG.CPP), some don't. There is also the matter of dealing with several source files compiled together. While debugging large programs, you might want to print the name of each source file being processed. __FILE__ enables you to do just that.

Listing 2.15. Using __LINE__ and __FILE__.

```
 1:  // Filename: LINEFILE.CPP
 2:  // Program that uses __LINE__ and __FILE__ identifiers
 3:  #include <stdio.h>     // For printf()
 4:
 5:  main()
 6:  {
 7:     printf("Line %d being processed...\n", __LINE__);
 8:     printf("This source code is named %s.\n", __FILE__);
 9:     printf("Line %d being processed...\n", __LINE__);
10:
11:
12:     return 0;
13:  }
```

```
Line 7 being processed...
This source code is named C\:LINEFILE.CPP.
Line 9 being processed...
```

C++ Is Superior!

> **Note:** You don't have to include a header file for the Visual C++ predefined identifiers. The identifiers are available to all programs.

DO / DON'T

DO use `__LINE__` during debugging if you want to know when certain lines are executing. (Visual C++'s on-line debugger is better to use, but `__LINE__` is especially helpful to print line numbers on output that goes to paper.)

DON'T use `__DATE__` and `__TIME__` to print the *current* date or time when the program runs. All the identifiers are set to compile-time values, not runtime values.

DON'T ever define your own variables or constants with the same names as the predefined identifiers.

Summary

This chapter gave you a taste of the differences in C++ over C. Throughout this book, as you learn OOP you will see why the designers of Visual C++ chose to include the features discussed here. Nevertheless, even if you never learn OOP, the material in this chapter is useful and should help improve your code over regular C code.

From comments to `inline` functions, the goal of Visual C++ is to make your programming easier, not harder. Whereas some of the differences between C++ and C are trivial (such as the linkage of global `const` values), most help you by speeding your program development.

The next chapter dives into Visual C++'s I/O (input/output) features. Visual C++ is a language that takes I/O to levels not achievable in C. You will find that I/O is much simpler in Visual C++.

Q&A

Q. How can regular C comments get you in trouble?

A. The problem with the enclosing /* and */ is that you cannot nest them. During debugging sessions, programmers like to comment out the correctly working code to help spot code with errors. They also like to comment out the code with errors to test the rest of the program for consistency. When you place C-style comments to the right of statements, you cannot just insert an opening comment, /*, and then several lines later insert the closing comment, */, and expect Visual C++ to work things out.

When using the C++ comment, you only have to insert // at the beginning of every line you want to comment out regardless of what else is on the line.

Q. How does C++ save you time when writing with struct, enum, and union?

A. You don't have to repeat the struct, enum, or union keywords when defining variables. The data type, such as your structure, is almost a part of the Visual C++ language after you declare what the aggregate data type looks like.

Q. Are C++'s strict prototype requirements a drawback to using C++?

A. Not at all. Despite the extra work needed to prototype every function and include all needed header files, prototypes are for your own good. By prototyping your functions, you tell Visual C++ exactly how you want to execute those functions later. If you break this contract by passing to a function data types that you should not, Visual C++ will not want to compile the program.

Q. Why is inline only a suggestion to Visual C++?

A. If the body of an inline function does too much, Visual C++ makes an executive order and ignores your inline request. The reason that you specify inline is to save function call overhead without letting the drawbacks of parameterized macros creep into your code. If the function is too long or complicated, that long or complicated code would have to be placed inline everywhere the function is called. Making such a replacement could make the code too large, so inline is only a hint to Visual C++ (as is register if you are familiar with that) that you want a function inlined where it is called.

Day 2: C++ Is Superior!

Workshop

The Workshop offers quiz questions and exercises to hone your skills and give you feedback on today's lesson. You'll find some proposed answers in Appendix D.

Quiz

1. A C++ comment begins with `//`. What ends a C++ comment?
2. What is a function's signature?
3. True or False: The following function prototypes are equivalent:

    ```
    float fun(int a, float b, char * c);
    ```

    and

    ```
    float fun(int, float, char *);
    ```

4. True or False: The following functions' first lines are equivalent:

    ```
    float fun(int a, float b, char * c)
    ```

    and

    ```
    float fun(int, float, char *)
    ```

5. True or False: Visual C++ considers the following prototypes equivalent:

    ```
    int fun();
    ```

    and

    ```
    int fun(void);
    ```

6. What two predefined identifiers are useful for debugging?
7. If a program is compiled on January 1, 1994, and is run on September 7, 1994, what value would the program's `__DATE__` identifier produce?

Exercises

1. Rewrite the following code with the two `printf()`s commented out:

    ```
    #include <stdio.h>
    main()
    {
    ```

```
    printf("Welcome to Visual C++.\n");   // Output
    printf("The power is yours!\n");
    return 0;
}
```

2. Rewrite the following code without using #define:

```
// Filename: NODEFINE.CPP
#include <stdio.h>
#define PI 3.14159
#define cirArea(r) PI * (r * r)

main()
{
  float radius;
  printf("What is the circle's radius in inches? ");
  scanf(" %f", &radius);
  printf("The area of the circle is %.2f inches.\n",
cirArea(radius));

  return 0;
}
```

DAY 3

Simple I/O

Simple I/O

Input and output, or *I/O*, occur when you send data from the computer to an output device such as a printer, or when your computer receives data from an input device such as a keyboard or disk.

I/O is nothing new to you, but the way Visual C++ handles I/O will be new. Visual C++ provides one of the easiest I/O systems available in any language. What's more, after you learn more about OOP, you'll be able to extend Visual C++'s I/O capabilities so that they behave exactly the way you want them to, and so that they work with your own data types.

Although some of Visual C++'s I/O syntax will be new to you, after you get used to it, you'll wonder how you ever wrote a program without it. You can easily format your output using simple Visual C++ specifiers. Today, you learn about the following topics:

- Visual C++ stream I/O
- Outputting with cout <<
- Inputting with cin >>
- Error displaying with cerr <<
- The I/O manipulators and format flags

Output Your Data with *cout* and <<

Before going any further, get used to using the following header file at the top of all your Visual C++ programs:

```
#include <iostream.h>
```

IOSTREAM.H is the header file that replaces STDIO.H in Visual C++. If you use a function such as gets() (but there is almost always a better Visual C++ method of I/O than C's old I/O functions), you'll have to include STDIO.H for those functions. However, for the C++ I/O to work the way this chapter explains, you'll want to include IOSTREAM.H in every Visual C++ program you write (before main() is the best place to include the file).

You are used to using the printf() function for output. Instead of using a function, Visual C++ uses an *object*. Yes, that's the same object as in *object-oriented programming*, but you don't have to understand objects to use Visual C++'s output object. The name of Visual C++'s output object is cout.

> **Note:** For the time being, think of cout as being your screen. Actually, cout might be your screen, your printer, or anywhere else you redirect your computer's standard output through DOS. If you are unfamiliar with redirecting of output, you're not missing much—there now are better ways to route output to various devices that you'll learn about throughout this book.

Figure 3.1 simplifies the concept of cout as much as possible. If you want to send something to your screen, whether that something is a string, an integer, or a floating-point value, send that data to cout. Figure 3.1 also shows a new Visual C++ operator not found in the C language. The << operator is called the *inserter* operator, but C++ programmers rarely call it that. (Many programmers talk as if cout is the output operator, as in "Next, you *cout* the value.")

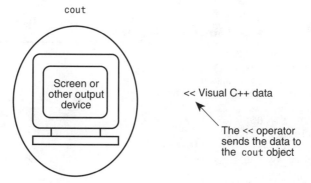

Figure 3.1. The screen is the cout object.

As long as you think of your screen as being the cout object, and as long as you know that the inserter operator, <<, is the output operator, you can send data to the screen by routing the data into the cout object using <<. You might have seen << used as the C bitwise left-shift operator; << is still the bitwise left-shift operator in Visual C++, but << is also used for output. Visual C++ decides the correct usage of << from the context in which you use it.

Simple I/O

For example, the following statement prints `I'm learning OOP!` on-screen:

`cout << "I'm learning OOP!";`

> **Note:** Can't you just picture Visual C++ sending the message `I am learning OOP!` to the cout object? The cout is the screen, so the << operator sends that message directly to the screen. The format of `cout` and `<<` looks just like their resulting actions.

You already know that printing this same message in C is about as easy. Here is a `printf()` that does just that:

`printf("I'm learning OOP!");`

The big difference and advantage of cout comes to light when you print values other than strings. With `printf()` you must specify format codes such as `%d` and `%f`. You don't need to specify formats when outputting with cout. Consider the program in Listing 3.1.

Listing 3.1. Output with cout.

```
 1:  // Filename: COUT1ST.CPP
 2:  // Demonstrates cout
 3:  #include <iostream.h>
 4:  main()
 5:  {
 6:     int i = 65;
 7:     float f = 1.234567;
 8:     double d = -9485.675544;
 9:     cout << "Here is i: ";
10:     cout << i;
11:     cout << "\n";
12:     cout << "Here is f: ";
13:     cout << f;
14:     cout << "\n";
15:     cout << "Here is d: ";
16:     cout << d;
17:     cout << "\n";
18:     return 0;
19:  }
```

```
Here is i: 65
Here is f: 1.23457
Here is d: -9485.68
```

The \n works in Visual C++ just as it does in C and sends the cursor to the next line.

The nice thing about cout is that you don't have to specify %d and %f when printing numeric values. More important, you can combine the output of more than one value on a single line. Listing 3.2 illustrates how you can group the cout in Listing 3.1 into a more compact form.

Listing 3.2. Combining the output.

```
1:  // Filename: COUT2ND.CPP
2:  // Demonstrates grouped cout
3:  #include <iostream.h>
4:  main()
5:  {
6:     int i = 65;
7:     float f = 1.234567;
8:     double d = -9485.675544;
9:     cout << "Here is i: " << i << "\n";
10:    cout << "Here is f: " << f << "\n";
11:    cout << "Here is d: " << d << "\n";
12:    return 0;
13: }
```

```
Here is i: 65
Here is f: 1.23457
Here is d: -9485.68
```

Not only does this syntax take fewer lines of code, but it is easier to understand. You can group as many output values as you like into the cout object. Later sections in this chapter will show you how to control the output format, such as the number of decimal places printed.

DO	DON'T

DO include IOSTREAM.H in all your Visual C++ programs that take advantage of C++ input/output.

DO use cout and the inserter operator, <<, for all your Visual C++ output.

> **DON'T** use format specifiers such as `%f` with `cout`. There are ways to control formatted output, but `cout` usually guesses correctly as to how you want your data to look.

Input Is Just as Easy with *cin* and >>

Toss away `scanf()`! Although most seasoned C programmers stop using `scanf()` when they collect better input routines from bulletin boards, from friends, and when they write their own, C programmers still throw in a `scanf()` here and there. Visual C++ rises above the rigors of `scanf()` and finally makes input as easy as output with the `cin` object and the *extractor* operator, >>.

Just as you can picture `cout` as being the screen, `cin` is your keyboard. More accurately, `cin` is the standard input device usually routed to your keyboard unless you change that routing through DOS (which we rarely do anymore). Figure 3.2 illustrates `cin` and >>. Notice the data-flow direction indicated by the >>—data is going from the keyboard into variables.

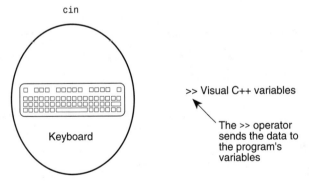

Figure 3.2. The keyboard is the `cin` object.

Suppose that you needed to ask the user for an inventory quantity. Here is how you can do that:

```
int quant;
cout << "How many items are in the inventory? ";
cin >> quant;
```

The third line takes the keyboard input (the `cin` object) and sends the keyboard's data to the quant variable. If the variable is floating-point, there is no difference. Consider this:

```
float price;
cout << "How much does the item cost? ";
cin >> price;
```

Visual C++ stores whatever the user enters for the price in `price`. You can group together more than one input variable using a single `cin`, as Listing 3.3 shows.

Listing 3.3. Input with `cin`.

```
 1:  // Filename: MULTICIN.CPP
 2:  #include <iostream.h>
 3:  main()
 4:  {
 5:    int quant;
 6:    float price;
 7:    cout << "What is the number and price? ";
 8:    cin >> quant >> price;   // Combine the input with caution!
 9:    cout << "\n\nNumber: " << quant << "\nPrice: " << price << "\n";
10:    return 0;
11: }
```

What is the number and price? **3 4.56**

Number: 3
Price: 4.56

Requesting more than one input value in a single `cin` can be confusing to the user, so avoid doing this. The user might not separate the two values by a whitespace (a space, an Enter, or a tab) and might try to put commas between the values, which would mess up the input.

`cin` is not capable of inputting strings of more than one word. Although a string ends with a null terminating zero, `cin` only accepts strings up to the first space. The space tells `cin` (arguably incorrectly) that the current string ends, and then Visual C++ saves the rest of the string in the input buffer until the next `cin` executes. There are ways to input strings that contain spaces; you'll see how later in this chapter.

Simple I/O

> **DO** use `cin` and the extractor operator, `>>`, for your Visual C++ input.
>
> **DON'T** group more than one input value together. If you want to ask the user for three values, use three separate `cin` statements.
>
> **DON'T** use `cin` to input strings that might have spaces in them (most do).

How to Display Error Messages

In a perfect world, with perfect programmers, perfect programs, and perfect users, you could skip this section. Nevertheless, you are well aware of the importance of good error checking and helpful, clear, and concise error messages when appropriate.

Most computer applications in use today consist of error-checking and error-message-handling code. Some estimate that 35 percent of the lines in all programs used today are error checks and handling for when things go wrong at the user's end. Throughout this book, you'll see why OOP is so advantageous to programmers. Petty details of programming are lifted off your programming back so that you can concentrate on the application and not as much on error checking and other details.

You still have to check for errors, but you can teach your data to check itself through OOP practices you'll learn a little later. You'll find that the `main()` function and all the functions that `main()` calls shrink dramatically in size when you move to object-oriented programming because your data takes over a lot of tedious tasks and your code is not as burdened with mundane tasks such as user-input checking.

Nevertheless, *somewhere* in your programs, you'll have to display warnings and errors to your users. When you write the code for your active data objects, you'll have to write the output statements that display the errors. OOP, however, enables you to write this kind of code once, and your data will automatically trigger that code when needed.

Rather than `cout`, most Visual C++ programmers route their error messages to the `cerr` object. `cerr`, which is the screen, works just like `cout`. (`cerr` is always unbuffered, in case you are interested. Being unbuffered means that your user sees the error as soon as it's generated, not later when it might be too late as with buffered output.)

Suppose that you wanted to calculate an average price for the user, but the user's input wouldn't enable you to (you cannot divide by zero). The following code checks the user's input value and prints an error message accordingly:

```
cout << "What was the total dollar amount of last month's sales? ";
cin >> sales;
cout << "How many units did you sell? ";
cin >> num;
if (num == 0)
   { cerr << "The average cannot be computed.\n"; }
else
   { avgSales = sales / num;
     cout << "The average selling price per unit was ";
     cout << avgSales << "\n";
   }
```

Of course, the program could have sent the error to `cout`. However, just in case the user routed the standard output to another device, `cerr` always prints to the screen so that the user can see the message immediately. `cerr` is equivalent in every way to C's `stderr`.

Note: A fourth I/O object named `clog` is sometimes used for error messages. `clog`, however, is buffered, and it's possible that error messages might not display if a serious error occurs. The error itself might involve the output device or put the computer in an infinite loop, and the buffered `clog` error message might never get displayed. Always use `cerr` and you won't have the problem.

DO / DON'T

DO use the unbuffered `cerr` for displaying error messages.

DON'T use `clog` because the buffering can keep error messages from displaying.

Using the I/O Objects: *cout, cin,* and *cerr*

```
cout << dataValue [<< formatSpecifiers] [<< dataValue...];
cin >> variable [<< formatSpecifiers] [>> variable...];
cerr << errorMessage [<< formatSpecifiers] [<< errorMessage];
```

You can follow the << or >> with multiple values to group output and input into single statements, but it is generally agreed that you should group only output and not more than one input value together.

Day 3: Simple I/O

You do not have to use any format specifiers. You can control the way the data is output or input by inserting data-manipulating objects and format control before the data being input or output. If you do not specify any formatting, Visual C++ displays the data in its native format, and often no format control is necessary.

Example

```
// Filename: IOTHREE.CPP
// Demonstrates the I/O objects and operators
#include <iostream.h>
#include <stdlib.h>
// stdlib.h has prototype for exit()
main()
{
  int age;
  cout << "How old are you? ";         // Ask a question
  cin >> age;
  if ((age < 0) || (age > 150))        // Check for extremes
    { cerr << "You can't be that age!\n";
      exit(1);   // Stop program
    }
  if (age < 18)
    {cout << "Go to school.\n"; }
  else
    { cout << "Go to work.\n"; }
  return 0;
}
```

What's Down the Road?

The most important reason to switch to Visual C++'s I/O is not its ease of use but the extensibility of the I/O objects and operators. You can set up the operators, using the object-oriented capabilities that you'll learn throughout this book, so that they work on your own data types and behave exactly as you want them to behave.

What if you want to send the contents of a huge structure to the screen? Suppose you wanted to print the contents of this structure:

```
struct Person {
  char    last[15];
  char    first[15];
  int     age;
  double  salary;
  int     dependents;
  char    address[25];
  char    city[15];
  char    state[3];
```

```
    char    zip[6];
    long    yearBegan;
    int     extension;
    int     officeNumber;
} employee[1000];    // Defines 1,000 employee records
```

Normally, you would call a function to display each member in the structure variable being printed. In Visual C++, however, you have to do only this:

```
cin >> employee[i];    // Get the next employee's data
```

That single `cin` prompts the user for each member and retrieves the user's input. It can even check for input errors and display error messages if needed!

Obviously, Visual C++ cannot read your mind; you have to set up `cin` and `>>` so that they behave the way you want them to. On Days 11 and 12, you'll learn how to extend the way Visual C++ operators work and make them work seamlessly with your own data types, such as the structure shown here. You still have to write the code that Visual C++ needs so that Visual C++ knows what to do when you want to fill a structure variable. However, after you teach Visual C++ how to retrieve such data in the format you want, you only have to use the single-line `cin` just shown to get data into any variable derived from this structure.

All the mysteries of such input will be solved as you progress through this book. This section is not trying to tease you with material you're not ready for; in fact, this section is attempting to explain a supportable, concrete, and extremely helpful reason for learning the I/O techniques in this chapter.

By the way, you can make the `cout` and `<<` work on your own data as well. If you want, you can instruct Visual C++ to display the full-screen display shown in Figure 3.3 when the following simple statement executes:

```
cout << employee[2];    // Outputs the structure variable's members
```

Note: You have already read several times in this book that Visual C++ helps speed your program development. After you set up the I/O to work with your data types, isn't it easier to write `cout` every time you want to display an output screen or `cin` every time you want to get the user's input than to remember function names or place the I/O code everywhere you want it executed?

Simple I/O

```
                    *** Employee Entry Screen ***
                    - - - - - - - - - - - - - - - -
```

| Last name: Johnson | First: Fred | Age: 34 |

| Address: 1013 S. Illinois Ave. |

| City: St. Louis | State: MO | ZIP: 63043 |

| Salary: $54,245.10 | Dependents: 2 |

| Year began: 1985 | Phone ext: 421 | Office: 52 |

Figure 3.3. A simple cout can produce this output screen.

Manipulating the Output

Visual C++ includes many helpful *manipulators* that manipulate your output so that the data looks the way you want it to look. As you saw earlier in this chapter, you don't have to format Visual C++ output, but there will be times when you want exactly two decimal places or when you want to specify a certain output justification that a cout by itself will not provide.

Table 3.1 lists all the I/O manipulators, and Table 3.2 lists some support values, called *format flags*, that go with some of the manipulators. The data that you input or output is called a *stream*, and these manipulators are formally called *stream manipulators*. You embed the manipulators inside cout as shown next. (On Day 12, you'll learn how to write your own I/O manipulators and use them just as though they were built into Visual C++.)

Note: Include IOMANIP.H when you use any of these manipulators. In Visual C++, the IOMANIP.H header file automatically includes IOSTREAM.H if IOSTREAM.H isn't already included. Therefore, you

don't have to include IOSTREAM.H in programs that include IOMANIP.H, although many C++ programmers include both out of habit. If you include both header files, IOSTREAM.H will be included only once and won't be repeated in your program.

Table 3.1. The I/O stream manipulators.

Manipulator	Description
dec	Sets decimal conversion base.
hex	Sets hexadecimal conversion base.
oct	Sets octal conversion base.
endl	Inserts newline and flush stream.
ends	Inserts null zero in string.
flush	Flushes an output stream.
resetiosflags(long f)	Clears the format specified by f. f is a format flag from Table 3.2.
setiosflags(long f)	Sets the format specified by f. f is a format flag from Table 3.2.
setfill(int c)	Sets the fill character to c.
setprecision(int n)	Sets the floating-point precision to n.
setw(int n)	Sets the field width to n.

Note: All the manipulators with parentheses accept arguments and are called *parameterized manipulators*.

Day 3 Simple I/O

Table 3.2. Format flag values for `resetiosflags()` and `setiosflags()`.

Format Flag Name	Description
`ios::left`	Left-justifies output within the `setw()` width.
`ios::right`	Right-justifies output within the `setw()` width.
`ios::scientific`	Formats output in scientific notation.
`ios::fixed`	Formats numbers in decimal format (rather than scientific notation).
`ios::dec`	Formats numbers in base 10.
`ios::hex`	Formats numbers in base 16.
`ios::oct`	Formats numbers in base 8.
`ios::uppercase`	Formats all hexadecimal and scientific notation value characters in uppercase (such as `1.32E+03` rather than `1.32e+03`).
`ios::showbase`	Prints a leading numeric base prefix (either `0x` for hexadecimal or `0` for octal).
`ios::showpos`	Outputs a plus sign, `+`, when printing positive numbers. (The plus sign is suppressed otherwise.)
`ios::showpoint`	Displays trailing zeroes when needed for precision.

Note: The format flags look odd with the embedded scope-resolution operator in them. These values are just constants (as `#define` produced named constants in C) that trigger a certain action depending on their values. The format flags work in the two functions `resetiosflags()` and `setiosflags()`.

The program in Listing 3.4 shows how the base-conversion manipulators `dec`, `hex`, and `oct` output the same number in different bases.

74

Listing 3.4. Using each of the base-conversion manipulators.

```
 1:  // Filename: BASES.CPP
 2:  // Prints numbers in three bases
 3:  #include <iostream.h>
 4:  #include <iomanip.h>
 5:  main()
 6:  {
 7:    int num = 211;
 8:    cout << "The decimal num: " << num << "\n";  // Base 10
 9:    cout << "The hexadecimal num: " << hex << num << "\n";  // Base 16
10:    cout << "The octal num: " << oct << num << "\n";  // Base 8
11:    return 0;
12:  }
```

```
The decimal num: 211
The hexadecimal num: d3
The octal num: 323
```

The decimal number 211 is equivalent to the hexadecimal number d3 and the octal number 323 (octal is rarely used anymore). Visual C++ remembers each of the base-conversion manipulators until the program ends or until you supply a different value. Therefore, if you want all of your integer values to print in hexadecimal format, specify hex in the first cout and all subsequent cout statements will also output in hexadecimal.

> **Note:** You don't have to specify dec, because Visual C++ defaults to base 10 output. However, if you print in a different base and then want to change back to base 10, use dec.

Table 3.1 contains some end-of-output manipulators that you might use occasionally. You often see the endl, ends, or flush manipulators used at the end of data being output. endl does the same thing as the newline character, '\n', followed by flush, by sending a newline and flushing the output buffer. These statements all do the same thing:

```
cout << "Hello there\n" << flush;
cout << "Hello there" << '\n' << flush;
cout << "Hello there" << endl;
```

> **Note:** If you are writing to the screen, you rarely need these manipulators.

The `ends` manipulator outputs a null zero at the end of a string of characters. You might need to terminate a string of individual characters with the terminating zero if you print the characters to a disk file or modem. Although the following statement appears to print individual characters, it actually prints a string because a string is always a group of characters terminated by a null zero.

```
cout << 'a' << 'b' << 'c' << ends;
```

The `ends` manipulator produces an extra blank when you output it to the screen.

> **Sticky Manipulation**
>
> All the I/O manipulators in Table 3.1, except for `setw()`, are sometimes called *sticky manipulators*. All but `setw()` remain in effect for the rest of the program unless you override them by specifying new manipulators.
>
> The `setw()` manipulator works only for the `cout` in which it appears.

The `setw()` manipulator specifies exactly how wide of a field to use for output data. Often when printing tables of data, you want the data to print uniformly within the same number of spaces so that your columns align with each other. Specify `setw()` on every cout line for which you want a width set. Visual C++ always defaults to variable-width output in `cout` lines that don't contain `setw()`.

> **Note:** All values are right-justified within the `setw()` field width unless you use format flags from Table 3.2 as shown later in this section. If the data is wider than the argument in `setw()`, Visual C++ ignores the `setw()` width and prints the entire value.

The program in Listing 3.5 prints various data values within different field widths so that you can see how the width specifier controls the placement of the data within their printed fields.

Listing 3.5. Printing within different field widths.

```
1:  // Filename: WIDTHS.CPP
2:  // Prints data using different field widths
3:  #include <iostream.h>
4:  #include <iomanip.h>
5:  main()
6:  {
7:    cout << "Without a field width set:\n";
8:    cout << "abcdefg" << "\n";
9:    cout << 12345 << "\n";
10:   cout << 123.45 << "\n";
11:   cout << "With a 10-character field width set:\n";
12:   cout << setw(10) << "abcdefg" << "\n";
13:   cout << setw(10) << 12345 << "\n";
14:   cout << setw(10) << 123.45 << "\n";
15:   return 0;
16: }
```

```
Without a field width set:
abcdefg
12345
123.45
With a 10-character field width set:
   abcdefg
     12345
    123.45
```

Warning: Some versions of Visual C++ produce this warning message when you compile programs using I/O manipulators: `test.cpp(14) : warning C4270: 'initializing' : do not initialize a non-const 'class ::__SMANIP_int __near &' with a non-lvalue 'class ::__SMANIP_int ' function return`. You can safely ignore this Visual C++ quirk because it is a known minor compiler bug recognized by Microsoft's support staff.

As you can see, the fill character that Visual C++ uses to pad justified fields is a blank. The `setfill()` manipulator enables you to change the fill character. By placing the statement

```
cout << setfill('x');
```

Simple I/O

before the `cout` statements in Listing 3.5, you force the program to produce this output:

```
Without a field width set:
abcdefg
12345
123.45
With a 10-character field width set:
xxxabcdefg
xxxxx12345
xxxx123.45
```

`setfill('*')` would be useful for printing payroll check amounts so that the numbers could not be altered.

After learning `setw()`, you're ready to learn about `setiosflags()` and `resetiosflags()` (and you'll also wonder why the designers of C++ wrote names that long!). If you want to left-justify data within the width, use `setiosflags()` with the `ios::left` format flag. Using the `ios::right` parameter with `ios::setiosflags` resets the justification to the right. Listing 3.6 prints the Listing 3.5 values left-justified, rather than right-justified as is the default.

Note: If you left-justify output, the fill character will fill from the right rather than from the left.

Listing 3.6. Printing left-justified within different field widths.

```
 1:  // Filename: WIDTHLFT.CPP
 2:  // Prints data using different field widths
 3:  #include <iostream.h>
 4:  #include <iomanip.h>
 5:  main()
 6:  {
 7:     cout << "Without a field width set:\n";
 8:     cout << "abcdefg" << "abcdefg" << "\n";
 9:     cout << 12345 << 12345 << "\n";
10:     cout << 123.45 << 123.45 << "\n";
11:     cout << "With the default right-justified 10-character ";
12:     cout << "field width set:\n";
13:     cout << setw(10) << "abcdefg" << setw(10) << "abcdefg" << "\n";
14:     cout << setw(10) << 12345 << setw(10) << 12345 << "\n";
15:     cout << setw(10) << 123.45 << setw(10) << 123.45 << "\n";
```

```
16:     // Force left-justification
17:     cout << setiosflags(ios::left);
18:     cout << "With a left-justified 10-character field width set:\n";
19:     cout << setw(10) << "abcdefg" << setw(10) << "abcdefg" << "\n";
20:     cout << setw(10) << 12345 << setw(10) << 12345 << "\n";
21:     cout << setw(10) << 123.45 << setw(10) << 123.45 << "\n";
22:     return 0;
23: }
```

```
Without a field width set:
abcdefgabcdefg
1234512345
123.45123.45
With the default right-justified 10-character field width set:
   abcdefg   abcdefg
     12345     12345
    123.45    123.45
With a left-justified 10-character field width set:
abcdefg   abcdefg
12345     12345
123.45    123.45
```

Unlike several previous program listings, Listing 3.6 prints two columns of data using three different methods: no width set, a right-justified width set, and a left-justified width set. This listing enables you to see the effects of setw() and setiosflags().

The ios::dec, ios::hex, and ios::oct flags enable you to use setiosflags() to set the numeric base rather than the other base-conversion manipulators described earlier. For example, the following statement prints the 44 in base 16 as 2c:

```
cout << setiosflags(ios::hex) << 44;  // Outputs 2c
```

The setiosflags() accepts more than one argument if you separate the arguments with a bitwise OR operator, |. Suppose that you wanted a hexadecimal value printed left-justified in a width of 10. The following statement does just that:

```
cout << setw(10)<<setiosflags(ios::hex|ios::left) << 44 << 45 << endl;
```

Here is the output from this cout:

```
2c        2d
```

The ios::uppercase ensures that all alphabetic hexadecimal values print in uppercase. The following statement prints 2C because of the ios::uppercase inside the setiosflags() along with the ios::hex parameter:

```
cout << setiosflags(ios::hex | ios::uppercase) << 44;
```

Simple I/O

The `resetiosflags()` resets any or all of the parameters in effect. For example, if you used the preceding `cout` to print 44 in an uppercase hexadecimal format, the following statement would reset (turn off) the `ios::uppercase` format but keep the `ios::hex` in effect:

```
cout << resetiosflags(ios::uppercase) << 44;
```

Of course, not all hexadecimal numbers have alphabetic characters in them. Therefore, you can request that Visual C++ output the hexadecimal or octal base prefix characters, `0x` and `0`, so that the user knows what base to use for interpreting the numbers. Listing 3.7 prints the number 10 in three different bases with their appropriate base prefixes.

Listing 3.7. Printing with base prefix characters.

```
 1:  // Filename: BASESHOW.CPP
 2:  // Prints  different bases with base prefix characters
 3:  #include <iostream.h>
 4:  #include <iomanip.h>
 5:  main()
 6:  {
 7:     cout << setiosflags(ios::showbase);
 8:     cout << 10 << endl;                              // Base 10
 9:     cout << setiosflags(ios::oct) << 10 << endl;     // Base 8
10:     cout << setiosflags(ios::hex) << 10 << endl;     // Base 16
11:     return 0;
12:  }
```

```
10
012
0xa
```

To print a number in scientific notation, use the `ios::scientific` parameter in `setiosflags()`. The lines

```
cout << 12345.678 << endl;
cout << setiosflags(ios:: scientific) << 12345.678 << endl;
```

produce this output:

```
12345.67
1.234567e+04
```

If you want to see a plus sign before a positive number, use the `ios::showpos` flag as Listing 3.8 illustrates.

Listing 3.8. Printing the plus sign.

```
1:  // Filename: SHOWPOS.CPP
2:  // Prints plus signs before positive numbers
3:  #include <iostream.h>
4:  #include <iomanip.h>
5:  main()
6:  {
7:    int i = 7, j = -8;
8:    cout << "i is " << i << " and j is " << j << endl;
9:    cout << setiosflags(ios::showpos);  // Turn on plus sign
10:   cout << "i is " << i << " and j is " << j << endl;
11:   return 0;
12: }
```

```
i is 7 and j is -8
i is +7 and j is -8
```

One of the most important formatting requirements for numbers is the capability to limit decimal places. Use setprecision() to set the precision of your output. Listing 3.9 prints the number 1.2345678 using nine different precision settings.

Listing 3.9. Printing precisions.

```
1:  // Filename: PRECNINE.CPP
2:  // Prints nine different precisions of same number
3:  #include <iostream.h>
4:  #include <iomanip.h>
5:  main()
6:  {
7:    cout << setiosflags(ios:: fixed);
8:    cout << "The original number is " << 1.234567 << endl;
9:    for (int i=0; i<=7; i++)
10:     { cout << setprecision(i) << 1.234567 << endl; }
11:   return 0;
12: }
```

```
The original number is 1.234567
1
1.2
1.23
1.235
1.2346
```

81

Day 3: Simple I/O

```
1.23457
1.234567
1.2345670
```

Notice that `setprecision()` dictates how many places to the right of the decimal point, from none to seven. The initial `setiosflags(ios::fixed)` on line 7 ensures that Visual C++ prints trailing zeros if needed to fill all the places (as shown in the last line of the output that prints one more decimal place than there are digits in the number).

Tip: If you print dollars and cents values, always precede your first `setprecision(2)` with `setiosflags(ios::fixed)` so that both digits in the cents appear even if one or both are zeroes.

DO	DON'T

DO include IOMANIP.H when using the I/O manipulators.

DO combine several format flags inside a single `setiosflags()` or `resetiosflags()` by separating them with a bitwise OR operator, |.

DO combine `setprecision()` and `setiosflags(ios:: fixed)` if you want a fixed number of decimal places printed with trailing zeros when appropriate.

DON'T specify `dec` for base 10 numbers unless in the same program you set the output to a different base. Decimal output is the default.

DON'T use `ios::uppercase` for text data. `ios::uppercase` prints only hexadecimal and scientific notation letter values in uppercase rather than their lowercase default.

Looking at Input

The discussions in the preceding section were concerned with output. User input is just as important. C was never known for extremely accurate user input control. Visual C++'s `cin` accepts user input, and you can basically control the way the user enters that input. Still, Visual C++ provides only a limited framework for input, and you'll have

to write a lot of input routines or use one written by someone else (the computer magazines and bulletin boards are full of C++ I/O libraries that you can order).

Using cin and >>, Visual C++ reads the next character into the character variable after >> or the next value (string or number) into the non-character variable after >>. Either way, Visual C++ skips whitespace characters such as newlines, tabs, and spaces to get the input.

The program in Listing 3.10 shows how Visual C++ treats single-character input. Remember that cin >> skips all whitespace, unlike regular C.

Listing 3.10. Inputting single characters.

```
 1:  // Filename: INPUTSIN.CPP
 2:  // Gets five single characters
 3:  #include <iostream.h>
 4:  #include <iomanip.h>
 5:  main()
 6:  {
 7:    char  c;
 8:    for (int i=0; i<5; i++)
 9:      { cout << "What is the next character? ";
10:        cin >> c;
11:        cout << "You typed " << c << endl;
12:      }
13:
14:    return 0;
15: }
```

```
What is the next character? a
You typed a
What is the next character? b
You typed b
What is the next character? c
You typed c
What is the next character? d
You typed d
What is the next character? e
You typed e
```

This program seems trivial unless you are used to getting single-character input with regular C's scanf() or getchar() functions. When the user enters a single character, such as a, the user must press Enter to end the data-entry of the a. Therefore, it appears that a \n goes to the input buffer, and it does. (In C, you would have to add another cin that accepted the \n and discarded the \n just to get the \n out of the way for the next character's input.) The next time this program inputs a character, however, cin skips the preceding character's \n because that's what cin does.

If you want to get whitespace characters into the character variable, you must use the get() function. The get() function's syntax doesn't look like anything you are used to, but by the time you finish learning Visual C++, you'll understand why the syntax looks the way it does. In the meantime, here is how you can get a single character into a character variable *without* skipping the whitespace:

```
cin.get(myInit);    // Waits for user to type a letter
```

The Enter key ends user input. Therefore, pressing a single key (other than Enter) is not enough to store that key's character into the myInit variable. When using cin.get(), you must add a second cin.get() to discard the Enter's newline character. The following code does store the user's entered character in myInit:

```
cin.get(myInit);    // Get's user's first letter
cin.get(nl);        // The variable nl will hold '\n'
```

The bottom line is this: If you want to get individual characters and skip whitespace characters, use cin >>, and if you want to read all characters typed, even those that are whitespace characters, use cin.get().

get() is actually a multiple-purpose function. You can get characters and strings depending how you use it. get() is known as an *overloaded function,* meaning that you can pass it a different number and type of arguments and it behaves differently. You'll learn how to write your own overloaded functions in Day 6's chapter, "Communicating with Functions."

get() is useful for getting strings of data. Unlike simple cin >>, get() does not stop at the first whitespace. Therefore, you can get the user's strings with embedded spaces with get(). Here are the arguments for get() when used to get string input:

```
get(char * cp, int len [, char terminator])
```

The terminator's default is \n, but you can change it by passing the third parameter to get(). The *terminator* tells Visual C++ which character to input up to and stop.

The program in Listing 3.11 asks for the user's entire name and then prints it.

 Listing 3.11. Getting strings with get().

```
1:  // Filename: STGET.CPP
2:  // String-input program
3:  #include <iostream.h>
```

```
4:  #include <iomanip.h>
5:  main()
6:  {
7:    char name[80];   // Will hold user's full name
8:    cout << "What is your full name? ";
9:    cin.get(name, 80);  // The function uses at most 79 characters of
10:                       // input and leaves the rest on input buffer
11:    cout << "Your name is " << name << endl;
12:    return 0;
13: }
```

What is your full name? **William Harper Littlejohn**
Your name is William Harper Littlejohn

If you used cin >> to get the name, Visual C++ would receive only the first name, William, and the rest would be left in the input buffer. Also, if the user were to enter a string longer than 79 characters (80 with the terminator), Visual C++ would store only the first 79 characters in the name array and would leave any remaining characters on the input buffer for the next input. The second argument protects your arrays so that the user does not overwrite the array.

The getline() function works like get(), except getline() discards the terminating newline keystroke whereas get() leaves the newline on the input buffer. The program in Listing 3.12 demonstrates the problems that can occur when you use get() followed by a second get().

Listing 3.12. Having two get() functions in a row causes problems.

```
1:  // Filename: GETBAD.CPP
2:  // String-input program with a bad get()
3:  #include <iostream.h>
4:  #include <iomanip.h>
5:  main()
6:  {
7:    char name[80];   // Will hold user's full name
8:    char city[25];   // Supposed to hold user's city name
9:    cout << "What is your full name? ";
10:   cin.get(name, 80);  // The function uses at most 79 characters of
11:                       // input and leaves the rest on input buffer
12:   cout << "Your name is " << name << endl;
13:   cout << "What is your city? ";   // Will NOT wait for user!
14:   cin.get(city, 25);
15:   cout << "Your city is " << city << endl;  // Nothing prints!
16:   return 0;
17: }
```

Day 3 Simple I/O

```
What is your full name? Theodore Marley Brooks
Your name is Theodore Marley Brooks
What is your city? Your city is
```

Notice that the second get() does not wait for the user to type anything. That's because the first get() left a \n on the input stream and get() does not skip whitespace characters, so the second get() malfunctions. Changing the get() functions to getline()s fixes everything, as Listing 3.13 shows.

Listing 3.13. Two getline() functions in a row work fine.

```
 1: // Filename: GETLINE.CPP
 2: // String-input program with getline()s
 3: #include <iostream.h>
 4: #include <iomanip.h>
 5: main()
 6: {
 7:   char name[80];   // Will hold user's full name
 8:   char city[25];   // Will hold user's city name
 9:   cout << "What is your full name? ";
10:   cin.getline(name, 80);  // The function uses at most 79 characters
11:                           // of input and leaves the rest on input buffer
12:   cout << "Your name is " << name << endl;
13:   cout << "What is your city? ";
14:   cin.getline(city, 25);
15:   cout << "Your city is " << city << endl;  // The city prints
16:   return 0;
17: }
```

```
What is your full name? Theodore Marley Brooks
Your name is Theodore Marley Brooks
What is your city? New York
Your city is New York
```

When getting numbers, you can specify which base you want to accept for numeric input. In other words, if you expect the user to enter a hexadecimal or octal number, you can use a base manipulator directly inside the cin >> line to accept that base. If you don't specify a base manipulator, Visual C++ defaults to decimal input. The following statement expects the user to type a decimal value:

```
cin >> num;
```

The following statement expects the user to type an octal value:

```
cin >> oct >> num;
```

If the user does not type an octal number (for example, f8 is not an octal number), num retains the same value it had before the cin. The following statement expects the user to type a hexadecimal value:

```
cin >> hex >> num;
```

If the user enters anything but a hexadecimal number, num does not change. In all numeric input, if the first part of the value is valid but the last is not, Visual C++ stops reading until the invalid value. For example, if the user entered **12v** in response to the following cin >>

```
cin >> num;
```

the 12 would go into num and the v\n would be left on the input stream.

DO	DON'T
DO use cin >> if you want Visual C++ to ignore whitespace. **DO** use get() if you want Visual C++ to read whitespace characters into character variables.	**DON'T** use cin >> to get string input that contains spaces. cin >> can get only one word at a time. **DON'T** let the user overwrite character array boundaries; use getline() to keep input strings within their target array limits.

Summary

Visual C++ programmers rarely use printf(), scanf(), or the family of the getchar() functions because cin and cout are so much easier and faster to code. Outputting data with cout and inputting data with cin makes a lot of sense when you picture the cout object as being your screen and cin as being the keyboard.

The overloaded << and >> operators send data to and from your screen and keyboard in conjunction with the cout and cin objects. All the regular C I/O functions are available for your Visual C++ programs, but you rarely need them.

Always include IOSTREAM.H when using cout and cin, and also include IOMANIP.H when formatting with the manipulators and format flags.

Simple I/O

Q&A

Q. Why does thinking about `cout` and `cin` as screen and keyboard objects make sense?

A. The look of output statements using `cout`, as in `cout << "Visual C++";`, actually makes you think that Visual C++ is being pushed into the `cout` screen device and `cin >> myName;` shows, through the >> direction indicator, that data is coming from the keyboard and being pushed into the variable `myName`.

Technically, `cout` and `cin` are your standard output and standard input device, which can be rerouted to devices other than your screen and keyboard. However, Visual C++ programmers rarely redirect their output from these devices.

Q. What is wrong with this statement:

```
cout >> age;
```

A. The direction of << is wrong. If you picture `cout` as being the screen, you can see that the screen cannot send data to variables, but variables *can* go to the screen. Although the `cin` and `cout` inserter and extractor operators, << and >>, point in different directions, their directions are easy to remember if you remember that `cout` represents the screen and `cin` represents the keyboard.

Q. Why would I write to `cerr` when the screen is `cout`?

A. In your programs, send all error messages to the `cerr` error device. `cerr` will always be your screen. Under the slim chance that the user has redirected `cout` output somewhere else, `cerr` will still be pointing to the screen, and your error messages will be read.

Q. Can I specify more than one format flag with `setiosflags()` and `resetiosflags()`?

A. Yes, you can, by separating the format flags with the bitwise OR, |, operator. For example, if you wanted to print a number in octal format, left-justified within a field width of 8 with the base prefix showing, you could do so in a single `setiosflags()` manipulator like this:

```
cout << setw(8) << setiosflags(ios::left | ios::octal|ios::
↪showbase) << i;
```

Q. Why would you ever use getline() over cin >> when inputting strings?

A. cin >> gets only a word at a time, stopping at the first whitespace character including a blank. cin >> leaves all input to the right of blanks on the input stream.

Often, you'll want to input strings of data that contain blanks. You can by using getline(). getline() keeps reading a string until the user presses the terminator character (usually the \n unless you've specified the optional third parameter of getline()) or types the maximum number of characters allowed by the getline().

Workshop

The Workshop offers quiz questions and exercises to hone your skills and give you feedback on today's lesson. You'll find some proposed answers in Appendix D.

Quiz

1. What is the header file you must include to use cout, cin, and cerr?
2. What is the header file you must include to use the I/O manipulators?
3. How does setw() behave differently from all the other manipulators?
4. When you specify a width with setw(), will the subsequent numeric value print left-justified or right-justified within the width?
5. True or False: The following statements print three numbers right-justified within a column of eight characters:

   ```
   cout << setw(8) << setiosflags(ios::right) << 25 << endl;
   cout << 26 << endl;
   cout << 27 << endl;
   ```

6. How does endl differ from ends and flush?
7. When would you use cin >> over get()?
8. True or False: Using getline(), you can keep the user from overwriting character array boundaries.

Simple I/O

Exercises

1. Convert the following three `cout` statements into a single `cout` statement.

   ```
   cout << "Hi!";
   cout << "\n";
   cout << setprecision(2) << setiosflags(ios::showpoint) << amt;
   ```

2. Write the `cin` statement that reads the data 234A and stores the 234 in an integer variable and the A in a character variable.

3. Write a Visual C++ program that uses `cin` and `cout` to ask the user for three prices. Print the dollar total of those prices on-screen. Print the total within a field of 20 spaces and left-fill the leftover spaces with asterisks. Also, be sure that the total prints to two decimal places as dollars and cents should print.

Powerful Pointers

Powerful Pointers

Pointers separate the *real* programmers from all the rest. Actually, some people view pointers as difficult to master, but if you've used them at all, you've probably found them to be powerful and straightforward.

The true power of pointers comes to light when you use pointers to pass arguments between functions and to allocate memory dynamically on the heap. Today, you'll learn about Visual C++ pointer manipulation, especially honing in on the differences between Visual C++'s pointer and that of C. Most of what you already know about C pointers holds true in Visual C++ programs with little exception.

This chapter will concentrate on pointer issues that affect object-oriented programming the most. Today, you learn about the following topics:

- How Visual C++ handles `void` pointers
- What reference variables are
- The differences between pointer constants and pointers to constants
- How to declare a read-only alias to a variable
- The advantage of `const` definitions

Working with *void* Pointers

A `void` pointer is a pointer variable that can point to *any* data type. Some mistakenly think that a `void` pointer points to null zero, but a *null pointer* points to null zero. (To keep people really confused, C and C++ programmers also call the null zero *ASCII zero, binary zero,* and *terminating zero.*) Figure 4.1 helps clarify the distinction between `void` pointers and null pointers.

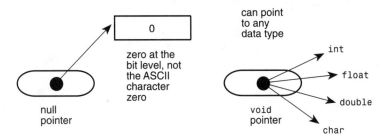

Figure 4.1. Don't confuse `void` pointers with `null` pointers.

 Note: void pointers are sometimes called *generic pointers*.

You have probably used void pointers in your C programming, but void pointers are even more important in Visual C++ than in C. Visual C++ is a stronger data type-checking language than C, and sometimes you'll need the freedom that void pointers allow.

You can assign any pointer variables—*other than* const or volatile pointers—to void pointers. Visual C++ even enables you to assign function pointers to void pointers as well, although not all C++ compilers enable you to do so.

As you know, to define a pointer, you must use the dereferencing operator to let the compiler know that you are defining a pointer and not a regular variable. For example, the following statement defines an integer:

```
int i;
```

The following statement, however, defines a *pointer* to an integer (loosely called an *integer pointer*):

```
int * ptrI;
```

As with every other kind of variable, pointers are not initialized with valid data until you store something in them. In the preceding statements, you don't know what value i or ptrI holds. To store a value in i, assign it a value, and to store a value in ptrI, assign it an address because pointers can hold only addresses of other values. The following statements store 10 in i and the address of i in ptrI:

```
i = 10;
ptrI = &i;    // & is the "address of" operator
```

The reason you have walked through this review is that defining a void pointer takes no more effort than defining a pointer of any other data type, except you use the keyword void rather than data types. The following statement defines a void pointer named vPtr:

```
void * vPtr;   // Defines a void pointer
```

Integer pointers can point *only* to integers, floating-point pointers can point *only* to floating-points, and character pointers can point *only* to characters. void pointers can point to *any* data type; they don't even have to typecast to a specific data type.

Powerful Pointers

Listing 4.1 defines two void pointers, an integer pointer, and a floating-point pointer. Even experienced C pointer users might have to think twice about some of the statements, especially the last two couts.

Listing 4.1. Working with several kinds of pointers.

```
 1:  // Filename: LOTSPTRS.CPP
 2:  // Defines several pointers and assigns them values
 3:  #include <iostream.h>
 4:  #include <iomanip.h>
 5:  main()
 6:  {
 7:     void   * vPtr1;      // Define two void pointers
 8:     void   * vPtr2;
 9:     int i = 15;          // Defines a regular integer variable
10:     int    * iPtr;       // Defines an integer pointer
11:     float f = 4.68;      // Defines a regular floating-point variable
12:     float * fPtr;        // Defines a floating-point pointer
13:
14:     // Assign the pointers in several ways
15:     iPtr = &i;           // iPtr points to i
16:     fPtr = &f;           // fPtr points to f
17:     vPtr1 = &i;          // A void pointer points to an integer
18:     vPtr2 = &f;          // A void pointer points to a float
19:     vPtr1 = fPtr;        // Directly assigns a float pointer to a void
20:     vPtr1 = iPtr;        // Assign to that same void pointer an integer
21:
22:     // Print values using typecast void pointers
23:     cout << "vPtr1 points to " << *((int *)vPtr1) << "\n";
24:     cout << "vPtr2 points to " << *((float *)vPtr2) << "\n";
25:
26:     return 0;
27: }
```

```
vPtr1 points to 15
vPtr2 points to 4.68
```

Lines 15–20 show you ways to assign values to pointer variables. iPtr and fPtr are assigned the address of regular variables in lines 15 and 16. The two void pointers are assigned the address of the two regular variables in lines 17 and 18, showing that a void pointer can point to any address no matter what kind of data is stored in that address. Lines 19 and 20 also show that you can directly assign the values of pointers to void pointers.

The strange syntax (and luckily, the syntax that programmers don't use a lot!) appears in lines 23 and 24. You can assign any type of pointer to a void pointer, but when it's time to do anything with the data stored in the void pointer, you usually have to typecast that void pointer to the proper data type. It would be nice if you could print the value pointed to by vPtr1 and vPtr2 by a simple dereference like this:

```
cout << "vPtr1 points to " << *vPtr1 << "\n";
cout << "vPtr2 points to " << *vPtr2 << "\n";
```

You cannot, however, print the dereferenced simple void pointer, because Visual C++ cannot magically read your mind and know what type of data the void pointers point to. Visual C++ does not know how to print void pointer data. Technically, if a void pointer is pointing to an integer, Visual C++ would have to print the two bytes pointed to by the void pointer, and if a void pointer is pointing to a floating-point value, Visual C++ would have to print the four bytes pointed to by the void pointer. The couts cannot determine exactly how much memory to dereference by the dereference symbol alone; you must typecast the void pointer to the proper pointer data type before dereferencing. Figure 4.2 helps illustrate how the typecast works.

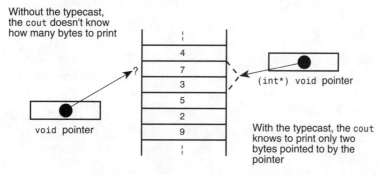

Figure 4.2. The pointer typecast tells Visual C++ how much memory to dereference.

As with most convoluted expressions in Visual C++, just read the expression *((int *)vPtr1) from right to left and you'll understand it. The void pointer vPtr1 is typecast to an integer pointer with (int *). (Without the *, you would be typecasting the pointer to a regular integer, which wouldn't work.) By typecasting, you tell Visual C++ how much memory to dereference. After you've properly typecast the pointer, the dereference operator, *, knows to grab the integer (two bytes) at vPtr's address. Line 24 then typecasts the floating-point pointer before dereferencing it.

Powerful Pointers

> **Don't Assign void to non-void**
>
> Not only must you typecast `void` pointers before dereferencing them, but you must also typecast `void` pointers before assigning them to pointers of other data types. The following statement is invalid:
>
> ```
> iPtr = vPtr1;     // Not allowed
> ```
>
> As long as you typecast `iPtr`, you can make the assignment. This statement is OK:
>
> ```
> iPtr = (int *)vPtr1;    // Allowed
> ```
>
> You can, as you saw in Listing 4.1, assign regular pointer variables to `void` pointers. This statement is fine:
>
> ```
> vPtr1 = iPtr;     // Allowed
> ```
>
> When typecasting pointers, you must include the asterisk in the typecast and use the C style of typecasting. This statement is a bad typecast and is not allowed:
>
> ```
> iPtr = int *(vPtr1);    // Bad typecast syntax
> ```
>
> All of this discussion dealing with the assignment of `void` pointers to regular pointers and vice versa pertains to passing arguments between functions as well. You cannot pass a `void` pointer to a non-`void` pointer unless you typecast the void pointer to the target pointer's data type first. You can, however, pass non-`void` pointers to `void` pointers.

> **Note:** C allows implicit conversion from a non-`void` to a `void` pointer so that `malloc()`'s syntax was eased a bit and you didn't *have* to typecast the return value of `malloc()`. You can assign a non-`void` pointer to a `void` pointer without a typecast, and C attempts to resolve the pointers. However, Visual C++ requires that you explicitly typecast the assignment as shown in this section when assigning a non-`void` pointer to a `void` pointer. By the way, after Day 5, you'll never use `malloc()` again, so requiring explicit `void` typecasting won't present problems anyway.

DO	DON'T

DO use `void` pointers when you want to store several kinds of pointers in a single pointer throughout the program.

DO typecast `void` pointers before assigning them to non-`void` pointers or dereferencing them in any way.

DON'T typecast regular pointers before assigning them to `void` pointers.

DON'T confuse `void` pointers with null pointers. A `void` pointer can point to any data type, whereas a null pointer points to zero (a terminating zero).

DON'T attempt to assign a `const` or `volatile` pointer to a `void` pointer.

References Refer to Data

References are new to C++ and don't appear in C. It is easy to confuse pointers and references, so right off the bat, here is the best definition of a reference that you'll see: A reference is a pointer that is automatically dereferenced for you. That definition almost seems circular, but as you learn more about references, you'll see that the definition fits the term perfectly.

References are basically pointer variables. You use them like pointer variables, but references are easier to work with. Being *automatically dereferenced* means, on one level, that you don't have to use the dereference operator, *, to get to a reference's value. References also enable you to create *aliases* for other variables. The true power of references, however, appears when you pass and return references between functions.

Before going too far, you should know how to define reference variables. The following statements define a regular integer variable, a pointer to an integer variable, and a reference to an integer:

```
int i=19;            // Regular integer variable
int * iPtr = &i;     // Pointer to the integer
int & rPtr = i;      // Reference to the integer
```

Notice that you use the *address of* operator, &, to define references. The address of operator appears in the definition line just to differentiate the reference definition from other kinds of variables. In other words, the & lets the compiler know that you are defining a reference, but the & is not part of the variable name just as the * is not part of `iPtr`'s name.

Powerful Pointers

Never define a reference without initializing it. The initialization links the reference to its associated value. rPtr is now an *alias* for i, and anything you do to rPtr will be done to i (and vice versa) until you change rPtr to reference a different variable.

> Some Visual C++ programmers prefer to remove the spaces from between the * and & and the variable names. These two statements do the same thing as the last two statements in the preceding code:
>
> ```
> int *iPtr = &i;    // Pointer to the integer
> int &rPtr = i;     // Reference to the integer
> ```
>
> The following statements contain no spaces between the data type and the operator, which is legal as well:
>
> ```
> int* iPtr = &i;    // Pointer to the integer
> int& rPtr = i;     // Reference to the integer
> ```
>
> Use whichever style you prefer because Visual C++ doesn't care.
>
> If you want to use the value of i through the iPtr pointer variable, you must dereference the pointer variable with *. If you want to use the value of i through the rPtr reference variable, you don't have to do anything special because rPtr is already dereferenced. The program in Listing 4.2 shows what happens when you change a variable and the reference to that variable.

Listing 4.2. If you change a reference, the reference's aliased variable changes also.

```
1:  // Filename: REFINTRO.CPP
2:  // Introduces references
3:  #include <iostream.h>
4:  main()
5:  {
6:     int i=19;
7:     int *iPtr = &i;   // Pointer to the integer
8:     int &rPtr = i;    // Reference to the integer
9:     iPtr = &i;
10:    rPtr = i;
11:    cout << "i is " << i << endl;
12:    cout << "*iPtr is " << *iPtr << endl;
13:    cout << "rPtr is " << rPtr << endl;      // rPtr is alias to i
14:    i = 25;
15:    cout << "After changing i to 25:\n";
16:    cout << "i is " << i << endl;
```

```
17:     cout << "*iPtr is " << *iPtr << endl;
18:     cout << "rPtr is " << rPtr << endl;
19:     rPtr = 100;     // Store 100 in i as well!
20:     cout << "After changing rPtr to 100:\n";
21:     cout << "i is " << i << endl;
22:     cout << "*iPtr is " << *iPtr << endl;
23:     cout << "rPtr is " << rPtr << endl;
24:     return 0;
25: }
```

```
i is 19
*iPtr is 19
rPtr is 19
After changing i to 25:
i is 25
*iPtr is 25
rPtr is 25
After changing rPtr to 100:
i is 100
*iPtr is 100
rPtr is 100
```

This output shows how a reference acts like an alias to a variable. The variable i can be changed and used in three ways: by working directly with i, by dereferencing the iPtr pointer, and by changing the reference rPtr. The reference is a pointer to i in every sense of the word except that you don't have to dereference the reference as you would a pointer. Figure 4.3 shows the computer's memory right before Listing 4.2 finishes. As Figure 4.3 shows, rPtr is more than a pointer; rPtr is an alias to i.

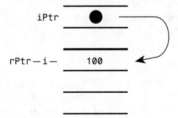

Figure 4.3. A reference is an alias and is always attached to its variable.

References lighten your coding burden because you don't have to include the dereferencing symbol, *, every time you use the reference's value.

Powerful Pointers

A reference is always attached to a single variable. For example, if the program in Listing 4.2 contained an integer variable named j and you assigned the reference to j like

```
rPtr = j;    // Assigns the referenced i the value of j
```

you have not made `rPtr` a reference to j but have simply changed the value of i. As Figure 4.3 showed, the reference is an attached alias to the variable it refers to, and that attachment lasts for the entire scope of the reference variable.

Now that you understand references, you might be asking yourself why you need them. After all, pointers still work as usual in Visual C++. And pointers seem to have the advantage over references in that you can make pointers point to different memory locations whereas references are always fixed to their original referenced location. The advantage that references provide is that you can use them as pointers without dereferencing them *when passing and returning parameters* from one function to another. Day 6's chapter, "Communicating with Functions," will show you how to streamline Visual C++ functions using references.

Defining References

dataType & refName expression

`dataType` is any intrinsic data type such as `int` or `float`, or a user-defined data type created with `struct`, `union`, `enum`, or `class`. `refName` is any valid variable name, and `expression` is the variable or expression you want to reference.

Example

```
// Filename: REFSYN.CPP
// Illustrates a reference to a variable
#include <iostream.h>
#include <iomanip.h>
main()
{
  float value = 123.45;      // Regular floating-point
  float value2 = 87.12;      // 2nd regular float
  float & ref1 = value;      // Reference to value
  cout << setprecision(2);
  cout << setiosflags(ios::showpoint);
  cout << "value is " << value << "\n";
  cout << "ref1 is also " << ref1 << "\n";
  ref1 = value2;
  cout << "Both value and ref1 now refer to " << value << "\n";
  return 0;
}
```

DO	DON'T

DO define a reference using the & operator.

DO use a reference as an automatically dereferenced pointer.

DO use references for pointers to pointers in order to ease the complicated double-dereferencing syntax needed when pointing to pointers or arrays.

DON'T define a reference without initializing it at the same time.

DON'T ever dereference a reference variable with *. References are automatically dereferenced, and Visual C++ generates an error if you attempt to dereference a reference variable.

DON'T use references just for aliasing variables. Although a reference in effect gives you a second name to the same variable, calling the same variable two different names can create interesting debugging sessions. The true advantage of references appears when you use references for passing and returning parameters shown in Day 6's chapter.

Constants Stay *const*

A constant defined with const remains constant, and Visual C++ makes sure of it. Visual C++ protects the programmer better than C did. Look at the program in Listing 4.3 that attempts to change a const value through a pointer.

Type

Listing 4.3. There's no way to change a const value through a pointer.

```
 1:  // Filename: CONSTPTR.CPP
 2:  // Visual C++ doesn't let you change constants
 3:  #include <iostream.h>
 4:  main()
 5:  {
 6:     const int minAge = 18;      // A constant integer
 7:     int * agePtr;                // An integer pointer
 8:     agePtr = & minAge;           // Error happens here
 9:     return 0;
10:  }
```

Powerful Pointers

If you attempt to compile Listing 4.3's program, Visual C++ displays the following error message:

```
error C2446: '=' : no conversion from 'const int __near *' to 'int
➥__near *'
```

This fancy error message is Visual C++'s attempt at trying to associate a regular pointer to a constant value. Only pointers to const can point to const values.

> **Note:** Visual C++ will enable you to typecast away a const, but be careful if you do so and question yourself three times before doing such a thing. If you find yourself typecasting away a const, perhaps the value should not have been const to begin with.

Why do you think Visual C++ does not allow line 8? Such code would allow for sneaky manipulation of a const value. For example, you already know not to change minAge because it is a const value. You could never attempt this:

```
minAge = 16;    // Cannot change a const
```

Visual C++ knows that if you could make a pointer variable point to a const value, you could change the const through the pointer. If line 8 in Listing 4.3 were allowed, you could change the const like this:

```
*agePtr = 16;    // Thankfully, Visual C++ guards against this!
```

To help clarify pointers and constants further, the next section describes everything you ever wanted to know about pointers and constants— but were afraid to code.

Don't Forget Constant Arrays

If you define an array and want to keep the rest of the program (or another programmer who might maintain the program) from changing the array, use const when you define the array. The following statement defines a constant array of integers:

```
const int monthDays[] = {31, 28, 31, 30, 31, 30, 31, 31, 30, 31,
➥30, 31};
```

> Throughout the rest of the program, you can use the array, but you can never change the array with statements such as this:
>
> ```
> monthDays[2] = 31;     // Not allowed
> ```
>
> Visual C++ will not even compile the program if you attempt to change one of the array elements.

const Used with Pointers and References

You will find that Visual C++ programmers use const more faithfully than C programmers do. Visual C++ programmers are more accustomed to C++'s strictness; using const for values that don't change clarifies code and makes the intent of the constants better known. As mentioned in Day 2's chapter, "C++ Is Superior," Visual C++ programmers use const rather than #define, so const is seen more by Visual C++ programmers and they are more accustomed to using it than many C programmers are.

Nevertheless, using the const keyword can add confusion for programmers just beginning to use it. When mixing pointers, constants, and references, newcomers to Visual C++ programming can get confused enough to eliminate the const keyword from their programs when the compiler starts complaining too much. Removing const is not a good solution to compiler errors and warnings. Learning how to use const with pointers is easy and is a better approach.

There are three combinations of pointers and const value:

- Pointers to constants
- Constant pointers
- Constant pointers to constants

All of these items are different to Visual C++, but they sometimes seem to run together for people using them. The following sections explain them one at a time.

Powerful Pointers

Pointers to Constants

A *pointer to a constant* is just that: a pointer variable points to a `const` value. In the section called "Constants Stay const," you learned that you cannot directly assign a pointer variable to a `const`, but you can use the `const` keyword to do so. Using `const` tells the compiler that you are aware of the `const` but still want to point to the `const` with the pointer. The compiler will enable you to point to a constant as long as you specify `const` when defining the pointer like this:

```
const minAge = 18;              // Regular constant
const int * aPtrAge = minAge;   // Pointer to a constant
```

Always read variable definitions from right to left starting at the equal sign. This definition of `aPtrAge` tells Visual C++ this:

> *"Define a variable named* `aPtrAge` *that points to an integer constant. Initialize* `aPtrAge` *by making it point to* `minAge`.*"*

Without `const`, Visual C++ would not enable you to define `aPtrAge` because the compiler fears that you might try something like this:

```
*aPtrAge = 16;    // Not allowed
```

With `const`, however, you are making the commitment to Visual C++ that you will never change the constant that the pointer points to, and if you try to, the compiler complains and does not allow it.

Figure 4.4 shows the computer's memory being defined by `aPtrAge`. The bold box around `minAge` indicates that `minAge` is a constant and cannot be changed.

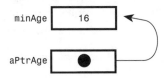

Figure 4.4. `aPtrAge` can change but `minAge` cannot, even through the pointer.

You *can* change the value of `aPtrAge`! `aPtrAge` is a regular pointer variable, but it just happens that `aPtrAge` points to a constant. `aPtrAge` is a pointer *to* a constant, not a *constant pointer*. This statement is allowed in the program:

```
aPtrAge = & newAge;    // Changes aPtrAge
```

However, you can never change that value pointed to by `aPtrAge` using `aPtrAge`.

> **Note:** You can use pointers to constants as lvalues, but you cannot use *dereferenced* pointers to constants as lvalues. An lvalue is a variable that cannot be changed.

Technically, aPtrAge does not have to point to a constant, but Visual C++ acts as though any value pointed to by aPtrAge is a constant. Listing 4.4 shows a regular integer pointed to by a pointer to a constant.

Listing 4.4. You can change the integer, but not with the pointer.

```
1:  // Filename: REGCONST.CPP
2:  // A regular integer that acts like a constant when pointed to
3:  #include <iostream.h>
4:  main()
5:  {
6:    int i = 7;
7:    const int * pi = &i;
8:    cout << "*pi is " << *pi << "\n";
9:    // Now change the integer but not with the pointer.
10:   // You could NEVER do this:
11:   // *pi = 18;
12:   i = 18;
13:   cout << "*pi is now " << *pi << "\n";
14:   return 0;
15: }
```

```
*pi is 7
*pi is now 18
```

Although line 7 defines a pointer to an integer constant, the integer i is not really an integer constant. Nevertheless, Visual C++ learns in line 7 that you'll never attempt to change i through pi (as shown in lines 9–11). You can change i as done in line 12, however, because i is a regular integer variable.

Constant Pointers

Just as the name implies, a *constant pointer* never changes—but the value that it points to can change. As with all constants, you have to initialize a constant pointer when you define it or you'll never have another chance because constants can never change.

Powerful Pointers

Here is the definition of a constant pointer:

```
int age = 20;              // Regular integer
int * const pAge = &age;   // Pointer constant
```

Notice that the keyword `const` appears on the right side of the *, whereas it appeared on the left when defining pointers to constants. Reading from right to left before the equal sign, the second statement tells Visual C++ that you want this:

> *"Define a variable named pAge that is a constant pointer to an integer. Initialize the pointer constant with the address of age."*

age can change because age is not a constant. However, you can do nothing to change pAge or Visual C++ will complain. By creating a constant pointer, you have created a fixed pointer that can never move even though the data it points to might change. Figure 4.5 shows memory after the previous definitions are in place.

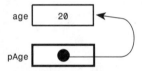

Figure 4.5. age can change but pAge cannot.

Sometimes, *embedded* Visual C++ programmers use constant pointers to change external events. Embedded programs often control non-computer devices. For instance, the computer inside a late-model car is controlled by a program. The program is burned into the computer's ROM (*read-only memory*), and the program controls external devices attached to the car's computer. The devices throughout the car, such as the transmission sensor, are attached to actual memory locations in the computer chip's memory. The sensor wire's location leading from the transmission never changes, but its signal can change. The program would contain a constant pointer to that sensor's location. Through the pointer, the program could read and set the sensor wire's signal, but the pointer's address would never change because the location of the sensor wire would never change.

 Note: An array name is a constant pointer. You cannot use an array name as a lvalue but you can change the contents of an array. An array name is just a constant pointer that points to the first element in an array. If you want to reserve heap memory (as shown in tomorrow's chapter) and use that heap memory as if it were an array, point to the heap with a constant pointer.

Constant Pointers to Constants

The epitome of constants (and confusion) appears when you define constant pointers to constant values. There is nothing inherently difficult in the concept of constant pointers to constants; they simply form a combination of the previous two subjects: pointers to constants and constant pointers.

A constant pointer to a constant is a pointer that cannot change and is pointing to a value that cannot change. To define a constant pointer to a constant, you must first define the constant and then define the constant pointer. The following statements define an integer constant named ic and a constant pointer to that integer constant named pc:

```
const int ic = 10;           // A constant
const int const * pc = & ic; // Constant pointer to a constant
```

The second statement tells Visual C++ this:

> *"Define a variable named pc that is a constant pointer to an integer constant. Initialize the pointer constant with the address of ic."*

Figure 4.6 shows how Visual C++ defines ic and pc.

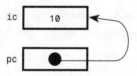

Figure 4.6. Defining a constant pointer to a constant.

As with the previous figures, Figure 4.6's dark boxes indicate memory that cannot change. Nothing you do in code can change the value of pc; you cannot make pc point to any other address in memory, which means that pc can never be an lvalue. Neither can you change the integer constant ic.

Actually, `ic` doesn't have to be defined as a constant. In the definition

```
int ic = 10;                    // A regular integer
const int const * pc = & ic;    // Constant pointer to a constant
```

`ic` is a regular variable. However, the second statement tells the compiler that you will never attempt to change `pc` and that you will never attempt to change `ic` through the pointer named `pc`.

DO	DON'T
DO use `const` for safety to protect those values that should not change. **DON'T** ever attempt to change a `const` value through a pointer. **DON'T** ever attempt to change a `const` pointer after it is defined. **DON'T** ever attempt to change a `const` pointer *or* the `const` it points to if you define a constant pointer to a constant.	

Read-Only Aliases

Closely related to constant pointers are *read-only aliases*. A read-only alias is a reference to a constant value. Earlier in this chapter, you learned how to create references to variables and use either the reference or the variable name to change the value in the variable. When you create a read-only reference, you can change the variable but not with the reference.

The following statements define one integer variable named `iv` and a read-only alias reference to that variable named `rv`:

```
int iv = 25;              // Regular integer variable
const int & rv = iv;      // Read-only alias
```

Visual C++ enables you to change `iv` as long as you use the variable's actual name. However, the reference is a reference to a constant. Even though `iv` is not really a constant, the second statement tells this to Visual C++:

> *"Define a reference named* `rv` *to the constant named* `iv`*. I will never use the reference to change* `iv` *because I am defining a reference* to a constant *(a read-only reference)."*

The following statement stores 89 in iv:

```
iv = 89;
```

If you want to print the value of iv, you can use either the variable or its reference. Both of the following statements print 89:

```
cout << iv << "\n";
cout << rv << "\n";
```

You cannot change iv through the reference, however, as you would be able to do if rv were a regular integer reference. Visual C++ will not enable you to do this:

```
rv = 45;    // You cannot use rv as an lvalue!
```

> **Advantageous Constants**
>
> const values are always constant…unless you override their "constantness" with typecasting. Programmers often create constants to protect the program's variables from themselves as much as other programmers who might come along later and maintain the program.
>
> Defining a value as constant creates a contract between you and Visual C++. Without using tricky typecasts, you cannot break your end of the contract, and Visual C++ will never enable you to change a constant value.
>
> If somebody wants to come along later and remove const from your data's definition, the programmer then has the freedom to change the value as much as he or she wants to. Therefore, you can do nothing to ensure that your const data remain constant, but const is a very strong suggestion.
>
> When you explicitly define a value as constant, you put the burden of constant-checking onto Visual C++'s back—where it belongs. Being able to catch errors at compile time is much more productive than trying to find errors that show up at runtime. Runtime errors produce incorrect results that you must trace, but the errors generated at compile time are much easier to fix. When you enter into a contract with Visual C++ and define a variable as constant, and then you break that contract by trying to change the constant, Visual C++ catches the error before your program finishes compiling.

Summary

Today's chapter has been a data-oriented chapter with an emphasis on references and constants. If you pick up virtually any C++ book or magazine, you'll see references defined and used all the time. A reference is an automatically dereferenced pointer. Unlike with pointers, you never have to dereference a reference variable.

A reference is an alias to another variable. You can use either the name of the variable or the name of the reference, and you'll be printing or changing the same value. Most Visual C++ programmers don't define references for aliases; instead, Visual C++ programmers define references to help clarify their pointer usage and the passing and returning of parameters between functions, as you'll see in future daily lessons.

As you saw on a previous day, `#define` is used much less frequently in C++ than in C. Many Visual C++ programmers have eliminated all `#define` preprocessor directives from their programs. The replacement, `const`, is often misunderstood when used with pointers and references.

When you want to point to a constant but not change the constant through the pointer, create a pointer to the constant. When you want a pointer to point to the same place in memory at all times, define a constant pointer. When you want both—a constant pointer that never changes pointing to data that cannot change—define a constant pointer to a constant.

There is a special kind of reference you can create that generates read-only aliases. When you define a reference to a constant, you define a read-only alias. You can read the value being aliased with the alias name, but you cannot change the value via the alias name. You can always change the variable using its original name as long as the variable is not defined with `const`.

Q&A

Q. What is a `void` pointer?

A. A `void` pointer is a pointer that can point to *any* data type. Non-`void` pointers such as `int` pointers and `float` pointers can point only to `int`s and `float`s, respectively. `void` pointers are generic; you can assign a `void` pointer the address of any data type.

Q. What is a reference?

A. Simply stated, a reference is a pointer that is always dereferenced. A reference closely resembles a pointer, and you can use a reference anywhere you would use a dereferenced pointer. A reference acts like an alias, a second name for a variable.

Aliases aren't the primary reason for using references. References simplify programming because they eliminate the need for the dereferencing operator, *, and they simplify the passing and returning of parameters between functions, as you'll see in Day 6's chapter, "Communicating with Functions."

Q. How do I define a reference?

A. Use the address of operator, &, to define a reference. Because a reference closely resembles a pointer, you usually create a reference that points to a value of the same data type. In other words, you could create an int reference to a float, but Visual C++ does not generate a true reference when you do. (Visual C++ creates a reference to an integer temporarily created from the float.)

To define a reference to a char variable named c, you would use this statement:

```
char & rc = c;    // rf is a reference to c
```

You must initialize a reference when you define it. Visual C++ will not enable you to use this statement:

```
char & rc;        // Not allowed
```

Q. What is the difference between a constant pointer and a pointer to a constant?

A. A constant pointer cannot be changed. Therefore, you cannot redirect a constant pointer to a different memory location from its original value when you defined it. A pointer to a constant is just that—a pointer variable that points to a value that cannot change. You can redirect the pointer to any other memory location that you want, but you cannot change the memory location through the pointer.

Combining a constant pointer with a pointer to a constant creates the most solid of all data ties possible in Visual C++; a constant pointer to a constant is a pointer that cannot change pointing to a value that cannot change.

Powerful Pointers

Q. What is a read-only alias?

A. In Visual C++, an alias is a reference. A read-only alias is a reference to a constant. More accurately, a read-only alias is a reference defined as if it were pointing to a constant, but in reality, the value being referenced was not defined with `const`. You can use the reference name to retrieve the reference's value, but you must use the variable's original name to change the value stored in the variable.

Q. How does the use of `const` clarify my code?

A. By specifying `const` for every variable in your program that will not change (including arguments when you receive them), you protect yourself from inadvertently changing those variables. You also help ensure that other programmers who might later maintain your program don't inadvertently change values that shouldn't change.

When you violate the contract of `const` values by trying to change a `const`, Visual C++ issues an error when you compile the program. Fixing compile-time errors is much easier than debugging program errors at runtime.

Workshop

The Workshop offers quiz questions and exercises to hone your skills and give you feedback on today's lesson. You'll find some proposed answers in Appendix D.

Quiz

1. True or False: The following statement defines a pointer variable and a reference variable:

   ```
   char * pPtr;
   char & rPtr;
   ```

2. How would you change the value of `i` through a reference variable named `ri`?

3. Each of the following v variable definitions fits into one of the following categories:

   1. Regular integer variable
   2. Constant integer variable
   3. Reference to an integer
   4. Pointer to an integer
   5. Pointer to an integer constant
   6. Constant pointer to an integer
   7. Constant pointer to a constant integer
   8. Read-only alias

   Which of these descriptions best fits the following definitions?

   A. `const int v = 9;`

   B. `const int * v = &anotherInt;`

   C. `int * const v = &anotherInt;`

   D. `const int const * v = &anotherInt;`

   E. `int v = anotherInt;`

   F. `int & v = anotherInt;`

   G. `const int & v = anotherInt;`

   H. `int * i = &anotherInt;`

4. True or False: The following statement initializes a void pointer:

   `ptr = 0;`

Exercises

1. Write a program that initializes a regular integer array with the days in each of the 12 months in each element. (Ignore leap years.) After defining and initializing the array, create a constant pointer that points to the first element of the array. Write a loop that prints the elements of the array by using the constant pointer, not by using the array name.

Powerful Pointers

2. Write a program that defines, initializes, and prints the value of each of these:
    - ☐ Integer constant variable
    - ☐ Reference to an integer
    - ☐ Read-only alias
    - ☐ Pointer to an integer
    - ☐ Pointer to an integer constant
    - ☐ Constant pointer to an integer
    - ☐ Constant pointer to a integer constant

Day 5

Memory Allocation: There When You Need It

Memory Allocation: There When You Need It

Dynamic memory allocation enables you to use as much or as little memory as you need. Not only that, but you can get the memory or release it whenever your program is ready for it.

If you have done much C programming, you are accustomed to using the `malloc()` and `free()` functions to allocate and deallocate memory. `malloc()`, as with all its related functions such as `calloc()` and `realloc()`, requires practice and is prone to programmer errors because of its cryptic nature.

Visual C++ programmers don't use `malloc()` and `free()` because Visual C++ includes two new operators, `new` and `delete`, that take the place of `malloc()` and `free()`, respectively. `new` and `delete` are extremely easy to use and do much more behind-the-scenes work than their corresponding functions.

If you never learn the OOP parts of Visual C++, you will probably still switch to Visual C++ when you see how easy and powerful `new` and `delete` are. When you master OOP, however, you'll see how to use `new` and `delete` to work with objects, and you will even learn to write your own memory-allocation operators using `new` and `delete`. Today, you learn about the following topics:

- How to allocate memory with `new`
- How to deallocate memory with `delete`
- How to allocate arrays and matrixes on the heap
- How to write event-driven programs that automatically check for allocation errors using Visual C++'s exception handling routine

Note: Although the words `new` and `delete` do not look like regular operators such as + and *, they are operators in the same way that `sizeof()` is an operator, even though `sizeof()` often looks and acts like a built-in function.

new to Allocate, *delete* to Eliminate

As with most of the C functions, Visual C++ supports the `malloc()` and `free()` functions if you want to use them, but there is little reason for either function in Visual

C++ programs. `malloc()` and `free()` are cumbersome and require detailed syntax. To use `malloc()` properly, you must include the STDLIB.H header file and always typecast the return pointer from `malloc()` to a data type pointer that you are working with.

`malloc()` returns a `void` pointer, and as you learned from the preceding day's chapter, you must typecast all `void` pointers before doing much with them—`malloc()`'s return value is no exception.

`malloc()` becomes especially difficult when you have to allocate an array of structures on the heap. Here is a `malloc()` function call that allocates 75 structure variables named `players` on the heap:

```
players = (struct players *)malloc(75 * sizeof(struct players));
```

Visual C++ does not require the repetition of the `struct` keyword that is shown here, which offers a slight improvement over C's `malloc()`, but that improvement by itself doesn't justify changing to `new`. The other drawbacks of `malloc()` discussed in this chapter justify using `new` rather than `malloc()` because `new` and Visual C++ take much of the work off your back.

How Important Is Allocation, Really?

Every day, computer memory and disk space are getting cheaper and more abundant. Whereas 256K was considered plenty of room a short time ago, 4 *megabytes* of memory is considered squeezing things today.

Many PC computer systems come equipped with 8 to 16 megabytes of RAM and hundreds of megabytes of disk space. With disk-doubling technologies and with the prices of RAM decreasing as fast as the density of RAM increases, you might tend to think that memory allocation problems would go away; after all, when you've got *tons* of memory and you use only a fraction of it, why bother with allocating memory for variables? Why not just use local variables and not worry about freeing the memory later in the program?

Experts agree that more memory in your systems requires even *more* reason to allocate memory when and only when you need it. With more powerful computer systems, people use more powerful programs, especially networked, windowing, multitasking, and multi-user computers and programs. As soon as your program begins sharing the same resource space (especially

Memory Allocation: There When You Need It

memory) with another task, memory becomes a premium, and both tasks need all they can get to maintain speed and functionality. If your program needs a large amount of memory for a short time, your program should use memory only during that time and free that memory for other tasks which might need the memory next.

Given that memory allocation is more important than ever, a good case can be made for learning Visual C++'s easy memory allocation operators new and delete.

To summarize Visual C++ memory allocation operators, keep the following two points in mind as you read the rest of this chapter:

new is Visual C++'s heap allocation operator replacement for the malloc() function.

delete is Visual C++'s heap deallocation operator replacement for the free() function.

The Concept of Memory Allocation

It might be prudent to review the process of dynamic memory allocation briefly so that all readers will be on common ground. The heap is a large chunk of unused memory in your PC (see Figure 5.1). The size of the heap changes when you (or another task running such as MS-DOS or Windows) allocate variables and deallocate variables.

Note: The word *dynamic* means changing, so *dynamic memory allocation* refers to the changing heap size as you allocate and deallocate memory.

Some people mistakenly believe that using local variables eliminates the need for dynamic memory allocation. After all, the variables go into scope when needed, and when they are no longer needed (when their block ends), they go out of scope and are no longer available.

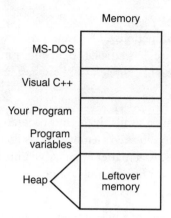

Figure 5.1. The heap is memory left over after DOS, Visual C++, and your program have taken all they need.

Local variables are no longer visible when they go out of scope, but they still consume memory for the life of the program. When you run a Visual C++ program, the program loader makes room for all global *and* local variables needed in the program. The local variables are reserved on the *stack* (an area of memory that changes somewhat like the heap but on a smaller scale), and the global variable space is already attached to your executable program. (Visual C++ actually appends global variable space to your executable program, which is one reason why programs with global variables take more disk space than the same program with fewer or no global variables.)

Given this background, you'll understand why learning about dynamic memory allocation is so critical. Although you should use local variables as much as possible, they do not improve your use of memory during runtime.

You would never want to allocate *every* variable on the heap. And in reality, you couldn't allocate every variable on the heap because you have to define nonheap pointers that point to heap data to get to the heap's data. Most arrays are perfect candidates for heap allocation because you rarely use every element in every array throughout an entire program. Using dynamic memory allocation, you can grab more array elements from the heap when you need them and put them back when you are through with them.

Note: Some fixed arrays, such as day-of-the-week names, are better left as local arrays (and arguably global arrays, but only if you use them

Memory Allocation: There When You Need It

> throughout many functions). Dynamic memory allocation is fairly efficient, but it is still less efficient than allocating local and global arrays. Small arrays that don't change in size are best left as regular arrays.

Memory that you allocate is available to your program just like variables are, except that you can only point to allocated memory, not assign names to heap memory as you do with regular variables. As a matter of fact, dynamic memory allocation is perhaps the most important reason for learning about pointers in the first place; you can't access the heap without pointers.

It helps to think of the heap as a pile of memory, not a sequential listing of memory as it is in reality. When you deallocate memory, your program releases the data from the reserved heap and puts that memory back to the heap so that another process (either your program or another, such as the operating system) can get to that memory when needed. The reason it helps to view the heap as a big pile of memory is that when you deallocate memory, you must assume that you no longer know where that memory is. In other words, if you deallocate memory (with `delete` or `free()`), for a few microseconds and maybe longer that memory will probably still be at the same place on the heap with the values you left in it. However, you must assume that the memory is no longer where you first allocated it because another task could have taken the memory as soon as you released it. That's the entire idea of deallocation anyway—the memory is thrown back to the free heap (sometimes called the *free store*) so that the resource is given back to other tasks that might need it.

Figure 5.2 shows three kinds of data allocated on the heap. A character array, an integer, and a floating-point value are all allocated. Notice that pointers (through dereferencing) are the only means for getting to the heap values.

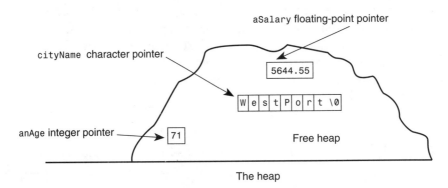

Figure 5.2. After allocating three kinds of data.

When you deallocate heap memory, your pointers are, in effect, disconnected from the heap, and the heap manager knows to give up the freed portion of the heap if another process wants it.

Note: Don't ever mix `new` and `free()` or `malloc()` and `delete`. Although some combinations seem to work, the results are unpredictable and could wreak havoc in large programs. If you allocate with `malloc()`, use `free()` to deallocate; if you allocate with `new`, use `delete` to deallocate.

Specifying *new* for a Heap of Memory

When you allocate with `new`, you don't have to typecast the return pointer. Visual C++ is smart enough to determine the right kind of pointer you need.

Suppose that you want to allocate a new integer on the heap. First, you must define an integer pointer such as this:

```
int * anAge;     // Define an integer pointer
```

Then you must allocate the heap memory. To tell Visual C++ that you want a new integer from the heap and you want `anAge` to point to that integer, you can use this statement:

```
anAge = new int;    // Allocates a new integer
```

Notice why you don't need a typecast: the `int` keyword tells Visual C++ exactly what kind of heap data you want. You can combine the pointer definition with the heap allocation in one statement if you want memory allocated close to the pointer's definition like this:

```
int * anAge = new int;    // Defines pointer and allocates heap
```

Because you can define variables anywhere in a Visual C++ program (as long as you define them before using them), you don't have to allocate a heap pointer ahead of the time you want it.

To define a floating-point pointer and allocate a `float` value on the heap, you can use this statement:

```
float * aSalary = new float;    // Define and allocate pointer
```

121

Day 5

Memory Allocation: There When You Need It

Of course, allocating single variables isn't that beneficial; the pointers to the data take almost as much space as the integers and floating-point values themselves do. However, when allocating arrays, you can allocate as many elements as you like and still point to the elements with a regular pointer like this:

```
char * cityName = new char[9];    // Allocate a character array
```

To allocate an array, simply put the number of array elements (including room for the null zero if you allocate a character array that will hold a string) in brackets after the data type. Visual C++ will reserve that many elements as long as the free heap has a large enough space for the array at the time of the new.

After the preceding three definitions are completed, you'll have the heap reserved like the one you saw in Figure 5.2. The following three statements initialize the heap memory to Figure 5.2's values:

```
*anAge = 17;              // Use dereferencing to initialize
*aSalary = 5644.55;       // the values on the heap
strcpy(cityName, "Westport");
```

Note: The heap is not automatically initialized for you, so be sure to initialize the heap with data yourself.

The program in Listing 5.1 allocates strings for as long as the user wants to enter new names. The program does not free the allocated memory, but it should. The program relies on DOS to take care of putting memory back to normal when the program ends. When you learn the details of delete a little later in the chapter, you'll see how to properly deallocate memory. (In other words, this program is to illustrate new, but it stinks when it comes to cleaning up after itself. As a master Visual C++ programmer, you'll *always* deallocate heap memory when you finish with it, even if the last line in the program contains a delete.)

Listing 5.1. Allocating strings for the user's input.

```
1:  // Filename: NAMENEW.CPP
2:  // Allocates strings on the heap
3:  #include <iostream.h>
4:  #include <string.h>
5:  main()
6:  {
7:      const int MAX = 50;     // We'll hold up to 50 names on heap
8:      char inputName[80];     // A place to hold name entered
```

```
 9:    // Each of the names[] pointers will point to a different name
10:    char * names[MAX];
11:    cout << "** Name Entering Program **\n";
12:    for (int num=0; num<MAX; num++)
13:    {  cout << "Please enter a name (End quits) --> ";
14:       cin.getline(inputName, 80); // Get a string up to 80 characters
15:       if (!stricmp(inputName,"END"))    // Continue only if not END
16:          { break; }
17:       // The following statement does a lot of work. It allocates
18:       // just enough characters to hold the name entered by the user
19:       // along with a null zero at the end of the string.
20:       names[num] = new char[strlen(inputName)+1];
21:       // Copy the entered name to the heap
22:       strcpy(names[num], inputName);
23:    }
24:    cout << "\nHere are the names you entered:\n";
25:    for (int j=0; j<num; j++)
26:      { cout << names[j] << "\n"; }
27:    return 0;
28: }
```

```
** Name Entering Program **
Please enter a name (End quits) --> Sam Spade
Please enter a name (End quits) --> Doc Savage
Please enter a name (End quits) --> Steve Austin
Please enter a name (End quits) --> Heath Barkley
Please enter a name (End quits) --> end

Here are the names you entered:
Sam Spade
Doc Savage
Steve Austin
Heath Barkley
```

This program asks for up to 50 names. (You can easily increase the maximum number of names by changing the MAX constant in line 7 to a different value.) One character array is defined in line 8 to hold the user's input of each name. After the user enters a name, strlen() determines the length of the name. The result is then sent to the new operation on line 20 to allocate enough heap memory for that string plus one for the string terminator. When the user types end (in either uppercase or lowercase because stricmp() is not case-sensitive), the program stops asking for user input and allocates the strings on the heap.

Figure 5.3 shows what the strings look like when the program allocates them, given the output just shown. Each element in the character pointer array called names points to a different string on the heap. As Figure 5.3 shows, the strings don't necessarily appear on the heap in the order in which they were allocated.

Memory Allocation: There When You Need It

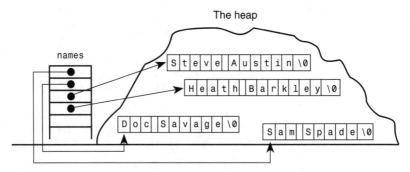

Figure 5.3. The look of the heap after allocating the user's strings.

> **Note:** Notice on line 26 that you don't dereference character pointers when printing them with cout. All strings are passed as pointers to the operators, and Visual C++ knows to dereference the pointer for you.

Initializing While Allocating

If you want to specify an initial value for your allocated data, Visual C++ supports a special syntax that enables you to. You can initialize the allocated heap memory with a value only when you allocate the memory.

To initialize heap memory at the time you allocate it, enclose the initial value inside parentheses at the right of the statement with new. For example, to initialize an integer value you are allocating on the heap, you can use this statement:

```
int * myVal = new int (0);   // Allocates and initializes
```

Visual C++ puts a zero in the myVal on the heap. Initializing with the parenthetical value is similar to using calloc(), except that calloc() always initializes with zero and you can initialize with any value you want when using new.

> **Note:** The initialization syntax looks odd, but it works efficiently and is better than using an assignment later to initialize the value on the heap.

You cannot automatically initialize array values on the heap. Later in the book, you'll see how to write your own array initialization new operator. (Yes, in Visual C++, you can change the way operators work with your data!)

The program in Listing 5.2 shows several kinds of values being allocated on the heap, and all are initialized at the time of their allocation. As with the program in Listing 5.1, the allocated memory is not freed as it should be (putting the burden on DOS's back). But the next section will demonstrate how to free heap memory properly with Visual C++.

Listing 5.2. Allocating and initializing heap data.

```
1:  // Filename: ALLINIT.CPP
2:  // Allocates and initializes several values on the heap
3:  #include <iostream.h>
4:  main()
5:  {
6:     // Allocate single data values
7:     char * cPtr = new char ('X');
8:     int * iPtr = new int (0);
9:     float * fPtr = new float(1.1);
10:    double * dVal = new double (12345.678);
11:    // Print the values to show the initialization
12:    cout << "cPtr is " << *cPtr << "\n";
13:    cout << "iPtr is " << *iPtr << "\n";
14:    cout << "fPtr is " << *fPtr << "\n";
15:    cout << "dVal is " << *dVal << "\n";
16:    return 0;
17: }
```

```
cPtr is X
iPtr is 0
fPtr is 1.1
dVal is 12345.67
```

As you can see in lines 7 through 10, you can initialize any kind of heap data with any value you want at the time of the allocation.

Using *new*

pointerVar = new *datatype* [[*numElements*]] [(*initialVal*)]

The brackets within brackets indicate that the number of elements is optional if you want to allocate an array on the heap. If you do allocate an array, you must specify the initial number of elements in the array, and you must enclose the number of elements

Memory Allocation: There When You Need It

within brackets. You must enclose the initial value in parentheses, and you cannot specify an initial value if you allocate an array on the heap.

Example

```
// Examples of using the new operator
main()
{
  // Allocate single data values
  char * cPtr1 = new char;    // Allocate without initialization
  int * iPtr1 = new int;
  float * fPtr1 = new float;
  // Allocate with initialization
  char * cPtr2 = new char('a');
  int * iPtr2 = new int(40);
  float * fPtr2 = new float(-5.7);
  // Allocate arrays of any data type
  char * cAra = new char [100];
  int * iAra = new int [60];
  float * fAra = new float [35];
  // Be sure to deallocate when you are done with the data
  // Rest of program would follow
```

Deallocating with *delete*

The `delete` operator deallocates memory allocated with `new` just as the `free()` function deallocates memory allocated with `malloc()`. To free memory, simply list the pointer's name of the allocated memory after `delete`. For example, the following statement deallocates a section of the heap pointed to by `aPtr`:

```
delete aPtr;   // Give the memory back to the heap
```

When you delete heap memory, the size of the free heap expands by the amount of the deleted memory (along with a little extra for overhead). When you delete memory, you release that memory back to the heap so that other tasks running will have access to the heap.

The Heap Is Efficient—But Not Perfect

As you allocate and deallocate, fragmented holes can begin to appear in your heap and slow down tasks that use the heap. Visual C++ does not defragment the heap (by collecting all the unused holes of memory into a contiguous chunk at the end of the heap) because doing so would slow down a running program greatly during the heap's clean-up process.

Heap fragmentation occurs if you allocate and deallocate lots of small chunks of heap memory. Although you'll rarely notice that heap fragmentation is occurring, you could reach a point at which you have heap memory left but cannot allocate any more because there is not one single block of free heap left as large as you want to allocate. Figure 5.4 shows how the heap can become cluttered with small chunks of free memory that used to be allocated.

Through the years, C and C++ programmers have offered solutions to heap fragmentation. If you plan to allocate and deallocate hundreds of small blocks from the heap, consider allocating one big chunk and using an array of your own pointers within that heap memory to simulate allocation for the rest of the program. Doing so is not a trivial programming task, but the speed improvement might be worth it to you.

As computers get faster and faster, Microsoft might consider offering a heap defragmentation routine or Visual C++ might defragment automatically. At this time, however, programmers are happier having the efficiency of speed at the trade-off of fragmentation.

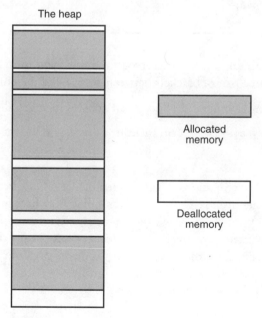

Figure 5.4. The heap can become full of unused memory holes too small to be used for later allocations.

Memory Allocation: There When You Need It

The program in Listing 5.3 properly deallocates the memory first allocated in Listing 5.2.

Listing 5.3. Freeing heap memory when done.

```
 1: // Filename: ALLINIT2.CPP
 2: // Allocates and deallocates several values on the heap
 3: #include <iostream.h>
 4: main()
 5: {
 6:   // Allocate single data values
 7:   char * cPtr = new char ('X');
 8:   int * iPtr = new int (0);
 9:   float * fPtr = new float(1.1);
10:   double * dVal = new double (12345.678);
11:   // Print the values to show the initialization
12:   cout << "cPtr is " << *cPtr << "\n";
13:   cout << "iPtr is " << *iPtr << "\n";
14:   cout << "fPtr is " << *fPtr << "\n";
15:   cout << "dVal is " << *dVal << "\n";
16:   delete cPtr;   // Free memory for other tasks
17:   delete iPtr;
18:   delete fPtr;
19:   delete dVal;
20:   return 0;
21: }
```

When deallocating memory reserved for arrays, you must use a special syntax for `delete`. Insert a pair of brackets between `delete` and the pointer to the heap's array.

The following statement deallocates an array of memory allocated with `new`:

```
delete [] myName;    // Deallocates an array from the heap
```

Note: Older versions of C++ (those before AT&T version 2.1) required a number inside `delete`'s brackets telling C++ how many elements to delete. Visual C++, as with most modern C++ compilers, keeps track of the allocated elements for you so that you type only the empty brackets and Visual C++ knows how many elements to deallocate based on how many elements you allocated previously.

The brackets tell Visual C++ that you want to deallocate an array of values and not just a single pointer's value from the heap. For example, suppose you allocated an array of 16 characters on the heap and assigned the heap array a value like this:

```
char * lotsOfText;
lotsOfText = new char [16];   // Allocate 16 characters
strcpy(lotsOfText, "Dan's Bake Sale");
```

If you attempted to deallocate the array like

```
delete lotsOfText;     // Only a partial deallocation
```

then only the first of the 16 allocated characters will be deallocated. However, if you properly deallocated the array like

```
delete [] lotsOfText;    // Full deallocation
```

then all 16 characters would properly be returned to the free heap. Figure 5.5 shows the difference between the two deallocations.

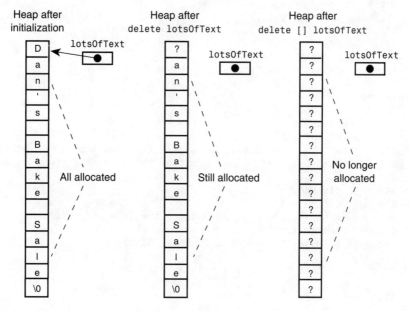

Figure 5.5. Be sure to deallocate everything!

Not deallocating all the memory defeats the purpose of dynamic memory allocation. Being able to release all your memory back to the rest of the system is the primary reason to use `new` and `delete`.

Memory Allocation: There When You Need It

The program in Listing 5.4 demonstrates dynamic memory allocation and deallocation with new and delete for television show data. A structure is declared, and an array holds pointers to the initialized allocated structure variables as the user enters data. A menu controls whether the user wants to add data or see the data. Before the program ends, all the memory is freed from the heap.

Listing 5.4. A television show program demonstrating allocation and deallocation.

```
1:   // Filename: TVSHOWS.CPP
2:   // Uses the heap for allocating and deallocating structures
3:   #include <iostream.h>
4:   #include <string.h>
5:   struct show {
6:      char * showName;
7:      int dayNum;        // 0-Sun, 1-Mon, ..., 6-Saturday
8:      int length;        // In minutes
9:   };
10:  // Program prototypes follow
11:  void dispMenu(void);
12:  void addShows(show * shows[], int * showCnt);
13:  void prShows(show * shows[], int showCnt);
14:  void errPrint(void);
15:  void delAll(show * shows[], int showCnt);
16:
17:  main()
18:  {
19:     char ans, cr;
20:     const int MaxShows = 100;
21:     show * shows[MaxShows];   // All TV shows are stored on heap
22:     int showCnt = 0;       // Count of the number of shows on heap
23:     do
24:     { dispMenu();
25:        cin >> ans;
26:        cin.get(cr);       // Discard the Enter keystroke
27:        switch (ans)
28:        { case '1' : addShows(shows, &showCnt);
29:                     break;
30:          case '2' : prShows(shows, showCnt);
31:                     break;
32:          case '3' : break;
33:          default  : errPrint();
34:                     break;
35:        }
36:     } while (ans != '3');
37:     delAll(shows, showCnt);   // Must free both names and structures
38:     return 0;
39:  }
40:  //////////////////////////////////////////////////////////////////
```

```
41: // Function to display a menu
42: void dispMenu(void)
43: {
44:    cout << "\n** Television Show Program **\n";
45:    cout << "\n\nDo you want to:\n";
46:    cout << "1. Add a television show to the list\n";
47:    cout << "2. Print the current list of shows\n";
48:    cout << "3. Exit the program\n";
49:    cout << "What is your choice? ";
50:    return;
51: }
52: //////////////////////////////////////////////////////////////
53: // Function to add shows to the heap
54: void addShows(show * shows[], int * showCnt)
55: {
56:    char inLine[80];            // Need a temporary place to hold
57:                                // the user's entered data
58:    cout << "\nWhat is the next show's name? ";
59:    cin.getline(inLine, 80);
60:    shows[*showCnt] = new show;   // Allocate the structure
61:    // The structure holds a character pointer to the show's
62:    // name so allocate data for the show name as well
63:    shows[*showCnt]->showName = new char[strlen(inLine) + 1];
64:    strcpy(shows[*showCnt]->showName, inLine);
65:    cout << "What day is the show on?\n";
66:    cout << "(0=Sunday, 1=Monday, 2=Tuesday, ..., 6=Saturday) ";
67:    cin >> shows[*showCnt]->dayNum;
68:    cout << "How long is the show (in minutes)? ";
69:    cin >> shows[*showCnt]->length;
70:    (*showCnt)++;
71:    return;
72: }
73: //////////////////////////////////////////////////////////////
74: // Function to print the shows from the heap
75: void prShows(show * shows[], int showCnt)
76: {
77:    char * weekDay[] = {"Sunday", "Monday", "Tuesday", "Wednesday",
78:                        "Thursday", "Friday", "Saturday"};
79:    char cr;    // Key Enter keystroke
80:    if (showCnt == 0)
81:    {
82:       cout << "\n** There are no shows entered yet...\n";
83:    }
84:    else
85:    {  for (int cnt=0; cnt<showCnt; cnt++)
86:       { cout << "\nShow name: " << shows[cnt]->showName << "\n";
87:         cout << "Day of show: " << weekDay[shows[cnt]->dayNum];
88:         cout << "\nShow length: " << shows[cnt]->length << "\n";
89:       }
90:    }
91:    cout << "\nPress Enter to continue...";
```

continues

Day 5
Memory Allocation: There When You Need It

Listing 5.4. continued

```
 92:    cin.get(cr);    // Let user press Enter to resume program
 93:    return;
 94: }
 95: //////////////////////////////////////////////////////////////////
 96: // Function to print an error if the user enters a bad menu choice
 97: void errPrint(void)
 98: {
 99:    char * enterPress = 0;    // Just to discard the newline
100:    cout << "\n\n*** You did not enter a correct menu option...\n";
101:    cout << "Press Enter to return to the menu and try again.\n";
102:    cin.getline(enterPress, 2);
103:    return;
104: }
105: //////////////////////////////////////////////////////////////////
106: // Function to deallocate all the heap data
107: void delAll(show * shows[], int showCnt)
108: {
109:    for (int cnt=0; cnt<showCnt; cnt++)
110:    {
111:       // First delete the name pointed to by
112:       // the structure's first member
113:       delete [] shows[cnt]->showName;
114:       // Now delete the memory of the rest of the structure
115:       delete [] shows[cnt];
116:    }
117:    // Now only the array of pointers is left
118:    return;
119: }
```

```
** Television Show Menu **

Do you want to:
1. Add a television show to the list
2. Print the current list of shows
3. Exit the program
What is your choice? 1

What is the next show's name? The C Programmer's Comedy Club
What day is the show on?
(0=Sunday, 1=Monday, 2=Tuesday, ..., 6=Saturday) 2
How long is the show (in minutes)? 30

** Television Show Menu **

Do you want to:
1. Add a television show to the list
2. Print the current list of shows
```

```
3. Exit the program
What is your choice? 1

What is the next show's name? The Computerist's Kitchen
What day is the show on?
(0=Sunday, 1=Monday, 2=Tuesday, ..., 6=Saturday) 5
How long is the show (in minutes)? 120


** Television Show Menu **

Do you want to:
1. Add a television show to the list
2. Print the current list of shows
3. Exit the program
What is your choice? 2

Show name: The C Programmer's Comedy Club
Day of show: Tuesday
Show length: 30

Show name: The Computerist's Kitchen
Day of show: Friday
Show length: 120

Press Enter to continue...

** Television Show Menu **

Do you want to:
1. Add a television show to the list
2. Print the current list of shows
3. Exit the program
What is your choice? 3
```

This program is the most extensive so far in the book, but like most programs, its look is worse than its *byte* (sorry about the pun...). As Figure 5.6 shows, not only are the structure variables allocated, but data within each allocated structure points to other allocated memory. Notice that within each allocated structure is a pointer to showName that also points to allocated memory. The only memory taken by the program for its entire run (other than a few working variables) is the array of 100 pointers. The structure data that each pointer points to is not allocated until the user is ready to enter a new show.

Although the days of the week could have been put on the heap as well, there was not a good reason for taking the coding and execution time to do so. The days of the week never change, and there are always seven of them. The heap is best left for changing data, such as new values being entered by the user over time as the program runs.

Memory Allocation: There When You Need It

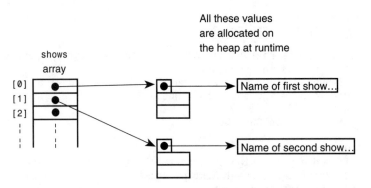

Figure 5.6. Each allocated structure points to an allocated name.

Note: You will also note that showCnt had to be passed by address to the addShows() function. Tomorrow's chapter will show you a much better way of passing data than by address when you have a function that must change a value passed to it.

Using *delete*

delete [[]] *pointerVar*;

The brackets within brackets indicate that brackets are optional. You specify the brackets only when you want to deallocate array memory on the heap. Visual C++ always deallocates the proper amount of memory. For example, if *pointerVar* is a pointer to double, delete deallocates enough memory for the double value being pointed to.

Example

```
// Examples of using the delete operator
main()
{
  // First allocate data values
  char * cPtr1 = new char;
  int * iPtr1 = new int (8);
  float * fPtr1 = new float;
  char * cPtr2 = new char[100];
  // Deallocate the data
  delete cPtr1;     // Deallocates a single character
```

```
delete iPtr1;    // Deallocates a single integer
delete fPtr1;    // Deallocates a single floating-point
delete [] cPtr2; // Deallocates all 100 characters
```

Multidimensional Arrays

Although arrays with more than one or two dimensions seem rare, there might be times when you must keep track of data that fits best within a *matrix* (a matrix is an array with more than one dimension, also called a *table*).

The most important part of allocating matrixes with new is to define the array properly. After you define the array, allocating the space for the array with new is trivial.

The general format of defining a matrix variable is

dataType (**matrixName*)[*numEls*]...

in which *dataType* is any data type, such as int, double, or a user-defined data type such as a structure. The *matrixName* is a variable name you want to give the matrix. Following the *matrixName*, list one or more sets of subscripts enclosed in brackets. Each subscript should be the maximum possible dimension size. *Don't specify the first subscript, however.* List only the remaining subscripts after the first one.

> **Note:** The matrix variable definition does not yet reserve space for the matrix, but only the pointer to the matrix. You'll use new for allocating the entire matrix in a moment. The matrix variable definition simply tells Visual C++ that the pointer will eventually point to a matrix of more than one dimension.

The following statement defines a two-dimensional matrix of floating-point values. The first dimension is unspecified, and the second holds six elements for each of the first dimension's elements.

```
float (*table)[6];   // Define the matrix name
```

After you define the matrix, you can allocate the matrix with new like this:

```
table = new float[5][6]; // Allocate 30 floating-point values
```

It is only when you allocate the memory on the heap that you specify the first dimension.

Memory Allocation: There When You Need It

You can combine the two statements like this:

```
float (*table)[6] = new float[5][6];   // Define and allocate
```

Figure 5.7 shows what the resulting heap's matrix looks like.

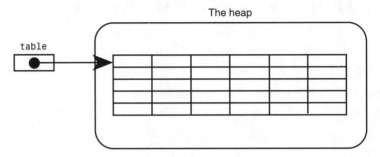

Figure 5.7. The matrix allocated on the heap.

As with arrays, you need only to specify a single bracket when deallocating a matrix, and Visual C++ takes care of deallocating the entire matrix. The following statement deallocates the `table` matrix defined earlier:

```
delete [] table;   // Frees all 30 floating-point values
```

The program in Listing 5.5 allocates three regions' sales. Each region contains five salespeople, and the table holds 12 months' worth of data for the five salespeople. The program simply allocates the three-dimensional matrix, fills the matrix with random values, and then deallocates the matrix.

> **Note:** Rarely, if ever, will you need more than two dimensions. If your programming up to this point required only single-dimensional arrays, you'll probably not have much need for them in the future. A lot of scientific and mathematical programs require multidimensional tables.

Listing 5.5. Allocating and deallocating a three-dimensional matrix.

```
1:  // Filename: SALESMAT.CPP
2:  // Allocates, initializes, and deallocates a three-dimensional table
3:  #include <iostream.h>
4:  #include <stdlib.h>
```

```
5:  main()
6:  {
7:    float (*sales)[5][12];
8:    sales = new float [3][5][12];   // Allocates 180 heap elements
9:    for (int region=0; region<=3; region++)
10:   {
11:     for (int people=0; people<5; people++)
12:     {
13:       for (int months=0; months<12; months++)
14:       {
15:         // Store a random number in each element
16:         sales[region][people][months] = float(rand());
17:       }
18:     }
19:   }
20:   // Now, deallocate the data with a single statement
21:   delete [] sales;    // Deallocates all 180 elements
22:   return 0;
23: }
```

Here is what line 7 actually says:

"Define a pointer to floating-point values. The pointer will eventually point to a matrix with a second dimension of 5 elements and a third dimension of 12 elements."

DO	**DON'T**

DO use new and delete rather than malloc() and free().

DO initialize heap values with the parenthetical syntax if you want the same initial value stored in the element you are allocating.

DO free heap arrays using the bracket syntax.

DO be careful to define the matrix pointer properly before allocating the matrix from the heap.

DON'T assume that Visual C++ initialized or zeroed heap memory for you; you must initialize your heap data yourself.

DON'T ever mix new with free() or malloc() with delete. The results are unpredictable and even disastrous in Visual C++.

Memory Allocation: There When You Need It

If the Heap Has a Problem

There is a physical limit to the size of your heap no matter how much memory your computer holds. Instead of blindly allocating memory in the hope that there will be enough when you need it, you should always make sure that new did its job. One way to determine whether the heap allocation was successful is to see whether new's pointer points to NULL (the same as 0 in Visual C++, but this does not always hold true for all C++ compilers) after the new statement.

Suppose that you requested 500 floating-point elements from the heap, but Visual C++ cannot find 500 continuous floating-point heap values. The following code would print a warning message and terminate the program if the heap space was not available:

```
float * values = new float[500];   // Attempt allocation
if (values == NULL)
{
  cerr << "Cannot allocate the requested memory.\n";
  exit (1);   // Terminate the program
}
// The rest of the program would continue if the
// heap allocation was successful.
```

new never produces a NULL pointer value unless the allocation failed. Many factors affect allocation, and you should *always* check that the allocation attempt worked (by comparing the pointer to NULL) every time you use new.

There is a problem with checking new's success, however. The problem is that you are busy writing an application that deserves your attention, and every time you allocate memory, you have to check for the success or failure of that allocation.

Luckily, Visual C++ makes your programming life easier by providing an *automatic* method for checking new's success. As you learn more and more of Visual C++, you'll see how Visual C++ takes the tedium out of programming and takes care of a lot of the petty details that you would have to handle yourself in other programming languages such as C.

Visual C++ offers a new *exception handler*. An exception handler is simply a function that you write which contains code you want executed when and if an allocation fails. The function can be as long or short as you like. Many Visual C++ programmers just print an error message and terminate the program such as in the previous code you saw. After you set up the failed allocation function, you never have to check for allocation success again; Visual C++ automatically calls the function when and if an

allocation fails. (Day 19's chapter, "Introduction to Throwing and Catching Exceptions," describes other methods that Visual C++ provides for exception handling.)

Here is the previous allocation-failure code turned into a function that the exception handler can recognize:

```
int newError(size_t size)
{
  cerr << "Cannot allocate the requested memory.\n";
  exit (1);   // Terminate the program
  return 0;
}
```

Your memory error function must receive a `size_t` argument. `size_t` is a built-in data type used for byte counts. In reality, you could use `unsigned int` because a `typedef` statement in the NEW.H header file defines `size_t` as an `unsigned int`. Your function doesn't have to use the `size_t` argument (this `newError()` function does not), but the `size_t` value is the number of bytes of heap memory requested in the new that triggered the error.

You must now tell your Visual C++ program that this function, `newError()`, is to execute when and if an allocation fails. Visual C++ includes a special allocation-failure testing routine prototyped in NEW.H called `_set_new_handler()`. (Don't forget the leading underscore.) This function takes as its only argument the name of your error-handling function. For example, the following statement sets up the link between Visual C++'s internal handler and your function named `newError()`:

```
_set_new_handler(newError);   // Sets up your error function
```

That's it on your part, and now Visual C++ does the rest behind your program's back during execution of the program. If a new ever fails, Visual C++ immediately calls your `newError()` function, but your function never executes if all the program's new statements work.

Listing 5.6 shows how to install the exception-handler function in a program that allocates more memory than can be gotten from the heap to show the resulting error message.

Listing 5.6. Forcing the allocation-failure function's execution.

```
1:  // Filename: ALLFAIL.CPP
2:  // Attempts a bad heap allocation
3:  #include <iostream.h>
4:  #include <new.h>
5:  #include <stdlib.h>      // For exit() function call
```

continues

Day 5

Memory Allocation: There When You Need It

Listing 5.6. continued

```
 6:   int newError(size_t size);
 7:   // Regular program appears next
 8:   main()
 9:   {
10:     _set_new_handler(newError);
11:     // Now, attempt to allocate memory
12:     char * c1 = new char[2];
13:     cout << "First allocation worked properly...";
14:     // Now, attempt a bad allocation
15:     char * c2 = new char[64000U];
16:     if (c2)
17:       { cout << "Second allocation worked properly.\n";
18:         delete [] c1;  // Deallocate if previous ones worked
19:         delete [] c2; }
20:     else
21:       { delete [] c1; // It's a good assumption that the 1st
22:                       // allocation worked so clean its memory
23:       }
24:     return 0;
25:   }
26:   ///////////////////////////////////////////////////////////
27:   // The following function executes only if new fails
28:   int newError(size_t size)
29:   {
30:     cerr << "Cannot allocate the requested memory.\n";
31:     return 0;
32:   }
```

First allocation worked properly.
Cannot allocate the requested memory.

The first allocation in line 12 works, but the second, in line 15, fails because too many heap characters are being allocated. The second line of output was produced from line 30 because Visual C++ automatically called the `newError()` function when it realized that the new request can't be filled successfully.

As you can see, the `newError()` function returns a 0 on line 31. Your error function should return an integer. If you return a zero from the error function, Visual C++ will not attempt to retry the new that failed. If, however, you return a nonzero value, Visual C++ will again attempt to allocate the memory that failed originally. You might want Visual C++ to try the allocation again if you were able to free some heap space in the error handler.

Summary

You now have the tools to allocate and deallocate memory using Visual C++'s `new` and `delete` functions. There are many advantages to `new` and `delete` over the older `malloc()` and `free()` functions. `new` and `delete` are easier to type, use, and understand than their function counterparts.

Because `new` and `delete` are operators, you don't have to specify the `sizeof()` operator as with `malloc()`. You can easily reserve arrays and matrixes on the heap by inserting the maximum subscript in brackets after `new`. If you like, you can initialize allocated non-array values by enclosing the initial value in parentheses at the end of the `new`.

One of the most useful and time-saving features of `new` and `delete` is Visual C++'s automatic execution of your allocation-failure function. It is this exception handler that enables you to concentrate more on the problem you are programming and less on the tedious coding for details such as error checking.

Q&A

Q. Why is dynamic memory allocation becoming even more important as time goes by?

A. More and more people are using multitasking and networked multi-user PCs. Your running program should use only those resources it needs so that other tasks and users can have all the free resources they might need.

Q. Why is new better than `malloc()`?

A. `new`'s syntax is cleaner than `malloc()`'s. `malloc()` is a function and not an operator, so `malloc()` cannot automatically recognize storage requirements of heap values. You have to specify your own `sizeof()` operator when using `malloc()`, whereas `new` can figure out the size of your data for you.

With `new`, you can also specify your own error-handling function that Visual C++ executes if the allocation fails.

Q. Why is `delete` better than `free()`?

A. Given that `new` is better than `malloc()`, `delete` is the corresponding deallocation operator to `new`. You cannot properly `free()` memory allocated with `new`, so when using `new`, you should always use `delete` to deallocate the memory.

Memory Allocation: There When You Need It

Later in this book, you'll learn how to change the behavior of new and delete so that they work exactly the way you want them to, a claim that cannot be made about malloc() and free().

Q. What is an exception handler?

A. The term *exception handler* is a general term applied to functions that automatically execute when an error (the *exception*) occurs. Visual C++'s exception handler function, _set_new_handler(), executes automatically when a new allocation fails. You can force the exception handler to execute your own error function if a memory allocation fails, and you don't have to check each individual use of new for errors because the _set_new_handler() automatically monitors all new attempts and intervenes if needed.

Workshop

The Workshop offers quiz questions and exercises to hone your skills and give you feedback on today's lesson. You'll find some proposed answers in Appendix D.

Quiz

1. What are the Visual C++ equivalents of malloc() and free()?

2. What is wrong with the following code's outline:

    ```
    // First part of program here
    int * i = new int;
    // Middle of program
    free(i);
    // Last part of program
    ```

3. True or False: The following statement both allocates and initializes an integer on the heap to zero:

    ```
    int * myVal = new int (0);
    ```

4. True or False: The following statement both allocates and initializes an integer array on the heap to zero:

    ```
    int * myArray = new int[40] (0);
    ```

5. How many table values are reserved with the following definition?

   ```
   float (*table)[6];   // Define the matrix name
   ```

   A. 6

   B. 30

   C. Cannot be determined

6. What is the name of new's exception handler?

7. Why won't the following delete operation delete an array with 50 values from the heap?

   ```
   delete [50] heapPtr;
   ```

Exercises

1. Write a program that asks the user for his or her age (for a maximum of 100). Allocate a string for each year in the user's age that contains the words Make every year a good one!. Print the strings on-screen, then deallocate them before the program ends.

2. Write an exception handler function that displays Memory Problem! and terminates the program when a memory allocation fails. (**Hint:** Use the exit() function prototyped in STDLIB.H to exit the program from the error handler instead of returning to the main() code.)

DAY 6

Communicating with Functions

Communicating with Functions

Visual C++ promotes the building-block approach to programming by supporting function calls and parameter passing better than its predecessor, C. Some of the Visual C++ features you learned in earlier days' chapters prepared you for today's chapter. Today's chapter goes hand-in-hand with tomorrow's as well. Visual C++ supports so many features related to functions that it takes two days to cover them all.

Visual C++ eases the syntax needed when passing and returning values from one function to another by enabling you to pass *by reference*. Whereas C enables you to pass parameters by address and by value, Visual C++ adds the third method of passing by reference that provides the same capabilities of passing by address but cuts down on the messy syntax involved.

When you're writing multipurpose functions, you will sometimes need to work with *command-line arguments* (values typed at the DOS prompt and passed to your program) and variable-length argument lists using unspecified argument lists. Visual C++ implements some of these features in a manner similar to C, but there are some differences related to the following topics worth noting:

☐ Passing reference values

☐ Returning reference values

☐ Using default arguments when receiving parameters

☐ Visual C++ and command-line arguments

☐ Unspecified arguments and variable-length argument lists

Passing by Reference

In the past, the terms *passing by address* and *passing by reference* were synonymous. Although some of the predecessors to C, such as Algol, offered three ways to pass parameters (by address, by value, and by reference), C offered only two. And somehow, passing by address was referred to by some C programmers as passing by reference. Anyway, all that has changed because Visual C++ supports the third, separate, and distinct parameter-passing version called *passing by reference*.

When you pass by value (also called *by copy*), you pass a copy of a non-array variable's value. When you pass by address, you pass an array or a pointer to a function. To pass by reference, you only need to pass a reference variable. Adding the third method does not add a great deal of confusion, as you'll soon see. As a matter of fact, there is little reason to pass by address after you learn how to pass by reference, so you are still left with two primary means of communicating between functions in Visual C++: passing by value and passing by reference.

A quick background won't hurt. The sole reason you pass values has to do with the nature of local variables. Global variables cause too many problems due to name clashes, which can occur when two or more programmers write routines for the same program. Local variables are preferred over global variables because they offer safety. Local variables are visible only within the block they are defined. A function that does not have access to a variable cannot change it. Therefore, if you want two or more functions to work with the same variable, you must somehow pass that variable from one function to the next.

The difference between the two older methods of passing parameters (by value and by address) lies in the way the receiving function changes or does not change the parameters sent. You might recall the following rules:

- If the receiving function is to change parameters sent to it, and if those parameters are to be known in the calling function, pass by address.

- If the calling function's parameters are to remain unchanged by the receiving function, pass by value.

Listing 6.1 demonstrates the difference between the two methods.

Listing 6.1. Passing by address and by value to the same function.

```
 1:  // Filename: VALADD.CPP
 2:  // Passes and receives parameters by value and by address
 3:  #include <iostream.h>
 4:  void passVals(int * canChange, int cannotChange);
 5:  main()
 6:  {
 7:     int canChange = 10;
 8:     int cannotChange = 50;
 9:     cout << "Before calling passVals:\n";
10:     cout << "canChange is " << canChange << "\n";
11:     cout << "cannotChange is " << cannotChange << "\n";
12:     passVals(&canChange, cannotChange);
13:     cout << "After calling passVals:\n";
14:     cout << "canChange is " << canChange << "\n";
15:     cout << "cannotChange is " << cannotChange << "\n";
16:     return 0;
17:  }
18:  //////////////////////////////////////////////////////////////
19:  // Receive two parameters using two different passing values
```

continues

Listing 6.1. continued

```
20: void passVals(int * canChange, int cannotChange)
21: {
22:    *canChange = 99;     // Must use * everywhere it appears
23:    cannotChange = 99;
24:    cout << "Inside passVals:\n";
25:    cout << "canChange is " << (* canChange) << "\n";
26:    cout << "cannotChange is " << cannotChange << "\n";
27:    return;
28: }
```

```
Before calling passVals:
canChange is 10
cannotChange is 50
Inside passVals:
canChange is 99
cannotChange is 99
After calling passVals:
canChange is 99
cannotChange is 50
```

In this program, canChange and cannotChange are two integers local to main(). It is because the variables are local that they must be passed to passVals() before passVals() can work with them. On line 12, canChange is passed by address. (More specifically, the address of canChange is passed.) Because canChange is passed by address, if passVals() changes the variable, it will also be changed back in main(). It is because cannotChange is passed *by value* that passVals() cannot affect the value when main() resumes.

When you receive a parameter that is passed by address, you must dereference the parameter everywhere you use it in the receiving function. Therefore, if passVals() were 30 lines long, and 20 of those lines used the variable canChange, you would have to dereference canChange by putting the dereferencing operator, *, before the variable name in each of those lines.

 Note: If you do not dereference variables passed by address, the receiving function will work with the *addresses* and not the values stored in those addresses. (This discussion holds true for non-array variables passed by address. You'll learn about passing arrays in a moment.)

Figure 6.1 helps demonstrate the results of passing by each method. The arrow heads show you that passing values by address is a two-way pass because the changed values are known in both functions.

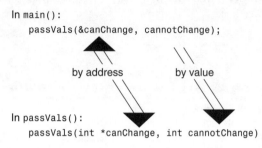

Figure 6.1. When you pass variables by value, the original contents are left unchanged.

When you pass variables by value, you pass them more safely than when passing them by address because there is no way the receiving function can modify the calling function's variables.

> **Not Just Easier, but Safer Too!**
>
> This book is not intended to be a rehash of your C learning, but this background is crucial to understanding some of the upcoming OOP issues. In these first few chapters, you have been reading how Visual C++ takes a lot of tedious details out of your hands and frees you to concentrate on the more important tasks related to your application.
>
> Visual C++ brings an additional improvement over its language predecessors. Visual C++ adds a layer of safety to your programs. When following proper coding techniques, you will not overwrite unintended variables as easily as in C.
>
> Make sure that you understand local variables and the issues related to passing them before moving into the second week of this book, which begins the deeper OOP concepts.

Communicating with Functions

All arrays are automatically passed by address, and you cannot pass arrays by value. Remember that an array name is a pointer and a pointer always contains the address of data. As long as you receive arrays with their array brackets or a dereferencing operator in the receiving parameter list, you can change passed arrays in the receiving function, and those arrays will also be changed in the calling function, as Listing 6.2 shows.

Listing 6.2. Arrays are always passed by address.

```
 1: // Filename: ARRADD.CPP
 2: // Passes and receives an array by address
 3: #include <iostream.h>
 4: #include <string.h>
 5: void addFun(char compName[]);
 6: main()
 7: {
 8:    char compName[] = "C Compiler";
 9:    cout << "Before calling addFun():\n";
10:    cout << "compName[] holds: " << compName << "\n";
11:    addFun(compName);    // Pass the array by address
12:    cout << "After calling addFun():\n";
13:    cout << "compName[] holds: " << compName << "\n";
14:    return 0;
15: }
16: //////////////////////////////////////////////////////////////
17: // Receive the array and change it both here and in main()
18: void addFun(char newArrayName[])
19: {
20:    strcpy(newArrayName, "Visual C++");
21:    return;
22: }
```

```
Before calling addFun():
compName[] holds: C Compiler
After calling addFun():
compName[] holds: Visual C++
```

The array's value after calling addFun() is different from its original value before calling addFun(). Visual C++ passes the array by address, so main()'s array is changed when the array changes in the called function. Notice that it doesn't matter whether you change the array name in the receiving parameter list (line 18). The contents of the array change because the address is passed.

When you're passing by address, arrays have a definite advantage over non-array variables. You don't have to dereference an array every time you use it. (Technically,

using array subscripts dereferences the array for you.) The syntax of passing non-array variables by address is cumbersome. That is, it *was* cumbersome until Visual C++ came along!

Pass by Address Cleanly by Passing Reference Variables

Visual C++ enables you to pass non-array values from one function to another as if by address and without the mess of dereferencing each variable. You might have already guessed that if you pass a reference variable, Visual C++ automatically dereferences the reference pointer for you. Automatic dereferencing is the primary purpose for using reference variables, as you learned in Day 4's chapter, "Powerful Pointers."

Any non-array variable can be passed by reference. The variable does not have to be a reference variable to begin with. Indicate that a variable is passed by reference by inserting an ampersand, &, in the receiving parameter list.

Note: Actually, you don't *pass* by reference as much as you actually *receive* by reference. You can pass either reference variables or nonreference variables, but as long as the receiving parameter list contains the ampersand, the variables will be received by reference.

There is little or no reason for passing by address again, except for the natural by-address method used for passing arrays and pointers. The `main()` function in Listing 6.3 passes the same variable by reference that was passed in Listing 6.1 by address. Notice that you don't have to dereference `canChange` everyplace it appears in the receiving function.

Listing 6.3. Passing by reference is cleaner than passing by address.

```
1:  // Filename: ADDREF.CPP
2:  // Passes and receives parameters by address and by reference
3:  #include <iostream.h>
4:  void passVals(int * canChange1, int & canChange2);
5:  main()
6:  {
7:     int canChange1 = 10;
```

continues

Communicating with Functions

Listing 6.3. continued

```
 8:     int canChange2 = 50;
 9:     cout << "Before calling passVals:\n";
10:     cout << "canChange1 is " << canChange1 << "\n";
11:     cout << "canChange2 is " << canChange2 << "\n";
12:     // Nothing special needed for reference
13:     passVals(& canChange1, canChange2);   // & before address parameter
14:     cout << "After calling passVals:\n";
15:     cout << "canChange1 is " << canChange1 << "\n";
16:     cout << "canChange2 is " << canChange2 << "\n";
17:     return 0;
18: }
19: /////////////////////////////////////////////////////////////////
20: // Receive two parameters using two different passing values
21: void passVals(int * canChange1, int & canChange2)
22: {
23:    * canChange1 = 99;
24:    canChange2 = 99;     // No need for the * here, but result is same!
25:    cout << "Inside passVals:\n";
26:    cout << "canChange1 is " << (* canChange1) << "\n";
27:    cout << "canChange2 is " << canChange2 << "\n";
28:    return;
29: }
```

```
Before calling passVals:
canChange1 is 10
canChange2 is 50
Inside passVals:
canChange1 is 99
canChange2 is 99
After calling passVals:
canChange1 is 99
canChange2 is 99
```

Both versions—the pass-by-address variable, `canChange1`, and the pass-by-reference variable, `canChange2`—are changed by the `passVals()` function. To indicate that `canChange2` is being passed by reference, only an ampersand was needed on line 21.

Note: Although passing by reference produces the same result as passing by address, the syntax is cleaner because you don't have to keep the dereferencing operator, *, in front of the receiving function's variable everywhere the variable appears.

Efficiency and Safety with Reference Passing

You can precede received reference parameters with const to keep the function from inadvertently changing reference parameters.

At first, you might wonder why you would want to pass parameters by reference if you didn't want the receiving function to change the calling function's values. It might seem that passing the parameters by value would be easier and would ensure that the receiving function couldn't touch the sending function's values.

Passing parameters by value adds some inefficiency to your programs. When passing variables by value, especially large structure variables, Visual C++ has to take some needed runtime to make a local copy of the variable. (That's why the term *by value* is often called *by copy*.)

However, when you pass variables by address or by reference, a pointer is passed to the data rather than the data itself. (The pointer is automatically dereferenced when you are passing by reference.) Therefore, if efficiency is important—and it is a lot of times—you'll want to pass by reference but precede the receiving value with the const modifier if the receiving function is not supposed to change the parameters.

Receiving Reference Parameters

`functionName(& parameter [, & parameter])`

Precede each parameter being received by reference with an ampersand symbol. In the rest of the function, don't carry the ampersand or dereferencing operator in front of the variable because Visual C++ automatically dereferences the variable for you. Also, the parameters being sent don't have to be reference variables in the calling function. If the receiving function changes a reference parameter, the parameter will still be changed when the calling function regains control.

Example

```
// Filename: REFSYNT.CPP
// Examples of passing by reference
void doubIt(int & i);
#include <iostream.h>
main()
{
```

Communicating with Functions

```
  int i = 20;
  doubIt(i);     // Double i in the function
  cout << "i is now " << i << "\n";  // Prints a 40
  return 0;
}
void doubIt(int & i)
{
  i *= 2;    // Multiply i by 2
}
```

Returning a Reference

Another advantage to learning about reference variables appears when you see how to return a reference value from a function. As with most programming languages, you can return a maximum of one value from a function. (If a function is to change more than one value, you have to pass those parameters by address or by reference so that they will be changed when the calling function regains control.)

Here is the prototype of a function that accepts three reference parameters and returns a reference to a character:

```
char & refFun(int & i, char & c, float & f);
```

Most programmers are used to using functions as *rvalues* and not *lvalues* (loosely speaking, values that can appear on the left side of an assignment). That is, you are used to something like

```
ans = refFun(num, initial, amt);   // Assign the return value
```

but you have not put a function call on the *left* side of an equal sign like this:

```
refFun(num, initial, amt) = hisInitial;
```

In this statement, the function is used as an lvalue. The reason you can use the `refFun()` function as an lvalue is that it returns a reference to a variable. A reference is always a dereferenced pointer. In other words, the return variable from the function is assigned the value in the assignment statement.

When you first see a function used as an lvalue, you can easily become confused by the syntax, but the program in Listing 6.4 will help clarify what takes place. The program zeroes the minimum and maximum of two values returned from functions.

Listing 6.4. Returning references to functions.

```
 1: // Filename: MINMAX.CPP
 2: // Returns references to functions and changes those return values
 3: #include <iostream.h>
 4: int & max(int & num1, int & num2);
 5: int & min(int & num1, int & num2);
 6: main()
 7: {
 8:    int num1, num2;
 9:    cout << "Enter the first number: ";
10:    cin >> num1;
11:    cout << "Enter the second number: ";
12:    cin >> num2;
13:    max(num1, num2) = 0;    // Zero-out the maximum number
14:    cout << "\nAfter putting zero in the largest, the numbers are";
15:    cout << "\n" << num1 << " and " << num2 << "\n";
16:    cout << "\nNow, please enter two more numbers.\n";
17:    cout << "Enter the first number: ";
18:    cin >> num1;
19:    cout << "Enter the second number: ";
20:    cin >> num2;
21:    min(num1, num2) = 0;    // Zero-out the minimum number
22:    cout << "\nAfter putting zero in the smallest, the numbers are";
23:    cout << "\n" << num1 << " and " << num2 << "\n";
24:    return 0;
25: }
26: //////////////////////////////////////////////////////////////
27: // Find and return the greatest number
28: int & max(int & num1, int & num2)
29: {
30:    return (num1 > num2) ? num1: num2;  // Return the greatest
31: }
32: //////////////////////////////////////////////////////////////
33: // Find and return the smallest number
34: int & min(int & num1, int & num2)
35: {
36:    return (num1 < num2) ? num1: num2;  // Return the smallest
37: }
```

```
Enter the first number: 27
Enter the second number: 98

After putting zero in the largest, the numbers are
27 and 0
```

Day 6: Communicating with Functions

```
Now, please enter two more numbers.
Enter the first number: 34
Enter the second number: 85

After putting zero in the smallest, the numbers are
0 and 85
```

Without the advantage of returning by reference, you would have to expand lines 13 and 21 into a multiple-line `if-else` statement. For example, you would have to find the maximum number and assign zero to that number, then do the same for the minimum. Returning reference values becomes especially critical on Days 11 and 12 when you learn how to change the way operators work on your user-defined data types.

Please realize that lines 30 and 36 *do not* return integer values! Lines 30 and 36 return references to integer values so that you can change the return value's contents of the function calls themselves.

DO	DON'T
DO pass by reference rather than by address because the syntax is easier to use and less error-prone. **DO** insert ampersands (&) in front of parameters when receiving them by reference. **DO** return a reference value when the calling function needs to change the return value directly. **DO** use the `const` modifier when receiving values by reference that you don't want changed.	**DON'T** pass by value when efficiency is important. When passing by value, Visual C++ must make a copy of each parameter, and that takes runtime away from the program.

Default Arguments Speed Program Development

Have you ever written functions that almost always receive the same value? For instance, suppose you write a function that computes sales tax for your store's point-of-sale computer. A large majority of the time, you'll be calling the function to compute sales tax for your city. Every once in a while, however, the mail-order portion of the program will call the function, and the sales tax routine will have to compute tax for an out-of-town purchase.

Many times, you can simplify the *calling* of functions by specifying *default argument lists*. A default argument list is a function's argument list that does not have to be sent values; if you call the function without passing values, the default values are accepted. If, however, you call the function and pass values, the values you pass override the default values.

Default argument lists are always specified in the receiving function. Here is the prototype for the sales tax function just described:

```
sTax(float taxRate = .07);  // Use 7% unless another value is passed
```

Note: Specify the default argument list in the prototype, not in the function's actual first line. The prototype is sometimes called the *function declaration,* and the function's first line is sometimes called the *function definition.*

You've probably never seen an assignment in a parameter list before this one. The assignment to taxRate tells Visual C++ to use .07 for the value of taxRate in the function *if another value is not passed to override it.* If main() or another function calls sTax() like

```
sTax();    // Call the sales tax function with default tax rate
```

then Visual C++ executes the sTax() function as though you had passed it .07 for the tax rate. If, however, you call sTax() like

```
sTax(.12); // Call the sales tax function with a nondefault rate
```

Visual C++ executes the sTax() function and passes the value of .12 to the taxRate parameter.

Does This Really Save Me Work?

Default argument lists *do indeed* save you work. You do not have to type the parameter if you want the default value to be passed. As you will soon see,

Communicating with Functions

> specifying more than one default value in functions that accept multiple parameters enables you to call the same functions in several different ways without having a different function for each combination of parameters.
>
> Default argument lists are just another entry in the long list of advantages and shortcuts that Visual C++ provides to help lessen the details of writing programs.

Listing 6.5 includes a complete program that calculates a sales tax computation based on either the default sales value or one that is passed.

Listing 6.5. Calling the sales tax function two different ways.

```
1:  // Filename: STAXDEF.CPP
2:  // Calls a sales tax function using a default argument value
3:  #include <iostream.h>
4:  #include <iomanip.h>
5:  float sTax(float taxRate=.07);
6:  main()
7:  {
8:    float salesTotal;
9:    salesTotal = sTax();    // Uses the default .07 value
10:   cout << setprecision(2) << setiosflags(ios::fixed); // Proper
      ➥cents
11:   cout << "Your first total is " << salesTotal << "\n\n";
12:   // Now call the function using a passed value for the tax rate
13:   salesTotal = sTax(.11); // Uses .11 for the passed value
14:   cout << "The second total is " << salesTotal << "\n";
15:   return 0;
16: }
17: //////////////////////////////////////////////////////////////
18: // Function that uses either default argument value or passed one
19: float sTax(float taxRate)
20: {
21:   float sales;
22:   cout << "What is the total sales? ";
23:   cin >> sales;
24:   return (sales + (sales * taxRate));   // Send the total sales back
25: }
```

```
What is the total sales? 1.00
Your first total is 1.07
```

```
What is the total sales? 1.00
The second total is 1.11
```

Notice that the same *function*, sTax(), produces a different result even though the same sales value in Line 23 is entered (1.00) both times the function is called.

Using Multiple Default Arguments

Visual C++ does not limit you to one default argument. You can specify as many default argument values as you require. Not all of your parameters to any given function have to be default or otherwise; you are free to mix default arguments and regular arguments.

Note: Technically, you *pass arguments* and *receive parameters*. The calling function passes a value (the argument), and the receiving function receives that value (the parameter when it is received) by value, by reference, or by address. Among friends (and we are friends), the distinction between an argument and a parameter is rather trivial. The value inside a function's parentheses can be called either name without too much confusion. When the distinction is important so that you can clarify the difference between a calling function's list of values inside the parentheses and that of a receiving function, this book uses the terms *calling function* or *receiving function* in addition to *parameter* or *argument* so that you'll know which is being discussed.

Although you can mix default and regular arguments, you must mix them in a required order. Visual C++ requires that all default arguments go at the end of the argument list.

Figure 6.2 shows a function prototype with four arguments, two of which are regular arguments and two of which are default arguments.

Notice that you can specify any type of argument, including character arguments, to be default arguments. Here are three different ways to call this function:

```
defFun(2, 30.2, 17, 'A');  // Pass all four values
defFun(2, 30.2, 17);       // Pass three values
defFun(2, 30.2);           // Pass two values
```

Communicating with Functions

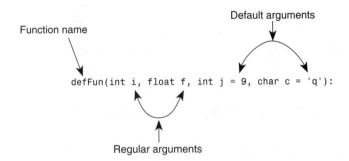

Figure 6.2. Mixing regular arguments with default arguments.

If you pass all four arguments, the default values are not used. If you pass three arguments, Visual C++ uses the default value of `'q'` for the fourth argument. If you pass only two arguments, Visual C++ uses the default values for both j and c. In regular C, you would have to write three different functions to accomplish the same thing, calling one of the three depending on the values you have to pass at the time. More functions mean more memory work on your part. You don't need lots of details getting in the way of a running program—you need fewer petty details slowing you down.

You are not allowed to list default values anywhere but at the end of an argument list. The following function prototype is invalid because one of the default arguments (j) doesn't appear at the end of the prototype:

```
defFun(int i, int j=9, float f, char c='q');   // Cannot do this!
```

There is just no way to specify values for the first and third regular arguments when calling `defFun()`. The following statement could not correctly call `defFun()` if the preceding prototype were allowed, because Visual C++ would not know whether it should use 67 for j or skip the j because it has a default value and propagate the 67 to a 67.0 and pass the 67.0 to the floating-point argument f.

```
defFun(1, 67);   // Where does 67 go?
```

> **Note:** As with all prototypes, you don't have to list variable names after the default argument data types. Here is a perfectly good prototype for the `defFun()` being described in this section:
>
> ```
> defFun(int, float, int=9, char='q');
> ```
>
> Most Visual C++ programmers include variable names in prototypes because they copy and paste the function's first line to the prototype

section of the program before compiling. The variable names are required in a function's first line (the function's definition), but the default values are not allowed in the function definition.

The function shown in Listing 6.6 calculates payroll for hourly employees and those salespeople who get commission. If the function is passed a commission value, that commission is added to the total pay. If, however, the commission is not passed to the function, the function's default commission value of 0 is used, and no commission is added into the pay.

Listing 6.6. A function that contains two regular arguments and a default argument.

```
1:  // Function that returns a total pay and optionally uses a
2:  // commission in the calculation if one is passed.
3:  float computePay(int hours, float rate, float commission=0.0)
4:  {
5:      float totalPay;
6:      totalPay = (hours * rate) + commission;
7:      return totalPay;
8:  }
```

If you were to embed Listing 6.6's function inside another program, computePay()'s prototype should list the default values rather than the function's definition line. If this function is called with a statement such as

`payAmt = computePay(40, 10.00);   // Compute hourly payroll`

then the payAmt variable will receive 400.00 because no commission is added into the calculation (the commission is assumed to be zero). If, however, the function were called like

`payAmt = computePay(40, 10.00, 50.00);   // Compute sales payroll`

then the payAmt variable will receive 450.00 because Visual C++ uses the commission passed in the function call.

A Built-In Function That Uses Default Arguments

Back in Day 3's chapter, "Simple I/O," you learned about the getline() function that accepts a line of keyboard input. Although the syntax for

Communicating with Functions

getline() is strange to a newcomer of Visual C++, the function is easy enough to use. The following statement receives up to 25 characters of input from the user and stores that input in the character array named city:

```
cin.getline(city, 25);
```

The getline() function contains *three* arguments, but usually, you'll use just the two shown here. The third argument to getline() is a default argument that specifies the character that ends the input. Most of the time, the newline character produced by the Enter keystroke is used to signal that the user is done with data entry. However, if you were to call the getline() function like

```
cin.getline(city, 25, '#');
```

the Enter keystroke is still required to end the data entry, but Visual C++ stops storing the input in city as soon as a # is reached. If the user types Joplin, the entire city name is stored in city, but if the user types Jop#lin, only Jop is stored in city and the remaining input characters remain on the buffer to be read at the next input statement.

Rarely will you specify a non-newline terminating character when getting user input. A lot of times, a different terminating character is used to read data from disk files whose records might not be delimited with newline characters.

Syntax

Specifying Default Arguments

functionName(type arg [= defaultVal] [, type arg [= defaultVal]]);

The function prototype always contains the default values. When you specify a default argument, that argument must appear at the end of the prototype. Therefore, if you mix several default and nondefault arguments, you must place the default arguments at the end of the argument list.

Example

```
myFun1(int i=10);   // A single default argument

myFun2(int i, int j=20);   // A regular and default argument
myFun2(int i, float x=9.1, char x='*');  // 1 regular, 2 default
```

DO	DON'T

DO use default arguments instead of writing more than one function that differs only in numbers of arguments passed.

DO put all default arguments at the *end* of their prototypes. You cannot insert default arguments in the middle of a prototype and place nondefault arguments at the end.

DO pass the `getline()` function a third argument (a character argument) if you want `getline()` to stop reading input when it reaches a character other than newline.

DON'T include the default values in the function's definition line (the actual first line of the function), but rather specify the default values in the function's prototype.

Visual C++ and Command-Line Arguments

Sometimes, you'll write a Visual C++ program that needs to get values from outside its domain, DOS to be exact. Perhaps a batch file or another Visual C++ program executes your program, and values from the batch file or program must be sent to your program's variables. Maybe you wrote a DOS-based Visual C++ program that compresses a file and the filename comes from the user at the DOS prompt.

Values sent to a program on its start-up are called *command-line arguments*. As you are aware, even the `main()` function has argument parentheses. `main()`, however, is the first function that executes in any Visual C++ program, so how can you send `main()` arguments? You can send `main()` command-line arguments from the DOS prompt or from within the Visual C++ editing environment.

Note: If you run your program from within Visual C++'s environment, as most programmers do, you'll see in a moment how to use the Visual C++ menu system to send command-line arguments to `main()`. Many Visual C++ programmers test their programs within the editor before distributing their programs as .EXE files.

Communicating with Functions

When you type one or more command-line arguments, they are described to your program by two variables: an integer that holds the number of arguments you typed and an array of character pointers that holds the arguments, one argument pointed to by each array element.

For example, suppose you compiled your program as a DOS program and called it MYPROG.EXE. If you wanted to pass three arguments to MYPROG.EXE when you started the program, you could do so by typing this at the DOS prompt:

```
C:\>MYPROG.EXE 17.8 George 15
```

Separate command-line arguments by at least one space. The three arguments, 17.8, George, and 15, are sent to main(), which must be set up to receive the arguments. Here is the way to code main() to receive such command-line arguments:

```
main(int argc, char *argv[])
```

> **Note:** The *argv[] is an array of pointers. An array name is really just a constant pointer, so argv is actually a pointer to other pointers. You'll sometimes see Visual C++ programs written to receive the arguments like this:
>
> ```
> main(int argc, char ** argv)
> ```
>
> The double-dereference operator seems to add confusion. If you stay with an array of pointers, you'll find that your code is slightly easier to write and maintain.

As you know, when a function receives an array of any kind, you don't have to specify the number of elements in that array. Therefore, the empty brackets let Visual C++ know that main() is receiving arguments and that they will be stored in the array of pointers by the program loader, but you don't know ahead of time how many command-line values are passed to main(). The first argument, argc, contains the number of arguments actually passed plus one extra for the DOS path and program name.

By the way, the names argc and argv are industry-standard names, but you can call the command-line arguments anything you like. Sticking to the industry-accepted standard, though, makes your program more maintainable to those who might have to change it later.

Figure 6.3 shows the contents of main()'s two arguments after typing the DOS line shown previously. Although you'll rarely care about the first argument (the DOS command needed to start the program), it sometimes comes in handy, especially when you need to inform the user of a program error during the development of several programs chained together in a batch file.

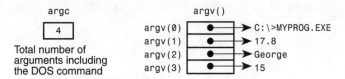

Figure 6.3. After passing command-line arguments to main().

The program in Listing 6.7 echoes the user's command-line arguments to the screen.

Listing 6.7. Printing the command-line arguments.

```
 1:  // Filename: CMDARGS.CPP
 2:  // Accepts command-line arguments and prints them back to the user
 3:  #include <iostream.h>
 4:  main(int argc, char * argv[])
 5:  {
 6:    cout << "\nYou typed these words to begin this program:\n";
 7:    for (int i=0; i < argc; i++)
 8:      { cout << argv[i] << "\n";}    // Prints one per line
 9:    return 0;
10:  }
```

C:\>**CMDARGS 17.8 George 15** ◄──────── User typed this line from the DOS prompt
You typed these words to begin this program:
C:\>CMDARGS.EXE
17.8
George
15

Note: Although you don't have to type the .EXE extension when running this program, the first command-line argument always points to a string containing the path and full filename of the executable program.

Communicating with Functions

If you want to supply command-line arguments from within Visual C++'s editor, select **O**ptions Debug... from the pull-down menus, and type the command-line arguments in the **P**rogram Arguments dialog box like the one shown in Figure 6.4.

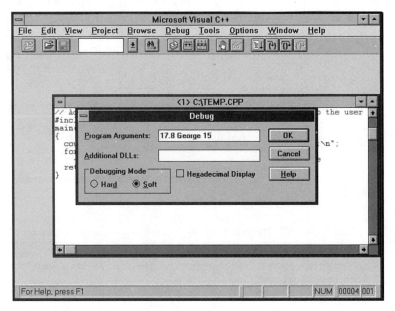

Figure 6.4. Specifying command-line arguments inside the editor.

It often helps to add an error-checking routine to the command-line arguments in case the user does not supply enough arguments. For example, the program in Listing 6.8 attempts to print the average of the three command-line argument values. If the user types fewer than three numbers, the program displays an error message and shows the user what he or she should have typed.

Listing 6.8. Making sure the user types the right number of arguments.

```
1:  // Filename: CMDCHK.CPP
2:  // Displays error if the user doesn't enter a
3:  // correct number of command-line arguments.
4:  #include <iostream.h>
5:  #include <iomanip.h>
6:  #include <stdlib.h>
7:  main(int argc, char * argv[])
8:  {
9:    float avg;
```

```
10:     if (argc != 4)    // User MUST enter 3 values after program name
11:        { cerr << "\n** You did not start this program correctly!\n";
12:          cerr << "The program requires three arguments like this:\n";
13:          cerr << "C:\\>CMDCHK 32 45 21\n";
14:        }
15:     else
16:        { avg = (atoi(argv[1]) + atoi(argv[2]) + atoi(argv[3])) / 3;
17:
18:          cout << setprecision(2);
19:          cout << "The average of your three numbers is " << avg
              ↪<< "\n";
20:        }
21:     return 0;
22: }
```

```
C:>CMDCHK 10 20 30 40  ◄
** You did not start this program correctly!
Type three numbers after the program name like this:
    C:>CMDCHK 32 45 21
C:>CMDCHK 10 20 30  ◄
The average of your three numbers is 20
```

— User typed these lines from the DOS prompt

Notice that the built-in atoi() function is used on line 16 to convert the command-line argument strings to their numeric integer equivalents. All the ato...() functions are useful for converting strings to various types of numbers. (The name atoi() stands for *alpha-to-integer*.) The ato...() functions are prototyped in the STDLIB.H header file.

Using Variable-Length Argument Lists

Programmers don't program variable-length argument lists too often because of their cryptic nature, but you might at some time want to offer an open-ended function that can take as many parameters as the calling program wants to send. The old printf() and scanf() functions are variable-length argument functions because you can pass one or more arguments to them.

> **Note:** Because of the cryptic nature of variable-length argument lists, consider passing an array of character pointers to a function instead of using variable-length argument lists.

Communicating with Functions

When passing a variable number of arguments, you must somehow signal to Visual C++ that it has come to the end of the list of values. For example, if -99 will never be a value that you pass to the function, use -99 for the end-of-argument signal. The next program explains how to use this signal value.

Visual C++ includes the same set of variable-length argument macros as C does. You must prototype the argument lists with an ellipsis, a series of three periods (...). Always include the STDARG.H or VARARGS.H header files when working with variable-length argument lists so that Visual C++ will recognize the macros that you use. Although you, as a programmer, should use `inline` functions in place of `#define` macros, as Day 2's chapter pointed out, the variable-length argument macros are supplied by Microsoft and work fine if you want to use them.

Table 6.1 lists the macros you need and their descriptions to help you pick off each argument passed and use the argument in a function. You must pass at least one fixed argument (that is, at least one regular argument must precede the ellipsis in the variable-length argument list).

Table 6.1. The variable-length argument macros.

Name	Parameters	Description
`va_list`	`ap`	Defines a special variable that holds the variable-length argument list, called `ap` in this table.
`va_arg()`	`va_list ap, type`	Picks off the next parameter from the argument list and converts it to the `type` specified. (The `type` cannot be `char`, `unsigned char`, or `float`.)
`va_end()`	`va_list ap`	Cleans up the variable-length argument work and is required bookkeeping when you are through grabbing all the arguments from the list.
`va_start()`	`va_list ap, lastfix`	Initializes the `ap` variable defined with `va_list` and requires that you send the last-named argument as well so that `va_list()` knows when to begin.

Name	Parameters	Description
		In other words, if there were three fixed arguments specified before the ellipses, you must pass the last of those three arguments to va_start() so that va_start() can find the first variable-length argument that comes next.

Suppose you wanted to write a function that returned the largest value from a list of arguments passed to it. The function is to be called from several places throughout a program, and the number of arguments sent to the function changes depending on what part of the program calls it. Listing 6.9 contains such a function.

Type

Listing 6.9. Finding the maximum argument in a list.

```
1:  // Filename: VARARGS.CPP
2:  // Program that contains a variable argument list.
3:  // The end of list is signaled by the -99 at the end
4:  // of the function calls.
5:  #include <iostream.h>
6:  #include <stdarg.h>
7:  void totNums(int numPassed, ...);
8:  main()
9:  {
10:    // -99 is used to trigger the end of the variable arguments
11:    totNums(23, 43, 1, 3, 45, 66, 8, 5, 5, 23, 55, 77, -99);
12:    totNums(1, 2, -99);
13:    totNums(4, 5, 77, 32, 4, 77, 87, 13, -99);
14:    totNums(1, -99);
15:    return 0;
16: }
17: /////////////////////////////////////////////////////////////
18: // Variable-length argument function
19: void totNums(int numPassed, ...)
20: {
21:    int total;
22:    int num;
23:    va_list ap;    // Points to the list of arguments
24:    va_start(ap, numPassed); // Tells Visual C++ where to begin
25:    total = numPassed;       // Store the first argument to total
26:    while ((num = va_arg(ap, int)) != -99)
27:    {
```

continues

Communicating with Functions

Listing 6.9. continued

```
28:      total += num;    // Add next value to grand total
29:    }
30:    va_end(ap);        // Cleanup that is always needed
31:    cout << "The total of this list is " << total << "\n";
32: }
```

```
The total of this list is 354
The total of this list is 3
The total of this list is 299
The total of this list is 1
```

Line 26 is the most difficult line in the program. The va_arg() macro picks off the next integer from the list. That value is stored in num and then compared to -99 to control the termination of the while loop.

Note: The prototype on line 7 indicates that totNums() contains an *unspecified number of arguments*. In regular C, you can get by with using empty argument lists in the prototype to indicate an unspecified number of arguments, but as you learned in Day 2's chapter, "C++ Is Superior," Visual C++ interprets an empty argument list as if you specified void.

You can sometimes send the total number of arguments when calling the variable-length argument function. Listing 6.10 shows the same program as in Listing 6.9, but the number of arguments passed at each function call is specified by the first argument.

Listing 6.10. Another way to find the maximum argument in a list.

```
1:  // Filename: VARARG2.CPP
2:  // Program that contains a variable argument list
3:  // with an argument that tells how many arguments follow
4:  #include <iostream.h>
5:  #include <stdarg.h>
6:  void totNums(int numPassed, ...);
7:  main()
8:  {
9:     totNums(12, 23, 43, 1, 3, 45, 66, 8, 5, 5, 23, 55, 77);
10:    totNums(2, 1, 2);
11:    totNums(8, 4, 5, 77, 32, 4, 77, 87, 13);
12:    totNums(1, 1);
13:    return 0;
```

```
14: }
15: //////////////////////////////////////////////////////////////
16: // Variable-length argument function
17: void totNums(int numPassed, ...)
18: {
19:    int total=0;
20:    int num;
21:    va_list ap;     // Points to the list of arguments
22:    va_start(ap, numPassed); // Tells Visual C++ where to begin
23:    for (int i=0; i<numPassed; i++)
24:    {
25:      num = va_arg(ap, int);    // Get next integer
26:      total += num;    // Add next value to grand total
27:    }
28:    va_end(ap);         // Cleanup that is always needed
29:    cout << "The total of this list is " << total << "\n";
30: }
```

The output of Listing 6.10 is identical to that of Listing 6.9. The only difference between the two programs is that Listing 6.10 picks off arguments from the list as determined by the first value, which tells the function how many arguments follow.

Note: You might wonder how the `printf()` function knows how to end. When you call `printf()`, you don't have to specify a trailing value, and you don't have to tell `printf()` how many values are in the list. Actually, the first argument in `printf()`, the format argument, indirectly tells the `printf()` code how many arguments follow. The `printf()` function scans the format to determine how many arguments are supposed to follow. The code inside `printf()` knows to stop calling `va_arg()` when all the arguments are read that satisfy the format.

Summary

Today's chapter is the first of two that prepare you for Visual C++'s use of function calls and parameter passing. You learned in this chapter how to pass and return reference values. Actually, you receive parameters by reference instead of passing them by reference, despite what the description *pass by reference* would lead you to believe.

Day 6: Communicating with Functions

When passing by reference, you get all the benefit of passing by address without the extra dereferencing operator preceding your variables throughout the function. If you want the efficiency of passing by reference, but you want the safety of passing by value, pass references and receive with the `const` modifier so that the receiving function cannot change the reference arguments.

By returning reference values, you can save a step or two while programming. Suppose that you want to assign the return value of a function a specific value. Returning a reference returns an actual dereferenced variable so that you can assign a function call a value (when that function call returns a reference). The return value, stored in a reference variable, will be assigned the new value.

Default argument lists save you time when you're programming. If you often write functions that receive the same values *most* of the time, consider making those values default arguments. Specify default arguments in the function prototype. If you choose to call the function but not pass a value to an argument, the default will be used for that argument.

Command-line arguments become important when you pass to a compiled program values from a DOS batch file or from another program that calls yours. `main()` can receive arguments just like any other function can. `main()` receives those arguments in an array of pointers that you have to convert to the proper data type. For extra safety, you can check to ensure that the user passed the correct number of arguments and print an error message if needed.

Today's chapter ended with an explanation on variable-length argument lists. As with the `printf()` function, you might need to pass a function a different number of arguments every time you call that function. The syntax for the variable-length argument macros is a little strange, and many programmers stay away from variable-length argument lists. Using variable-length arguments is not difficult, but you are perhaps better off passing an array of pointers when sending varying amounts of data to a function.

Q&A

Q. How do I pass by reference?

A. Actually, you receive by reference by preceding all parameters with an ampersand, &, like this:

```
recFun(int & i, char & c)
```

Q. What is the advantage of learning yet another way to pass parameters in addition to *by address* and *by value*?

A. Although passing by address is sometimes dangerous (because a function might inadvertently change a sending function's value that it should not change), passing by address is more efficient than passing by value. It's more efficient because a copy of the data is not passed, only the address is passed. Nevertheless, when you pass by address, you must use a dereferencing operator before all non-array variables. The dereferencing operator is syntactically messy and sometimes error prone.

When you pass by reference, you don't have to repeat the dereference operator in front of all the parameters in the receiving function, but you still receive the same efficiency gains offered by address passing.

One of the nice side effects of reference variables is in the *returning* of reference variables from functions. When you return a reference variable, you can actually assign the function call a new value (use a function call as an *lvalue*). When the function call finishes, its return variable will be assigned the new value.

Q. Why can I not put default arguments at the beginning of an argument list when I also have nondefault arguments in the list?

A. There would be no way for Visual C++ to know which defaults to use. For example, study this function prototype (an incorrectly written one):

```
fun(char i=8, int j, int k=10);   // Not allowed
```

How could you pass the middle variable, j, a value? If you called the function like

```
fun(10);
```

then Visual C++ could not tell whether the 10 was to replace the default for i or whether j was supposed to receive the value. Visual C++ does not support the use of extra commas such as this:

```
fun(, 10);   // Not allowed
```

Q. What are command-line arguments, and why would I need them?

A. Command-line arguments are passed to your program (via main()) from DOS or another program. Sometimes, a program must use values gotten from outside its code.

Communicating with Functions

When you receive command-line arguments, Visual C++ passes the number of command-line arguments as an integer followed by an array of character pointers to the individual arguments. Your program can then search the array and convert each of the arguments to a different data type if needed.

Q. What is the difference between command-line arguments and variable-length arguments?

A. In one sense, command-line arguments are variable-length arguments because a program cannot tell in advance how many command-line arguments will be passed to it. Nevertheless, command-line arguments are supplied by the program loader at runtime, and command-line arguments are slightly easier to use than variable-length arguments.

When writing functions that use variable-length arguments, you must prototype the functions with ellipses (called an *unspecified argument list*) rather than argument descriptions. You must use the variable-length argument macros supplied in the STDARG.H header file to set up and retrieve variable-length arguments in the function that receives them.

Workshop

The Workshop offers quiz questions and exercises to hone your skills and give you feedback on today's lesson. You'll find some proposed answers in Appendix D.

Quiz

1. Which is more efficient: passing by value or passing by reference?
2. Is this a function declaration or definition?

    ```
    void fun(int i);
    ```

3. Is this a function declaration or definition?

    ```
    void fun(int i)
    ```

4. True or False: You can pass arguments to `main()`.
5. When you are passing by reference, if the receiving function changes a parameter, does that same value change in the sending function?
6. What do ellipses signify in a function prototype?

7. What is the *first* argument passed to main() when it is receiving command-line arguments?

8. How can you protect reference parameters so that they cannot be changed by the receiving function?

Exercises

1. Write a program with one function that accepts two arguments: a character and an integer. The function prints a line of characters as many times as specified by the integer. If a pound sign and 40 are passed to the function, the function is to print 40 pound signs on a line. If no character is passed, the function is to print an asterisk. If no integer is passed either, the function is to print a line of 10 asterisks (the default). In main(), pass several combinations of values to the function to see the results.

2. Write a program that prints the product (the multiplied total) of all the values that are passed to it from the command line. (Hint: You must convert the arguments to integers after you retrieve them and store the result in a long int in case the answer is large.)

3. Write a function that accepts variable-length arguments and prints the average of those arguments. (Hint: Assume that the first argument passed holds the number of values that follows.)

DAY 7

Overloaded Functions Lessen Your Load

Overloaded Functions Lessen Your Load

Today's chapter concludes yesterday's chapter, which discussed Visual C++–specific function mechanisms. Today's chapter teaches you a new concept that has become one of the most important OOP concepts that exists in Visual C++.

Visual C++ enables you to write more than one function with the same name. Although this sounds a little strange, and possibly even error-prone, today's chapter shows you why *overloading functions* helps take more of the tedious details out of your programming job while enabling you to concentrate on the application you are programming.

As you will see, being able to overload functions requires that Visual C++ perform a little trick behind your back. In doing so, Visual C++ makes it a little harder for you to use the C functions you have written for other programs that you might want to port to Visual C++. However, when you inform Visual C++ that you want to use a C function, using the notation explained in today's chapter, Visual C++ bypasses its usual C++ mechanism for your C functions and enables you to integrate old C and new C++ within the same Visual C++ program.

One of the most important reasons to learn about overloaded functions is so that you can write your own *overloaded operators*. An overloaded operator is one that works on your own data types in the way *you* describe, not the way the compiler-writers describe. Although the true power of overloaded operators will not become apparent until Days 11 and 12, you'll get an introduction here, involving the following topics:

- Overloading functions of the same name
- Using C functions in Visual C++ programs
- Simple operator overloading

Overloading Functions

Visual C++ extends your control of functions by offering *overloaded functions*. Overloaded functions are functions you write that have the same name but contain different code. At first, the idea of overloaded functions in the same program seems at worse dangerous and at best confusing for the programmer. After all, if you call a function whose name appears on several function definitions in the same program, how would Visual C++ know which function to execute?

You are already used to overloading functions because you did something similar in your past C programs! For example, what does the * do in this statement?

```
a = 8 * 3;
```

Of course, the * means multiply. What does the * do here?

`f = *ptr;`

In this statement, the * is used for dereferencing a pointer's value. Although you used the same operator, neither you nor Visual C++ got confused because the *context* of the operator's use clearly showed which version, multiply or dereference, you wanted to use at the time.

In the same manner, you can give similar functions the same name. Here's the only rule to remember:

> *"Overloaded functions of the same name must differ in their argument lists by number of arguments, type of arguments, or both."*

The argument list is how Visual C++ knows which version of the function to call. A function's name and argument list is called the function's *signature.* As long as you change the argument list, Visual C++ recognizes that specific function's signature and calls the proper function. When you write prototypes for programs with overloaded functions, you must supply the prototype for each function. Each of the prototypes will have the same function name, but their argument lists will differ somehow.

Note: Notice that changing the return data type has no impact when you want to overload two or more functions. In other words, something in the parameter lists and *not* return values must differ between functions before Visual C++ knows which function call to resolve and execute.

Overloaded functions are the primary reason that Visual C++ considers a `char` data type to be different from an `int` although regular C compilers convert `char`s to `int`s and store them the same way. When two overloaded functions differ by only a single argument, one being `char` and the other `int`, Visual C++ must be able to distinguish between the two data types and make a correct decision as to which version of the function to call.

The program in Listing 7.1 returns to the maximum/minimum problem similar to one you saw in yesterday's lesson (Listing 6.4). The `main()` function initializes three arrays, all with different types of values in them, and calls `maxFind()` and `minFind()`. Visual C++ calls the appropriate function based on the data type of the arrays being passed.

Day 7

Overloaded Functions Lessen Your Load

Listing 7.1. A function that contains two regular arguments and a default argument.

```
 1: // Filename: MAXMINAR.CPP
 2: // Finds the maximum and minimum values in
 3: // arrays based on their data type.
 4: #include <iostream.h>
 5: #include <iomanip.h>
 6: int maxAra(int iAra[]);     // Only two function names in
 7: float maxAra(float fAra[]);   // these six functions
 8: double maxAra(double dAra[]);
 9: int minAra(int iAra[]);
10: float minAra(float fAra[]);
11: double minAra(double dAra[]);
12: main()
13: {
14:    int   iAra[10] = {5, 8, 4, 2, 1, 10, 9, 3, 5, 7};
15:    float fAra[10] = {45.5, 2.3, 63.2, 19.3, 70.1,
16:                      35.4, 51.2, 53.7, 39.4, 59.2};
17:    double dAra[10] = {45.54323, 2.46763, 63.29876, 19.67863,
18:         80.34541, 35.44009, 51.20392, 53.40967, 39.80604, 59.11112};
19:    cout << setprecision(5);  // 5 digits maximum precision in output
20:    cout << "Largest value in the iAra is " << (maxAra(iAra)) << "\n";
21:    cout << "Largest value in the fAra is " << (maxAra(fAra)) << "\n";
22:    cout << "Largest value in the dAra is " << (maxAra(dAra)) << "\n";
23:    cout << "Smallest value in the iAra is " << (minAra(iAra))<< "\n";
24:    cout << "Smallest value in the fAra is " << minAra(fAra) << "\n";
25:    cout << "Smallest value in the dAra is " << minAra(dAra) << "\n";
26:    return 0;
27: }
28: //////////////////////////////////////////////////////////////
29: // Overloaded functions follow
30: int maxAra(int iAra[])
31: {
32:    int max=0;  // Trigger value for first element in the array
33:    for (int i=0; i<10; i++)
34:    { if (iAra[i] > max)
35:        { max= iAra[i]; }
36:    }
37:    return max;
38: }
39: float maxAra(float fAra[])
40: {
41:    float max=0.0;  // Trigger value for first element in the array
42:    for (int i=0; i<10; i++)
43:    { if (fAra[i] > max)
44:        { max= fAra[i]; }
45:    }
46:    return max;
47: }
48: double maxAra(double dAra[])
```

```
49: {
50:     double max=0.0;   // Trigger value for first element in the array
51:     for (int i=0; i<10; i++)
52:     {  if (dAra[i] > max)
53:         {  max= dAra[i]; }
54:     }
55:     return max;
56: }
57: int minAra(int iAra[])
58: {
59:     int min=9999;    // Trigger value for first element in the array
60:     for (int i=0; i<10; i++)
61:     {  if (iAra[i] < min)
62:         {  min= iAra[i]; }
63:     }
64:     return min;
65: }
66: float minAra(float fAra[])
67: {
68:     float min=9999.9;   // Trigger value for first element in the array
69:     for (int i=0; i<10; i++)
70:     {  if (fAra[i] < min)
71:         {  min= fAra[i]; }
72:     }
73:     return min;
74: }
75: double minAra(double dAra[])
76: {
77:     double min=99999.9;   // Trigger value for first item in the array
78:     for (int i=0; i<10; i++)
79:     {  if (dAra[i] < min)
80:         {  min= dAra[i]; }
81:     }
82:     return min;
83: }
```

```
Largest value in the iAra is 10
Largest value in the fAra is 70.1
Largest value in the dAra is 80.345
Smallest value in the iAra is 1
Smallest value in the fAra is 2.3
Smallest value in the dAra is 2.4676
```

In these minimum and maximum functions, a standard algorithm is used to find the largest and smallest values in the arrays. Before the program looks for the largest value in the maximum functions, a zero is stored in the max variables (lines 32, 41, 50) so that the first array element is always larger than max and the rest of the function compares the remaining elements to that first element. Before the

Overloaded Functions Lessen Your Load

program looks for the smallest value in the minimum functions, an extremely large value is stored in the min variables (lines 59, 68, 77) so that the first array element is always smaller than max and the rest of the function compares the remaining elements to that first element.

At this time, the most important point to note about this program is that its last six functions share two names, maxAra() and minAra(). Visual C++ knows which function to call by looking at the argument you pass. The argument's data type determines which function executes. When you have similar functions, you don't have to give each function a slightly different name as you do in C because Visual C++ steps in and does a little extra compile-time work for you to figure out which function to call.

> **Wrangle with Name-Mangling**
>
> Visual C++ uses an interesting method for differentiating overloaded functions at compile-time. Visual C++ *name-mangles* your function signatures. *Name-mangling* is fancy computer lingo for changing the function names after the compiler sees them.
>
> To mangle the names, Visual C++ combines the overloaded functions' original names with their argument data types and creates new names for the functions. Everywhere in the program one of these functions is prototyped, called, and defined, Visual C++ refers to the function by its mangled name.
>
> For example, if you used two functions prototyped like
>
> ```
> int myAns(float x, int j);
> int myAns(int i, char c);
> ```
>
> and if you called them with statements such as
>
> ```
> ans1 = myAns(14.2, 25);
> ans2 = myAns(62, 'x');
> ```
>
> then Visual C++ might change the names, after the source code leaves your hands but before the code is compiled, to these:
>
> ```
> int myAnsFLTINT(float x, int j);
> int myAnsINTCHA(int i, char c);
> ```

Visual C++ would also change the places these functions are called, such as these:

```
ans1 = myAnsFLTINT(14.2, 25);
ans2 = myAnsINTCHA(62, 'x');
```

Given these new names (Visual C++ uses a slightly more extensive naming algorithm, but you get the idea), Visual C++ has no problem calling `myAnsFLTINT()` when it's requested and `myAnsINTCHA()` when it's requested. After your program is compiled, the names are back the way you left them. Visual C++ mangles the names only so that it can distinguish between them when you overload functions.

Note: Visual C++ mangles *all* C++ function names, even those that are not overloaded. Therefore, if you want to link to Visual C++ program functions that you wrote and compiled using a C compiler, you'll have to request that the compiler not mangle the C function names when the C++ program calls them. Otherwise, Visual C++ will never find the C functions, because they were compiled without a name-mangling compiler. The next section in this chapter explains how to combine C and C++ code in one Visual C++ program so that name-mangling affects only the C++ functions.

DO · DON'T

DO overload functions that are similar but require a different type or number of arguments. You'll have fewer function names to remember.

DO prototype all your overloaded functions.

DON'T change only the return value of two overloaded functions, or Visual C++ will balk at the name clash that results. The parameter list is all that differentiates one overloaded function from another.

Overloaded Functions Lessen Your Load

Calling Your C Functions

There is little need to rewrite your libraries of C code just because you move to Visual C++. As you have seen so far, Visual C++ supports just about everything in the C language. However, you might have written or purchased some routines that are compiled and thoroughly tested, such as some fancy input/output functions, that you want to call from your Visual C++ programs.

As you read in the preceding section, Visual C++ calls functions with names that are different (mangled) from the names you wrote. You give a function a name, and Visual C++ mangles that name into something completely different, using the parameters, so that overloaded versions of the functions can be distinguished from each other.

Note: Day 14's chapter, "Loose Ends: *static* and Larger Programs," delves more fully into multiple-module programs and separate compilation and linking. You'll learn how to use Visual C++ to handle multiple code modules.

If you want to keep Visual C++ from mangling C function calls, you must include a statement at the top of your Visual C++ program (somewhere before `main()` is best, or perhaps in a header file) telling Visual C++ to keep a list of function calls nonmangled.

If you want to call a C function named `cFun()` from a Visual C++ program, include the following `extern` statement:

```
extern "C" void cFun(int i, float x);
```

If you had two or more C functions to call, you could declare them individually like this:

```
extern "C" void cFun1(int i, float x);
extern "C" float cFun2(float x, float y);
extern "C" double cFun3(char c);
```

Or you could group them into a single `extern` statement with a pair of braces like this:

```
extern "C" {
   void cFun1(int i, float x);
   float cFun2(float x, float y);
   double cFun3(char c);
}
```

The `main()` function shown in Listing 7.2 calls these three functions. The `extern` statement tells Visual C++ not to mangle the function calls because the C functions will eventually be linked to the current source code, and the names must be left intact.

Listing 7.2. A `main()` function that calls three C functions.

```
 1:  // Filename: CALLC.CPP
 2:  // main() function that calls three C functions already
 3:  // compiled and waiting to be linked to this program.
 4:  #include <iostream.h>
 5:  extern "C" {
 6:      void cFun1(int i, float x);
 7:      float cFun2(float x, float y);
 8:      double cFun3(char c);
 9:  }
10:  main()
11:  {
12:      float ans1;
13:      double ans2;
14:      cFun1(10, 20.5);            // Call first C function
15:      ans1 = cFun2(43.2, 905.3);  // Call second C function
16:      ans2 = cFun3('x');          // Call third C function
17:      cout << "ans1 and ans2 are " << ans1 << " and " << ans2;
18:      return 0;
19:  }
```

This program compiles with no errors, but Visual C++ refuses to link the program due to the missing functions named `cFun1()`, `cFun2()`, and `cFun3()`. To compile the program without linking, press Ctrl+F8 (rather than the usual Ctrl+F5) to select Project Compile File. This program will not successfully link unless you link the three compiled C functions to them. (The three C functions are not listed here because their contents are trivial to understanding the problem at hand, name-mangling.)

Note: The reason Visual C++ successfully compiles Listing 7.2's source code, even though the code is missing three function listings, is that the `extern` statement tells Visual C++ that the three functions reside outside the current source file. The `extern` statement also informs Visual C++ that the functions are C functions so that their function calls in lines 14, 15, and 16 will not be mangled.

Overloaded Functions Lessen Your Load

Calling C Functions

```
extern "C" {
  prototypeForCfunction;
       ;
}
```

This `extern` statement is needed when you want to call C functions from your Visual C++ code. The C functions are assumed to be already compiled and will be linked to the current Visual C++ program. Otherwise, if you insert the C code directly into your Visual C++ program source code, there is no need to use the `extern` because Visual C++ mangles both the function calls and the function definitions; Visual C++ cannot mangle a definition for functions already compiled.

Example

```
extern "C" {
  void compAmt(float sales, float tax);
  int skyIt(int t);
}
```

Simple Operator Overloading

It's time to introduce a concept that you'll read about in more depth on Days 11 and 12. Starting tomorrow, you'll begin to explore the true OOP capabilities of Visual C++. This section is going to whet your appetite a bit and hint at what's ahead.

Operators such as plus (+) and less-than (<) operate on data. (It's a good thing they're called *operators,* isn't it?) Even function-call parentheses, type casts, and `sizeof` are operators. You can overload almost all the operators, making them work on your data the way you define.

> **Note:** The most notable operator that you cannot overload is the conditional operator (?:). The *ternary arguments* (fancy computer lingo meaning that the operator requires three values to work, whereas most require only two) make overloading the conditional operator impossible. You also cannot overload the scope resolution operator (::), the dereference operator (*), and the member dot operator (.).

Appendix C lists all the Visual C++ operators and their precedence. You cannot change the precedence of the Visual C++ operators. (Just because you can change the way the operators work doesn't mean you can change their precedence.) Also, you cannot change the way operators work on the built-in data types such as int and char. You can only change the way the operators work with your user-defined data types such as struct variables.

> **You Use Overloaded Operators All the Time**
>
> Although the term *overloaded operator* might be new to you, you have used overloaded operators when writing C programs. You know that * is the multiplication operator *and* the dereferencing operator. Visual C++ uses a few additional overloaded operators, such as the << for output when << is also used for bitwise left-shifting.
>
> Visual C++ knows when * means multiplication by the *context* in which you use the *. When you write your own overloaded operators, Visual C++ knows to use your overloaded operator routine in place of the one that is built in because of the context of the data types you use. Visual C++ looks for your overloaded operator when you apply an operator to your own data types, and it uses its built-in operator code when you apply operators to built-in data types.

The most important reason to overload operators is to perform seemingly built-in operations on your own data types. Suppose you defined your own data type called People and defined two People variables like this:

```
struct People {
  int age;
  char name[25];
  int numKids;
  float salary;
} emp1, emp2;
```

Suppose you want to add these two structure variables, emp1 and emp2, together. How about the following statement?

```
total = emp1 + emp2;    // I don't think so!
```

What's wrong with the addition of the two variables? The answer is that the two variables are not built-in data types but are user-defined data types. Visual C++ knows how to add two integers and even knows how to add a float to a double, but Visual C++ does not have any idea what you want done when you attempt to add two People variables. Visual C++ complains with this error message:

Overloaded Functions Lessen Your Load

```
Illegal structure operation
```

Think for a moment what could be accomplished if you *could* add two People variables together. You could get a total of their salaries if you wanted. Salary totals are used all the time for payroll budgeting and reporting. You would probably not have a use for adding the ages, unless you wanted to compute an average employee age. Therefore, when you want to add two People variables, you really don't want to add one entire structure variable to another, you just want to add a piece of each one.

Of course, you can use the addition operator along with the dot operator to add two salaries like this:

```
total = emp1.salary + emp2.salary;   // Add the two salaries
```

Adding two specific People variables has always required extra work. Until operator overloading, you would probably write a function to add these two kinds of variables together. The function might look something like this:

```
double addPeople(struct People p1, struct People p2)
{
  double temp;
  temp = p1.salary + p2.salary;
  return temp;    // Return the combined salaries
}
```

When using Visual C++, you don't have to use the struct keyword as long as the People structure is already defined in the program as shown a little earlier. Also, for efficiency and safety, you might want to pass const reference values to addPeople(). Here is a better version of the same function:

```
double addPeople(const People & p1, const People & p2)
{
  double temp;
  temp = p1.salary + p2.salary;
  return temp;    // Return the combined salaries
}
```

The function enables you to define what is meant by "add two People variables together." By definition, when you want to add two People variables, you really just want their salaries added together. To add two People salaries, you can now do this:

```
total = addPeople(emp1, emp2);   // Add the salaries
```

In ordinary programming languages, the dilemma is solved because you can now "add" two People variables using the function. However, Visual C++ is no ordinary programming language. Visual C++ acts as if you've just slowed yourself down by writing that function, and in a way you have. You now have two different ways to perform a similar operation. When you want to add two built-in data types, you must remember to use the plus sign, and when you want to add two `People` variables, you must remember the function name. The problem becomes even worse when you write an addition function for all your structure variables because you have to remember a different name for each user-defined data type.

Improving the Situation with Overloading

You might be thinking that function overloading would help. After all, you can name each of the adding functions the same name, and your different `struct` data types will distinguish which one gets called when the compiler sees something like this:

```
total = addPeople(emp1, emp2);   // Add the salaries
```

The designers of Visual C++ did not stop at function overloading. The designers of Visual C++ actually thought you should be able to make operators work the way you want them to. Why should you have to remember *any* function name when you want to add something? You already know the + operator, so that's what you should be able to use for both your own and the compiler's built-in data types. By extending function overloading to *operator overloading,* you can add practically anything you need with built-in operators.

The *operator...()* Functions

Visual C++ provides an interesting mechanism for overloading operators. You must write functions named `operator` followed by the operator that you want to overload. Therefore, to overload the plus sign, you would write a function named `operator+()`. All the other overloaded operators would be named in a similar manner, as Figure 7.1 suggests.

These functions…	Perform these operations
`operator+()`	Addition
`operator-()`	Subtraction
`operator*()`	Multiplication
`operator/()`	Division
`operator<()`	Less than
…and so on	

Figure 7.1. It's easy to see which operator triggers the operator functions.

Overloaded Functions Lessen Your Load

Whenever Visual C++ encounters a function named operator...() (replace the ellipses with the operator of your choice), Visual C++ looks at the data types passed to the function. If Visual C++ ever sees those data types on either side of the operator, *your function* will execute, not the built-in operator's regular routine.

Renaming the preceding addition function produces this:

```
double operator+(const People & p1, const People & p2)
{
  double temp;
  temp = p1.salary + p2.salary;
  return temp;   // Return the combined salaries
}
```

The two parameters inside the parentheses determine when Visual C++ calls this function. Whenever a plus sign appears between two People data types, Visual C++ calls this operator+() function. Therefore, rather than

```
total = operator+(emp1, emp2);   // Adds 2 structures
```

you can do this:

```
total = emp1 + emp2;   // Adds 2 structures
```

Figure 7.2 shows how Visual C++ decides when to call operator+(). When a People variable appears on each side of a +, Visual C++ automatically calls operator+().

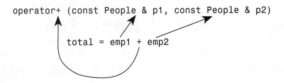

Figure 7.2. operator+() is called when you add two People variables.

Isn't that much better? The program in Listing 7.3 uses the People structure and operator+() function to add two salaries.

Listing 7.3. Using operator+().

```
1:  // Filename: ADDEMP.CPP
2:  // Overloading the plus operator
3:  #include <iostream.h>
4:  #include <iomanip.h>
5:  struct People {
6:    int age;
7:    char name[25];
```

```
 8:    int numKids;
 9:    float salary;
10: };
11: float operator+(const People & p1, const People & p2);
12: main()
13: {
14:    // Define and initialize two structure variables
15:    People emp1 = {26, "Robert Nickles", 2, 20933.50};
16:    People emp2 = {41, "Don Dole", 4, 30102.32};
17:    float totalSal;
18:    totalSal = emp1 + emp2;
19:    cout << setprecision(2) << setiosflags(ios::fixed);
20:    cout << "The total salary is " << totalSal << "\n";
21:    return 0;
22: }
23: //////////////////////////////////////////////////////////////
24: // Overloaded plus operator function appears next
25: float operator+(const People & p1, const People & p2)
26: {
27:    // Parameters were renamed from emp1 and emp2 just to show you
28:    // that the names used don't matter. When you pass by reference,
29:    // you work with the same data no matter what you call it in
30:    // both the calling and the receiving functions.
31:    float temp;
32:    temp = p1.salary + p2.salary;
33:    return temp;
34: }
```

The total salary is 51035.82

Notice that the People structure had to be declared (lines 5–10) before the operator+() function could be prototyped because operator+() referred to the People structure.

Expanding the Power of Operator Overloading

If you want to take operator overloading to an extreme, you might consider changing the operator+() function slightly to look like this:

```
People operator+(const People & p1, const People & p2)
{
  People tempEmp;
  tempEmp.salary = p1.salary + p2.salary;
  return tempEmp;   // Return the combined salaries
}
```

Overloaded Functions Lessen Your Load

The return value in this function differs from the one in the preceding function. Rather than a `double` being returned, a `People` structure variable is returned. The only member in the returned structure variable that is initialized is `salary`, but you can now stack several additions together like this:

```
People totalEmps;    // Define a structure variable
totalEmps = emp1 + emp2 + emp3 + emp4;
```

You can perform operator overloading on any of the operators (except for the handful mentioned earlier) in a similar manner. You can even write an overloaded operator function that works with both your own data type and a built-in data type. Consider the following function:

```
People operator+(const People & p1, int i)
{
  People temp;
  temp.age = p1.age + i;
  return temp;
}
```

Note: Notice that the first parameter is a `People` parameter. This function determines what you mean when you add an integer to a `People` variable. The following statement causes this `operator+()` to execute:
```
olderEmp = emp1 + factor;
```

However, the statement

```
olderEmp = factor + emp1;   // Not yet coded
```

would not execute the previous function because the arguments are reversed.

If you want to define the combination that adds a `People` variable to an integer, write another function reversing the two arguments. If you want to overload the function using reversed arguments, Visual C++ will know which one to call when you add a `People` and an integer value using either order.

In this function, it is `age`, not `salary`, that Visual C++ uses for the primary `operator+()` goal. The idea is that you can make `operator+()` do anything you want with your own data types. You can even force some kind of subtraction to take place if you coded `operator+()` to subtract (although you should stick to the spirit of the operator's original meaning).

If you included this `operator+()` with `People` and `int` arguments in the same program as the preceding `operator+()`, Visual C++ would call the appropriate one when the time came because the functions' signatures differ. Combining your data types with built-in data types could be useful for adding or multiplying a single value on every element of an array with a single + or * operation.

Your overloaded operator functions do what you define them to do. Just to drive the point home a little more clearly, this function appears to be a modulus (%) operator function, but it actually prints a message:

```
People operator %(const People & p1, const People & p2)
{
  cout << "\n\n** Just doing a modulus **\n\n";
  return p1;
}
```

If Visual C++ were to reach a statement such as

```
total = emp1 % emp2;
```

this is what would print:

```
** Just doing a modulus **
```

Some Final Warnings

If you want to learn more about operator overloading, you'll get more than you bargain for on Days 11 and 12. For now, today's chapter is an attempt to show you what Visual C++ can really do. Before expanding on operator overloading any further, you should get some OOP concepts behind you. After you learn OOP, you'll overload your program's operators a little differently from the way they are described in this chapter, because you'll be able to take advantage of some of the OOP mechanisms that improve upon overload overloading.

Don't violate the spirit of the original operator. Don't make a * perform division. You also will not have to overload every operator for all your own data types. Not only would that be a waste of your time, but you'll soon learn how Visual C++ and OOP make it easy for you to extend your programs later if you need additional operators.

Listing 7.4 gives you a feel for some additional ways to overload operators. Look through the program to get some ideas of other operator overloadings you can try. If you've ever explicitly called a function to perform a standard operation on your own data types, you'll appreciate this bonus feature (operator overloading) that Visual C++ provides to make your code cleaner; you'll now have to do less work and remember fewer function names.

Overloaded Functions Lessen Your Load

Type **Listing 7.4. Overloading several operators.**

```
1:  // Filename: OVRLOTS.CPP
2:  // Demonstrates overloading of several operators
3:  #include <iostream.h>
4:  #include <iomanip.h>
5:  struct People {
6:    int age;
7:    char name[25];
8:    int numKids;
9:    float salary;
10: };
11: double operator+(const People & p1, const People & p2);
12: int operator-(const People & p1, const People & p2);
13: int operator>(const People & p1, const People & p2);
14: main()
15: {
16:   // Define and initialize two structure variables
17:   People emp1 = {26, "Robert Nickles", 2, 20933.50};
18:   People emp2 = {41, "Don Dole", 4, 30102.32};
19:   double totalSal;
20:   int ageDiff;
21:   if (emp1 > emp2)
22:     { cout << "The first employee makes more than the second.\n"; }
23:   else
24:     { cout << "The second employee makes more than the first.\n"; }
25:   totalSal = emp1 + emp2;
26:   ageDiff = emp2 - emp1;
27:   cout << setprecision(2) << setiosflags(ios::fixed);
28:   cout << "The total of the salaries is " << totalSal << ".\n";
29:   cout << "The age difference is " << ageDiff << ".\n";
30:   return 0;
31: }
32: //////////////////////////////////////////////////////////////
33: // Overloaded function to add two People variables
34: double operator+(const People & p1, const People & p2)
35: {                    // You cannot stack these
36:   return (p1.salary + p2.salary);
37: }
38: //////////////////////////////////////////////////////////////
39: // Overloaded function to subtract two People variables
40: int operator-(const People & p1, const People & p2)
41: {                    // You cannot stack these
42:   return (p1.age - p2.age);
43: }
44: //////////////////////////////////////////////////////////////
45: // Overloaded function to compare two People variables
46: int operator>(const People & p1, const People & p2)
47: {                    // You cannot stack these
48:   if (p1.salary > p2.salary)
```

```
49:        { return 1; }
50:    else
51:        { return 0; }
52: }
```

The second employee makes more than the first.
The total of the salaries is 51035.82.
The age difference is 15.

Isn't it a lot clearer to compare two `People` variables with a simple > operator (line 21) than to write a function or do the memberwise comparison in the `main()` function? Of course, you still have to write the code that tests the individual members (lines 46–52), but after you've written the overloaded `operator>()` function, the rest of the program only has to use a simple comparison operator to compare two `People` variables.

The `operator>()` function must return an integer result because the > operator returns an integer 1 or 0 for true or false. When you overload operator functions, try to mirror their regular operator counterparts as closely as possible.

DO	DON'T

DO overload operators when you want to perform a built-in operation on your own data types.

DO return the proper kind of object if you want to string together operators such as multiply three or more of your data types in a single statement.

DO think about future maintenance to your programs. If you overload -, you might also consider overloading the -=.

DON'T overload a plus operator to perform subtraction. Stay with the original spirit of the operators when you write your own.

DON'T overload every operator unless your program actually needs that many operators defined.

Summary

After you learn to overload functions, you are on your way to simplifying your programs. Instead of remembering a bunch of names for functions that behave the

Overloaded Functions Lessen Your Load

same but work on different data types, you can now use the *same* function names. You then eliminate extra memory work on your part because Visual C++ takes over for you and calls the appropriate functions. As long as the function arguments differ, you can overload two or more functions.

To achieve operator overloading, Visual C++ combines a function name with its arguments and mangles the name. Every function prototype, function call, and function definition in Visual C++ is mangled right before the program is compiled so that the compiler can properly execute overloaded functions.

The name-mangling can cause problems if you attempt to link C functions you wrote and call those C functions from your Visual C++ program. To keep Visual C++ from mangling a function name, include an `extern` statement that lists all the C functions called by your program, and Visual C++ then leaves those functions alone.

When you define an overloaded operator function, you are defining operations for your own data types. You cannot rewrite the way an operator works on built-in data, and you cannot change the natural order of precedence from that of Appendix C's Visual C++ operator precedence table.

In your overloaded operator function, you can make the function do anything you want. The function is *your* definition of what that operator means when applied to your data types. You do not even have to code a math operation. For instance, you can print a message when two specific kinds of variables are added, subtracted, multiplied, or whatever.

One of the biggest advantages of overloaded operators appears in Day 12's chapter, "Extending Operator Overloads," when you see how to overload >> and << to make the input and output of your structure variables as simple as getting and printing integers.

Please remember that overloading an operator in one program doesn't overload it in all the rest. The program that contains the overloaded operator function is the program that works the operator on those data types. The foundation laid here will be greatly expanded on in later chapters, starting tomorrow, when you'll tackle some OOP concepts.

Q&A

Q. What is the advantage of overloaded functions?

A. You often run across the need for writing several functions that differ only in their argument lists. Some programmers have to write lots of functions that perform the same math calculation on all the different data types. Before Visual C++ came along, all those functions had to have different names. Now, if you want to perform the cubed root on an integer, floating-point, and double, you only have to call `cube()` (if that's the name you gave the three overloaded functions) rather than something like `cubeInt()`, `cubeFlt()`, and `cubeDoub()`.

Even more important, overloaded functions give you the ability to overload operators as well. Operator overloading is the epitome of Visual C++'s elimination of petty details from your programs. Instead of writing functions that apply common operations on your built-in data types, you can overload operator functions—named `operator...()` in which ... is one of the built-in operators—and apply the regular operators to your own data. The operators will behave the way you defined them in the overloaded operator functions.

Q. I've never seen a function name mangled. When does it happen?

A. When you send your program to be compiled, Visual C++ then mangles the function prototypes, function calls, and function definitions. After the name-mangling, all the overloaded functions have different names (the compiler made sure of it), so Visual C++ can then properly resolve the function calls.

After your program is compiled and you again look at the source code, the function names are back the way you left them. Visual C++ name-mangles in the same way that the old `#define` constants were changed—the change is made after the source code leaves your editor to go be compiled, and everything is restored before you see it again. The idea of name-mangling is that you have to mess with only *one* function name and then you let Visual C++ figure out how to differentiate the functions.

Q. I wrote a program that overloaded the division operator, but each time I try to use that division operator in other programs, I get an `Illegal structure operation` error. What am I doing wrong?

A. An overloaded operator function remains in effect for only the program in which it appears. Therefore, you have to include the overloaded operator function in each program that needs it.

Q. How can I mix C and C++ functions, and why would I need to?

A. You might never need to mix C and C++ functions within the same Visual C++ program. However, most programmers migrate to C++ from C, and

Overloaded Functions Lessen Your Load

those programmers have written many libraries of functions over the years. They don't want to recompile the functions using C++ code because it would take too much time and would not be worth the effort.

To link those C functions seamlessly to your C++ programs, you must tell the C++ code, via an `extern "C"` declaration, the names of all the C code used in the program. When Visual C++ compiles the source program that calls the external C function, Visual C++ will not mangle the function calls. (The C compiler did not mangle the function names when you compiled the functions, so Visual C++ would not be able to match the function calls with the functions if you didn't stop Visual C++ from mangling the C function calls.)

Q. What is the difference between overloaded functions and default argument lists?

A. Often, you can use either default arguments or overloaded functions to do the same job. However, as you progress into OOP, each has a better purpose than the other at different times. You'll see as you go along where each is best used.

To see their sometimes-confusing similarities, consider these function calls:

```
fun();
fun(10);
fun(20, 'c');
```

Are these function calls calling one function with default arguments prototyped like this:

```
void fun(int = 50, char = 'x');
```

Or are these function calls calling one of these three overloaded functions:

```
void fun(void);
void fun(int);
void fun(int, char);
```

The answer is that you cannot tell from the information given. This shows you how the distinction and use of overloaded functions and default argument lists are not always easy to determine.

Workshop

The Workshop offers quiz questions and exercises to hone your skills and give you feedback on today's lesson. You'll find some proposed answers in Appendix D.

Quiz

1. How does Visual C++ differentiate one overloaded function from another?

2. True or False: All the following statements properly overload the same function:

   ```
   int  fun(int, char, float);
   void fun(int, int, int, float);
   int  fun(float);
   ```

3. True or False: All the following statements properly overload the same function:

   ```
   int   fun(int, char, float);
   void  fun(int, int, int, float);
   float fun(int, char, float);
   ```

4. If you wanted to overload the operators &&, ||, and *=, what is the name of the functions you would have to write?

5. What do you have to do to change the + to work differently for integer data types?

6. What do you have to do to stack several overloaded operators together (that is, add three or more structure variables together in a single statement)?

7. Why would you need an `extern "C"` statement in some of your Visual C++ programs?

8. Here is a short program with two overloaded functions. There is a problem with the code. See whether you can spot it.

   ```
   void prFun(int i);      // Prototypes
   void prFun(float f);
   #include <iostream.h>
   main()
   {
     prFun(7);
   ```

Overloaded Functions Lessen Your Load

```
    prFun(7.35);
    return 0;
}
void prFun(int i=0)        // First overloaded function
{
    cout << "i is now " << i << "\n";
}
void prFun(float f=999.9) // Second overloaded function
{
    cout << "f is now " << f << "\n";
}
```

9. Rewrite the following C function call declarations as a single `extern` statement:

```
extern "C" char * getName(void);
extern "C" float amtDoub(float x);
```

Exercises

1. Write a program with two functions that have the same name. The first function is to return the average of an integer array passed to it, and the second function is to return the average of a floating-point array.

2. Add two overloaded operator functions to Listing 7.4's program. Overload both the += and the -= operators to add compound addition and subtraction.

Week 1 in Review

Now that you've finished the first week, you might like to see a long program that brings together much of the material from the first seven days. The program in Listing WR1.1 illustrates several Visual C++ features you now understand.

Listing WR1.1. Week one review listing.

```cpp
 1: // Filename: TRVAGNCY.CPP
 2: // Program that reviews the first week's lessons. This program
 3: // defines an array of client structures for a travel agency.
 4: // After the user enters data for the array, the program prints
 5: // the data and performs some calculations based on overloaded
 6: // operator functions.
 7: #include <iostream.h>
 8: #include <iomanip.h>
 9: #include <ctype.h>
10: #include <string.h>
11: const int TOTCUST = 25;
12: struct Client {
13:    char * name;
14:    int trips;        // Number of trips booked so far
15:    float balance;    // Total balance owed, if any
16:    double totHist;   // Total spent with agency to date
17: };
18: void prTitles(void);
19: void fillAra(Client clients[], int & numCur);
20: void getData(char * cName);
21: void getData(int & trips);
22: void getData(float & balance);
23: void getData(double & totHist);
```

continues

Week 1 in Review

Listing WR1.1. continued

```
24: int compAvgTrips(const Client clients[], const int & numCur);
25: float compAvgBal(const Client clients[], const int & numCur);
26: double compToDateTot(const Client clients[], const int &
       ➥numCur);
27: void delAllNames(Client client[], const int numCur);
28: void operator+=(double & temp, const Client & client);
29: void operator+=(float & temp, const Client & client);
30: void operator+=(int & temp, const Client & client);
31: main()
32: {
33:    int numCur = 0;            // Holds current number of
       ➥clients
34:    int avgTrips;
35:    float avgBal = 0;
36:    double totalToDate = 0.0;
37:    Client clients[TOTCUST];   // Define enough places for
       ➥clients
38:    prTitles();      // Print some opening titles
39:    fillAra(clients, numCur);   // Fill the arrays
40:    avgTrips = compAvgTrips(clients, numCur);
41:    avgBal = compAvgBal(clients, numCur);
42:    totalToDate = compToDateTot(clients, numCur);
43:    cout << setprecision(2) << setiosflags(ios::fixed);
44:    cout << "\nThe average number of trips taken per customer is
       ➥";
45:    cout << avgTrips << "\n";
46:    cout << "The average balance owed per customer is $";
47:    cout << avgBal << "\n";
48:    cout << "The total income to date is $" << totalToDate <<
       ➥"\n";
49:    delAllNames(clients, numCur);  // Deallocate the name heap
50:    return 0;
51: }
52: /////////////////////////////////////////////////////////////
53: // Function that prints an opening title
54: void prTitles(void)
55: {
56:    cout << "** Travel Agency Computation System **\n\n";
57:    cout << "This program will ask for some travel agency data
              ➥and\n";
58:    cout << "compute some statistics for you.\n\n";
59:    cout << "Buon Viaggio! Andiamo Italia!\n\n";
60: }
61: /////////////////////////////////////////////////////////////
62: // Function that controls the input of data
```

```
 63: void fillAra(Client clients[], int & numCur)
 64: {
 65:   char ans, cr;
 66:   do {
 67:     getData(clients[numCur].name);   // Overloaded input
                                          ↳routines
 68:     getData(clients[numCur].trips);
 69:     getData(clients[numCur].balance);
 70:     getData(clients[numCur].totHist);
 71:     numCur++;
 72:     cout << "Are there more clients? (Y/N) ";
 73:     cin.get(cr);   // Discard the newline from previous input
 74:     cin.get(ans);
 75:     cin.get(cr);   // Discard the newline
 76:   } while (toupper(ans) == 'Y');
 77: }
 78: //////////////////////////////////////////////////////////////
 79: // Each of the following overloaded functions gets a different
 80: // client structure member, and the data type dictates which
 81: // version of the function Visual C++ calls.
 82: // This program does not do anything with the client names, but
 83: // routines could be added later that do.
 84: void getData(char * cName)
 85: {
 86:   // Get the client's name by allocating enough spaces
 87:   char buffer[80];   // Local holding place for input
 88:   cout << "What is the client's name? ";
 89:   cin.getline(buffer, 80);
 90:   cName = new char[strlen(buffer) + 1];
 91:   strcpy(cName, buffer);   // Copy entered name
 92: }
 93: //////////////////////////////////////////////////////////////
 94: void getData(int & trips)
 95: {
 96:   // Get the client's number of trips taken so far
 97:   cout << "How many trips has the client taken from this
              ↳agency? ";
 98:   cin >> trips;
 99: }
100: //////////////////////////////////////////////////////////////
101: void getData(float & balance)
102: {
103:   // Get the client's balance owed if any
104:   cout << "How much does the client owe from previous trips?
           ↳";
105:   cin >> balance;
106: }
```

continues

Week 1 in Review

Listing WR1.1. continued

```
107: ////////////////////////////////////////////////////////////
108: void getData(double & totHist)
109: {
110:    // Get the client's balance owed if any
111:    cout << "How much has the client spent on all trips to date? ";
112:    cin >> totHist;
113: }
114: ////////////////////////////////////////////////////////////
115: // Overloaded operator so the program can average
116: // the number of trips per client
117: int compAvgTrips(const Client clients[], const int & numCur)
118: {
119:    int avg = 0;
120:    for (int i=0; i<numCur; i++)
121:    {  avg += clients[i]; }  // Call overloaded operator function
122:    avg /= numCur;
123:    return (avg);   // Discard partial trip (if any) in the
                        ➥average
124: }
125: ////////////////////////////////////////////////////////////
126: void operator+=(int & temp, const Client & client)
127: {
128:    temp += client.trips;
129: }
130: ////////////////////////////////////////////////////////////
131: // Overloaded operator so the program can average
132: // the outstanding balances
133: float compAvgBal(const Client clients[], const int & numCur)
134: {
135:    float avg = 0.0;
136:    for (int i=0; i<numCur; i++)
137:    {  avg += clients[i]; }  // Call overloaded operator function
138:    avg /= numCur;
139:    return avg;
140: }
141: ////////////////////////////////////////////////////////////
142: void operator+=(float & temp, const Client & client)
143: {
144:    temp += client.balance;
145: }
146: ////////////////////////////////////////////////////////////
147: // Function to add each client's total history
148: double compToDateTot(const Client clients[], const int &
       ➥numCur)
149: {
150:    double temp = 0.0;
```

```
151:      for (int i=0; i<numCur; i++)
152:       { temp += clients[i]; }   // Call overloaded operator
                                     ↪function
153:      return temp;
154: }
155: //////////////////////////////////////////////////////////////
156: void operator+=(double & temp, const Client & client)
157: {
158:    temp += client.totHist;
159: }
160: //////////////////////////////////////////////////////////////
161: // Function to deallocate each client's name from the heap
162: void delAllNames(Client client[], const int numCur)
163: {
164:    for (int i=0; i<numCur; i++)
165:     { delete client[i].name; }
166: }
```

The program computes simple statistics for a travel agency using many of the concepts you learned in your first week with this book. Comments explain a lot of this program, and all the comments use the Visual C++ // style rather than the older /* */ style.

Lines 12–30 declare the client structure and prototype the functions in the program. This section of code would probably be better put in a header file and included in this code. Include this kind of declaration section in your programs when possible to keep the "real" program from getting too cluttered.

Line 11 uses const to define a constant and not #define as C programmers would do. Visual C++ programmers avoid using #define.

Although the program does nothing with the client names except ask for them and store them, you'll notice in lines 84–92 that the new operator is used to reserve heap memory for each client's name. The program then deallocates those names in lines 161–166 right before the program ends.

The most important thing to note about the code is its extensive use of overloaded functions. Notice that getData() is called in lines 67–70. Because each member of the client's structure is a different data type, and each member is passed to getData() every time getData() is called, a different getData() executes due to the differences in the argument data types.

Week 1 in Review

You'll also notice toward the end of the program that there are several overloaded operator+=() functions. To allow this, each set of arguments to the operator+=() functions is different.

When an argument is left unchanged in a receiving function, the receiving function receives that argument as a constant (such as in line 148). Also, when a variable such as numCur is changed by the receiving function, that variable is passed by reference (as in line 63), so the calling function's value changes along with it. There is little reason to pass such values by address now that you know how to pass by reference.

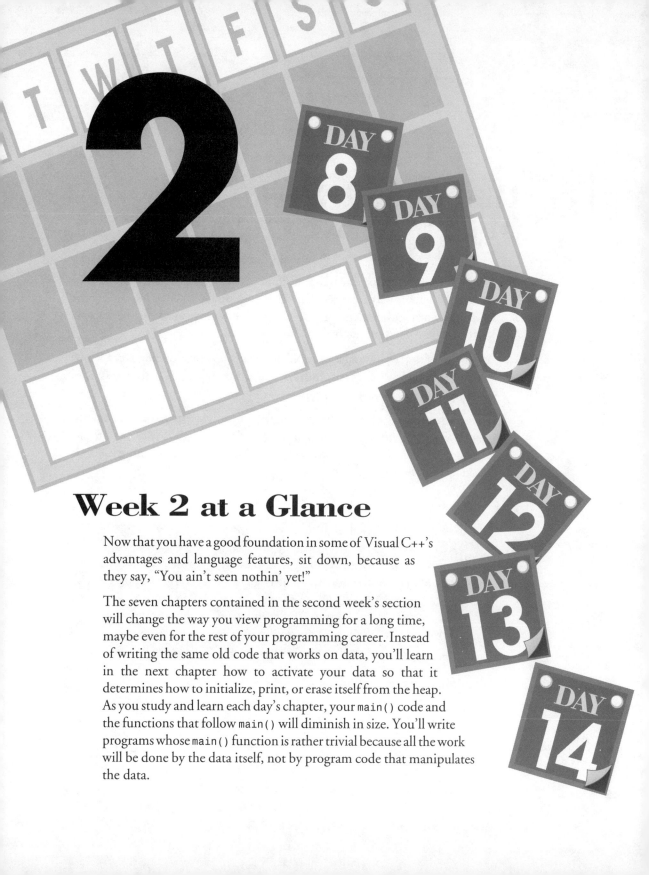

Week 2 at a Glance

Now that you have a good foundation in some of Visual C++'s advantages and language features, sit down, because as they say, "You ain't seen nothin' yet!"

The seven chapters contained in the second week's section will change the way you view programming for a long time, maybe even for the rest of your programming career. Instead of writing the same old code that works on data, you'll learn in the next chapter how to activate your data so that it determines how to initialize, print, or erase itself from the heap. As you study and learn each day's chapter, your `main()` code and the functions that follow `main()` will diminish in size. You'll write programs whose `main()` function is rather trivial because all the work will be done by the data itself, not by program code that manipulates the data.

In a nutshell, you're about to learn what the *object* in *object-oriented programming* really means.

The Second Week's Objectives Are Objects

The next seven days will provide you with a newcomer's introduction to OOP concepts without talking down to you. Tomorrow's Day 8 chapter explains how to write Visual C++ structures in the way that Visual C++ likes best: using the `class` keyword rather than `struct` to provide data protection unlike data protection you've ever seen before.

At the end of the second week, you will be an expert at overloading every Visual C++ operator, and you'll learn how to take advantage of C++ mechanisms to write better overloaded operator functions than you were able to write last week.

After six heavy OOP chapters (heavy, challenging, but extremely fun), Day 14's chapter will wrap up some loose ends and give you a slight breather from the bombardment of OOP concepts. You'll learn more about combining multiple program functions into one program.

Note: If you've tried to tackle OOP before but failed (it happens to all of us the first time, it seems), you'll be pleasantly surprised at the approach taken by this book. There is nothing unusual about the methodology of the teaching, but you'll see that many examples and topics are explained as fully as possible before you are moved to the next topic. OOP topics build on themselves; you have to know the early concepts fully before moving to the more advanced ones. If you learn the basics well, the "harder" material never seems hard.

DAY 8

Add Some *class* to Your Data

Add Some *class* to Your Data

Today's chapter begins your exploration of object-oriented programming. The groundwork laid today forms the basis of all your future programming in Visual C++. This chapter is the first to show you what a Visual C++ *object* really is.

Technically, an object is any variable at all, but today, you'll learn how to create objects called *class variables*. A class variable is what most Visual C++ programmers think of when they hear the word *object*.

After you're done with this chapter, you'll rarely or never use `struct` again. A `class` variable takes the place of structure variables in most Visual C++ programs.

Perhaps the most important reason to learn about OOP and class variables is that class variables provide better data protection than anything you've ever seen in programming. Local variables are *far* more visible than many class variables. If a certain section of code shouldn't have access to a variable, Visual C++ ensures that no access is given.

Before getting too far ahead, this chapter slows down and shows you lots of overlapping examples. When learning C++, many people jump in too fast, but this chapter won't permit that. You're here for the entire day, and it will be a full day.

Today, you learn about the following topics:

- Abstract data types
- The `class` keyword
- True data hiding and protection provided with `class`
- Access specifiers `private` and `protected`

Abstract Data Types

An abstract data type is a data type that you create. An abstract data type is not one of the built-in data types, although you combine built-in data types to create your own abstract data types.

The following data types aren't abstract because they are all built into the Visual C++ language:

```
int     long     float     double
```

Abstract data types exist in both the C and the C++ languages. You have used the `struct` keyword to create abstract data types in the past. When you build abstract data types, you combine the built-in data types to form a new "look."

Building an Abstract Data Type

Suppose that you have to keep track of an employee's weekly salary and you have to determine the best way to hold that salary in a program. Although you could create an abstract data type (a `struct`) to hold the salary, you probably shouldn't. After all, one of the built-in data types works fine, as shown here:

```
float wkSal;    // Holds the weekly salary
```

Suppose that you have to store 100 employees' weekly salaries. You could define an array of floating-point salaries as done here:

```
float wkSal[100];    // Holds 100 weekly salaries
```

You could also define a pointer and let the heap hold the 100 salaries like this:

```
float * wkSal = new float[100];   // Holds 100 weekly salaries
```

All the previous definitions have one thing in common: there is no need to define an abstract data type to hold the salaries because the built-in data types worked just fine. Defining structures would be redundant and less memory-efficient, and would cause the program to run slower, so there is no need to bother with structures for the salaries.

There is another point worth making here that most programmers take for granted. You never have to tell Visual C++ (or C for that matter) what a `float` is. It's built in. It's there, you can use it—why even worry about it?

To move into the OOP-like way of thinking, consider for a moment what you would have to do if you were required to tell Visual C++ what a `float` is before defining a `float` variable. You would have to decide how much memory each `float` could take. You wouldn't want to use too much memory or memory would be wasted, and you wouldn't want to use too little memory for each `float` or the program couldn't store very large `float` values. You would have to tell the compiler that floating-point values have decimal points (they are *real numbers*) and that the fraction is always carried in addition to the whole portion of the number.

Aren't you glad you don't have to tell Visual C++ what a `float` is before using one? If so, you might be surprised to learn that some OOP languages such as Smalltalk do not even know what a `float` is. If you write in those languages, you must define *all* data types, including integer and floating-point data types, before you can define your first variable. These languages are called *pure object-oriented languages* because every data type is an abstract data type and every data type builds on data types already defined in the program.

Add Some *class* to Your Data

Visual C++ is known as a *hybrid object-oriented programming language,* although the additional term *hybrid* is usually dropped. Being a hybrid OOP language does not imply that Visual C++ is inferior to the pure OOP languages (although some pure OOP proponents make good arguments that the hybrid languages are inferior to the pure ones).

One reason so much emphasis is placed on the term *abstract data type* in Visual C++, whereas it was not emphasized as much in C, is that the abstract data types in Visual C++ become extremely important when you are writing OOP programs.

> **They're Less Abstract in Visual C++!**
>
> Unlike in C, in C++ the term *abstract* is a little misleading. When you define a new data type using a `struct` (and `class`, as you'll see later today), you basically add that data type to Visual C++'s built-in list of data types.
>
> Do you remember all the way back in Day 2's chapter, "C++ Is Superior," when you learned that you don't have to repeat the keyword `struct` every time you refer to a structure data type? Only when you first declare a structure do you have to use `struct`. When you've declared a structure, Visual C++ recognizes that structure and doesn't require the redundant `struct` keyword.
>
> In a way, Visual C++ is the best of both the hybrid and the pure OOP world. With Visual C++, you get a lot of common built-in data types. You therefore don't have to mess with defining them when you almost always will need some or all of them in every program. You can also define your own data types and use those new data types almost as though they were built in. Through the next two weeks, you'll learn ways to teach Visual C++ how to recognize and work with your abstract data types more and more. The more that Visual C++ recognizes and reacts to your abstract data types as though they were built in, the less abstract those data types become and the more fine-tuned the resulting program is when working with your data.

Going back to the weekly salary example introduced earlier in the chapter, suppose that you want to keep track of each employee's salary and employee code. You could keep track of two separate arrays, one with floating-points and one with a character-pointer array to the employee codes, but a structure makes a more natural holding vehicle for this kind of data. Here is a structure declaration:

```
struct empData {
  char empCode[8];
  float wkSalary;
};
```

The structure named empData is an abstract data type. By declaring the structure, you told Visual C++ exactly what an empData value looks like. You've now told Visual C++ that all empData values have an eight-character array followed by a floating-point value. Visual C++ now recognizes empData as easily as ints and floats.

Before, you saw a floating-point variable defined like this:

```
float wkSal;    // Holds the weekly salary
```

An empData variable is defined like this:

```
empData emp1;   // Holds employee data
```

Look at the similarities in the two variable-definition statements. They each have a data type, float and empData, and a variable that is to take on that data type's characteristics. You don't have to tell Visual C++ what empData means because you told it earlier in the structure declaration. You don't have to tell Visual C++ what a float is because Visual C++ already knew that.

Listing 8.1 creates, initializes, and displays a few empData values and offers a structure variable refresher before taking structures to their next logical OOP level.

Listing 8.1. Using a structure variable and pointer to a structure.

```
 1: // Filename: STREVIEW.CPP
 2: // Simple program that demonstrates abstract data type structures
 3: #include <iostream.h>
 4: #include <string.h>
 5: #include <iomanip.h>
 6: struct empData {
 7:   char empCode[8];
 8:   float wkSalary;
 9: };
10: main()
11: {
12:   empData emp1;    // Regular structure variable
13:   empData * emp2;  // Pointer to a structure
14:   // Initialize the structure variable with the dot operator
15:   strcpy(emp1.empCode, "ACT08");
16:   emp1.wkSalary = 1092.43;
17:   // Allocate and initialize a structure on the heap
18:   emp2 = new empData;
```

continues

213

Add Some *class* to Your Data

Listing 8.1. continued

```
19:    strcpy(emp2->empCode, "MKT21");   // Use structure-pointer operator
20:    emp2->wkSalary = 1932.23;
21:    // Print the data
22:    // Without setiosflags(ios::fixed), Visual C++ tends to print
23:    // floating-point data in scientific notation
24:    cout << setprecision(2) << setiosflags(ios::fixed);
25:    cout << "Employee 1:\n";
26:    cout << "Code:\t" << emp1.empCode << "\n";
27:    cout << "Salary:\t" << emp1.wkSalary << "\n\n";
28:    cout << "Employee 2:\n";
29:    cout << "Code:\t" << emp2->empCode << "\n";
30:    cout << "Salary:\t" << emp2->wkSalary << "\n\n";
31:    delete emp2;
32:    return 0;
33: }
```

```
Employee 1:
Code:   ACT08
Salary: 1092.43

Employee 2:
Code:   MKT21
Salary: 1932.23
```

This program is fairly basic. As a review, remember to use the dot operator, (.), to access structure variable members, and the structure pointer operator, ->, to access structure members when the structure is pointed to (as in lines 29 and 30). Otherwise, you have to dereference the structure pointer and use the dot operator.

From the Abstract to the Abstract

There's one more subject to review before reaching the point of no return (that is, before ending your use of struct forever!). Defining a structure that contains another structure is perhaps the most obvious example showing that when you define a structure, you have added a new data type to Visual C++.

Suppose that a company wants to track more than the employee's salary and code. The company wants to track the employee name, age, and number of years of service. At the same time, the company needs to track the employee code and weekly salary separately for some of its functions. The company needs to keep the employee structure but then include that structure *within* another structure.

Note: Structures within structures are called *nested abstract data types* or *nested structures*. When you define a structure, you can then use that structure as a member of another as if that structure were a built-in data type.

The program in Listing 8.2 defines this structure within a structure and assigns data to it. Pay attention to the fact that a structure becomes just another data type after you define it.

 Listing 8.2. Using a structure to define another structure.

```
1:  // Filename: STRINSTR.CPP
2:  // When defined, a structure is available to be used inside others
3:  #include <iostream.h>
4:  #include <string.h>
5:  #include <iomanip.h>
6:  struct empData {
7:     char empCode[8];
8:     float wkSalary;
9:  };
10: // Now, define a second structure using the previous one as a member
11: struct employee {
12:    char name[25];
13:    int age;
14:    int yrsServ;
15:    empData workData;
16: };
17: main()
18: {
19:    employee empl1;    // Regular structure variable
20:    employee * empl2;  // Pointer to a structure
21:    // Initialize the structure variable with the dot operator
22:    strcpy(empl1.name, "George Wilbur");
23:    empl1.age = 42;
24:    empl1.yrsServ = 3;
25:    strcpy(empl1.workData.empCode, "ENG11");
26:    empl1.workData.wkSalary = 1439.08;
27:    // Allocate and initialize a structure on the heap
28:    empl2 = new employee;
29:    strcpy(empl2->name, "Julie Meyers");
30:    empl2->age = 29;
31:    empl2->yrsServ = 6;
32:    strcpy(empl2->workData.empCode, "SEC50");
33:    empl2->workData.wkSalary = 2711.57;
```

continues

Add Some *class* to Your Data

Listing 8.2. continued

```
34:    // Print the data
35:    // Without setiosflags(ios::fixed), Visual C++ tends to print
36:    // floating-point data in scientific notation
37:    cout << setprecision(2) << setiosflags(ios::fixed);
38:    cout << "Employee 1:\n";
39:    cout << "Name:\t" << empl1.name << "\n";
40:    cout << "Age:\t" << empl1.age << "\n";
41:    cout << "Years:\t" << empl1.yrsServ << "\n";
42:    cout << "Code:\t" << empl1.workData.empCode << "\n";
43:    cout << "Salary:\t" << empl1.workData.wkSalary << "\n\n";
44:    cout << "Employee 2:\n";
45:    cout << "Name:\t" << empl2->name << "\n";
46:    cout << "Age:\t" << empl2->age << "\n";
47:    cout << "Years:\t" << empl2->yrsServ << "\n";
48:    cout << "Code:\t" << empl2->workData.empCode << "\n";
49:    cout << "Salary:\t" << empl2->workData.wkSalary << "\n\n";
50:    delete empl2;
51:    return 0;
52: }
```

```
Employee 1:
Name:    George Wilbur
Age:     42
Years:   3
Code:    ENG11
Salary:  1439.08

Employee 2:
Name:    Julie Meyers
Age:     29
Years:   6
Code:    SEC50
Salary:  2711.57
```

Figure 8.1 shows what the `employee` structure looks like. The fourth member of `employee` (line 15) is separately defined earlier in the program (lines 6–9). Please keep in mind that the `employee` structure has only four members: a character array, two integers, and an `empData` structure. The members within `empData` don't count in the `employee` member list. If you want to access data in a member in the embedded structure, you have to use two dot operators, as done in line 42, or combine the dot operator and structure pointer operator, as done in line 48.

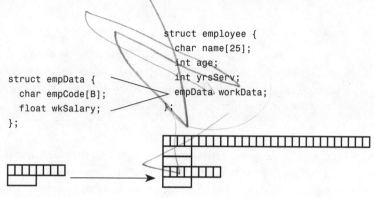

Figure 8.1. A defined structure becomes a new abstract data type that you can use inside other structures.

Nothing proves better that a defined structure is a new data type than a nested structure. After you define a structure, you can use it along with other built-in data types to "build" a new structure.

Out with *struct*—In with *class*

You might be asking, "So why spend all that time reviewing structures?" That's a good question, especially when you learn that the rest of this book tells you to eliminate the use of struct from your programming toolkit!

Actually, you don't have to eliminate struct, but the more modern Visual C++ replacement offers better safety than struct. Visual C++ programmers almost exclusively use class in place of struct.

Here's an example of using a class. This statement declares a class that looks like the empData structure declared earlier:

```
class empData {
  char empCode[8];
  float wkSalary;
};
```

Note: As with structure declarations, most Visual C++ programmers declare their classes globally and their class variables locally. Over time you'll write many class declarations. If you put the class declarations in header files (grouping the ones that go together in the same header files)

Day 8

Add Some *class* to Your Data

> and include those headers when needed (with `#include`), you'll be able to keep your programs cleaner. If your class declarations change, you'll only have to change one header file and recompile instead of changing every source program in which the same class declaration appears.

There's not a lot of deep-level thinking needed at this time to understand the `class` keyword. You can define variables of the `empData` type now because `class`, just as `struct`, declares new data types. The following statement defines a variable named `employ`:

```
empData employ;
```

As with `struct`, you can carry the `class` keyword down on the variable definition line if you prefer, such as this:

```
class empData employ;   // class is redundant
```

There is little need to do so, however. `class` adds a new data type to Visual C++, just as `struct` did, as was explained throughout the first part of today's chapter.

If you were to look in memory at the description of the `employ` variable, you would see a new variable that looks *exactly* like that of a `struct` variable of the same configuration. In fact, other than an extremely minor difference (minor, but not trivial), `class` does everything that `struct` does by declaring new aggregate data types—or more accurately for this discussion, `class` declares abstract data types and declares them to Visual C++ so that the compiler can recognize data in the format you require.

As with structures, after you declare a new class abstract data type, you can then use that class data type as a member of a new class like this:

```
class empData {
  char empCode[8];
  float wkSalary;
};
// Now, define a second class using the previous one as a member
class employee {
  char name[25];
  int age;
  int yrsServ;
  empData workData;
};
```

Figure 8.1's structure-within-a-structure looks just like the class-within-a-class created here. In memory, both the structure and the class look the same, and you can point to a class or define a class variable on the heap exactly as you do with structures.

Note: As with structures, always add a trailing semicolon at the end of a `class` declaration's closing brace. The semicolon is always required, whether you declare just the `class`, as just done, or define variables along with the `class` like this:

```
class empData {
  char empCode[8];
  float wkSalary;
} emp1, emp2;
```

Getting into Objects—Finally!

Guess what? You can now define an object! Actually, if you take the technical definition of *object* literally, all variables are objects. However, Visual C++ programmers like to reserve the term *object* for their class variables. Define class variables just as you do structures. Listing 8.3 contains a simple program that defines object variables from the employee class described earlier.

Listing 8.3. Defining objects from a class.

```
1:  // Filename: CLASSOBJ.CPP
2:  // Define objects from a class and an embedded class definition
3:  #include <iostream.h>
4:  #include <string.h>
5:  #include <iomanip.h>
6:  class empData {
7:     char empCode[8];
8:     float wkSalary;
9:  };
10: // Now, define a second class using the previous one as a member
11: class employee {
12:    char name[25];
13:    int age;
14:    int yrsServ;
15:    empData workData;
```

continues

Add Some *class* to Your Data

Listing 8.3. continued

```
16: };
17: main()
18: {
19:    empData employed;    // First class variable
20:    employee fullEmp;    // Nested class variable
21:    return 0;
22: }
```

Analysis

When you compile this program, Visual C++ issues two warnings that let you know you are creating variables (in lines 19 and 20) that aren't used for anything. Ignore the warnings for now. The important thing to notice is that creating class variables is the same as creating structure variables. Those variables (`employed` and `fullEmp`) are objects.

After you declare the `class`, that `class` becomes a new abstract data type to Visual C++. There was no data type that looked like an eight-character array followed by a `float` until lines 6–9 added one to the compiler's repertoire. (The abstract data type, however, only stays around for the scope of this program, whereas the built-in data types are permanent.)

> **Have a Little Faith**
>
> The advantage of using `class` to create objects is not yet known to you. The advantage will be known soon enough. For now, get used to `class` and realize that `class` and `struct` do *basically* the same things and that their minor difference (which you'll learn about in a moment) makes `class` the preferred choice for Visual C++ programmers.
>
> Later sections of the book will refer to parts of this in-depth discussion, and you'll see that your time was well-spent here.

Figure 8.2 helps further clarify the difference between a `class` and a class's *object*. The `class` is the declaration that describes a new abstract data type to Visual C++, and the object is the creation of an *instance* of that `class`.

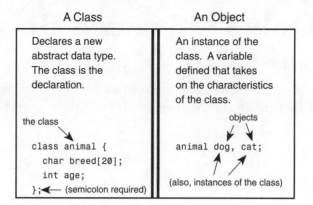

Figure 8.2. A `class` declares what eventually becomes the object variable.

> **Note:** Many Visual C++ programmers use the term *instance;* this book will be no exception. Objects are the definition of variables from classes, but a specific object is often called an instance of the `class`. Visual C++ programmers further expand their vocabulary (and confuse others more) by saying that *a class is instantiated,* meaning that you've defined an instance of the class—or in simpler terms, you've just defined a new variable for the `class`.

DO / DON'T

DO use classes in place of structures. With classes, you can create the objects that most Visual C++ programmers refer to when they use the term *object-oriented programming*.

DON'T forget the semicolon that must go at the end of all `class` declarations whether or not you define variables along with the `class`.

DON'T let new terms throw you. An *instance* of a `class` is just a variable that you define from that `class`. An *object* is the same thing as an instance or `class` variable as well. All three terms, *object, instance,* and `class` *variable,* will be used throughout this book as is done in the C++ community.

Add Some *class* to Your Data

The Only Difference Between *class* and *struct*

There is only a tiny difference between a `class` declaration and a `struct` declaration. Suppose that you define some `class` variables like this:

```
class abc {
  int i;
  float x;
  char c;
};
main()
{
   abc var1, var2, var3;
// Rest of program would follow
```

`main()` cannot use the variable. `main()` cannot initialize the `class` variable, `main()` cannot print the `class` variable, `main()` cannot use the `class` variable in a calculation. More specifically, `main()` cannot access *any* of the members of the `class` variable! (Are any warning sirens going off in your head yet?)

It's true that `class` variables are not usable in `main()` because `class` members are *private* by default. `struct` variables are *public* by default. The public/private difference is the only thing that differentiates a `class` instance of a variable from a `struct` instance of a variable.

You are familiar with two kinds of visibility: local and global (the technical name for local visibility is *block scope,* and the technical name for global visibility is *file scope*). There are also other kinds of scope that some C programmers are aware of, such as *prototype scope,* but the two most important ones for most programs are local and global scopes. A local variable is visible only within the block in which it's defined. In Listing 8.4, the variable `i` cannot be printed by the `cout` at the bottom of the program because `i` is local to `main()`'s inner block and `i` is not visible when its block ends at its terminating brace.

 Listing 8.4. Incorrect use of a local variable.

```
1:  // Filename: LOCGLB.CPP
2:  // Define a global and local object
3:  #include <iostream.h>
4:  int g = 7;    // Global variable
5:  main()
6:  {
7:     cout << "g is " << g << "\n";
```

```
 8:    // Open a new block to limit i's scope
 9:    {
10:      int i = 10;
11:      cout << "Inside the inner block, i is " << i;
12:      cout << " and g is still " << g << "\n";
13:    }  // When the block ends, i goes away completely
14:    cout << "After the inner block, i is " << i;   // Error!
15:    cout << " and g is " << g << "\n";
16:    return 0;
17: }
```

If you were to compile this code, Visual C++ would generate this error message:

```
error C2065: 'i' : undeclared identifier
```

The problem occurs at line 14. The program attempts to print i, but because i is no longer in scope, the variable cannot be printed. There is no problem with printing g because g is visible for the entire file. Because g is global, it could be printed on line 15 if you removed line 14 so that the program could compile properly.

Visual C++ introduces a new kind of scope to your repertoire called *class scope*. When a variable has class scope, that variable can be used only *within the class*. Look again at this section of code while reading the discussion that follows.

```
1: class Abc {
2:    int i;
3:    float x;
4:    char c;
5: };
6: main()
7: {
8:     abc var1, var2, var3;
9: // Rest of program would follow
```

As mentioned earlier, you are extremely limited as to what you can do with the class variables. You can define them by reserving their storage on the heap, you can define an array or a table of the class variables, you can pass the variables between functions, and you can deallocate their storage, but you cannot use the members of the class because of class scope. Notice where the members are declared: inside the class section of the program. As with structures, you declare class members inside the class, but when you do, those members can be used only within the class because all class members have class scope. Even though main() "owns" the class variables, and even though the class variables are local to main(), main() can only define, pass, and deallocate the variables, but main() has no access to the members within the class variables.

Add Some *class* to Your Data

Do you see how Visual C++ protects your data? As reviewed earlier, local variables are well-protected within their block (Listing 8.4), but `class` variables are even more protected. Because they have class scope, `class` variables are so protected that their members aren't available to functions even though the `class` variables are local to those functions.

> **Note:** Many Visual C++ programmers prefer to capitalize the first letter of `class` names. Throughout most of this book, the standard will be followed. All variable names, however, whether they are `class` variables or non-`class` variables, will not have capitalized first letters.

Listings 8.5 and 8.6 differ in only a single keyword. Listing 8.5 uses `struct` and Listing 8.6 uses `class`. As expected, Listing 8.5's `main()` can access the structure members, but Listing 8.6's `main()` cannot.

Listing 8.5. A program with a struct works OK.

```
 1:  // Filename: STRUCT.CPP
 2:  // Program that uses a structure and its members
 3:  #include <iostream.h>
 4:  struct Time {
 5:    int hours;
 6:    int minutes;
 7:    int seconds;
 8:  };
 9:  main()
10:  {
11:    Time clock;
12:    Time * watch;
13:    clock.hours = 10;
14:    clock.minutes = 23;
15:    clock.seconds = 47;
16:    watch = new Time;
17:    watch->hours = 11;
18:    watch->minutes = 41;
19:    watch->seconds = 19;
20:    cout << "The clock says " << clock.hours << ":" << clock.minutes;
21:    cout << ":" << clock.seconds << "\n";
22:    cout << "The watch says " << watch->hours << ":"
         ➥<< watch->minutes;
23:    cout << ":" << watch->seconds << "\n";
24:    delete watch;
25:    return 0;
26:  }
```

```
The clock says 10:23:47
The watch says 11:41:19
```

Listing 8.6. The same program with a `class` seems useless because it doesn't work.

```cpp
1:  // Filename: CLASS.CPP
2:  // Program that attempts to use a class and its members
3:  #include <iostream.h>
4:  class Time {
5:    int hours;
6:    int minutes;
7:    int seconds;
8:  };
9:  main()
10: {
11:   Time clock;
12:   Time * watch;
13:   clock.hours = 10;
14:   clock.minutes = 23;
15:   clock.seconds = 47;
16:   watch = new Time;
17:   watch->hours = 11;
18:   watch->minutes = 41;
19:   watch->seconds = 19;
20:   cout << "The clock says " << clock.hours << ":" << clock.minutes;
21:   cout << ":" << clock.seconds << "\n";
22:   cout << "The watch says " << watch->hours << ":"
        ↪<< watch->minutes;
23:   cout << ":" << watch->seconds << "\n";
24:   delete watch;
25:   return 0;
26: }
```

When you compile this program, you'll get these error messages:

```
    error C2248: 'hours' : cannot access private member declared in class 'Time'
    error C2248: 'minutes' : cannot access private member declared in class 'Time'
error C2248: 'seconds' : cannot access private member declared in class 'Time'
error C2248: 'hours' : cannot access private member declared in class 'Time'
error C2248: 'minutes' : cannot access private member declared in class 'Time'
error C2248: 'seconds' : cannot access private member declared in class 'Time'
```

Add Some *class* to Your Data

```
error C2248: 'hours' : cannot access private member declared in class 'Time'
error C2248: 'minutes' : cannot access private member declared in class 'Time'
error C2248: 'seconds' : cannot access private member declared in class 'Time'
error C2248: 'hours' : cannot access private member declared in class 'Time'
error C2248: 'minutes' : cannot access private member declared in class 'Time'
error C2248: 'seconds' : cannot access private member declared in class 'Time'
```

The error messages are Visual C++'s way of letting you know that the `class Time`'s members cannot be accessed by `main()`. Visual C++ doesn't display undefined variable error messages because the `Time` variables are visible to `main()`. It's just that `main()` cannot use any members of variables defined from the `Time` class.

> **Here's the Bottom Line**
>
> The members of a structure are public by default; the members of a class are private by default. Although `class` variables are local to whatever block defines them, the members of those variables are protected with their private access.
>
> The public and private access defaults are the only difference between variables defined with `class` and variables defined with `struct`.
>
> Luckily, you can change these defaults if and when you need to.

Overriding Public and Private Access

Visual C++ introduces two new keywords, `public` and `private`, that change the default status of `class` and `struct` members. The `public` and `private` keywords must appear before the members that you want to have public or private access. Structures don't need the `public` keyword because their members are public by default. Classes don't need the `private` keyword because their members are private by default.

Here is a `class` declaration whose members are all public:

226

```
class Time {
public:                 // All members are now available
  int hours;
  int minutes;
  int seconds;
};
```

Note: Notice that `public:` must end with a colon, `:`. If you use `private`, terminate it too with a colon.

`public` tells Visual C++ to make *every* member that follows the `public` keyword available to all blocks in the program that use the `class` variable. If `private` appears later in the list of members, all members following `private` then have private access. Although you can intersperse several occurrences of `public` and `private` within the same `class` declaration, good coding practices dictate that you keep all `private` members together and all `public` members together in the same `class` declaration.

Listing 8.7 contains a fixed version of the `Time` class program shown earlier. A single insertion of the `public` keyword at the top of the `class` lets `main()` access all the members.

Listing 8.7. Finally, `Time` class variables that `main()` can use.

```
 1: // Filename: CLASSPUB.CPP
 2: // Program that fixes access to the class members
 3: #include <iostream.h>
 4: class Time {
 5: public:        // Make the members available
 6:   int hours;
 7:   int minutes;
 8:   int seconds;
 9: };
10: main()
11: {
12:   Time clock;
13:   Time * watch;
14:   clock.hours = 10;
15:   clock.minutes = 23;
16:   clock.seconds = 47;
17:   watch = new Time;
18:   watch->hours = 11;
19:   watch->minutes = 41;
20:   watch->seconds = 19;
```

continues

Add Some *class* to Your Data

Listing 8.7. continued

```
21:    cout << "The clock says " << clock.hours << ":" << clock.minutes;
22:    cout << ":" << clock.seconds << "\n";
23:    cout << "The watch says " << watch->hours << ":"
       ➥<< watch->minutes;
24:    cout << ":" << watch->seconds << "\n";
25:    delete watch;
26:    return 0;
27: }
```

```
The clock says 10:23:47
The watch says 11:41:19
```

The output shows that main() now has access to the members of Time object variables. The public keyword on line 5 lets *any* function with access to Time variables access the members as well.

Although this might seem trivial now, Listing 8.8 shows the same program as Listing 8.7, except that a struct is used with the private access keyword inserted before the structure's first member.

Listing 8.8. A private struct is protected just like a class.

```
1:  // Filename: STRPRIV.CPP
2:  // Program that keeps main() away from structure access
3:  #include <iostream.h>
4:  struct Time {
5:  private:            // Make the members unavailable
6:     int hours;
7:     int minutes;
8:     int seconds;
9:  };
10: main()
11: {
12:    Time clock;
13:    Time * watch;
14:    clock.hours = 10;
15:    clock.minutes = 23;
16:    clock.seconds = 47;
17:    watch = new Time;
18:    watch->hours = 11;
19:    watch->minutes = 41;
20:    watch->seconds = 19;
21:    cout << "The clock says " << clock.hours << ":" << clock.minutes;
22:    cout << ":" << clock.seconds << "\n";
```

```
23:     cout << "The watch says " << watch->hours << ":"
    ➥<< watch->minutes;
24:     cout << ":" << watch->seconds << "\n";
25:     delete watch;
26:     return 0;
27: }
```

 Analysis If you compile this program, you'll get "cannot access" error messages because the `private` keyword keeps `main()` from accessing members of the structure.

 Note: The `private` and `protected` keywords are called *access specifiers*. Although the term is new, it makes sense because `private` and `public` determine whether you can access members of structures and classes. There is a third access specifier called `protected` that you'll read about in future chapters.

Mix and Match Access Specifiers

Figure 8.3 illustrates two sets of structure and class declarations that are equivalent. Depending on the default access and the access specifier that you specify, classes act like structures and structures act like classes.

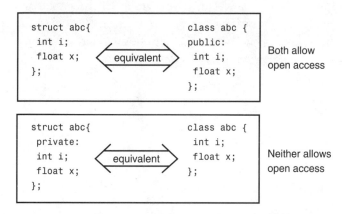

Figure 8.3. A `class` can mirror a `struct` when you use the appropriate access specifiers.

DAY 8
Add Some *class* to Your Data

> **If They're the Same, Why Use *class*?**
>
> That's a good question for which there is a reasonable answer. Visual C++ programmers prefer `class` over `struct` because of the default safety that classes provide.
>
> It might seem as though the `class` default (`private`) is too limiting because the program cannot access the members. However, along with the lack of access comes true data protection.
>
> Private members are as protected from access as possible in the Visual C++ programming language. Through some function mechanisms that you'll learn in tomorrow's chapter, you can get to private members, but only through strictly controlled methods (and, it just so happens, the technical term for those access ways are indeed named *methods*).
>
> To take advantage of the OOP philosophy, you've got to be able to achieve this powerful data protection. You don't have to specify `private` explicitly when using `class` declarations, and it is because the default is `private` that programmers prefer `class` over `struct` declarations.
>
> Here's an additional note to ponder: Even though `class` defaults to `private`, and that's the most important reason to use `class`, many Visual C++ programmers *still* insert `private` before their `class` members just to show their intent to make the `class` members private.

Although you can specify more than one `private` or `public` access specifier in the same class, your code will be clearer if you group all the public and private members together, preferably putting the private ones at the top of the class (their usual location) and the public members at the bottom. Here is a sample class that includes a mixture of `private` and `public` access specifiers:

```
class MixedBad {
public:
  float x;
private:
  char name[25];
public:
  int * atom;
private:
  int age;
public:
  double * amount;
```

```
private:
  char initial;
};
```

Obviously, the following declaration is preferred even though it does the same thing as the preceding class:

```
class MixedBetter {
private:
  char name[25];
  int age;
  char initial;
public:
  float x;
  int * atom;
  double * amount;
};
```

Note: Get in the habit of listing the private member group at the top of the class and leave the public members at the bottom. If you forget to specify private, you'll still have the default private class protection.

Figure 8.4 shows a diagram of the `MixedBetter` class and illustrates how the program has access only to the last three members.

```
class MixedBetter {
private:
    char name[25];      ┐  These data members cannot be
    int age;             │  used outside this class.
    char initial;       ┘
public:
    float x;            ┐  The rest of the program
    int*atom;            │  can access these members.
    double*amount;      ┘
};
```

Figure 8.4. The program can access only members designated as `public`.

Note: Visual C++ programmers often use the term *data hiding* to refer to the private mechanism available in classes (and structures if you use them with private specified). The data-hiding capabilities provided with classes go far beyond those of regular local variables.

231

Add Some *class* to Your Data

Listing 8.9 includes a program that defines two class object variables with both public and private members.

Type **Listing 8.9. Using the public members in a class.**

```
 1: // Filename: CARSCLSS.CPP
 2: // Program that declares private and public members of a class
 3: // that describes an automobile inventory. Until access mechanisms
 4: // to private members are learned, all access to the class variables
 5: // (called objects) can be for only the public members, not the
 6: // private ones.
 7: #include <iostream.h>
 8: #include <iomanip.h>
 9: #include <string.h>
10: // Class declaration next
11: class Car {
12: private:
13:    float wholesalePrice;
14:    int maxMPH;
15: public:
16:    char make[10];
17:    char model[25];
18:    int year;
19:    float retailPrice;
20: };
21: main()
22: {
23:    Car sedan, roadster;
24:    // Initialize the public members
25:    strcpy(sedan.make, "Chord");
26:    strcpy(sedan.model, "RushMobile");
27:    sedan.year = 1994;
28:    sedan.retailPrice = 28675.99;
29:    strcpy(roadster.make, "Gee 'Em");
30:    strcpy(roadster.model, "Sprinter");
31:    roadster.year = 1967;   // Really used car!
32:    roadster.retailPrice = 24344.01;
33:    // Print the data
34:    cout << setprecision(2) << setiosflags(ios::fixed);
35:    cout << "Cars:\n";
36:    cout << "Make:\t" << sedan.make << "\n";
37:    cout << "Model:\t" << sedan.model << "\n";
38:    cout << "Year:\t" << sedan.year << "\n";
39:    cout << "Price:\t$" << sedan.retailPrice << "\n\n";
40:    cout << "Make:\t" << roadster.make << "\n";
41:    cout << "Model:\t" << roadster.model << "\n";
42:    cout << "Year:\t" << roadster.year << "\n";
```

```
43:     cout << "Price:\t$" << roadster.retailPrice << "\n\n";
44:     return 0;
45: }
```

```
Cars:
Make:   Chord
Model:  RushMobile
Year:   1994
Price:  $28675.99

Make:   Gee 'Em
Model:  Sprinter
Year:   1967
Price:  $24344.01
```

If you run this program, Visual C++ issues neither errors nor warnings, even though you declare members but never use them (`wholesalePrice` and `maxMPH`). Visual C++ knows that you cannot use these two members in the normal sense of the word as you do with regular members.

DO / DON'T

DO use `class` in place of `struct` to protect your data as much as possible. The two can offer the same protection if you specify the appropriate access specifiers, but the default `private` access of classes provides safer protection and you don't risk forgetting to specify `private` as you would to protect `struct` private members.

DO insert the `public` keyword in front of those members that must be accessed directly in `main()` and the rest of the program. Leave the rest specified as `private`. You'll learn how to get at those private members in tomorrow's chapter.

DO explicitly specify `private` for private class members even though they default to private because doing so shows your intent and helps document the code. However, leaving off `private` at the top of a `class` does no harm (whereas forgetting `private` when working with structures could expose members that shouldn't be exposed).

DON'T mix lots of private and public members throughout a class. Keep all your private members in one place (at the top of the class is best) and all the public members in another place.

Add Some *class* to Your Data

Summary

If you think that a lot of this discussion is elementary, you're right—it is. But remember one thing: *all* of Visual C++ is elementary. Learning Visual C++ doesn't take an advanced degree in computer science!

> **Note:** If you learn the basics well (these next few days), you'll have no problem tackling some of the more advanced OOP topics. If, however, you skim through the basics as a lot of newcomers to OOP concepts do, you'll lack the deeper understanding needed to master OOP concepts.

This chapter began with a review that was intended to drive home the point that structures create abstract data types. In Visual C++, unlike its C predecessors, the `struct` keyword (and also the `class` keyword) doesn't have to precede the variable being defined.

In reality, the term *abstract data type* is a little misleading. To Visual C++, there is very little about your declared data types that is abstract. As you learn more about OOP, you'll learn more ways to make your abstract data types mimic the built-in data types even more. Perhaps the most obvious application which shows that an abstract data type becomes like a built-in data type is when you nest structures and classes. After you've defined a class, you can use that class as a member of another class.

The last part of today's chapter explained the access specifiers that enable you to use the `class` keyword to create very well-protected data—so well, in fact, that `main()` cannot have access to that data.

All data protection is done at the member level by the access specifiers `private` and `public`. In other words, you cannot protect an entire class variable, just its members. The ordinary rules for local and global variables apply to class variables.

Q&A

Q. What is an *abstract data type*?

A. An abstract data type is a data type that you define and add to your program. You are probably used to adding structure variables to a program. Before creating structure variables, you have to tell C and Visual C++ what the format of your structure looks like. You don't, however, have to tell C or

Visual C++ what an `int` looks like because, unlike abstract data types, built-in data types are already understood by the compiler.

After you add an abstract data type to a program, the rest of that program treats the abstract data type *almost* as if it were a supplied built-in data type.

Q. What is the difference between `struct` and `class`?

A. Despite all the articles and books written about classes, there is one and only one difference: class members are private by default, whereas structure members are public by default. In every other way, `struct` and `class` do the very same thing.

The class was introduced in C++ to handle special data-hiding protection needed when programming with objects. The designers of C++ added to the capabilities of structures (tomorrow's chapter will explain the new capabilities) and gave those same capabilities to classes. Structures can now do more than hold members of data, as can classes. However, Visual C++ programmers prefer to use class variables because they add an extra layer of data-protection by default.

Q. Can I keep using the familiar `struct` keyword because I am most used to it? (I'll keep everything `private` that should be.)

A. You can keep using `struct`, as long as you place the `public` and `private` keywords properly. If, however, you leave off `private` when data hiding is critical, a structure offers no protection whereas a class does.

It's best to begin using `class` and eliminate `struct` from your programming vocabulary because you'll rarely see an OOP-like C++ program that uses structures but not classes.

Q. Can I define an abstract data type with a `class`?

A. Of course you can because a class is no different from a structure except for the default access provided. After you declare a class, you don't have to use the `class` keyword to define variables for that class. Assuming that you've declared a class named `Child`, both of the following statements define variables for that class:

```
Child girl;
```

and

```
Child boy;
```

235

Add Some *class* to Your Data

Q. If I cannot get to private members, why define them?

A. Beginning in tomorrow's chapter, you'll learn why most Visual C++ programmers specify *all* `class` members as `private`. Although putting members out of reach of the program seems absurd, the data protection afforded by the hiding of members will eventually provide you with less debugging time when writing programs.

There are some well-defined ways to get at those private members, but beginning in tomorrow's chapter, you'll have to learn a brand-new OOP concept called *member functions*.

(In Visual C++, a `class`—and `struct` because they are the same thing—can have *both* data *and* functions, as you'll see tomorrow.)

Workshop

The Workshop offers quiz questions and exercises to hone your skills and give you feedback on today's lesson. You'll find some proposed answers in Appendix D.

Quiz

1. What is an object?

2. Questions 2 A through 2 E refer to this class and defined variables at the bottom of the class:

```
class computer {
   int RAM;
   int ROM;
public:
   float price;
   char * name;
   int yrBuilt;
} PC, Mac;
```

   A. How many members are private?

   B. What is the name of the class?

   C. How many objects are defined?

D. If you were to add the `private` specifier without changing the meaning of the class now, where would `private` go?

E. If the keyword `class` were replaced with `struct`, how many private members would then be defined?

3. True or False: Access to a member is determined by the access to the class or structure variable itself; if `main()` has access to a class variable, `main()` also has access to the private members within that class.

4. True or False: These are equivalent in every way:

```
struct abs {
  int i;
public:
  float x;
};
```

and

```
class abs {
private:
  int i;
public:
  float x;
};
```

5. True or False: These are equivalent in every way:

```
struct abs {
  int i;
public:
  float x;
};
```

and

```
class abs {
public:
  int i;
public:
  float x;
};
```

Add Some *class* to Your Data

Exercise

1. Rewrite the structure program from Listing 8.1 using class in place of struct on line 6. You don't need to modify the program very much to make it produce the same output using a class rather than a structure.

DAY 9

Member Functions Activate *class* Variables

Member Functions Activate *class* Variables

Today's chapter shows you how to use the private, hidden data inside your classes. Through *member functions,* you can access all of your program's private data.

Visual C++ doesn't keep you from getting to the private members totally; if it did, the private section would be worthless. After yesterday's chapter, you know how to protect data by making it private, and after today's, you'll appreciate how Visual C++ keeps private data protected while still offering access to that data. The access to private data is achieved through a well-defined *controlled* access you can supply.

When you learn how to get to private data through the controlled access offered by member functions, you'll begin to shift the way you think about data. You'll begin to see how Visual C++ data is *active* data that "knows" how to manipulate itself. When you want a variable printed, you won't print the variable, but the variable will print itself! This magical data activity is all performed through an object's member functions.

Today, you learn about the following topics:

- How to specify member functions
- How to call member functions
- The way to activate objects
- Using the scope resolution operator to code member functions outside a `class`
- Member function argument lists
- How member functions work inside the class scope
- That *encapsulation* is little more than a long word
- What the `*this` pointer is all about

> **Note:** A member function is sometimes called a *method* because it provides a strict method that dictates how to access private data. This book sticks to the more obvious term *member function.* You'll see why the term *member function* is clearer when you see how to place member functions inside a class.

Member Functions Combined with Data Members

You are already well-aware of what data members are. The following class has three of them:

```
class Abc {
   char a;        // A character data member
   int b;         // An integer data member
   float c;       // A floating-point data member
};
```

You could say that this class has *characteristics*. The characteristics describe the format of the class. The characteristics include a character member, an integer member, and a floating-point member. All of these members compose the characteristics of the Abc class.

OK, hang on to your hats because here comes the single most important concept that differentiates Visual C++ from other non-OOP languages:

> *You can insert functions directly inside a* class *(or* struct*) declaration!*

Here is a function located inside the Abc class:

```
class Abc {
   char a;        // A character data member
   int b;         // An integer data member
   float c;       // A floating-point data member
   void pr(void)
   {
      cout << "a is " << a << "\n";
      cout << "b is " << b << "\n";
      cout << "c is " << c << "\n";
   }
};
```

Isn't that the strangest thing you've ever seen? The Abc class now has *four* members, three data members and one member function. The data items inside the class declaration are called data members. If there are functions inside class declarations, they are called *member functions* (the name makes sense because functions are members of the class).

All four members are private because the default protection offered by classes is private, unless you override that protection with a public access specifier. It is said that the Abc class still has the same characteristics described earlier: three data members.

Member Functions Activate *class* Variables

The Abc class now has *behavior* as well. It is this behavior that really distinguishes Visual C++ OOP objects. In its practical definition, an object variable has both characteristics and behaviors.

Note: Structures won't be mentioned much for the remainder of this book, but as yesterday's chapter taught, a struct is *exactly* the same as a class in Visual C++, and you can add functions to structures just as you can to classes. The only difference is the default public access provided by structures versus the private access provided by classes. (Structures could not contain member functions in C.)

When your member functions are private, the rest of the program cannot access them. Therefore, you usually see member functions in the public section of classes. (There are some member functions best left in the private section, and this chapter explains when that is appropriate.)

DO	DON'T
DO insert member functions directly inside a class definition to add behaviors to the class.	
DON'T put needed member functions in the private section of a class if the nonclass portion of the program is going to use them.	

Using Public Member Functions

Although the Abc class is simple, there are some modifications that make the class usable by the program that contains the Abc class. For starters, it would be smart to keep all the data members in the private section and put some member functions in a public section.

What are some of the things programmers do with class data? Defining an Abc class variable is simple because main(), and any other function, can define Abc variables as long as the class declaration remains global (but the data members won't be available).

There must be a way to initialize the data by putting values in the members. Also, the data members must be printable to see what they contain.

Listing 9.1 contains a program that includes the Abc class with two public member functions. One function initializes the data and the other prints the data. The main() function executes the member functions and the Analysis section after the program explains how the member functions are triggered.

Listing 9.1. Looking at a class with data members and member functions.

```
 1: // Filename: CLSFUN.CPP
 2: // First program with data members and a member
 3: // function in the same class.
 4: #include <iostream.h>
 5: class Abc {
 6: private:          // Not needed but recommended
 7:   char a;
 8:   int b;
 9:   float c;
10: public:           // main() can "see" the rest of the class
11:   void init(void)
12:     { a = 'x';    // Assign the data members some values
13:       b = 100;
14:       c = 12.345;
15:     }
16:   void prAbc(void)
17:     { cout << "a is " << a << "\n";
18:       cout << "b is " << b << "\n";
19:       cout << "c is " << c << "\n";
20:     }
21: };
22: main()
23: {
24:    Abc aVar;         // Defines an Abc variable
25:    aVar.init();      // Initialize the variables
26:    aVar.prAbc();     // Print the data
27:    return 0;
28: }
```

```
a is x
b is 100
c is 12.345
```

Although the program initializes and prints data, main() is extremely small. One of the characteristics of object-oriented Visual C++ programs is that main() and the rest of the nonclass portion of the program shrink in size from a comparable

Member Functions Activate *class* Variables

non-OOP program. The entire program's size is about the same as that of a non-OOP program, but much of the code moves up into the `class` section.

The only members of the class that `main()` can access are the two public member functions. If there were public data members, `main()` could access those members. Lines 25 and 26 trigger the execution of each of the public member functions. Notice that the dot operator executes the member functions; you use the dot operator to access data members of class variables and to execute member functions of class variables as well.

Before getting too far ahead (and the questions in your head are probably flying, but they'll be answered shortly), take a look at a variation on this program that assigns random values, rather than constants, to the data members. Rather than one class variable, the program in Listing 9.2 defines two variables, each having different data due to the random values assigned to each.

Listing 9.2. Defining two class variables.

```
1:  // Filename: CLSFUN2.CPP
2:  // Program with two class variables
3:  #include <iostream.h>
4:  #include <stdlib.h>
5:  class Abc {
6:  private:         // Not needed but recommended
7:     char a;
8:     int b;
9:     float c;
10: public:          // main() can "see" the rest of the class
11:    void init(void)
12:      { a = (rand() % 27) + 65;   // Random ASCII from 'A' to 'Z'
13:        b = rand() % 100;
14:        c = float(rand() * .25);
15:      }
16:    void prAbc(void)
17:      { cout << "a is " << a << "\n";
18:        cout << "b is " << b << "\n";
19:        cout << "c is " << c << "\n";
20:      }
21: };
22: main()
23: {
24:    Abc aVar1, aVar2;     // Defines two Abc variables
25:    aVar1.init();         // Initialize the first variable
26:    aVar1.prAbc();        // Print the first variable
27:    aVar2.init();         // Initialize the second variable
28:    aVar2.prAbc();        // Print the second variable
29:    return 0;
30: }
```

```
a is W
b is 30
c is 2745.5
a is K
b is 56
c is 1779.25
```

Lines 25 through 28 show that the member functions apply to the object variables that trigger those functions. In other words, init() is applied to the aVar1 or aVar2 objects depending on which variable appears in front of the dot operator. (Your output might differ due to the rand() function calls.)

It is important to note that there is not really a separate copy of the member functions in each object, although there are separate copies of the data members. Figure 9.1 shows that the object variables share the same member functions (through some internal pointers) but have their own copies of data members to make good use of memory.

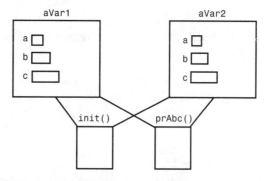

Figure 9.1. Visual C++ acts as if each object variable contains its own data and member functions.

Note: For all practical purposes, consider that the objects have their own copies of the member functions even though they don't. As the next section points out, thinking of the objects as containers of both data and functions helps objects mirror the real world they represent.

If you defined pointers to classes rather than class variables, you can use the structure pointer operator to trigger the execution of member functions. For example, suppose you created a pointer to the Abc class like this:

Member Functions Activate *class* Variables

```
Abc * avarPtr;
```

And then you allocated the class data space on the heap like this:

```
avarPtr = new Abc;
```

You could then initialize the heap with the `init()` function, and then print the heap space with the `prAbc()` function like this:

```
avarPtr->init();    // Initialize the heap object
avarPtr->prAbc();   // Print the heap data
```

That's What Objects Are All About

You might be wondering what was gained by adding member functions to objects. Certainly, the length of the program was not reduced, just the length of `main()`. (In longer programs, you will see some shortening of the code, but brevity does not always occur and is not the OOP goal by any means—readability and maintainability are the goals of OOP.)

By adding member functions to the objects, you have just added behaviors to the data. You have a smart variable that is active and not passive as non-OOP variables are. For example, consider what you are requesting when you type this:

```
aVar1.init();
```

Although the syntax of the dot operator preceding a function call is new to you, the actual execution of the `init()` function is not really that big of a deal, and you can figure out what is going on. You are doing more than just telling Visual C++ to execute a function, however—you are telling a *variable* to execute that function. You are telling the `aVar1` variable, "Go initialize yourself."

After your data contains behaviors as well as characteristics, your data can manipulate itself. You still have to write the code that tells the data what it can do. The member function, in effect, teaches the data how to behave.

As mentioned briefly in yesterday's chapter, a member function is sometimes called a *method*. The method is what the variable uses to fulfill your request. Perhaps this other common term for the execution of the member function is even more appropriate: *passing a message to an object*.

Use your imagination and picture the statements

```
aVar1.init();
aVar1.prAbc();
```

as instructing the aVar1 object variable to go initialize and print itself. In effect, you are whispering a message to the objects directing them to go off on their own and do something.

After your objects "know" how to behave, they become active parts of your program. You have to train them by writing their code, code that would usually appear in the body of the program, but after you write the code for those behaviors, *the rest of your program becomes simply a director that directs when objects are to do their thing.*

An object-oriented programmer does not so much write code as write directions for objects. The code that describes the behaviors of the objects, the member functions, could conceivably take more source-code real estate than the entire rest of the program. This could happen because all the details are contained in the class so that the objects know what to do. Most of the program's details rise to the class level. You are left with a handful of directions that are *much* more manageable than if the details were left in the main body of the code.

Again consider the program back in Listing 9.2. The main() function, the primary body of the program, is much shorter than the class itself. The size of main() shrank considerably. Also, the simpleness of main() increased.

In other words, when you take the details out of main(), you write programs at an abstraction level *above* that of regular structured programming techniques. All the details are taken out of your primary program's hands and put into the class's hands.

Assembly-Line Programming

For years, the backlogs in programming departments kept programmers working frantically to produce the programs demanded. Although manufacturing of almost every product has been automated into a smooth assembly-line process, programming remains too personal and detail-prone to automate to the level where production gains can be made that equal those of other industries.

Finally, OOP brings that assembly-line automation to programming. It is because of the efficiency improvements offered by OOP that the programming backlogs might tend to level off eventually and cost efficiencies in

Member Functions Activate *class* Variables

programming can finally be achieved. (Some estimate that OOP improves programmer productivity by factors of 10 or more.)

When a plant builds an automobile, the employees take prefabricated parts and put those parts into place. The car makers don't have to make the windshield glass, attach the rubber to the wiper blades, and tread the tires because all those details are left up to the experts who make those items. The car experts do what they do best: assemble the cars.

Some day, you'll be able to buy classes that contain all the details (member functions for the behaviors and data members for the storage) for specific applications, such as accounting classes, payroll classes, and inventory classes. Your program will only have to direct the objects and order their creation and manipulation without having to understand all the petty details inside the classes. The car builder doesn't know or care how the windshield was made; the OOP programmer does not have to know about all the petty details inside a class to use a store-bought class. Programmers will be able to pick and choose classes to build their programs just as an assembly-line picks and chooses parts that go into the production of a product.

In addition, businesses are already popping up that write classes you can buy and use in your own programs. Someday, you might write classes for others to use.

You Now Have Controlled Access

The private data and public member functions compose a fully protected data class. The data within the class is protected, much more than with regular non-OOP local variables, because *nothing* in the rest of the program can change the data members. The data members can be changed only through the member functions.

The primary purpose of member functions is to control access to data for the rest of the program. When you want data initialized, you don't directly initialize the data, you initialize the data through member functions. When you want to see values in variables, you have to call displaying member functions that show the values.

Figure 9.2 shows that all access to and from the data members is to be handled by the member functions. The member functions, sometimes called *access functions* for obvious reasons, access the data for the rest of the program. The access to all data will now be controlled access. If data is not to be changed, don't provide a member function which changes that data. If data is to be used for calculations but never printed, don't provide a printing member function for the data, but provide only a function that returns the value of the data so that the data can be used in other calculations.

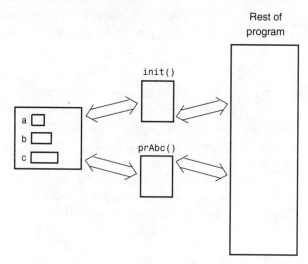

Figure 9.2. The member functions provide all access to objects throughout the rest of the program.

The next section shows you how to use the member functions to pass values to objects from the rest of the program. The member functions provide the vehicle that the rest of the program uses to change class data. The advantage with OOP programming, as you'll see, is that bad values *never* end up in your variables, whereas there is no way to control such occurrences in regular non-OOP programming without bulky and cumbersome error-checking routines after each assignment statement.

Less Abstraction

Here's another OOP difference to keep a lookout for: Notice that the program doesn't really need to know what a class's member function code

Member Functions Activate *class* Variables

> looks like. Someday when you buy off-the-shelf classes, you'll be provided with a `class` header that shows the private data members and the public member function *prototypes,* but you won't be privy to the code inside the member functions (you'll see how to set up such a class later in today's chapter). There is no reason why the programmer who uses a member access function has to know the contents of that function. The programmer needs to know only what kind of access (initialization, displaying, or allocating) the function provides. When you use a microwave oven, you don't have to know what wires are behind the button panel in order to use the High setting; when you use a class, you don't have to know the code underneath the access functions to use the access functions and manipulate the class data.
>
> Our object data values are becoming more like the real-world objects they represent. There is less abstraction between your program objects, such as an employee object, and real-world counterparts. An employee clocks in, works so many hours, gets paid, and so forth. Your employee objects can now take on those kinds of behaviors too because OOP objects have behaviors provided by member functions. You can tell an employee object to go home (by passing a message such as `emp.goHome()`), and the `goHome()` function executes on that employee's data, stopping the hour totaling for that employee.
>
> The more you learn about Visual C++ and OOP, the more you'll see your programming reflect the real-world behaviors and the easier your programs will be to write and maintain.

main() Can Pass Data to an Object

If an initialization member function always assigned the same value to an object, or if a member function always assigned random values to an object (as today's earlier listings did), the whole OOP concept would be worthless. Luckily, however, there is nothing that says a member function cannot initialize an object with user input or through data passed from `main()`.

The program in Listing 9.3 shows the Abc class program with two different initialization member functions. The first one, getVals(), asks the user for the three values from within the member function and assigns the data members those values. The second initialization member function named init() assigns values passed from main() to the data members for whatever object gets the message to initialize. The program shows how member functions act to transfer values from main() to your data members.

Listing 9.3. Passing values to member functions.

```
 1:  // Filename: INIT2.CPP
 2:  // A class that initializes itself from outside sources.
 3:  #include <iostream.h>
 4:  #include <iomanip.h>
 5:  // Class declaration next
 6:  class Abc {
 7:  private:
 8:     char a;
 9:     int b;
10:     double c;
11: public:
12:    void getVals(void)
13:    {  cout << "What is the value of a? ";
14:       cin >> a;
15:       cout << "What is b? ";
16:       cin >> b;
17:       cout << "What is c? ";
18:       cin >> c;
19:    }
20:    void init(char mainA, int mainB, double mainC)
21:    {  a = mainA;   // Assign the data members whatever
22:       b = mainB;   // values are passed from main().
23:       c = mainC;
24:    }
25:    void prAbc(void)
26:    {  cout << "here are the values:\n";
27:       cout << "a is " << a << "\n";
28:       cout << "b is " << b << "\n";
29:       cout << "c is " << c << "\n";
30:    }
31: };
32: main()
33: {
34:    Abc aVar1, aVar2;
35:    aVar1.getVals();   // User will initialize these members
36:    aVar2.init('x', 12, 56.6565);   // main() initializes these
```

continues

Member Functions Activate *class* Variables

Listing 9.3. continued

```
37:     cout << "\nFor aVar1, ";
38:     aVar1.prAbc();
39:     cout << "\nFor aVar2, ";
40:     aVar2.prAbc();
41:     return 0;
42: }
```

What is the value of a? **q**
What is b? **12**
What is c? **3.4**

For aVar1, here are the values:
a is q
b is 12
c is 3.4

For aVar2, here are the values:
a is x
b is 12
c is 56.656

Line 35 calls a member function that first asks the user for three values and then assigns those values to the data members. Visual C++ knows which object variable, aVar1, to initialize because in main()'s line 35, aVar1 was sent the message to initialize using the getVals() member function. Line 36 passes values directly from main() to the member function, and the member function assigns those three values to the data members of the class variable. main() could not directly assign values to the three data members, so the access function initializes the data for main().

Again, notice that main() is becoming little more than an outline of a program. main() is just a high-level set of instructions that directs the objects and tells them what to do by passing them messages (via member functions).

Note: Notice that there is no need to prototype the member functions because they are seen by the compiler before main() triggers their execution. In regular C programs, main() usually physically appears in the program before the first function that it calls, so you have to prototype non-OOP functions called by main(). (Member functions are sometimes called *self-prototyping functions* because their definition appears before they are called, even though they are not called in the usual way.) There are

> exceptions, however, and you'll see a little later in today's chapter why you should prototype some member functions.

It's interesting to see the way some Visual C++ programmers would program the arguments for the `init()` function. Consider this rewritten version of `init()`:

```
void init(char A, int B, float C)
{ a = A;   // Assign the data members whatever
  b = B;   // values are passed from main().
  c = C;
}
```

The only difference between this version and the one on lines 20–24 is that the parameter names differ. Notice that uppercase versions of the data member names are used. The case of variable names is critical to Visual C++ just as it is to C. An uppercase variable named A is different from a lowercase variable named a. The parameters are named with the same names, with the case differences, as the data members they initialize. You'll find that such parameter names are common throughout the C++ community.

Many Visual C++ programmers take full advantage of default argument lists. If you put default values in member function argument lists (in the class header), the data members will be initialized to those default values unless `main()` or another user of the initialization function passes values to override those defaults. As with all Visual C++ functions, you can overload member functions as well. Throughout this book, you'll read all about overloaded member functions and default argument lists in them.

> **Don't Attempt to Initialize Class Definitions!**
>
> There is no way to initialize class data members like this:
>
> ```
> class Abc {
> private:
>   char a = 'q';       // Can't do because there are no
>   int b = 33;         // class variables defined yet!!
>   float c = 98.76;
> public:
>   // Rest of class goes here
> };
> ```

253

Member Functions Activate *class* Variables

> You can store data only after defining variables. The `class` is being defined here, but no storage is reserved that can hold data until later when you define variables with statements such as these:
>
> ```
> Abc aVar1, aVar2;    // Defines 2 class variables
> ```
>
> Although most programmers know not to initialize structure members inside the structure definition, it helps for you to be reminded that classes work the same way.

DO / DON'T

DO add arguments to your member functions if you want the rest of the program to be able to pass values to the member functions.

DON'T prototype member functions such as the ones you have seen. Later in today's chapter, you'll see how to move member function code from the class to an area outside the class, and you'll have to prototype the functions when you do that.

DON'T attempt to initialize class members inside the `class` definition. The `class` definition defines the format of the class; you can store data only after you define variables for that class.

Returning from Member Functions

Member functions are not just one-way data tunnels to your objects. A member function can return a value to `main()` very easily as long as you set up a return value from the member function.

The program in Listing 9.4 is the same as the one in Listing 9.3 with one exception. `main()` needs to total the object variables' double floating-point values. Therefore, `main()` must be given the capability to read the contents of the data members.

Note: Often, you'll write a member function that does nothing more than return the value of one of the data members. Again, main() cannot directly read the data members, so a public access function has to be written to return the value to main(). These kinds of member functions are read-only member functions; they return values but do no initialization of data members.

Listing 9.4. A member function might need to return member values to the rest of the programs.

```cpp
1:  // Filename: INITRET.CPP
2:  // A class that initializes itself from outside sources
3:  // and returns a value to main().
4:  #include <iostream.h>
5:  #include <iomanip.h>
6:  // Class declaration next
7:  class Abc {
8:  private:
9:     char a;
10:    int b;
11:    double c;
12: public:
13:    void getVals(void)
14:    { cout << "What is the value of a? ";
15:      cin >> a;
16:      cout << "What is b? ";
17:      cin >> b;
18:      cout << "What is c? ";
19:      cin >> c;
20:    }
21:    void init(char mainA, int mainB, double mainC)
22:    { a = mainA;   // Assign the data members whatever
23:      b = mainB;   // values are passed from main().
24:      c = mainC;
25:    }
26:    void prAbc(void)
27:    { cout << "here are the values:\n";
28:      cout << "a is " << a << "\n";
29:      cout << "b is " << b << "\n";
30:      cout << "c is " << c << "\n";
31:    }
32:    float getC(void)     // Does nothing more than return a data member
33:    { return c; }
34: };
```

continues

Member Functions Activate *class* Variables

Listing 9.4. continued

```
35: main()
36: {
37:   Abc aVar1, aVar2;
38:   double total;
39:   aVar1.getVals();   // User will initialize these members
40:   aVar2.init('x', 12, 56.6565);  // main() initializes these
41:   cout << "\nFor aVar1, ";
42:   aVar1.prAbc();
43:   cout << "\nFor aVar2, ";
44:   aVar2.prAbc();
45:   // Now, get the total of the floats
46:   total = aVar1.getC() + aVar2.getC();  // Adds the return values
47:   cout << "\nThe total of the c's is " << total << ".\n";
48:   return 0;
49: }
```

```
What is the value of a? u
What is b? 6
What is c? 76.5

For aVar1, here are the values:
a is u
b is 6
c is 76.5

For aVar2, here are the values:
a is x
b is 12
c is 56.6565

The total of the c's is 133.157.
```

Although `main()` cannot directly access the data members of `aVar1` and `aVar2`, the `getC()` access function hands `main()` the values of the appropriate floating-point values so that `main()` can use them.

Note: Some programmers automatically add a read-only member function, such as the one shown in Listing 9.4's lines 32 and 33, for every data member. Although having read-only access for every member is sometimes overkill, you'll find yourself writing lots of them. Letting `main()` (and the rest of the program) read public values directly does not offer as much control (and safety) as providing access functions that return values when appropriate.

Cleaning Up the Class

The Abc class is getting quite large. Pretty soon, the class will be as big as an entire equivalent non-OOP program! Actually, you are doing little more than moving details out of the main() program and into the class. Although the amount of coding is not less, the way you are beginning to look at programs is extremely different. Fairly soon, you'll hardly remember putting details of a class's manipulation down into the primary part of the program because the class member functions will seem so natural. After all, it is the objects that should do all the work, even though non-OOP procedural programming has made the roles of variables passive. A small shift in thinking can activate variables, putting that activity where it belongs.

There is a common way to clean up a class definition using the scope resolution operator, ::, that you read about back in Day 2's chapter, "C++ Is Superior!" You can prototype your member functions in the class, leaving only a *class header* (an outline of the class with data members and member function prototypes) and put the body of the member functions following the class (but before main() as is usually done).

Listing 9.5 contains the same program as Listing 9.4 except that the class is cleaned up greatly; only the class header is left in the class definition. The body of the member functions follows the Abc class. Notice the definition lines of each member function; you'll see the :: operator used on each line. The analysis section after the program explains how the scope resolution operator helps the Abc class find its member functions.

Listing 9.5. Cleaning up the class and leaving only a class header.

```
 1:  // Filename: CLSSHEAD.CPP
 2:  // After cleaning up the class.
 3:  #include <iostream.h>
 4:  #include <iomanip.h>
 5:  // Class declaration next
 6:  class Abc {
 7:  private:
 8:     char a;
 9:     int b;
10:     double c;
11: public:
12:    void getVals(void);
13:    void init(char mainA, int mainB, double mainC);
14:    void prAbc(void);
15:    float getC(void);
```

continues

Listing 9.5. continued

```
16: };
17: void Abc::getVals(void)
18:    { cout << "What is the value of a? ";
19:      cin >> a;
20:      cout << "What is b? ";
21:      cin >> b;
22:      cout << "What is c? ";
23:      cin >> c;
24:    }
25: void Abc::init(char mainA, int mainB, double mainC)
26:    { a = mainA;   // Assign the data members whatever
27:      b = mainB;   // values are passed from main().
28:      c = mainC;
29:    }
30: void Abc::prAbc(void)
31:    { cout << "here are the values:\n";
32:      cout << "a is " << a << "\n";
33:      cout << "b is " << b << "\n";
34:      cout << "c is " << c << "\n";
35:    }
36: float Abc::getC(void)  // Does nothing more than return a data member
37:    { return c; }
38: //////////////////// Class ends here ////////////////////////////
39: main()
40: {
41:    Abc aVar1, aVar2;
42:    double total;
43:    aVar1.getVals();   // User will initialize these members
44:    aVar2.init('x', 12, 56.6565);  // main() initializes these
45:    cout << "\nFor aVar1, ";
46:    aVar1.prAbc();
47:    cout << "\nFor aVar2, ";
48:    aVar2.prAbc();
49:    // Now, get the total of the doubles
50:    total = aVar1.getC() + aVar2.getC();  // Adds the return values
51:    cout << "\nThe total of the c's is " << total << ".\n";
52:    return 0;
53: }
```

Analysis

The scope resolution operators seem strange at first. After all, without the `Abc::` in front of the `getVals()` function on line 17, wouldn't Visual C++ still be able to find `getVals()`? It turns out that *class scope*, introduced in yesterday's chapter, plays a role here that requires the use of the class name followed by :: in front of every function you define outside a class.

Every member of a class has class scope. If you wanted, you could define many more classes in Listing 9.5's program, *all with the same member function names.* The function names can be the same because each name is scoped to the class in which it is prototyped or defined.

It is because more than one function could have a function named getVals() that you must resolve the scope of the getVals() function along with every other function defined after the class. The fact that there is only a single class in this program has no bearing on the need to resolve the class scope of getVals(). If you define the body of a member function directly inside the class header, there is no need to resolve its scope, but if you place the body of the member function outside the class, you must resolve its scope as shown in lines 17, 25, 30, and 36.

Most Visual C++ programmers leave their member function definitions outside their class headers. When a class header is left without member function code, the class is cleaner and easier to maintain.

Many Visual C++ programmers prefer to type their class headers in their source code, but they include (with the #include directive) the member function definitions. These programmers' class header (or headers if more than one class is used by the program, as is frequently done) is then available for them to peruse while programming, and the details are left in the included files for compilation.

Perhaps the most important reason for separating class headers from their member function code is for class distribution. It is possible to compile (but not link) class member function code by itself and store that compiled object code as a stand-alone file. Whenever you write programs which use that class, the programs need only a copy of the class header (which is usually included with #include), and the member functions are then linked to the compiled program which uses that class.

Separate compilation of classes lets class vendors (people who write classes for a living) sell their class code without distributing source code to their classes. When you purchase math or I/O classes to use with your own programs, the class vendor usually supplies you with the following three items:

- ☐ A class header amply commented
- ☐ A compiled object file with the class's member function definitions
- ☐ Documentation that tells how to use the class and what the class provides

The class header (and sample documentation) is all you need in order to write programs with other people's classes. As mentioned earlier in this chapter, you need

Member Functions Activate *class* Variables

not know the details of a class to use the class just as you need not know the inside components of your monitor to plug it in and use it. Classes are going to be available, if predictions are correct, for all kinds of professions and computing needs. When you want to write OOP programs, you won't *write* them as much as you'll *build* them with parts (other people's classes as well as classes you have written).

This building-block approach is why the programming industry is so gung-ho about OOP. Perhaps there really might be an end to the programming backlog that plagues data processing departments across the country.

DO / **DON'T**

DO write access member functions that do nothing more than return member values when `main()` or another part of the program needs to use one of the members.

DO write clean class headers by placing the member function definitions beneath the class. An even better practice would be to place all class definitions in a header file and include the class code with an `#include` directive. The best practice of all is to supply the class header but compile the class member functions and link the compiled code to your programs which use that class.

DON'T forget to resolve the scope of all member function definitions you place outside the `class`. You must precede *every* member function with its class name and scope resolution operator before Visual C++ can match the function to the class in which it belongs.

Use *inline* for Efficiency

There is one simple addition you can make to your classes that improves their efficiency. Add the `inline` keyword to your class member functions. You learned in Day 2's chapter that `inline` suggests to the compiler (Visual C++ can ignore the suggestion) that it expand the function call into the function code itself.

When Visual C++ is able to inline your member function code successfully, your class member function executions become more efficient. Inlining class member functions requires nothing more than adding the `inline` keyword before the member function names, as shown in Listing 9.6. Listing 9.6 does the same thing as Listing 9.5. The only differences are the `inline` keywords on lines 17, 25, 30, and 36.

Listing 9.6. Improving your program's efficiency with `inline`.

```
 1:  // Filename: CLSSINL.CPP
 2:  // Adding inline to improve efficiency.
 3:  #include <iostream.h>
 4:  #include <iomanip.h>
 5:  // Class declaration next
 6:  class Abc {
 7:  private:
 8:    char a;
 9:    int b;
10:    double c;
11: public:
12:   void getVals(void);
13:   void init(char mainA, int mainB, double mainC);
14:   void prAbc(void);
15:   float getC(void);
16: };
17: inline void Abc::getVals(void)    // First inlined function
18:    { cout << "What is the value of a? ";
19:      cin >> a;
20:      cout << "What is b? ";
21:      cin >> b;
22:      cout << "What is c? ";
23:      cin >> c;
24:    }
25: inline void Abc::init(char mainA, int mainB, double mainC)
26:    { a = mainA;   // Assign the data members whatever
27:      b = mainB;   // values are passed from main().
28:      c = mainC;
29:    }
30: inline void Abc::prAbc(void)
31:    { cout << "here are the values:\n";
32:      cout << "a is " << a << "\n";
33:      cout << "b is " << b << "\n";
34:      cout << "c is " << c << "\n";
35:    }
36: inline float Abc::getC(void)
37:    { return c; }
38: /////////////////////// Class ends here ///////////////////////////
39: main()
40: {
41:    Abc aVar1, aVar2;
42:    double total;
43:    aVar1.getVals();    // User will initialize these members
44:    aVar2.init('x', 12, 56.6565);  // main() initializes these
45:    cout << "\nFor aVar1, ";
46:    aVar1.prAbc();
47:    cout << "\nFor aVar2, ";
```

continues

Member Functions Activate *class* Variables

Listing 9.6. continued

```
48:     aVar2.prAbc();
49:     // Now, get the total of the doubles
50:     total = aVar1.getC() + aVar2.getC();   // Adds the return values
51:     cout << "\nThe total of the c's is " << total << ".\n";
52:     return 0;
53: }
```

Note: You don't have to specify `inline` if you list member function code directly inside the class. Visual C++ automatically inlines those functions.

Make Classes Self-Protecting

Although the Abc class has been useful for illustrating class fundamentals, there has been very little advantage to creating the private Abc class data and making all the class data public. After all, main() could initialize the class members with any value at all, in effect, through the access member functions, giving main() full write-access to the class data.

Most of the time, member functions ensure that *proper* data gets sent to the class members. If any values could be assigned, through member functions, the member function does little more than add overhead to programs.

The program in Listing 9.7 provides a little more class functionality to Abc data by showing you how the member functions can act as data protectors to the class. The member functions ensure that only lowercase letters of the alphabet are passed to the a data member, that only the values from 1 to 10 are passed to the b data member, and that only positive values below 100.0 are passed to c. Notice how main() doesn't change in length even though you've added all this checking—the objects themselves now "know" how to initialize with good values and reject bad ones.

Listing 9.7. Adding error checking to member functions.

```
1:  // Filename: CLSSCHK.CPP
2:  // Access member functions should check to make sure that
3:  // data members never get out-of-range values.
4:  #include <iostream.h>
5:  #include <iomanip.h>
```

```cpp
 6: #include <stdlib.h>
 7: // Class declaration next
 8: class Abc {
 9: private:
10:    char a;
11:    int b;
12:    double c;
13: public:
14:    void init(char mainA, int mainB, double mainC);
15:    void prAbc(void);
16: };
17: inline void Abc::init(char mainA, int mainB, double mainC)
18:    { if (mainA >= 'a' && mainA <= 'z')
19:         {  a = mainA;  } // Assign the data members only correct
                    ↪values
20:      else
21:         { cerr << "a cannot be initialized with " << mainA << ".\n";
22:           exit(1);
23:         }
24:      if (mainB >= 1 && mainB <= 10)
25:         { b = mainB; }
26:      else
27:         { cerr << "b cannot be initialized with " << mainB << ".\n";
28:           exit(1);
29:         }
30:      if (mainC >= 0.0 && mainC < 100.00)
31:         { c = mainC; }
32:      else
33:         { cerr << "c cannot be initialized with " << mainC << ".\n";
34:           exit(1);
35:         }
36: }
37: inline void Abc::prAbc(void)
38:    { cout << "here are the values:\n";
39:      cout << "a is " << a << "\n";
40:      cout << "b is " << b << "\n";
41:      cout << "c is " << c << "\n";
42:    }
43: ///////////////////// Class ends here /////////////////////////
44: main()
45: {
46:    Abc aVar1, aVar2;
47:    aVar1.init('x', 3, 56.6565);
48:    cout << "\nFor aVar1, ";
49:    aVar1.prAbc();
50:    // aVar2 will get a bad value
51:    aVar2.init('a', 12, 33.0);   // 12 will trigger the error
52:    cout << "\nFor aVar2, ";
53:    aVar2.prAbc();
54:    return 0;
55: }
```

Member Functions Activate *class* Variables

```
For aVar1, here are the values:
a is x
b is 3
c is 56.6565
b cannot be initialized with 12.
```

The error checking done in lines 18–35 makes sure that the data members get only the values that fall within their range. When a bad value, the 12, is sent to the data members in line 51 (via the init() member function call), the error-checking member function keeps the bad data from getting to the class variable by stopping the program instead of letting the values get through.

It's worth noting that another member function could have been called just to do the checking. The more you break down your class into separate member functions with their own unique tasks, the easier it will be to spot bugs and the more general-purpose your classes become. For instance, consider this class (the entire program is not listed here, just the class), which lets another member function handle the error correction:

```cpp
class Abc {
private:
  char a;
  int b;
  double c;
public:
  void init(char mainA, int mainB, double mainC);
  void prAbc(void);
  void checkData(char mainA, int mainB, double mainC);
};
inline void Abc::init(char mainA, int mainB, double mainC)
  { checkData(mainA, mainB, mainC);
    // Code gets here only if checkData() didn't terminate
    a = mainA;
    b = mainB;
    c = mainC;
  }
inline void Abc::checkData(char mainA. int mainB, double mainC)
  { if (mainA < 'a' || mainA > 'z')
      { cerr << "a cannot be initialized with " << mainA << ".\n";
        exit(1);
      }
    if (mainB < 1 || mainB > 10)
      { cerr << "b cannot be initialized with " << mainB << ".\n";
        exit(1);
      }
    if (mainC < 0.0 || mainC >= 100.00)
      { cerr << "c cannot be initialized with " << mainC << ".\n";
        exit(1);
```

```
    }
  }
inline void Abc::prAbc(void)
  { cout << "Here are the values:\n";
    cout << "a is " << a << "\n";
    cout << "b is " << b << "\n";
    cout << "c is " << c << "\n";
  }
```

The checkData() member function exists only for internal use within the class. init() calls checkData(), and as long as checkData() finds no data out of bounds, init() regains control and initializes the data members. However, if checkData() finds a bad data value, init() will never regain control, and the program will terminate via an exit() call.

Can you see any reason why checkData() should remain in the public section of the class? There is no reason why it should. Another member in the class calls checkData(), not main(). If a function outside the class has no need for access to a class member, make that member private. Therefore, the better way of arranging the previous class would be like this:

```
class Abc {
private:
  char a;
  int b;
  float c;
  void checkData(char mainA, int mainB, double mainC);
public:
  void init(char mainA, int mainB, double mainC);
  void prAbc(void);
};
inline void Abc::init(char mainA, int mainB, double mainC)
  { checkData(mainA, mainB, mainC);
    // Code gets here only if checkData() didn't terminate
    a = mainA;
    b = mainB;
    c = mainC;
  }
inline void Abc::checkData(char mainA. int mainB, double mainC)
  { if (mainA < 'a' || mainA > 'z')
      { cerr << "a cannot be initialized with " << mainA << ".\n";
        exit(1);
      }
    if (mainB < 1 || mainB > 10)
      { cerr << "b cannot be initialized with " << mainB << ".\n";
        exit(1);
      }
```

Member Functions Activate *class* Variables

```
        if (mainC < 0.0 || mainC >= 100.00)
          { cerr << "c cannot be initialized with " << mainC << ".\n";
            exit(1);
          }
    }
inline void Abc::prAbc(void)
  { cout << "Here are the values:\n";
    cout << "a is " << a << "\n";
    cout << "b is " << b << "\n";
    cout << "c is " << c << "\n";
  }
```

The sixth line is the first time you've seen a member function in the private section of a class, but it makes sense to keep the member function there. Only another member function calls checkData(), so checkData() should remain hidden from the rest of the program that has no need to use it.

> **To Correct, or Not to Correct...**
>
> When an error occurs in a class member function, such as main() attempting to initialize with out-of-range values, should the member function terminate the program as done in the previous program, or should it assign a good value that falls in the range and continue?
>
> Your specific application's needs must dictate the answer to that. Most of the time, you will probably want to terminate the application with appropriate error messages if a bad value is sent to a data member. However, you might have a situation in which the member function can fix values. For instance, if the smallest value that is to go in a data member is zero, and the initialization member function gets a negative initial value, the function might assign a zero and continue as though nothing bad had happened.
>
> Only you know whether a function should change a bad initial value to one that is correct because you know the consequences of such data when you write your programs. Handling an error or correcting the problem is secondary to the overall charge of controlled access member functions; such functions should provide the access to the private data members and be the gateway through which other parts of the program access the data.

DO	DON'T

DO use `inline` on your shorter member functions so that Visual C++ will eliminate the function call overhead when possible.

DO provide data protection through your member functions so that `class` data is not sent incorrect values. The more protection you add to a class, the less work you have to do when *using* that class. That's one reason why you'll become a much faster programmer as you create classes that you can reuse; the classes will contain their own error checking, and you can concentrate on the more important details of the application without putting error checks throughout your programs.

DON'T forget to write two-way access classes. `main()` (and the rest of the program) must have a way to look at and change data members. A read-only access function simply returns the value of a data member so that `main()` can work with the value.

DON'T use `inline` on functions you completely define inside a class header. Visual C++ inlines those functions automatically.

A More Useful Example

The program in Listing 9.8 contains a class that keeps track of lemonade sales for a kid's neighborhood lemonade stand (if the kid needs a computer to track lemonade sales, it must be good lemonade!). There are two kinds of lemonade sold: sweetened for 50 cents a glass and unsweetened for 45 cents a glass.

The `Lemon` class contains a data member that keeps track of the total dollar amount of lemonade sold and the number of glasses left to sell (beginning with 100 at the start of the day). The amount of sugar teaspoons left (each sweetened lemonade consumes two) is tracked as well. The member function `showTot()` prints the grand total sold.

As customers come to buy lemonade, the member function `buySweet()` adds 50 cents to the total income, and `buyUnSweet()` adds 45 cents. Either way, the number of glasses remaining is decreased automatically.

One `switch` statement and menu controls the program. Notice how `main()` is extremely simple now that the class does all the work. `main()` acts only as a guide

Member Functions Activate *class* Variables

ordering the events and directing the objects just as a movie director would direct actors who know how to act.

Listing 9.8. An OOP class program that tracks lemonade sales.

```
 1:  // Filename: LEMONS.CPP
 2:  // Child's lemonade-sale tracking program
 3:  #include <iostream.h>
 4:  #include <iomanip.h>
 5:  #include <stdlib.h>
 6:  // Lemonade class declaration next
 7:  class Lemon {
 8:  private:
 9:     int totalLeft;         // Will start at 100
10:     int sugarTeasp;        // Starts at 80
11:     float total;           // Income for day
12:  public:
13:     void init(void);       // Initialize members upon program start-up
14:     void showTot(void);    // Print the day's total income
15:     void buySweet(void);   // Executes when customer buys sweetened
16:     void buyUnSweet(void); // Executes when customer buys unsweetened
17:  };
18:  void Lemon::init(void)
19:  {  totalLeft = 100;
20:     sugarTeasp = 80;
21:     total = 0.0;
22:  }
23:  void Lemon::showTot(void)
24:  { cout << setprecision(2) << setiosflags(ios::fixed);
25:    cout << setiosflags(ios::showpoint); // Ensure that decimal prints
26:    cout << "\nTotal so far today is $" << total << "\n\n";
27:  }
28:  void Lemon::buySweet(void)
29:  {
30:     if (totalLeft == 0)
31:        { cerr << "Sorry, no more lemonade is left.\n\n";}
32:     else
33:        if (sugarTeasp == 0)
34:           { cerr << "No more sugar is left. Sorry.\n\n"; }
35:        else
36:           { cout << "Enjoy your drink!\n\n";
37:             totalLeft--;        // One less glass left
38:             sugarTeasp -= 2;    // Each glass takes 2 teaspoons
39:             total += (float).50;
40:           }
41:  }
42:  void Lemon:: buyUnSweet(void)
43:  {
44:     if (totalLeft == 0)
```

```
45:       { cerr << "Sorry, no more lemonade is left.\n\n";}
46:    else
47:       { cout << "Enjoy your drink!\n\n";
48:         totalLeft--;      // One less glass left
49:         total += (float).45;
50:       }
51: }
52: /////////////////////// Class ends here /////////////////////////////
53: main()
54: {
55:   Lemon drink;
56:   int ans;
57:   drink.init();   // Initialize data members to start of day
58:   do {
59:     cout << "What's happening?\n";
60:     cout << "  1. Sell a sweetened.\n";
61:     cout << "  2. Sell an unsweetened.\n";
62:     cout << "  3. Show total sales so far.\n";
63:     cout << "  4. Quit the program.\n";
64:     cout << "What do you want to do? ";
65:     cin >> ans;
66:     switch (ans)
67:       { case 1 : drink.buySweet();
68:                  break;
69:         case 2 : drink.buyUnSweet();
70:                  break;
71:         case 3 : drink.showTot();
72:                  break;
73:         case 4 : drink.showTot();   // Print total one last time
74:                  exit(1);
75:       }
76:     } while (ans >=1 && ans <= 4);
77:   return 0;
78: }
```

```
What's happening?
   1. Sell a sweetened.
   2. Sell an unsweetened.
   3. Show total sales so far.
   4. Quit the program.
What do you want to do? 3

Total so far today is $0.00

What's happening?
   1. Sell a sweetened.
   2. Sell an unsweetened.
   3. Show total sales so far.
   4. Quit the program.
```

DAY 9

Member Functions Activate *class* Variables

```
What do you want to do? 1
Enjoy your drink!

What's happening?
  1. Sell a sweetened.
  2. Sell an unsweetened.
  3. Show total sales so far.
  4. Quit the program.
What do you want to do? 3

Total so far today is $0.50

What's happening?
  1. Sell a sweetened.
  2. Sell an unsweetened.
  3. Show total sales so far.
  4. Quit the program.
What do you want to do? 2
Enjoy your drink!

What's happening?
  1. Sell a sweetened.
  2. Sell an unsweetened.
  3. Show total sales so far.
  4. Quit the program.
What do you want to do? 1
Enjoy your drink!

What's happening?
  1. Sell a sweetened.
  2. Sell an unsweetened.
  3. Show total sales so far.
  4. Quit the program.
What do you want to do? 3

Total so far today is $1.45

What's happening?
  1. Sell a sweetened.
  2. Sell an unsweetened.
  3. Show total sales so far.
  4. Quit the program.
What do you want to do? 4

Total so far today is $1.45
```

Analysis

The program tracks sales of lemonade through a lemonade class that is fairly smart. Although `main()` cannot directly access any data member, all the member functions of the class take care of initialization, updating, and printing when needed. `main()` simply guides the `drink` object and tells it what to do based on user response to the menu.

If more than 40 glasses of sweetened lemonade are sold, the user sees the message

```
No more sugar is left. Sorry.
```

and the total sales is not updated. When all 100 glasses of the lemonade are sold, the message from line 31 or 45 prints, depending on the type of lemonade someone is trying to buy.

Here's a Tongue-Twister: Encapsulation

A capsule is an enclosed shell that usually contains several items. A space capsule contains people and equipment. A cold capsule contains granules of cold medicine.

Do you see how a class can be thought of as a capsule? The data members and the member functions are all stored in this capsule called an object.

As you peruse object-oriented programming magazines and reference manuals, you'll run across the term *encapsulation* often. It seems that computer people never use an easy word when a difficult one will do nicely and confuse more people. Nevertheless, the term *encapsulation* will not throw you now because it is obvious to you what encapsulation means: encapsulation is the binding together of data members and member functions in classes (and also structures) so that smart objects that contain both characteristics and behaviors can be created.

The `Lemon` class in Listing 9.8 is said to be encapsulated with code and data. You'll not be thrown by that word if you read it again!

The Hidden *this* Pointer

If you are the curious kind, you've probably wondered how Visual C++ matches up the correct objects to data members. (If you haven't wondered why, you'll still be intrigued at the answer.) In other words, when a `main()` function in the Visual C++ `class Abc` program initializes a variable like

```
aVar1.init('x', 3, 56.65);
```

you should understand how Visual C++ applies the `init()` function to `aVar1` and not to other variables in the program. Visual C++ pulls some sleight-of-hand during compilation. The reason that you should know about the method is that at times you will need to use this knowledge to make a program behave in a way that you otherwise could not.

Member Functions Activate *class* Variables

Visual C++ converts the preceding `init()` function call to this:

`init(&aVar1, 'x', 3, 56.65);`

In other words, Visual C++ passes the object variable to the function (by address). The `init()` function's prototype, however, doesn't have a place for the extra variable. The prototype looks like this:

`void init(char mainA, int mainB, float mainC);`

Although that's the prototype you entered, Visual C++ changes it to this during the compilation of your program:

`void init(Abc * this, char mainA, int mainB, float mainC);`

The pointer variable, called the **this pointer,* lets the function modify the object in question because pass-by-address lets a called function modify its calling function's values. You never have to remember that this extra argument is being sent. Try to think of statements such as

`aVar1.init('x', 3, 56.65);`

as messages being sent to objects. In this case, the statement says, "Hey, aVar1, go initialize yourself with the data values x, 3, and 56.65." The hidden *this pointer ensures that aVar1 keeps any changes made to it by the `init()` member function call.

> **Note:** If you ever need to return an object from a function (and you do need to at times), return the *this value with the following statement:
>
> `return (*this);`
>
> Returning the *this pointer ensures that whatever object triggered this function is returned. You don't know ahead of time whether the function will act on aVar1 or aVar2 (keeping the same variable names used in this chapter's examples), but *whatever* object variable triggers the function will be returned by the `return` statement shown here.

One more thing: Never modify the *this pointer in a member function. Although the data members can change, consider the *this pointer a constant, and you'll always be safe in explicitly referring to it inside a member function if the need arises.

Summary

Today's chapter taught you a lot, and you're probably ready for a break. If so, take a siesta because you have just cleared a major hurdle in the object-oriented programming learning curve.

Member functions are functions that you place directly inside a class (or structure). It is the member function that gives a class its behavior and activates that class by making objects operate on their own.

You don't have to define the entire function inside the class. Most Visual C++ programmers declare a class header with member function prototypes and then code the function definitions later in the code or include (or link) the member function's code.

Although data members are almost always private to maintain the data protection that Visual C++ is known for, most of your member functions will be public to allow controlled access to your private data. Instead of the rest of the program being able to access data directly, the program will be able to call public member functions when a data value has to be changed or printed.

You'll end up with several member functions in each class. Often, the member functions will expand your classes so that they are larger than the rest of the program that contains them. The more member functions you write, the more kinds of access the rest of the program has to your private data.

When you add argument lists to member functions, the rest of the program can pass values directly to private data via the member functions. When the rest of the program needs to use one of the private data values, you can supply an access function that returns a private value, all the while protecting the value from modification outside the class.

Visual C++ programmers have coined a word for the canning together of both data and functions into class objects: *encapsulation*. Encapsulation describes the process of binding together the functions and data into capsule-like forms and giving objects their active role in OOP programs.

In today's chapter, you also learned how a hidden *this pointer works behind the scenes to properly give access to objects and their member functions. Every time you pass a message to a member function by triggering one of its member functions, a pointer to that object is secretly passed to the member function so that Visual C++ will have the object inside the function to work with. Most of the time, you can ignore the hidden *this pointer and act as if you know nothing about it.

Member Functions Activate *class* Variables

Q&A

Q. Why are objects said to be active rather than passive?

A. Objects are said to be active because, compared to non-OOP programs, objects do seemingly take on behaviors and intelligence by initializing themselves, printing themselves, and even allocating themselves. This activity is accomplished by appropriate member functions inside the class.

When you write member functions instead of putting those functions throughout the rest of the program, you bind the member functions to the objects defined. The rest of the program (from `main()` down) then becomes a director, directing objects that take care of themselves instead of manipulating the variables as in non-OOP programs.

After the class is written, the resulting program's details are reduced considerably. Over time, as you write more and more classes that provide for active data, you'll reuse those classes and build programs much more quickly than before because you'll leave error checking and other tedious details for the class's member functions to handle.

Q. Is there an advantage to separating my member function code from my class headers?

A. By separating your member function code from the class, leaving just a class header that contains prototypes to those functions, you not only clean up the class but also allow for separate compilation of member function code.

Separate compilation is how class vendors supply their classes. Suppose you want to write programs that produce 3-D graphics and you find an advertisement that sells a top-notch 3-D graphics class library you can use in your own programs. When you order the class, you'll get the source code for the class header, documentation for using the class, and an object file (the compiled class member functions) that you can link your program to.

Q. How can public access member functions protect my private data?

A. If your program uses public access functions to access private class data members, those public access functions can check to ensure that data passed to the public functions are inside the boundary limits required by the class. For example, if you need to initialize an age data member, the access function can keep negative ages from being stored in the member by printing an appropriate error message when needed (ages cannot be negative).

Often, as shown in today's chapter, an access function calls a private member function to do the data checking.

Q. How is a *layer of abstraction* removed when I program with objects?

A. Objects mirror the real world they represent better than regular non-OOP variables in other kinds of programs. If you were writing a Visual C++ program that simulated a stoplight, you would write a class that contains a data member, lightColor, and member functions such as turnOnGreen(), turnOnYellow(), and turnOnRed(). The object variable, perhaps aptly named stopLight, would actually seem to change colors on its own when you told it to do so with statements such as this one:

stopLight.turnOnRed();   // Tell the light to go red

An equivalent non-OOP program would have to set up codes or enumerated data types that set appropriate color codes to the stoplight variable, and functions would have to be called with the light passed to them before the light could change color. In other words, there would be more abstraction between the real-world counterpart and the program.

The closer your program mirrors the real world that it represents, the faster you will be able to code because your programs will more accurately reflect their real-life counterparts.

Q. What exactly is a *this pointer?

A. The *this pointer, which is secretly passed to all member functions, is a pointer that points to the object triggering the member function call.

By passing the *this pointer, Visual C++ gives member functions access to whatever object variable is triggering the member function at the time. There will be some instances in which you will have to work directly with the *this pointer, but most of the time you can ignore the pointer completely.

Workshop

The Workshop offers quiz questions and exercises to hone your skills and give you feedback on today's lesson. You'll find some proposed answers in Appendix D.

Member Functions Activate *class* Variables

Quiz

1. Describe two ways to call member functions.
2. Why must you use a scope resolution operator when coding member function bodies outside class headers?
3. What is meant by the phrase *sending messages to objects*?
4. True or False: You can use default argument lists but not overloaded functions in member functions.
5. How does main() access private data members when data has to be printed?
6. True or False: You can change the *this pointer's data members through a member function, but not the *this pointer itself.

Exercises

1. Write the beginnings of a grading program for a teacher. Create a class named LetterGrades that contains a single character data member named grade. Write two public member functions, one that passes a letter grade to the class variable from main() and one that prints the letter grade. Make sure the first function contains a default argument of A so that the program doesn't have to pass an A, just other grades. Define several variables (representing different student scores), and initialize and print them.

2. Add a private member function to the LetterGrades class which ensures that the letter grade falls in the range from A to F (convert lowercase letters a through f to uppercase if needed). Call the member function from the public initialization function before initializing the grade with a value.

3. Add another private function to the lemonade program in Listing 9.8 so that the program prints a warning message when fewer than five glasses are left. Call the function from both sales functions so that a message prints when either the sugar or the lemonade runs low. Optionally, add a fifth menu option that enables the user to supply another 80 spoons of sugar and another 100 glasses of lemonade when needed (the answer to the optional portion is not included in the Appendix D answers).

DAY 10

Friends When You Need Them

Friends When You Need Them

Yesterday's chapter was the most important chapter in the book. All knowledge of Visual C++ and OOP that you gain from this point on will be based on the foundation you learned yesterday.

If you understood everything in yesterday's chapter, it is all downhill from here. If you are still a little unsure about the material, please give it some review before continuing. Newcomers to OOP will give up about here if they haven't mastered yesterday's material because everything else in the language is based on member function access to private data. Nothing else will seem difficult if you understand member functions.

To give you some breathing room and time for review, today's chapter lightens things a bit. Today, you'll learn about friend functions and classes, specified by the `friend` keyword. Today's chapter is a little shorter than yesterday's; you need the extra time to review yesterday's chapter. You'll find that friend functions and friend classes are, well, *friendly* and fairly easy to learn.

Friend functions give you a back door to private data that you would otherwise not have access to except through member functions. Although you shouldn't rely on friend functions to bypass normal private access, you'll see some uses for friend functions as this book progresses, especially on Days 11 and 12 (starting tomorrow) when you learn how to overload operators using OOP member functions.

Today, you learn about the following topics:

- ☐ When and how to use friend functions
- ☐ When and how to use friend classes

Why Use Friends?

Suppose that you create a class properly by putting the data members in a private section and member functions in a public section only to find that you need to give data access to certain functions in the program that aren't in the class. There are basically three ways to get around the private specification.

You can insert the `public` keyword at the top of the class, but that defeats the whole purpose of proper data hiding, and you might as well return to non-OOP programming for good if you find yourself eliminating the privatization of data. You can write access functions for the data that return, change, or display the values that the other function needs. Access functions are an important part of OOP programs, as you saw in yesterday's chapter and as you'll see throughout this book.

However, there are some non-member functions and secondary classes which must have intimate access to data that should remain private to other parts of the program. Sometimes, a function needs to have access to data that no other part of the program, outside the class, needs. *Friend functions* and *friend classes* provide access to certain functions and classes without giving up the safety of privatization of the data in general.

Note: As you progress through this book, especially during Days 11 and 12, you'll see when friend functions are needed most. Some Visual C++ programmers shy away from using friend functions as much as possible because they believe, and rightfully so, that declaring a function as a `friend` defeats the class mechanism that protects data so well. For now, learn how to specify and use friend functions and friend classes. This book points out when their use is appropriate and when it's inappropriate. Limit your use of the `friend` keyword to those cases described by this book. Unless otherwise needed, reserve all other uses of friends for your social get-togethers.

Friend Functions

A function specified as a `friend` has access to class members but doesn't have to be a part of that class. For example, in the following set of classes, each class has its own printing and initialization member functions:

```
class girlsSoftball {
  char name[25];
  int age;
  float batAvg;
public:
  void prData(void);
  void init(void);
};

class boysSoftball {
  char name[25];
  int age;
  float batAvg;
public:
  void prData(void);
  void init(void);
};
```

Friends When You Need Them

There's nothing incorrect about using the same function name in both classes because member functions have class scope and there's no discrepancy in the use of the same name twice. (The same class, however, cannot have two members with the same name.)

Suppose that the person who manages both softball teams was computerizing the two teams' records. Sometimes the manager wants to print the girls' roster and sometimes the manager wants to print the boys' roster. Sometimes, however, the manager wants to print a combined list of both rosters. That's where you encounter the problem that you cannot solve with your current bag of OOP knowledge (without incorrectly inserting `public` at the top of the classes).

It is possible to set up a friend function that accesses both classes at the same time while still keeping the classes private to all other parts of the program. Before getting into the specifics of adding a friend to both classes, the next section shows you how to write a friend for a single class.

Use *friend* to Specify Friend Functions

Here is a smaller version of the `girlsSoftball` class shown earlier. The `prData()` member function is left out. Given the class as it now stands, there is no way for the program to print the contents of the class data because the data is in the `private` section of the class.

```
class girlsSoftball {
  char name[25];
  int age;
  float batAvg;
public:
  void init(void);
};
```

If you want to add a function to print the data members, that function has to be either a member of the class or a friend function. Remember that a friend function is *not* a member of the class, but is a function completely outside the class scope.

To specify a friend function, insert the function prototype inside the class just as if the function were a member function. Precede the prototype with the `friend` keyword like this:

```
class girlsSoftball {
  char name[25];
  int age;
  float batAvg;
```

```
public:
  void init(void);
  friend void prData(girlsSoftball pl);   // Friend function
};
```

The `prData()` is now the *only* function besides the member function `init()` that can access the class's private data. If you noticed that `prData()` no longer contains a `void` argument list (it did when `prData()` was a member function), you'll learn why the argument list had to be passed in a moment.

> **The Class Decides the Friendship**
>
> The class itself must offer the friendship. In other words, without the `friend` keyword in front of the function's prototype in the class, no function can be a friend of the class.
>
> Although friend functions slightly bend the data-protection rules, it is the class that contains the `friend` declaration, and therefore it is the class that dictates who is its friend and who is not. Functions cannot gain access to a class's private members unless the class contains the `friend` declaration.
>
> Therefore, the rules are bent in that although a function outside the class can gain private access, the friend is limited to those functions specifically listed as a friend, and a function cannot on its own gain access to a class unless the class contains the `friend` keyword.

The friend function declaration can appear in either the private or the public sections of a class. The location does not matter because the friend function is not a member function. The friend function is just a function outside the class (neither public nor private) that can access the data within the class. The best place to put friend function declarations is along with the rest of your member functions. Many Visual C++ programmers put friend function declarations at the end of the public section because the function is not really part of the class, and the end placement helps distinguish the function from the member functions that come before it.

Listing 10.1 contains a working program with the girls' softball class and the friend function described earlier. Notice that `prData()`'s function definition appears after `main()` and `main()` calls the function. Unlike most non-member functions called by `main()`, you don't have to prototype `prData()` because it is already prototyped in the class at the `friend` declaration.

281

Friends When You Need Them

Listing 10.1. The friend function accesses private data.

```
 1: // Filename: FRND1.CPP
 2: // First program that uses a friend function to access a class's
 3: // private data members.
 4: #include <iostream.h>
 5: #include <iomanip.h>
 6: #include <string.h>
 7: class girlsSoftball {
 8:   char name[25];
 9:   int age;
10:   float batAvg;
11: public:
12:   void init(char N[], int A, float B);
13:   friend void prData(const girlsSoftball pl);
14: };
15: void girlsSoftball::init(char N[], int A, float B)
16: {
17:   strcpy(name, N);
18:   age = A;
19:   batAvg = B;
20: }
21: ////////////////Primary Program Code Follows////////////////////
22: main()
23: {
24:   girlsSoftball player1, player2, player3;
25:   player1.init("Stacy", 12, .344);
26:   player2.init("Judith", 13, .326);
27:   player3.init("Leah", 12, .468);
28:   prData(player1);   // Call friend function
29:   prData(player2);
30:   prData(player3);
31:   return 0;
32: }
33: // Friend function's code appears next
34: void prData(const girlsSoftball pl)   // Friend function
35: {
36:   cout << setprecision(3);
37:   cout << "Player name:    " << pl.name << "\n";
38:   cout << "Player age:     " << pl.age << "\n";
39:   cout << "Player average: " << pl.batAvg << "\n\n";
40: }
```

```
Player name:     Stacy
Player age:      12
Player average:  0.344

Player name:     Judith
Player age:      13
Player average:  0.326

Player name:     Leah
Player age:      12
Player average:  0.468
```

The first place to start the analysis is on line 13, the declaration of the friend function named prData(). The friend function requires an argument list so that prData() knows which object variable to print. The following rule holds true for all friend functions, and it is critical that you understand it:

> *Because friend functions are not member functions, they don't get a copy of the* *this *pointer whereas regular member functions do.*

It is because prData() doesn't get a copy of a *this pointer to the object that you have to pass the object to prData() just as you would any other non-member function. A friend function is not a member function in any sense of the word; a friend function has access to a class's data, but that's its only advantage over non-friend functions. Friend functions always contain some kind of argument list because you have to get object data to them that they can work with.

Never attempt to execute a non-member function with the dot operator like

`player1.prData();`

or Visual C++ will issue this compiler error message:

`error C2039: 'prData' : is not a member of 'girlsSoftball'`

Only member functions can execute by the dot operator; all other functions must be called explicitly and passed any data they have to work with.

A Friend of Two Classes

As mentioned earlier, friend functions are often used to access data from more than one class. Suppose that the softball manager wanted to print a list of players' names from *both* teams, the girls' and boys'. A stand-alone prData() function could do so, but only if it were a friend of both classes. Listing 10.2 shows a program in which such is the case.

Friends When You Need Them

Listing 10.2. A friend of two classes.

```
1:  // Filename: FRND2.CPP
2:  // First program that uses a friend function to access
3:  // two different class's private data members.
4:  #include <iostream.h>
5:  #include <iomanip.h>
6:  #include <string.h>
7:  class boysSoftball;   // Forward reference (prototype)
8:
9:  class girlsSoftball {
10:    char name[25];
11:    int age;
12:    float batAvg;
13: public:
14:    void init(char N[], int A, float B);
15:    friend void prData(const girlsSoftball plG,
          ➥const boysSoftball plB);
16: };
17: void girlsSoftball::init(char N[], int A, float B)
18: {
19:    strcpy(name, N);
20:    age = A;
21:    batAvg = B;
22: }
23: class boysSoftball {
24:    char name[25];
25:    int age;
26:    float batAvg;
27: public:
28:    void init(char N[], int A, float B);
29:    friend void prData(const girlsSoftball plG,
          ➥const boysSoftball plB);
30: };
31: void boysSoftball::init(char N[], int A, float B)
32: {
33:    strcpy(name, N);
33:    age = A;
35:    batAvg = B;
36: }
37:
38: /////////////////Primary Program Code Follows///////////////////
39: main()
40: {
41:    girlsSoftball Gplayer1, Gplayer2, Gplayer3;
42:    boysSoftball Bplayer1, Bplayer2, Bplayer3;
43:    Gplayer1.init("Stacy", 12, .344);
44:    Gplayer2.init("Judith", 13, .326);
45:    Gplayer3.init("Leah", 12, .468);
46:    Bplayer1.init("Jim", 11, .231);
```

```
47:     Bplayer2.init("Michael", 13, .543);
48:     Bplayer3.init("Larry", 12, .345);
49:     prData(Gplayer1, Bplayer1);   // Call friend function
50:     prData(Gplayer2, Bplayer2);
51:     prData(Gplayer3, Bplayer3);
52:     return 0;
53: }
54: // Friend function's code appears next
55: void prData(const girlsSoftball plG, const boysSoftball plB)
56: {
57:     cout << setprecision(3);
58:     cout << "Player name:    " << plG.name << "\n";
59:     cout << "Player age:     " << plG.age << "\n";
60:     cout << "Player average: " << plG.batAvg << "\n\n";
61:     cout << "Player name:    " << plB.name << "\n";
62:     cout << "Player age:     " << plB.age << "\n";
63:     cout << "Player average: " << plB.batAvg << "\n\n";
64: }
```

```
Player name:    Stacy
Player age:     12
Player average: 0.344

Player name:    Jim
Player age:     11
Player average: 0.231

Player name:    Judith
Player age:     13
Player average: 0.326

Player name:    Michael
Player age:     13
Player average: 0.543

Player name:    Leah
Player age:     12
Player average: 0.468

Player name:    Larry
Player age:     12
Player average: 0.345
```

In general, if you understood the program in Listing 10.1, there is not much more to look at here. The friend function now receives two arguments, one for each object it works with. If the friend function were to work with three classes at the same time (there are only two in this program), then all three class variables would have to be passed to the friend function.

285

Friends When You Need Them

Perhaps the most important part of Listing 10.2 is the simple-looking but strangely placed statement on line 7. Line 7 looks as if the boysSoftball class is about to be defined, but as you can see, the statement doesn't define anything. Line 23 begins the definition of the boysSoftball class.

Line 7 is required because of line 15. The friend function requires two different class variables, and one of those variables is a boysSoftball class object; the boysSoftball class, however, is not defined until later in the program. To eliminate a compile-time error, you often have to give a *forward reference* telling Visual C++ that a class will be defined later. Between the forward reference and the class definition, you can use the class to declare arguments and so forth without getting an error on line 15.

In a way, the forward reference is a prototype for a class. Rearranging the boysSoftball class with the girlsSoftball class will not help because the boysSoftball prData() prototype would then contain a forward reference to the girlsSoftball class before it is defined.

Keep in mind that prData() is a regular stand-alone function in the program, callable from main() or from any other function in the program. The friend keyword gives the function access to the private data, but that's the only thing special about the function.

Figure 10.1 shows a diagram of the relationship that prData() has with the two classes. Although prData() lies outside both classes, it has access to the data members.

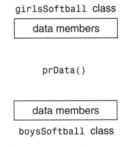

Figure 10.1. The prData() function is a friend of both classes but not a member of either class.

Listing 10.3 adds three more friend functions to the softball program. Each class has its own individual friend function that computes the batting average of each class. And each class shares two friend functions, one that prints the average of both class averages and the prData() friend function shown previously.

286

Type **Listing 10.3. Adding more friend functions.**

```cpp
1:  // Filename: FRND3.CPP
2:  // Adding more friend functions.
3:  #include <iostream.h>
4:  #include <iomanip.h>
5:  #include <string.h>
6:  class boysSoftball;   // Forward reference (prototype)
7:
8:  class girlsSoftball {
9:     char name[25];
10:    int age;
11:    float batAvg;
12: public:
13:    void init(char N[], int A, float B);
14:    friend void gAvg(const girlsSoftball plG[]);
15:    friend void combAvg(const girlsSoftball plG[],
        ↪const boysSoftball plB[]);
16:    friend void prData(const girlsSoftball plG,
        ↪const boysSoftball plB);
17: };
18: void girlsSoftball::init(char N[], int A, float B)
19: {
20:    strcpy(name, N);
21:    age = A;
22:    batAvg = B;
23: }
24: class boysSoftball {
25:    char name[25];
26:    int age;
27:    float batAvg;
28: public:
29:    void init(char N[], int A, float B);
30:    friend void bAvg(const boysSoftball plB[]);
31:    friend void combAvg(const girlsSoftball plG[],
        ↪const boysSoftball plB[]);
32:    friend void prData(const girlsSoftball plG,
        ↪const boysSoftball plB);
33: };
34: void boysSoftball::init(char N[], int A, float B)
35: {
36:    strcpy(name, N);
37:    age = A;
38:    batAvg = B;
39: }
40: ////////////////Primary Program Code Follows////////////////////
41: main()
42: {
43:    girlsSoftball Gplayers[3];
```

continues

Friends When You Need Them

Listing 10.3. continued

```
44:      boysSoftball Bplayers[3];
45:      Gplayers[0].init("Stacy", 12, .344);
46:      Gplayers[1].init("Judith", 13, .326);
47:      Gplayers[2].init("Leah", 12, .468);
48:      Bplayers[0].init("Jim", 11, .231);
49:      Bplayers[1].init("Michael", 13, .543);
50:      Bplayers[2].init("Larry", 12, .645); // New value to raise
                                              ➥average
51:      // Call the friend functions
52:      gAvg(Gplayers);
53:      bAvg(Bplayers);
54:      combAvg(Gplayers, Bplayers);
55:      for (int i=0; i<3; i++)
56:         { prData(Gplayers[i], Bplayers[i]); }
57:      return 0;
58:   }
59: //////////////////////////////////////////////////////////////
60: // Friend functions are listed next
61: void gAvg(const girlsSoftball plG[])
62: {
63:      float gAvg = 0.0;
64:      for (int i=0; i<3; i++)
65:        { gAvg += plG[i].batAvg; }
66:      gAvg /= (float)3.0;
67:      cout << setprecision(3);
68:      cout << "The girls' average is " << gAvg << "\n";
69: }
70: //////////////////////////////////////////////////////////////
71: void bAvg(const boysSoftball plB[])
72: {
73:      float bAvg = 0.0;
74:      for (int i=0; i<3; i++)
75:        { bAvg += plB[i].batAvg; }
76:      bAvg /= (float)3.0;
77:      cout << "The boys' average is " << bAvg << "\n";
78: }
79: //////////////////////////////////////////////////////////////
80: void combAvg(const girlsSoftball plG[], const boysSoftball plB[])
81: {
82:      float totalAv = 0.0;
83:      for (int i=0; i<3; i++)
84:        { totalAv += (plG[i].batAvg + plB[i].batAvg); }
85:      totalAv /= (float)6.0;
86:      cout << "The total average of all six players is " << totalAv
           ➥<< "\n\n";
87: }
88: //////////////////////////////////////////////////////////////
89: void prData(const girlsSoftball plG, const boysSoftball plB)
90: {
91:      cout << "Player name:       " << plG.name << "\n";
```

```
92:     cout << "Player age:     " << plG.age << "\n";
93:     cout << "Player average: " << plG.batAvg << "\n\n";
94:     cout << "Player name:    " << plB.name << "\n";
95:     cout << "Player age:     " << plB.age << "\n";
96:     cout << "Player average: " << plB.batAvg << "\n\n";
97: }
```

Output

```
The girls' average is 0.379
The boys' average is 0.473
The total average of all six players is 0.426

Player name:    Stacy
Player age:     12
Player average: 0.344

Player name:    Jim
Player age:     11
Player average: 0.231

Player name:    Judith
Player age:     13
Player average: 0.326

Player name:    Michael
Player age:     13
Player average: 0.543

Player name:    Leah
Player age:     12
Player average: 0.468

Player name:    Larry
Player age:     12
Player average: 0.645
```

Figure 10.2 shows the relationship of the friend functions and classes in Listing 10.3.

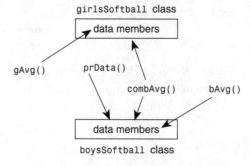

Figure 10.2. The relationship of Listing 10.3's friend functions.

Friends When You Need Them

DO	DON'T

DO use friend functions when a non-member function must work with private data from one or more classes.

DO place the `friend` keyword in the class that is offering the friendship.

DON'T repeat the `friend` keyword before the function's definition itself.

DON'T forget that a friend function cannot be passed a `*this` pointer. Therefore, you must pass object variables to friend functions.

DON'T overdo friend functions, because they are not intended to bypass the safety mechanisms of `private` class declarations.

Friend Classes

In rare instances, you might want to make one class a friend of another class. Doing so gives all the friend class members access to the other class at once. Specifying a friend class requires trickier logic and doesn't lend itself to extremely readable code. Limit your use of friend classes to those classes that need full access to another class.

> **Good Design Might Be at Risk**
>
> Don't overdo the use of friend functions and classes. If you find that one class needs access to all of another class's members, study your class design to make sure that you can't combine the two classes into one.
>
> The `friend` keyword breaks down the private barriers set up by the `class` designation. Friends are needed in some programs, especially when certain operators are being overloaded, as you'll see in tomorrow's chapter. Also, friends help you write functions that work with more than one class.
>
> Nevertheless, if you write enough access functions that return private values from within classes, you can write functions that work with data from more than one class while still maintaining the class barriers.
>
> Some Visual C++ programmers cringe at the use of friends, but they realize that friends do fill a need sometimes (we all get lonely...). Therefore, they

write friend functions, but they use access functions to get private data even though they could access the private data directly. About the only generally accepted use of friend functions is for operator overloading, as you'll see in tomorrow's chapter. There is widespread agreement that one rarely if ever needs to define friend classes.

Listing 10.4 shows a program that contains a class named regClass and one named frndClass. The frndClass is a friend of the other class and therefore has total access to all the members. Notice that the frndClass prData() member function is able to print anything it wants from the other class and can also call a private function from the other class.

Listing 10.4. A friend class has full access to everything.

```
1:  // Filename: FRNDCLS.CPP
2:  // Working with a friend class
3:  #include <iostream.h>
4:  #include <iomanip.h>
5:  #include <string.h>
6:  // First regular class follows
7:  class regClass {
8:    int num;
9:    void trip(void);
10:   // Notice there are NO public members!
11:   void init(int i);
12:   friend class frndClass;
13: };
14:
15: void regClass::trip(void)      // Member function definitions
16: {
17:   cout << "Before the triple, num is " << num << "\n";
18:   num = num * 3;
19:   cout << "num is now " << num << " after tripling.\n";
20: }
21: void regClass::init(int i)
22: {
23:   num = i;
24: }
25: // Friend class follows
26: class frndClass {
27:   regClass classVar;    // A member is another class!
28: public:
29:   void prData(int mainI);
```

continues

Friends When You Need Them

Listing 10.4. continued

```
30: };
31:
32: void frndClass::prData(int mainI)   // Member function definitions
33: {
34:   classVar.init(mainI); // Calls regular class's private function
35:   classVar.trip();
36: }
37: ////////////////////////////////////////////////////////////////////
38: // main() isn't much now because the classes do all the work
39: main()
40: {
41:   frndClass item;
42:   item.prData(25);
43:   return 0;
44: }
```

```
Before the triple, num is 25
num is now 75 after tripling.
```

There are all sorts of tricky things going on here, and trickiness is often a part of embedding friend classes. As you know, your goal should be readable code, not tricky code, but if you find yourself writing lots of friend functions to get around private walls, perhaps a friend class with its own functions could maintain the privatization from the rest of the program while getting to the private members it needs.

In main(), a frndClass object named item is defined on line 41, and that object is used to call the prData() routine on line 42. prData() does little in itself. It takes the value passed from main() and on line 34 calls a private function named init() from the other class. prData() acts like a buffer class between main() and regClass. main() cannot initialize regClass data because there are no public functions in the regClass class. prData() collects main()'s value and passes that value on to the private functions in regClass.

In a way, the frndClass is the go-between between main() and a class whose members are all private. Would it have been better to add some public member functions to regClass? Probably so, but if there were other reasons to keep a class fully private, a friend class could get into that class for other parts of the program and still maintain some kind of controlled integrity to the private class.

 Note: The `frndClass` did not have to be a friend to declare a class member on line 27, but `frndClass` couldn't get to the private parts of `regClass` if it weren't a friend.

Friend classes are one-way paths. In other words, `regClass` is *not* a friend of `frndClass` even though `frndClass` is a friend of `regClass`. If two classes are to be friends of each other, both have to include a friend declaration for the other class. Doing so often creates the need to declare the second class (as done on line 7 of Listing 10.2) before its definition.

DO	DON'T

DO declare friend classes when one class needs access to several or all of the private data members and private member functions of another class.

DON'T forget that the `friend` declaration generates tricky code, and if you find yourself using friend classes a lot, you might need to combine two classes together into one.

Summary

Today's chapter introduces friend functions and friend classes. The chapter is short to give you a breather from yesterday's chapter, but also there is little to friend functions and classes.

Friend functions are useful when a function is to access more than one class. A regular member function can access only the class in which it is defined. However, a friend function of two or more classes can work with the data in all those classes.

A friend function is a function that has full access to a class's private and public members. The friend designation is always described with the `friend` keyword in the class giving the friendship. A friend function is an ordinary function in all respects except for its access to members that it would otherwise not have access to. Therefore, Visual C++ never passes the `*this` pointer to friend functions; if you want a friend function to work with an object (and you usually do), you'll have to pass that object to the friend function.

Friends When You Need Them

A friend class is a class used as a member of another class. If the class that contains the embedded class wants access to the private members (and it usually does), the embedded class must offer its friendship to the class.

The most important reason for limiting `friend` declarations is this: Friend declarations can produce tricky code and create hard-to-follow programs. There are times when overloading operators (explained in tomorrow's chapter) require the use of friends, and you'll learn for certain in those cases when to use friends and when not to. However, for other times, friends generally offer little more than logic problems except when you *must* write functions that use members from more than one class.

Q&A

Q. What is a friend function?

A. A friend function is a function that has access to another class's private members but is not a member function. Friend functions are designated by the `friend` keyword in the class giving its friendship. A function or class cannot be a friend to another class unless that class clearly defines the friend relationship.

Friend functions are most useful when they must access members from more than one class.

Q. Why do I have to pass objects to friend functions but I don't have to pass objects to member functions?

A. Friend functions are *not* member functions. If they were, there would be no need to specify them as a `friend` because they already have access to the private members of the class.

Visual C++ does not automatically pass a `*this` pointer to friend functions, so you'll have to pass all data to a friend that it needs to work with. Keep in mind that friend functions are regular non-member functions, often called by `main()`. Friend functions cannot be triggered by using the dot operator or structure pointer operator as member functions can.

Q. What is the difference between a friend function and a friend class?

A. As the name implies, a friend function is a function that has access to a class's private and public members. That friend function can access, change, and print any data from within the class. A friend class is a separate class that can access all the members of another class.

A friend class contains a member whose type matches that of the original class providing the friendship. If the friend class were not a friend, the friend class could include members of the other class but not access the private members of that other class.

Workshop

The Workshop offers quiz questions and exercises to hone your skills and give you feedback on today's lesson. You'll find some proposed answers in Appendix D.

Quiz

1. If you were writing a program and a function needed to have access to private data members of a class, would you put the `friend` keyword before the function declaration, before the function definition, or inside the class itself?

2. True or False: A friend function can have access to a class's public members but not the private members.

3. Why do you sometimes need to declare a class in advance?

4. Where must a friend function or friend class declaration go: in the private or public section of a class?

5. True or False: Friends often improve the readability of a program.

6. Assuming that `doInit()` is a friend function of a class, why could you not execute `doInit()` like this:

   `aClassVar.doInit();`

Exercise

1. Rewrite Listing 10.2 so that `main()` defines an array of three pointers to each class. Allocate the players on the heap instead of defining individual object variables. Optionally, allocate a linked list with private pointers that point to the next item so that you can eliminate the array of three pointers. Doing so improves your memory usage and enables you to easily add to the program functions and add extra players when needed. (The answer to the optional portion is not trivial and is also not included in the Appendix D answers because of its advanced nature; the linked-list algorithm is outside the scope of this book's goals.)

DAY 11

Introduction to Overloading Operators

Day 11: Introduction to Overloading Operators

Way back on Day 7, you learned about overloaded functions and got a glimpse of overloaded operators. Perhaps you were amazed that you could make Visual C++'s operators behave the way you want them to behave. Operator overloading is one of the primary reasons why programmers move to Visual C++.

Nevertheless, when overloaded operators were introduced on Day 7, you did not know anything about classes, the *this pointer, member functions, and all the parts of Visual C++ that form the basis for OOP. Without OOP, you can overload operators as you read on Day 7, but with OOP, you can really get down to business!

You'll learn starting today (there are so many operators that it takes two days to cover them all) how to overload Visual C++ operators the OOP way. After you understand member functions and friend functions, you'll be able to use overloaded operators that are easier to write than before your introduction to OOP concepts. Virtually every useful Visual C++ program that takes advantage of OOP uses operator overloading because of its power, but more important, because of the ease with which you manipulate class data after you overload operators.

When you increase the capability of Visual C++—and that is exactly what you are doing when you teach the language how to operate on data types that you write—you are *extending* the language. The term *extensibility* is one of those long buzzwords that Visual C++ programmers use a lot. It simply means that you aren't limited to the base language but you can extend the language's behavior.

Today, you learn about the following topics:

- ☐ How to overload math operators using member functions
- ☐ How the *this pointer affects operator overloading
- ☐ How to overload compound operators that update their first operand
- ☐ How to overload the relational and logical operators
- ☐ How to overload increment and decrement operators
- ☐ How to distinguish between increment and decrement operator postfix and prefix functions

Note: You cannot overload the conditional operator, ?:, the scope resolution operator, ::, the dereference operator, *, or the member dot operator, ..

A Quick Review

Recall that Visual C++ enables you to overload operators by writing overloaded functions whose names begin with `operator` and end with the actual operator. For example, the overloaded operator function for addition is `operator+()`, and the overloaded operator for modulus is `operator%()`.

You cannot change the way Visual C++ operators work on built-in data types. You cannot make the plus sign do anything to two integers except add the integers together. Unless you write overloaded operator functions, Visual C++ does not have the capability to operate on your class (or structure) data. You cannot add two class variables together by inserting the plus sign between them because Visual C++ wouldn't understand what it means to add two data types that you created.

> **Note:** It might help to think of the built-in operators as having their own `operator...()` functions. For instance, think of Visual C++ as having an internal `operator+(int, int)` function, an internal `operator/(float, float)` function, and so on. When you write operator functions that contain your own class data types as arguments, you simply overload those functions already built into the compiler. It is through the overloading capability that Visual C++ knows what to do when it sees a plus sign between two integers and a plus sign between two class variables.

However, after you write overloaded operator functions for your classes, then Visual C++ *does* know how to add two class variables or perform any other operation on your class variables because you teach Visual C++ what to do when you write overloaded operator functions.

Listing 11.1 contains a simple class and overloaded `operator+()` function that lets one class variable be added to another. The `operator+()` function is set up to add the integer members together and ignore the floating-point members. Again, an overloaded operator does *whatever* you program it to do. You don't even have to add when overloading the plus sign, but obviously, your programs are more maintainable if you keep the spirit of the original operator intact.

Introduction to Overloading Operators

Note: The class members were all kept public for this example. The next section explains how to write overloaded operator functions using safer private members.

Listing 11.1. A simple overloaded operator program.

```
1:  // Filename: OVCLSMP.CPP
2:  // Simple overloading of a class.
3:  #include <iostream.h>
4:  class aClass {
5:  public:          // All members are public
6:     float x;
7:     int i;
8:     char c;
9:     void init(float X, int I, char C)
10:    {  x = X;
11:       i = I;
12:       c = C;
13:    }
14: };
15: int operator+(const aClass & v1, const aClass & v2);
16: //////////////////////////////////////////////////////////////////
17: main()
18: {
19:    aClass aVar1, aVar2;
20:    int total1, total2;
21:    aVar1.init(12.34, 10, 'a');   // Put data in both class variables
22:    aVar2.init(56.78, 20, 'b');
23:    total1 = operator+(aVar1, aVar2);   // Add them one way
24:    cout << "total1 is " << total1 << "\n";
25:    total2 = aVar1 + aVar2;       // Add the better way
26:    cout << "total2 is " << total2 << "\n";
27:    return 0;
28: }
29: //////////////////////////////////////////////////////////////////
30: // Overloaded plus operator function follows
31: int operator+(const aClass & v1, const aClass & v2)
32: {
33:    return v1.i + v2.i;
34: }
```

```
total1 is 30
total2 is 30
```

Notice that the class variables are added using two different styles in lines 23 and 25. Obviously, it makes more sense to add the class variables using the simple plus sign (line 25) because Visual C++ calls operator+() for you when it sees two class variables between the plus sign.

The arguments are passed to operator+() by reference for efficiency and as constants because operator+() does not modify the variables.

Note: Although it doesn't promote extremely good coding habits, many of the member functions in this book don't receive const arguments, and many don't receive their arguments by reference when it might seem prudent to do so. Lines can get extremely long when argument lists contain the const and & qualifiers. The length of those lines, especially those so long they must be wrapped to the next line, would detract more from your understanding the point at hand than they would help. When writing your own functions, use const for any arguments left unmodified by their receiving functions, and pass by reference whenever you can to improve efficiency.

OOPing the Operator Overloads

The operator...() functions generally are *not* listed outside a class as shown in Listing 11.1. It makes sense to specify overloaded operator functions as members of a class because specific operator functions work on individual class data.

Remember that the primary difference between a member function and a regular non-member function is that the member function is automatically passed the *this pointer. When you first read about the *this pointer on Day 9, you probably didn't think it would keep cropping up as much as it has in today's and yesterday's chapters.

Day 11: Introduction to Overloading Operators

Nevertheless, although you don't directly use the `*this` pointer much, it is vital that you remember it is there passing object data to member functions. The member function call

```
cVar.prData();
```

actually looks like this when the compiler analyzes it:

```
prData(&cVar);
```

And the implementation of the `prData()` member function that you typed like

```
void prData(void)
{
   cout << "The first data item is " << a << "\n";
   cout << "The last data item is " << b << "\n";
}
```

looks like this when the compiler analyzes it:

```
void prData(myClass *this)
{
   cout << "The first data item is " << this->a << "\n";
   cout << "The last data item is " << this->b << "\n";
}
```

Without the `*this` pointer, Visual C++ would not know which object's `a` and `b` to print. Luckily, Visual C++ adds the `*this` pointer behind your back. This way, you can code generic member functions that work on data members by the member names and let the compiler send the appropriate object when compiling the program.

The way that Visual C++ calls overloaded operator functions becomes critical if you really want to master overloaded operators and know them well enough to code them without remembering a bunch of rules. The `operator+()` prototype

```
int operator+(aClass v1, aClass v2);
```

declares what happens when two `aClass` variables appear on each side of the plus sign (the `const` and reference operator are left out to keep the prototype simpler). As Listing 11.1 pointed out, when you add two `aClass` variables together like

```
total = aVar1 + aVar2;
```

Visual C++ actually calls the `operator+()` function like this:

```
total = operator+(aVar1, aVar2);
```

The variable on the left of the plus sign (or whatever operator is being overloaded) is sent as the first argument to `operator+()`, and the variable on the right of the plus sign is sent as the second argument to `operator+()`.

Note: You'll want to make operator...() functions member functions when possible (sometimes, as explained later, the operator...() functions cannot be member functions) because the operator...() functions often work with private data members.

When an operator...() function becomes a member function, the look of the function changes slightly, even though the same method is used to accomplish the overloading. Consider the following class, which contains operator+() as a member function:

```
class aClass {
  float x;   // Private members
  int i;
  char c;
public:
  void init(float X, int I, char C);  // Defined later in code
  int operator+(aClass v2)    // No more first argument!!!
  {
     return i + v2.i;   // this pointer helps out
  }
};
```

Look at the i variable sitting by itself in the operator+() member function. How does Visual C++ know *which* object's i to add to v2's i? The answer is easy if you recall the *this pointer. The Visual C++ compiler acts as though you typed the following class:

```
class aClass {
  float x;   // Private members
  int i;
  char c;
public:
  void init(float X, int I, char C);  // Defined later in code
  int operator+(aClass * this, aClass v2)    // No more first argument!!!
  {
     return this->i + v2.i;   // this pointer helps out
  }
};
```

Never specify the first argument when writing overloaded operator member functions because the first argument of *all* member functions is the *this pointer. (If you were to code the first argument, Visual C++ would see *three* arguments because the *this pointer is always passed to member functions no matter what else you pass to the member functions.) All occurrences of i by itself are preceded with the hidden (and dereferenced) *this pointer, and all occurrences of v2.i are left alone because the v2 overrides the insertion of the *this pointer.

Introduction to Overloading Operators

Now, when you code something like

```
total = var1 + var2;   // Assume var1 and var2 are aClass objects
```

to trigger the execution of the function, Visual C++ converts your statement into the following function call:

```
total = var1.operator+(var2);
```

This function call is actually the following when you rearrange the function call as will the compiler:

```
total = operator+(&var1, var2);
```

Figure 11.1 illustrates this behind-the-scenes behavior more fully.

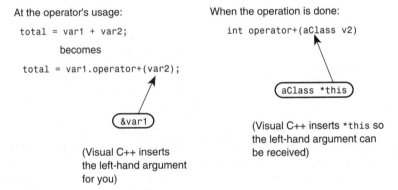

Figure 11.1. The hidden *this pointer provides the lefthand argument for the operator.

Keep Going!

It helps to look at and write a few simple overloaded operator functions before you can fully appreciate the *this pointer background on operator member functions. Use this chapter's overloaded operator...() functions as patterns for your own.

After you write a few overloaded operator member functions, reread the preceding few paragraphs, and you'll perhaps better understand how Visual C++ uses the *this pointer and eliminates your specific receiving of the class variable at the left of the operator's argument list.

Listing 11.2 contains a rewritten version of Listing 11.1 with the operator+() function as a member function inside the class. The class data members can now be private because the operator+() has full access to the class's private data now that operator+() is a member of the class.

Listing 11.2. Using an overloaded member operator+().

```
1:  // Filename: OVCLMEM.CPP
2:  // Using a member function to overload the plus sign.
3:  #include <iostream.h>
4:  class aClass {
5:     float x;    // Private data
6:     int i;
7:     char c;
8:  public:
9:     void init(float X, int I, char C);
10:    int operator+(const aClass & rightArg)
11:    {
12:       return (i + rightArg.i);
13:    }
14:    // The operator+() definition could also be listed outside
15:    // the class using the scope resolution operator as init() is.
16: };
17: void aClass::init(float X, int I, char C)
18:    {  x = X;
19:       i = I;
20:       c = C;
21:    }
22: //////////////////////////////////////////////////////////////
23: main()
24: {
25:    aClass aVar1, aVar2;
26:    int total;
27:    aVar1.init(12.34, 10, 'a');   // Put data in both class variables
28:    aVar2.init(56.78, 20, 'b');
29:    total = aVar1 + aVar2;        // Add using member function
30:    cout << "total is " << total << "\n";
31:    return 0;
32: }
```

```
total is 30
```

Day 11: Introduction to Overloading Operators

 The most important part of the program for you to focus on at this time is in lines 9–13. The left side of the plus sign in line 29 is passed to operator+() as the *this pointer, so you only have to tell the function that the second argument is coming. Every time you reference the i member of the first argument, just use i because there will be a hidden this-> placed in front of the i. You have to specifically tell the member function on line 12 to use the righthand argument when referring to its i inside the function.

> **Don't Forget to Allow Stacking**
>
> You might recall that Day 7's chapter taught you how to write overloaded operator functions that you stack together several times.
>
> For instance, in Listing 11.2's operator+() function, the function returns an integer, so you can use the overloaded plus sign only when an integer result is needed. However, what if you had several objects and wanted to add them all together like this:
>
> ```
> totalCl = aVar1 + aVar2 + aVar3;
> ```
>
> To stack several operations together, you must return a class variable, not a built-in data type. The preceding stacked assignment becomes a nested operator+() function call that gets changed by the compiler to look like this:
>
> ```
> totalCl = operator+(aVar1, operator+(aVar2, aVar3));
> ```
>
> If the innermost operator+() returned an int, Visual C++ would fail trying to find a prototype for this:
>
> ```
> operator+(class aClass, int);
> ```
>
> Therefore, the operator+() has to return a class variable so that the outside operator+() works. The big problem *then* is that you cannot assign the stacked values to an integer, but you have to assign them to another class variable (called totalCl here) unless you have overloaded another member operator+() function whose righthand operand argument is an integer.

Listing 11.3 begins to show the real power of overloaded operators. The nClass contains three integer data members and four floating-point data members. Five class object variables are defined and then added together using stacked plus signs. The program defines the plus sign so that an nClass total variable contains the total of all seven members from the five objects, as illustrated in Figure 11.2.

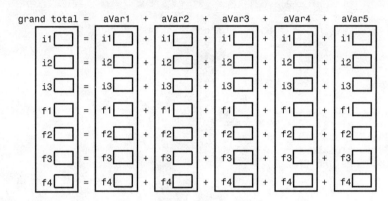

Figure 11.2. The meaning of adding together nClass object variables.

Listing 11.3. Overloading the addition operator and stacking additions together.

```
 1:  // Filename: OVFULL.CPP
 2:  // Overloading (with stacking capability) the plus operator.
 3:  #include <iostream.h>
 4:  #include <iomanip.h>
 5:  class nClass {
 6:    int i1, i2, i3;
 7:    float f1, f2, f3, f4;
 8:  public:
 9:    inline void init(int I1, int I2, int I3, float F1, float F2,
         ➥float F3, float F4);
10:    inline nClass operator+(const nClass & rightArg);
11:    int getI1(void) { return i1; }   // Must have read-access member
12:    int getI2(void) { return i2; }   // functions to print the members
13:    int getI3(void) { return i3; }   // of the total object variable.
14:    float getF1(void) { return f1; }
15:    float getF2(void) { return f2; }
16:    float getF3(void) { return f3; }
17:    float getF4(void) { return f4; }
```

continues

Introduction to Overloading Operators

Listing 11.3. continued

```
18: };
19: void nClass::init(int I1, int I2, int I3, float F1, float F2,
    ➥float F3, float F4)
20: {
21:    i1 = I1; i2 = I2; i3 = I3;
22:    f1 = F1; f2 = F2; f3 = F3; f4 = F4;
23: }
24: nClass nClass::operator+(const nClass & rArg)
25: {
26:    nClass gTotal;
27:    gTotal.i1 = i1 + rArg.i1;
28:    gTotal.i2 = i2 + rArg.i2;
29:    gTotal.i3 = i3 + rArg.i3;
30:    gTotal.f1 = f1 + rArg.f1;
31:    gTotal.f2 = f2 + rArg.f2;
32:    gTotal.f3 = f3 + rArg.f3;
33:    gTotal.f4 = f4 + rArg.f4;
34:    return gTotal;
35: }
36: ////////////////////////////////////////////////////////////////
37: main()
38: {
39:    nClass aVar1, aVar2, aVar3, aVar4, aVar5;
40:    nClass grandTotal;   // Class variable that will hold the total
41:    // Put data in the object variables
42:    aVar1.init(4, 2, 5, 12.34, 10.4, 7.6, 5.3);
43:    aVar2.init(2, 5, 9, 2.47, 7.52, 5.06, 6.2);
44:    aVar3.init(8, 3, 8, 2.03, 11.67, 4.4, 3.9);
45:    aVar4.init(3, 6, 7, 5.3, 4.30, 7.5, 2.1);
46:    aVar5.init(1, 3, 1, 2.8, 5.23, 4.2, 7.7);
47:    // Add using operator member function
48:    grandTotal = aVar1 + aVar2 + aVar3 + aVar4 + aVar5;
49:    cout << setprecision(2) << setiosflags(ios::fixed);
50:    cout << "After adding the objects together, here are";
51:    cout << "\nthe contents of the total variable's members:\n";
52:    cout << "i1: " << grandTotal.getI1() << "\n";
53:    cout << "i2: " << grandTotal.getI2() << "\n";
54:    cout << "i3: " << grandTotal.getI3() << "\n";
55:    cout << "f1: " << grandTotal.getF1() << "\n";
56:    cout << "f2: " << grandTotal.getF2() << "\n";
57:    cout << "f3: " << grandTotal.getF3() << "\n";
58:    cout << "f4: " << grandTotal.getF4() << "\n";
59:    return 0;
60: }
```

```
After adding the objects together, here are
the contents of the total variable's members:
i1: 18
i2: 19
i3: 30
f1: 24.94
f2: 39.12
f3: 28.76
f4: 25.20
```

At first glance, this program might seem intimidating, but the concepts in it are simple. Most of the code is contained in four repetitive sections: the read-access member functions in lines 11–17 (coded inline because they are so short), the adding together of matching members in lines 27–33, the initialization of data in lines 42–46, and the printing of the total object's members in lines 52–58.

The operator+() function in lines 24–35 adds the plus sign's right argument to the *this pointer's variable, which produces the grandTotal value in line 48. Notice how easy it is to add nClass variables.

The local class variable defined on line 26 is needed to hold and return a class value so that operators can be stacked together. After you've learned how to write special functions called *constructors* in Day 13's chapter, "Constructing and Destructing," you'll learn a cleaner way to return class values from overloaded operator functions.

Remember that Visual C++ knows to call the operator+() function whenever an nClass object appears on each side of the plus sign. Later in today's chapter (in the section "Mixing Class and Built-In Data Types"), you'll learn how to write overloaded operator functions that execute when Visual C++ encounters an operator surrounded by your data type and also a built-in data type.

Note: The overloaded operators offer just one additional proof that Visual C++ improves your coding productivity and eliminates the tedious details. Sure, you still have to write the operator...() functions and "define" what you want done when you perform an operation on one of your data types. After you've written an overloaded operator function, however, the rest of the program can use the familiar operator when you want an operation performed, rather than having to remember a bunch of different function names.

Introduction to Overloading Operators

DO	DON'T
DO use overloaded operator functions when you want to perform operations on your own data types that are similar to the built-in operations on built-in data types. **DO** overload as many operator...() functions as you need to in order to perform that operation on all the combinations of data that will appear on each side of the operator.	**DON'T** pass too many arguments when overloading operator member functions. Visual C++ takes care of sending and receiving the *this pointer as it does with all member functions. **DON'T** swerve too far from an operator's original meaning when you overload an operator...() function.

The Remaining Simple Math Operators

There is very little more that can be said about overloading the regular math operators, -, *, /, and %. They overload in a manner similar to the operator+() described in the preceding section. Again, the operator+() function does *whatever* you define it to do, and so do all the other overloaded operator functions.

Just so you can see an example of each overloaded operator, Listing 11.4 expands the preceding listing to include overloaded functions for all five standard math operators (+, -, *, /, and %). The program performs the arithmetic on each member in the class. For example, when you subtract an nClass variable from another, Visual C++ subtracts all the members of one class from the other and stores the resulting values in the class variable being assigned to the answer inside main(). Other than the additional overloaded operator functions, Listing 11.4 includes an extra printing member function to eliminate the class's need for a lot of get...() member functions that simply return single values.

Note: It is because the modulus operator, %, is defined just for integers that the operator%() function works only with integers and returns zeros for the floating-point members in the object answer.

Listing 11.4. Overloading +, -, *, /, and %.

```
1:  // Filename: OVFALL.CPP
2:  // Overloading (with stacking capability) the math operators.
3:  #include <iostream.h>
4:  #include <iomanip.h>
5:  class nClass {
6:     int i1, i2, i3;
7:     float f1, f2, f3, f4;
8:  public:
9:     inline void init(int I1, int I2, int I3, float F1, float F2,
        ➥float F3, float F4);
10:    inline void prData(void);
11:    inline nClass operator+(const nClass & rightArg);
12:    inline nClass operator-(const nClass & rightArg);
13:    inline nClass operator*(const nClass & rightArg);
14:    inline nClass operator/(const nClass & rightArg);
15:    inline nClass operator%(const nClass & rightArg);
16: };
17: void nClass::init(int I1, int I2, int I3, float F1, float F2,
    ➥float F3, float F4)
18: {
19:    i1 = I1; i2 = I2; i3 = I3;
20:    f1 = F1; f2 = F2; f3 = F3; f4 = F4;
21: }
22: void nClass::prData(void)
23: {
24:    cout << setprecision(2) << setiosflags(ios::fixed);
25:    cout << "i1: " << i1 << "\n";
26:    cout << "i2: " << i2 << "\n";
27:    cout << "i3: " << i3 << "\n";
28:    cout << "f1: " << f1 << "\n";
29:    cout << "f2: " << f2 << "\n";
30:    cout << "f3: " << f3 << "\n";
31:    cout << "f4: " << f4 << "\n";
32: }
33: nClass nClass::operator+(const nClass & rArg)
34: {
35:    nClass gTotal;
```

continues

Introduction to Overloading Operators

Listing 11.4. continued

```
36:      gTotal.i1 = i1 + rArg.i1;
37:      gTotal.i2 = i2 + rArg.i2;
38:      gTotal.i3 = i3 + rArg.i3;
39:      gTotal.f1 = f1 + rArg.f1;
40:      gTotal.f2 = f2 + rArg.f2;
41:      gTotal.f3 = f3 + rArg.f3;
42:      gTotal.f4 = f4 + rArg.f4;
43:      return gTotal;
44: }
45: nClass nClass::operator-(const nClass & rArg)
46: {
47:      nClass gTotal;
48:      gTotal.i1 = i1 - rArg.i1;
49:      gTotal.i2 = i2 - rArg.i2;
50:      gTotal.i3 = i3 - rArg.i3;
51:      gTotal.f1 = f1 - rArg.f1;
52:      gTotal.f2 = f2 - rArg.f2;
53:      gTotal.f3 = f3 - rArg.f3;
54:      gTotal.f4 = f4 - rArg.f4;
55:      return gTotal;
56: }
57: nClass nClass::operator*(const nClass & rArg)
58: {
59:      nClass gTotal;
60:      gTotal.i1 = i1 * rArg.i1;
61:      gTotal.i2 = i2 * rArg.i2;
62:      gTotal.i3 = i3 * rArg.i3;
63:      gTotal.f1 = f1 * rArg.f1;
64:      gTotal.f2 = f2 * rArg.f2;
65:      gTotal.f3 = f3 * rArg.f3;
66:      gTotal.f4 = f4 * rArg.f4;
67:      return gTotal;
68: }
69: nClass nClass::operator/(const nClass & rArg)
70: {
71:      nClass gTotal;
72:      gTotal.i1 = i1 / rArg.i1;
73:      gTotal.i2 = i2 / rArg.i2;
74:      gTotal.i3 = i3 / rArg.i3;
75:      gTotal.f1 = f1 / rArg.f1;
76:      gTotal.f2 = f2 / rArg.f2;
77:      gTotal.f3 = f3 / rArg.f3;
78:      gTotal.f4 = f4 / rArg.f4;
79:      return gTotal;
80: }
81: nClass nClass::operator%(const nClass & rArg)
82: {
```

```
 83:    nClass gTotal;
 84:    gTotal.i1 = i1 % rArg.i1;
 85:    gTotal.i2 = i2 % rArg.i2;
 86:    gTotal.i3 = i3 % rArg.i3;
 87:    gTotal.f1 = 0.0;
 88:    gTotal.f2 = 0.0;
 89:    gTotal.f3 = 0.0;
 90:    gTotal.f4 = 0.0;
 91:    return gTotal;
 92: }
 93:
 94: /////////////////////////////////////////////////////////////////////
 95: main()
 96: {
 97:    nClass aVar1, aVar2, aVar3, aVar4, aVar5;
 98:    nClass grandTotal;   // Class variable that will hold the total
 99:    // Put data in the object variables
100:    aVar1.init(4, 2, 5, 12.34, 10.4, 7.6, 5.3);
101:    aVar2.init(2, 5, 9, 2.47, 7.52, 5.06, 6.2);
102:    aVar3.init(8, 3, 8, 2.03, 11.67, 4.4, 3.9);
103:    aVar4.init(3, 6, 7, 5.3, 4.30, 7.5, 2.1);
104:    aVar5.init(1, 3, 1, 2.8, 5.23, 4.2, 7.7);
105:    // Add using operator member function
106:    grandTotal = aVar1 + aVar2 + aVar3 + aVar4 + aVar5;
107:    cout << "After adding the objects together, here are";
108:    cout << "\nthe contents of the total variable's members:\n";
109:    grandTotal.prData();
110:    grandTotal = aVar3 - aVar5;
111:    cout << "After subtracting the fifth object from the third,
       ➥here";
112:    cout << "\nare the contents of the total variable's members:\n";
113:    grandTotal.prData();
114:    grandTotal = aVar1 * aVar2 * aVar3;
115:    cout << "After multiplying the first three objects, here are";
116:    cout << "\nthe contents of the total variable's members:\n";
117:    grandTotal.prData();
118:    grandTotal = aVar4 / aVar2;
119:    cout << "After dividing the 2nd object from the 4th objects, ";
120:    cout << "\nhere are the total variable's members:\n";
121:    cout << "(the integers were divided using integer division)\n";
122:    grandTotal.prData();
123:    grandTotal = aVar3 % aVar4;
124:    cout << "After performing modulus on the 3rd and 4th objects, ";
125:    cout << "\nhere are the total variable's members:\n";
126:    grandTotal.prData();
127:    return 0;
128: }
```

Introduction to Overloading Operators

```
After adding the objects together, here are
the contents of the total variable's members:
i1: 18
i2: 19
i3: 30
f1: 24.94
f2: 39.12
f3: 28.76
f4: 25.20
After subtracting the fifth object from the third, here
are the contents of the total variable's members:
i1: 7
i2: 0
i3: 7
f1: -0.77
f2: 6.44
f3: 0.20
f4: -3.80
After multiplying the first three objects, here are
the contents of the total variable's members:
i1: 64
i2: 30
i3: 360
f1: 61.87
f2: 912.69
f3: 169.21
f4: 128.15
After dividing the 2nd object from the 4th objects,
here are the total variable's members:
(the integers were divided using integer division)
i1: 1
i2: 1
i3: 0
f1: 2.15
f2: 0.57
f3: 1.48
f4: 0.34
After performing modulus on the 3rd and 4th objects,
here are the total variable's members:
i1: 2
i2: 3
i3: 1
f1: 0.00
f2: 0.00
f3: 0.00
f4: 0.00
```

The operator...() member functions coded in lines 33–92 are fairly routine. You'll write lots of them using the same format that you see here. Remember to return the object's data type if you want to stack operators. When you stack them, you'll have to collect the answer in a designated total object (as in line 110) and print what you want from that total variable. Of course, the code body of your own operator...() functions for the common math operators will differ from that in Listing 11.4 depending on your application's specific needs.

It's interesting to note that Visual C++ doesn't even care if you put the *same* variable name on each side of an overloaded operator. If you were to code

```
grandTotal = aVar3 - aVar3;
```

then Visual C++ would put zeros in all of grandTotal's members. You can even zero an object's contents like this:

```
aVar3 = aVar3 - aVar3;   // Subtract from itself
```

The only requirement of Listing 11.4's operator...() functions is that you collect the answer to the operation in a class variable, or stack the operations together with other class variables.

In Listing 11.4, you could never attempt

```
grandTotal = aVar3 - 5;
```

or

```
grandTotal = 3 + aVar3;
```

because there are no overloaded operator member functions that accept both a class variable and an integer. (You'll see how to code such functions in a moment, but it's worth pointing out that friend functions are required to combine built-in data types with your own.)

Overloading Relational and Logical Operators

The relational and logical testing operators return a 1 or 0 indicating whether the test was true or false. Table 11.1 reviews the relational and logical operators. These comparison operators are often used to test to see whether two class variables are equal, greater than, or less than each other. Depending on the format of your class, when a comparison is made, you might want to base the true-false result on only an individual data member out of several other members.

Introduction to Overloading Operators

Table 11.1. The relational and logical operators.

Operator	Name
>	Greater than
<	Less than
==	Equal to
!=	Not equal to
>=	Greater than or equal to
<=	Less than or equal to
&&	AND (logical)
||	OR (logical)

You'll find that you won't overload the logical operators much because they usually fall between two relationals that already return 1 or 0. In other words, the following statement's logical && operator combines two overloaded relational operators:

```
if ((costOfFruit < costOfMeat) && (moneyInPocket <= 10.00))
```

If you properly overload these relational < and <= operators, they return 1 or 0 integers. The built-in && is already designed to work with 1s and 0s without overloading an `operator&&()` function.

After you overload the relational operators, you use the built-in operators to perform comparisons on your own data types. For instance, you might want to compare payroll objects to see whether one employee makes more than another. Although an employee class variable might have 100 members, the comparison could be made on only a single salary member.

Note: Although the bitwise operators aren't included in Table 11.1, you overload them in the same way as shown here for their counterparts. You'll manipulate your own data types using the bitwise operators according to the meaning you want to apply to the overloaded bitwise operators.

If you want to stack several relational and logical operators together, you don't have to do anything different from overloading them for single uses. As shown earlier in this chapter, the regular math operators are often overloaded to return different data types depending on your using them stacked together or individually. A comparison operator in Visual C++ (as in C) always returns an integer result of 1 or 0, and if you stack several, a 1 or 0 return value always works just as it does when you use one of the comparison operators by itself.

The biggest decision you have to make when writing comparison operators is which members are to be included in whatever comparison is being made at the time.

There is one efficiency loss that occurs when you overload logical && and || operators. When Visual C++ sees the `if` statement

```
if (2 == 2) || (a < b)    // Rest of 'if' would follow
```

Visual C++ will *not* evaluate the a < b test because it will compute a True result with the equality comparison of the 2s, and True OR anything else is still True. Short-circuiting logical tests can also occur with the && like this:

```
if ((2 < 2) && (a < b))    // Rest of 'if' would follow
```

In this statement, the 2 < 2 is False, and False AND any other value is False. Visual C++ ignores the a < b and saves a microsecond or two of execution time by bypassing the expression.

No short-circuiting is done when class data appears on either side of the logical operators. Therefore, if `stuff1` and `stuff2` in the statement

```
if (stuff1 || stuff2)    // Rest of 'if' would follow
```

are class variables, Visual C++ will always evaluate both sides of the ||, even if it determines that the left side is True.

The program in Listing 11.5 defines a few payroll objects and then uses overloaded conditional operators to compare the payroll objects to each other. Notice how clean `main()` can become when the comparisons begin. In C or any programming language that includes record data types such as classes and structures, you would have to call functions to compare aggregate data types or individually compare members every time you compared.

Introduction to Overloading Operators

Type Listing 11.5. Overloading the relational operators.

```
1:  // Filename: PAYCOMP.CPP
2:  // Overload comparison relational operators.
3:  #include <iostream.h>
4:  #include <string.h>
5:  class payClass {
6:    char name[25];
7:    float salary;
8:  public:
9:    inline void init(char N[], float S);
10:   inline char * getName(void);
11:   inline int operator<(const payClass & emp);   // Relational
12:   inline int operator>(const payClass & emp);   // operators
13:   inline int operator==(const payClass & emp);
14:   inline int operator!=(const payClass & emp);
15:   inline int operator>=(const payClass & emp);
16:   inline int operator<=(const payClass & emp);
17: };
18: void payClass::init(char N[], float S)
19: {
20:   strcpy(name, N);
21:   salary = S;
22: }
23: char * payClass::getName(void)
24: {
25:   return name;     // Return pointer to the name
26: }
27: // All the comparison operators will compare the salary members
28: int payClass::operator<(const payClass & emp)
29: {
30:   // For review: This function is called like this:
31:   //    if (emp1 < emp2) ...
32:   // The emp1 is passed and dereferenced automatically (as this)
33:   // so its salary member is directly referred to, but emp2's has to
34:   // be received and specified like emp.salary
35:   if (salary < emp.salary)
36:     return 1;      // True
37:   else
38:     return 0;      // False
39: }
40: int payClass::operator>(const payClass & emp)
41: {
42:   if (salary > emp.salary)
43:     return 1;      // True
44:   else
45:     return 0;      // False
46: }
47: int payClass::operator==(const payClass & emp)
48: {
49:   if (salary == emp.salary)
```

```
50:       return 1;        // True
51:    else
52:       return 0;        // False
53: }
54: int payClass::operator!=(const payClass & emp)
55: {
56:    if (salary != emp.salary)
57:       return 1;        // True
58:    else
59:       return 0;        // False
60: }
61: int payClass::operator<=(const payClass & emp)
62: {
63:    if (salary <= emp.salary)
64:       return 1;        // True
65:    else
66:       return 0;        // False
67: }
68: int payClass::operator>=(const payClass & emp)
69: {
70:    if (salary >= emp.salary)
71:       return 1;        // True
72:    else
73:       return 0;        // False
74: }
75: //////////////////////////////////////////////////////////////////
76: main()
77: {
78:    payClass emp1, emp2, emp3, emp4;
79:    // Put data in the object variables
80:    emp1.init("Stacy Miller", 4323.45);
81:    emp2.init("Dean Hiquet", 6534.56);
82:    emp3.init("Richard Short",9345.67);
83:    emp4.init("Lloyd Swadley", 2932.41);
84:    // Perform comparisons
85:    if (emp1 < emp3)
86:       { cout << emp3.getName() << " makes less than "
         ➥<< emp1.getName();
87:         cout << "\n";
88:       }
89:    if (emp2 != emp4)
90:       { cout << emp2.getName() << " and " << emp4.getName()
         ➥<< " don't make ";
91:         cout << "the same salary.\n";
92:       }
93:    if (emp3 > emp4)
94:       { cout << emp3.getName() << " makes more than "
         ➥<< emp4.getName();
95:         cout << "\n";
96:       }
```

continues

Introduction to Overloading Operators

Listing 11.5. continued

```
 97:    if (emp1 >= emp3)
 98:       { cout << emp1.getName() << " makes at least as much as ";
 99:         cout << emp3.getName() << "\n";
100:       }
101:    // Didn't have to overload && to use it between two comparisons
102:    if ((emp3 > emp2) && (emp4 < emp2))
103:       { cout << emp3.getName() << " makes more than "
             << emp2.getName();
104:         cout << " and so does " << emp4.getName() << "\n";
105:       }
106:
107:    return 0;
108: }
```

```
Richard Short makes less than Stacy Miller
Dean Hiquet and Lloyd Swadley don't make the same salary.
Richard Short makes more than Lloyd Swadley
Richard Short makes more than Dean Hiquet and so does Lloyd Swadley
```

Although all the relational operators are overloaded in this program, `main()` doesn't happen to use them all (such as <=). However, you can see how the relational operators (and the logical operators if you had data that needed to be compared with them) are overloaded.

`main()` is just a controller for the comparisons now. It is as easy to compare class objects as it is to compare two integers, demonstrated by lines 85, 89, 93, 97, and 102. All the overloaded relational operator functions return integers to mimic the built-in relational operators as much as possible.

> **Be Careful When Comparing *floats***
>
> As in any programming language, comparing floating-point values for equality is tricky and usually error-prone. The `operator==()` and `operator!=()` functions coded in Listing 11.5 are kept short and consistent with the surrounding overloaded operator functions to help you learn overloading operators.
>
> However, when comparing floating-point values in "real life," compare a range of values instead of comparing for exact equalities or inequalities. For example, the following comparison would catch any internal rounding differences and compare two floating-point values as being "about

equal," which is about all you can do. (The smaller the range of the comparison, the more accurate the equality test will be.)

```
int payClass::operator==(const payClass & emp)
{
  // Make sure salaries are approximately equal
  // due to the natural internal rounding of
  // real numbers inside the computer.
  if ( ((salary - .001) < emp.salary)
        && ((salary + .001) > emp.salary))
    return 1;      // True
  else
    return 0;      // False
}
```

Now, the Compound Operators Are a Snap!

The compound math operators, listed in Table 11.2, are just as easy to overload as the other math operators. When writing overloaded operator functions, think about what is happening with the operators. Although the following statements use different operators, they are equivalent:

```
c = c + 24;
```

and

```
c += 24;
```

(If you add other expressions and variables to the expression, however, the + differs from += because of their different placements in the operator hierarchy.) When you code two values on either side of a compound operator, you want the math operation to be performed and the result to be placed inside the variable on the left. (The left operand to any of the compound operators must be an lvalue.)

Introduction to Overloading Operators

Table 11.2. The compound math operators.

Operator	Name
+=	Compound addition
-=	Compound subtraction
*=	Compound multiplication
/=	Compound division
%=	Compound modulus

Note: The compound bitwise operators aren't discussed in this text, but their overloading is just as straightforward.

The program in Listing 11.6 again shows a class (defined earlier in Listing 11.4) with several integer and floating-point members. Compound operators are overloaded to achieve the same effect as that shown in Figure 11.2. You might want to overload the compound operators so that updating object values is easier to code. Also, if you overload the standard math operators, consider overloading their compound operator equivalents for completeness, although the regular overloaded operators aren't included in Listing 11.6 for the sake of brevity.

There is one difference to look for in this program that didn't appear in any previous overloaded operator. The overloaded compound operator functions require that you specifically return a dereferenced *this pointer.

Listing 11.6. Overloading the compound operators.

```
1:  // Filename: COMPOV.CPP
2:  // Overloading the compound math operators.
3:  #include <iostream.h>
4:  #include <iomanip.h>
5:  class nClass {
6:     int i1, i2, i3;
7:     float f1, f2, f3, f4;
8:  public:
9:  inline void init(int I1, int I2, int I3, float F1, float F2,
    ↪float F3, float F4);
```

```cpp
10:     inline void prData(void);
11:     inline nClass operator+=(const nClass & rightArg);
12:     inline nClass operator-=(const nClass & rightArg);
13:     inline nClass operator*=(const nClass & rightArg);
14:     inline nClass operator/=(const nClass & rightArg);
15:     inline nClass operator%=(const nClass & rightArg);
16: };
17: void nClass::init(int I1, int I2, int I3, float F1, float F2,
    ➥float F3, float F4)
18: {
19:   i1 = I1; i2 = I2; i3 = I3;
20:   f1 = F1; f2 = F2; f3 = F3; f4 = F4;
21: }
22: void nClass::prData(void)
23: {
24:   cout << setprecision(2) << setiosflags(ios::fixed);
25:   cout << "i1: " << i1 << "\n";
26:   cout << "i2: " << i2 << "\n";
27:   cout << "i3: " << i3 << "\n";
28:   cout << "f1: " << f1 << "\n";
29:   cout << "f2: " << f2 << "\n";
30:   cout << "f3: " << f3 << "\n";
31:   cout << "f4: " << f4 << "\n";
32: }
33: nClass nClass::operator+=(const nClass & rArg)
34: {
35:   i1 += rArg.i1;    // Compound adding to  this pointer's data
36:   i2 += rArg.i2;
37:   i3 += rArg.i3;
38:   f1 += rArg.f1;
39:   f2 += rArg.f2;
40:   f3 += rArg.f3;
41:   f4 += rArg.f4;
42:   return *this;
43: }
44: nClass nClass::operator-=(const nClass & rArg)
45: {
46:   i1 -= rArg.i1;    // Compound subtracting from this pointer's data
47:   i2 -= rArg.i2;
48:   i3 -= rArg.i3;
49:   f1 -= rArg.f1;
50:   f2 -= rArg.f2;
51:   f3 -= rArg.f3;
52:   f4 -= rArg.f4;
53:   return *this;
54: }
55: nClass nClass::operator*=(const nClass & rArg)
56: {
57:   i1 *= rArg.i1;    // Compound multiplying to this pointer's data
```

continues

Introduction to Overloading Operators

Listing 11.6. continued

```
58:        i2 *= rArg.i2;
59:        i3 *= rArg.i3;
60:        f1 *= rArg.f1;
61:        f2 *= rArg.f2;
62:        f3 *= rArg.f3;
63:        f4 *= rArg.f4;
64:        return *this;
65: }
66: nClass nClass::operator/=(const nClass & rArg)
67: {
68:        i1 /= rArg.i1;      // Compound dividing to  this pointer's data
69:        i2 /= rArg.i2;
70:        i3 /= rArg.i3;
71:        f1 /= rArg.f1;
72:        f2 /= rArg.f2;
73:        f3 /= rArg.f3;
74:        f4 /= rArg.f4;
75:        return *this;
76: }
77: nClass nClass::operator%=(const nClass & rArg)
78: {
79:        i1 %= rArg.i1;      // Compound modulus on this pointer's data
80:        i2 %= rArg.i2;
81:        i3 %= rArg.i3;
82:        f1 = 0.0;
83:        f2 = 0.0;
84:        f3 = 0.0;
85:        f4 = 0.0;
86:        return *this;
87: }
88: /////////////////////////////////////////////////////////////////////
89: main()
90: {
91:     nClass aVar1, aVar2, aVar3, aVar4, aVar5;
92:     // Put data in the object variables
93:     aVar1.init(4, 2, 5, 12.34, 10.4, 7.6, 5.3);
94:     aVar2.init(2, 5, 9, 2.47, 7.52, 5.06, 6.2);
95:     aVar3.init(8, 3, 8, 2.03, 11.67, 4.4, 3.9);
96:     aVar4.init(3, 6, 7, 5.3, 4.30, 7.5, 2.1);
97:     aVar5.init(1, 3, 1, 2.8, 5.23, 4.2, 7.7);
98:     // Use the overloaded operator member functions
99:     aVar1 += aVar2;
100:    cout << "After updating aVar1 with aVar2's values (using +=),";
101:    cout << "\nhere are the contents of aVar1's members:\n";
102:    aVar1.prData();
103:    // Put aVar1 back the way it was
104:    aVar1 -= aVar2;
105:    cout << "\nAfter updating aVar1 with aVar2's values (using -=),";
106:    cout << "\nhere are the contents of aVar1's members:\n";
```

```
107:    aVar1.prData();
108:    // Update aVar2 by multiplying
109:    aVar2 *= aVar3;
110:    cout << "\nAfter updating aVar2 with aVar3's values (using *=),";
111:    cout << "\nhere are the contents of aVar2's members:\n";
112:    aVar2.prData();
113:    // Put them back by dividing
114:    aVar2 /= aVar3;
115:    cout << "\nAfter updating aVar2 with aVar3's values (using /=),";
116:    cout << "\nhere are the contents of aVar2's members:\n";
117:    aVar2.prData();
118:    // Perform a modulus update on the integer members of aVar4
119:    aVar4 %= aVar1;
120:    cout << "\nAfter updating aVar4's members with aVar1's values ";
121:    cout << "(using %=), \nhere are aVar2's members:\n";
122:     aVar4.prData();
123:    return 0;
124:}
```

```
After updating aVar1 with aVar2's values (using +=),
here are the contents of aVar1's members:
i1: 6
i2: 7
i3: 14
f1: 14.81
f2: 17.92
f3: 12.66
f4: 11.5

After updating aVar1 with aVar2's values (using -=),
here are the contents of aVar1's members:
i1: 4
i2: 2
i3: 5
f1: 12.34
f2: 10.4
f3: 7.6
f4: 5.3

After updating aVar2 with aVar3's values (using *=),
here are the contents of aVar2's members:
i1: 16
i2: 15
i3: 72
f1: 5.01
f2: 87.76
f3: 22.26
f4: 24.18
```

Introduction to Overloading Operators

```
After updating aVar2 with aVar3's values (using /=),
here are the contents of aVar2's members:
i1: 2
i2: 5
i3: 9
f1: 2.47
f2: 7.52
f3: 5.06
f4: 6.2

After updating aVar4's members with aVar1's values (using %=),
here are aVar2's members:
i1: 3
i2: 0
i3: 2
f1: 0.00
f2: 0.00
f3: 0.00
f4: 0.00
```

Every overloaded compound operator function shown here returns a dereferenced this value (lines 42, 53, 64, 75, and 86). Think about what's going on, and you'll understand the need to return the object (via *this). By their definitions, compound operators assign values to their left operands. When Visual C++ executes the statement

```
a += b;
```

Visual C++ takes the left operand, the a, and then adds the right operand, b, to a. The left operand is always changed (and, therefore, always must be an lvalue). Although the member functions you saw previously could access the left operand's members, they didn't need to return a modified left operand.

Also, don't be concerned that member functions sometimes use *this but never define the *this pointer explicitly. Visual C++ passes the *this pointer, receives it, and properly defines it for you. Usually, the *this pointer stays behind the curtains from the cover of your source, but you sometimes have to use the *this pointer directly as shown here.

Where's the Assignment Operator, =?

You won't find an overloaded equal sign in this chapter. There are many times, however, when you want to assign objects to other objects in ways that aren't defined by the memberwise default assignment performed by

Visual C++. You can overload the equal sign, but there are extra considerations when doing so that you're not quite ready for. You'll learn how to overload the equal sign on Day 13.

Although overloading the equal sign is fairly straightforward, it is too close in nature to two other Visual C++ topics, regular constructors and copy constructors, to discuss here. You'll learn about all these topics together where they logically belong, on Day 13, "Constructing and Destructing."

DO | DON'T

DO overload compound operators if you overload their regular equivalent operators. In other words, if you overload multiplication, *, also overload compound multiplication, *=. Doing so is not a requirement, but you'll improve the richness of the class.

DO return a dereferenced *this pointer when overloading compound operators. Compound operators must return a modified copy of their lefthand operand.

DON'T expect perfect results when comparing floating-point (or double floating-point) values. It is difficult representing real numbers at the computer's binary level. Compare against a small range of values so that you'll test for "approximate equality" rather than exact equality.

DON'T overload the logical operators and then expect to see the short-circuiting efficiency feature that occurs when && or || are surrounded with built-in operators. Visual C++ must evaluate both sides of overloaded logical operators, even though it doesn't have to for regular built-in data types using the same operators.

DON'T attempt to overload the assignment operator, =, just yet. That comes on Day 13.

Introduction to Overloading Operators

Mixing Class and Built-In Data Types

Although you cannot change the way operators work on built-in data types, you *can* change the way operators work on combinations of your data types and the built-in data types. Consider for a moment that you have customer objects defined in a program and that each customer is assigned a special discount based on his or her buying history and economic conditions. The customer class might look something like this:

```
class Cust {
  char name[25];
  char custCode[5];
  float outBalance;
  int timesPurchased;
  float discPercent;       // We're interested in this now
public:
  // The public member functions would go here
};
```

You could create an array of customer objects like this:

```
Cust customers[100];
```

Assuming that you are having an exceptional year, you decide to increase each customer's discount by 10 percent over current levels. To increase a value by 10 percent, you multiply it by 1.10. For example, 25 times 1.10 is 27.5. The following loop would increase each customer's discount by 10 percent, assuming that you overloaded the * operator to handle the discount increase:

```
for (int c=0; c<100; c++)
  { customers[c] = customers[c] * 1.10; }
```

(Of course, a compound *= operator would be cleaner, but we're keeping this extra simple just to demonstrate the current topic.)

Here is another way to accomplish the same discount increase:

```
for (int c=0; c<100; c++)
  { customers[c] = 1.10 * customers[c]; }
```

The only difference between the two routines is the location of the 1.10 constant. In the first routine, the 1.10 appears after the * operator, and in the second routine, the 1.10 appears before the *.

What kind of overloaded operator*() member function is needed? You'll have to define an operator*() function to receive a Cust and a float value for the first routine.

That's easy. When Visual C++ sees customers[c] * 1.10, it calls the function operator*(&customers[c], 1.10) and looks for a corresponding operator*(*this, float) function. (When you wrote the function, you didn't specify *this, but you knew that the compiler would add it for you.) Here's an overloaded * operator member function that might handle the first routine:

```
Cust operator*(float f)
{
  Cust tempCust;
  tempCust.discPercent = discPercent * f;
  return tempCust;   // (You could have used *this also)
}
```

By now, it should come as no surprise to you that Visual C++ changes this member function into this during compilation:

```
Cust operator*(Cust *this, float f)
{
  Cust tempCust;
  tempCust.discPercent = this->discPercent * f;
  return tempCust;   // (You could have used *this also)
}
```

It turns out that to write an overloaded operator function for the second routine takes a completely different kind of overloaded operator function! To overload the second operator, with a float as the first argument and a Cust class as the second, you must use a friend function and not a member function.

The following member function is just a mirror-image of the preceding one, but it will not work for multiplying a float times a Cust:

```
Cust operator*(float f, Cust c)     // INVALID!
{
  Cust tempCust;
  tempCust.discPercent = c.discPercent * f;
  return tempCust;   // (You could have used *this also)
}
```

Think for a moment why this function won't work. Here's a hint: It's a *member* function. Visual C++ sticks the *this pointer in *every* member function, even when you don't want the *this pointer there! Visual C++ would convert the preceding function, if it were a member function, to this:

```
Cust operator*(Cust *this, float f, Cust c)     // INVALID!
{
  Cust tempCust;
  tempCust.discPercent = c.discPercent * f;
  return tempCust;   // (You could have used *this also)
}
```

Introduction to Overloading Operators

After the *this pointer is added, there is no way that Visual C++, through function overloading, will match this operator*() with the expression 1.10 * customers[c]. Therefore, you need a function that is *not* passed the *this pointer but one that still has access to private members of the class. Friend functions fill that need nicely.

Remember that friend functions have full access to private class members, but they never get passed a *this pointer. Although this means you must specifically receive both arguments in the friend function whereas most operator member functions need only one argument from you, the friend function always enables you to combine a built-in data type with a derived data type when the built-in data type appears to the left of the operator.

Here is the class and friend function that enables you to multiply 1.10 times a Cust object:

```
class Cust {
  char name[25];
  char custCode[5];
  float outBalance;
  int timesPurchased;
  float discPercent;    // We're interested in this now
public:
  friend Cust operator+(float f, Cust c);
  // The public member functions would go here
};
// The following function is NOT part of the class
friend Cust operator+(float f, Cust c)
{
  Cust tempCust;
  tempCust.discPercent = f * c.discPercent;
  return tempCust;   // (You could have used *this also)
}
```

The bottom line is this: If you ever need a built-in data type on the left side of an operator and your own data type on the right, you'll have to overload a friend operator function so that the *this pointer doesn't get in your way.

Overloading ++ and --

The increment and decrement unary operators are easy to overload. The most important consideration to give them is that they require only one operand (only a single lvalue is incremented or decremented by the ++ and -- operators), and that operand is always a dereferenced *this pointer. You therefore never explicitly pass arguments to operator++() and operator--() functions unless you write them as friend functions.

However, there are two sets of increment and decrement operators: postfix and prefix. Visual C++ (beginning back in version 2.0) enables you to distinguish between overloaded increment and decrement operators by inserting the int keyword in the overloaded increment and decrement member functions' argument lists. The int is there only to distinguish between postfix and prefix. Therefore, most Visual C++ programs that include overloaded increment and decrement operator member functions include four of them, prototyped here:

```
className operator++(void);      // Prefix ++
className operator++(int);       // Postfix ++
className operator--(void);      // Prefix --
className operator--(int);       // Postfix --
```

You can code each set the same or differently depending on whether you want a different routine to execute when the user uses postfix or prefix. Again, the int is there just for the determination of postfix and prefix. You'll *never* pass an integer to these functions. Therefore, if you increment an nClass variable named aVar1 like

```
aVar1++;        // Postfix
```

then Visual C++ calls the member function prototyped like this:

```
className operator++(int);       // Postfix ++
```

But if you increment aVar1 like

```
++aVar1;        // Prefix
```

then Visual C++ calls the member function prototyped like this:

```
className operator++(void);      // Prefix ++
```

The program in Listing 11.7 includes a set of increment and a set of decrement operator member functions for the nClass class used in some previous listings. The increment and decrement are applied to all integer members within the class. The overloaded member functions could have been written to increment the floating-point members as well, but the next section of the chapter explains more about applying these overloaded operators to floats.

Just to show you that the compiler distinguishes between prefix and postfix, a message is printed to let you know which is called, even though the same operation code appears in both increment functions and both decrement functions.

Introduction to Overloading Operators

> **Note:** As with the compound operators, both ++ and -- operate on an lvalue (they change the operand that triggers their execution). Therefore, overloaded increment and decrement member functions always return *this.

Listing 11.7. Overloading increments and decrements.

```
1:  // Filename: INCDECOV.CPP
2:  // Overloading increments and decrements
3:  #include <iostream.h>
4:  #include <iomanip.h>
5:  class nClass {
6:    int i1, i2, i3;
7:    float f1, f2, f3, f4;
8:  public:
9:    inline void init(int I1, int I2, int I3, float F1, float F2,
        float F3, float F4);
10:   inline void prData(void);
11:   inline nClass operator++();  // No argument needed for prefix
12:   inline nClass operator--();
13:   inline nClass operator++(int);  // int argument needed for postfix
14:   inline nClass operator--(int);
15:   };
16: void nClass::init(int I1, int I2, int I3, float F1, float F2,
       float F3, float F4)
17: {
18:   i1 = I1; i2 = I2; i3 = I3;
19:   f1 = F1; f2 = F2; f3 = F3; f4 = F4;
20: }
21: void nClass::prData(void)
22: {
23:   cout << setprecision(2) << setiosflags(ios:: fixed);
24:   cout << "\ni1: " << i1 << "       " << "i2: " << i2 << "        ";
25:   cout << "i3: " << i3;
26:   cout << "\nf1: " << f1 << "     " << "f2: " << f2 << "     ";
27:   cout << "f3: " << f3 << "\n";
28:   cout << "f4: " << f4 << "\n";
29: }
30: nClass nClass::operator++()       // No argument needed for prefix
31: {
32:   cout << "(prefix ++ being done...)\n";
33:   i1++;
34:   i2++;
```

```
35:     i3++;    // Leave all float members alone
36:     return *this;
37: };
38: nClass nClass::operator--()      // No argument needed for prefix
39: {
40:     cout << "(prefix -- being done...)\n";
41:     i1--;
42:     i2--;
43:     i3--;    // Leave all float members alone
44:     return *this;
45: };
46: nClass nClass::operator++(int)    // Ignore the postfix int argument
47: {
48:     cout << "(postfix ++ being done...)\n";
49:     i1++;
50:     i2++;
51:     i3++;    // Leave all float members alone
52:     return *this;
53: };
54: nClass nClass::operator--(int)    // Ignore the postfix int argument
55: {
56:     cout << "(postfix -- being done...)\n";
57:     i1--;
58:     i2--;
59:     i3--;    // Leave all float members alone
60:     return *this;
61: };
62: //////////////////////////////////////////////////////////////
63: main()
64: {
65:     nClass aVar1, aVar2, aVar3, aVar4;
66:     // Put data in the object variables
67:     aVar1.init(4, 2, 5, 12.34, 10.4, 7.6, 5.3);
68:     aVar2.init(2, 5, 9, 2.47, 7.52, 5.06, 6.2);
69:     aVar3.init(8, 3, 8, 2.03, 11.67, 4.4, 3.9);
70:     aVar4.init(3, 6, 7, 5.3, 4.30, 7.5, 2.1);
71:     aVar1++;
72:     ++aVar2;
73:     aVar3--;
74:     --aVar4;
75:     // Show that overloaded functions worked
76:     aVar1.prData();
77:     aVar2.prData();
78:     aVar3.prData();
79:     aVar4.prData();
80:     return 0;
81: }
```

Introduction to Overloading Operators

```
(postfix ++ being done...)
(prefix ++ being done...)
(postfix -- being done...)
(prefix -- being done...)

i1: 5        i2: 3         i3: 6
f1: 12.34    f2: 10.40     f3: 7.60
f4: 5.30

i1: 3        i2: 6         i3: 10
f1: 2.47     f2: 7.52      f3: 5.06
f4: 6.20

i1: 7        i2: 2         i3: 7
f1: 2.03     f2: 11.67     f3: 4.40
f4: 3.90

i1: 2        i2: 5         i3: 6
f1: 5.30     f2: 4.30      f3: 7.50
f4: 2.10
```

Look in the initialization lines 67–70 to find the original values for the `i1` through `i3` variables. The increment and decrement operators were not overloaded here to do anything with the floating-point values. You can see from the four printed messages at the top of the output that each postfix and prefix version of the increment and decrement operators were called.

The overloaded postfix operator functions don't use the `int` argument because it is there just to let Visual C++ know that the function is postfix.

More Hints of Extensibility

Have you ever wished you could apply the increment and decrement operators to floating-point and double floating-point variables? You can by creating specialized classes that contain the data type (`float` or whatever) for which you want to apply a customized operator. After you see some of the ways that Visual C++ customizes how operators work with your data, you'll understand why the entire data processing industry seems to be migrating to C++.

The program in Listing 11.8 contains two classes: `Float` (the first letter is capitalized to distinguish it from the built-in `float`) and `charAlph`. You can apply increment and decrement to any variable defined as a `Float` because a set of overloaded operators (prefix only to retain some brevity here) is included to handle the incremented and decremented floating-point values. Also, `charAlph` objects show how incrementing and decrementing *character* data is possible. When a charAlph object is incremented or decremented, the next highest or lowest alphabetic character is stored in the object. If an attempt is made to decrement before A or increment after Z, the appropriate overloaded operator wraps around to the last or first of the alphabet (A decrements to Z, and Z increments to A).

Listing 11.8. Extending the normal operation of floats and chars.

```
1:  // Filename: FLTCHAR.CPP
2:  // Overload a float-like class and a special alphabetic-only class
3:  #include <iostream.h>
4:  #include <iomanip.h>
5:  class Float {       // Will simulate a special floating-point
6:     float f;
7:  public:
8:     void init(float F) {f = F;}   // Inline because it is short
9:     inline Float operator++(void);
10:    inline Float operator--(void);
11:    float getFloat(void) { return f; };
12: };
13: Float Float::operator++(void)    // Adds 1 to the float
14: {
15:    f += (float)1.0;
16:    return *this;
17: }
18: Float Float::operator--(void)    // Subtracts 1 from the float
19: {
20:    f -= (float)1.0;
21:    return *this;
22: };
23: // Second class next
24: class charAlph {
25:    char c;
26: public:
27:    void init(char C) {c = C;}   // Inline because it is short
28:    inline charAlph operator++(void);
29:    inline charAlph operator--(void);
30:    char getAlph(void) { return c; }
31: };
32: charAlph charAlph::operator++(void)
33: {
34:    if (c == 'Z')
35:       c = 'A';
36:    else
37:       c++;      // Visual C++ will add an ASCII 1 to the character
38:    return *this;
39: }
```

continues

Day 11: Introduction to Overloading Operators

Listing 11.8. continued

```
40: charAlph charAlph::operator--(void)
41: {
42:   if (c == 'A')
43:     c = 'Z';
44:   else
45:     c--; // Visual C++ will subtract an ASCII 1 from the character
46:   return *this;
47: }
48: ///////////////////////////////////////////////////////////////////
49: main()
50: {
51:   Float fVal;
52:   charAlph initial;
53:   fVal.init(34.5);
54:   cout << "Before increment, fVal is " << fVal.getFloat() << "\n";
55:   ++fVal;
56:   cout << "After increment, fVal is " << fVal.getFloat() << "\n";
57:   --fVal;
58:   cout << "After decrement, fVal is " << fVal.getFloat() << "\n\n";
59:   initial.init('Y');
60:   cout << "Before increment, initial is " << initial.getAlph()
        ➥<< "\n";
61:   ++initial;
62:   cout << "After increment, initial is " << initial.getAlph()
        ➥<< "\n";
63:   ++initial;
64:   cout << "Incrementing initial again produces "
        ➥<< initial.getAlph() << "\n";
65:   --initial;
66:   cout << "After decrementing, initial is " << initial.getAlph()
        ➥<< "\n";
67:   return 0;
68: }
```

```
Before increment, fVal is 34.5
After increment, fVal is 35.5
After decrement, fVal is 34.5

Before increment, initial is Y
After increment, initial is Z
Incrementing initial again produces A
After decrementing, initial is Z
```

Perhaps little more has to be said about this program than that it gives you some insight in writing your own *type-safe* data types. That is, you now have the power to create data classes that protect themselves and act the way you want them to.

In a couple of days, you'll learn how to write completely self-governing classes, such as charAlph here, that never accept values other than those that fall within the ranges you specify. For example, you could write your own integer class that prints an error message if any value is assigned that is outside the normal range of int data. You will also be able to write true alpha-like data types that accept and work only with alphabetic characters, just as Listing 11.8 begins to do with the increment and decrement operator member functions.

DO	DON'T

DO feel free to overload operators so that they work with a built-in data type and your own data type. Many Visual C++ programs contain three sets of overloaded operator functions: one set handles two class variables of the same type, one set handles a built-in data type used as the left operand, and the third set handles a built-in data type used as the right operand.

DO write friend functions when the left operand is a built-in data type. You cannot use a member function to overload such operations because the *this pointer gets in the way.

DON'T overload the prefix increment and decrement functions without overloading postfix as well, unless you're sure that both kinds won't be used.

DON'T use an argument name after int in postfix increment and decrement functions or you'll receive a compiler warning from Visual C++.

Summary

You've mastered the primary discussion about overloaded operators. About 75 percent of all the operators you ever overload will use code that mirrors the examples from this chapter. Although there is more to learn about operator overloading (and the remaining operator overloading material will be saved for tomorrow's chapter), you now have a good part of operator overloading behind you.

In today's chapter, you learn how to overload all the primary math operators, using them as member functions. When using member functions, don't pass the first operand because of the *this pointer that's passed for you by Visual C++. As long as you want to use operators that work with your data types, or a combination of your data type and a built-in data type, Visual C++ enables you to overload functions to handle the job.

It makes sense to use member functions for overloaded operator functions as much as possible because the functions must have access to private data members.

Overloading the relational and logical operators simply requires that you return an integer True or False (1 or 0) value. The comparison operator functions actually compare internal members from the class variables on either side. Remember, though, that the short-circuiting feature of the built-in logical operators won't apply to expressions you've overloaded.

Although this chapter didn't show a specific example, you can overload an operator to operate on variables from two different classes. Simply make sure that the argument in the overloaded operator function contains the second class's data type.

Finally, overloading increment and decrement operations is easy. You don't even have to specify an argument because these operators are unary operators and `*this` is passed automatically. By inserting the `int` keyword inside the argument list (with no argument name after `int`), you indicate that the function is postfix rather than the default prefix.

Q&A

Q. What's the difference between overloading using regular functions, as learned on Day 7, and overloading using member functions?

A. Member functions never need to be passed the first operand. Visual C++ always passes the first operand as the hidden `*this` pointer, so you specify only the right operand (if you aren't overloading the unary increment and decrement operators that take only one operand) in the overloaded operator function's argument list.

There are times when you'll still use non-member functions to overload operators (when using friend functions). However, the increment and decrement operators, as well as operators that work solely on two of your own data types, should always be member functions; you won't have to worry about passing the left operand as an argument.

Q. Why do some overloaded operator member functions return *this?

A. You must always remember that some operators, such as the compound operators and the increment and decrement operators, change their left operand. The statement

aVar += aVarNew;

changes aVar. It is said that the compound operators (and the increment and decrement as well) *update* one of their operands. The *this pointer always holds a pointer to the first operand. After updating the first operand, you must return that operand with its new value so that the compiler will retain the newly updated value in the program's variable.

Q. When would I ever use a friend function for an overloaded operator function?

A. Remember that the *this pointer is never passed to friend functions because friend functions are stand-alone non-member functions. The only difference between a friend function and any other function that appears after main() is that a friend function has access to a class's private members.

When you want to overload an operator to work on a built-in data type as the left operand and one of your own data types, you have to specify that the function be a friend function or else the *this pointer that is always passed as a first argument will get in the way.

Q. How does Visual C++ distinguish between postfix and prefix increment and decrement overloaded operator functions?

A. If you want to overload an increment or decrement operator using a member function, insert int inside the parentheses of the function like this:

```
aClass operator++(int)     // Postfix
{
  member1++;
  member2++;
  member3 += 1.0;
  return *this;
}
```

The int lets Visual C++ know that it should call this increment when a postfix operator is applied to an aClass object like this:

aVar++;   // Add 1 with a postfix operator function

Introduction to Overloading Operators

Workshop

The Workshop offers quiz questions and exercises to hone your skills and give you feedback on today's lesson. You'll find some proposed answers in Appendix D.

Quiz

1. How many arguments do most overloaded operator member functions take (not counting increment and decrement member functions)?
2. How does Visual C++ know which operator function to call if you've coded more than one?
3. What are the names of the prefix increment overloaded function and the postfix increment overloaded function?
4. Explain why overloaded logical operators don't always perform as efficiently as regular built-in logical operators.
5. What data type should overloaded relational and logical operators have to return?
6. Would the following prototype be used for prefix or postfix decrement?

    `aClass operator--(int);`

7. What is usually the return data type of overloaded operators that you want to stack together like this:

    `aClassVar = aClassVar1 + aClassVar2 + aClassVar3 + aClassVar4;`

8. What does the return statement usually look like for overloaded compound operator and overloaded increment/decrement functions?
9. How does *this sometimes get in your way?
10. Why shouldn't you put an argument name after int when overloading postfix operators?

Exercises

1. Rewrite the program in Listing 11.8 so that lowercase letters will be "safe" as well (the a would wrap around to z, and z would wrap around to a).
2. Write a program with a class that has two private integer values. Overload the logical operators, && and ||, so that True or False results if both integers of objects on both sides of the logical operators have non-zero values.

DAY 12

Extending Operator Overloads

Day 12: Extending Operator Overloads

Today's chapter explains how to overload the remaining operators, including I/O operators such as <<, >>, and the I/O manipulators. You'll also see some additional ways you can use overloading to make Visual C++ do exactly what you want it to do.

The primary reason for overloading operators is to make your programming life easier. When you overload operators, you can concentrate on the application details of your program (the program's goals) instead of worrying about lots of details.

Isn't it easier to use + than to remember `addEmps()`, `addCusts()`, `addVendors()`, `addInventory()`, and so on? Of course, you have to initially write the code that performs the overloading details on the class data, but after you do, the rest of the program is much more straightforward, and you'll find yourself reusing the same code from certain overloaded operator functions among several programs.

Today, you learn about the following topics:

- ☐ How to overload << to output your own class data
- ☐ How to overload >> to input your own class data
- ☐ How to write your own I/O manipulators
- ☐ How to overload subscripts

Note: Some of the concepts in today's chapter will be improved on after you learn the material in tomorrow's chapter, "Constructing and Destructing." Many of the details found so far in the book, such as long initialization routines in the primary part of the program, will be eliminated after tomorrow's chapter.

Overloading Input and Output Operators

Overloading I/O forms the epitome of operator overloading. After you learn how to overload << and >>, you'll be inputting and outputting entire class variables in single statements such as

```
cin >> employee;   // This cin could possibly ask for 50 members
```

and

```
cout << employee;
```

In one sense, << and >> are already overloaded. Consider this statement:

```
i = u << 3;    // Bitwise left-shift
```

The << used in this statement is a bitwise left-shift operator. You might have never used the bitwise operators in your programming career. Many C and C++ programmers program for years and never need them. Nevertheless, the statement shown here works at the internal bit level of memory. The internal bit representation of u is shifted to the left three places (zeros fill in from the right), and the result is stored in the variable i (u is left unchanged).

Now, consider how this next statement differs from the preceding bitwise statement:

```
cout << i << u << 3;
```

You now know that the cout object is the standard output device, normally the screen. Therefore, the << insertion operator tells Visual C++ to send the values of i, u, and then 3 to the screen. (There won't be any spacing between the output values.)

How does Visual C++ know that the first use of << meant bitwise left-shift and the second use of << meant output? Visual C++ contains its own built-in overloaded operator functions. Although you cannot access the code, internally Visual C++ contains these overloaded operator function prototypes:

```
friend int operator<<(int, int);
```

and

```
ostream & operator<<(int);
```

Note: These prototypes are intentionally left simpler than the true internal prototypes really appear.

You can guess that the bitwise << is a friend function (unless you write an overloaded << that takes a class for an operand), because an integer appears as the left operand. You learned in yesterday's chapter that a friend function is needed any time an operator's left operand is a non-class variable.

The second prototype implies that a simple output statement such as

```
cout << 10;
```

343

Day 12: Extending Operator Overloads

actually becomes this overloaded operator function:

```
cout.operator<<(10);
```

(The compiler would then insert the `cout` object into the argument list and receives it as a `*this` pointer as usual.)

Way back in Day 3's chapter, "Simple I/O," you learned that `cout` and `cin` are *objects*, but you were told not to concern yourself with that term yet because you had yet to be exposed to class variables and objects. Now, however, the term *object* should make perfect sense. Somewhere inside the compiler, there are classes for `cout` and `cin` (and other I/O objects). When you apply the `<<` or `>>` operators to them, Visual C++ calls overloaded `operator<<()` and `operator>>()` functions that use those I/O objects.

> ### Object or Class?
>
> If the `cout` and `cin` objects are really objects, they must be instantiated (be created) from some I/O class within Visual C++, and they are. The `cout` object is from the output class called `ostream`, and `cin` is from the input class named `istream`. That's why the overloaded `<<` function prototype in the file IOSTREAM.H always returns a reference `ostream` object. Because a reference to an object is returned, you can stack `cout` with multiple `<<`'s.
>
> If you fail to include the file IOSTREAM.H at the top of your Visual C++ programs, you'll get a message similar to this one if you attempt to use `cout`:
>
> ```
> Undefined symbol 'cout'.
> ```

Before looking at the specific details of I/O overloading, consider how Visual C++ handles these kinds of statements:

```
cout << i << u << 3;
```

Visual C++ first notices that `cout` is a member of the `ostream` class. Finding the overloaded `operator<<()` function that accesses an `ostream` object as its first argument, Visual C++ first changes the statement to look something like this:

```
cout.operator<<(i) << u << 3;
```

As shown a moment ago, `operator<<()` returns a reference to an `ostream` object, which is just a fancy (and more accurate) way of saying that `cout` is returned from `operator<<()`. When Visual C++ interprets the second `<<` in this `cout`, the compiler then changes the statement to this:

```
cout.operator<<(cout.operator<<(i), u) << 3;
```

Using the same logic, Visual C++ then changes the statement to this to handle the third <<:

```
cout.operator<<(cout.operator<<(cout.operator<<(i), u), 3);
```

Right before the program is compiled, Visual C++ converts this nested overloaded function call to the *this pointer notation, moving cout inside the function parentheses as the first argument. Figure 12.1 shows yet an additional way of interpreting the actions of Visual C++ when the previous cout executes.

```
                                 cout << i << u << 3;
                                       \  /
  Left-to-right associativity of <<:   cout << u << 3
                                           \  /
                                           cout << 3;
```

Figure 12.1. Each pair of operands surrounding << must return a cout object (more accurately, a reference to one) to successfully stack together output values.

Note: By the way, this discussion has attempted to offer a background on how the overloading of >> and << works, but if you aren't sure you fully understand the ostream and istream classes, they will become more obvious to you the more you overload << and >>. Today's chapter now has the theory out of the way and can concentrate on the coding necessary to get the job done.

The Details of Overloading << for Output

Here's output overloading in a nutshell: Almost every overloaded << output function you write will have the format

```
ostream & operator<<(ostream & out, yourClass & object)
{
  // Body of function goes here
  return out;
}
```

Extending Operator Overloads

This overloaded function must be a friend function. If you could create it as a member function, you wouldn't have to specify the first argument (the one that receives cout) because Visual C++ would send a pointer to cout as *this. However, you must specify overloaded I/O operator functions as friend functions because they have to work with the IOSTREAM.H header file in a way that requires the friend availability. The nice thing also about making them friend functions is that you can output like

```
cout << myObject << 2;
```

and like

```
cout << 2 << myObject;
```

Limiting overloaded << outputs to those whose left operands are class objects, as you would have to do with member functions, would be too constraining.

The body of the operator<<() function contains *whatever* code you want executed when the rest of the program (often called the *user of the* class) uses the overloaded operator with cout. Listing 12.1 contains a class with six members. The program initializes an object of the class and then outputs all six members with appropriate titles using a single cout output statement.

Listing 12.1. Overloading a class for easy output of objects.

```
1: // Filename: SIXOUT.CPP
2: // Outputs an object using overloading
3: #include <iostream.h>
4: #include <string.h>
5: class aClass {
6:    char c;
7:    char s[25];
8:    int i;
9:    long l;
10:   float x;
11:   double d;
12: public:
13:    inline void init(char, char [], int, long, float, double);
14:    friend ostream & operator<< (ostream &, aClass);
15: };
16: void aClass::init(char C, char S[], int I, long L, float X,
    ➥double D)
17:    { c = C; strcpy(s, S); i = I; l = L; x = X; d = D; }
18:    // Overloaded output function next
19:    ostream & operator<<(ostream & out, aClass obj)
20: {
21:    out << "Here's the object:\n";
```

```
22:     out << "c is " << obj.c << "\n";
23:     out << "s is " << obj.s << "\n";
24:     out << "i is " << obj.i << "\n";
25:     out << "l is " << obj.l << "\n";
26:     out << "x is " << obj.x << "\n";
27:     out << "d is " << obj.d << "\n";
28:     return out;      // Allows stacking
29: }
30: //////////////////////////////////////////////////////////////
31: main()
32: {
33:    aClass anObject;
34:    anObject.init('Q', "Visual C++", 14, 54234L, 6.75, 456.5432);
35:    cout << anObject;    // ALL output done here!
36:    return 0;
37: }
```

```
Here's the object:
c is Q
s is Visual C++
i is 14
l is 54234
x is 6.75
d is 456.543
```

The entire output of the aClass object is done using a single, simple cout on line 35. Why do you think the operator<<() class contains out << and not cout << (lines 21–27)? The reason is that the class must send its output to the local object named out, the data being output. That local object is the same thing as main()'s cout. Remember that when Visual C++ sees

```
cout << anObject;
```

in main(), Visual C++ changes it to this after rearranging the object as the first argument:

```
operator<<(cout, anObject);
```

The function operator<<() contains a local ostream object variable named out that receives by reference main()'s cout object when operator<<() is called.

The out object is returned on line 28 so that stacking of the << operator could occur. If main() defined two object variables and printed them like

```
main()
{
  aClass anObject1, anObject2;
  anObject1.init('Q', "Visual C++", 14, 54234L, 6.75, 456.5432);
```

Extending Operator Overloads

```
    anObject2.init('W', "OOP's easy!", 25, 98455L, 8.01, 90210.90210);
    cout << anObject1 << anObject2;    // ALL output done here!
    return 0;
}
```

then you would see this output:

```
Here's the object:
c is Q
s is Visual C++
i is 14
l is 54234
x is 6.75
d is 456.543
Here's the object:
c is W
s is OOP's easy!
i is 25
l is 98455
x is 8.01
d is 90210.9
```

Note: Do you see how `main()` collapses down to virtually nothing? The lines of output consume more programming statements than all of `main()`. Again, overloading the << operator is just one way to rid the primary sections of your programs of typical tedious details. After you overload the I/O, you use standard >> and << to input and output complete class data.

The program in Listing 12.2 takes the output of the `aClass`'s six member functions to an extreme. Using textual line-drawing characters, the output of the class object outputs using text boxes. Figure 12.2 shows what the output from the program looks like. Despite the advanced control of the screen, all the output is accomplished, just as it was back in Listing 12.1, with this simple statement:

```
cout << anObject;
```

You ought to be imagining how easy it will be to write programs after the output of complicated class data becomes as easy as outputting an integer. Sure, you still have to write the output code. But you separate it from the primary part of the program, and you're then able to see the application's direction without lots of messy details getting in the way. As you write your programs, you'll be coding simple statements for major output instead of keeping track of lots of function names that do the work. Object-oriented programming promotes a much more natural way of getting your job done.

```
+====================+
| Here's the object |
+====================+

+-------+
| c is W |
+-------+
+------------------+
| s is OOP's easy! |
+------------------+
+---------+
| i is  25 |
+---------+
+-----------+
| l is 98455 |
+-----------+
+-----------+
| x is 8.01 |
+-----------+
+--------------+
| d is 90210.9 |
+--------------+
```

Figure 12.2. No matter how fancy your output, overload << to handle it easily.

Listing 12.2. Drawing boxes around output.

```
 1: // Filename: FANCYOUT.CPP
 2: // Outputs an object using overloading
 3: #include <iostream.h>
 4: #include <iomanip.h>
 5: #include <string.h>
 6: class aClass {
 7:    char c;
 8:    char s[25];
 9:    int i;
10:    long l;
11:    float x;
12:    double d;
13: public:
14:    inline void init(char, char [], int, long, float, double);
15:    friend ostream & operator<< (ostream &, aClass);
16:    };
17: void aClass::init(char C, char S[], int I, long L, float X,
    ➥double D)
18:    { c = C; strcpy(s, S); i = I; l = L; x = X; d = D; }
```

continues

Extending Operator Overloads

Listing 12.2. continued

```
19:  // Overloaded output function next
20:  ostream & operator<<(ostream & out, aClass obj)
21:  {
22:    out << "\n\t\t" << '+';     // Title's corner
23:    for (unsigned int i=0; i<19; i++) // Double-lined top of box
24:       { out << '='; }
25:    out << "+\n";
26:    out << "\t\t| Here's the object |\n";
27:    out << "\t\t" << '+';     // Corner
28:    for (i=0; i<19; i++)
29:       { out << '='; }        // Double-line bottom of box
30:    out << "+\n";
31:    for (i=0; i<79; i++)
32:       { out << '-'; }        // Straight line across the screen
33:    out << "\n\t+";           // c's output (upper-right corner)
34:    for (i=0; i<8; i++)
35:       { out << '-'; }        // Top of straight-lined box
36:    out << "+\n";             // Upper-right corner of c's box
37:    out << "\t| c is " << obj.c << " |\n";
38:    out << "\t+";             // Left-bottom corner of c's box
39:    for (i=0; i<8; i++)
40:       { out << '-'; }        // Bottom line of c's box
41:    out << "+";               // Right-bottom corner of c's box
42:    out << "\n\t+";           // s's output (upper-right corner)
43:    for (i=0; i<(7+strlen(obj.s)); i++)
44:       { out << '-'; }        // Top of straight-lined box
45:    out << "+\n";             // Upper-right corner of s's box
46:    out << "\t| s is " << obj.s << " |\n";
47:    out << "\t+";             // Left-bottom corner of s's box
48:    for (i=0; i<(7+strlen(obj.s)); i++)
49:       { out << '-'; }        // Bottom line of s's box
50:    out << '+';               // Right-bottom corner of s's box
51:    out << "\n\t+";           // i's output (upper-right corner)
52:    for (i=0; i<10; i++)
53:       { out << '-'; }        // Top of straight-lined box
54:    out << "+\n";             // Upper-right corner of i's box
55:    out << "\t| i is " << setw(3) << obj.i << " |\n";
56:    out << "\t+";             // Left-bottom corner of i's box
57:    for (i=0; i<10; i++)
58:       { out << '-'; }        // Bottom line of i's box
59:    out << "+";               // Right-bottom corner of i's box
60:    out << "\n\t+";           // l's output (upper-right corner)
61:    for (i=0; i<12; i++)
62:       { out << '-'; }        // Top of straight-lined box
63:    out << "+\n";             // Upper-right corner of l's box
64:    out << "\t| l is " << setw(5) << obj.l << " |\n";
65:    out << "\t+";             // Left-bottom corner of l's box
66:    for (i=0; i<12; i++)
```

```
67:      { out << '-'; }       // Bottom line of l's box
68:     out << "+";             // Right-bottom corner of l's box
69:     out << "\n\t+";         // x's output (upper-right corner)
70:     for (i=0; i<11; i++)
71:      { out << '-'; }       // Top of straight-lined box
72:     out << "+\n";           // Upper-right corner of x's box
73:     out << "\t¦ x is" << setw(5) << obj.x << " ¦\n";
74:     out << "\t+";           // Left-bottom corner of x's box
75:     for (i=0; i<11; i++)
76:      { out << '-'; }       // Bottom line of x's box
77:     out << "+";             // Right-bottom corner of x's box
78:     out << "\n\t+";         // d's output (upper-right corner)
79:     for (i=0; i<14; i++)
80:      { out << '-'; }       // Top of straight-lined box
81:     out << "+\n";           // Upper-right corner of d's box
82:     out << "\t¦ d is" << setw(8) << obj.d << " ¦\n";
83:     out << "\t+";           // Left-bottom corner of d's box
84:     for (i=0; i<14; i++)
85:      { out << '-'; }       // Bottom line of d's box
86:     out << "+";             // Right-bottom corner of d's box
87:     return out;     // Allows stacking
88: }
89: //////////////////////////////////////////////////////////////
90: main()
91: {
92:     aClass anObject;
93:     anObject.init('W', "OOP's easy!", 25, 98455L, 8.01, 90210.90210);
94:     cout << anObject;   // ALL output done here!
95:     return 0;
96: }
```

After double-clicking on the output screen's title bars to expand the output window to full screen, you see the output that was shown in Figure 12.2.

Warning: Remember that Visual C++ versions 1.0 and 1.5 generate compiler warnings whenever you compile a program with I/O manipulators, such as Listing 12.2. You'll get the following warning message for each I/O manipulator:

```
warning C4270: 'initializing' : do not initialize a non-const
'class
```

Microsoft recognizes that there is a problem with this warning (the warning does not appear in the Visual C++ compiler for NT).

Day 12: Extending Operator Overloads

 Lines 22–87 might initially look confusing, but their primary purpose is to draw the boxes around the member data. There is not much going on here; the ASCII hex values of appropriate box-drawing characters are printed to surround the member data values.

Notice that, other than different initial data, main() didn't change at all from the main() in Listing 12.1, yet the two outputs from the programs differ greatly. The beauty of Visual C++ is its maintainability and extensibility. If you want to change the look of your program's output, you no longer have to sift through all the code looking for function names and change how they are called. *You only have to change the class that outputs the data using overloaded functions.*

> **Note:** By the way, using dashes and plus signs to box output is a little outdated, although using the text characters here serves the purpose of showing how easily you can output fancy text. You'll want to explore the graphics capabilities of the supplied MFC classes for more powerful Windows-based graphics, as described in the fourth Extra Credit Bonus chapter of this book.

Overloading << to Streamline Class Output

```
ostream & operator<<(ostream & out, yourClass & object)
{
  // Body of function goes here
  return out;
}
```

out is the received argument name for the output object cout, and *object* is the function's local name for the class variable being output. Always return the out object if you want to stack several couts together in succession.

Example

```
ostream & operator<<(ostream & out, Date & d)
{
  out << "\n";
  out << "The day is " << d.day << "\n";
  out << "The month is " << d.month << "\n";
  out << "The year is " << d.year << "\n";
  return out;
}
```

The Details of Overloading >> for Input

Overloading the >> character for input requires a mirror-image overloaded function from the output's operator<<() function. The whole purpose of overloading operators is to make your data types (declared with classes) behave as the built-in ones do. Suppose you want to ask the user for the six member values from the aClass shown in the previous listings. You could have separate member functions that request each member, but main() would have to call them individually or would have to call a public member function, which in turn would print the data.

Why not overload >> so that a simple statement such as

```
cin >> anObject;
```

produces all the prompting and input needed to fill the members with data?

To overload >>, you'll have to write an operator>>() function that looks something like this:

```
istream & operator>>(istream & in, yourClass & object)
{
  // Body of function goes here
  return in;
}
```

Note: Whereas the reference symbol, &, before the second argument was optional when overloading output, it is required for *both* arguments in operator>>().

You'll need to return a reference to the istream input object, just as you did with the output object before, so that you can stack several inputs together like this:

```
cin >> anObject1 >> anObject2;
```

As with the operator<<() function, your operator>>() functions must be friend functions so that they interact with the IOSTREAM.H file properly.

Listing 12.3 contains a version of Listing 12.1 that does not initialize the object directly; instead, this version asks the user for the initialization inside an overloaded operator>>() function. (Listing 12.2's box-drawing commands were left out of this operator<<()'s code for brevity.)

Day 12: Extending Operator Overloads

 Listing 12.3. Overloading a class for easy input of objects.

```
1:  // Filename: SIXIN.CPP
2:  // Both inputs and outputs an object using overloading
3:  #include <iostream.h>
4:  #include <iomanip.h>
5:  #include <string.h>
6:  class aClass {
7:     char c;
8:     char s[25];
9:     int i;
10:    long l;
11:    float x;
12:    double d;
13: public:
14:    friend ostream & operator<< (ostream &, aClass);
15:    friend istream & operator>> (istream &, aClass &);
16: };
17: // Overloaded output function next
18: ostream & operator<<(ostream & out, aClass obj)
19: {
20:    out << "\nHere's the object:\n";
21:    out << "c is " << obj.c << "\n";
22:    out << "s is " << obj.s << "\n";
23:    out << "i is " << obj.i << "\n";
24:    out << "l is " << obj.l << "\n";
25:    out << "x is " << obj.x << "\n";
26:    out << "d is " << obj.d << "\n";
27:    return out;      // Allows stacking
28: }
29: istream & operator>>(istream & in, aClass & obj)
30: {
31: // This function does a lot of work
32:    cout << "I need some data for the class.\n";
33:    cout << "What is the value of c? ";
34:    in >> obj.c;
35:    cout << "What is s? ";
36:    in.ignore();
37:    in.get(obj.s, 25);
38:    cout << "What is i? ";
39:    in >> obj.i;
40:    cout << "What is l? ";
41:    in >> obj.l;
42:    cout << "What is x? ";
43:    in >> obj.x;
44:    cout << "What is d? ";
45:    in >> obj.d;
46:    return in;       // Allows stacking
47: }
48: //////////////////////////////////////////////////////////////////
```

```
49: main()
50: {
51:    aClass anObject;
52:    cin >> anObject;      // Easy, right?
53:    cout << anObject;
54:    return 0;
55: }
```

```
I need some data for the class.
What is the value of c? r
What is s? Visual C++
What is i? 3
What is l? 4
What is x? 5.6
What is d? 7.8

Here's the object:
c is r
s is Visual C++
i is 3
l is 4
x is 5.6
d is 7.8
```

This program introduces the use of the `ignore()` input member function included in Visual C++. `ignore` (on line 37) gets rid of the newline character that is left on the input stream (`istream`) buffer after the single character is input. The `in` object is used rather than `cin` because `in` is receiving all the input in this function. As you can see, the `cin`'s member function named `get()` works for `in` and enables the user to enter a full string with embedded spaces (up to 25 characters in length) on line 38, rather than only a single word.

Now that you've mastered I/O overloading, check out Listing 12.4. It asks the user for the time inside an overloaded `operator>>()` function, performing input error checking. You now can write classes that prevent the user from entering bad values!

Listing 12.4. Creating a time class that checks itself.

```
1: // Filename: TIMECHK.CPP
2: // Requires that the user enter correct time values
3: #include <iostream.h>
4: class Time {
5:    int hour;
6:    int minute;
7:    int second;
8: public:
```

continues

Day 12: Extending Operator Overloads

Listing 12.4. continued

```
9:     friend ostream & operator<< (ostream &, Time);
10:    friend istream & operator>> (istream &, Time &);
11: };
12: // Overloaded output function next
13: ostream & operator<<(ostream & out, Time t)
14: {
15:    out << "\nHere's the time:\n";
16:    out << t.hour << ":" << t.minute << ":" << t.second << "\n";
17:    return out;    // Allows stacking
18: }
19: istream & operator>>(istream & in, Time & t)
20: {
21:    cout << "Please enter the time as follows:\n";
22:    do {
23:       cout << "What is the hour (0-23)? ";
24:       in >> t.hour;
25:    } while ((t.hour < 0) || (t.hour > 23));
26:    do {
27:       cout << "What is the minute (0-59)? ";
28:       in >> t.minute;
29:    } while (t.minute < 0 || t.minute > 59);
30:    do {
31:       cout << "What is the second (0-59)? ";
32:       in >> t.second;
33:    } while (t.second < 0 || t.second > 59);
34:    return in;    // Allows stacking
35: }
36: /////////////////////////////////////////////////////////////////
37: main()
38: {
39:    Time now;
40:    cin >> now;         // Get the time
41:    cout << now;        // Print it
42:    return 0;
43: }
```

Output

```
Please enter the time as follows:
What is the hour (0-23)? 34
What is the hour (0-23)? 332
What is the hour (0-23)? 5454
What is the hour (0-23)? 565
What is the hour (0-23)? 21
What is the minute (0-59)? 50
What is the second (0-59)? 31

Here's the time:
21:50:31
```

— It took the user five tries to enter a correct hour.

This program's Time class is a smart class that prevents the user from entering values that are out of range. Throughout this book, you'll see other ways that objects can be made smart like this. Eventually, you'll be able to write classes that never, through assignment or user input, allow bad data to get into the class, thus creating fully safe and protected classes.

Through a series of do-while loops (such as the one in lines 22–25), the program ensures that the user enters correct values into the 24-hour Time members. main() is about as simple as it can be.

Overloading >> to Streamline Class Input

```
istream & operator>>(istream & in, yourClass & object)
{
  // Body of function goes here
  return in;
}
```

in is the received argument name for the output object cin, and *object* is the function's local name for the class variable being input. Always return the in object if you want to stack several cins together in succession. You *must* receive *object* by reference—operator>>() will not work properly if you don't.

Example

```
istream & operator>> (istream & in, Date & d)
{
  cout << "\n";
  cout << "What is the month (1-12)? ";
  in >> d.month;
  cout << "What is the day (1-31)? ";
  in >> d.day;
  cout << "What is the year (1980-2100)? ";
  in >> d.year;
  return in;
}
```

DO	DON'T

DO specify your overloaded I/O operator functions as friend functions.

DO use all the I/O manipulator and input functions that you want when overloading input with operator>>(). Just be sure to use the istream object's name and not cin inside the function. ignore(), getline(), and get() all work inside overloaded operator>>() functions.

Day 12 Extending Operator Overloads

> **DO** return a reference to the input or output object if you want to stack several `cin`s or `cout`s together in sequence.
>
> **DON'T** forget to add error-checking routines to your overloaded input operations. Your data becomes self-policing, and therefore the main part of the program has to do much less at each input.

Creating Your Own I/O Manipulators

Although you might not have a daily need to do so, you can overload the I/O manipulators so that they modify your output the way you want it modified. You might find it easier to overload a manipulator (which usually means writing your own manipulator and naming it yourself).

To create your own manipulators, all you have to do is write a friend function that takes an `ostream` object as its only operator. Although doing this does not qualify the function as an overloaded operator function, the use of `ostream` fits in neatly with the first part of this chapter that introduced `ostream`. `ostream` is just the output stream. (You can also define manipulators for the input stream, `istream`, although these are rarer.)

Suppose that you wanted to create an I/O manipulator named `ring` that rang the PC's speaker whenever it appeared in an output stream. In other words, when you typed

```
cout << ring;
```

the speaker would beep. You would also want the capability to embed the `ring` manipulator inside stacked outputs such as this:

```
cout << oldMessage << ring << newMessage << ring << "\n";
```

It turns out that ringing the PC's bell inside a QuickWin application is not simple. Unlike with DOS-based C programs, you cannot output the `\a` alarm escape sequence or even the ASCII code for the alarm, 7, because QuickWin cannot deal with control characters other than a handful such as `\n` and `\t`. You'll have to resort to assembly language programming to sound the PC's alarm from within QuickWin. Therefore, a `ring` I/O manipulator comes in handy because, instead of calling the assembler code every time you want to ring the bell, you can insert a `ring` manipulator after a `cout`. Visual C++ enables you to embed inline assembly language programs directly inside your C or C++ application. The following assembly code is needed to sound the PC's alarm:

```
__asm { \
  __asm    sub   bx, bx     \
  __asm    mov   ax, 0E07h  \
  __asm    int   10h        \
}
```

You can call the assembler code inside a `ring` manipulator like this:

```
ostream & ring(ostream & out)
{
__asm { \
  __asm    sub   bx, bx     \
  __asm    mov   ax, 0E07h  \
  __asm    int   10h        \
  }
  return out;
}
```

You could insert this code together with other manipulators you write and place them in a header file that you include at the top of your programs.

Note: Code your manipulator functions as friend functions so that all classes can use them.

Listing 12.5 includes the `ring` manipulator as well as three tabbing manipulators, called `tab5`, `tab10`, and `tab15`. Each of the `tab...` manipulators tabs a different number of spaces when you embed them in an output stream.

Listing 12.5. Defining new manipulators.

```
 1: // Filename: MANIP.CPP
 2: // Includes several user-defined output manipulators
 3: #include <iostream.h>
 4:
 5: ostream & ring(ostream & out);
 6: ostream & tab5(ostream & out);
 7: ostream & tab10(ostream & out);
 8: ostream & tab15(ostream & out);
 9:
10: main()
11: {
```

continues

Day 12: Extending Operator Overloads

Listing 12.5. continued

```
12:     cout << "Hi. Here's a bell." << ring << "\n";
13:     cout << "tab..." << tab5 << "5 spaces later." << "\n";
14:     cout << "tab..." << tab10 << "10 spaces later." << "\n";
15:     cout << "tab..." << tab15 << "15 spaces later." << "\n";
16:     return 0;
17: }
18: //////////////////////////////////////////////////////////////////
19: ostream & ring(ostream & out)
20: {
21:     __asm
22:     { sub  bx, bx
23:       mov  ax, 0E07h
24:       int  10h       // End of the assembler code
25:     }
26:     return out;  // Pass control through the output stream
27: }
28: ostream & tab5(ostream & out)
29: {
30:     out << "     ";
31:     return out;
32: }
33: ostream & tab10(ostream & out)
34: {
35:     out << "          ";
36:     return out;
37: }
38: ostream & tab15(ostream & out)
39: {
40:     out << "               ";
41:     return out;
42: }
```

```
Hi. Here's a bell.
tab...     5 spaces later.
tab...          10 spaces later.
tab...               15 spaces later.
```

The program in Listing 12.5 doesn't happen to have classes, but if there were classes in the program, as well as overloaded operator>>() and operator<<() functions, any of them could use the manipulators coded there. (The classes, of course, would have to list the manipulator functions as friends if the manipulator needed access to any of the class's private members.)

Lines 5–8 include function prototypes because main() calls, albeit indirectly, the manipulator functions, and all functions called by main() must be prototyped.

When you compile Listing 12.5, you'll receive the following compiler warning from Visual C++:

```
warning C4704: 'ring':in-line assembler precludes global optimizations
```

Visual C++ is simply letting you know that no optimization will take place for your assembler code. (Visual C++ will, however, continue to optimize the C++ code everywhere it can.)

Creating I/O Manipulators

```
ostream & manipName(ostream & out)
{
  // Output manipulator code goes here
  return out;
}
```

and

```
istream & manipName(istream & in)
{
  // Input manipulator code goes here
  return in;
}
```

out and in receive the output or input of the manipulation code that you write.

Example

```
ostream & line20(ostream & out)
{
  for (int i=0; i<19; i++)    // Outputs 20 hyphens
    { out << "-"; }
  return out;
}
```

Subscript Overloading

If you want to, you can overload the subscript operator to work the way you need with your own data types. Consider this class named Sales:

```
class Sales {
  char compName[25];
  float divisionTotals[5];    // 5 divisions
public:
  // Public members go here
};
```

Extending Operator Overloads

The company is divided into five divisions, and the sales totals of each of the divisions are stored in the object's floating-point array.

The most important members of the class are stored in the division total values. In using the class, you'll be initializing, printing, and calculating with the five division totals. Instead of writing some kind of access function for each of the five divisions, you can overload the subscript operator to ease your programming considerably.

> **Note:** You'll often overload subscript operators so that they return members, or individual array elements of members, from inside your class.

For example, you could overload the subscript operator so that using it with a `Sales` object returns that subscript from the `divisionTotals` array. Listing 12.6 does just that.

 Listing 12.6. Overloading subscripts.

```
1:  // Filename: SUBOV.CPP
2:  // Overload subscript operators so that accessing a class object
3:  // via a subscript returns one of the members.
4:  #include <iostream.h>
5:  #include <iomanip.h>
6:  #include <string.h>
7:  class Sales {
8:     char compName[25];
9:     float divisionTotals[5];
10: public:
11:    inline void init(char [], float []);
12:    inline float & operator[](const int);
13:    char * getName(void) { return compName; };
14: };
15: void Sales::init(char CN[], float DT[])
16: {
17:    strcpy(compName, CN);
18:    for (int i=0; i<5; i++)
19:       { divisionTotals[i] = DT[i]; }
20: }
21: float & Sales::operator[](const int sub)
22: {
23:    return divisionTotals[sub];
24: }
25: //////////////////////////////////////////////////////////////////
26: main()
```

```
27: {
28:   float totalSales=0.0, avgSales;
29:   float divs[5] = {3234.54, 7534.45, 6543.23, 5665.32, 1232.45};
30:   Sales company;
31:   company.init("Swiss Cheese", divs);
32:   cout << setprecision(2) << setiosflags(ios::showpoint);
33:   cout << setiosflags(ios::fixed);
34:   cout << "Here are the sales for " << company.getName();
35:   cout << "'s divisions:\n";
36:   for (int i=0; i<5; i++)
37:     { cout << company[i] << "\n"; }  // Overloaded subscript
38:   // Add the sales for the divisions
39:   for (i=0; i<5; i++)
40:     { totalSales += company[i]; }
41:   cout << "The total sales are $" << totalSales << "\n";
42:   // Compute average sales
43:   avgSales = totalSales / (float)5.0;
44:   cout << "The average sales are $" << avgSales << "\n";
45:   return 0;
46: }
```

```
Here are the sales for Swiss Cheese's divisions:
3234.54
7534.45
6543.23
5665.32
1232.45
The total sales are $24209.99
The average sales are $4842.00
```

Accessing the company object with a subscript would normally make no sense in this program because there is no array of company objects. Nevertheless, the subscript is overloaded here to work in a special way when applied to the company object. The subscript will always return the division's total that matches the subscript number.

The reason it is important to return a reference to a floating-point value is that you might want to *assign* a value to one of the division totals from within main(). The overloaded subscript operator is one way of doing that. Therefore, instead of using the init() function, main() can directly assign divisionSales[] values even though the divisionSales[] array is private. Here is just one example of how main() can initialize the divisionSales[] array:

```
company[0] = 1234,56;
company[1] = 4234.09;
company[2] = 9248.63;
company[3] = 5434.94;
company[4] = 9242.45;
```

Extending Operator Overloads

You know by now that `main()` probably isn't the best place in a program to be assigning values to private values. What if `main()` were to do something like this:

```
company[64] = 4009.81;    // Not possible!
```

If `main()` attempted to assign a value to the element numbered 64, the `operator[]()` function would insert the value in the 64th element of `divisionSales[]`—of which there is none. We're back to letting `main()` damage values that it shouldn't be able to damage in spite of their private access. However, it's extremely easy to modify the `operator[]()` function so that it does not allow bad subscripts! Doing so provides a self-protected class that still allows limited modifying access from within `main()`.

Listing 12.7 shows a modified version of the previous program. This time, the overloaded subscript operator includes code that checks for array boundary problems.

Listing 12.7. Overloading smarter subscripts.

```
 1: // Filename: SUBOV2.CPP
 2: // Overload subscript operators so that accessing a class object
 3: // via a subscript returns one of the members.
 4: #include <iostream.h>
 5: #include <iomanip.h>
 6: #include <string.h>
 7: #include <stdlib.h>
 8: class Sales {
 9:    char compName[25];
10:    float divisionTotals[5];
11: public:
12:    inline void init(char []);   // No longer needed float array
13:    inline float & operator[](const int);
14:    char * getName(void) { return compName; };
15: };
16: void Sales::init(char CN[])
17: {
18:    strcpy(compName, CN);
19: }
20: float & Sales::operator[](const int sub)
21: {
22:    if (sub < 0 || sub > 4)    // Subscript checking routine
23:      { cerr << "Bad subscript! " << sub << " is not allowed.\n";
24:        exit(1); }
25:    return divisionTotals[sub];
26: }
27: //////////////////////////////////////////////////////////////////
28: main()
29: {
30:    float totalSales=0.0, avgSales;
31:    Sales company;
```

```
32:     company.init("Swiss Cheese");
33:     company[0] = 3245.76;    // Assign values to individual
34:     company[1] = 2900.93;    // and private members.
35:     company[2] = 9455.32;
36:     company[3] = 3447.11;
37:     company[4] = 7533.01;
38:     cout << setprecision(2) << setiosflags(ios::showpoint);
39:     cout << setiosflags(ios::fixed);
40:     cout << "Here are the sales for " << company.getName();
41:     cout << "'s divisions:\n";
42:     for (int i=0; i<5; i++)
43:        { cout << company[i] << "\n"; }   // Overloaded subscript
44:     // Add the sales for the divisions
45:     for (i=0; i<5; i++)
46:        { totalSales += company[i]; }
47:     cout << "The total sales are $" << totalSales << "\n";
48:     // Compute average sales
49:     avgSales = totalSales / (float)5.0;
50:     cout << "The average sales are $" << avgSales << "\n";
51:     return 0;
52: }
```

```
Here are the sales for Swiss Cheese's divisions:
3245.76
2900.93
9455.32
3447.11
7533.01
The total sales are $26582.13
The average sales are $5316.43
```

The `operator[]()` function no longer allows bad values to be sent to the company object, but `main()` can assign values to the division totals (as in lines 33–37). If, however, `main()` were to *incorrectly* assign a value using a bad subscript like

```
company[64] = 4009.81;   // Not possible!
```

then the program would produce this error message:

```
Bad subscript! 64 is not allowed.
```

Note: Visual C++ does not include array bounds-checking. Neither C nor C++ checks for array subscripts boundary problems because doing so would slow down the execution and reduce efficiency. Now that you know how to overload the subscript operator, you should consider putting all your arrays in their own classes and adding array

Extending Operator Overloads

> bounds-checking code, such as that shown in Listing 12.7. The third exercise at the end of the chapter helps illustrate this point further.

Summary

Today's chapter concludes the direct discussion of overloading operators. In tomorrow's chapter, you'll see how to overload the assignment operator because the assignment operator's overloading relates to the material presented there. Other than the assignment operator, you've now seen how to overload virtually any operator you'll ever need to overload to make that operator work on your class data.

Being able to overload the insertion, <<, and extraction, >>, operators means that you can in yet another way get rid of tedious details from `main()` and leave the details to your classes. By coding a simple overloaded `operator<<()` function, you can display a fancy boxed screen with a class's complete list of members and titles with a simple `cout`. Conversely, you can get the contents of a complete class from the user with a single `cin`.

While reading about the ins and outs (should we say, *cins and couts*?) of operator overloading, you learned that the `istream` and `ostream` objects are connected to the input and output data streams. Being able to access those streams enables you to write your own I/O manipulators.

The subscript operator is an operator you can overload that lets the rest of the program access individual members or a member's array elements. Using the subscript operators, you can create safe arrays that check for their own array boundary problems.

Q&A

Q. How can overloaded I/O operators save me time?

A. By overloading the << and >> operators, you can input or output complete classes with simple `cout` and `cin` objects, just as you input or output built-in data types such as integers and floating-point values.

The overloaded I/O operator functions provide one more reason for needing reference operators. When overloaded I/O operator functions return the I/O streams by reference, they then enable you to stack several inputs and

outputs in succession while still ensuring that your I/O code executes to produce the I/O.

Q. How can overloading a subscript operator help me?

A. Overloading subscript operators lets `main()` (and the rest of the program) access individual object array elements or individual object members with subscripts. Even if your classes don't contain arrays, you can write an overloaded subscript operator function that returns any of the members based on the array subscript used.

Not only will overloading subscript operators give your programs more controlled access to private object members, but it also will give you the ability to define safe arrays.

Q. What is meant by the term *safe array*?

A. A safe array is one that checks for its own array boundary limitations, or rather the overloaded subscript function checks for array boundary subscripts problems. When `main()` or another part of the program uses a good array subscript, the `operator[]()` function uses the subscript to return an appropriate value from the class.

Workshop

The Workshop offers quiz questions and exercises to hone your skills and give you feedback on today's lesson. You'll find some proposed answers in Appendix D.

Quiz

1. What are the names of the overloaded operator functions that overload input and output?
2. Why should overloaded operator functions be friend functions?
3. True or False: When you write an I/O manipulating function, you must use function parentheses after the manipulator's name in the I/O stream that uses the manipulator.
4. What is the name of the function that overloads the subscript operator?
5. True or False: The second argument of `operator>>()` should always be received with a reference operator, &.

Extending Operator Overloads

6. How can you ensure that overloaded I/O operations can be stacked together?

7. Why does Visual C++ not provide for array bounds-checking automatically?

8. True or False: If you overload the subscript operator for a class, that class must contain an array as one of its members.

Exercises

1. Write a simple date class that asks the user for a date and prints the correct date. Ask the user for the date in the format *dd, mm,* and *yy,* in which *dd* represents the day number (1–31), *mm* represents the month number (1–12), and *yy* represents a year (1980–2100). Add error checking to the overloaded input routine. Print the date with a full month name inside the overloaded output operator.

2. Write a simple overloaded operator function that overloads the comma operator so that it can take the place of << in integer output statements. Rather than

   ```
   cout << 12 << "\t" << 'c' << amount << "\n";
   ```

   you can do this:

   ```
   cout , 12 , "\t" , 'c' , amount , "\n";
   ```

3. Write a class that holds the total number of days in each of the 12 months.

DAY 13

Constructing and Destructing

Day 13
Constructing and Destructing

Most of the programs you've seen so far that contained class data included initialization member functions that assigned initial values to the class objects. The initialization functions were needed because `main()` could not directly access and initialize private data members, and the public initialization function allowed `main()` just enough access to get initial data into the objects.

Visual C++ offers a much better way for initializing objects. With *constructors,* you can both define and initialize an object's data members at the same time.

Constructors are member functions, just as any other initialization function is. However, when you specify a function as a constructor function, Visual C++ recognizes the function as being different from the others. You'll find that you can use constructors to initialize data in ways that other member functions cannot easily provide.

When you are done with object data, you can provide *destructors* that get rid of the data in the way that you specify. A destructor is a special member function you write that "cleans up" your program's data.

Throughout this second week's chapters, you've not seen object data that contained members initialized on the heap. Of course, you'll often want to use the heap with objects, but constructors and destructors are the perfect vehicle functions for allocating and deallocating your objects. Although public member functions can allocate and deallocate, you'll learn in today's chapter how constructors and destructors do more automatically for you than other functions can do.

After you learn how constructors and destructors work, you'll understand a few remaining Visual C++ function overloading advantages, including the overloading of the assignment operator and how to write your own typecasting functions.

Today, you learn about the following topics:

- How to code and use constructor functions
- How to code and use destructor functions
- How to specify overloaded constructors
- How to overload the assignment operator
- How to write your own typecast operators
- How to write copy constructors

Note: Throughout this chapter, remember that constructors and destructors are nothing more than member functions that create, initialize, and get rid of object data. You can overload constructor functions, so there might be more than one for a class because some classes might need to be constructed in one of several ways. (You cannot overload destructor functions, however, but you won't ever need to.)

Defining Constructors

Constructors and destructors are best learned by seeing them in use. Therefore, instead of reading a lot of theory in advance, you need to learn how to specify constructor and destructor functions. That's where today's chapter begins.

A constructor function is a member function that has the same name as the class itself. Therefore, if a class is named `aClass`, the constructor function will be named `aClass()`. If the class is named `Customer`, the class constructor will be named `Customer()`.

Constructors never have return values, and you cannot specify a return type, not even `void` (this is true for destructors as well). When you overload functions, only the argument lists differentiate, in number of arguments or data types, one overloaded function from another.

Here is a class header that includes three constructor functions:

```
class Children {
  char name[25];
  int age;
  float weight;
public:
  void prData(void);
  char * getName(void);
  int getAge(void);
  float getWeight(void);
  Children(void);              // Three constructors begin here
  Children(int, float);
  Children(char *, int, float);
};                             // No destructor specified
```

371

Constructing and Destructing

Note: Constructors can have default arguments if needed.

You'll see later that you rarely call constructors explicitly. Visual C++ calls them for you when you define an object.

Defining Destructors

A destructor function is a member function that has the same name as the class itself preceded by a tilde character, ~. Therefore, if a class is named aClass, the destructor function will be named ~aClass(). If the class is named Customer, the class destructor will be named ~Customer().

A class can contain at most one destructor function. Destructor functions are member functions that have no return data type *and no arguments* (not even void). It is because destructors are not allowed argument lists that you cannot overload destructors.

Here is the Children class you saw earlier with a destructor function added:

```
class Children {
  char name[25];
  int age;
  float weight;
public:
  void prData(void);
  char * getName(void);
  int getAge(void);
  float getWeight(void);
  Children(void);                 // Three constructors begin here
  Children(int, float);
  Children(char *, int, float);
  ~Children();                    // Here's the destructor
};
```

If you supply a constructor function that allocates memory for data members, you'll always want to supply a destructor that deallocates the memory. You then won't have to worry about the heap in the main part of your program.

Why Constructors and Destructors Are Needed

Visual C++ already contains several built-in constructor functions. There is a constructor function that "knows" how to create an integer variable. When you use the statement

```
int abc;
```

the constructor function finds an empty place in memory, reserves storage the size of an integer, and names that storage location abc. Whatever values happened to be in that variable's location before the constructor began are left there after construction. Therefore, uninitialized variables have garbage in them when you define them.

> **Why Didn't They Do More?**
>
> The designers of Visual C++'s predecessor C language could have chosen to initialize variables with a value, but they didn't do so for two reasons: The more the compiler does for you, the more that efficiency is lost. Also, how could the designers of C know what initial values you would want in all your variables? They could not. You don't always want your variables zeroed out when you first use them.
>
> Even if Visual C++ were to initialize your variables with zeros for you, good coding practices dictate that you explicitly initialize data yourself. By doing so, you make your intentions known and you eliminate uncertainties during program maintenance (such as, "Did I really intend to use this variable's initial value, or did I just forget to initialize it with another value?").
>
> Constructors enable you to write your own initializer routines so that you can create initialized data with whatever values you want the data to have.

When you use the statement

```
int abc=25;
```

the constructor function not only reserves and names an integer location, but the constructor also inserts a 25 there, as Figure 13.1 shows.

Day 13
Constructing and Destructing

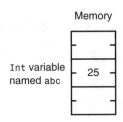

Int variable named abc — 25

Figure 13.1. The internal integer constructor function created and initialized abc for you.

All the constructors for `float`, `int`, and the other built-in data types are invisible to you. The variables' values remain reserved and available in memory as long as they remain in scope. When a variable goes out of scope, Visual C++ calls a built-in destructor function which returns that memory space to the available pool of memory.

> **Note:** All local variables are reserved on the stack. The stack is an accordion-like area in memory whose data space grows and shrinks as programs work with data. The stack is different (although similar in concept as far as the compiler and DOS are concerned) from the heap in that you cannot specifically allocate and deallocate the stack unless you call internal assembly-language code. All global variables are reserved in the name space of your executable program.

As you learn how to write your own constructors and destructors, keep in mind that these tasks are nothing new to the compiler, but they're new to you. You've probably never thought much about how Visual C++ creates variables when you've defined variables. When moving to OOP, you must be made more aware of data creation because you will not always like the way Visual C++ creates objects for you; many times you'll want to replace Visual C++'s default constructors with your own.

Although this information might surprise you, Visual C++ even contains a built-in constructor function for your own class data as the preceding paragraph implied. For example, when you create a class variable like

```
main()
{
  Children kid;
  // Rest of program follows
```

Visual C++ calls its internal *default constructor function* and creates a class variable for you by reserving the space in free memory and assigning the name kid to that space. As with built-in constructors for the built-in data types, Visual C++ cannot and does not make any guesses about initial values. Whatever happened to be located in kid's memory space before you defined the variable is still there after kid is defined.

When main()'s block ends, kid goes out of scope. "Going out of scope" is a fancy way of saying that a variable's default destructor is called. The destructor function releases the kid from memory and returns the space to the free pool of memory. If kid were a variable local to an internal block of code inside main(), kid would go out of scope, meaning the destructor function would be called, as soon as the block ends.

The reason you are learning how to code constructors and destructors is that Visual C++ sometimes has to guess how you want class data reserved, and sometimes Visual C++ doesn't guess well! Many times, you'll want Visual C++ to construct a class variable in a special way, and if so, you'll probably need to destruct that variable in a special way as well. When you write your own constructor and destructor functions for class data (you cannot write constructors and destructors for built-in data types), your constructor functions will override the default constructor functions, and your destructor functions will override the default destructor functions.

The Bottom Line

Visual C++ already contains *default constructor functions* and *default destructor functions*. When you define a variable, whether that variable is a class variable or a variable of a built-in type, a default constructor is called to reserve the variable's space and to assign the variable name to the variable.

When a variable goes out of scope, the default destructor function is called that releases that memory back to the free memory pool.

You'll learn in the rest of this chapter how to *override* the default constructor and destructor functions. When you specify your own constructor, Visual C++ executes it and not the default constructor. When you specify your own destructor, Visual C++ executes it and not the default destructor.

When are default constructors called? When a variable is *first* defined. When are default destructors called? As soon as a variable goes out of scope. When you replace default constructors and destructors with your own specific versions, Visual C++ calls your constructors when the variables are first

Day 13: Constructing and Destructing

defined, and Visual C++ calls your destructors when the variables go out of scope. You don't explicitly call constructors or destructors because Visual C++ automatically calls them as soon as data goes in and out of scope.

DO	DON'T

DO give constructors the same name as the class they reside in.

DO give destructors the same name as the class they reside in, but precede their name with a tilde (~).

DON'T specify a return type, even void, for constructors and destructors.

DON'T attempt to write constructors and destructors for the built-in data types. Visual C++ has to use its own default constructors and destructors for its built-in data types.

Timing Is the Key

The timing of constructor member functions takes place automatically. Visual C++ calls them for you when you define variables. Visual C++ calls destructor member functions when variables go out of scope.

Constructor and destructor functions can do anything any other functions can do. They can initialize, print, loop, read and write to disk, and so forth. Usually, though, constructor functions initialize data members and possibly allocate member data on the heap when dynamic memory allocation is required. Destructors then deallocate heap memory when required.

Note: Even if dynamic memory allocation isn't being used, always define a destructor if your program has a constructor function. You're more likely to use the destructor if you change to memory allocation, and in the advanced OOP that you'll read about in next week's chapters, destructors are sometimes required.

Constructors and destructors should be made public member functions. Even though they are called by Visual C++ when it creates your objects, Visual C++ knows that main() (or whatever other function defines the class variable) triggered the constructor's execution, and therefore, the constructor must have public access. In a way, you *do* call constructors, but you do so indirectly by defining new object variables. (You'll see later today some cases in which you will actually call constructor functions by name just as you would a regular member function—another reason to keep them public.)

The program in Listing 13.1 demonstrates the timing of constructor and destructor calls. The constructor doesn't really construct anything, but instead, it prints a message letting you know that it has been called. The destructor function also prints a message. In main(), a class object variable had to be defined to trigger the execution of the constructor.

Listing 13.1. Printing messages to show constructor and destructor timing.

```
 1: // Filename: CONSMESG.CPP
 2: // Demonstrates the timing of constructors and destructor
 3: // functions by printing messages when each is called.
 4: #include <iostream.h>
 5: class aClass {
 6:   int i;    // Nothing's done with i
 7: public:
 8:   aClass(void);    // Constructor
 9:   ~aClass(void);   // Destructor
10: };
11: aClass::aClass(void)    // Constructor's implementation code
12: {
13:   cout << "The constructor is being called...\n";
14: }
15: aClass::~aClass(void)   // Destructor's implementation code
16: {
17:   cout << "The destructor is being called...\n";
18: }
19: //////////////////////////////////////////////////////////////
20: main()
21: {
22:   aClass var;           // Automatically calls constructor
23:   return 0;
24: }
```

Day 13: Constructing and Destructing

> **Note:** Constructor and destructor function bodies can be coded inside the class if they are short, but most Visual C++ programmers opt to keep their class header files clear of code except for data members and member function prototypes.

```
The constructor is being called...
The destructor is being called...
```

If the constructor and destructor functions had not been included with the `aClass` class, Visual C++ would have executed its default constructor and destructor. The `var` variable would still be created and would still go out of scope, but no messages would print.

Line 22 forces the execution of the `aClass` constructor because an `aClass` class object variable is being defined. The constructor and destructor messages prove that those member functions are executing even though `main()` does very little except define a variable and return to the operating system.

> **Note:** As this program demonstrates, if you start at `main()` and trace through the program line by line, OOP programs don't follow the normal sequential progression that other programs do. It seems as if events are triggered on their own accord—and they are! That's the nice thing about OOP; objects initialize themselves so that you don't have to in the main part of the program.

The constructor function is typically used to initialize data, and that's just what the program in Listing 13.2 does. The constructor function assigns the `i` data member a value. In previous chapters, `main()` called an initialization member function, but the constructor is a better place for initialization because `main()` doesn't have to do anything special to initialize data when it defines variables. (Therefore, you don't have to remember to initialize data either! Using constructors for data initialization is safer than relying on `main()` or other functions to execute member functions.)

Listing 13.2. Initializing data in the constructor.

```cpp
1: // Filename: CONSINIT.CPP
2: // Uses a constructor to initialize a data member
3: // and the destructor then zeroes out the member when done.
4: #include <iostream.h>
5: class aClass {
6:    int i;      // i will be initialized by the constructor
7: public:
8:    void prClass(void);
9:    aClass(void);     // Constructor
10:    ~aClass(void);    // Destructor
11: };
12: void aClass::prClass(void)
13: {
14:    cout << "The value of i inside the class is " << i << "\n";
15: }
16: aClass::aClass(void)     // Constructor's implementation code
17: {
18:    cout << "The constructor is being called...\n";
19:    i = 25;    // Initialize the data member
20: }
21: aClass::~aClass(void)    // Destructor's implementation code
22: {
23:    cout << "The destructor is being called...\n";
24:    i = 0;     // Zero out the 25
25: }
26: //////////////////////////////////////////////////////////////
27: main()
28: {
29:    aClass var;              // Automatically calls constructor
30:    var.prClass();           // Print the initialized data member
31:    return 0;
32: }
```

```
The constructor is being called...
The value of i inside the class is 25
The destructor is being called...
```

The first question you might ask is why the destructor function assigns a zero to the object's data member, overwriting the original 25 assigned in the constructor, even though the variable is about to go out of scope never to be used again.

The destructor assigns the zero on line 24 just to show you that a destructor could be used for anything you want it to be used for. Instead of zeroing-out data, destructors are often used to close files, close windows, deallocate heap memory, and so forth.

Constructing and Destructing

Having a destructor assign zeros to data members right before their object goes out of scope is not an efficient use of execution time, but we're more concerned here with your understanding the timing of destructors than the overall timing efficiency of the program.

One more iteration will really improve this program, and that's a version that uses the heap for storage. The program in Listing 13.3 includes the class shown earlier, but the `i` data member is now a pointer to an array on the heap rather than a stand-alone integer variable. (Notice that `main()` did absolutely nothing to allocate the data on the heap!) The output messages are removed from Listing 13.3 because you now understand when constructors and destructors are called.

Type

Listing 13.3. Allocating within the constructor.

```
1:  // Filename: CONSHEAP.CPP
2:  // Uses a constructor to allocate and initialize data members on
3:  // the heap and the destructor then deallocates the heap memory.
4:  #include <iostream.h>
5:  class aClass {
6:     int * i;      // i is pointer to heap
7:  public:
8:     void prClass(void);
9:     aClass(void);    // Constructor
10:    ~aClass(void);   // Destructor
11: };
12: void aClass::prClass(void)
13: {
14:    cout << "Here's the memory at i:\n";
15:    for (int ctr=0; ctr<25; ctr++)
16:       { cout << i[ctr] << " "; }
17: }
18: aClass::aClass(void)    // Constructor's implementation code
19: {
20:    i = new int[25];     // Allocate the data member
21:    for (int ctr=0; ctr<25; ctr++)
22:       { i[ctr] = ctr; }  // Initialize heap with 0-24
23: }
24: aClass::~aClass(void)   // Destructor's implementation code
25: {
26:    delete [] i;          // Deallocate all the heap
27: }
28: /////////////////////////////////////////////////////////////
29: main()
30: {
31:    aClass var;           // Automatically calls constructor
```

```
32:    var.prClass();         // Print the initialized data member
33:    return 0;
34: }
```

Here's the memory at i:
0 1 2 3 4 5 6 7 8 9 10 11 12 13 14 15 16 17 18 19 20 21 22 23 24

Does object-oriented programming really make your programming life easier? You bet it does. Think for a moment about the implications of Listing 13.3. If you decide to store the class data on disk and read the initial values into the class array, or if you decide to ask the user for the initial values, or whatever you want to do to change the way the array in aClass is stored and initialized, main() *never* changes! Only the constructor changes. main() goes about its merry way not knowing or caring how the data got to the array.

Even in the best well-structured non-OOP programs, data storage techniques are combined with the code that accesses the data. There is no separation of the data storage (lines 18–23) from the nonclass part of the program that uses the class (lines 31–33). Often, a few changes in a non-OOP data structure can wreak havoc in a program because the data structure is referenced throughout the entire program.

DO	**DON'T**
DO all class cleanup, such as deallocation, in the destructor function. **DO** let the constructor initialize your data so that main() doesn't have to.	**DON'T** forget to deallocate with a destructor if you allocate with a constructor.

Constructing with Arguments

By passing data to constructors, and by allowing for default argument lists, you can write constructor functions that interact better with the surrounding program than the three programs shown so far.

You might want to perform some calculations with user input in main() (or another function called by main()) and then construct an object using results from those calculations. You learned in Day 2's chapter, "C++ Is Superior!" that Visual C++,

Constructing and Destructing

unlike regular C, enables you to define variables anywhere in a program that you need the variables, not just at the top of a block.

The only trouble with adding argument lists to constructor functions is that there must be some way for you to pass the arguments to the constructor, but you never explicitly called constructor functions. The way you pass data to a constructor function is to put those parameters after the object's name when you define the object. Visual C++ then constructs the object and passes the parameters.

Without arguments, you would call the Group class constructor like this:

Group people;   // Define only

With four constructor arguments (an int, a char, a float, and another int for example), you could call Group's constructor like this:

Group people(14, 'A', 21.44, 100);   // Define and initialize

When you want to define and initialize class data at the same time, use a constructor with an argument list. Visual C++ constructs the object and passes the arguments to the constructor function.

Listing 13.4 contains a program that defines and initializes four automobile objects by sending initial values to the constructor function. Note also that the << is overloaded to print the four cars. main() is almost as optimized and about as high-level now as it can be despite the fact that there's lots going on behind the scenes in the class.

Listing 13.4. Constructing with arguments.

```
1:  // Filename: CONSARG.CPP
2:  // Constructor arguments that are passed from main().
3:  #include <iostream.h>
4:  #include <iomanip.h>
5:  #include <string.h>
6:  class Auto {
7:    char name[25];
8:    float price;
9:    char styleCode;
10:   int miles;
11: public:
12:   friend ostream & operator<<(ostream & out, Auto & car);
13:   Auto(char [], float, char, int);   // Constructor with arguments
14:   ~Auto(void);   // Destructor
15: };
16: Auto::Auto(char N[], float P, char S, int M)
17: {
18:   strcpy(name, N);
```

```
19:    price = P;
20:    styleCode = S;
21:    miles = M;
22: }
23: Auto::~Auto(void)    // Destructor's implementation code
24: {
25:    // Nothing to deallocate, but future maintenance
26:    // could be easier with a destructor.
27: }
28: ostream & operator<<(ostream & out, Auto & car)
29: {
30:    out << setprecision(2) << setiosflags(ios::fixed);
31:    out << "Here's a car's statistics:\n";
32:    out << "Name:\t" << car.name << "\n";
33:    out << "Price:\t" << setw(8) << car.price << "\t";
34:    out << "Style:\t" << car.styleCode << "\t";
35:    out << "Miles:\t" << car.miles << "\n\n";
36:    return out;
37: }
38: ////////////////////////////////////////////////////////////////
39: main()
40: {
41:    Auto car1("PowerHorse", 18334.32, 'D', 2592);
42:    Auto car2("Go Get'um", 7334.32, 'S', 30901);
43:    Auto car3("Mover", 19123.45, 'A', 93);
44:    Auto car4("ZoomZoom", 23112.32, 'I', 627);
45:    // Print the objects using overloaded operator
46:    cout << car1 << car2 << car3 << car4;
47:    return 0;
48: }
```

```
Here's a car's statistics:
Name:    PowerHorse
Price:   18334.32        Style:  D       Miles:  2592

Here's a car's statistics:
Name:    Go Get'um
Price:   7334.32         Style:  S       Miles:  30901

Here's a car's statistics:
Name:    Mover
Price:   19123.45        Style:  A       Miles:  93

Here's a car's statistics:
Name:    ZoomZoom
Price:   23112.32        Style:  I       Miles:  627
```

Day 13: Constructing and Destructing

Analysis: On lines 41–44, the program defines four `Auto` objects and initializes them at the same time. You're used to defining and initializing regular variables at the same time like this:

```
char Company[] = "XYZ Industries";
```

Now you can do the same for object variables. Each of the four arguments is passed from `main()` to the public constructor function.

Note: The car's name was not initialized on the heap, but it could have been, and the destructor could then deallocate the heap's name. The destructor on lines 23–27 had nothing to do, but the shell was left there in case the constructor is changed later and needs cleanup by the destructor.

You won't always know the values of each member when you construct an object variable. Sometimes, you might know all the values, and if you do you can use arguments such as the ones in the preceding program. If you know *some* of the arguments, you can use a constructor default argument list such as the ones used in Listing 13.5. The constructor shown in this program contains default values for each member. In `main()`, none, one, two, three, or all four initial values are sent to the constructor when the five objects are defined.

Listing 13.5. Constructing with default arguments.

```
1:  // Filename: CONSARG2.CPP
2:  // Constructor default arguments
3:  #include <iostream.h>
4:  #include <iomanip.h>
5:  #include <string.h>
6:  class Auto {
7:    char name[25];
8:    float price;
9:    char styleCode;
10:   int miles;
11: public:
12:   friend ostream & operator<<(ostream & out, Auto & car);
13:   Auto(char []="Standard Stock", float=20000.0,
14:        char='X', int=0);   // 4 default arguments
15:   ~Auto(void);  // Destructor
16: };
17: Auto::Auto(char N[], float P, char S, int M)
```

```
18: {
19:     strcpy(name, N);
20:     price = P;
21:     styleCode = S;
22:     miles = M;
23: }
24: Auto::~Auto(void)    // Destructor's implementation code
25: {
26:     // Nothing to deallocate, but future maintenance
27:     // could be easier with a destructor.
28: }
29: ostream & operator<<(ostream & out, Auto & car)
30: {
31:     out << setprecision(2) << setiosflags(ios::fixed);
32:     out << setiosflags(ios::showpoint);   // Always show decimal point
33:     out << "Here's a car's statistics:\n";
34:     out << "Name:\t" << car.name << "\n";
35:     out << "Price:\t" << setw(8) << car.price << "\t";
36:     out << "Style:\t" << car.styleCode << "\t";
37:     out << "Miles:\t" << car.miles << "\n\n";
38:     return out;
39: }
40: //////////////////////////////////////////////////////////////////
41: main()
42: {
43:     Auto car1;                    // Use all defaults
44:     Auto car2("Go Get'um");       // Override 1 default
45:     Auto car3("Mover", 19123.45); // Override 2 defaults
46:     Auto car4("ZoomZoom", 23112.32, 'W');  // Override 3 defaults
47:     Auto car5("Fireball", 17528.41, 'F', 823);  // All overridden
48:     // Print the objects using overloaded operator
49:     cout << car1 << car2 << car3 << car4 << car5;
50:     return 0;
51: }
```

```
Here's a car's statistics:
Name:   Standard Stock
Price:  20000.00        Style:  X       Miles:  0

Here's a car's statistics:
Name:   Go Get'um
Price:  20000.00        Style:  X       Miles:  0

Here's a car's statistics:
Name:   Mover
Price:  19123.45        Style:  X       Miles:  0

Here's a car's statistics:
Name:   ZoomZoom
Price:  23112.32        Style:  W       Miles:  0
```

Day 13: Constructing and Destructing

```
Here's a car's statistics:
Name:    Fireball
Price:   17528.41       Style:  F       Miles:  823
```

This program defines five `Auto` object variables in lines 43–47. Each one of the objects uses a different combination of default arguments. The `car1` object is constructed using all four default arguments, and `car5` is constructed using four values that override the default arguments.

As with all default argument lists, the constructor's prototype on lines 13 and 14 contains the default values that are used when and if needed. Using constructor default arguments is useful because you sometimes know initial values and other times you want to accept defaults, such as zeros or some other helpful initial value.

> **Note:** Do you see that the program in Listing 13.5 could *not* contain a constructor prototyped as `Auto(void);`? If there were a prototype with a void argument list, Visual C++ could not know which one to call, it or the prototype with all four default arguments, when you defined an object like this:
>
> `Auto car1;    // Take the default or void?`
>
> You can certainly code a constructor with a `void` argument list, but if you do, you cannot also code one with all default arguments.

Nowhere in `main()` could the statement

`Auto car();    // Not allowed`

appear because Visual C++ would look for a matching constructor function with `void` as an argument list, and it would find none. Remember that in C++, an empty argument means the same as `void`. When defining an object without initializing that object at the same time, leave the parentheses off the object unless you do code a constructor that defines `void` as its argument list.

You Can Now Overload Typecasts!

You now have all the tools you need in order to overload the typecast operator! Although you might not have thought about it, you'll need to typecast data from

built-in data types to your class data, and also you'll need to typecast your class data to the built-in data types.

Actually, writing typecasts to convert built-in data types to your class data is the easiest to do. Using the Auto class with default constructor lists shown in Listing 13.5, what happens when Visual C++ sees this?

```
Auto car2("Go Get'um");
```

As you know from the previous program, Visual C++ creates a car2 object with the string as the name, and the default arguments fill the rest of the data members. This statement is a typecast, although you probably didn't think of it in that way. The statement typecasts a string to an Auto class variable!

Remember that in Visual C++, these statements are both the same:

```
i = int(5.42);   // New style
```

and

```
i = (int)5.42;   // Old style
```

The new style is easier to read, but even more important, the new style lends itself to overloading typecasts yourself. When the compiler sees the statement

```
Auto car2("Go Get'um");
```

Visual C++ knows that it must take the string Go Get'um and convert that string to an Auto object.

What if you wanted to overload the int typecast operator so that an integer can be converted to an Auto variable? You'll only have to write a constructor function that takes a single integer as its argument like this:

```
Auto(int M)
{
   miles = M;              // Here's the argument
   strcpy(name, "Stock");  // Place initial values
   price = 20000.00;
   styleCode = 'A';
}
```

When you typecast an integer to an Auto variable like

```
cout << Auto(32);
```

Visual C++ calls the overloaded constructor function, uses the integer for the miles data member, and initializes the remaining members as dictated by the function.

Constructing and Destructing

Note: If you like the old style of typecasts, you can accomplish the same conversion from integer to `Auto` by coding the typecast like this:

```
cout << (Auto)32;    // Not as clear, but more familiar
```

It's only slightly more difficult to typecast from a class data type to a built-in data type. The first thing you must do is write the operator typecast function. An operator typecast function for built-in data types takes the name of the data type. However, because data types use words and not operators, you have to separate the `operator` from the data type before the function parentheses. For example, here are the three overloaded operator function prototypes that convert to `int`, `float`, and `char`:

```
int & operator int(void);        // Note the space
float & operator float(void);    // after operator and
char & operator char(void);      // before ()
```

Note: Don't overload an `int` data type and call the operator function `operatorint()` because Visual C++ will never realize (without the space before the `int` keyword) that you want to overload the `int` typecast operator.

You must then decide what you want done when the typecasting occurs in the program. For example, if a program typecasts an `Auto` object to a `float`, that programmer might want to return the floating-point member named `price` from the typecast. Here's the short function that accomplishes the `Auto` to `float` overloading:

```
float operator float(void)
{
  return price;     // The "converted" value
}
```

When to Call Constructors Explicitly

There are times when you might directly call a constructor by its name. One of those times appears when you want to return an object from a function, such as an overloaded operator function. Any time a function returns a class value, you can save a step if you use a constructor (assuming that you've defined one with arguments) instead of defining a stand-alone local class variable.

For example, in Day 11's chapter, "Introduction to Overloading Operators," you saw the following operator*() function:

```
Cust operator*(float f)
{
  Cust tempCust;
  tempCust.discPercent = discPercent * f;
  return tempCust;   // (You could have used *this also)
}
```

The function handles operations such as

```
newCustomer = oldCustomer * 1.23;
```

in which a class Cust object is multiplied by a floating-point constant. The local variable tempCust is unneeded. Take a look at this rewritten version of the operator*() function that does the same thing in a more elegant way:

```
Cust operator*(float f)
{
  float tempDiscount;
  tempDiscount = discPercent * f;
  return Cust(tempDiscount);
}
```

To make this function work, there has to be a Cust constructor that takes one floating-point value as its argument. This constructor is called explicitly in the return statement. In other words, an object is created and initialized with the computed floating-point value, and return's newly created object (one that is nameless) exists just long enough for the multiplication to complete in the statement that triggered operator*(). The newly created Cust object then goes away when operator*()'s closing brace appears.

It is slightly more efficient, especially if your class has many members, to create local variables for the needed calculations (as done with tempDiscount) and construct a nameless object using those local variables in the return, as shown here.

The constructor is also useful to call directly when you want to define and initialize heap data in the same statement. For example, the following statement initializes a new Auto (from Listing 13.5) on the heap and also initializes that heap space with the values in the parentheses:

```
Auto *car = new Auto("Roadster", 42123.43, 'A', 12);
```

Constructing and Destructing

If the Auto constructor has all default arguments, those defaults will be sent to the heap if you don't override them with other values.

DO	DON'T
DO specify default argument values for your constructors if you don't want to initialize all arguments every time you call the constructor. **DO** call the constructor by name only when returning temporary objects or allocating heap data. **DO** use constructors to convert from a built-in data type to a class data type. **DON'T** forget the space when overloading a typecast operator that converts from a class value to a built-in data type. **DON'T** use parentheses after an object when you define it unless you are passing parameter values to the object's constructor. **DON'T** define both a constructor that takes no arguments and one that includes all default arguments, or Visual C++ won't know which one to call when you define an object without initializing it.	

Default Constructor Function Considerations

You read earlier in this chapter that Visual C++ uses a built-in constructor if you don't supply one. If you specify any constructor with arguments, you *must* construct using those arguments unless all of them are default arguments. In other words, after you define a constructor that receives arguments, you can no longer define a class variable like this:

```
Auto car1;   // Invalid if at least one argument is required
```

Even though Visual C++ uses its internal constructor if you don't supply one, if you *do* supply one, Visual C++ uses only yours. The next section of the book expands on this a bit. The bottom line is that if you write your own constructor or set of overloaded constructors, your object definition must be such that one of your constructors can be used to initialize the object. If you supply no constructor, Visual C++ creates the object for you, but you lose the advantage of automatic heap allocation and other important constructor advantages that you'll read about later.

As long as you supply a constructor with *all* default arguments or one with *no* arguments specified, you can define a variable without initial values as just shown.

> **Note:** Any time Visual C++ can create an object without your supplying an initial value of any kind, Visual C++ is using a *default constructor*. A default constructor is one with `void` in the argument list or with all arguments in the argument list given default values.

Constructing Arrays of Objects

All the constructor examples so far have constructed only a single object at a time. What if the programmer of the `Auto` class wanted to allocate an array of 50 cars? The constructor function would be applied to each object in the array. It is this array mechanism that assures you that every element of every object array is initialized when you use constructors (and the reverse happens with destructors).

> **Note:** If you supply no constructor, the array of objects will still be defined by Visual C++'s internal default constructor, but each object's members will hold garbage until you assign them something. Supplying your own default constructor with default values enables you to initialize every element in the object array at the time that you define the array.

The program in Listing 13.6 expands on the `Auto` class program a bit by defining an array of five cars. The default arguments in the constructor are assigned to each of the five array elements when they are defined. The program could then change the data in each of the array elements, but it's not done here for brevity. Notice that the `name` member is now allocated on the heap (by the constructor), so the destructor has to deallocate each car's name. The destructor is called when `main()` deallocates the array with `delete`.

Constructing and Destructing

> **Note:** The program in Listing 13.6 demonstrates one of the most important reasons to use constructors and destructors rather than `malloc()` and `free()` (besides the obvious notational advantages). Visual C++ automatically calls constructors and initializes data for you as soon as the data is defined or as soon as you allocate new occurrences of that data on the heap. Visual C++ automatically calls destructors for you when an object goes out of scope or when you deallocate an object. `malloc()` and `free()` are never called automatically.

Listing 13.6. Constructing and destructing an array of objects.

```
1:  // Filename: CONSDEST.CPP
2:  // Constructor and destructor program using the heap.
3:  #include <iostream.h>
4:  #include <iomanip.h>
5:  #include <string.h>
6:  class Auto {
7:     char * name;    // Now must be allocated by constructor
8:     float price;
9:     char styleCode;
10:    int miles;
11: public:
12:    friend ostream & operator<<(ostream & out, Auto & car);
13:    Auto(char []="Standard Stock", float=20000.0,
14:        char='X', int=0);   // 4 default arguments
15:    ~Auto(void);   // Destructor
16: };
17: Auto::Auto(char N[], float P, char S, int M)
18: {
19:    name = new char[25];   // Allocate name space
20:    strcpy(name, N);
21:    price = P;
22:    styleCode = S;
23:    miles = M;
24: }
25: Auto::~Auto(void)   // Destructor's implementation code
26: {
27:    // Must deallocate what main() allocated
28:    delete [] name;   // Brackets required
29: }
30: ostream & operator<<(ostream & out, Auto & car)
31: {
```

```
32:     out << setprecision(2) << setiosflags(ios::fixed);
33:     out << setiosflags(ios::showpoint);  // Always show decimal point
34:     out << "Here's a car's statistics:\n";
35:     out << "Name:\t" << car.name << "\n";
36:     out << "Price:\t" << setw(8) << car.price << "\t";
37:     out << "Style:\t" << car.styleCode << "\t";
38:     out << "Miles:\t" << car.miles << "\n\n";
39:     return out;
40: }
41: //////////////////////////////////////////////////////////////////
42: main()
43: {
44:    Auto * cars = new Auto[5];    // Allocates 5 cars on the heap
45:    // Print the objects using overloaded operator
46:    cout << cars[0] << cars[1] << cars[2] << cars[3] << cars[4];
47:    delete [] cars;
48:    return 0;
49: }
```

Because all five cars are initialized with the same default arguments, the output consists of five repetitions of the following lines:

```
Here's a car's statistics:
Name:   Standard Stock
Price:  20000.00        Style:  X       Miles:  0
```

Figure 13.2 shows the data structure of the Auto data after the constructor finishes its job. main() allocates the five car objects, and then each object's individual constructor allocates the name space for the car's name. Both main() and the destructor's delete (in lines 47 and 28) have to delete arrays. The destructor must delete the name array, and main() must delete the cars array of objects.

You might wonder why main() has to deallocate the cars array. main() allocated the object array, just not the individual names within each object. Therefore, good programming practices dictate that main() deallocate what it allocated.

Note: main()'s delete could not deallocate the name member heap space because main() didn't allocate the name space.

393

Day 13: Constructing and Destructing

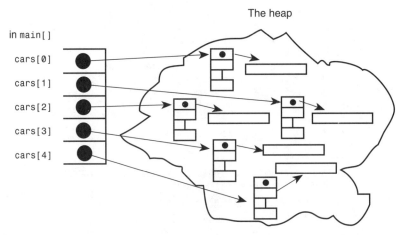

Figure 13.2. Showing how the objects and heap relate.

operator=() and the Copy Constructor

A special kind of constructor, called the *copy constructor*, defines exactly what happens when you define an object from another object. It is easy to confuse the copy constructor with regular constructors and with the assignment operator, but all three are different. Often, programs contain both a copy constructor and an overloaded assignment. The operator=() was saved for this section of the book because it makes the most sense to discuss it and the copy constructor at the same time.

All three of the following statements are different:

```
Auto car1;          // Use the default constructor
Auto car2 = car1;   // Use the copy constructor
car3 = car2;        // Use the overloaded assignment statement
```

In the first statement, a regular default constructor is used to create car1. If the Auto class contains no defined constructor, the compiler's built-in default constructor will be used to create car1. If the Auto class contains a constructor with all default arguments such as

```
Auto(char []="Standard Stock", float=20000.0, char='X', int=0);
```

then that constructor will be used to create car1. If the Auto class contains a constructor with no arguments specified such as

```
Auto(void);    // Simple constructor
```

then that constructor will be used to create `car1`. Both of these constructors, the one with four default arguments and the one with a `void` argument list, are default constructors because they can be used without passing arguments to the constructor.

The second statement, `Auto car2 = car1;` is different from the first statement because a new object is being created from the old. By definition, Visual C++ uses the copy constructor to create `car2`. The copy constructor is different from the default constructor and is used whenever one object is created from another. The `operator=()` is not used here because a new object is being created.

If you don't write a copy constructor, Visual C++ copies all the members from `car1` to `car2`. This *memberwise copy* occurs by default by the compiler if you don't supply a copy constructor. If you supply a copy constructor, your copy constructor will be called when you create a new object from an existing object. A copy constructor always has this format:

```
className(className &);
```

Therefore, the prototype of the copy constructor for the `Auto` class always looks like this:

```
Auto(Auto &);    // Copy constructor
```

This special syntax of the copy constructor, with a reference to the class as the argument, tells the compiler to use this copy constructor whenever one `Auto` object is created from another. As with all constructors, never code a return value for copy constructors.

> **Note:** Although it's easy to forget, the copy constructor is also called when objects are passed by value or returned by value. Your copy constructor determines how the copy of the value is made, either through memberwise copy or via your copy constructor if you code one.

Many times, the default copy constructor works fine, but if your class contains pointers, the memberwise copy of the default copy constructor won't produce correct results. For example, if `car1` contains a `name` member that points to its name on the heap, and a memberwise copy is performed to create `car2`, both cars will have the same name. That's OK, because when you create one object from another like

```
Auto car1 = car2;
```

Day 13: Constructing and Destructing

you expect both objects to have the same data. The problem occurs later when you deallocate car1 (by car1 going out of scope or if you explicitly change the data located at car1's name pointer). When that name changes, so does car2's. But when you created car2 from car1, you wanted them to have the same data values but different occurrences of those values. Therefore, a copy constructor usually contains a straight memberwise copy of all the non-pointer members and the creation of separate pointers for members that are pointers. The following rule holds true when copying objects that contain pointer members:

> *When you are copying objects using memberwise copy, the pointers get copied, but not the data getting pointed to.*

When you create one object from another but the second object does not point to a copy of the first one's data, you'll have problems because when you change one object's pointed-to data, the other object's data changes as well. The next example program demonstrates a copy constructor's body.

The operator=() is a third kind of function you can write. When your compiler runs across a statement such as

```
car3 = car2;
```

an assignment is being performed. car2 must already be constructed, so neither a default constructor nor a copy constructor is used here. Visual C++ uses a default operator=() function unless you supply your own. As with the default copy constructor, the default operator=() function performs a memberwise copy of the data, which is fine in many cases, but not when pointers are involved. Most programmers code their own operator=() function in case they ever add pointers as members later when they expand the class.

The operator=() function takes on the following format except in extremely rare cases:

```
className & operator=(const className &)
```

- ☐ Destructor code for the target object. When you assign car2 to car1 with car1 = car2;, car1 is the *target* object and car2 is the *source*. Before destructing the target object, check to make sure that the target and the source objects aren't the same thing.

- ☐ The copy constructor code.

- ☐ A return of *this (to allow stacked assignments).

The destruction ensures that the target is properly deallocated if needed. Usually pointers are involved, or you wouldn't be worrying about operator=() because the regular memberwise copy works fine on non-pointer data. However, because pointers are involved, you often have to clean up the target pointer on the heap before assigning new data to the target pointer.

Right before you destruct, however, you'll want to check to make sure that the user code hasn't called operator=() like this:

```
car1 = car1;   // OK to do, but watch out for it in operator=()
```

You will want to check to make sure the target is not the same as the source. If you don't, you'll destruct the source and, therefore, destruct the target at the same time.

The program in Listing 13.7 contains all three kinds of functions described in this section: a default constructor, a copy constructor, and an overloaded operator=() function. Almost all your programs that contain pointers as members will contain these functions as does Listing 13.7.

No C++ book would be complete without a version of a String class program. Listing 13.7 contains a simple but workable implementation of a string class to show you what true power you have with Visual C++. There is no string data type in Visual C++ and its predecessor C, although there is in just about every other programming language. You must use functions to copy strings when simple assignment statements are all that's needed in other programming languages. Now, by using this String class, you can have a string class that operates almost exactly like strings in other languages. You can overload = to assign one string to another, and you can overload operators such as + to concatenate strings without resorting to strcpy() and strcat(). All string data is stored on the heap in the program.

Type

Listing 13.7. A String class that overcomes string deficiencies in Visual C++.

```
 1:  // Filename: STRCLASS.CPP
 2:  // Program that contains a string class and a main() that
 3:  // uses the class. The highlights of this program are
 4:  //    1. A safe string class is provided for string initialization,
 5:  //       assignment, and concatenation.
 6:  //    2. A copy constructor is provided to show the format of such
 7:  //       constructors.
 8:  //    3. An operator=() is provided to show how destruction should
 9:  //       first take place before assignment of objects that contain
10:  //       pointers for members.
11:  #include <iostream.h>
```

continues

Constructing and Destructing

Listing 13.7. continued

```
12:    #include <string.h>
13:    class String {
14:      char *st;          // Points to the heap
15:    public:
16:      String & operator=(const String &);   // Overloaded assignment
17:      friend String operator+(const String &, const String &);
18:      friend ostream & operator<<(ostream &, const String &); // Output
19:      String();                  // Default constructor
20:      String(const char *);      // Initializer constructor
21:      String(const String &);    // Copy constructor
22:      ~String();                 // Destructor
23:    };
24:    String & String::operator=(const String & s) // Overloaded
                                                    ↪assignment
25:    {
26:      // The overloaded assignment makes sure that a copy of data is
27:      // made, not just a copy of pointers as would otherwise be
28:      // the case.
29:      if (this == &s)    // Make sure you don't destroy target
30:         { return *this; }  // No need for operator=() after all
31:      delete [] st;     // Deallocate target string to clean it up
32:      // The next two lines are just like the copy constructor
33:      st = new char[strlen(s.st)+1];  // Allocate target based on length
34:                                      // of source string plus string terminator
35:      strcpy(st, s.st);  // Now that room is made, copy the source
                                                    ↪string
36:      return *this;     // Always allow for stacked assignments
37:    }
38:    String::String()     // Default constructor
39:    {
40:      st = '\0';   // Creates a null string
41:    }
42:    String::String(const char * s)
43:    {
44:      // Allocate heap space and copy initialization string
45:      st = new char[strlen(s) + 1];
46:      strcpy(st, s);
47:    }
48:    String::String(const String & s)    // Copy constructor
49:    {
50:      st = new char[strlen(s.st) + 1];
51:      strcpy(st, s.st);
52:    }
53:    String::~String()    // Destructor
54:    {
55:      delete [] st;   // Deallocate memory used by string
56:    }
```

```
57: String operator+(const String & source, const String & tar)
58: {
59:    // Concatenate two strings
60:    // First, see if concatenation is really necessary
61:    if (!strlen(source.st))       // If there's nothing to append to,
62:        return tar;               // don't do concatenation
63:    else if (!strlen(source.st))  // If there's nothing to append,
64:      return source;              // don't do concatenation
65:    String temp;      // Uses default constructor
66:    // Reserve room for both strings and the null
67:    temp.st = new char[strlen(source.st) + strlen(tar.st) + 1];
68:    strcpy(temp.st, source.st);   // Copy source first
69:    strcat(temp.st, tar.st);      // Append target onto source
70:    return temp;
71: }
72: ostream & operator<<(ostream & out, const String & s) // Output
73: {
74:    out << s.st << "\n";
75:    return out;
76: }
77: //////////////////////////////////////////////////////////////////
78: main()
79: {
80:    String myName;        // Use default constructor
81:    String yourName("Sandy");     // Use initializer constructor
82:    String hisName = yourName;    // Use copy constructor
83:
84:    myName = "Terry";   // Use operator=()
85:    // By the way, isn't it nice to assign directly to strings?
86:    cout << "My name is " << myName;
87:    cout << "Your name is " << yourName;
88:    cout << "His name is " << hisName;
89:    hisName = "Jim";
90:    cout << "Oops! I mean his name is " << hisName;
91:    // Now combine them all
92:    String ourName;
93:    ourName = myName + yourName + hisName;
94:    cout << "Our names are " << ourName;
95:    return 0;
96: }
```

```
My name is Terry
Your name is Sandy
His name is Sandy
Oops! I mean his name is Jim
Our names are TerrySandyJim
```

Day 13: Constructing and Destructing

Analysis: Although `main()` is kept simple, that's the beauty of the program! Look how easy it is for `main()` to assign, change, and concatenate strings!

The program contains lots of comments to walk you through the code. Basically, the default constructor enables you to safely create empty strings, and the heap allocation is done for you (lines 38–41). The copy constructor enables you to create one string from another (lines 48–52) and ensures that the second string contains not only a new pointer, but a new copy of the data as well (all on the heap). The assignment operator (lines 24–37) enables you to assign strings to one another after those strings are created as done on lines 84 and 89.

Actually, line 93 uses *both* the overloaded plus sign for concatenation and the overloaded assignment operator for the assignment of the concatenated strings.

Tip: By the way, the strings could have been assigned embedded spaces, but the example happened not to use any spaces in the names.

Note: Looking at the design of a string class gives you lots of opportunity to study classes, constructors, and destructors. There is a lot of debate over the "best" way to write a string class. In reality, looking at a string class's design while learning C++ is advantageous, but C++ compilers often supply a ready-to-go, debugged, and full-functioning string class—and Visual C++ is no exception. In the second bonus chapter at the end of the book, you'll learn about Visual C++'s string class supplied as part of the MFC (Microsoft Foundation Classes) supplied with Visual C++.

DO	DON'T
DO write constructors and destructors when you define arrays of objects. Visual C++ applies the constructor to every element of the object array when the array is created, and the destructor cleans up all the objects when they go out of scope or when you delete them.	

DO write overloaded assignment and copy constructor functions when you create objects that contain pointers as members.

DON'T write an overloaded assignment operator without first checking to see that the two operands are different.

DON'T forget to destruct the first operand in operator=() before performing the assignment.

Summary

Today's chapter strengthens your OOP skills by teaching you constructors and destructors. The constructor takes all the work out of your hands when you define new objects. Whether you define single objects or arrays of objects, the constructor automatically executes for you when those objects go into scope. When objects go out of scope, whether their block ends or you deallocate them, the destructor is called.

Constructors and destructors are nothing more than member functions. Constructors always have the same name as the class. So do destructors, except you must precede destructors with the tilde, ~.

If you do not write constructors and destructors, Visual C++ uses built-in default constructors and destructors. Usually, however, if you want allocation or initialization performed automatically, you should code your own constructors and destructors for the cleanup.

There is a special type of constructor known as the copy constructor. The copy constructor takes as its argument a reference to a class variable. The copy constructor is called when you initialize one object from another or when you pass and return objects by reference. Again, if you don't define a copy constructor, Visual C++ uses its own, but if your class has pointer members, you should probably write your own copy constructor.

This chapter ended with a program demonstrating a string class. With the string class, you can create, initialize, copy, and concatenate strings as if they were built-in data types. The program demonstrated how to overload the assignment operator so that string data, not just pointers to the data, gets copied.

Constructing and Destructing

Q&A

Q. Why do I need constructors and destructors?

A. You don't really *have* to have constructors and destructors if you're willing to do all the work in main() and in functions that main() calls. Constructors set up or create object data in the way you want automatically when the data goes into scope, and destructors destroy data automatically when the data goes out of scope.

With constructors and destructors, you'll have to worry about all the details of creating and initializing your objects. The beauty of classes is that after you write them, all your programs that use those classes become much more simple and easier to write (consider the string class program's main() function in Listing 13.7). The more you let Visual C++ do in the class, the less you'll ever have to do again.

Q. What is a default constructor?

A. A default constructor takes no arguments and tells the compiler exactly what to do when you define an object without initialization.

Visual C++ includes its own default constructors and destructors. That's why you were able to define objects before this chapter. However, when you write your own constructors and destructors, Visual C++ uses your functions rather than its own, and you understand your data needs much better than Visual C++.

Q. What if I want to construct an entire array of objects?

A. The nice thing about Visual C++ constructors is that if you want to construct an array of objects, you don't have to do anything special. Visual C++ applies the constructor on every element in the array!

Q. What is the copy constructor?

A. The copy constructor describes what happens when you define a class variable and assign that variable a value at the time of definition. The copy constructor is used whenever one object is created from another. For example, if you have created a Book class object called title, you can construct a new title from the current one with this statement:

```
Book newTitle = title;   // Use copy constructor
```

operator=() is not called here. The newTitle is created from title using the copy constructor. When a new object is created from an existing one, all members from the existing object are copied to the new object. The copy is performed either the way you've defined with an explicit copy constructor or member-by-member (the compiler's default). A copy constructor always follows the same syntax, and as with all constructors, copy constructors never return values.

Q. What's the difference between the copy constructor and the assignment operator?

A. Both perform memberwise copies of data unless you provide your own versions of them. You learned in today's chapter that memberwise assignment becomes troublesome when pointers are involved. If you change one object's pointed-to data, the other's changes as well. Therefore, you'll often write your own copy constructor and operator=() functions to create new copies of pointed-to data whenever a copy or assignment is made.

The operator=() usually contains a destruction of the argument being assigned to, followed by the copy constructor's code, followed by a return of *this so that stacked assignments can be made.

Workshop

The Workshop offers quiz questions and exercises to hone your skills and give you feedback on today's lesson. You'll find some proposed answers in Appendix D.

Quiz

1. True or False: A class can contain more than one constructor function.
2. What is the maximum number of destructors a class can contain?
3. When are default constructors called?
4. When are your class constructors called?
5. When are destructors called?
6. True or False: When using constructors and destructors, main() never has to allocate and deallocate again.

Constructing and Destructing

7. What is called when the following statement executes: a copy constructor, a default constructor, or an operator=()?

   ```
   classVar2 = classVar1;
   ```

8. What is called when the following statement executes: a copy constructor, a default constructor, or an operator=()?

   ```
   class CV ClassVar2;
   ```

9. What is called when the following statement executes: a copy constructor, a default constructor, or an operator=()?

   ```
   class CV classVar3 = classVar2;
   ```

10. When should you code a copy constructor and operator=()?

Exercises

1. Add two member functions that return the lefthand or righthand portion of a string created with the String class. The function should receive a value that determines how many characters must be returned.

2. Write a program for a beverage company that contains a class called Drinks. Include a member for the individual drink name, wholesale price, and retail price. Create a default constructor and copy constructor, and overload the assignment so that main() can create and manipulate drink objects with ease. Keep all string data on the heap. Also, overload the << and >> operators so that input and output are easy (even though your input will be limited to one word at a time). Have main() initialize, assign, and print several objects to the screen. Be sure that the destructors properly clean up the objects before the program finishes.

DAY 14

Loose Ends: *static* and Larger Programs

Loose Ends: *static* and Larger Programs

Object-oriented programs don't execute in the sequential-like fashion of non-OOP programs. Even if a non-OOP program contains loops and branches, you can generally follow the code and trace the path of the execution line by line.

You can do the same with Visual C++ OOP programs, but the act gets trickier because so many things, such as constructors and destructors, occur automatically. That's the *nice* thing about OOP, however. As you've seen, your objects take on more active roles and do things on their own, and sometimes, as is the case with constructors, they do so behind your back.

Learning OOP is not always an easy task because there are so many pieces of the OOP puzzle, and it's difficult to learn them sequentially. Today's chapter tries to wrap up this week's material by tying up some loose ends. Today, you'll learn about `static` objects and functions, and you'll also see how to work with multipart programs that require separate compilation and linking.

Many of the concepts presented here are not covered in other books because it is assumed that you already know them or that you'll learn them elsewhere. The problem is that not everybody knows how to compile multipart programs, and there isn't always another resource that tells you why you would want to work with several source programs scattered over more than one file.

There might be some topics in this chapter that you've already learned. If so, feel free to skip those topics. Today's chapter is an attempt to give you some rest from the grueling overloaded operators and constructor chapters of the past few days. Although the `static` objects and functions are OOP-like, much of this chapter gives you a better feel for Visual C++'s capabilities as a compiler and perhaps introduces you to some parts of the compiler you weren't aware of previously.

Today, you learn about the following topics:

- ☐ How `static` affects local and global variables
- ☐ How `static` affects non-member functions
- ☐ How to define and use `static` data members
- ☐ The need for `static` member functions
- ☐ The advantages of Visual C++'s project manager when working with multipart programs

All About *static*

You have probably used the `static` keyword in your C programs. The `static` keyword ensures that local variables aren't destroyed when their blocks end. `static` goes before `int`, `float`, or any of the other data types, and you can put `static` before your own data types as well. Later sections in today's chapter illustrate `static` and class data more fully.

For built-in data, Visual C++ handles the `static` keyword in the same way as C. Here's a quick review of `static` to get you in the `static` thinking mode before introducing new `static` topics a little later today.

static Maintains Values

`static` is sometimes called *duration* because being static affects how long (the duration) a variable retains its value. The opposite of `static` duration is `auto` duration. You've probably never seen `auto` in a C program because `auto` is the default. The following three variables are all automatic variables:

```
int i=25;
float f = 76.543;
char c = 'Q';
```

The following three variable definitions are exactly the same as the former three definitions because the former ones were `auto` by default and these are explicitly specified auto:

```
auto int i=25;
auto float f = 76.543;
auto char c = 'Q';
```

 Note: The placement of `auto` and `static` before the data type is a standard but not a requirement. `auto` and `static` can go after the data type if it makes more sense to you to place them there.

Some people confuse `static` and `auto` with `local` and `global`. `static` and `auto` dictate how durable a variable is, meaning that they determine how long a variable retains its value. `local` and `global` determine how visible variables are from other parts of the program. If a variable is `auto`, that variable loses its value when its block ends. If a variable is `static`, it retains its value when its block ends.

Day 14

Loose Ends: *static* and Larger Programs

Consider the program in Listing 14.1. The program contains a static variable named st and an auto variable named a. Variables declared as static are initialized *only* the first time their block begins. This means that the line assigning 25 to st occurs only the first time main() calls the function named seeVars().

Listing 14.1. static variables retain their values; auto variables are always reinitialized.

```
 1: // Filename: STAUTO.CPP
 2: #include <iostream.h>
 3: void seeVars(void);
 4: main()
 5: {
 6:   seeVars();
 7:   seeVars();
 8:   seeVars();
 9:   seeVars();
10:   return 0;
11: }
12: //////////////////////////////////////////////////////////////
13: void seeVars(void)
14: {
15:   static int st = 25;
16:   int a = 10;   // auto by default. a is always assigned the 10
17:   cout << "st is " << st << "\n";
18:   cout << "a is " << a << "\n\n";
19:   // Change both variables
20:   st += 25;
21:   a += 20;
22: }
```

```
st is 25
a is 10

st is 50
a is 10

st is 75
a is 10

st is 100
a is 10
```

main() calls seeVars() four times. Inside seeVars() the st and a integer variables are printed and then updated with new values in lines 20 and 21. If you trace the output, you'll see that a's updated value is not carried through to the next seeVars() function call, but st's new value is. In other words, even though 10 is added to a each time seeVars() executes, the value doesn't remain in a because a is automatic. The duration of a's value is much shorter than that of st because a is defined as auto and st is defined as static.

To see why you shouldn't confuse static and auto with local and global, consider the visibility of the two variables in seeVars(). Both variables are local, and main() could not print seeVar()'s local variables because both are local to seeVars().

To drive the point home further, the program in Listing 14.2 contains a global variable. Although defining global variables between two functions is not the best thing you can do (the global variable definitions are too difficult to find when looking through the program), you'll see that the global variable named g must be static, and it is. All global variables are static, and a global variable can never be defined as auto.

Listing 14.2. The global variable named g is static.

```
1:  // Filename: GLOBST.CPP
2:  #include <iostream.h>
3:  void doSomething(void);
4:  main()
5:  {
6:    doSomething();
7:    doSomething();
8:    doSomething();
9:    doSomething();
10:   doSomething();
11:   return 0;
12: }
13: //////////////////////////////////////////////////////////////////
14: //     *** Look at the next line for a global variable ***
15: int g = 100;
16: //     *** g is static because all globals are static
17: //////////////////////////////////////////////////////////////////
18: void doSomething(void)
19: {
20:   cout << "g is " << g << "\n\n";
21:   // Change global variable
22:   g += 100;
23: }
```

```
g is 100

g is 200

g is 300

g is 400

g is 500
```

Loose Ends: *static* and Larger Programs

If the global variable g were not `static`, it would not retain its value every time `doSomething()` is called. However, the global variable is `static`. Global variables cannot be defined with `auto` because they are initialized at compile time, not at runtime.

Think about the placement of the variable on line 15. No part of the program actually executes line 15; the program executes *around* line 15 because functions surround the variable. Visual C++ could not initialize g at runtime because no execution of line 15 really takes place. Therefore, g is defined at compile time, and when g changes during runtime, its value is retained.

Note: g is global but not visible to `main()` because all global variables are defined from their point of definition *down* in the source file.

Here's the bottom-line rule for distinguishing between `local` and `global`:

All global variables are `static` by default and cannot be defined as `auto`. All local variables are `auto` by default, but you can define local variables with `static`. Whether `static` or `auto`, local variables are always local to the block in which they are defined, but local `static` variables retain their values when their blocks end.

There's One Slight Variation with *static* Globals

As you read in the last section, all global variables have static duration, and there's nothing you can do to make global variables `auto`. However, the following global variable definitions do not quite do the same thing:

```
int gSta = 5;
```

and

```
static int gSta = 5;
```

If `gSta` were a local variable, these would be two different statements indeed because local variables are automatic unless you override their duration with `static`.

When you explicitly define a global variable with the `static` keyword, you are telling Visual C++ to give that global variable single file scope. In other words, if you link another set of functions to the program with the static global variable (as will be explained later in today's chapter), those other functions will not be able to use your file's global variable. An explicit static definition tells the compiler not to let other files have access even when linked to the current source file.

If you do not give a global variable static duration, all other files linked to yours can access the global variable as long as they contain the extern keyword like this:

```
extern int gSta;    // Use another file's global variable
```

Functions Can Be *static* Too!

As with global variables, you can limit a function's visibility from other source files that might be linked to yours by preceding the function's definition with static. Listing 14.3 shows a program that contains both a static global and a static function. If another program is linked to this one that uses the same names, there will not be a name clash.

Listing 14.3. static before a function name limits the use to the current source file.

```
 1: // Filename: STATFN.CPP
 2: // Includes a static function and global variable
 3: #include <iostream.h>
 4: // Global variable comes next
 5: static char gc = 'Q';
 6: // Static function's prototype appears next
 7: static void doFun(void);
 8: main()
 9: {
10:    cout << "In main(), gc is " << gc << "\n";
11:    doFun();  // Never pass global variables because they don't
12:              // have to be passed.
13:    return 0;
14: }
15: //////////////////////////////////////////////////////////////
16: // Static function is next and can be called only in this file
17: void doFun(void)
18: {
19:   cout << "Welcome to doFun() where gc is still " << gc << "\n";
20: }
```

Loose Ends: *static* and Larger Programs

```
In main(), gc is Q
Welcome to doFun() where gc is still Q
```

If other functions written in separately compiled source files are to be linked and called from this one, they could never access gc or doFun(), even if an extern statement were included in their listings. When all the code is linked together, the functions from the other files that call doFun() or that use the gc variable will get an error because of this file's static keywords on lines 5 and 7. Notice that the static keyword doesn't have to be listed again in front of the function definition (line 17) as long as it appears in the function's prototype.

By the way, if you want a second source file to be able to call another file's non-static function after you link them together, you must prototype the function in all files that call your file's function with the function's prototype preceded by extern like this:

```
extern void prData(int, char *);   // Call another file's function
```

> **Using Another File's Globals and Functions**
>
> Using multiple source files and determining which global variables and functions can be shared and which ones must be limited with static becomes an important topic in programming departments in which several programmers might work on different parts of the same program.
>
> You just cannot arbitrarily name variables and functions when your code will be linked to someone else's to produce single executable modules. There must be communication between all programmers, and a central repository of variable and function names (sometimes called the *data dictionary*) must be kept so that programmers don't use duplicate names that clash when all the separate files are linked together.
>
> If you want to create a variable or function that will never clash with those of another programmer who might link files with yours, add static before the global variables and file names. In this way you'll ensure that those names are available only from within your source file. (You must, however, be sure to compile your source file separately before linking to the other files.)

It is said that non-static functions and non-static global variables have *external linkage*. That is, other source code external to the current source file can use the non-static definitions. static data and functions have *internal linkage* because only internal routines to the current source file can use them.

Objects Are No Exception

Just because you're now putting data into `class` objects doesn't mean that the rules of local, global, `auto`, and `static` change. You can create `static` object variables that have internal linkage and `static` local object variables that retain their values when their block is reentered.

Listing 14.4 contains a program that defines a local object variable in a second function called by `main()`. Every time the function is called, its object variable's previous value is still known.

Listing 14.4. You can define objects to be static too.

```
1:  // Filename: STATOBJ.CPP
2:  // Objects can be static too
3:  #include <iostream.h>
4:  static void doFun(void);
5:  class aClass {
6:     int i;
7:     float f;
8:  public:
9:     aClass(int I, float F) {i = I; f = F;}
10:    ~aClass() {};         // Nothing needed in destructor
11:    void setI(int I) { i = I; }
12:    void setF(float F) {f = F; }
13:    int getI(void) { return i; }     // Access functions
14:    float getF(void) { return f; }
15: };
16: main()
17: {
18:   for (int i=0; i<5; i++)
19:   { doFun(); }
20:   return 0;
21: }
22: ////////////////////////////////////////////////////////////////
23: // The next function contains a static object
24: void doFun(void)
25: {
26:    static aClass aVar(10, 65.0);
27:    // Print the object
28:    cout << "aVar contains the member values of " << aVar.getI();
29:    cout << " and " << aVar.getF() << "\n";
30:    // Change the value of the data
31:    aVar.setI(aVar.getI()*3);   // Multiply member by 3
32:    aVar.setF(aVar.getF()*(float)2.5);  // Multiply member by 2.5
33: }
```

Loose Ends: *static* and Larger Programs

```
aVar contains the member values of 10 and 65
aVar contains the member values of 30 and 162.5
aVar contains the member values of 90 and 406.25
aVar contains the member values of 270 and 1015.63
aVar contains the member values of 810 and 2539.06
```

There was not enough of a program here to overload an output operator, so some access member functions were added to get the member data for printing. From the output, you'll see that the class variable retained its former value and was never reinitialized when doFun() was called again. static kept the constructor on line 26 from constructing the object each time through the function.

You might wonder about the embedded function calls on lines 31 and 32. doFun() has no read or write access to the two data members of aVar. The inside function on lines 31 and 32 get the member's value, and the outside function stores that value after multiplying the value by another number.

If you were simply to remove static from the constructor on line 26, this would be the output of the program:

```
aVar contains the member values of 10 and 65
aVar contains the member values of 10 and 65
aVar contains the member values of 10 and 65
aVar contains the member values of 10 and 65
aVar contains the member values of 10 and 65
```

Without static, aVar is reconstructed (and, therefore, reinitialized) each of the five times main() calls doFun().

When you are defining global static objects (not that you'll do that a lot), Visual C++ defines the objects just like all other global variables. If you ever define global object variables, you should probably define them before main() and not sneak them in between two other functions.

The program in Listing 14.5 creates a global static object with a constructor that prints a message. Throughout this book, you've read how Visual C++ takes the details out of main() and moves those details into the class. Here's a program taking that to the extreme: main() has no code except a return, even though the program produces output! See whether you can tell why.

Listing 14.5. Global static object can take over the program (see main()).

```
1:  // Filename: GLOSTAOB.CPP
2:  // Interesting program with no main() but with output
3:  #include <iostream.h>
```

```
 4: class aClass {
 5:    int i;
 6: public:
 7:    aClass();    // Place all the program's output in constructor
 8:    ~aClass() {}; // Nothing needed in destructor
 9: };
10: // Constructor produces the output
11: aClass::aClass()
12: {
13:    i = 25;
14:    cout << "Here's the program output.\n";
15:    cout << "Let's generate some stuff...\n";
16:    for (int ctr=0; ctr<10; ctr++)
17:       { cout << "Counting at " << ctr << "\n"; }
18: }
19: ////////////////////////////////////////////////////////////////
20: // Global object next!
21: aClass anObject;
22: ////////////////////////////////////////////////////////////////
23: main()
24: {
25:    return 0;
26: }
```

```
Here's the program output.
Let's generate some stuff...
Counting at 0
Counting at 1
Counting at 2
Counting at 3
Counting at 4
Counting at 5
Counting at 6
Counting at 7
Counting at 8
Counting at 9
```

When is constructor code called? You know that constructor code is called at the time an object is defined. When is the anObject object defined? In line 21 before main(). Therefore, anObject's constructor is called before main() because all global variables that reside before main() must be created before main() begins. The constructor in lines 11–18 produces a lot of output that's unrelated to the object being created, but the point of all this is to study global objects.

You'd do best to stay away from global variables completely. As you see in Listing 14.5, global objects cause your program to behave a little differently than you might expect (including the suggested use of printf()...ugh!). Global objects also can cause name

Loose Ends: *static* and Larger Programs

clashes later if you're not careful about using static. However, global variables are sometimes useful, especially when virtually every function in a program needs access to the same variable. In that case, you would be foolish to pass the same local variable between every function.

DO	DON'T

DO define local variables with the static keyword if you want them to retain their values every time execution of the program reenters their block of code.

DO use static if you want to limit a global variable's access to the current file only.

DO put static before all functions if you don't want those functions to be called from other routines eventually linked to yours.

DON'T try to define global variables (or functions for that matter) with auto, or you'll get an error message. Global variables are always static by default.

Special Use of *static* Inside Classes

Perhaps some of the previous material was review for you, but putting static inside class headers will be new. By putting static in front of data members in your class header, you instruct Visual C++ to create just one instance of that member, even though there will be multiple instances of all the other data members.

Consider the following two sets of classes, the second differing from the first by a single static keyword:

```
class aClass {
  int i;
  float x;
  char c;
public:
  aClass(int, float, char);   // Constructor
  ~aClass();                  // Destructor
};
```

and

```
class aClass {
  int i;
  static float x;    // Here's the difference!
  char c;
public:
  aClass(int, float, char);  // Constructor
  ~aClass();                 // Destructor
};
```

In the second class, the x member is static. The static keyword before a member name has a different (but slightly related) use from using static in front of variable definitions. A static class member appears only once no matter how many object variables are created for the class.

If you define four class objects like

```
aClass var1, var2, var3, var4
```

Visual C++ creates four sets of three of the members for the class without the static, but there's only *one* occurrence of the member x, as Figure 14.1 illustrates. Although x is private, you can declare public data members static as well.

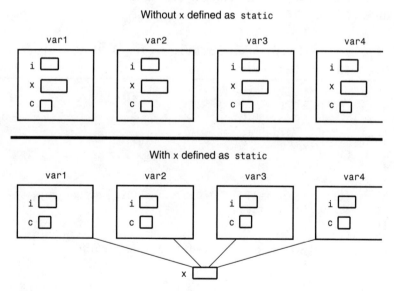

Figure 14.1. There is only one instance of a static member no matter how many objects there are.

Loose Ends: *static* and Larger Programs

Note: Although you can treat member functions as if a copy of each one appears in each object, Visual C++ creates only one member function for each class. Each object instantiated from the class then contains function pointers to its member functions.

`static` data members are often used to keep track of the number of objects defined. For example, a constructor could add one to the `static` member each time it is called. In the object's destructor function, you could subtract one from the count. At any time during program execution, the `static` member would hold the total count of how many objects have been constructed. (Other statistical values could also be calculated and stored in `static` members.)

There is no single object associated with `static` members. It is said that `static` members belong to the class, not to an object. Therefore, when referencing `static` members, you must precede the `static` member name with the class name and use the scope resolution operator (`::`) to resolve the member instead of using an object's name. The program in Listing 14.6 makes this point clear. It uses a public `static` member so that `main()` can more easily access the number of objects created at any one time.

Listing 14.6. Using `static` to track the number of objects created.

```
 1: // Filename: STATMEM.CPP
 2: // Members can be static too
 3: #include <iostream.h>
 4: #include <ctype.h>
 5: class aClass {
 6:    int i;
 7:    float f;
 8: public:
 9:    static int total;    // One per class, not per object
10:    aClass(int I, float F);
11:    ~aClass();
12: };
13: // Modify total in constructor and destructor
14: aClass::aClass(int I, float F)
15: {
16:    i = I;
17:    f = F;
18:    aClass::total++;    // Another object has been created
19: }
20: aClass::~aClass()
```

```
21: {
22:   aClass::total--;   // Another object has been destroyed
23: }
24: //////////////////////////////////////////////////////////////
25: // First, initialize the static total to zero
26: int aClass::total = 0;
27: //////////////////////////////////////////////////////////////
28: main()
29: {
30:   aClass var1(1, 2.2);
31:   aClass var2(1, 2.2);
32:   aClass var3(1, 2.2);
33:   cout << aClass::total << " objects created so far. ";
34:   cout << "\nConstructing another inside a new block...\n";
35:   {  // Ensures that a really local object is created temporarily
36:     aClass var4(1, 2.2);
37:     cout << aClass::total << " objects created so far.\n";
38:   }  // The last object will now go away
39:   cout << "... Now there are only " << aClass::total << " left.\n";
40:   return 0; // All the others will go away now also
41: }
```

```
3 objects created so far.
Constructing another inside a new block...
4 objects created so far.
... Now there are only 3 left.
```

The first place to begin studying Listing 14.6 is line 26. You'll be surprised by the placement of the initialization of `total`. At first glance, it looks as though `total` is a global variable, but it's not—it's a class member, and the scope resolution operator indicates so.

`static` members cannot be initialized inside the class because no memory is reserved in the class header. However, there might not be object variables defined in `main()` for a long time, and a programmer might need access to a `static` value long before the first object is defined.

Therefore, `static` data member values are initialized in never-never land before `main()` begins but after the class is declared. You have to repeat the data type of the `static` member (`int` in Listing 14.6's line 26), and you have to issue an initial value.

> **Note:** If the `static` member had been private in Listing 14.6, `main()` could access the `static` member only through the use of `static` member functions.

Loose Ends: *static* and Larger Programs

If you use *private* static data members, you'll need to use static member functions to manipulate those static data members. Visual C++ always passes the *this pointer to regular member functions, but no single object variable is associated with static data members because static members belong to the class, not to objects.

Another reason to define static member functions to access static data members is that you might want to work with the static value before you define any objects in a program. Listing 14.6 could have printed the total number of objects defined, zero, before any objects were actually defined. (Of course, Listing 14.6 contained a public static data member, so no access function was needed.)

Listing 14.7 shows the same program as Listing 14.6 with a static member function that accesses the now-private static data member. You can see that a little more work is needed to use private static data members, but as always, it is usually best to keep all data, even static data, private and away from other routines except through member functions.

Listing 14.7. static member functions access static members.

```
1:  // Filename: STATPRI.CPP
2:  // Use static member functions when your static data is private
3:  #include <iostream.h>
4:  #include <ctype.h>
5:  class aClass {
6:     int i;
7:     float f;
8:     static int total;     // One per class, not per object and private
9:  public:
10:    static int getTotal(void);   // The static function defined below
11:    aClass(int I, float F);
12:    ~aClass();
13: };
14: int aClass::getTotal(void)
15: {
16:    // Returns the total member so main() can print it
17:    return aClass::total;
18: }
19: // Modify total in constructor and destructor
20: aClass::aClass(int I, float F)
21: {
22:    i = I;
23:    f = F;
24:    aClass::total++;   // Another object has been created
25: }
26: aClass::~aClass()
27: {
```

```
28:    aClass::total--;   // Another object has been destroyed
29: }
30: /////////////////////////////////////////////////////////////////
31: // First, initialize the static total to zero
32: int aClass::total = 0;
33: /////////////////////////////////////////////////////////////////
34: main()
35: {
36:    aClass var1(1, 2.2);
37:    aClass var2(1, 2.2);
38:    aClass var3(1, 2.2);
39:    cout << aClass::getTotal() << " objects created so far. ";
40:    cout << "\nConstructing another inside a new block...\n";
41:    {  // Ensures that a really local object is created temporarily
42:      aClass var4(1, 2.2);
43:      cout << aClass::getTotal() << " objects created so far.\n";
44:    } // The last object will now go away
45:    cout << "... Now there are only " << aClass::getTotal()
      ➥<< " left.\n";
46:    return 0; // All the others will go away now also
47: }
```

```
3 objects created so far.
Constructing another inside a new block...
4 objects created so far.
... Now there are only 3 left.
```

Notice that when calling `static` member functions, you must resolve the scope of such functions with the scope resolution operator, just as you have to do when accessing `static` data members. On line 14, where the `static` function is defined, you don't repeat the `static` keyword; `static` appears before function names only in the class header.

Note: `static` members replace variables that used to be global before OOP came along. A global variable can be used to keep track of data as the data is allocated. However, if another programmer also works on your code and tries to define the same global variable—or even more surprising and harder to debug, if another programmer's code is linked to yours and both of you use the same global variable—a name clash will occur. The `static` member offers a much safer way of keeping count of data. The `static` member is more appropriate because it relates directly to the class. If you increment and decrement `static` members in constructors and destructors, the rest of the program never has to take care of the counts.

Loose Ends: *static* **and Larger Programs**

DO	DON'T

DO use the scope resolution operator, ::, to access static data members and function members. No object is associated with static members, so you must use the class to call a static function or access a static member.

DO use static member functions to manipulate private static data members.

DO initialize a static data member before main() begins. You must repeat the data type of the static data member before its name when defining it.

DO use static data members to track statistics about a class, such as totals and averages.

DON'T repeat the static keyword before the function definition. static goes before the function name only in the class header.

Multifile Processing

Visual C++ programmers almost always work with multiple source files when creating a large program. If breaking your programs into separate functions is good (and it is), breaking large programs into separate source files is good too. There are several logical places to break source files when they grow too large to manage individually.

This section of the book is not so much about OOP as it is about programming in Visual C++ in general. Nevertheless, OOP does add extra reasons for breaking programs into separate files, especially class header files and class implementation code.

> **Note:** To review, a class header is a class with data member declarations and member function prototypes. The implementation is the definition of all the member functions (the actual code in the functions). Figure 14.2 shows the difference.

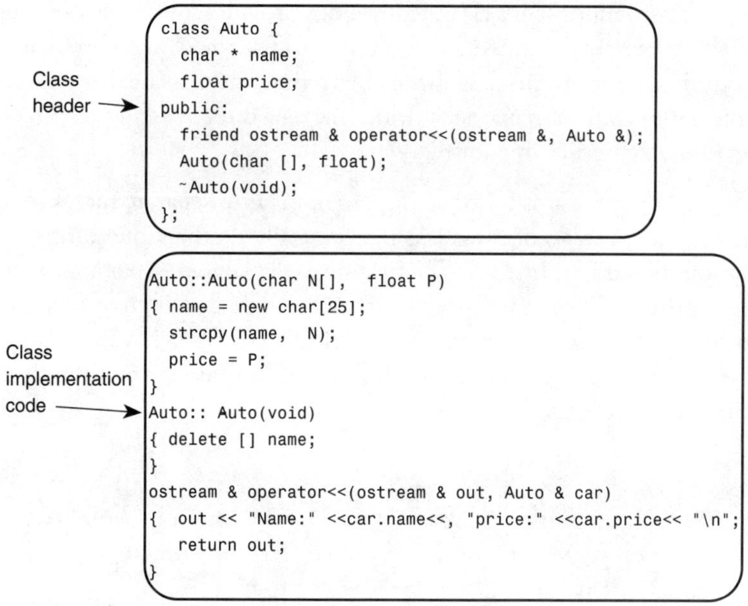

```
                    class Auto {
                      char * name;
                      float price;
     Class           public:
     header  ──▶       friend ostream & operator<<(ostream &, Auto &);
                      Auto(char [], float);
                      ~Auto(void);
                    };

                    Auto::Auto(char N[],  float P)
                    { name = new char[25];
                      strcpy(name,  N);
                      price = P;
     Class          }
     implementation Auto:: Auto(void)
     code    ──▶    { delete [] name;
                    }
                    ostream & operator<<(ostream & out, Auto & car)
                    {  out << "Name:" <<car.name<<, "price:" <<car.price<< "\n";
                       return out;
                    }
```

Figure 14.2. The difference between a class header and the class implementation.

As you've seen, classes provide building-block mechanisms for programmers. When you write a class, the program that uses the class neither knows nor cares how data is stored, initialized, and retrieved. As long as you write enough access member functions, the rest of the program uses the class data members any time it needs to. The member functions, however, provide the control and safety to ensure that the user program doesn't change the data when it shouldn't be able to do so.

There are now companies that sell only class libraries that you can incorporate into your own programs. You can purchase a class library to handle database-like file access, one to handle extended precision mathematics, and one that creates and works with text windows on the screen.

The class vendors do not offer source code when they sell their programs, because they don't want to give away their coding secrets and there is just not a good reason to do so. The vendor sells a compiled class implementation file (called an *object* file). A well-written class is usable by programs. That means that enough access functions were provided and the class was designed in such as way as to make the internal class code secondary to the objects you create with the class. You'll open and close colorful windows on your screen, for instance, without regard for how those windows were constructed. Your program just issues orders to the windows to display themselves, and they do it via the class code.

Loose Ends: *static* and Larger Programs

When a class vendor sells a class, that vendor provides source code for the class header and also probably documentation on how to use the class to build and manipulate objects derived from the class. Instead of typing the class header yourself, you'll just merge it into your source code with an `#include` directive and then link the compiled class implementation to your file.

There are other reasons for breaking programs into separate files. Often, you'll find that you have a series of programs that basically do the same thing except for a few functions that differ. Instead of compiling each program separately, you can compile the code that is alike in each program, then compile the different functions separately, and link each into its own executable file. If you later have to change one of the functions, you can recompile and link it without taking the time to recompile the entire source program.

Note: In a multifile source code that will eventually be linked into a single executable, there can be only one `main()` function because `main()` can exist only once in any executable program.

Tip: Advanced Visual C++ programmers especially rely on the project manager to tame the compilation and linking of Windows programs that sometimes consist of more than 10 files.

A Compile/Link Review Might Help

This book has often used terms such as *source code, object code, compilation, linking,* and *executable file* without lots of explanation because if you picked up this book and got past Day 1's chapter, you've probably worked with these terms before. You've certainly used all of them whether or not you knew the names of the terms. As a quick review to jog your memory, Table 14.1 explains the terms you need to know to continue in this chapter.

Table 14.1. A review of some multifile and compile-time terms.

Term	Description
Compile	Convert source code to object code. Selecting **P**roject+Com**p**ile File (Ctrl+F8) compiles your Visual C++ source program. Often, this term is loosely used to convert source code directly to executable (as happens when you select **P**roject+**Ex**ecute [Ctrl+F5] after typing or loading a C++ program). You must keep in mind, however, that an in-between linking step is being performed for you when you press Ctrl+F5.
Executable	The format of a program after all compiling and linking has taken place. An executable program is one that can be run, whereas source code and object code cannot be run until you convert them to an executable program.
Link	The linking step prepares the file for execution. As your program is compiled, Visual C++ transforms it into object code. If several parts of one program are scattered over several files on the disk, such as `main()` and a few functions in one source file, and other functions that `main()` calls in another source file, you must compile each separately into several object files. Each object file can then be linked to a single executable file, which can then run.
Object Code	The internal binary representation of your source program. In a way, the object file is your program in the format your PC understands, and your source code is in the format that you can read. Several object files can be linked together to form a single executable program that can be run.

Figure 14.3 helps illustrate the process of compiling and linking.

Day 14

Loose Ends: *static* and Larger Programs

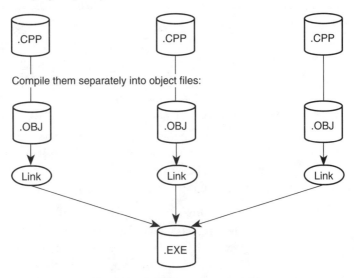

Figure 14.3. All separate source and object files must be linked into a single executable before you can run a program.

The nice thing about an environment such as Visual C++ is that you don't have to know anything about source and object files to write and execute programs. The **P**roject **E**xecute (Ctrl+F5) menu option converts your source file into an object file and then links the file into an executable file. Pressing Ctrl+F5 once more *then* runs the file (assuming there are no errors).

> **Note:** If you ever get linker errors when you press Ctrl+F5, you have probably misspelled a keyword, function, or variable name. Or you might have called a function from your program that doesn't exist and you failed to link another program to it that has the proper function—or you forgot to code the function altogether. The more you learn (with initial help from this chapter!) about compilation and linking, the better you'll understand error messages and the faster you'll program.

Visual C++ follows the standard file-naming rules when compiling your program. Source programs end with the filename extension .CPP. After Visual C++ compiles a program into object code, the object file ends with .OBJ. Linking the .OBJ file produces an executable file with the extension .EXE. (The first part of the filenames before .OBJ and .EXE will be the same as the source file unless you're combining several source files, in which case you'll have to specify the first names as described a little later.)

Clean Up Your Act!

Over time, you'll unknowingly build up a lot of .OBJ files on the disk as you compile. Visual C++ keeps the in-between object files on disk in case you want to use them later. Visual C++ also creates .BSC and .SBR browser database files (you'll read about the browser in the first Extra Credit Bonus chapter) when you compile programs.

When you write stand-alone programs that aren't part of multifile programs, you can delete these .OBJ, .BSC, and .SBR files from your program directory to free up space.

You'll also create a lot of .EXE program files over time. If you are finished with a program and you don't need it anymore, back it up onto a floppy disk or tape (just in case!) and then delete its executable and source file from your disk to free as much space as possible.

By the way, you can execute any Visual C++ .EXE directly from the Windows Program Manager. For instance, if you compile a program into an executable file and exit Visual C++, select **F**ile **R**un... from the Program Manager, and type the path and filename of the .EXE file.

Figure 14.4 shows how a larger multifile Visual C++ program might come together to form a single executable file. Such a system of files is called a *project*. Visual C++ contains special handling for projects that is explained in the next section. At any one time, the pieces of a project require different kinds of attention. For example, header files must be included, source files must be compiled, and object files must be linked.

Loose Ends: *static* and Larger Programs

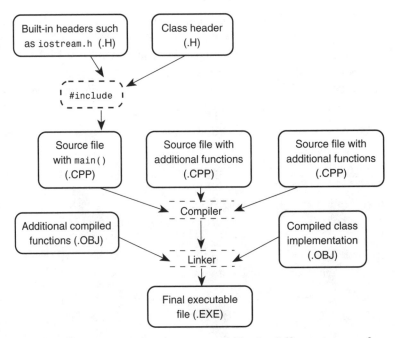

Figure 14.4. Large projects often have several files in different stages of compilation.

Programming departments aren't the only users of multifile source programs. Even when writing fairly small programs, you might want to separate the class header, the class implementation, the source program, and additional functions you have written in the past. When you write a general-purpose function that you'll want to use again, compile that function into its own .OBJ object file, and store it in a subdirectory you designate for such a library of functions. When you write a program that needs one or more of the functions you've compiled into objects, you can link those object files to the program that calls them, instead of including the source files and compiling the same functions over and over. You'll save time and finish your work faster if you compile the general-purpose functions once and link the already-compiled functions to the programs that need them.

Project Files Make Multifiles a Snap

As mentioned at the end of the preceding section, a collection of multiple files that you'll eventually combine into single executable files are called projects. Instead of having to find each file to link when you need it, you can set up a *project file* in Visual

C++ that does the necessary, including compiling and linking for you. You then have to worry about only the source code, and Visual C++ will take care of putting needed files together.

This section of the book walks you through building and using a project file. At the end of yesterday's chapter, exercise number 2 described a beverage program to construct and print beverage data. The answer for the program appears in Appendix D. The answer, however, appears as all one file, as most of the programs in this book will appear, because of space limitations. However, that program is easy to separate into separate files. This section explains how to use the Visual C++ project commands to work with the separate files.

To start with, Listing 14.8 contains the program code shown as one long program (*long* is relative here because as usual "real world" programs go, the beverage program is short). Because the program is simple and because you should have no problem with the code itself at this point, concentrate instead on the multipart program created from this long listing.

Type

Listing 14.8. The beverage program as a single long file.

```
 1: // Filename: BEV.CPP
 2: // Program to track, initialize, copy, and print beverage products.
 3: #include <iostream.h>
 4: #include <iomanip.h>
 5: #include <string.h>
 6: class Drinks {
 7:   char * name;
 8:   float whole;
 9:   float retail;
10: public:
11:   Drinks(char * = "Noname", float=0.0, float=0.0);
12:   ~Drinks();    // Destructor
13:   Drinks(const Drinks &);  // Copy constructor
14:   Drinks & operator=(const Drinks &);  // Assignment overload
15:   friend ostream & operator<< (ostream &, const Drinks &);
16:   friend istream & operator>> (istream &, Drinks &);
17: };
18: Drinks::Drinks(char * N, float W, float R)
19: {
20:   name = new char[strlen(N) + 1];
21:   strcpy(name, N);
22:   whole = W;
23:   retail = R;
24: }
25: Drinks::~Drinks()
26: {
```

continues

Loose Ends: *static* and Larger Programs

Listing 14.8. continued

```
27:    delete [] name;
28: }
29: Drinks::Drinks(const Drinks & d)      // Copy constructor
30: {
31:    int newLen = strlen(d.name) + 1;
32:    name = new char[newLen];
33:    strcpy(name, d.name);
34:    whole = d.whole;
35:    retail = d.retail;
36: }
37: Drinks & Drinks::operator=(const Drinks & d)   // Assignment overload
38: {
39:    if (this == &d)
40:       { return *this; }
41:    delete [] name;   // Deallocate old string
42:    name = new char[strlen(d.name) + 1];
43:    strcpy(name, d.name);   // Copy string member
44:    whole = d.whole;        // Copy float members
45:    retail = d.retail;
46:    return *this;
47: }
48: ostream & operator<< (ostream & out, const Drinks & d)
49: {
50:    out << setprecision(2) << setiosflags(ios::showpoint);
51:    out << setiosflags(ios::fixed);
52:    out << "Name: " << d.name << "\n";
53:    out << "Wholesale price: " << d.whole << "\tRetail price: ";
54:    out << d.retail << "\n\n";
55:    return out;
56: }
57: istream & operator>> (istream & in, Drinks & d)
58: {
59:    cout << "Please add to our line of beverage products.\n";
60:    cout << "What is the name of the next product? (one word
           ↪please)";
61:    char tempInput[80];     // Need to temporarily
62:    in >> tempInput;                  // store user input
63:    d.name = new char[strlen(tempInput) + 1];   // onto the heap.
64:    strcpy(d.name, tempInput);
65:    in.ignore();  // Remove carriage return
66:    cout << "What is the retail price of " << d.name << "? ";
67:    in >> d.retail;
68:    cout << "What is the wholesale price of " << d.name << "? ";
69:    in >> d.whole;
70:    return in;
71: }
72: /////////////////////////////////////////////////////////////////
73: main()
74: {
```

```
75:    Drinks * bevs = new Drinks[5];   // Array of 5 drinks on the heap
76:    for (int i=0; i<5; i++)
77:       { cin >> bevs[i]; };     // Ask the user for the beverages
78:    cout << "\n\nHere's what you entered:\n";
79:    for (i=0; i<5; i++)
80:       { cout << bevs[i]; };    // Show the user for the beverages
81:    bevs[3] = bevs[4];           // Test the overloaded assignment
82:    Drinks newBev = bevs[1];     // Test the copy constructor
83:    Drinks another("Diet Peach Flavored", .23, .67);
84:    cout << "After some changes:\n";
85:    cout << bevs[3] << newBev << another << "\n";   // Print new values
86:    cout << "Mmmm... Made from the best stuff on earth!";
87:    delete [] bevs;
88:    return 0;
89: }
```

 Note: Actually, the program in Listing 14.8 is *already* a multipart file because it includes several header files in lines 3–5.

The first place to begin breaking this program into separate files is with the class header, which could be stored on the disk as BEV.H:

```
1: // Filename: BEV.H
2: class Drinks {
3:    char * name;
4:    float whole;
5:    float retail;
6: public:
7:    Drinks(char * = "Noname", float=0.0, float=0.0);
8:    ~Drinks();    // Destructor
9:    Drinks(const Drinks &);   // Copy constructor
10:   Drinks & operator=(const Drinks &);   // Assignment overload
11:   friend ostream & operator<< (ostream &, const Drinks &);
12:   friend istream & operator>> (istream &, Drinks &);
13: };
```

You might want to give your class header files a different extension from the typical header files. Some Visual C++ programs name them with an .HPP extension, others with an .HCL extension. It doesn't matter what the filename extension is as long as you include the full filename in the source program that uses the class. After you enter BEV.H, close the editor's window with **F**ile **C**lose.

Loose Ends: *static* and Larger Programs

The class implementation could also be separated and turned into a stand-alone file. Here is the implementation file saved as BEVCLIMP.CPP:

```
1:  // Filename: BEVCLIMP.CPP
2:  #include <iostream.h>
3:  #include <iomanip.h>
4:  #include <string.h>
5:  #include <bev.h>
6:  Drinks::Drinks(char * N, float W, float R)
7:  {
8:     name = new char[strlen(N) + 1];
9:     strcpy(name, N);
10:    whole = W;
11:    retail = R;
12: }
13: Drinks::~Drinks()
14: {
15:    delete [] name;
16: }
17: Drinks::Drinks(const Drinks & d)      // Copy constructor
18: {
19:    int newLen = strlen(d.name) + 1;
20:    name = new char[newLen];
21:    strcpy(name, d.name);
22:    whole = d.whole;
23:    retail = d.retail;
24: }
25: Drinks & Drinks::operator=(const Drinks & d)   // Assignment overload
26: {
27:    if (this == &d)
28:       { return *this; }
29:    delete [] name;   // Deallocate old string
30:    name = new char[strlen(d.name) + 1];
31:    strcpy(name, d.name);   // Copy string member
32:    whole = d.whole;         // Copy float members
33:    retail = d.retail;
34:    return *this;
35: }
36: ostream & operator<< (ostream & out, const Drinks & d)
37: {
38:    out << setprecision(2) << setiosflags(ios::showpoint);
39:    out << setiosflags(ios::fixed);
40:    out << "Name: " << d.name << "\n";
41:    out << "Wholesale price: " << d.whole << "\tRetail price: ";
42:    out << d.retail << "\n\n";
43:    return out;
44: }
45: istream & operator>> (istream & in, Drinks & d)
46: {
47:    cout << "Please add to our line of beverage products.\n";
```

```
48:    cout << "What is the name of the next product? (one word
       ➥please)";
49:    char tempInput[80];      // Need to temporarily
50:    in >> tempInput;                 // store user input
51:    d.name = new char[strlen(tempInput) + 1];   // onto the heap.
52:    strcpy(d.name, tempInput);
53:    in.ignore();  // Remove carriage return
54:    cout << "What is the retail price of " << d.name << "? ";
55:    in >> d.whole;
56:    cout << "What is the wholesale price of " << d.name << "? ";
57:    in >> d.retail;
58:    return in;
59: }
```

Notice that the implementation file must include all the header files it needs to do its job. Built-in string functions and I/O stream routines are used, so the file must include all the support files required to prototype the built-in routines used. Also, on line 5, the BEV.H class header file had to be included because it contains the prototypes for all the class functions and the data members for the class implementation to work with.

The class implementation file is ready for compilation. You cannot link it, however, because there is no program code with main() here that uses the class, and all executable Visual C++ programs must have a main() function. Class implementations are usually compiled as explained earlier because the user program of the class and the programmer using the implementation code don't need to see the details of the implementation unless the programmer needs to change the implementation and has the source code to do so.

Compile BEVCLIMP.CPP by selecting **P**roject **C**ompile (Alt+F9) from the Visual C++ menu after entering the class implementation source code. Visual C++ compiles the program and adds the BEVCLIMP.OBJ object file to your disk (assuming there were no typing errors).

Note: If you get an error message such as Cannot open include file: 'bev.h', you should insert the full pathname of the BEV.H file before its name in the #include directive.

If you wanted to delete BEVCLIMP.CPP, now you could because a compiled object version is all you need to use the class. However, leave the implementation source file intact now for possible modifications in the future.

Loose Ends: *static* and Larger Programs

The only thing left to do is to put the rest of the program in its own file. The rest of the program is just a main() function, but because this function begins the execution and controls the class, it's vital that you use it along with the others. Here is the main() function saved as the file named BEVREST.CPP:

```
 1:  // Filename: BEVREST.CPP
 2:  #include <iostream.h>
 3:  #include <bev.h>
 4:  // Again, you may have to insert BEV.H's pathname before bev.h above
 5:  main()
 6:  {
 7:    Drinks * bevs = new Drinks[5];   // Array of 5 drinks on the heap
 8:    for (int i=0; i<5; i++)
 9:      { cin >> bevs[i]; };   // Ask the user for the beverages
10:    cout << "\n\nHere's what you entered:\n";
11:    for (i=0; i<5; i++)
12:      { cout << bevs[i]; };   // Show the user for the beverages
13:    bevs[3] = bevs[4];        // Test the overloaded assignment
14:    Drinks newBev = bevs[1];  // Test the copy constructor
15:    Drinks another("Diet Peach Flavored", .23, .67);
16:    cout << "After some changes:\n";
17:    cout << bevs[3] << newBev << another << "\n";   // Print new values
18:    cout << "Mmmm... Made from the best stuff on earth!";
19:    delete [] bevs;
20:    return 0;
21: }
```

You now have the following files that compose your project:

☐ The BEV.H class header source file

☐ The BEVCLIMP.OBJ object class implementation file

☐ The BEVREST.CPP source code that uses the class

You're now ready to compile the BEVREST.CPP source code and link the resulting object file with the BEVCLIMP.OBJ file into a single executable file by using the project feature of Visual C++.

Close all windows in Visual C++ and select **P**roject **N**ew. The **P**roject menu option controls all the project-building and editing commands in Visual C++. Type the name **BEV.MAK** (projects should have the .MAK extension), preceding the name with the pathname of your beverage file. Also, scroll the Project Type to the Quick Win Application (you'll see several types of files you can compile with Visual C++). When you press Enter or click OK, you'll see the project window shown in Figure 14.5.

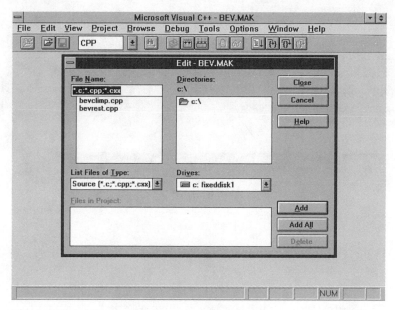

Figure 14.5. The newly opened project window.

All you now have to do is inform the project system of the two files needed, BEVREST.CPP and BEVCLIMP.OBJ. You don't specify the BEV.H class header file because #include in the source file takes care of the class header. To build your project, follow these steps:

1. Type **BEVREST.CPP** with a pathname specified to the location where you stored BEVREST.CPP earlier. (Optionally, you can select it from the dialog box's list.) You can type filenames in either uppercase or lowercase letters. Press Enter or click **A**dd. Visual C++ adds the file to the Files in Project text box.

2. Type **BEVCLIMP.OBJ** with the pathname, and select **A**dd.

3. Select Cl**o**se to quit entering project files.

You can now *build the project* (which means compile and link all necessary files as determined by the project's contents). If you press Shift+F8 (**P**roject **B**uild), Visual C++ builds the final executable file but does not run it. If you then press Ctrl+F5 (**P**roject E**x**ecute), Visual C++ builds the project and runs the program. (Ctrl+F5 would have built the file for you as well as Shift+F8.)

Loose Ends: *static* and Larger Programs

> **Tip:** Visual C++ includes two buttons on the toolbar that you can use to build your project, as shown in Figure 14.6. The Build Changed button recompiles and links only the files that have changed since the most recent build. The Rebuild All button compiles and links all files whether or not any changes were made.

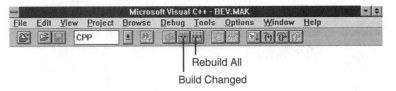

Figure 14.6. You can build your entire project with a single click.

Here's the great thing about projects: If you change the BEVREST.CPP source file, the project manager recompiles the program. If, however, you don't change the source code and want to run the program again, the project manager knows not to recompile and runs the executable file. If you *forgot* whether you changed the program, don't fret—the project manager recompiles only if needed to include the latest changes you make to the file.

If you change the BEVCLIMP.OBJ object file by recompiling, again, the project manager takes care of relinking the two object files, but it won't recompile BEVREST.CPP except when you modify it.

> **Note:** The project manager keeps accurate track of the project entries' date and time stamps, and compares against its records to determine what needs to be recompiled or relinked.

You can close the project file with **P**roject **C**lose.

DO	DON'T

DO break your programs into separate files, especially class header and class implantation files, to speed development and keep the user program of the class cleaner.

DO use the project manager to build your projects automatically.

DON'T include any of the built-in or class header files in the project listing because the individual source code files include header files automatically when they are compiled.

Summary

Today's chapter started with a review of static basics. The OOP-specific static declarations are similar to those of non-OOP programming. static variables, as opposed to auto variables, do not lose their values when their blocks end. Although a local static variable remains local to its block, it is not reinitialized if execution enters the block a second time.

static in front of global variables or function names forces internal linkage of those variables and functions, meaning that secondary source files cannot execute the static functions or use the static global variables even if extern is attempted in the secondary source files. Global variables cannot be declared with the auto keyword.

static data members exist *once* across all objects. In other words, the value of a static data member isn't affected by the number of other objects defined or even block scope (notice the similarity between static data members and static local variables).

You must define static variables before main() begins, and you can use those variables before class objects are defined. The static members are defined for the class, not for individual objects as are regular data members. Therefore, you must use the class name and the scope resolution operator to access static members.

After wrapping up static, today's chapter explored multifile processing. Often, you'll find it advantageous to break your programs into separate files, especially the class headers and class implementation code. You read a review of source files, object files, and executable files, and then you saw how Visual C++'s project manager makes the building of multifile projects easy.

Loose Ends: *static* and Larger Programs

Although it takes a little effort (not much with the interactive help of Visual C++) to set up a project, after you set one up, you'll never have to worry about compiling and linking the right files again. All your multifile projects will build faster because the project manager only recompiles and relinks those files needed to keep the executable file up-to-date.

Tip: An added advantage of using a project is that your previous project option settings are remembered each time you reopen a project. Not all the compiler options are saved between compiles if you compile a single program at a time.

Q&A

Q. Why should some local variables be `static` and some left as automatic?

A. Normally, local variables are automatic local variables (you can optionally put `auto` in front of their definitions). Local automatic values disappear when the block in which they're defined ends. If execution reenters the same block, the local variables are reinitialized again. If you do nothing special, these local variables remain automatic.

If you precede local variables with the `static` keyword, their values will not go away when the block ends. The variable is still local, but its value remains in the variable. If, therefore, the block is executed again, the previous value of the `static` variable remains. `static` local variables are great for keeping track of totals; the total doesn't get wiped out when the block ends.

Q. What is a `static` function?

A. If you write only stand-alone programs, `static` functions won't add any advantage to your programming. However, many people write multipart programs, and there are lots of programs written by teams of programmers. When working with multifile programs, you'll often want to ensure that a function name you place in one file doesn't clash with a name in another.

When you precede a function with `static`, the compiler limits that function to *internal linkage*, which means that other source files that are eventually linked to the current one can contain the same function names, and those function names won't conflict with yours.

Q. What is a `static` data member?

A. A `static` data member belongs to the class, not to an individual object. Visual C++ ensures that a `static` data member exists only once, no matter how many class objects are defined.

Visual C++ programmers often use `static` data members to keep track of the number of objects currently defined as well as other statistics, such as totals and averages of object data as a whole.

Q. When would I need a `static` member function?

A. `static` member functions manipulate `static` data members. You cannot call regular member functions until there is at least one object defined to associate with that member function. You might want to use a `static` data member before defining a `static` object. If so, write a public `static` member function, and call that function using the class name followed by a scope resolution operator.

Q. Why should I use Visual C++'s project manager?

A. The project manager manages your multifile projects. When writing programs that require several parts, or when programming in a programming department, you'll often work on pieces of a program inside stand-alone files rather than one large single source program.

When working with lots of files, both source and object files, the project manager eases your workload by streamlining the compilation and linking of files that need compiling and linking. The project manager searches the date and time of the project's pieces and rebuilds a project in a minimum amount of time.

Workshop

The Workshop offers quiz questions and exercises to hone your skills and give you feedback on today's lesson. You'll find some proposed answers in Appendix D.

Quiz

1. True or False: Local variables are auto by default.

2. True or False: `static` and `auto` are synonyms for local and global variables.

Loose Ends: *static* and Larger Programs

3. An object called thing is defined from a class named ClassStuff. The class contains a public static member named factor. Which of the following lines properly references the static member?

    A. ClassStuff::factor

    B. ClassStuff.factor

    C. thing.factor

4. What is *internal linkage*?

5. What is *external linkage*?

6. Should static data members remain public or private?

7. What is a project?

8. How does a project file speed your program development?

Exercises

1. Write a teacher's program that defines a class for students' names and grades. Add a static data member to the class to keep track of the class average. Define an array of five objects for the teacher's five students. Initialize the array through constructors that ask the user for the students' names and grade averages. After all the students' data is entered, print the average from the static data member variable.

2. Practice using the project manager by writing a stand-alone function to the beverage project described in this chapter that increases the wholesale and retail price of a beverage passed to it by 10 percent when a price increase occurs. Keep the function separate, and add it to the top of the BEV.MAK project list. Rebuild the project and test the program. Make a change to the function and rebuild again. Now, make a change to BEVREST.CPP by adding a centered title at the top of the screen before it prints anything. Rebuild the project. Notice that the project manager recompiles only those files you change, not the files you don't change.

Week 2 in Review

Now that you've finished the second week, you're ready for a program that brings together much of the material from the first two weeks. The programs in Listing WR2.1 (the class header file) and Listing WR2.2 (the class implementation and `main()`) illustrate several Visual C++ features you now understand, such as constructors, destructors, overloaded operators, and a `static` member. The programs define several house objects for a real-estate investor. The programs don't do a lot with the data so that you can better study their details, which exercise so many elements found in the first weeks of the book.

Listing WR2.1. Weeks one and two review class header listing.

```
1:  // Filename: RENTAL.H
2:  // Class header
3:  class Prop {   // Property Class
4:     char propCode[7];    // 6 characters plus null zero
5:     char * address;
6:     float askingPrice;
7:     int sqrFeet;
8:     int numRooms;
9:  public:
10:    static int number;    // Running total of Prop objects
11:    float getPrice(void) {return askingPrice; } // For average
12:    Prop();    // Default constructor
13:    Prop(const char [], const char *, const float &, const int &,
    ➥const int &);
14:    ~Prop();    // Destructor
15:    Prop(const Prop &);    // Copy constructor
16:    Prop operator=(const Prop &);    // Assignment overload
17:    // An overloaded addition so an average can be calculated
```

continues

Week 2 in Review

Listing WR2.1. continued

```
18:    Prop operator+(const Prop &);
19:    friend ostream & operator<< (ostream &, const Prop &);
20:    friend istream & operator>> (istream &, Prop &);
21: };
```

Listing WR2.2. Weeks one and two review class implementation listing.

```
1:  // Filename: RENTAL.CPP
2:  // Tracks, initializes, copies, and prints properties.
3:  #include <iostream.h>
4:  #include <iomanip.h>
5:  #include <string.h>
6:  #include <stdlib.h>
7:  #include <new.h>
8:  // You'll have to insert the path of RENTAL.H in the next
    ↪#include
9:  #include <rental.h>
10: Prop::Prop()
11: {
12:    Prop::number++;
13:    askingPrice = 0.0;      // Zeros mean no data yet
14:    sqrFeet = 0;
15:    numRooms = 0;
16: }
17: Prop::Prop(const char PC[], const char *A, const float & AP,
18:            const int & SQ, const int & NR)
19: {
20:    Prop::number++;    // Increase static value
21:    strcpy(propCode, PC);
22:    address = new char[strlen(A) + 1];
23:    strcpy(address, A);
24:    askingPrice = AP;
25:    sqrFeet = SQ;
26:    numRooms = NR;
27: }
28: Prop::~Prop()
29: {
30:    Prop::number--;    // Decrease static value
31: //   delete [] address;
32: }
33: Prop::Prop(const Prop & p)    // Copy constructor
34: {
35:    Prop::number++;    // Increase static value
36:    int newLen = strlen(p.address) + 1;
```

```
37:    address = new char[newLen];
38:    strcpy(address, p.address);
39:    strcpy(propCode, p.propCode);
40:    askingPrice = p.askingPrice;
41:    sqrFeet = p.sqrFeet;
42:    numRooms = p.numRooms;
43: }
44: Prop Prop::operator=(const Prop & p)   // Assignment overload
45: {
46:    if (this == &p)
47:       { return *this; }
48:    delete [] address;   // Deallocate old string
49:    int newLen = strlen(p.address) + 1;
50:    address = new char[newLen];
51:    strcpy(address, p.address);
52:    strcpy(propCode, p.propCode);
53:    askingPrice = p.askingPrice;
54:    sqrFeet = p.sqrFeet;
55:    numRooms = p.numRooms;
56:    return *this;
57: }
58: Prop Prop::operator+(const Prop & p)
59: {
60:    // This function returns an object with asking price
61:    // plus the 2nd operand's asking price
62:    askingPrice += p.askingPrice;
63:    return *this;
64: }
65: ostream & operator<< (ostream & out, const Prop & p)
66: {
67:    out << setprecision(2) << setiosflags(ios::showpoint);
68:    out << setiosflags(ios::fixed);
69:    out << "Code: " << p.propCode << "\t";
70:    out << "Address: " << p.address << "\n";
71:    out << "Asking price: $" << setw(9) << p.askingPrice
       ➥<<"\t";
72:    out << "Square feet: " << p.sqrFeet << "\t";
73:    out << "No. of rooms: " << setw(2) << p.numRooms;
74:    out << "\n\n";
75:    return out;
76: }
77: istream & operator>> (istream & in, Prop & p)
78: {
79:    cout << "Property Input:\n";
80:    char tempInput[80];    // Need to temporarily hold input
81:    do {
82:      cout << "What is the property code (6 character please)? ";
83:      in >> tempInput;     // store user input
84:      if (strlen(tempInput) != 6)
```

continues

Week 2 in Review

Listing WR2.2. continued

```
 85:        { cout << "\n*** The code can be only 6 characters ***
            ➥\n\n"; }
 86:     } while (strlen(tempInput) != 6);
 87:     strcpy(p.propCode, tempInput);
 88:     in.ignore();     // Ignore carriage return
 89:     cout << "What is the address? ";
 90:     in.getline(tempInput, 80);
 91:     p.address = new char[strlen(tempInput) + 1];
 92:     strcpy(p.address, tempInput);
 93:     cout << "What is the asking price? ";
 94:     in >> p.askingPrice;
 95:     cout << "What is the square feet? ";
 96:     in >> p.sqrFeet;
 97:     cout << "What is the number of rooms? ";
 98:     in >> p.numRooms;
 99:     return in;
100: }
101: int newProblem(size_t size)
102: {
103:     cerr << "\nMemory problem\n";
104:     exit(1);
105:     return 0;
106: }
107: int Prop::number = 0;
108: ////////////////////////////////////////////////////////////
109: main()
110: {
111:    _set_new_handler(newProblem);
112:    // First, construct a house with values already known
113:    Prop house1("HOUSE1", "220 E. Richmond", 9500.0, 800, 6);
114:    cout << house1;
115:    // Construct a house using copy constructor
116:    Prop house2 = house1;
117:    cout << house2;
118:    // Construct a house using default constructor
119:    Prop house3;
120:    cin >> house3;   // Ask user for values
121:    // Construct using default constructor,
122:    // then use operator=() to initialize
123:    cout << "\nYou entered this house:\n";
124:    cout << house3;
125:    Prop house4;
126:    house4 = house3;    // operator=() called
127:    cout << house4;
128:    // Use the static member to show total number of houses
129:    // constructed so far (even though it's obvious there are 4)
130:    cout << "\nThere are " << Prop::number << "\n";
131:    Prop total;
```

```
132:    Prop::number--;  // Don't include total variable in static
        ↳count
133:    total = house1 + house2 + house3 + house4;
134:    cout << "The average asking price is ";
135:    float avg = total.getPrice() / Prop::number;
136:    cout << avg;
137:    return 0;
138: }
```

main() first sets up the new handler. The newProblem() function automatically takes over if a memory allocation fails. The newProblem() code appears on lines 101–106, and if a problem occurs, the program quits via the exit() call on line 104.

The program then creates the house1 object with some data in it. The creation of house1 occurs through the constructor function that begins on line 17. The arguments passed to the constructor are assigned to the house1 variable inside the constructor. The overloaded << (lines 65–76) prints all the program's Prop objects to the screen.

Line 116 uses the copy constructor that starts on line 33 to create a new object, house2, from house1. The copy constructor and not the overloaded assignment is called because house2 is constructed and didn't exist before line 116.

The default constructor is used on line 119 to create house3. The default constructor that starts on line 10 simply assigns zeroes to the numeric data members. An overloaded >> function (lines 77–100) asks the user for the values of house3 before house3 is printed on line 124.

house4 is constructed on line 125 by the default constructor, and the overloaded = function then assigns all of house3's members to house4 before house4 is printed on line 127.

Although four houses are explicitly constructed (five if you count total on line 131), a static member named number initialized to 0 on line 107 keeps track of the object count. The default constructor (starting on line 10), the constructor with arguments (line 17), and the copy constructor (starting on line 33) all increment the static number variable so that an accurate count can be made for the average calculation on line 135. Of course, the average could have been explicitly divided by four because it's obvious that only four objects are defined. Using the static member, however, helps demonstrate the use of static. The destructor starting on line 28 must decrement the count so that number always holds the total number of objects created at any one time.

Week 3 at a Glance

You're now two-thirds of the way through teaching yourself OOP with Visual C++! The foundation you have now will make the next week seem easy. Despite all the OOP hype that you read about, there isn't that much to object-oriented programming—as long as you learn it carefully through a structured approach that explains each step fully without first throwing in a bunch of buzzwords.

There are just a few new concepts left for you to learn. Most of them, inheritance, virtual functions, containers, and file I/O, build on your current OOP knowledge of overloaded functions, overloaded operators, constructors, and public/private member access data and functions.

Reuse Speeds Programming

As its name implies, inheritance enables you to create new objects from existing objects and new classes from existing classes. Rather than the usual copy-and-paste methods to reuse code, inheritance forms a safer and more structured approach to the reuse of program sections. You'll find that when you need a class that's almost like another class you've already written, you can inherit that class and let Visual C++ do all the work of reusing the class without your having to copy code from one place to another.

This reuse of code is actually the cornerstone of the third week of this book. Containers provide mechanisms that enable you to use Visual C++-supplied classes in your own programs without having to worry about writing data structures to hold class data.

Note: The terms *inheritance, virtual functions,* and *containers* probably sound like difficult subjects. They sound that way because the terms are new to you. As you learned with the terms *class, object, instantiation, constructor functions,* and *destructor functions,* the language of OOP isn't as difficult as it sounds. The programming community doesn't often use a short easy word when a long one will do just as nicely and confuse more people! Relax. You'll understand inheritance, virtual functions, and the many other new topics in this third and last week because the OOP way of programming is the most natural way, and these terms describe extensions to programming that make a lot of sense.

The last chapter in the book explains Visual C++ file I/O. In a way, this chapter is a breather from the new OOP subjects that have taken you through the first and second weeks of material. The file I/O routines available in Visual C++ are class-related. As with cin and cout, you'll use built-in objects and classes as well as your own to write data to disk files and read data from disk files. You'll find that file I/O in Visual C++ is easier than in regular C (and most other programming languages) because the file I/O is just an extension of the I/O routines you already know.

DAY 15

It's Hereditary: Inheriting Data

Day 15
It's Hereditary: Inheriting Data

People learn things faster when new concepts are compared to ones they already know. For instance, when learning a foreign language, you see translations into the language you already know. When you're given directions, it helps when the new location is oriented with a site you already know. When you're learning OOP, it helps to relate new topics to the non-OOP ones you already know.

In data processing departments throughout the world, new programs are being designed and written all the time. When writing new programs, programmers often use code from existing programs. Although the cut-and-paste process is error prone, using parts of existing program source code is faster than rewriting all that code from scratch.

Companies merge and spin off all the time. Data processing departments are often swamped with programming projects that appear as the result of a corporate change. The new programs are rarely new systems to be put in place, but rather are modifications of existing business activities that take into account the new corporate form.

Through *inheritance,* object-oriented programming helps individuals and companies produce faster code by taking away many of the details of code reuse from the programmer while still allowing parts of one program to be used in another. More often than not, a single program contains related code because the program works with similar but different data. For example, a personnel program might track salaried and hourly employees. These two kinds of employees have similar information (names, addresses, phone numbers, ages, and so on) with some differences such as their pay determination. Those employees also share characteristics with the people variables already coded for customers in another program.

Data structures aren't the only kind of programming element from which you can inherit. You can inherit windows, screens, graphics, on-screen push-button controls, and a lot more. You can inherit anything that you can represent as an object.

Today's chapter begins a four-part tour into inheritance issues with Visual C++. Inheritance relieves you from the burden of cutting-and-pasting code from one part of a program to another when you want to share pieces of programs. Also, inheritance keeps your code clear of duplicate data and code definitions, leaving you with a cleaner program and one you can manipulate more easily than you otherwise could.

Today, you learn about the following topics:

- ☐ The structure of inheritance
- ☐ The terminology of inheritance

- Setting up a base class properly with the `protected` access specifier
- How to derive new classes from existing ones
- How to specify receiving access specifiers so that an inherited class contains the kind of members it needs in order to operate
- How to instantiate objects from both the original class and a derived class

Note: One of the reasons Visual C++ classes are called *classes* is because of the similar hierarchy that inherited class objects share with the classification found in the scientific community, such as mammal classifications, chemical classifications, medical classifications, and so forth.

The Structure of Inheritance

Although you cannot inherit from functions and regular variables, you can inherit from classes. (You can also inherit from structures in Visual C++ if you want to use structures.) As you know, you can include data and function members inside classes, so classes are really all you need to use for inheritance—if any kind of computer element appears inside a class, you can inherit the class, in effect inheriting the element itself.

When inheriting, you can reuse existing classes or add functionality to existing classes and thereby create more powerful classes. To ease the inheritance learning curve as much as possible, you need to learn some common terms used throughout Visual C++ inheritance.

The process of inheriting one class from another is called *derivation*. Derivation is the process of inheritance; that is, when you inherit one class from another, you *derive* the new class from the original class.

For example, the `Person` class

```
class Person {
  char * name;
  char * address;
  int areaCode;
  long int phone;
public:
  // Public member data and functions would follow
};
```

It's Hereditary: Inheriting Data

might be the original class from which you derive this `Customer` class:

```
class Customer {
  char * name;
  char * address;
  int areaCode;
  long int phone;
  char * custCode;        // Three new members not found
  double balanceOwed;     // in the original class
  int daysPastDue;
public:
  // Public member data and functions would follow
};
```

 Note: For now, concentrate on getting the inheritance terms down. You'll learn the C++ inheritance specifics later in today's chapter.

In inheritance terminology, the `People` class is called the *base* class, and the `Customer` class is called the *derived* class. Figure 15.1 helps illustrate the difference between the terms.

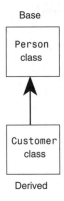

Figure 15.1. The derived class reuses and adds functionality to the base class.

Notice when looking at inheritance diagrams that the base class is usually listed at the top and all derived classes fall beneath the base class. The arrow showing the inheritance direction always points from the derived class (or classes).

More than one class can be inherited from another. Figure 15.2 shows three inherited classes derived from a single base class. As the figure's callouts show, the base class is sometimes called the *parent* class, and the derived classes are called *child* classes.

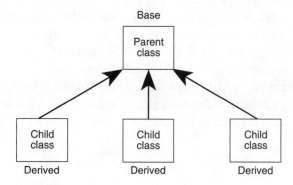

Figure 15.2. Three child classes are derived from a parent class.

> **Keeping It Simple Helps**
>
> You cannot easily take away functionality through inheritance. Therefore, the more generic the primary class from which you'll inherit is, the more fully you can use that class in later classes that you create through inheritance.
>
> You might recall that languages such as Smalltalk (as Day 8's chapter explained) don't come supplied with any built-in data types. You have to start with a generic object and build your own data types from that.
>
> Inheritance is the mechanism you use in such languages to create data types. Think for a moment about numeric data. You could create an integer class. Then you could inherit long integers from the integer because long integers have all the characteristics of regular integers plus some additional characteristics. You then could inherit floating-point from the long integer class, adding characteristics such as a decimal portion to the data. Double floating-point is then trivial.
>
> Requiring that you add functionality along the inheritance path isn't extremely limiting as long as you make sure your base class is generic enough to be inherited from. You'll learn some inheritance design tips in this week's chapters, but experience will be your best teacher.

It's Hereditary: Inheriting Data

The entire collection of derived classes, from the base class through all of its derived classes, is called the *inheritance hierarchy*. As with family traits, Visual C++ inheritance hierarchies might contain several layers. For instance, a parent class named `Person` might produce three child classes called `Employee`, `Customer`, and `Vendor`. The `Employee` class might in itself be used to derive two more classes, `Salaried` and `Hourly`. The `Hourly` class might also be used to derive two more classes named `PartTime` and `FullTime`. This entire class hierarchy is shown in Figure 15.3.

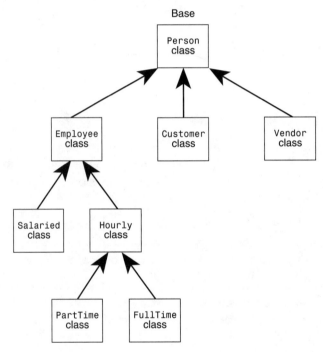

Figure 15.3. A class hierarchy might contain many derivations.

 Note: Although the `Person` class is the inheritance hierarchy's base class, the sublevel hierarchies falling beneath the `Person` class are minihierarchies in themselves. `Hourly` is the parent class or base class to the derived `PartTime` and `FullTime` classes.

The inheritance hierarchies described so far have all consisted of *single inheritance*. In single inheritance hierarchies, a derived class has one and only one parent. As you learn and read more about OOP, you'll run across the term *multiple inheritance*. A class hierarchy with multiple inheritance contains one or more derived classes with more than one parent class.

Visual C++ supports multiple inheritance, but you'll not find multiple inheritance taught in this or in some other Visual C++ books. The OOP industry wages endless debates on the merits or drawbacks of multiple inheritance. Many Visual C++ programmers say that any program and any class hierarchy can be written using only single inheritance. The multiple inheritance proponents argue that multiple inheritance streamlines some classes.

Programming with multiple inheritance adds lots of confusion and complexity to your code. Get comfortable with single inheritance before attempting to learn multiple inheritance. You will probably find that you never need to learn multiple inheritance, and you'll decrease the chance of long debugging sessions if you never use multiple inheritance.

The Smalltalk pure-OOP language does not support multiple inheritance, and Smalltalk programmers do not understand why a programmer would ever need multiple inheritance. If your base classes and derived classes are designed properly, you can write any program using solely single inheritance.

Figure 15.4 shows an example of multiple inheritance. The `PartnerClient` might be both a customer and a vendor. The biggest problem with multiple inheritance is that it is conceptually easy to understand, and therefore frighteningly easy to attempt to use in programs that don't need it. This author believes that a foundation in single inheritance will guide the OOP newcomer to become a solid Visual C++ programmer. Single inheritance gives you the power you need to write powerful OOP programs. The difficulties that come with multiple inheritance probably aren't worth your time at this point in your OOP career.

Day 15: It's Hereditary: Inheriting Data

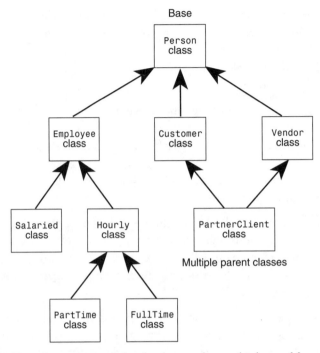

Figure 15.4. Some customers might also be vendors, which would produce this multiple inheritance relationship.

> **You Have Already Used Multiple Inheritance!**
>
> The IOSTREAM.H header file contains an input/output multiple inheritance hierarchy. Input and output stream classes combine to form new kinds of classes through a complicated use of multiple inheritance.
>
> Could the IOSTREAM.H class hierarchy be written using single inheritance? Yes it could, but the fact remains that Visual C++, and probably every other C++ compiler, contains the same multiple inheritance IOSTREAM.H header file class.
>
> The IOSTREAM.H header file is a well-written (as well-written as multiple inheritance can be) multiple inheritance hierarchy, and it is safe to use. As with all well-written class libraries, you don't have to know that the class contains multiple inheritance to use the class effectively.

> Some day, you might want to scan the IOSTREAM.H header file (don't change it!) and see how its multiple inheritance hierarchy works. Until then, keep it a secret that a class you use in every Visual C++ program contains multiple inheritance, and maybe nobody else will realize you use multiple inheritance!

Inheritance terms are easy to understand. Although this book shies away from introducing new terms before explaining the code beneath the terms, inheritance mirrors the way you classify real-life elements. OOP inheritance is not just a shortcut for programming; inheritance enables you to group like data into related units. When you use existing knowledge to learn new knowledge, you don't have to "reinvent the wheel."

Another reason for inheritance is the ease of change that inheritance provides. If you change a base class, all derived classes automatically change as well. If you were to use the old cut-and-paste approach to data processing, a change in the original class would mean a manual search and change of every other place where you use that code.

As you write object-oriented programs that require inheritance, you'll start with a basic framework class and derive new classes from that common class. With the common data and functions in the base class, you can then concentrate on programming only the changes that appear in all the derived classes that follow.

DO   DON'T

DO learn the terminology of inheritance. You'll learn inheritance specifics faster when common terms can be used.

DO use inheritance to speed your program development. It's easier and faster to inherit from a parent class than to rewrite a similar class from scratch.

DON'T use multiple inheritance for a while, if ever. Most Visual C++ programmers don't use multiple inheritance because it is thought that every inheritance hierarchy can be achieved through single inheritance. Multiple inheritance adds complexity that you don't need right now.

It's Hereditary: Inheriting Data

Diving into Visual C++ Inheritance

Some of the early inheritance examples that you study in today's chapter will use classes that contain all public members. The reason that public data members and member functions are shown is that inheritance of private members does *not* occur; in other words, a derived class can never inherit the private members of a base class.

> **Note:** After you see a few inheritance examples that contain all public classes, you'll see ways to maintain the data protection that the `private` keyword provides without giving up inheritance limitations of private members.

Returning to the `Person` class introduced earlier in the chapter, the `Person` class was the base class and described a generic person used throughout the rest of the company's class hierarchy. Here is the `Person` class that contains all public members:

```
class Person {
public:
  char * name;
  char * address;
  int areaCode;
  long int phone;
  Person();        // Public member functions follow
  ~Person();
  Person inputPerson(void);
  prPerson(void);
};
```

Of course, a person's address contains a city, state, and ZIP code, but this class is being kept as simple as possible to focus on the inheritance specifics described here. Also, you might want to override operators and constructors so that there could be several occurrences of them.

It is common for programmers never to instantiate a base class object variable. That is, sometimes a base class exists just to provide a format for all the more specific classes derived from the base class.

Deriving a child class from a parent class requires only that you specify the parent class to inherit from and the new members you want added to the derived class. When you declare a derived class, separate the name of the derived class from the base class with a colon. The following Employee class derives from the Person class shown earlier:

```
class Employee : Person {
public:          // Keeps things simpler for now
  int dependents;
  int yrsWorked;
  int testYears(void);   // Indicates True if employed
};                       // more than 10 years
```

Figure 15.5 shows the resulting Employee class. It first appears that Employee has only three members, but the Person after the Employee name in the class's first line tells Turbo C++ to inherit all public members from Person and bring them down into an Employee class.

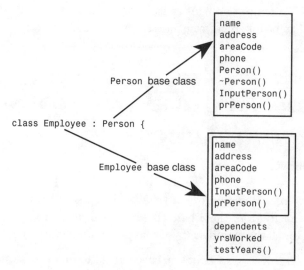

Figure 15.5. Inheriting the Person class.

You'll see from Figure 15.5 that constructors and destructors are not inherited. Each class must include its own constructor and destructor because the constructor and destructor functions must be so aligned with the class in which they appear. Tomorrow's chapter will explain how to create and call constructor and destructor functions when inheritance is involved.

All the public members, both data and member functions, drop down to the Employee class. No data is reserved yet because no objects are defined. But if the main() function in the program using these classes were to create a Person object, that object would

It's Hereditary: Inheriting Data

contain all the members of the `Person` class, and any `Employee` object would contain all the members of the `Person` class (except the constructor and destructor) as well as the three new members.

DO	DON'T

DO use a colon, `:`, to separate a new class name from the inherited class name.

DON'T design a base class with lots of private members unless the base class is to forbid inheritance of those private members. No derived class ever inherits a private member.

DON'T attempt to inherit constructors or destructors because neither of them can be inherited from a base class to a derived class.

Getting Around *private* with *protected* Access

Don't throw the `private` access specifier away just because derived classes cannot inherit private members. The data protection provided by private members is too critical to lose. However, if you write generic base classes and never plan to create objects directly from those base classes (just from derived classes), feel free to use `private` for all the members if you want to. However, there is a better alternative.

There is a third access specifier you haven't read about so far because you never needed it before inheritance came into the picture. The `protected` access specifier provides the best of both worlds: data protection and inheritability.

Here is a class with all three (there are only three) access specifiers: `private` (the default of a class until overridden), `protected`, and `public`:

```
class BaseCl {
    int a;              // Private by default
    int b;
protected:              // Available ONLY to inherited classes
    int c;
    int d;
public:                 // Available to ALL elements that access a member
    int e;
    int f;
};
```

As you can see, the protected keyword appears in the class at the location before the first protected member. All other members below protected remain protected until another access specifier changes the access. Figure 15.6 shows how the BaseCl makes the three groups of members available.

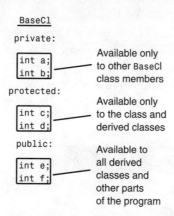

Figure 15.6. public is available to all, protected is available to the class and derived classes, and private is available to the class only.

Often, a base class contains only protected and public members because inheritance needs access to all the members. Here is the Person class rewritten using protected access for the members that need it:

```
class Person {
protected:
  char * name;
  char * address;
  int areaCode;
  long int phone;
public:           // Public member functions follow
  Person();
  ~Person();
  Person inputPerson(void);
  prPerson(void);
};
```

Now, if the Employee class attempted to inherit from Person, the derived Employee class would receive all the members of Person (except, as usual, the constructor and destructor) as if they were all public. However, no other underived part of the program could access the protected members because they are protected from access by all except derived classes.

It's Hereditary: Inheriting Data

Note: You cannot apply `private`, `protected`, and `public` to unions. Union members are always public, and you can neither derive them nor derive from them. (Unions, however, can contain constructors.)

To summarize this section, the `Person` class with protected members still contains members not available to any function *outside* the inheritance hierarchy. In other words, all derived classes can inherit the protected members, but neither `main()` nor any other non-member function can access the protected members. As always, all program elements (`main()`, functions called by `main()`, or derived classes) have access to the public members.

DO	DON'T

DO specify `protected` when you want to limit member access to the class and any derived classes.

DON'T forget that a derived class can never change the access of a parent class's member. If the parent class contains a private member, there is nothing the derived class can do to access that member.

DON'T expect all your base classes to be object classes. In other words, you might create a generic base class that will be used only to derive other classes. The base class offers a uniform foundation for all the derived classes. If you put the data members that are most likely to change in a parent class, if the change does occur, you won't have to change any of the derived classes as long as the parent class's access keyword was `protected` or `public` on the members that might change.

DON'T apply the access specifiers to unions because unions cannot be used in an inherited hierarchy.

How Derived Classes View Inherited Members

At first glance, it might seem that when a derived class inherits `protected` members, those members remain protected, and when a derived class inherits public members,

those members remain public. That's not always the case, however. Throughout this section, you'll learn how the derived class changes the access of members when it inherits them.

Note: Throughout the rest of the book, keep in mind that a derived class can change *nothing* about the base class. No matter what a derived class contains, the base class private members are always private, the base class protected members are always protected, and the base class public members are always public. This section shows how to receive such access so that it appears different in the derived class after inheritance takes place.

If you need to, you can add an access specifier, private, protected, or public, in front of the base class name when inheriting. Here are the first lines of three derived class definitions that do just that:

```
class DerivedCl1 : private BaseCl {
class DerivedCl2 : protected BaseCl {
class DerivedCl3 : public BaseCl {
```

This means that not only do you put the access specifiers in front of the base class members you want specified, but you also put the access specifiers in front of the base class name when deriving from the base class. When an access specifier appears in front of a derived class's base class name, it determines the method Visual C++ uses to merge the base class into the derived class.

The default method of *receiving* inherited members is private. This does *not* mean that all inherited members are private. It simply means that both of the following statements are exactly the same because the receiving access of a derived class is automatically private by default:

```
class DerivedCl1 : private BaseCl {
```

and

```
class DerivedCl1 : BaseCl {        // private not needed
```

Three possible access specifiers are available for base class members, and three are available for receiving base class members in derived classes, making a total of nine combinations possible. Luckily, most Visual C++ programmers either keep the default private derivation or specify public. The protected keyword is rarely used to receive derivations.

It's Hereditary: Inheriting Data

About the only way to tackle these access specifier combinations is to look at an example and explain each combination in turn. Listing 15.1 provides a class listing of the Person hierarchy, the top level of the one described earlier in Figure 15.3. The analysis section explains each of the derived class's receiving access specifiers. (There is no output because no main() appears in the listing.)

Type

Listing 15.1. Looking at the derived class specifiers.

```
 1: // Filename: ACCESS.CPP
 2: class Person {
 3:    long int interCode;  // Internal code is only private member
 4: protected:
 5:    char * name;         // Four protected members
 6:    char * address;
 7:    int areaCode;
 8:    long int phone;
 9: public:                 // Public member functions follow
10:    Person();
11:    ~Person();
12:    Person inputPerson(void);
13:    prPerson(void);
14: };
15: class Employee : private Person {   // Private receipt is default
16:    int dependents;
17: protected:
18:    int yrsWorked;
19: public:
20:    int testYears(void);  // True if employed more than 10 years
21: };
22: class Customer : protected Person {
23:    char * custNum;
24: protected:
25:    float custBalance;
26: public:
27:    int prCust(void);
28: };
29: class Vendor : public Person {
30:    char * vendNum;
31: protected:
32:    float vendOwed;
33: public:
34:    prVend(void);
35: };
```

Notice that the base class, Person, contains members that use all three access specifiers, private, protected, and public (lines 3–13). It is the access specifiers in the base class, Person, that determine how the rest of the program can see its members.

Note: The class hierarchy is more complicated than it would probably be in a regular program. Programmers don't generally write derived classes that receive using the protected or private keywords; most derived classes receive using public. This example is good, however, in that it shows you all the possibilities of sending and receiving derived classes throughout the hierarchy.

Neither main() nor any derived classes can access the interCode member in Person. interCode is private to the class; only the rest of the Person class can access it. When another class inherits Person, no matter what the other class's receiving access specifier is, interCode will never be accessible to another class.

The members name, address, areaCode, and phone are protected. They can never be accessed by main(), but all derived classes will receive those four members (unlike interCode). No matter how a derived class inherits from Person, the derived class will contain these four members of Person.

The members Person(), ~Person(), inputPerson(), and prPerson() are all public and therefore can be used from any other part of the program. main() can access these members. Also, all derived classes that derive from Person will contain those four public members as well.

Note: The fact that the four public members are member functions has nothing to do with their access. If two were data members and two were functions, all four still would be public and would be available to all parts of the program due to their public keyword.

All the access specifiers that appear in the base class dictate how other classes see the base class members. It's time to look at how each derived class *receives* the members available in the Person base class. Here is a review list:

- When a derived class inherits with the `private` keyword in front of the base class name, or when no access specifier appears before the base class name (`private` is the default), all inherited protected *and* public members appear in the derived class as private members.

- When a derived class inherits with the `protected` keyword in front of the base class name, all inherited protected *and* public members of the base class appear in the derived class as protected members.

- When a derived class inherits with the `public` keyword in front of the base class name, the inherited protected members remain protected when they get to the derived class, and all inherited public members remain public when they get to the derived class. The `public` keyword is the most commonly used access specifier in receiving inheritance hierarchies.

Figure 15.7 shows the derived `Employee` class after the inheritance takes place. The incoming members from `Person` are all received as private members, and the members explicitly listed in `Employee` (`dependents`, `yrsWorked`, and `testYears()`) retain their stated access.

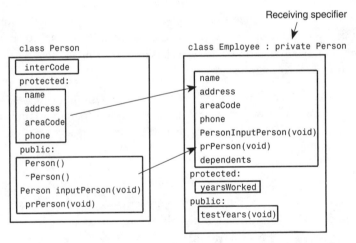

Figure 15.7. All inherited members from `Person` appear in `Employee` as private members.

`main()` has no access to any of the seven resulting private members of the `Employee` class. All six inherited members and the one explicitly stated member (`dependents`) are private to `Employee`. Only members of the `Employee` class have the capability to access the seven private members. If you were to derive another class from Employee, none of those seven members would be inherited.

 Note: The reason that seven members are inherited from Employee is that constructors and destructors are never inherited.

Because the yrsWorked member is protected, the Employee class and any derived class have access to yrsWorked, but main() does not. The public member testYears() can be both inherited and used by main().

Figure 15.8 shows the derived Customer class after the inheritance takes place. The incoming protected and public members from Person are all received as protected members, and the members explicitly listed in Customer (custNum, custBalance, and prCust()) retain their stated access.

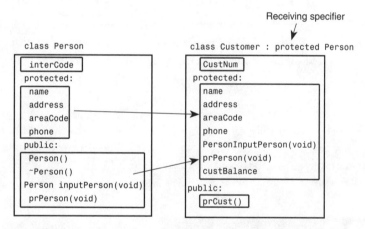

Figure 15.8. All inherited members from Person appear in Customer as protected members.

main() has no access to the private member of Customer (custNum) or to the seven protected members, but main() can access the public member prCust(). If you derive a new class from Customer, the derived class could have access to the seven protected members and to the public member prCust().

It's Hereditary: Inheriting Data

Figure 15.9 shows the derived Vendor class after the inheritance takes place. The incoming members from Person are received as either protected or public depending on their access in the Person class. The four protected Person members remain protected and the two public Person members remain public when they get to Vendor.

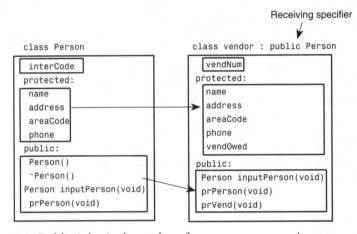

Figure 15.9. Public inherited members from Person appear in Vendor as public, and protected inherited members from Person appear as protected.

Note: Technically, private base class members are inherited but are not accessible in derived classes. The result is that private base class members don't appear to pass to their descendants.

DO	DON'T

DO give members private access if you want to keep all code outside the class, including derived classes from using the member.

DO specify a receiving access specifier if you want to override the default private access provided automatically when inheriting. Generally, programmers inherit using the public access specifier before the inherited base class name. In this way, all base class protected members remain protected in the derived class, and all base class public members remain public in the derived class.

> **DON'T** use the `protected` access specifier unless you want *both* protected and public inherited members to remain protected in the derived class.

Where You're Headed

Despite all the theory today's chapter taught, you've seen very little code. The reason is that constructing derived and base class objects takes some extra constructor review. Tomorrow's chapter will explore how to construct derived and base class objects and will explain how to destruct such objects as well.

For now, realize that a derived class, after all the inheritance has taken place, is just like any other class in that it has members (some are unseen in the code because they are inherited) that take on any of the three private, protected, or public access specifiers. You can instantiate objects from derived classes or from base classes.

Given the previous `Person` hierarchy, you can define a `Person` base class object like this:

```
main()
{
  Person human;
  // Rest of program would follow
```

The `human` object would include four private members and four public members. The `Person()` constructor would be used to construct the `human` object.

If you want to define an `Employee` object, you can do that as well. The following code defines three `Employee` objects:

```
main()
{
  Employee emp1, emp2, emp3;
  // Rest of program would follow
```

You don't have to define a base class object before defining a derived class object. In fact, you don't ever have to define base class objects if the base class is set up to be a common skeleton class for all the related and derived classes that derive from the base.

It is worth noting that the built-in *default constructor* is used to create the three employee objects. No constructor exists in the `Employee` class, so none can be used. Remember that neither constructors nor destructors are inherited.

Day 15

It's Hereditary: Inheriting Data

The instantiated objects behave as expected. If you want to execute the `testYears()` member function on one of the employee objects, you can do so like this:

```
emp1.testYears();
```

If you defined a `human` base class object, you can execute its `prPerson()` member function like this:

```
human.prPerson();
```

Remember, though, that you can also execute the `prPerson()` member function on the derived class objects because `prPerson()` is a public member function in the base class and so it always gets inherited. If you want an `Employee` object to execute the `prPerson()` member function, you can do so like this:

```
emp3.prPerson();
```

DO	DON'T
DO instantiate both derived and base class objects just as you do non-inherited objects. **DON'T** write constructors or destructors for derived classes until you've mastered tomorrow's material. You need to read some extra cautions and learn some other procedures before writing full-blown Visual C++ programs that contain inheritance.	

Summary

Today's chapter introduces inheritance and provides lots of insight on why you need inheritance. Inheritance gives Visual C++ a great capability to reuse class data. As you inherit from existing classes, you can add data and functionality to the inherited classes.

Terminology is important in discussions of inheritance. The class from which you inherit is called the base class or the parent class. The class produced by the inheritance is called the derived class or the child class. After deriving a child class, you can derive additional child classes from it.

This chapter introduces single inheritance. In single inheritance, every derived class has at most one parent class. Visual C++ does support multiple inheritance, but deriving classes with multiple parents is tricky, error prone, and especially difficult

when you're setting up constructors and destructors. Most of the programs you ever write will work faster if you stay with the simpler single inheritance. After you are comfortable with single inheritance, you can study classes that successfully use multiple inheritance.

When inheriting, the private members in the base class always remain private. There is nothing you can do to inherit private members, whether they are data members or member functions. (Of course, friend functions have access to private members, but they are a special case.)

The third (and last) access specifier, named `protected`, is needed when inheriting. When a base class contains protected members, those members remain private to everything outside the class except other derived classes (and friend functions, of course).

Not only do you have to worry about the access offered by a base class, but you also must concern yourself with the receiving access in the derived class. Depending on which of the three access specifiers you supply when inheriting, the incoming members appear in the private, protected, or public section of the derived class.

Q&A

Q. Why would I want to inherit?

A. Inheritance enables you to reuse classes that you've already written. Inheritance forms the perfect vehicle for extending programs while providing data protection. If you purchase class libraries from other sources, you can inherit your own classes from those supplied even if you don't have source code to the supplied class implementations. When you need a new window that behaves differently from the one your class creates, inherit a new window class that behaves slightly differently.

The nice thing about inheritance is that it enables you to write new code based on code you already know and understand. New classes are easily derived from existing classes that you've already written and debugged. Reusing code and data through inheritance is safer and faster than the old cut-and-paste methods used in non-OOP programming.

Q. What is the `protected` access specifier used for?

A. The `protected` access specifier had to be added to Visual C++ to allow inheritance while maintaining data protection. No derived class can use a base class's private member.

It's Hereditary: Inheriting Data

Making a base class member protected guards that member from use by outside procedures and classes but does allow derived classes access to the data. Protected data is still hidden from the rest of the program but is available to all derived classes.

Without the protected access specifier, there would be no way to keep data private while still allowing derived access.

Q. What can I change in a derived class from the base class?

A. You can add data members and functionality in derived classes. In a way, a child class always outperforms its parent class because a child class contains all the members and functions of the parent class and also adds some of its own.

Q. Why is single inheritance better than multiple inheritance?

A. Single inheritance is many times easier to code than multiple inheritance. The benefits of multiple inheritance just don't seem to be worth the effort involved in writing code with multiple inheritance. When faced with a programming situation that requires multiple inheritance, try to rework your class to work with single inheritance so that your programming is more productive and less error prone.

Q. Why must I supply an access specifier when deriving classes?

A. You don't *have* to supply an access specifier when receiving inherited classes because Visual C++ defaults to private inheritance. However, in private inheritance, all inherited members, both protected and public members, become private in the derived class. Most of the time, inheriting with private access is too limiting.

When you inherit with protected access, both incoming protected and public members become protected in the derived class.

When you inherit with public access (the most common way), incoming protected members remain protected, and incoming public members remain public.

Workshop

The Workshop offers quiz questions and exercises to hone your skills and give you feedback on today's lesson. You'll find some proposed answers in Appendix D.

Quiz

1. Which of the following classes is the base class, A or B?

   ```
   class A {
     int i;
   public:
     void getI();
   };
   class B : A {
     int j;
   public:
     void getJ();
   };
   ```

2. Which of the classes in question 1, A or B, is the derived class?

3. In the class hierarchy of question 1, is there any way that B can access A's member named i? If so, how?

4. Given the inheritance hierarchy

   ```
   class baseCl {
     int i;
   protected:
     int j;
   public:
     int k;
   };
   class derivedCl : public baseCl {
     float x;
   public:
     prDerived();
   };
   ```

   answer the following questions:

   A. How many of baseCl's members can derivedCl work with?

   B. Is j public, protected, or private when it gets to derivedCl?

   C. Is k public, protected, or private when it gets to derivedCl?

5. Where is the one safe place to use multiple inheritance?

It's Hereditary: Inheriting Data

Exercise

1. Add to Listing 15.1 so that it contains inheritance of all of Figure 15.3's classes.

DAY 16

Inherited Limits and Extensions

Inherited Limits and Extensions

Today's chapter shows you complete programs that use inheritance hierarchies. Before writing programs that use inheritance, you need to learn how constructors and destructors work in an inheritance environment. Constructor and destructor functions cannot be inherited. Simply adding a constructor and destructor to a base class does not ensure that Visual C++ will properly construct and destruct that class— you need to learn how to write inheritance-related constructors and destructors correctly.

The constructors used in inheritance hierarchies look slightly different from the simple ones you've seen so far. Actually, derived class constructors are just as simple as those for stand-alone classes, but the syntax used differs when inheritance is used.

The new syntax for inheritance-related constructors includes *constructor initialization lists*. Initialization lists provide constructor values outside the body of the constructor, as you'll learn about in today's chapter. You can use constructor initialization lists for all your constructors, not just for those classes you inherit. Therefore, for consistency and also to maintain the habit, many Visual C++ programmers use constructor initialization lists for all their constructors, even for those classes that do not contain inheritance.

Although inherited class destructor functions don't differ in syntax from their stand-alone class equivalents, you need to learn the timing of destructors when using inheritance. Today's chapter focuses on the timing of both constructors and destructors when you're working with base and derived classes.

Today, you learn about the following topics:

- The syntax of constructor initialization lists
- Constructing parent class objects from derived classes
- The order of constructing within an inheritance hierarchy
- The order of destructing within an inheritance hierarchy
- Some coding and maintenance advantages of inheritance

The Need for Initialization Lists

All the constructor functions you've seen so far have assigned initial values to members. There is a problem with a constructor doing this, however, and at first the problem seems trivial. Constructors should not assign data; assigning data is best left to overloaded assignment operator functions. (Copy constructors fall between the cracks, designed to be both a constructor and an assignor.)

Constructors should construct. The data constructed should be new objects with initial values in them at their creation. It is easy to come up with an example class that cannot be constructed with an assignment constructor like the ones you've seen so far. The class in Listing 16.1 contains a const member. You might never have seen a const member in a class or structure before, but it is perfectly acceptable and is needed for safety in many cases.

Listing 16.1. Individual members can be constants.

```
1: // Filename: CONSTCLS.CPP
2: // A class with a constant member
3: class Inventory {
4:   char name[25];
5:   int quantity;
6:   float price;
7:   const int initialQuantity;  // Original order's quantity
8: public:
9:   // Public members go here
10: };
```

Although the body of this class is not complete, you can attempt to compile it as you can all stand-alone class header files. When you try to compile the class header, Visual C++ produces this error message:

```
error C2610: class 'Inventory' can never be instantiated; user-defined
➥constructor is required
```

Visual C++ notices the constant member on line 7 and informs you that you need a constructor when a constant member appears in a class. The built-in default constructor is not enough to handle constant members.

Note: Remember that a built-in default constructor (as opposed to a default constructor that you supply) initializes its members with garbage values. Visual C++ knows that if it uses its own default constructor to create an object of the Inventory class, a garbage value remains fixed in the constant member for all objects constructed. Visual C++ wants you to supply your own constructor so that you can control the initial value placed in the initialQuantity member.

Inherited Limits and Extensions

Listing 16.2 shows the `Inventory` class with a constructor added.

Listing 16.2. Attempting to add a constructor.

```
1:  // Filename: CONSTCL2.CPP
2:  // A class with a constant member and attempted constructor
3:  #include <string.h>
4:  class Inventory {
5:    char name[25];
6:    int quantity;
7:    float price;
8:    const int initialQuantity;  // Original order's quantity
9:  public:
10:   Inventory(char N[], int Q, float P, int I)
11:   {
12:     strcpy(name, N);     // Assign each of the passed values
13:     quantity = Q;
14:     price = P;
15:     initialQuantity = I; // Oops, this is suspicious!
16:   }
17:   // Rest of public members go here
18: };
```

Lines 12–15 form the familiar constructor pattern that you've seen in some of the past few chapters. Of course, this constructor could have been placed outside the body of the class header, but for this short example, it was left inside the class.

The constructor is not a default constructor. The constructor is written assuming that `main()` will create an `Inventory` object and at the same time provide the initial values in a statement such as this:

```
Inventory item1("Red High stool", 16, 25.65, 10);
```

There's still a major problem with this nondefault constructor. If you attempt to compile the class header in Listing 16.2, Visual C++ gives you the error messages shown here:

```
error C2758: 'initialQuantity' : must be initialized in constructor
➥base/member initializer list
error C2166: l-value specifies const object
```

Perhaps these compiler messages seem incorrect because `initialQuantity` is assigned an initial value in the constructor, and other than the constructor, the class header doesn't assign the constant `initialQuantity` any values. However, Visual C++ cannot handle the statement on line 15 because this is the internal order of all constructors:

1. Construct the object by reserving memory, and attach the object name to the reserved memory location.
2. Execute the body of the constructor code after the object is reserved in memory.

Because the body of the constructor consists of assignment statements, Visual C++ refuses to compile the class header. At line 15, the object is already constructed, or at least memory is already reserved with the object's name attached. (Technically, *at runtime,* if this constructor were to execute, the memory would already be reserved before line 15.) The assignment statement is attempting to assign a value to a constant that is already in memory, and constants cannot be changed after they are in memory.

By using constructor initialization lists, your constructors more accurately *construct and initialize* rather than *construct and assign.* This doesn't mean that constructors should not and cannot contain assignment statements and other code, but they rarely do contain code unless dynamic memory allocation is involved.

> **Note:** Besides constructing objects with constant members, you'll reap additional side benefits of constructors after you learn how to use initialization lists rather than constructor code. Your constructors will be cleaner, and constructor initialization lists construct derived classes. Also, if a member is a reference variable, you'll face the same initialization-versus-assignment problem that you face with constants because references must be initialized at the time they are defined, just as constants must be.

When you use a constructor initialization list, Visual C++ will truly construct and initialize at the time an object is created. Not only can your constant members therefore be initialized, but so can your other members as well.

Constructor Initialization Style

Most of the time, a constructor initialization list contains a value for every assignment statement the constructor would otherwise have. A constructor initialization list actually looks as if it is constructing individual members, and in a way it is. Here is a constructor that uses a construction initialization list to construct the Inventory class shown earlier:

Inherited Limits and Extensions

```
Inventory(char N[], int Q, float P, int I) : quantity(Q), price(P),
                                              initialQuantity(I)
{
  strcpy(N, name);   // Couldn't work in initialization list
}
```

Notice that constructor initialization lists follow the constructor's closing argument list parenthesis and a colon, :. All non-array members can be initialized. In this constructor, the three members in the initialization list are *initialized,* not assigned in the sense that they would be assigned in the constructor's body. The initialization list gives the compiler the go-ahead to create the constant member `initialQuantity` with an initial value. The `const` locks that value into the member permanently. (This all happens at runtime when an object variable is instantiated from the class.)

It might look strange to include constructor-like syntax for members of built-in data types, but the syntax assures initialization rather than assignment.

Notice that the character array member must be assigned in the function body. Member character arrays and pointers are usually reserved on the heap, so they require the usual assignment syntax in the body of the constructor.

Just for review, here is a simple class that contains three members and a constructor that properly constructs the members when an object is created:

```
class C {
  int i;
  char c;
  float f;
public:
  C(int I, char C, float F) : i(I), c(C) , f(F) {};
};
```

This class contains no array or pointer members to keep its initialization simple. Figure 16.1 shows how the initialization lists work like assignments, but they are assignments that occur *as* the object is being constructed.

```
                                    i=I;        f=F;
                                     ↑           ↑
            C(int I, char C, float F) :i(I), c(C), f(F) {
                                            ↓
                                           c=C;
```

Figure 16.1. Initialization works like an assignment but occurs during construction.

The preceding class does exactly the same thing as the next one, except that C's members are initialized in the preceding code and are created and then assigned in this code:

```
class C {
  int i;
  char c;
  float f;
public:
  C(int I, char C, float F)
  { i = I;        // Assigns all the members
    c = C;
    f = F;
  }
};
```

With no arrays, constant members, or references to members, either of these two sets of code works fine. However, the first class with the initialization list is shorter and easier to code and maintains the spirit of constructors (initialization, not assignment). Most of the constructors in the rest of this book will use constructor initialization lists to initialize the members instead of doing the assignment in the body of the function. The only exception will occur when an array or the heap (or both) is involved.

> **Note:** The definition lines of constructors with constructor initialization lists often get to be lengthy. Often, Visual C++ programmers move the initialization list down to the line following the constructor's first line like this:
>
> ```
> C(int I, char C, float F) :
>   i(I), c(C) , f(F) {};
> ```
>
> The extra spacing doesn't help or hurt a free-form language such as Visual C++, but it sure helps the Visual C++ *programmer* keep a better focus on the code.

If the implementation of your constructor appears outside the class header, there is no change in the syntax for the constructor initialization list. Listing 16.3 contains a rewritten version of the Inventory class with the constructor implementation put below the class header.

Inherited Limits and Extensions

Listing 16.3. Moving the body of the constructor.

```
 1: // Filename: CONSTCL3.CPP
 2: // A class with a constant member and constructor initialization
 3: #include <string.h>
 4: class Inventory {
 5:    char name[25];
 6:    int quantity;
 7:    float price;
 8:    const int initialQuantity;   // Original order's quantity
 9: public:
10:    Inventory(char N[], int Q, float P, int I);
11:    // Rest of public members go here
12: };
13: // Notice that the initialization list must go with the
14: // constructor's implementation, not the prototype above
15: Inventory::Inventory(char N[], int Q, float P, int I)
16:           : quantity(Q), price(P), initialQuantity(I)
17: {
18:    strcpy(name, N);      // Array requires assignment
19: }
```

DO	DON'T

DO familiarize yourself with constructor initialization lists and use them for all member initialization when your classes contain non-array members.

DO use assignment statements inside constructors, even those constructors that contain initialization lists, if you want to store data members on the heap, in arrays, or both.

DON'T use assignment statements in constructors to initialize constant or reference members.

Construct Base Classes First

A child class must take care of its parent class. That is, when you construct a child (a derived) class object, the child constructor must call the parent's (the base's) class constructor. The interrelationships of hierarchical inheritance is critical to proper construction of your derived objects.

It's easy to construct a base class object. No matter how many classes are derived from a base class, if you want to create a base class object variable, you can use the standard constructors or constructor initialization lists described until now in the book. Listing 16.4 shows a parent class named Parent and two child classes named Son and Daughter. main() then ignores the two derived classes and creates a base class object with a constructor from the base class.

Note: Base class destructors are just as straightforward as base class constructors. All the constructor/destructor material you've read to this point in the book works for base classes no matter how many classes are then derived from the base class.

Listing 16.4. Construct and destruct base class objects as usual.

```
 1:  // Filename: PARENTCH.CPP
 2:  // Constructs and destructs base class objects
 3:  #include <iostream.h>
 4:  #include <string.h>
 5:  class Parent {
 6:  protected:            // To allow inheritance
 7:     char name[25];
 8:     int age;
 9:  public:
10:     Parent(char [], int);
11:     ~Parent() {};   // No body necessary because no heap work done
12:     void dispParent(void);
13:     // No overloaded output to keep program short
14:  };
15:  Parent::Parent(char N[], int A) : age(A) {
16:     strcpy(name, N);
17:  }
18:  void Parent::dispParent(void)
19:  {
20:     cout << "Parent's name is " << name << "\n";
21:     cout << "Parent's age is " << age << "\n";
22:  }
23:  class Son : Parent {
24:     int yrInSchool;
25:  public:
26:     void dispSon(void);
27:  };
28:  void Son::dispSon(void)
29:  {
30:     cout << "Son's name is " << name << "\n";
```

continues

Day 16

Inherited Limits and Extensions

Listing 16.4. continued

```
31:    cout << "Son's age is " << age << "\n";
32: };
33: class Daughter : Parent {
34:    int yrInSchool;
35: public:
36:    void dispDaughter(void);
37: };
38: void Daughter::dispDaughter(void)
39: {
40:    cout << "Daughter's name is " << name << "\n";
41:    cout << "Daughter's age is " << age << "\n";
42: };
43: ///////////////////////////////////////////////////////////////
44: main()
45: {
46:    Parent mom("Bettye", 58); // Construct 2 parent class objects
47:    Parent dad("Glen", 57);
48:    // Print them to show they were properly constructed
49:    mom.dispParent();
50:    dad.dispParent();
51:    return 0;
52: }
```

There's not much in this first rendition of the Parent hierarchy except for the normal constructor of the Parent on lines 15–17. The Parent constructor uses a constructor initialization list for the non-array member age and uses strcpy() to assign the initial name to the name member. The two Parent objects are constructed on lines 46 and 47 in the usual manner.

The next step to make this code compile properly would be to construct a Son and Daughter object. Notice that each of these derived objects contains an extra member named yrInSchool that will have to be dealt with via a constructor. Remembering that constructors are never inherited, you'll have to define a constructor for the derived objects.

Things are not always as they might seem. Listing 16.5 contains code that appears to construct a Son object properly. The extra member, yrInSchool, is passed to the Son constructor function, and the constructor initializes the new yrInSchool member and the two inherited members.

Listing 16.5. Attempting to construct a derived class.

```
1: // Filename: PARENTSO.CPP
2: // Attempts to construct derived class objects
```

```
 3:  #include <iostream.h>
 4:  #include <string.h>
 5:  class Parent {
 6:  protected:              // To allow inheritance
 7:    char name[25];
 8:    int age;
 9:  public:
10:    Parent(char [], int);
11:    ~Parent() {};   // No body necessary because no heap work done
12:    void dispParent(void);
13:    // No overloaded output to keep program short
14:  };
15:  Parent::Parent(char N[], int A) : age(A) {
16:    strcpy(name, N);
17:  }
18:  void Parent::dispParent(void)
19:  {
20:    cout << "Parent's name is " << name << "\n";
21:    cout << "Parent's age is " << age << "\n";
22:  }
23:  class Son : Parent {
24:    int yrInSchool;
25:  public:
26:    void dispSon(void);
27:    Son(char [], int, int);
28:  };
29:  Son::Son(char N[], int A, int Y)
30:  {
31:    age = A;
32:    strcpy(name, N);
33:    yrInSchool = Y;
34:  }
35:  void Son::dispSon(void)
36:  {
37:    cout << "Son's name is " << name << "\n";
38:    cout << "Son's age is " << age << "\n";
39:    cout << "Son's year in school is " << yrInSchool << "\n";
40:  }
41:
42:  class Daughter : Parent {
43:    int yrInSchool;
44:  public:
45:    void dispDaughter(void);
46:  };
47:  void Daughter::dispDaughter(void)
48:  {
49:    cout << "Daughter's name is " << name << "\n";
50:    cout << "Daughter's age is " << age << "\n";
51:  };
52:  ////////////////////////////////////////////////////////////////
```

continues

Day 16: Inherited Limits and Extensions

Listing 16.5. continued

```
53: main()
54: {
55:    Parent mom("Bettye", 58); // Construct 2 parent class objects
56:    Parent dad("Glen", 57);
57:    // Print them to show they were properly constructed
58:    mom.dispParent();
59:    dad.dispParent();
60:    Son boy("Luke", 17, 11);
61:    return 0;
62: }
```

The program in Listing 16.5 will not work. As a matter of fact, the program will not even compile. It looks as if line 60 properly constructs a Son object using the constructor on lines 29–34. The constructor is not accurate, however, because derived class constructors require extra considerations that base class constructors don't require.

When you attempt to compile this program, Visual C++ displays the following messages:

```
error C2512: 'Parent' : no appropriate default constructor available
error C2610: class 'Daughter' can never be instantiated; user-defined
➥constructor is required
```

The daughter class is not yet constructed, but the first error message is more revealing at this point. A derived class constructor cannot construct a derived object *until the parent is constructed*. A child class *must* construct the parent class.

> **Note:** It's easy to remember the parent-construction rule: in real life, a child cannot exist if the parent doesn't, and Visual C++ wants to imitate real life!

Requiring the base class construction makes sense technically. After all, a child object inherits members and member functions from a parent, and that parent *has* to exist before there is anything to bring into the derived object. This does *not* mean that you have to construct a stand-alone base class object before constructing a derived class object. Although two Parent objects are constructed in Listing 16.5's lines 55 and 56 (or they *would* be constructed if the program compiled), no stand-alone Parent *object* has to exist before a Son object is constructed. However, a derived class constructor must first call the base class constructor to avoid the error message shown earlier.

Note: If a derived class is itself derived from another derived class (as in Figure 16.2), each derived class has to worry only about constructing its immediate parent. That parent, in turn, is responsible for constructing *its* parent, and so on.

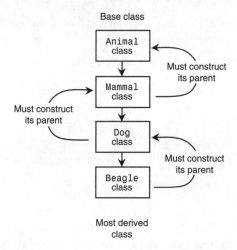

Figure 16.2. A derived class must construct its immediate parent class.

A derived class constructor must use constructor initialization lists to construct its parent class, or a default constructor must be supplied for the parent class. As is so often the case, a default constructor rarely works well because you want to initialize the members of the parent object that will appear in the derived object. Therefore, in most cases, a derived class will contain an initializer list item that is nothing more than a call to the parent class's constructor.

The Son constructor cannot directly assign values to the Parent class members as it is doing in Listing 16.5. Instead of trying to, like

```
Son::Son(char N[], int A, int Y)
{
  age = A;
  strcpy(name, N);
  yrInSchool = Y;
}
```

the Son constructor needs only to initialize a Parent class object like this:

Inherited Limits and Extensions

```
Son::Son(char N[], int A, int Y) : Parent(N, A)
{
  yrInSchool = Y;
}
```

List the order of the base class constructor arguments in the same order as the base class constructor function arguments. If you rearrange them, the base class constructor arguments will receive incorrect values.

The Son's yrInSchool member is not an array, so it too could be added to the initializer list like this:

```
Son::Son(char N[], int A, int Y) : Parent(N, A), yrInSchool(Y)
{ // No body is necessary
}
```

> **Note:** If the Son class contained additional members that were arrays or pointers to heap memory, the constructor body would contain additional code to set up those arrays and pointers.

After the Son constructor is properly set up, the following statement constructs a Son object because the base class constructor is now called during the Son's initialization:

```
Son boy("Luke", 17, 11);   // Construct a Son object
```

Adding a Daughter constructor is now trivial because it looks just like the Son class constructor. Listing 16.6 contains the proper base class initialization list for both the Son and the Daughter classes. The program also adds a character array member to the Daughter class to add code body to the Daughter's constructor.

Listing 16.6. The derived classes properly construct the base class.

```
 1:  // Filename: PARENTFX.CPP
 2:  // Constructs base class objects properly
 3:  #include <iostream.h>
 4:  #include <string.h>
 5:  class Parent {
 6:  protected:            // To allow inheritance
 7:    char name[25];
 8:    int age;
 9:  public:
10:    Parent(char [], int);
11:    ~Parent() {};   // No body necessary because no heap work done
```

```
12:     void dispParent(void);
13:     // No overloaded output to keep program short
14: };
15: Parent::Parent(char N[], int A) : age(A) {
16:     strcpy(name, N);
17: }
18: void Parent::dispParent(void)
19: {
20:     cout << "Parent's name is " << name << "\n";
21:     cout << "Parent's age is " << age << "\n";
22: }
23: class Son : Parent {
24:     int yrInSchool;
25: public:
26:     void dispSon(void);
27:     Son(char [], int, int);
28: };
29: Son::Son(char N[], int A, int Y) : Parent(N, A), yrInSchool(Y)
30: {
31: }
32: void Son::dispSon(void)
33: {
34:     cout << "Son's name is " << name << "\n";
35:     cout << "Son's age is " << age << "\n";
36:     cout << "Son's year in school is " << yrInSchool << "\n";
37: }
38:
39: class Daughter : Parent {
40:     int yrInSchool;
41:     char friendsName[25];
42: public:
43:     Daughter(char [], int, int, char []);
44:     void dispDaughter(void);
45: };
46: Daughter::Daughter(char N[], int A, int Y, char F[]) :
47:                   Parent(N, A), yrInSchool(Y)
48: {
49:     strcpy(friendsName, F);
50: }
51: void Daughter::dispDaughter(void)
52: {
53:     cout << "Daughter's name is " << name << "\n";
54:     cout << "Daughter's age is " << age << "\n";
55:     cout << "Daughter's year in school is " << yrInSchool << "\n";
56:     cout << "Daughter's friend is " << friendsName << "\n";
57: };
58: ////////////////////////////////////////////////////////////////
59: main()
60: {
61:     Parent mom("Bettye", 58); // Construct 2 parent class objects
```

continues

Day 16: Inherited Limits and Extensions

Listing 16.6. continued

```
62:    Parent dad("Glen", 57);
63:    // Print them to show they were properly constructed
64:    mom.dispParent();
65:    dad.dispParent();
66:    Son boy("Luke", 17, 11);
67:    boy.dispSon();
68:    Daughter girl("Jayne", 16, 10, "Melissa");
69:    girl.dispDaughter();
70:    return 0;
71: }
```

```
Parent's name is Bettye
Parent's age is 58
Parent's name is Glen
Parent's age is 57
Son's name is Luke
Son's age is 17
Son's year in school is 11
Daughter's name is Jayne
Daughter's age is 16
Daughter's year in school is 10
Daughter's friend is Melissa
```

From the output you can see that both `Parent` objects are properly constructed, and so are the `Son` and `Daughter` objects. The only way the two derived class objects could be constructed is for them to construct their parent class, and that's what they do. The `Son` constructs a `Parent` on line 29, and the `Daughter` constructs a `Parent` on line 47.

Notice how clean the two derived class listings are. Again, with inheritance, you don't have to repeat any of the members that appear in both classes as long as you properly construct the classes and make sure that a child class constructs a parent class.

Listing 16.7 contains an additional derived class named `GrandChild`. The `GrandChild` class derives from `Girl`. As you'll see in the `GrandChild` constructor, the `GrandChild` class has to worry only about properly constructing the `Daughter` class because the `Daughter` class is already set up to construct the `Parent` class properly.

Listing 16.7. Deriving a second class in the inheritance hierarchy.

```
1:    // Filename: GRANCHLD.CPP
2:    // Deriving classes from other derived classes
3:    #include <iostream.h>
4:    #include <iomanip.h>
```

```
 5:  #include <string.h>
 6:  class Parent {
 7:  protected:              // To allow inheritance
 8:    char name[25];
 9:    int age;
10:  public:
11:    Parent(char [], int);
12:    ~Parent() {};   // No body necessary because no heap work done
13:    void dispParent(void);
14:    // No overloaded output to keep program short
15:  };
16:  Parent::Parent(char N[], int A) : age(A) {
17:    strcpy(name, N);
18:  }
19:  void Parent::dispParent(void)
20:  {
21:    cout << "Parent's name is " << name << "\n";
22:    cout << "Parent's age is " << age << "\n";
23:  }
24:  class Son : public Parent {
25:    int yrInSchool;
26:  public:
27:    void dispSon(void);
28:    Son(char [], int, int);
29:  };
30:  Son::Son(char N[], int A, int Y) : Parent(N, A), yrInSchool(Y)
31:  {
32:  }
33:  void Son::dispSon(void)
34:  {
35:    cout << "Son's name is " << name << "\n";
36:    cout << "Son's age is " << age << "\n";
37:    cout << "Son's year in school is " << yrInSchool << "\n";
38:  }
39:
40:  class Daughter : public Parent {
41:  // 'protected' was removed
42:    int yrInSchool;
43:    char friendsName[25];
44:  public:
45:    Daughter(char [], int, int, char []);
46:    Daughter(char [], int);
47:    void dispDaughter(void);
48:  };
49:  Daughter::Daughter(char N[], int A, int Y, char F[]) :
50:                    Parent(N, A), yrInSchool(Y)
51:  {
52:    strcpy(friendsName, F);
53:  }
54:  Daughter::Daughter(char N[], int A) : Parent(N, A)
```

continues

Day 16: Inherited Limits and Extensions

Listing 16.7. continued

```
55: {  // No function body needed; the initialization list does it all
56: }
57: void Daughter::dispDaughter(void)
58: {
59:    cout << "Daughter's name is " << name << "\n";
60:    cout << "Daughter's age is " << age << "\n";
61:    cout << "Daughter's year in school is " << yrInSchool << "\n";
62:    cout << "Daughter's friend is " << friendsName << "\n";
63: };
64: class GrandChild : Daughter {
65:    float weightAtBirth;
66: public:
67:    GrandChild(char [], int, float);
68:    void dispGrand(void);
69: };
70: GrandChild::GrandChild(char N[], int A, float W) :
71:                        Daughter(N, A), weightAtBirth(W)
72: {  // Initialization list does it all
73: }
74: void GrandChild::dispGrand(void)
75: {
76:    cout << setprecision(1) << setiosflags(ios::fixed);
77:    cout << "Grandchild's name is " << name << "\n";
78:    cout << "Grandchild's age is " << age << "\n";
79:    cout << "Grandchild's weight at birth was " << weightAtBirth
             ➥<< "\n";
80: }
81: //////////////////////////////////////////////////////////////////
82: main()
83: {
84:    Daughter girl("Barbara", 22, 16, "Elizabeth");
85:    girl.dispDaughter();
86:    GrandChild baby("Suzie", 1, 7.5);
87:    baby.dispGrand();
88:    return 0;
89: }
```

```
Daughter's name is Barbara
Daughter's age is 22
Daughter's year in school is 16
Daughter's friend is Elizabeth
Grandchild's name is Suzie
Grandchild's age is 1
Grandchild's weight at birth was 7.5
```

A few changes had to be made to the Daughter class to allow the inheritance to the GrandChild class. The public receiving the access specifier was included when the Daughter inherited from the Parent in line 40 because the GrandChild had to have access to the Parent's members too. (The public receiving access specifier was added to the Son class as well on line 24, but no other class derives from Son. However, if derived classes are ever added to the Son class, a public or protected keyword will be needed as the receiving access specifier.)

Back in Listing 16.6, there was no need to change the Daughter's receiving access from the private default because all of Daughter's inherited members could remain private; no other class would need the members. After the GrandChild class was added that needed access to the Daughter's members, however, the public keyword ensured that all protected and public inherited members from Parent would remain protected and public respectively when they get to Daughter. The Daughter can then pass on those members (perhaps *traits* would be a more appropriate term) to the GrandChild.

> **Note:** Figure 16.3 shows the contents of the GrandChild class and explains where each member comes from.

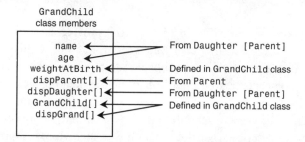

Figure 16.3. The origin of the GrandChild class members.

Figure 16.3 does raise a few questions that are easily answered. For example, all of Parent and Daughter's public member functions are inherited along with the data members. You would never want to apply the dispParent() or dispDaughter() function to a GrandChild object, but the inheritance makes these functions available anyway.

There is a simple solution to this situation. Give all the display functions, in each class, the *same name*. If all the functions were named display(), the following four statements would each produce different results:

```
mom.display();      // Call Parent class's display()
boy.display();      // Call Son class's display()
```

Day 16: Inherited Limits and Extensions

```
girl.display();  // Call Daughter class's display()
baby.display();  // Call GrandChild class's display()
```

The `display()` function in each derived class would replace the one that would otherwise be inherited if the display function names were all different, as they are in Listing 16.7. By using the same member function names for similar functions, you decrease the number of function names you have to deal with and thus simplify your programming. Visual C++ calls the correct function based on the object that triggers the call.

In a way, giving derived function names the same names as a parent's function names limits the inheritance. The derived class function replaces the one that would otherwise come from the parent. You can also limit the inheritance of data members by giving them the same name in a derived class.

Note: The common function names would not clash because all members of a class have class scope, not block, function, or file scope.

Doesn't the `main()` function in Listing 16.7 provide a very high-level view of the program? It's almost as if `main()` were written in a non-C-like language because of its style. After the screen clears, a `Daughter` object is created and displays, then a `GrandChild` object is created and displays. Besides making it easy to understand what each argument means (for instance, the second `Daughter` argument is the age, the third is the number of years in school), `main()` is such that a nonprogrammer can *almost* look at it and describe what the program is doing. More important, a programmer can look at `main()` and quickly and reliably interpret what the program is doing. The real value is not apparent understanding by nonprogrammers, but real understanding by actual programmers.

When you add functionality through inheritance to your classes, you can improve your programming productivity tremendously. All the petty details are gone. A huge benefit of inheritance appears during program maintenance. If the `Parent` class changes, the change ripples through the rest of the inheritance hierarchy. For example, if you decide to store the `Parent`'s name member on the heap, you only have to change the `Parent` constructor and recompile the program. No derived class changes, because Visual C++ keeps classes encapsulated and inherits whatever needs to be inherited automatically.

What About Destructors?

The example built throughout today's chapter doesn't concentrate on destructors for these two reasons:

- ☐ No destructor code was really needed because nothing was allocated on the heap.

- ☐ Visual C++ handles destructing the inheritance hierarchy for you, unlike constructors, which you must specifically construct in a sequential manner (up the hierarchy) as shown in today's chapter.

If you don't supply a destructor for any or all classes in a hierarchy, Visual C++ uses a default destructor to get rid of the objects when they go out of scope. If the heap is not involved in the program, the default destructor works fine. If you supply a destructor, however, for any or all objects, Visual C++ calls the one you supply.

As Figure 16.4 illustrates, Visual C++ automatically destructs the child before its parent. (The parent always outlives the child in OOP.) Destructors are called in the opposite order of constructor calls. You never call destructors explicitly, even when inheritance is involved, because there can be one and only one destructor for any class (either yours or a default destructor), and Visual C++ knows to call a class destructor when an object goes out of scope.

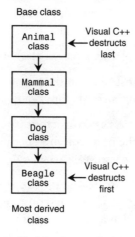

Figure 16.4. Destructors are called in the opposite sequence of constructors.

Day 16: Inherited Limits and Extensions

DO	DON'T

DO use the same order in constructor initialization argument lists as the parent class's constructor argument list so that the proper values are sent to the parent's constructor function.

DO construct base classes before derived classes.

DO use the same data member or member name in a derived class as in the parent class if you want to change or limit the functionality of the inherited member.

DON'T call destructors, even when inheritance is involved. Unlike with constructors, Visual C++ handles destructing your inherited objects automatically, from the most derived class to the parent class.

Summary

Today's chapter showed you how to utilize inheritance by constructing and destructing derived class objects. It is the job of the derived class to construct its parent. (Visual C++ makes sure that the derived class is destructed first.) Only after the parent class is constructed can a child class be constructed because only then will the parent's members be available to the derived class.

There are two ways to construct a parent class:

- ☐ Supply a default constructor in the parent class. When you do, Visual C++ calls the default constructor before a derived class object is constructed.

- ☐ Trigger the parent class's constructor through an initialization list. This approach is by far the most common because the parent constructor almost always needs values passed to it when a derived class object is constructed.

Initialization lists not only are helpful for constructing derived classes, but they also help you construct objects that contain constant members and reference members. Initialization lists ensure that an object's members are initialized when the object is defined, not afterward.

This chapter walked you through the building of an inheritance program by constructing the parent class using the second method just described. To keep things as obvious as possible, terms such as Parent, Son, Daughter, and GrandChild were used as class names so that you could more easily concentrate on the inheritance structure.

Without initialization lists, a child object could never be constructed (unless a more limiting default constructor was used). The parent must be constructed *before* the child, and initialization, not assignment, is the only way to accomplish this.

Inheritance plays a critical role in program writing and maintenance. Being able to inherit classes simplifies your programming after you master constructing specifics. You can make changes to a parent class without having to make those same changes to the child class.

Q&A

Q. Why must a child class worry about constructing a parent class?

A. A derived class cannot exist until the parent is constructed. The parent's members cannot be passed along to the child (the derived) class until the parent's members are constructed.

Whenever you write a constructor for a derived class, you must always provide a constructor initialization list or a default constructor in the parent class.

Q. Sometimes, the base class exists solely for deriving other classes, not for instantiating objects of its own. Do I still have to construct a parent class in the derived classes?

A. Yes. Even when a base class is not to be used for instantiating object variables, you must still provide a constructor initialization list in each derived class or provide a default constructor for the parent class. A parent class *must* be constructed before a derived class can exist.

Q. How can I ensure that destructors are called in the proper order?

A. You don't have to. That's the beauty of Visual C++. All destructors will automatically be called in the reverse order of the constructors. In other words, a child's destructor always executes before the parent's.

If you don't need a destructor, Visual C++ calls a default destructor for you. If you supply some destructors in an inheritance hierarchy, but not a destructor for all the classes in the inheritance chain, Visual C++ calls your destructor when one is there and calls the default destructor when it cannot find a destructor that you've coded.

Day 16: Inherited Limits and Extensions

Workshop

The Workshop offers quiz questions and exercises to hone your skills and give you feedback on today's lesson. You'll find some proposed answers in Appendix D.

Quiz

1. True or false: If a parent class *and* a child class contain default constructors, no explicit construction has to take place.

2. Why can't a regular constructor be used to construct when a class contains a constant member?

3. Where do initialization lists go?

4. True or false: Both constant members and reference members require constructor initialization lists.

5. What is wrong with this derived class's constructor?

```
class A {
  int i;
  float x;
public:
  A(int I, float X);
};
class B : public A {
  char c;
public:
  B(int I, float X, char C) : A(X, I), c(C) {};
};
```

6. What is the order of constructors in this inheritance hierarchy?

```
class A {
  int i;
public:
  A(int I);
};
class B : public A {
  int j;
public:
  B(int I, int J) : A(I), j(J) {};
};
```

```
class C : public B {
  int k;
public:
  C(int I, int J, int K) : B(I, J), k(K) {};
};
```

   A. A, B, C
   B. C, B, A
   C. Cannot be determined

7. In the inheritance hierarchy of question 6, what is the order of destructor calls?

   A. A, B, C
   B. C, B, A
   C. Cannot be determined

8. What do you do to make Visual C++ destruct an inheritance hierarchy properly?

Exercises

1. Change all the character arrays in the Parent inheritance hierarchy (Listing 16.7) to character pointers, and initialize the arrays on the heap. You'll need to add proper destructors that deallocate the heap memory when the program finishes with the objects. Create a Parent object, a Son object, a Daughter object, and a GrandChild object to test your program.

   It's important to realize that by changing the class storage mechanism from a memory array to the heap, main() doesn't require anything different from what it would require if you left the names arrays. By doing this exercise, you should begin to see how writing OOP programs increases your productivity tremendously. You can make changes to a class without changing the code that uses that class. When you begin programming database structures, linked lists, and double-linked lists, you'll soon realize that this separation of code (main() and the functions that main() calls) from the storage and implementation of the class decreases programming problems by many factors. If the storage method changed for a non-OOP program, the entire program would have to be scoured for every reference in the code to the storage mechanism used.

Inherited Limits and Extensions

Extra: Make the class extremely easy to use by naming all the object-printing routines with the same name, `display()`. (You could also overload << to output the objects, but the amount of data being displayed probably doesn't warrant an overloaded `operator<<` function for each class.)

2. Add a `Pet` class to the `Parent` hierarchy. Inherit a `Pet` from the `Parent` class (it's stretching things a bit, but that's OK), and add a new member to the `Pet` class named `peopleYears`. (We're assuming that the pet will always be a dog for this exercise to work as described.) In the `Pet` constructor, multiply the age of the `Pet` by seven, and store the result in the `peopleYears` member. All `Pet` objects will now carry their actual age in dog years and their corresponding age to people in `peopleYears`.

DAY 17

Data Composition

Data Composition

Today's chapter teaches a new concept that is closely related to inheritance and is often confused with inheritance: *composition*. Composition is nothing more than embedding one class within another.

The reason people confuse composition and inheritance is that they both rely on other classes to build new classes. When you're using composition, the new class does not inherit anything, but rather, the new class *contains* another class. Composition still builds new classes from existing ones, but instead of inheriting members, the new class *contains* the other class in its entirety.

This introduction might still leave you confused, but in a few pages, you'll have no trouble distinguishing between inheritance and composition. The syntax you use for each is different, and the design of your classes requires that you know the difference between inheritance and composition so that you'll know when and how to use one or the other.

Today, you learn about the following topics:

- When to use composition over inheritance
- The *is-a* and *has-a* questions
- How to compose one class from another
- Composition's construction and destruction concerns
- Assigning composed objects to one another

Note: As you saw in yesterday's inheritance chapter, the primary difficulty when using composition is getting the constructing and destructing done properly. The embedded class must be constructed properly before it can be used inside another class.

Composition vs. Inheritance

Consider for a moment a new Visual C++ programmer writing a program to keep track of a homemade ice cream parlor's inventory. The store specializes in Italian *gelato* ice-cream cones, the tastiest, richest ice cream on earth. In talking to the owners and in thinking about the components of the inventory, the programmer learns that the shop purchases cream in bulk to make the ice cream. The program is to keep track of the amount and quality of cream bought.

The store also purchases sugar, filtered water, and cones. Each of these ice-cream cone ingredients must be tracked separately (in its own class), and the program also must keep track of the number of ice-cream cones sold.

The programmer, knowing all the advantages of Visual C++ code reuse, knows that after a class for the cream is defined, and after a class for the sugar is defined, and after a class for all the rest of the ingredients is defined, it would be a waste of time to repeat all those members inside the ice-cream cone class. Therefore, after defining a class for each of the ingredients, the programmer decides to inherit an ice-cream cone class from those classes already defined.

What do you suppose the base class should be? Sugar? Cream? There's a problem here. None of the ingredients seems to be the "base" class, even though they do all make ice-cream cones in the long run. There is sugar in an ice-cream cone, but an ice-cream cone doesn't seem to derive from sugar.

Should the programmer code the ice-cream cone class and then derive all the other ingredient classes from it? No, because there are no ice-cream cones in sugar. The programmer is stumped and believes that he will throw out all the inheritance knowledge and write a separate but overlapping ice-cream cone class. The programmer gets the program to work and presents the inventory system to the owners, but the programmer opened himself up to more maintenance nightmares than would otherwise be the case because there was no reuse of code. If the store changes to fat-free yogurt and stops keeping cream in stock, the ice-cream cone class *and* the class that handles the cream must be revised. If code reuse had been programmed into the system, the cream class could be converted to a yogurt culture class, and the ice-cream cone instantly becomes a yogurt cone.

This ice cream parlor situation is more common than it might seem here, especially in inventory systems. Lots of times, component parts combine to form a larger item, and both the component parts and the items made from those parts must be tracked. Inheritance, however, is not the OOP solution to the duplication of class data. As you just saw, it is impossible to define a base class when all the classes seem to have equal significance. Also, many of the classes (for instance, sugar, cream, and empty cones) don't derive from each other, so they should not be part of a long inheritance hierarchy.

Day 17

Data Composition

> **Note:** If you are wondering whether multiple inheritance could offer a solution, you *could* possibly code the ice-cream cone class with all those ingredient classes as the multiple parent classes of the ice-cream cone class. If you do, however, good luck! Having two parent classes creates lots of programming difficulties. Having more than two parent classes creates lots of programming migraines! Luckily, you're about to see a way to resolve this seemingly unsolvable problem without using inheritance.

Instead of inheriting the ice-cream cone class from all the ingredients, the programmer correctly decides to try composition. A composed class contains members that are other classes. See whether composition works: An ice-cream cone is *composed* of cream, sugar, filtered water, and cones. Those raw ingredients are part of the ice-cream cone. An ice-cream cone has all of those ingredients, so therefore, an ice-cream cone is *composed* of those ingredients.

None of the previous paragraphs contained the awkwardness you found when trying to inherit an ice-cream cone from those ingredients. Remember that it was impossible to determine what the base class ingredient would be. However, when you change the wording and say the ice-cream cone contains, or more accurately is *composed* of, the ingredients, everything begins to sound fine.

The terms *is-a* and *has-a* explain in a nutshell the difference between inheritance and composition. The following axioms describe the relationship between *is-a* questions, *has-a* questions, *inheritance,* and *composition:*

- A class that has another class or more than one class inside it is a composed class. The has-a question tells you so. If one class has another class, use composition and embed the component class inside the surrounding class. An ice-cream cone contains sugar, but an ice-cream cone would never be thought of as an advanced form of sugar. See Figure 17.1.

- A class that derives from another class has all the properties of that first class plus a few additional properties. The is-a question tells you so. If the derived class is another class with a few extra members, use inheritance. The ice-cream cone is not the same thing as sugar with a few other ingredients thrown in because none of the properties of sugar matches that of ice cream. Ice cream is not room temperature. Ice cream is not granular. Ice cream is not always sugar-colored.

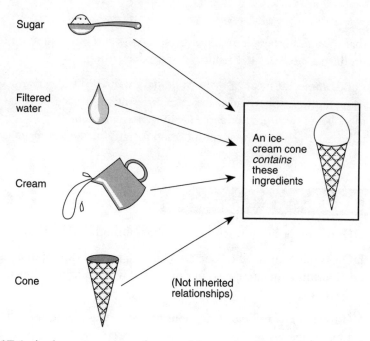

Figure 17.1. An ice-cream cone class would contain all the other classes, not be derived from them.

Consider an additional ice cream parlor requirement that the program track low-sugar ice-cream cones, regular ice-cream cones, and super-sugar ice-cream cones. A good case could be made that all three of these classes could be derived from each other. The base class could be low-sugar ice cream, and each derived class could add another sugar ingredient along the way. Such classes probably would benefit from inheritance, but the first class, the low-sugar class, would be formed through composition.

What about an ice cream sundae class? The sundae class would form best through composition because a sundae contains (*has-a*) ice cream and also contains (*has-a*) toppings.

Will Either Work?

It's true, especially if you're willing to use multiple inheritance (and spend some long nights of debugging instead of being home with the kids), that you *could* use either composition or inheritance to write virtually any class

Data Composition

that relates to other classes. However, the *is-a* and *has-a* question tests always produce a more natural result than guessing wrong.

For example, even though you could have written the ice-cream cone class using multiple inheritance, an ice-cream cone more accurately has all those ingredients and does not derive from those ingredients. The *has-a* question tells the programmer that composition is right for the ice-cream cones.

DO | **DON'T**

DO use composition when one class contains other classes.

DO use inheritance when one class forms a natural extension of another class, forming the same class but improved with additional functionality or characteristics.

DO use the *is-a* and *has-a* questions to decide whether to use inheritance or composition.

DON'T use multiple inheritance to replace the easier composition, even though both sometimes seem to work just as well for certain classes. Not only is composition clearer, but it is easier to code. (This book doesn't even show you how to code multiple inheritance because it's rarely if ever needed.)

Composing with Code

As with inheritance, the trickiest part of composition is knowing how to construct the embedded class objects. However, setting up a class with an embedded member is easy.

The next few example listings will compose a stereo class describing an electronics store's stereo inventory. A stereo is the perfect example of composition because it is composed of many parts that could stand apart by themselves such as a CD player, a turntable, a receiver, and speakers. As a matter of fact, the stereo industry calls those parts of a stereo system *components*.

Note: The ice cream class requires too many conversions such as gallons, scoops, number of cones, and so on to code easily here. Even for simple example listings, the details of coding the ice cream inventory would cloud the composition tutorial. The ice cream description, however, was a good introduction to composition and explained the problems involved with trying to inherit everything. In addition, it makes one's mouth water just thinking about it!

Starting with the individual component classes, Listing 17.1 contains the class code for receivers, CD players, and speakers.

Type

Listing 17.1. The components of a future stereo class.

```
 1:  // Filename: COMPHEAD.CPP
 2:  // Classes for stereo components
 3:  #include <iostream.h>
 4:  #include <iomanip.h>
 5:  #include <string.h>
 6:  class Receiver {
 7:     int watts;    // Watts per channel power
 8:     float price;
 9:     char * brand;
10:  public:
11:     Receiver(int, float, char *);
12:     ~Receiver();
13:     friend ostream & operator<<(ostream &, const Receiver &);
14:  };
15: Receiver::Receiver(int W, float P, char * B) : watts(W), price(P)
16: {
17:    brand = new char[strlen(B) + 1];
18:    strcpy(brand, B);
19: }
20: Receiver::~Receiver()
21: {
22:    delete [] brand;
23: }
24: ostream & operator<<(ostream & out, const Receiver & r)
25: {
26:    out << setiosflags(ios::fixed) << setiosflags(ios::showpoint);
27:    out << setprecision(2);
28:    out << "Receiver brand: " << r.brand << "\n";
29:    out << "Receiver price: $" << r.price << "   Watts per channel: ";
30:    out << r.watts << "\n";
```

continues

Data Composition

Listing 17.1. continued

```
31:       return out;
32: }
33: // Next class follows
34: class CD {
35:     int numOfCDs;   // Some combo CD players play 6 or more CDs
36:     float price;
37:     char * brand;
38: public:
39:     CD(int, float, char *);
40:     ~CD();
41:     friend ostream & operator<<(ostream &, const CD &);
42: };
43: CD::CD(int N, float P, char * B) : numOfCDs(N), price(P)
44: {
45:     brand = new char[strlen(B) + 1];
46:     strcpy(brand, B);
47: }
48: CD::~CD()
49: {
50:     delete [] brand;
51: }
52: ostream & operator<<(ostream & out, const CD & c)
53: {
54:     out << setiosflags(ios::fixed) << setiosflags(ios::showpoint);
55:     out << setprecision(2);
56:     out << "CD player brand: " << c.brand << "\n";
57:     out << "CD price: $" << c.price << "Number of CDs: ";
58:     out << c.numOfCDs << "\n";
59:     return out;
60: }
61: // Next class follows
62: class Speaker {
63:     int maxLoad;    // Amount of maximum wattage allowed
64:     float price;
65:     char * brand;
66: public:
67:     Speaker(int, float, char *);
68:     ~Speaker();
69:     friend ostream & operator<<(ostream &, const Speaker &);
70: };
71: Speaker::Speaker(int M, float P, char * B) : maxLoad(M), price(P)
72: {
73:     brand = new char[strlen(B) + 1];
74:     strcpy(brand, B);
75: }
76: Speaker::~Speaker()
77: {
78:     delete [] brand;
79: }
```

```
80: ostream & operator <<(ostream & out, const Speaker & s)
81: {
82:   out << setiosflags(ios::fixed) << setiosflags(ios::showpoint);
83:   out << setprecision(2);
84:   out << "Speaker brand: " << s.brand << "\n";
85:   out << "Speaker price (each): $" << s.price
       ➥<< "   Max. Num. of Watts: ";
86:   out << s.maxLoad << "\n";
87:   return out;
88: }
```

There is nothing new in this class that you haven't already seen. Each of the three stereo component classes contains three member functions that describe the characteristics of each class, Receiver, CD, and Speaker. Obviously, the next few listings will pull these three stand-alone classes into a combined composed stereo class.

> **Note:** Always include all the built-in header files, such as STRING.H, that your class needs to work correctly. The program using the class might not include those header files, and therefore, the target program would generate compile errors when it included your class and the needed prototyping built-in header files aren't brought in. Due to internal checking mechanisms inside each built-in header file, Visual C++ makes sure that a header file is not included more than once, even if both your class and the program using the class attempt to include the same header file.

Before working on the composition of the stereo class, can you see any improvement in these classes? Any time you see a big similarity between classes you've coded, consider using either inheritance or composition to streamline things. It turns out that the component classes can be improved through inheritance, and then that inheritance will be used inside another class for composition of a conglomerate class.

Each of these component classes contains a price and brand member. Therefore, all three of these components could come from a higher-level parent class named Component. The Component doesn't ever have to be instantiated into a class object, but it would remove a lot of the duplicity from the three component classes.

Before seeing the listing that contains a higher parent class, see whether you can write the code to do the same thing on your own. You know more than enough about access specifiers, receiving access specifiers, and constructor initialization lists to create a base class that contains the other classes' common code.

Day 17

Data Composition

Listing 17.2 contains rewritten stereo class hierarchy. Although there will never be a generic `Component` object, the `Component` base class helps group the other classes and makes updating easier if you ever want to increase the number of common members or change the storage mechanism of the `brand` member.

Type

Listing 17.2. Pulling similarities into a single base class.

```
1:  // Filename: STERINHE.CPP
2:  // Classes for stereo components with inheritance
3:  #include <iostream.h>
4:  #include <iomanip.h>
5:  #include <string.h>
6:  class Component {     // No objects of base class need
7:  protected:            // to ever be instantiated
8:    float price;
9:    char * brand;
10: public:
11:   Component(float, char *);
12:   ~Component();
13: };
14: // Only price can be initialized, the brand
15: // must be assigned in the body
16: Component::Component(float P, char * B) : price(P)
17: {
18:   brand = new char[strlen(B) + 1];
19:   strcpy(brand, B);
20: }
21: Component::~Component()
22: {
23:   delete [] brand;  // Isn't it nice that you don't have to
24: }                   // worry about deallocation in main()?
25: // Component classes begin next
26: class Receiver : public Component {
27:   int watts;     // Watts per channel power
28: public:
29:   Receiver(int, float, char *);
30:   ~Receiver() {}   // No destructor code needed
31:   friend ostream & operator<<(ostream &, const Receiver &);
32: };
33: // Use an initialization list to construct base object and member
34: Receiver::Receiver(int W, float P, char * B)
       ↪: Component(P, B), watts(W)
35: {  // The constructor gets easy
36: }
37: ostream & operator<<(ostream & out, const Receiver & r)
38: {
39:   out << setiosflags(ios::fixed) << setiosflags(ios::showpoint);
```

```
40:     out << setprecision(2);
41:     out << "Receiver brand: " << r.brand << "\n";
42:     out << "Receiver price: $" << r.price << "   Watts per channel: ";
43:     out << r.watts << "\n";
44:     return out;
45: }
46: // Next component class follows
47: class CD : public Component {
48:    int numOfCDs;   // Some combo CD players play 6 or more CDs
49: public:
50:    CD(int, float, char *);
51:    ~CD() {}   // No destructor code needed
52:    friend ostream & operator<<(ostream &, const CD &);
53: };
54: CD::CD(int N, float P, char * B) : Component(P, B), numOfCDs(N)
55: { // The constructor gets easy
56: }
57: ostream & operator<<(ostream & out, const CD & c)
58: {
59:    out << setiosflags(ios::fixed) << setiosflags(ios::showpoint);
60:    out << setprecision(2);
61:    out << "CD player brand: " << c.brand << "\n";
62:    out << "CD price: $" << c.price << "   Number of CDs: ";
63:    out << c.numOfCDs << "\n";
64:    return out;
65: }
66: // Next component class follows
67: class Speaker : public Component {
68:    int maxLoad;   // Amount of maximum wattage allowed
69: public:
70:    Speaker(int, float, char *);
71:    ~Speaker() {}   // No destructor code needed
72:    friend ostream & operator<<(ostream &, const Speaker &);
73: };
74: Speaker::Speaker(int M, float P, char * B)
      ➥: Component(P, B), maxLoad(M)
75: { // The constructor gets easy
76: }
77: ostream & operator <<(ostream & out, const Speaker & s)
78: {
79:    out << setiosflags(ios::fixed) << setiosflags(ios::showpoint);
80:    out << setprecision(2);
81:    out << "Speaker brand: " << s.brand << "\n";
82:    out << "Speaker price (each): $" << s.price
       ➥<< "   Max. Num. of Watts: ";
83:    out << s.maxLoad << "\n";
84:    return out;
85: }
```

Day 17: Data Composition

Analysis Figure 17.2 shows the inheritance hierarchy developed in Listing 17.2. The first half of the stereo class is now in place; the inheritance of each of the individual components forms a common base class component. The listing offers you nothing new yet, but the stereo (the composition of all the components) has yet to be defined.

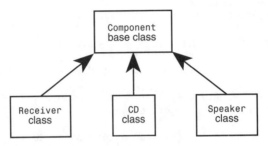

Figure 17.2. The Component class helps derive each of the specific stereo components.

 Note: Can't you see that now a receiver *is-a* component (pardon the grammar!), a CD player *is-a* component, and a set of speakers *is-a* component? Even newcomers to inheritance and composition find that the distinction is obvious when asked the *is-a* and *has-a* design questions. The final stereo class will contain both inheritance and composition as shown in the next program.

It's important to reinforce the idea that Stereo is not inherited from the component classes. If it were, you would have a tremendous multiple inheritance programming nightmare attempting to code the class as shown in Figure 17.3. Instead of being inherited from the component classes, Stereo contains the component classes.

Listing 17.3 contains the class header for the stereo class. Along with the integer, floating-point, and character pointer members, there are three members that are complete classes; in other words, three of the Stereo members are objects from other classes.

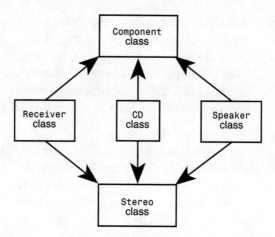

Figure 17.3. If Stereo were inherited, you would end up with a strange inheritance hierarchy.

Listing 17.3. Stereo class header composed of the other classes.

```
 1: class Stereo {
 2:   int wireLength;
 3:   float priceToInstall;
 4:   char * systemCode;      // For inventory
 5:   Receiver tuner;
 6:   CD discPlayer;
 7:   Speaker speakers;       // Notice spelling and case difference
 8: public:
 9:   // Member functions such as constructor and destructor go next
10: };
```

These members are other classes

If you're wondering what the fuss is all about, you've probably used composition before without even realizing it. In regular non-OOP C, you can embed a structure within another structure as done in this listing with classes.

Although the term *composition* is usually not used for embedded structures, composition is exactly what's going on. The reason so much attention to composition is being focused on here is that constructors and destructors must play a part in proper OOP composition. The following rule holds true:

> *An object composed of other objects, such as* Stereo, *cannot be constructed until all its member objects are constructed.*

Day 17
Data Composition

Notice that you don't have to face all the inheritance syntax when composing classes (lines 5–7 in Listing 17.3). You must, however, supply constructor initialization lists that take care of all the member objects before the composed object will be constructed. Therefore, composition is easier than inheritance because there is no inheriting class to contend with, but constructing composed classes involves some extra considerations that you don't have to worry with when working with non-composed classes.

When constructing a composed object, you must include each composed object's constructor initialization list inside the composed class definition line. Listing 17.4 shows a program that properly constructs a `Stereo` class. As you will see, the constructor's definition line is often longer than the body of the constructor. (Of course, long constructor definition lines are common after you begin using constructor initialization lists, even when no inheritance or composition is involved.) As you scan through Listing 17.4, watch for these things:

- ☐ The `main()` code must pass enough initial data to the constructor to construct the entire `Stereo` class. Later in today's chapter, you'll learn a shortcut that helps shorten such long initialization lists.

- ☐ Visual C++ makes sure that the initialization lists construct the member objects before the composed object's construction is begun.

- ☐ The `Stereo` class contains a huge constructor initialization list because of the three object class members: `Receiver`, `CD`, and `Speaker`. Although a smaller stereo system could have been created first to keep things simpler (perhaps composed on only a `Receiver` class), you should have little problem tracing the long `Stereo` constructor initialization list by now.

- ☐ If default constructors had been supplied for each of the components, no constructor initialization list would be necessary in the `Stereo` definition line. With the default constructors, Visual C++ could have constructed the object members without your doing anything special. However, such generic constructions are rare when using composition and would do little to teach you composition at this point.

Listing 17.4. Constructing and using `Stereo` objects that are composed of other objects.

```
1:  // Filename: STERCOMP.CPP
2:  // Classes for stereo components with inheritance
3:  #include <iostream.h>
4:  #include <iomanip.h>
```

```
 5:  #include <string.h>
 6:  class Component {      // No objects of base class ever
 7:  protected:             // need to be instantiated
 8:     float price;
 9:     char * brand;
10:  public:
11:     Component(float, char *);
12:     ~Component();
13:  };
14:  // Only price can be initialized, the brand
15:  // must be assigned in the body
16:  Component::Component(float P, char * B) : price(P)
17:  {
18:     brand = new char[strlen(B) + 1];
19:     strcpy(brand, B);
20:  }
21:  Component::~Component()
22:  {
23:     delete [] brand;  // Isn't it nice that you don't have to
24:  }                    // worry about deallocation in main()?
25:  // Component classes begin next
26:  class Receiver : public Component {
27:     int watts;    // Watts per channel power
28:  public:
29:     Receiver(int, float, char *);
30:     ~Receiver() {}   // No destructor code needed
31:     friend ostream & operator<<(ostream &, const Receiver &);
32:  };
33:  // Use an initialization list to construct base object and member
34:  Receiver::Receiver(int W, float P, char * B) :
     ➥Component(P, B), watts(W)
35:  { // The constructor gets easy
36:  }
37:  ostream & operator<<(ostream & out, const Receiver & r)
38:  {
39:     out << setiosflags(ios::fixed) << setiosflags(ios::showpoint);
40:     out << setprecision(2);
41:     out << "Receiver brand: " << r.brand << "\n";
42:     out << "Receiver price: $" << r.price << "  Watts per channel: ";
43:     out << r.watts << "\n";
44:     return out;
45:  }
46:  // Next component class follows
47:  class CD : public Component {
48:     int numOfCDs;  // Some combo CD players play 6 or more CDs
49:  public:
50:     CD(int, float, char *);
51:     ~CD() {}   // No destructor code needed
52:     friend ostream & operator<<(ostream &, const CD &);
53:  };
```

continues

Day 17: Data Composition

Listing 17.4. continued

```cpp
54: CD::CD(int N, float P, char * B) : Component(P, B), numOfCDs(N)
55: { // The constructor gets easy
56: }
57: ostream & operator<<(ostream & out, const CD & c)
58: {
59:   out << setiosflags(ios::fixed) << setiosflags(ios::showpoint);
60:   out << setprecision(2);
61:   out << "CD player brand: " << c.brand << "\n";
62:   out << "CD price: $" << c.price << "   Number of CDs: ";
63:   out << c.numOfCDs << "\n";
64:   return out;
65: }
66: // Next component class follows
67: class Speaker : public Component {
68:   int maxLoad;   // Amount of maximum wattage allowed
69: public:
70:   Speaker(int, float, char *);
71:   ~Speaker() {}   // No destructor code needed
72:   friend ostream & operator<<(ostream &, const Speaker &);
73: };
74: Speaker::Speaker(int M, float P, char * B) :
        ➥Component(P, B), maxLoad(M)
75: { // The constructor gets easy
76: }
77: ostream & operator <<(ostream & out, const Speaker & s)
78: {
79:   out << setiosflags(ios::fixed) << setiosflags(ios::showpoint);
80:   out << setprecision(2);
81:   out << "Speaker brand: " << s.brand << "\n";
82:   out << "Speaker price (each): $" << s.price
        ➥<< "   Max. Num. of Watts: ";
83:   out << s.maxLoad << "\n";
84:   return out;
85: }
86: class Stereo {
87:   char * systemCode;      // For inventory
88:   int wireLength;
89:   float priceToInstall;
90:   Receiver tuner;
91:   CD discPlayer;
92:   Speaker speakers;       // Notice spelling and case difference
93: public:
94:   Stereo(char *, int, float, int, float, char *,
95:          int, float, char *, int, float, char *);
96:   ~Stereo();
97:   friend ostream & operator<<(ostream &, const Stereo &);
98: };
99: // Here comes the HUGE constructor initialization list
100: Stereo::Stereo(char * SC, int WL, float PI, int RW, float RP,
```

```
101:          char * RB, int NCD, float CP, char * CB, int ML, float SP,
102:          char * SB) : tuner(RW, RP, RB), discPlayer(NCD, CP, CB),
              ➥speakers(ML, SP, SB),
103:          wireLength(WL), priceToInstall(PI)
104: {
105:   systemCode = new char[strlen(SC) + 1];
106:   strcpy(systemCode, SC);
107: }
108: Stereo::~Stereo()
109: {
110:   delete [] systemCode;
111: }
112: ostream & operator<<(ostream & out, const Stereo & s)
113: {
114:   // Can use overloaded functions from elsewhere
115:   out << "Here's the stereo system:\n";
116:   out << "System code: " << s.systemCode << "\n";
117:   out << "Wire length: " << s.wireLength;
118:   out << "\tInstallation price: $" << s.priceToInstall << "\n";
119:   out << "Components follow:\n";
120:   out << s.tuner << s.discPlayer << s.speakers;
121:   return out;
122: }
123: //////////////////////////////////////////////////////////////////
124: // It took a lot of work to get to main()!
125: main()
126: {
127:   Stereo system("HI42", 50, 75.00, 200, 450.00, "HiFi-HiTech", 6,
       ➥325.00,
128:                 "Disc Supreme", 350, 275.00, "Acoustic Output");
129:   cout << system;
130:   return 0;
131:}
```

```
Here's the stereo system:
System code: HI42
Wire length: 50   Installation price: $75
Components follow:
Receiver brand: HiFi-HiTech
Receiver price: $450.00   Watts per channel: 200
CD player brand: Disc Supreme
CD price: $325.00   Number of CDs: 6
Speaker brand: Acoustic Output
Speaker price (each): $275.00   Max. Num. of Watts: 350
```

The most important set of lines in the program is 100–107. These lines construct a `Stereo` object by actually constructing several components that make up the `Stereo` object. To help you understand what is going on in the constructor, Figure 17.4 labels the parts of the constructor to show you what all the arguments mean.

Day 17: Data Composition

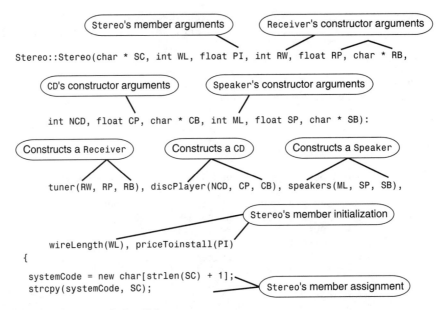

Figure 17.4. An analysis of the Stereo constructor.

Look at the output statement on line 129. The overloaded operator<<() function in lines 112–122 handles the output. You might think that line 129 is rather simplistic. All the Receiver, CD, and Speaker classes contain overloaded operator<<() functions, and those classes' objects (and therefore, their overloaded operator<<() functions) are already constructed. Therefore, the Stereo class's operator<<() can output the component objects using a simple << operator.

> **Note:** As a matter of fact, the Stereo class could not print the individual member values of the component parts any other way than through a function such as operator<<(). Stereo does *not* have access to the component members because they are private to their respective classes. Only through public member operator<<() functions can the Stereo class output the components.

As you might guess, the compiler takes care of destructing the composed class members before destructing the class itself. Each of the members must be destructed before the class, and each class contains its own destructor that Visual C++ calls. Visual

C++ calls a default constructor if you don't supply your own, but if the class contains heap data, the default destructor will not properly work and deallocate the heap. (Figure 17.5 shows the order of the constructors and destructors in the `Stereo` class.)

Constructing order:	1. Receiver	Destructing order:	1. Stereo
	2. CD		2. Speaker
	3. Speaker		3. CD
	4. Stereo		4. Receiver

Figure 17.5. The order of constructors and destructors for `Stereo`.

DO	DON'T

DO construct embedded class members with constructor initialization lists before constructing the overall class.

DO supply all the arguments needed to construct the entire composed class, including the arguments necessary to compose each component member in the class.

DON'T explicitly attempt to call destructors for embedded classes. When the composed object is destructed, Visual C++ destructs the embedded objects for you.

DON'T try to access the component class's private members from within the composed class. As with any code outside a class, a composed class can access private members of other classes (even embedded classes) only through access functions.

Shortening the Composition

All the arguments to the `Stereo` system in Listing 17.4 had to be passed to construct the entire system. Rather than using the stereo system, you could have constructed the components individually like this:

```
Receiver radio(200, 450.00, "HiFi-HiTech");
CD disco(6, 325.00,"Disc Supreme");
Speaker output(350, 275.00, "Acoustic Output");
```

Day 17

Data Composition

If you like, you can construct the individual components and then use those objects to construct the composed `Stereo` object. Doing this streamlines the construction of the `Stereo` and helps make the construction clearer than having a long list of arguments as done on lines 127 and 138 of Listing 17.4.

Listing 17.5 shows a new `Stereo` class and `main()` that could replace those in Listing 17.4 and produce the same output as before:

Listing 17.5. Creating the `Stereo` class from component objects.

```
1:  class Stereo {
2:    char * systemCode;      // For inventory
3:    int wireLength;
4:    float priceToInstall;
5:    Receiver tuner;
6:    CD discPlayer;
7:    Speaker speakers;       // Notice spelling and case difference
8:  public:
9:    Stereo(char *, int, float, int, float, char *,
10:           int, float, char *, int, float, char *);
11:   Stereo(char * SC, int WL, float PI, Receiver & r, CD & c,
           ➥Speaker & s);
12:   ~Stereo();
13:   friend ostream & operator<<(ostream &, const Stereo &);
14: };
15: // Here comes the HUGE constructor initialization list
16: Stereo::Stereo(char * SC, int WL, float PI, int RW, float RP,
17:          char * RB, int NCD, float CP, char * CB, int ML, float SP,
18:          char * SB) : tuner(RW, RP, RB), discPlayer(NCD, CP, CB),
           ➥speakers(ML, SP, SB),
19:          wireLength(WL), priceToInstall(PI)
20: {
21:   systemCode = new char[strlen(SC) + 1];
22:   strcpy(systemCode, SC);
23: }
24: // Shortened form of Stereo constructor that uses individual
25: // constructors that are already defined.
26: Stereo::Stereo(char * SC, int WL, float PI, Receiver & r,
27:                CD & c, Speaker & s) : tuner(r), discPlayer(c),
28:                speakers(s), wireLength(WL), priceToInstall(PI)
29: {
30:   systemCode = new char[strlen(SC) + 1];
31:   strcpy(systemCode, SC);
32: }
33: Stereo::~Stereo()
34: {
35:   delete [] systemCode;
36: }
```

```
37: ostream & operator<<(ostream & out, const Stereo & s)
38: {
39:   out << "Here's the stereo system:\n";
40:   out << "System code: " << s.systemCode << "\n";
41:   out << "Wire length: " << s.wireLength;
42:   out << "\tInstallation price: $" << s.priceToInstall << "\n";
43:   out << "Components follow:\n";
44:   out << s.tuner << s.discPlayer << s.speakers;
45:   return out;
46: }////////////////////////////////////////////////////////////////
47: // It took a lot of work to get to main()!
48: main()
49: {
50:   // First, construct the individual components
51:   Receiver radio(200, 450.00, "HiFi-HiTech");
52:   CD disco(6, 325.00,"Disc Supreme");
53:   Speaker output(350, 275.00, "Acoustic Output");
54:   cout << radio << disco << output;
55:   // Now, construct the whole system
56:   Stereo system("HI42", 50, 75.00, radio, disco, output);
57:   cout << system;
58:   return 0;
59: }
```

Analysis You might notice that in the prototype (line 11) and the definition lines (26–28), the character arrays are received by reference to make the code more efficient. In your own programs, passing all data by reference and preceding constant arguments with const improve your program efficiency and safety.

Line 56 directly constructs the composed Stereo class from already-instantiated objects. Although creating the component objects might not be as efficient as putting all the arguments in the Stereo constructor call (lines 127 and 128 of Listing 17.4), the code is easier to understand. A drawback to this method, however, is that you're creating two copies of the component objects: one stand-alone copy and another copy of the objects embedded within the Stereo object when it's created.

Assigning Composed Objects to One Another

The same assignment considerations take effect when you assign composed objects to one another as when you assign regular objects to one another. A member-by-member (called *memberwise*) assignment takes place. Memberwise assignment is fine as long as pointers aren't part of the object (which they are in the Stereo class). Even when

Data Composition

pointers are members of the objects, memberwise copying will not always produce side effects. However, because it does sometimes produce side effects, it's worthwhile to correct the situation.

For every member component class for which you supply an `operator=()` function, Visual C++ uses that function when it assigns those members. For every component member class for which you do not supply an overloaded `operator=()` function, Visual C++ performs memberwise copy.

Suppose you added a default constructor for `Stereo` that required no arguments. The constructor would exist just to create objects that you would later fill with data. Therefore, you could create a `Stereo` object like this:

```
Stereo saleSystem;  // Create an object using the default constructor
```

Suppose that earlier in the program you had created the `system` object as done in Listing 17.5's line 56, and you wanted to assign the `system` object to the new `saleSystem` just created. There is nothing technically wrong with making a direct assignment like this:

```
saleSystem = system;
```

Such a memberwise assignment, however, copies member pointers and not the data pointed to by the member pointers. This action will cause problems if one object is destroyed; the other object's pointers will point to deallocated heap memory.

Therefore, to make the composed `Stereo` class as usable as possible and to provide code that you can mirror when writing your own composed classes, Listing 17.6 contains `operator=()` code for each of the composed objects as well as for the `Stereo` object. A default `Stereo` constructor and a default constructor for each of the component classes are also included in the program to let the program create a second `Stereo` variable without the need for arguments.

Note: Remember that if you supply overloaded `operator=()` functions for only *some* of the composed object classes, only those members will copy properly when you assign one composed class variable to another. The classes without an overloaded `operator=()` will use memberwise copy.

Type **Listing 17.6. Adding overloaded operator=() functions to help the assignment of Stereo objects.**

```cpp
 1: // Filename: STEROPEQ.CPP
 2: // Classes for stereo components with inheritance
 3: #include <iostream.h>
 4: #include <iomanip.h>
 5: #include <string.h>
 6: class Component {      // No objects of base class ever
 7: protected:             // need to be instantiated
 8:    float price;
 9:    char * brand;
10: public:
11:    Component(float, char *);
12:    Component() {};     // Default constructor
13:    ~Component();
14: };
15: // Only price can be initialized, the brand
16: // must be assigned in the body
17: Component::Component(float P, char * B) : price(P)
18: {
19:    brand = new char[strlen(B) + 1];
20:    strcpy(brand, B);
21: }
22: Component::~Component()
23: {
24:    delete [] brand;    // Isn't it nice that you don't have to
25: }                      // worry about deallocation in main()?
26: // Component classes begin next
27: class Receiver : public Component {
28:    int watts;    // Watts per channel power
29: public:
30:    Receiver(int, float, char *);
31:    Receiver() {};     // Default constructor
32:    ~Receiver() {}     // No destructor code needed
33:    friend ostream & operator<<(ostream &, const Receiver &);
34:    Receiver & operator=(const Receiver &);   // Overload =
35: };
36: // Use an initialization list to construct base object and member
37: Receiver::Receiver(int W, float P, char * B) :
    ➥Component(P, B), watts(W)
38: {  // The constructor gets easy
39: }
40: ostream & operator<<(ostream & out, const Receiver & r)
41: {
42:    out << setiosflags(ios::fixed) << setiosflags(ios::showpoint);
43:    out << setprecision(2);
44:    out << "Receiver brand: " << r.brand << "\n";
45:    out << "Receiver price: $" << r.price << "   Watts per channel: ";
46:    out << r.watts << "\n";
```

continues

Data Composition

Listing 17.6. continued

```
47:    return out;
48: }
49: Receiver & Receiver::operator=(const Receiver & r)
50: {
51:    if (this == &r)
52:      { return *this; }
53:    watts = r.watts;         // Assign the righthand = operands
54:    price = r.price;         // to the lefthand = operands
55:    int newlen = strlen(r.brand) + 1;
56:    brand = new char[newlen];
57:    strcpy(brand, r.brand);
58:    return *this;
59: }
60: // Next component class follows
61: class CD : public Component {
62:    int numOfCDs;  // Some combo CD players play 6 or more CDs
63: public:
64:    CD(int, float, char *);
65:    CD() {};  // Default constructor
66:    ~CD() {}  // No destructor code needed
67:    friend ostream & operator<<(ostream &, const CD &);
68:    CD & operator=(const CD &);   // Overload =
69: };
70: CD::CD(int N, float P, char * B) : Component(P, B), numOfCDs(N)
71: { // The constructor gets easy
72: }
73: ostream & operator<<(ostream & out, const CD & c)
74: {
75:    out << setiosflags(ios::fixed) << setiosflags(ios::showpoint);
76:    out << setprecision(2);
77:    out << "CD player brand: " << c.brand << "\n";
78:    out << "CD price: $" << c.price << "  Number of CDs: ";
79:    out << c.numOfCDs << "\n";
80:    return out;
81: }
82: CD & CD::operator=(const CD & c)
83: {
84:    if (this == &c)
85:      { return *this; }
86:    numOfCDs = c.numOfCDs;     // Assign the righthand = operands
87:    price = c.price;           // to the lefthand = operands
88:    int newlen = strlen(c.brand) + 1;
89:    brand = new char[newlen];
90:    strcpy(brand, c.brand);
91:    return *this;
92: }
93: // Next component class follows
94: class Speaker : public Component {
95:    int maxLoad;  // Amount of maximum wattage allowed
```

```
96:  public:
97:    Speaker(int, float, char *);
98:    Speaker() {};
99:    ~Speaker() {}   // No destructor code needed
100:   friend ostream & operator<<(ostream &, const Speaker &);
101:   Speaker & operator=(const Speaker & );   // Overload =
102: };
103: Speaker::Speaker(int M, float P, char * B) :
     ➥Component(P, B), maxLoad(M)
104: { // The constructor gets easy
105: }
106: ostream & operator <<(ostream & out, const Speaker & s)
107: {
108:   out << setiosflags(ios::fixed) << setiosflags(ios::showpoint);
109:   out << setprecision(2);
110:   out << "Speaker brand: " << s.brand << "\n";
111:   out << "Speaker price (each): $" << s.price
     ➥<< "  Max. Num. of Watts: ";
112:   out << s.maxLoad << "\n";
113:   return out;
114: }
115: Speaker & Speaker::operator=(const Speaker & s)
116: {
117:   if (this == &s)
118:      { return *this; }
119:   maxLoad = s.maxLoad;       // Assign the righthand = operands
120:   price = s.price;           // to the lefthand = operands
121:   int newlen = strlen(s.brand) + 1;
122:   brand = new char[newlen];
123:   strcpy(brand, s.brand);
124:   return *this;
125: }
126: class Stereo {
127:   char * systemCode;        // For inventory
128:   int wireLength;
129:   float priceToInstall;
130:   Receiver tuner;
131:   CD discPlayer;
132:   Speaker speakers;         // Notice spelling and case difference
133: public:
134:   Stereo(char *, int, float, int, float, char *,
135:         int, float, char *, int, float, char *);
136:   Stereo(char * SC, int WL, float PI, Receiver & r, CD & c,
     ➥Speaker & s);
137:   Stereo() {};  // Default constructor
138:   ~Stereo();
139:   friend ostream & operator<<(ostream &, const Stereo &);
140:   Stereo & operator=(const Stereo & s);
141: };
142: // Here comes the HUGE constructor initialization list
```

continues

Day 17: Data Composition

Listing 17.6. continued

```cpp
143: Stereo::Stereo(char * SC, int WL, float PI, int RW, float RP,
144:         char * RB, int NCD, float CP, char * CB, int ML, float SP,
145:         char * SB) : tuner(RW, RP, RB), discPlayer(NCD, CP, CB),
              ↪speakers(ML, SP, SB),
146:             wireLength(WL), priceToInstall(PI)
147: {
148:   systemCode = new char[strlen(SC) + 1];
149:   strcpy(systemCode, SC);
150: }
151: // Shortened form of Stereo constructor that uses individual
152: // constructors that are already defined.
153: Stereo::Stereo(char * SC, int WL, float PI, Receiver & r,
154:                CD & c, Speaker & s) : tuner(r), discPlayer(c),
155:                speakers(s), wireLength(WL), priceToInstall(PI)
156: {
157:   systemCode = new char[strlen(SC) + 1];
158:   strcpy(systemCode, SC);
159: }
160: Stereo::~Stereo()
161: {
162:   delete [] systemCode;
163: }
164: ostream & operator<<(ostream & out, const Stereo & s)
165: {
166:   out << "Here's the stereo system:\n";
167:   out << "System code: " << s.systemCode << "\n";
168:   out << "Wire length: " << s.wireLength;
169:   out << "\tInstallation price: $" << s.priceToInstall << "\n";
170:   out << "Components follow:\n";
171:   out << s.tuner << s.discPlayer << s.speakers;
172:   return out;
173: }
174: Stereo & Stereo::operator=(const Stereo & s)
175: {
176:   if (this == &s)
177:     { return *this; }
178:   priceToInstall = s.priceToInstall;  // Assign righthand operands
179:   wireLength = s.wireLength;          // to the lefthand = operands
180:   int newlen = strlen(s.systemCode) + 1;
181:   systemCode = new char[newlen];
182:   strcpy(systemCode, s.systemCode);
183:   tuner = s.tuner;                    // Now, assign the component members
184:   discPlayer = s.discPlayer;
185:   speakers = s.speakers;
186:   return *this;
187: }
188: /////////////////////////////////////////////////////////////////////
189: // It took a lot of work to get to main()!
```

```
190: main()
191: {
192:    // First, construct the individual components
193:    Receiver radio(200, 450.00, "HiFi-HiTech");
194:    CD disco(6, 325.00,"Disc Supreme");
195:    Speaker output(350, 275.00, "Acoustic Output");
196:    // Now, construct the whole system
197:    Stereo system("HI42", 50, 75.00, radio, disco, output);
198:    // Now, create another Stereo object and assign
199:    // to it the first one's member data
200:    Stereo saleSystem;
201:    saleSystem = system;
202:    cout << saleSystem;    // Print to ensure it's OK
203:    return 0;
204: }
```

```
Here's the stereo system:
System code: HI42
Wire length: 50 Installation price: $75
Components follow:
Receiver brand: HiFi-HiTech
Receiver price: $450.00  Watts per channel: 200
CD player brand: Disc Supreme
CD price: $325.00  Number of CDs: 6
Speaker brand: Acoustic Output
Speaker price (each): $275.00  Max. Num. of Watts: 350
```

As you can see from the output, the assignment in line 201 works properly. A lot is going on under the hood at line 201. Four overloaded assign operators execute. The operator=() in Stereo first begins; then before it has a chance to finish, the component operator=() functions are triggered in lines 183–185.

Even the simple creation of a default object in line 200 forces several constructors (the Stereo, the individual components, and then the base class default constructor) to execute. However, it takes a lot of code in the class to streamline the user program. Is it worth the effort? Certainly, because after you write and debug your class, the rest of your application is transparent to the class, and your application programming involves manipulating objects at a high level instead of having to worry about programming details throughout your program.

Summary

This chapter is concerned with embedding one or more objects inside another. Often, a class contains another object. (You might have written structures that contain other structures as members back in your C programming days.)

Day 17: Data Composition

The problem with embedding class members is that you must properly construct each class member before constructing the composed class. To do that, you must add constructor initialization lists to the composed class constructor function.

Unlike with inheritance, you don't have to code special receiving access specifiers when composing because a composed class is not inherited from another—a composed class includes one or more other classes.

A composed class always follows the *has-a* question. If you can answer "yes" to the question "Does the composed class have a separate class for a member?" you must use composition. Inherited classes always answer positively to the *is-a* question, such as "Is this class another class with a little added functionality?" If so, inherit the new class from the existing one.

You should always include overloaded assignment functions for each of the component members if you don't want Visual C++ to perform a memberwise copy. Memberwise copy can leave you with two objects pointing to the same region in memory, giving your program fits if you deallocate one object and then attempt to use the other object.

Q&A

Q. What is the difference between inheritance and composition?

A. Inheritance takes place when one class is just like another except for added functionality or data members. Composition occurs when one class contains another class (or more than one other class), but the composed class is not just an extended version of another class.

As with inheritance, constructor initialization lists play important roles in the creation of class objects. When constructing the composed object, you must ensure that all the embedded component class members are constructed.

Q. Why must I worry about `operator=()` when assigning one composed object to another?

A. You don't always have to worry about overloading the assignment, but if your class or any of the composed classes have pointers as members, you're *strongly* advised to write an overloaded assignment.

You'll have to include an overloaded assignment for each embedded component class inside the composed class. If you fail to include an overloaded assignment function, Visual C++ must use memberwise assignment to create the new object's data, and if pointers are involved, you'll have two objects' pointers pointing to the same memory.

Workshop

The Workshop offers quiz questions and exercises to hone your skills and give you feedback on today's lesson. You'll find some proposed answers in Appendix D.

Quiz

1. What questions can you ask to determine whether you should use composition or inheritance?

2. Describe which works best, composition or inheritance, in each of the following situations:

   A. A tree class and a forest class.

   B. A dog class and a beagle class.

   C. A tire class, a motor class, and a car class.

   D. A dot class, a line-drawing class, a square-drawing class.

3. What is wrong with the following constructor?

   ```
   class A {
     int i;
     float j;
     char * c;
   public:
     A(int I, float J, char C) : i(I), j(J), c(C) {};
     ~A();
   };
   ```

4. If you include an overloaded assignment for one but not all composed classes, how does Visual C++ perform the assignments for the classes missing an operator=() function?

5. What side effect can occur if you fail to include an overloaded assignment function?

Data Composition

Exercises

1. Rewrite the following class's constructor using a constructor initialization list.

   ```
   class House {
     int sqFeet;
     char * address;
     float cost;
     int numRooms;
   public:
     House(int, char *, float, int);
     ~House();
   };
   House::House(int S, char * A, float C, int N)
   {
     sqFeet = S;
     int newlen = strlen(A) + 1;
     address = new char[newlen];
     strcpy(address, A);
     cost = C;
     numRooms = N;
   };
   House::~House()
   {
     delete [] address;
   }
   ```

2. The program in Listing 17.6 allocates data in lots of places. To brush up on your skills and add safety to the program, add a memory allocation error handler to the code so that a message prints and the program quits early if an allocation error occurs.

DAY 18

Virtual Functions: Are They Real?

Virtual Functions: Are They Real?

You have not seen pointers to objects mentioned much in the past few chapters. Pointers work with objects just as they do with other variables. However, there are extra considerations to learn about when you combine both pointers and inheritance. Pointers used inside inheritance hierarchies often require special handling that other pointers don't require.

Throughout today's chapter, lots of emphasis is placed on a *family of classes*. In this context, a family of classes refers to a single inheritance tree. In other words, if two child classes extend down from a single parent class, those three classes form an inheritance class family.

When using inheritance and pointers, you often have to write *virtual* functions. Virtual functions are member functions, all with the same name, that reside in an inheritance family of classes. Through the virtual interpretation techniques described in today's chapter, Visual C++ can wait until runtime to determine exactly which function to call when you execute member functions through pointers.

You'll also learn today how to set up an array of pointers, and also how to store a family of classes on the heap. The virtual-function mechanism sounds difficult, but as with most object-oriented programming techniques, you'll see that virtual functions save you programming time and effort by taking details out of your hands and placing those details on Visual C++'s back.

Today, you learn about the following topics:

- What a class family is
- The difference between early binding and late binding
- The way to define pointers to a class family of objects
- The need for virtual functions
- The difference between a virtual function and a pure virtual function
- How to define abstract base classes

Note: As you read and learn more about C++ and OOP, you might run across the term *virtual base classes*. Virtual base classes aren't related to virtual functions. You often write virtual base classes when programming inside multiple inheritance hierarchies. This book doesn't cover multiple inheritance, so you won't see virtual base classes described. You'll never need to learn about virtual base classes if you stay with single inheritance, as you can and probably should do.

For Ease of Discussion: This Is a Class Family

The term *class family* is often used in different ways. This chapter uses *class family* or *family of classes* to refer to related classes inside the same inheritance hierarchy. After you master *abstract base classes* at the end of today's chapter, you'll see why the term *family* makes a lot of sense.

A family of classes consists of classes somehow related by a common base class. The classes might or might not be sequentially related to one another. Figure 18.1 shows a class family. In the figure, a derived class derives from another derived class, which in turn derives from a base class. Figure 18.2 shows a different kind of class family. Several classes extend from the same parent in different combinations, and the entire hierarchy of classes forms a family of classes.

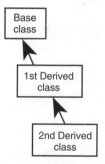

Figure 18.1. A class family can extend on the same inheritance line.

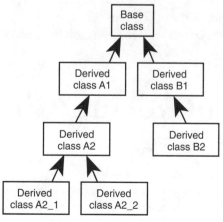

Figure 18.2. A class family always extends from the same parent class.

Virtual Functions: Are They Real?

Figure 18.3 shows two *separate* class families. There are two base classes in the figure that define two separate class hierarchies. Although it might seem obvious that these are two separate class families, it's important to point out that any one Visual C++ program might contain several different class families, and a different set of virtual functions would have to exist for each class family. Virtual functions would never span two different inheritance hierarchies like those shown in Figure 18.3. (Figure 18.3 does not show multiple inheritance, just two separate families of classes. Multiple inheritance takes place when a single class is derived from more than one parent class.)

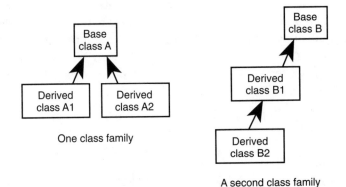

Figure 18.3. Virtual functions don't span two class families at one time.

 Note: Don't get too concerned with the term *class family* because, as mentioned earlier, the term has several meanings depending on the context in which you use it. However, the next few sections describe virtual functions, and you must understand that virtual functions play an important role only with the same inheritance tree (class family).

When to Execute? Early and Late Binding

Early binding, sometimes called *static binding,* is the process of determining at compilation time what functions to call. Early binding might sound complicated, but it is exactly what you are already used to. Virtually every C program you've written (and every program in any other programming language) uses early binding for all function and subroutine calls.

With early binding, you write a function call and supply the function. Again, this is exactly what you've always done but probably never stopped to think about. You perhaps didn't even know that the process had a name.

When a program is compiled, Visual C++ sets up all the program data and functions in a specific order. At compile time, Visual C++ cannot know in advance exactly where in memory a program will be loaded for execution. You might compile a program on one computer and then run the program on a different computer with a different version of DOS, different drivers loaded into memory, a different memory manager, and so forth. The first available memory address differs on each computer configuration.

Therefore, when Visual C++ compiles a program, it stacks the compiled functions sequentially inside the compiled file. When `main()` calls a function, the address of the called function has to go in `main()`'s function call statement. Visual C++ inserts the location of the function relative to the start of the file. In other words, when `main()` calls a function, `main()` knows exactly where that function will reside when the program loads. Therefore, if the function happens to begin at location 35 relative to the start of the program, `main()` contains a function call to address 35.

When you finally run a program, the .EXE program loader determines the first available free space in memory where the program can execute from and adds that address to all function calls. Therefore, whatever address Visual C++ puts in the function call is adjusted at runtime to the exact address needed. When the program is compiled, all addresses are relative, and those addresses become absolute when a program runs.

All this background is actually not essential to understanding early binding. If anything, it almost distracts from the discussion, but you should understand the way programs compile and run. It appears that function call addresses always change from the time a program is compiled to the time it runs. Function call addresses do change, but only so that they execute properly when the program is loaded. The program loader blindly adds the program's starting address to all function call addresses, but those function addresses remain relative to the position they were in when the program was compiled.

Consider the simple program in Listing 18.1. `main()` calls a function called `tripleIt()`, and in turn, `tripleIt()` calls a function named `prName()`. The program uses early binding for the execution of its two function calls.

Day 18

Virtual Functions: Are They Real?

Type Listing 18.1. Using early binding for function calls.

```cpp
1:  // Filename: REGBINDG.CPP
2:  // Use early binding to resolve function calls at compilation time
3:  #include <iostream.h>
4:  void tripleIt(int num);
5:  void prName(int num);
6:  main()
7:  {
8:    int num;
9:    do {
10:       cout << "Please type a number from 1 to 10: ";
11:      cin >> num;
12:    } while ((num < 1) || (num > 10));
13:    tripleIt(num);   // Triple the number
14:    return 0;
15: }
16: void tripleIt(int num)
17: {
18:   int trip;
19:   prName(num);   // Prints the number's word
20:   trip = num * 3;
21:   cout << " tripled is " << trip << "\n";
22: }
23: void prName(int num)
24: {
25:   switch (num)
26:   { case(1) : cout << "One";
27:               break;
28:     case(2) : cout << "Two";
29:               break;
30:     case(3) : cout << "Three";
31:               break;
32:     case(4) : cout << "Four";
33:               break;
34:     case(5) : cout << "Five";
35:               break;
36:     case(6) : cout << "Six";
37:               break;
38:     case(7) : cout << "Seven";
39:               break;
40:     case(8) : cout << "Eight";
41:               break;
42:     case(9) : cout << "Nine";
43:               break;
44:   };
45: }
```

```
Please type a number from 1 to 10: 7
Seven tripled is 21
```

When Visual C++ compiles this program, the tripleIt() function might happen to fall 25 bytes from the start of the program, and prName() might happen to fall 38 bytes from the start of the program. Therefore, line 13 compiles as a function call executing the function at address 25, and line 19 compiles as a function call executing the function at address 38.

The important thing to note about this program is that all function calls are adjusted but never changed from their relative position in the file. The relative function addresses are bound *early* in the process, during compilation. Figure 18.4 shows that the compiled program's relative function call addresses never change from their relative positions when the program loads for execution.

Relative address	When compiled:	If program loads at address 340000:	If program loads at address 450500:

0	main()
	{
	
	execute 25
	
	}
		main()
		{
		
		execute 340025
		
		}
			main()
			{
			
			execute 450525
			
			}

25	tripleIt()
	{
	
	execute 38
	
	}
		tripleIt()
		{
		
		execute 340038
		
		}
			tripleIt()
			{
			
			execute 450538
			
			}

38	prNames()
	{
	}
		prNames()
		{
		}
			prNames()
			{
			}

Figure 18.4. Program calls compile with relative starting addresses.

Note: Always keep in mind that early binding (and late binding too) is focused on function *calls,* not the function definitions themselves. Binding is the insertion of the proper address into a function call. Early binding means that a function's relative address position is known during compilation. No matter what binding method takes place, function

Virtual Functions: Are They Real?

> definitions themselves don't rearrange in memory; they always stay in the order they were compiled in and always remain in their relative positions in the compiled file.

Late binding occurs when nothing is stored in a function call until the program actually runs. You might wonder how Visual C++ can even compile a program if it cannot store addresses in function calls, but if you've ever seen a program that used pointers to functions, you've seen late binding in action.

Listing 18.2 contains a program that includes an array of pointers to five functions that compute math results. The program defines an array of pointers to the five math functions and then uses a `for` loop to execute each of the functions.

Listing 18.2. Using function pointers to demonstrate late binding.

```
1:  // Filename: FUNPTR.CPP
2:  // Program that contains an array of pointers to functions
3:  #include <iostream.h>
4:  #include <iomanip.h>
5:  #include <math.h>
6:  // Must prototype all functions before defining pointers to them
7:  void doSin(float number);
8:  void doCosin(float number);
9:  void doTangent(float number);
10: void doArcsin(float number);
11: void doArcosin(float number);
12: // Define an array of pointers to each function
13: void (*fun[])(float)={doSin, doCosin, doTangent, doArcsin,
    ➥doArcosin};
14: main()
15: {
16:    float number;
17:    cout << setprecision(3) << setiosflags(ios::fixed);
18:    cout << "*** Math Program ***\n";
19:    cout << "\n\nEnter a floating-point number and I'll print\n";
20:    cout << "some calculations from it: ";
21:    cin >> number;
22:    for (int ctr=0; ctr<5; ctr++)
23:       {
24:          fun[ctr](number);      // Here's where late binding occurs
25:       }
26:    return 0;
27: }
```

```
28: void doSin(float number)
29: {
30:     cout << "\nThe sine of " << number << " is " << sin(number)
        ➥<< "\n";
31: }
32: void doCosin(float number)
33: {
34:     cout << "The cosine of " << number << " is " << cos(number)
        ➥<< "\n";
35: }
36: void doTangent(float number)
37: {
38:     cout << "The tangent of " << number << " is " << tan(number)
        ➥<< "\n";
39: }
40: void doArcsin(float number)
41: {
42:     cout << "The arc sine of " << number << " is " << asin(number)
        ➥<< "\n";
43: }
44: void doArcosin(float number)
45: {
46:     cout << "The arc cosine of " << number << " is " << acos(number)
        ➥<< "\n";
47: }
```

```
*** Math Program ***

Enter a floating-point number and I'll print
some calculations from it: .45
The sine of 0.45 is 0.435
The cosine of 0.45 is 0.9
The tangent of 0.45 is 0.483
The arc sine of 0.45 is 0.467
The arc cosine of 0.45 is 1.104
```

Five math functions, defined in lines 28–47, contain simple built-in function calls that perform various trigonometric calculations. After the user enters a floating-point value in line 21, that value is passed to each of the five math functions in the for loop of lines 22–25.

The for loop steps through the array of function pointers defined on line 13. The first time through the loop, the program executes fun[0](number); the second time through the loop, the program executes fun[1](number); and so on.

Virtual Functions: Are They Real?

Note: If you've shied away from ever using pointers to functions, don't let this review frighten you. Most Visual C++ programmers don't use pointers to functions because virtual functions often replace the need for function pointers.

During compilation, what address does Visual C++ insert at line 24? Does Visual C++ insert the address of `doSin()`? What about `doCosin()`? It turns out that Visual C++ cannot insert *any* address when it compiles this program! Visual C++ cannot determine which of the five functions to call until runtime. (Determining which functions to call is also referred to as *resolving the functions*.)

The value of the loop counter, `ctr`, determines which function is called and when. Therefore, runtime data determines which function is called. During compilation, Visual C++ can do little more than place a *hint* of a function call at line 26. Visual C++ places an indirect call to a location in memory and at runtime. Visual C++ then fills this location with the proper function's address when it's finally determined what function the program is to execute.

Late binding is the process of waiting until runtime, not compile time, to decide which function to call at a given point in the program. Late binding takes place any time you use a pointer to execute a function, as done in Listing 18.2. Late binding must also take place when you program in OOP and use inheritance and pointers to objects, as the next section explains.

DO / DON'T

DO learn the difference between early binding and late binding. Early binding is what you have always been used to when calling regular functions from within your programs. Late binding takes place when function calls cannot be resolved until runtime, as happens when you define pointers to functions.

DON'T give up pointers to functions in Visual C++ if you see the need to use them. They provide lots of power, and if you're comfortable with them, use them when you want to.

DON'T get too worried if you, like many C programmers, have never used pointers to functions. As a Visual C++ programmer, you'll use virtual functions more often to achieve the same late binding that pointers to functions provide in C.

Virtual Functions

Virtual functions provide a late binding mechanism for OOP that truly makes your programs seem to think for themselves. At runtime, your programs decide which functions to call. Before you go any further, you need to remember a simple rule that explains when virtual functions, as opposed to the regular member functions you've seen, are needed:

> *When you define pointers to several objects from a class family, and more than one class within the family contains functions with common names, use virtual functions.*

As you already know, you can define pointers to objects. If you create an inheritance class, you can define a pointer (or array of pointers) to the base class and then point to *any derived class objects from that base class.* Figure 18.5 shows what is meant here; if you define a pointer to a base class, you can then point to *any* object instantiated from any derived class of that base class.

Note: If you define a pointer to a derived class, you cannot point to base class objects with the pointer; the pointer through inherited class families works only from the base class down the inheritance hierarchy.

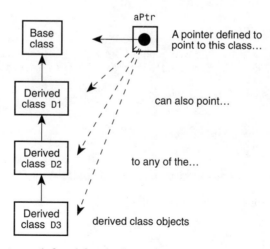

Figure 18.5. A pointer defined for the base class can point to any derived class object.

Virtual Functions: Are They Real?

As you know, an array name is nothing more than a pointer to a list of objects. You can define an array of objects, defined with the base class name, and then store derived class objects in the same array.

A quick example will demonstrate the need for virtual functions. The program in Listing 18.3 contains a program that almost works properly, but *almost* doesn't count in this business!

Listing 18.3. A program with pointers that doesn't quite work properly.

```
1:  // Filename: NOVIRT.CPP
2:  // Program to demonstrate pointers through a hierarchy and also
3:  // to show the problems if you don't use virtual functions
4:  #include <iostream.h>
5:  #include <iomanip.h>
6:  #include <string.h>
7:  class Building {
8:  protected:
9:     int sqFt;
10:    char address[25];   // Don't worry about city, state, ZIP
11: public:
12:    Building(int, char []);
13:    void prData(void);
14: };
15: Building::Building(int S, char A[]) : sqFt(S)
16: {
17:    strcpy(address, A);
18: }
19: void Building::prData(void)
20: {
21:    cout << "The building has " << sqFt << " square feet.\n";
22:    cout << "The building's address is " << address << ".\n\n";
23: }
24: class Shed : public Building {
25:    char useCode;
26: public:
27:    Shed(int, char[], char);
28: };
29: Shed::Shed(int S, char A[], char U) : Building(S, A), useCode(U)
30: { // No body necessary duc to initialization lists
31: }
32: class House : public Building {
33:    int numRooms;
34:    float cost;
35: public:
36:    House(int, char [], int, float);
37:    void prData(void);
38: };
```

```
39: House::House(int S, char A[], int N, float C) : Building(S, A),
40:             numRooms(N), cost(C)
41: { // No body necessary due to initialization lists
42: }
43: void House::prData(void)
44: {
45:    cout << "The house has " << sqFt << " square feet.\n";
46:    cout << "The house address is " << address << ".\n";
47:    cout << "The house has " << numRooms << " number of rooms.\n";
48:    cout << "The house cost " << cost << "\n\n";
49: }
50: class Office : public Building {
51:    int zoneCode;
52:    float rent;
53: public:
54:    Office(int, char [], int, float);
55:    void prData(void);
56: };
57: Office::Office(int S, char A[], int Z, float R) : Building(S, A),
58:                zoneCode(Z), rent(R)
59: {  // No body necessary due to initialization lists
60: }
61: void Office::prData(void)
62: {
63:    cout << "The office has " << sqFt << " square feet.\n";
64:    cout << "The office address is " << address << ".\n";
65:    cout << "The office is zoned for " << zoneCode << " code.\n";
66:    cout << "The office rents for " << rent << ".\n\n";
67: }
68: main()
69: {
70:    // Define pointers to class objects. Notice that the base
71:    // class is used to define the pointers, not any derived class
72:    Building * properties[3];
73:
74:    // Reserve heap and initialize with a constructor
75:    Shed aShed = Shed(78, "304 E. Tenth", 'x');
76:    House aHouse = House(2310, "5706 S. Carmel", 8, 121344.00);
77:    Office anOffice = Office(1195, "5 High Rise", 'B', 895.75);
78:    properties[0] = &aShed;
79:    properties[1] = &aHouse;
80:    properties[2] = &anOffice;
81:
82:    // Prepare output now that objects are constructed
83:    cout << setprecision(2) << setiosflags(ios::showpoint);
84:    cout << setiosflags(ios::fixed);
85:    // Print the objects using a loop
86:    for (int ctr=0; ctr<3; ctr++)
87:    {
88:       properties[ctr]->prData();   // Which prData() prints?
```

continues

Day 18: Virtual Functions: Are They Real?

Listing 18.3. continued

```
89:    }
90:
91:    // Deallocate the memory
92:    delete properties[0];
93:    delete properties[1];
94:    delete properties[2];
95:    return 0;
96: }
```

The building has 78 square feet.
The building's address is 304 E. Tenth.

The building has 2310 square feet.
The building's address is 5706 S. Carmel.

The building has 1195 square feet.
The building's address is 5 High Rise.

Study the class hierarchy (Figure 18.6 will help) to get an idea of the class makeup before studying `main()`. As you can see, the `useCode` is not accessed after it's initialized in the `Shed` constructor. The generic `Building`'s `prData()` function, inherited from `Building`, is all that's needed to print the `Shed`'s data.

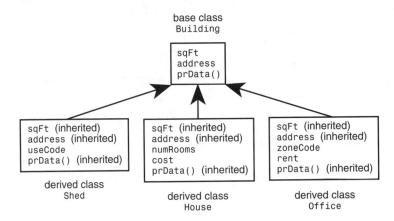

Figure 18.6. The class hierarchy of `Building` and its descendants.

`main()` is extremely compact, considering all that takes place at the class level. The pointers to the data on the heap all point to different kinds of objects (within the same class family). As you can see, however, there is something wrong with the output from this program.

Why didn't the House prData() function execute when line 88's properties pointer executed the prData() member function with the House object? The same question could be asked for the Office object as well. In other words, even though the prData() function was overridden in the two derived classes (lines 37 and 55), the base class prData() (line 14) executed instead.

You already know that derived classes can override their inherited data and member functions. It appears that both Office and House override Building's prData() member function. And yet, the Building's prData() member function executes for all objects pointed to by the pointer.

Note: It's OK that the Shed object prints with the Building's prData() because the Shed class made no attempt to override the prData() function but instead uses the one it inherits directly from Building.

Early binding is the reason for the problem. When Visual C++ compiles Listing 18.3, it must do something with line 88. After all, line 88 calls a prData() function. It is because the properties[] array is defined to point to the base class that the base class prData() executes. Instead, there has got to be a way to request that Visual C++ *not* bind the function calls early, but rather bind them at runtime when the objects pointed to can determine the correct functions to call.

In other words, there needs to be a way for you to give the compiler the following information:

> *If properties[] is pointing to a base class object, or to a derived class such as Shed that doesn't override prData(), use Building's prData() function. If, however, properties[] is pointing to a derived class, use that derived class's copy of prData() (unless there is none, as in the Shed class).*

There is a way to request that Visual C++ perform late binding when such pointers to objects are involved. As you might have guessed, using virtual functions solves the problem.

Specifying Virtual Functions

To fix the problem with Listing 18.3, you only need to tell Visual C++ exactly which functions in the base class are to be virtual by inserting the virtual keyword in front of those functions. By inserting virtual before the base class prData() function name,

Virtual Functions: Are They Real?

you inform Visual C++ that you only want the base class prData() function called if the object that triggers the member function, the *this object, is from the base class or from a derived class such as Shed that doesn't override prData().

Here is a rewritten version of the Building class with virtual properly specified:

```
1:  // Filename: VIRT.CPP
2:  class Building {
3:  protected:
4:     int sqFt;
5:     char address[25];   // Don't worry about city, state, ZIP
6:  public:
7:     Building(int, char []);
8:     virtual void prData(void);    // Here's the fix!
9:  };
```

The simple addition of virtual makes all the difference in the world. When you add virtual before the Building's prData() prototype as done here, you'll receive this output from the program:

```
The building has 78 square feet.
The building's address is 304 E. Tenth.

The house has 2310 square feet.
The house address is 5706 S. Carmel.
The house has 8 number of rooms.
The house cost 121344.00

The office has 1195 square feet.
The office address is 5 High Rise.
The office is zoned for 66 code.
The office rents for 895.75.
```

As you can see, line 88 (from Listing 18.3) now properly calls the correct prData() function. The function call is resolved at runtime, not compile time.

Polymorphism: "Many Forms"

The Greek for *many forms* is *polymorphism*. You might have seen this term in OOP literature, and that single word might have kept you away from learning OOP! Polymorphism makes learning OOP sound like slightly less fun than losing your job.

The fact is that the preceding section utilized polymorphism, only you didn't know the term. The prData() function is polymorphistic. After all, there are many forms (three) of prData() in Listing 18.3. When Listing 18.3 is corrected with the virtual keyword, Visual C++ takes care of figuring out which polymorphistic function to execute based on the type of value of the pointer on line 88.

Why is all this such a big deal? Well, if nothing else, learning to use the `virtual` keyword takes care of the programming problem shown in this chapter. When you want to point to objects throughout an inheritance class family, and when one or more of those objects share the same name as a base class function, you've got to tell Visual C++ to wait until runtime to resolve the function call.

An even better reason for using `virtual` is that you can again forget about messing with details and concentrate on the overall goal of your programming application. You don't have to name similar functions different names between inherited class families! Instead of worrying about `prOffice()`, `prBuilding()`, `prHouse()` and `prShed()`, you only have to remember `prData()` and let Visual C++ figure out at runtime which version of the `prData()` function to call! Isn't a simple `for` loop like the one on lines 86–89 (Listing 18.3) easier to code than four distinct function calls? What if there were 20 levels of hierarchy in the `Building` class? If there were, you would only change the `for` loop's `3` to `20`, but if you had not used virtual functions, you would have to code 17 more distinct function calls!

There's yet another reason for needing the `virtual` keyword before inherited function names. The same early binding problem occurs as it did originally in Listing 18.3 when you use references to invoke inherited member functions.

For example, suppose that you wrote a function called `printAll()` that applied the `prData()` function to whatever object is passed by reference as shown here:

```
void printAll(Building & place)
{
  place.prData();    // Hopefully, prData() is virtual!
  // Other code could follow
}
```

If `prData()` is listed as `virtual` in the base class, then whatever kind of object, `Building`, `Shed`, `House`, or `Office`, is passed to `printAll()` gets printed properly. However, if `prData()` is not listed in the base class as `virtual`, the base class `prData()` always executes no matter what kind of object is passed to `printAll()`.

Efficient or Not?

Visual C++ uses an elaborate system of indirect function call tables to resolve the `prData()` addresses at runtime. A table of virtual-function addresses, called the *vtable*, contains the addresses (with relative locations until the program is loaded for execution) of the functions that could be called polymorphically. Each class has a copy of the vtable. When the program

Virtual Functions: Are They Real?

runs, the vtables are used as go-between vehicles to find correct member functions from the inheritance hierarchy.

It is true that using virtual functions is slightly less efficient than using regular member function calls. If you don't point to objects, but rather you define objects with their own names, you won't have to use virtual functions. However, pointers are an important part of Visual C++, especially when using the heap. Therefore, you must remember to name all member functions between classes differently (which is not elegant or always wise), or you must remember to insert `virtual` before the base class functions that need to be resolved at runtime.

The slightly less efficient nature of virtual functions is the reason why the designers of C++ decided not to make `virtual` the default environment for all base class functions. The designers of C++ wanted efficiency in all programs, especially those that don't need polymorphism.

Depending on your application, at times you might not want the inherited function to execute when it otherwise would because of `virtual`. For example, suppose you expand on the `Building` program described in this chapter and add several functions and routines that print data for customers, real estate brokers, builders, and developers.

In the customer routines, you might not want the extra `House` members to print, but you'll still want the address and square feet to print. (You want to interest the customer, but not disclose the price except in person by a human agent.) In that function, you might want to use the base class `prData()` by overriding the `virtual` keyword like this:

```
properties[num]->Building::prData();   // Use base class version
```

Any time you override the virtualization, Visual C++ will perform early binding and insert the base class function's address at the function call during compilation and will always execute the base class version of the function when this function call is reached during execution.

Note: If your inheritance class hierarchy contains destructors, make the base class destructor virtual. Making the base class destructor virtual ensures that the proper destructor will be called when you delete an object through a pointer or reference using the `delete` operator.

If your base class virtual functions contain no code, those base class virtual functions are called *pure virtual functions.* They exist only to derive subsequent classes. No objects should be instantiated from a class that contains a pure virtual function. Therefore, if you design a high-level base class that is a model for derived classes, and you don't put any code in the base class virtual functions, don't instantiate base class objects. There will be trouble if you attempt to execute the member functions from the base object when no member function exists. Base classes with pure virtual functions are called *abstract base classes* because they are abstract and they model the rest of the inheritance family, but they should never be used to instantiate objects.

You can ensure that Visual C++ enforces your abstract base class by assigning 0 to all pure virtual functions in your programs like this:

```
virtual void prData(void) = 0;   // Can never instantiate now
```

Although the syntax is strange (assigning 0 to a function definition), the 0 tells the Visual C++ compiler to never enable you to instantiate base class objects. Without the setting to 0, you could compile a program that instantiated base class objects and then have trouble running it. It's a lot easier to debug compile-time errors (generated with the `= 0` format) than runtime errors that would occur if you used an object of an abstract base class.

DO	DON'T

DO define pointers or arrays to the base class if you want to point to or hold in an array several kinds of objects from the same class family.

DO use `virtual` when you point to objects in a class family and the same function name is used throughout the inheritance.

DO use `virtual` when receiving reference parameters that trigger inherited and overridden base class member functions.

DO override the virtualization if a base class function is supposed to execute when `virtual` would normally allow the derived class function to execute.

DO virtualize the base class destructor (or any class that contains a `virtual` function) so that your objects are always properly destructed. (Constructors cannot be virtualized—they don't ever need to be.)

DON'T apply `virtual` to friend functions.

DON'T apply `virtual` to regular member functions.

DON'T instantiate a base class that contains a pure virtual function.

Virtual Functions: Are They Real?

Summary

Today's chapter showed you the proper way to set up member functions when you define pointers to inherited objects. By specifying virtual functions, you let Visual C++ decide at runtime (late binding), and not at compile time (early binding), how to resolve function references. The effect of late binding is that your objects seem to decide for themselves which member functions to call.

In learning about late binding, you saw how early binding takes place in common C and C++ programs. At compile time, the compiler inserts function addresses into function calls so that the correct function can be found.

When you define pointers to several objects in an inheritance hierarchy, you define the pointers to be base class pointers. You then can assign those pointers to any derived object in the hierarchy. The only problem that remains is letting Visual C++ know which member functions to call, via the object pointers, when more than one class uses a function name that is the same as a base class function name.

If you insert `virtual` before each function prototype in the base class, Visual C++ uses late binding to look at the type of object being pointed to and to execute that object's class member function. However, without `virtual`, Visual C++ always executes the base class function, even if the pointer is pointing to an object derived several layers down in the family class.

Q&A

Q. What is the difference between early and late binding?

A. Early binding takes place in most programs that don't provide for virtual functions. Unless you use pointers to functions, or unless you use virtual functions, all C and Visual C++ compilers compile programs using early binding.

Early binding is the process of resolving function calls at compile time rather than runtime. The more the compiler can finish at compile time, the more efficient the compiled runtime program will be because there is less overhead the program has to take care of at runtime.

Late binding occurs when function call resolutions are delayed until runtime. The OOP need for late binding appears when you point to objects throughout an inherited family of class. The pointer could be pointing to a base class or derived class, and the compiler will not know exactly which class the pointer will point to until the program runs. Adding `virtual` tells the compiler to wait until runtime to determine which function should be executed, the base class's or a derived class's function.

Q. How does Visual C++ achieve late binding? What is the internal mechanism that allows for virtual functions?

A. When Visual C++ compiles a program, it knows that there has to be *some* function call code inserted at the location of every function call. Therefore, when you request late binding with `virtual`, Visual C++ inserts an indirect pointer at the function call that points not to a function (that would be a direct pointer) but to a table of functions called the *vtable* (or sometimes, the *virtual table*).

At runtime, the object pointer that triggers the member function provides the offset needed in the vtable to execute the correct function.

Q. Why doesn't Visual C++ default to virtual functions instead of requiring the `virtual` keyword? It seems as if one would always want virtual functions.

A. You won't always want to execute virtual functions when pointing to a class hierarchy of objects, but it's true that you *usually* want to. As a previous answer explained, slightly more overhead is needed to resolve virtual function calls than for regular function calls. This additional overhead is needed because the compiler must make decisions and access an internal table at runtime that doesn't have to be accessed if early binding occurs.

However small the efficiency loss is, the designers of the C++ language felt that you should make the decision to use virtual functions, so they did not make late binding the default function resolution when pointers to objects are used.

Q. What is the difference between a pure virtual function and a regular virtual function?

A. A pure virtual function contains no code. You can optionally assign a zero to a pure virtual function to make the compiler issue errors if you try to instantiate an object from a class that contains a pure virtual function.

Any base class that contains one or more pure virtual functions is called an abstract base class and cannot be used to instantiate objects. There is no code for the pure virtual functions, so the object's member function would be empty and useless.

Virtual Functions: Are They Real?

Q. What good is an abstract base class?

A. Although you cannot instantiate an abstract base class, you can use it as a high-level model of the inheritance that follows. Such a base class provides an outline of all the family of classes that you derive from the base class. An abstract base class can list all the common data members and member functions of all classes derived from the abstract base class.

Workshop

The Workshop offers quiz questions and exercises to hone your skills and give you feedback on today's lesson. You'll find some proposed answers in Appendix D.

Quiz

1. Can a family class (as used in this chapter) contain more than one base class and hierarchy?

2. Name two places where late binding takes place in Visual C++. (Hint: One can occur in both C and C++.)

3. True or False: When you define pointers to functions, data not code determines exactly which function to call.

4. Which of the following function prototypes correctly defines a pure virtual function?

   A. ```
      class A {
      protected:
        int i;
      public:
        calcIt(void) { i = i * 23 - 7; }
      };
      ```

   B. ```
      class B {
      protected:
        int i;
      public:
        calcIt(void) = 0;
      };
      ```

C. ```
class C {
  protected:
    int i;
  public:
    pure calcIt(void) { i = i * 23 - 7; }
};
```

5. Which of the classes in question 4 is an abstract base class?

6. How can you tell whether a base class is an abstract base class?

7. How does assigning a zero to a pure virtual function change your program's compilation?

8. Why would you need a virtual destructor?

# Exercises

1. Write a program that executes a function based on a menu choice using functions to pointers. The function executed doesn't have to do anything but print a message showing the user that the correct function was triggered by the function pointer.

2. Rewrite Listing 18.3 with virtual functions needed in the base class so that the base class is an abstract base class. (Hint: You'll have to add a prData() function to the Shed class.)
```

DAY 19

Introduction to Throwing and Catching Exceptions

Day 19: Introduction to Throwing and Catching Exceptions

Throughout the past few years, there has been anticipation, some attempts, and few successes to include exception handling in C++ compilers. An exception is anything unexpected that happens during a program's execution. Exceptions usually result in an error message being displayed on-screen.

When you write an exception handler, you are telling the compiler to follow your code, as opposed to the usual error message, when an exception (error) occurs. The actions you want taken in the exception handler depend on both the severity and the recoverability of the error.

You can write a different exception handling routine for different kinds of exceptions that might take place. If an error occurs and you've written a handler for that error, your handler automatically takes control. If the error does not take place, your exception handler is ignored. It's true that some errors are so severe that you don't want to do anything more than close files and shut down the program. Also, some errors are so unlikely to happen that you won't want to write a separate exception handler for each one.

Today, you learn about the following topics:

- ☐ Why exceptions are needed
- ☐ How exception handling was designed
- ☐ The different types of errors
- ☐ C-style exceptions
- ☐ How to implement Windows/Visual C++ exceptions
- ☐ Looking ahead to the MFC exception types

Warning: You might feel that this chapter is incomplete. In today's chapter, you'll learn all there is about the concept of exceptions. A problem arises because using all the exception-handling capabilities of Visual C++ requires that you know more about the advanced Microsoft Foundation Classes (MFC) that comes supplied with Visual C++. You cannot learn about the MFC classes related to Visual C++ exceptions until the bonus section at the end of this book. Therefore, you'll learn a lot about exception handling in today's chapter, and you'll see how to apply exception handling as you progress through the remainder of this book.

> As you'll see before you're done with this book, the MFC classes make your programming job even easier than it already is with regular C++. Microsoft has written and debugged thousands of lines of code and encapsulated that code into the Microsoft Foundation Classes. The MFC supplies prewritten member functions you can use for exceptions, data storage structures, file I/O, strings, and Microsoft Windows programming.
>
> The biggest limitation of the QuickWin programs you've written throughout the entire book so far is that QuickWin programs do not support the MFC classes! Of course, the primary goal of this book is to teach the non-OOP programmer how to program in OOP using Visual C++, and to that end, the book is successful. However, the bonus section at the end of this book will introduce you to MFC classes and give you a preview of Microsoft Windows programming with MFC. It is there that you will learn more about exception handling in Visual C++.

The Need for Exception Handling

Before looking at exception-handling specifics, you should gain more insight into the need for exception handling. Exception handling is yet another way C++ lightens the workload from the C++ programmer's back. After writing error routines and tying those error routines to specific exceptions, you can go about programming your application without tediously checking for errors throughout the code the way you might be used to doing now.

Exception handling forces Visual C++ to look over your program's shoulder during execution. If an exception takes place (a specified error), Visual C++ then promptly and safely executes your error routine for you.

The Genesis of Exception Handling

Exception handling was not a part of the original C++ language repertoire. Bjarne Stroustrup (the original designer of C++) and Andrew Koenig (an industry-recognized expert in C++) introduced the C++ exception-handling concept in April of 1990, and the ANSI C++ committee adopted exceptions just seven months later.

Introduction to Throwing and Catching Exceptions

Although the proposed ANSI C++ language specification has included exceptions for a while now, only recently have compiler vendors jumped on the exception bandwagon and started offering exception handling in some form.

Sadly, Visual C++ does not specifically support exception handling using the same commands as the proposed ANSI C++ standard. As you might know, deviating from ANSI compatibility means that the program you write today might not compile correctly on tomorrow's computers. (Even though there is no official ANSI C++ specification at the time of this writing, most agree that the proposed ANSI C++ specification is close to the final ANSI C++ standard.) Nevertheless, the advantages of using exceptions in your programs now outweigh writing error routines in a more primitive manner. Also, the design of the Visual C++ exception handling implementation is closely tied to the proposed ANSI C++ behavior, so the programs you write today will probably easily convert to whatever final exception standard is adopted by the ANSI committee.

As you'll learn in this chapter and throughout the rest of the book, Visual C++ supports exceptions in more than one way. The first method, described in this chapter, enables you to use Windows programming functions that somewhat conform to the ANSI C++ exception-handling standard. In addition, there are several Visual C++–supplied exception macros you can use as you progress into the Microsoft Foundation Classes that come with Visual C++. Actually, the macros offer more power and flexibility than the Windows functions shown here, but the macros are Visual C++ specific and aren't supported by the ANSI committee or any other C++ compiler.

It is true that inline functions and the const identifier virtually eliminate the need for you as a programmer to write macros. For some reason, Microsoft decided to implement the MFC exception-handling features as macros. Perhaps implementing the actual commands within the language would cause a delay in the compiler's release, so Microsoft decided on the macro approach. In defense of Microsoft, however, the people there probably felt that macros were the safest implementation they could write at the time because the ANSI C++ draft is only a draft and not a final specification. By using macros, Microsoft is free in the future to change the behavior of those macros so that their underlying code conforms to whatever standard ANSI C++ decides on. And in the meantime, all the programs you write will still function properly. You'll learn Visual C++'s macro support for exceptions in the bonus section at the end of the book.

> **You Mean QBasic Includes Exception Handling?**
>
> It is sometimes embarrassing for major language developers to admit that QBasic (and many of the BASIC precursors), which is notably a beginner's programming language, supports a kind of exception handling that more mainstream programming languages fail to support. QBasic's `ON ERROR` statements trigger the automatic execution of a particular section of code (the exception-handler) if a runtime error occurs. For example, you can set up a divide-by-zero handler routine and a file-not-found handler routine and then go about writing the rest of the application. If either of those errors occurs during the program's execution, QBasic calls the appropriate handler.
>
> QBasic contains several `ON ERROR` options that enable you to continue with program execution before, at, or after the error took place. Before modern BASIC languages, the mainframe PL/I language was virtually the only other language that offered some kind of programmer-supplied support for handling runtime error conditions.

Kinds of Errors

Not all errors are alike. Most programmers agree that software errors fall into the following categories:

- Faulty hardware-triggered errors that occur when a hardware failure keeps the program from carrying out a given task.

- Design errors (sometimes called logic errors) that occur because the program designer failed to understand the full needs of the program. Design errors might not be noticed until after the user runs the application for a while.

- Syntax errors that occur because of the programmers' poor typing and spelling. Syntax errors appear quickly and are the easiest of all the errors to correct. The compiler tells you of your syntax errors every time you compile a program.

- Runtime errors that occur only during a program's execution. Sometimes, another kind of error, such as a hardware failure or a design error, causes a runtime error. If you do not check for runtime errors, or if you fail to

Introduction to Throwing and Catching Exceptions

include exception handling for all runtime errors that take place, the program might abort, data could be lost, and the computer could freeze up and require a complete restart. Common runtime errors include memory problems, file-not-found problems, attempting to read past the end of file, and division by zero.

The more exception handlers you place in a program, the more elegantly your program can recover from a runtime error. At the very least, handling runtime errors prevents your computer from locking up by allowing a graceful exit back to the operating system with as much data as possible intact. Many times, an exception handler can correct the cause of the error and put the program back on track again. If so, the user never has to know that a problem occurred.

Note: The more runtime errors you write exception handlers for, the less likely an unexpected event will cause your program to abort. Try to handle as many errors as possible. The opposite extreme, however, is a waste of time, too; writing an exception for every possible error would be ridiculous. In addition, you cannot predict every possible error that might happen. Luckily, there are well-known and common actions in most programs that could cause runtime errors, such as disk I/O, division, and memory-allocation problems. You'll want to set up exception handlers for the particular actions in your code that could trigger specific errors.

The World Without Exception Handling

You don't have to use exception handlers to handle runtime errors that occur during program execution. Before you divide, after you attempt to open a file, or immediately after allocating memory, you can check to see whether an error took place. However, having to check explicitly for all these possible errors, each time they might appear, is time-consuming and does not blend well with the C++ philosophy that tedious work should be off-loaded from the programmer's back and made the responsibility (through defined programmer-supplied methods) of the compiler.

> If you don't use exceptions, you must check for some runtime errors in advance, and others after the error takes place but before more damage is done. To guard against divide-by-zero, for example, you must first check the dividend (the number being divided into) to ensure that it's not zero. If you don't check for the zero before dividing, you'll get an unrecoverable runtime error at the point that division by zero is attempted. (Division by zero is undefined in mathematics, and a real number solution is not possible.)
>
> If you need to check for file-opening problems (and almost any other I/O error), you must check a return value after the I/O is attempted. C++ rarely displays error messages at the time I/O errors take place because the designers of the language hope that you properly check all return codes and handle the problem as you see fit. Only if you ignore a file I/O error and continue with the rest of the program do you risk unrecoverable error messages that are related to the I/O problem earlier.

Not only is typical error checking cumbersome, but real coding problems are associated with trying to write elegant error-handling code. After you write the code to take care of a divide-by-zero error, you'll want to call that code if you ever see that division by zero is about to take place.

The next few paragraphs describe how C language programmers sometimes simulate exceptions. The large review of this C concept is included here for two reasons. If you have used the C method for exceptions before, this discussion offers a good review and prepares you for tacking exceptions in the last part of this chapter and in the bonus chapters at the end of the book. Also, if you've never used the C-like exception handling described here, you might find that the terminology is more familiar than true exception handling terminology would be at first. Therefore, you'll probably adapt more to Visual C++ exceptions after this initial review of C.

The reason C simulates and now C++ includes support for exceptions is that problems often arise when the programmer is trying to handle error conditions. Consider the set of nested functions shown in Figure 19.1.

Introduction to Throwing and Catching Exceptions

```
main()
{ int errRtn = aFun();
  if (errRtn == -1) errorFun();
  // main() continues
}
int aFun()
{ int errRtn = bFun();
  if (errRtn == -1) return errRtn;
  // bFun() continues
  return 0; // No error
}
int bFun()
{ int errRtn = cFun();
  if (errRtn == -1) return err Rtn;
  // bFun() continues
  return 0; // No error
}
int cFun()
{ // Start up code
  if (userAns == 0) return -1; // Error
  avg = total / userAns;
  // Rest of cFun
  return 0;  // No error

}
```

Return error code to handle error

Return error code to handle error

Return error code to handle error

Figure 19.1. If `cFun()` fails, a long return chain is needed to get back to the error-handling code.

During the execution of Figure 19.1's innermost function, `cFun()`, if it's determined that a divide-by-zero is about to happen, the program returns from the function immediately and handles the error. Returning from the function means you have to return an error code throughout the entire set of nested routines until you reach a point where the error handler can be called.

Instead of dealing with all the code to return an error code through a long chain of nested functions, you would prefer to return directly to the error handler as shown in Figure 19.2. If the data is about to cause a divide-by-zero, control passes directly to the error-handling code.

```
main()
{ int errRtn = aFun();
  if (errRtn == -1) errorFun();
  // main() continues
}
int aFun()
{ int errRtn = bFun();
  if (errRtn == -1) return errRtn;
  // bFun() continues
  return 0; // No error
}
int bFun()
{ int errRtn = cFun;
  if (errRtn== -1) return errRtn;
  // bFun() continues
  return 0; // No error
}
int cFun()
{ // Start up code
  if (userAns == 0) return -1;
  avg = total / userAns;
  // Rest of cFun
  return 0;   // No error
}
```

Return error code directly to handler in main()

Figure 19.2. If cFun() fails now, the error handler takes over immediately.

Unless you've seen a similar discussion before, you might wonder how a C-like language can support such a return around all the other functions. In reality, a GOTO-like construct is required to bypass the normal function-return mechanism. The functions setjmp() and longjmp() provide the way for C to return over called functions to an original calling function such as main(), shown here.

Here is a description of the setjmp() and longjmp() functions (both are prototyped in C's SETJMP.H header file):

> setjmp(): setjmp() takes a snapshot of your computer's registers and important areas of memory. Later in the program, if a longjmp() occurs, the state of your program at the setjmp() resets (in effect, removing the layers of returns needed otherwise). You can test the value sent to setjmp() from the longjmp() to determine which particular error occurred if you want to set up a setjmp() call that handles more than one kind of error.

> longjmp(): Call longjmp() if an error occurs (or if you can tell that an error, such as divide by zero, is about to happen). Calling longjmp() forces immediate transfer of the program's control to the location of the setjmp().

Introduction to Throwing and Catching Exceptions

Listing 19.1 shows a simple C program that uses `setjmp()` to prevent bad user input and a bad `fopen()`. Something as common as user input probably doesn't warrant a `setjmp()` because the code to correct data-entry typically resides around the input code. However, Listing 19.1 shows you how to set up `setjmp()` to handle more than one kind of error.

Listing 19.1. Using `setjmp()` to handle two error conditions.

```
 1: /* Filename: SETJMP.C
 2:    C is used because setjmp() and longjmp() demonstrate C's
 3:    exception handling, and C++ exception handling makes setjmp()
 4:    and longjmp() now obsolete */
 5: #include <stdio.h>
 6: #include <setjmp.h>
 7: #include <stdlib.h>
 8: void inBetween(void);
 9: void getUserInput(void);
10: void openAFile(void);
11:
12: jmp_buf jmpBufStruct;   /* You must define this global buffer so
13:    C has a place to store the system's state at the setjmp() */
14:
15: main()
16: {
17:    int badVal;  /* Holds a value determining which error occurred */
18:
19:    /* You must set up a setjmp() handler for each error that must be
20:       controlled. If a longjmp() is never called later in the program,
21:       this setjmp() code is ignored. Only if a longjmp() forces a
22:       branch back to this setjmp() will the next switch activate */
23:    badVal = setjmp(jmpBufStruct);  /* The system's state is saved
24:                             here in case a longjmp() happens later */
25:    switch (badVal)
26:    {
27:       /* A return value of 1 means bad input, 2 means file not found */
28:       case (1): { printf("You are more than zero years old!\nRestart");
29:                   printf(" the program and type your true age.\n");
30:                   exit(99); }   /* Stop program */
31:       case (2): { printf("There is a problem. The data file");
32:                   printf(" cannot be found.\nSee your system");
33:                   printf(" administrator.");
34:                   exit(99); }   /* Stop the program */
35:    }
36:    /* NONE of these switches executes if longjmp() is not triggered*/
37:
38:    /******** The rest of main() is just straight common code */
39:    inBetween();  /* Call an intermediate function */
40:    return 0;
```

```c
 41: }
 42: /*******************************************************************/
 43: void inBetween(void)
 44: {
 45:    getUserInput();         /* This inBetween() function exists solely */
 46:    openAFile();            /* to add an extra layer of function calls */
 47:    return;                 /* between main()'s handlers and any error */
 48: }
 49: /*******************************************************************/
 50: void getUserInput(void)
 51: {
 52:    int age;
 53:    printf("How old are you? ");
 54:    scanf(" %d", &age);     /* Enter a 0 to trigger error */
 55:    if (age <=0)
 56:    {
 57:       longjmp(jmpBufStruct, 1);   /* Branch directly to setjmp() */
 58:    }
 59:    if (age < 18)
 60:    {
 61:       printf("Go to school.\n");
 62:    }
 63:    else
 64:    {
 65:      printf("Go vote in the next election.\n");
 66:    }
 67:    return;
 68: }
 69: /*******************************************************************/
 70: void openAFile(void)
 71: {
 72:    FILE *fp;
 73:    /* Open a file that you know doesn't exist to test setjmp() */
 74:    fp = fopen("nothere.abc", "r");
 75:    if (!fp)
 76:    {
 77:       longjmp(jmpBufStruct, 2);   /* Branch directly to setjmp() */
 78:    }
 79:    /* The file processing would normally take place
 80:       here IF it existed */
 81:    printf("Now closing file.\n");   /* This will never be reached */
 82:    fclose(fp);
 83:    return;
 84: }
```

Introduction to Throwing and Catching Exceptions

Note: The output shows two runs of the program so that you can see when the age data entry triggers an exception and when the file-open error triggers an exception.

```
How old are you? 4
Go to school.
There is a problem. The data file cannot be found.
See your system administrator.

How old are you? 0
You are more than zero years old!
Restart the program and type your true age.
```

As you can see, Listing 19.1 contains two error possibilities. The handler routine for both errors resides in `main()`, and the errors occur two nested function calls later. All programs that use `setjmp()` must define a buffer area as shown in line 12. (The buffer is global because one of several functions might later trigger the `setjmp()`.) Don't worry about the data type of `jmp_buf` objects; `jmp_buf` is typedefed in the SETJMP.H header file included in line 6. The `jmp_buf` buffer, named `jmpBufStruct` here, is where C stores the program's memory and register states at the `setjmp()`.

Line 23 begins the error-handling routine. That line tells the C compiler that if a `longjmp()` function is ever called, control is to branch immediately back to line 23 and the state of the system is to be restored to what it was when line 23 was first reached. Any subsequently defined local variables and nested function calls are eliminated upon a `longjmp()` function call if one occurs.

The return value of `setjmp()` enables you to handle more than one error. (You'll soon see how Visual C++'s exception handlers also enable you to handle more than one error.) The `switch` statement checks the return value of `setjmp()` (if and only if `setjmp()` is triggered by a subsequent `longjmp()`) and handles the error accordingly. The return value of `setjmp()` is determined by you when you eventually code the `longjmp()`. You could return a different value from several different `longjmp()` calls and handle a wide range of error conditions.

`main()`'s true execution begins at line 38. `main()` is short; it controls a single function call. The `inBetween()` function (lines 43–48) simply adds an extra layer between `main()` and the resulting error so you can see that the `longjmp()` distance can easily span multiple functions.

The getUserInput() function triggers an exception if the user enters an age that is less than zero. You might think that a less-than-zero error is not an exception because it is not a divide-by-zero or any other kind of runtime error. But if you were eventually to divide another value by the user's age input, a divide-by-zero error would occur. (In Visual C++'s exception handling, you'll see that a divide-by-zero can actually be attempted, and Visual C++ automatically executes your error handler.) Line 57 forces a branch back to the state of the setjmp() if the user enters a bad age value. longjmp() requires two simple arguments: the global system buffer you defined before main(), followed by an error number that you check for up in the setjmp() code. If the user doesn't enter a bad age, the longjmp() does not execute.

The openAFile() function attempts to open and immediately close a data file. If the file does not exist (and it's doubtful there is a file in your program named nothere.abc), the function calls longjmp(), and control is passed back to the setjmp() code so that the error can be handled by the second case of the switch statement in main().

The goal of this book is to teach you Visual C++, not C, but the old setjmp() routines are perfect introductions to exception handling because using setjmp() calls is the way programmers used to program exception-like code. setjmp() has a few problems that cannot be overcome, so it's good that Visual C++ contains other methods for handling exceptions.

The most important reason to stay away from setjmp() when you're writing Visual C++ programs is that Visual C++ doesn't support setjmp() (unless you save, compile, and run the program as a DOS-based C program from within Visual C++). Nevertheless, as mentioned earlier, this discussion of setjmp() is a good introduction to exception handling. Although fairly primitive compared to all the exception-handling macros that Visual C++'s MFC provides, the setjmp()/longjmp() philosophy is a good way to learn about exceptions because the goto-like concept of setjmp()/longjmp() is easy to grasp.

Warning: Although you've probably learned to stay away from goto, you might think a simple goto would send the control to whichever label you executed at the time of the error instead of messing with setjmp() and longjmp(). You must remember that goto labels must reside within the same function scope as the goto. You could never use a simple goto to send control to a statement in a completely different function.

Introduction to Throwing and Catching Exceptions

Note: The following discussion on Visual C++ exception handling can be shorter and more direct now that you understand the need of exception handling and now that you've seen the more primitive way C can simulate the same technique.

DO / DON'T

DO set up exception handling to handle your common errors.

DON'T attempt the C-style `setjmp()` in Visual C++ programs (unless you write DOS-based C programs within Visual C++), although learning how `setjmp()` works gives you all the background you need in order to dive directly into exception handlers next.

DON'T try to set up an exception for every possible runtime error that can occur. You know from your program's design which runtime errors are most likely to creep into the program.

Some Terminology

There are two ways to handle exceptions in Visual C++:

Using Microsoft Windows API function calls. The API (which stands for Application Programming Interface) is a set of more than 1,000 functions you can call from your Visual C++ program. Some of the API, such as its set of exception handling functions, is available to non-Windows programs, including the limited-Windows programs you write with QuickWin.

Using Visual C++'s Microsoft Foundation Class (MFC) macros. Most Visual C++ programmers write exception-handling routines using these macros. However, you'll have to put off their discussion until you learn more about MFC classes later in the book.

The rest of this chapter teaches you how to handle exceptions using Microsoft Windows programming functions supplied with Visual C++. You don't have to know anything about writing advanced Windows applications to use these functions. Basically, using the Windows functions will be a one-for-one conversion from the way

`setjmp()` and `longjmp()` worked earlier in the chapter. In using these functions, you'll be one step closer to Visual C++'s MFC macro implementation.

Warning: Be sure that you include the WINDOWS.H header file in all programs you write that use the exception-handling functions described in the rest of this chapter.

Visual C++ exception handling uses a new set of terms. When a statement generates a runtime error, whether that error occurs from within the runtime system or you generate one of your own, an exception is thrown. Not coincidentally, the function name for throwing exceptions is `Throw()`.

The error-handling code that you write is caught when an exception is thrown. The function name for catching thrown exceptions is `Catch()`. Using the C-style terminology, a `longjmp()` throws an error exception, and the `setjmp()` code catches the exception and handles it.

You must tell Visual C++ which code to include in your exception handling. In other words, there might be a critical section of code that could generate errors you want to handle, whereas other parts of the program could generate errors you could not handle. You must therefore tell Visual C++ which sections of code are to include exception handling, just as you had to do with `setjmp()` and `longjmp()`.

Warning: Keep in mind that when you learn how to code exceptions using the Windows functions `Catch()` and `Throw()`, you're still missing one piece of the puzzle before you'll fully master Visual C++ exceptions. Only after mastering more MFC material in the remainder of this book will you fully see when and why exceptions improve your programming muscle. C++ often brings on the cart-before-the-horse syndrome, and you often have to learn a subject in pieces as you're doing here.

Should I Use an Exception Handler or _set_new_handler()?

You already know how to write one kind of exception handler. In Day 5's chapter, "Memory Allocation: There When You Need It," you saw how to

Introduction to Throwing and Catching Exceptions

write the _set_new_handler() function. _set_new_handler() is an easy-to-write function call that automatically executes a given function if any of the rest of the program produces an allocation error with new.

You might wonder whether you should continue using the _set_new_handler() or the exception-handling techniques presented in today's chapter. Part of your choice of allocation options depends on your own style and skills. Although many people feel that _set_new_handler() is easier than exceptions to learn and use, you must remember that _set_new_handler() takes care only of problems surrounding C++'s new operator and not allocations requested with the C-style functions such as malloc() and realloc(). You might think that you'll never use malloc() again, and maybe you won't, but you might use someone else's code sometime that happens to use malloc().

Exceptions also provide a more uniform approach to handling exceptional conditions, and you can check for many more problems using exception handling than you can with _set_new_handler(). Learning about exceptions will therefore benefit you, and the sooner you begin using exceptions, the sooner you'll see the true power available with them. If, however, you want only to handle a new allocation and you aren't using the MFC classes, using _set_new_handler() works well until you need the power the MFC exception handlers can provide.

Coding an Exception

As promised earlier, using the Catch() and Throw() exception functions will seem anticlimactic to you because they are almost mirror-image partners with setjmp() and longjmp(). This section concludes this chapter on exceptions by showing you how to code the Windows API-based Visual C++ exceptions.

Catch() is to setjmp() what Throw() is to longjmp(). With only some slight changes, the program in Listing 19.2 works just like the one in Listing 19.1, except that the program contains Catch() and Throw() rather than setjmp() and longjmp().

 Day 20's chapter, "Easy File I/O," explains how to access files using Visual C++. Don't worry about the specific file I/O mechanisms in Listing 19.2. Instead, concentrate on the exception handling.

Listing 19.2. Using `catch()` and `throw()` to handle two exceptions.

```
 1: // Filename: cathrow.cpp
 2: // Catch() and Throw() demonstrate Visual C++'s exception handling
 3: #include <iostream.h>
 4: #include <windows.h>
 5: #include <stdlib.h>
 6: #include <fstream.h>
 7: void inBetween(void);
 8: void getUserInput(void);
 9: void openAFile(void);
10:
11: CATCHBUF jmpBufStruct;   // You must define this global buffer so
12: // Visual C++ has a place to store the system's state at the Catch()
13:
14: main()
15: {
16:   int badVal;  // Holds a value that determines which error occurred
17:
18:   // You must now set up a catch handler for each error that must be
19:   // controlled. If Throw() is never called later in the program,
20:   // this Catch() code is ignored. Only if a Throw() forces a branch
21:   // back to this Catch() will the subsequent switch activate
22:   badVal = Catch(jmpBufStruct);  // The system's state is saved
23:                                  // here in case a longjmp() happens later
24:   switch (badVal)
25:   {
26:   // A return value of 1 means bad input, 2 means file not found
27:     case (1): { cerr << "You are more than zero years old!\nRestart";
28:                 cerr << " the program and type your true age.\n";
29:                 exit(99); }   // Stop program
30:     case (2): { cerr << "There is a problem. The data file";
31:                 cerr << " cannot be found.\nSee your system";
32:                 cerr << " administrator.";
33:                 exit(99); }   // Stop the program
34:   }
35:   // NONE of the above switches executes if Throw() is not triggered
36:
37:   //******** The rest of main() is just straight common code
38:   inBetween();  // Call an intermediate function
```

continues

Introduction to Throwing and Catching Exceptions

Listing 19.2. continued

```
39:    return 0;
40: }
41: /////////////////////////////////////////////////////////////////
42: void inBetween(void)
43: {
44:    getUserInput();      // This inBetween() function exists solely
45:    openAFile();         // to add an extra layer of function calls
46:    return;              // between main()'s handlers and any error
47: }
48: /////////////////////////////////////////////////////////////////
49: void getUserInput(void)
50: {
51:    int age;
52:    cout << "How old are you? ";
53:    cin >> age;   // Enter a 0 to trigger error
54:    if (age <=0)
55:    {
56:       Throw(jmpBufStruct, 1); // Throw to the catch function
57:                               // wherever it is
58:    }
59:    if (age < 18)
60:    {
61:       cout << "Go to school.\n";
62:    }
63:    else
64:    {
65:      cout << "Go vote in the next election.\n";
66:    }
67:    return;
68: }
69: /////////////////////////////////////////////////////////////////
70: void openAFile(void)
71: {
72:    ifstream inpfile("nothere.abc");
73:
74:    // Open a file that you know doesn't exist to test catch()
75:    if (!inpfile.bad())
76:    {
77:      Throw(jmpBufStruct, 2);  // Throw to the Catch function
78:    }                          // wherever it is
79:    // File processing would normally take place here IF it existed
80:    cout << "Done with file.\n";  // This will never be reached
81:    return;
82: }
```

Note: The output shows two runs of the program so that you can see when the age data entry triggers an exception and when the file open error triggers an exception.

```
How old are you? 4
Go to school.
There is a problem. The data file cannot be found.
See your system administrator.

How old are you? 0
You are more than zero years old!
Restart the program and type your true age.
```

As you can see, throwing and catching exceptions with Catch() and Throw() works just as C's setjmp() did, with only minor differences.

Other than the WINDOW.H include file on line 4, you'll notice that the typedefed CATCHBUF (line 11) defines the buffer that will hold the system's state at the time of the thrown exception, whereas the jmp_buf structure defined the buffer area in the C version.

That wraps up exceptions for the time being. The Catch() and Throw() functions will keep you occupied for a while until you master the MFC-related exception macros.

Summary

Today's chapter introduced you to exception handling. There are several kinds of errors, and the most tedious errors to check for are runtime errors. Without the more structured approach that exceptions offer, you will find it difficult, time-consuming, and sometimes too much of a hassle to check for every runtime error that might arise.

You probably learned something in today's chapter about C that you had not known before. C's setjmp() and longjmp() functions enable you to simulate exceptions. The setjmp() saves the PC's state (registers and important memory areas). Then, if and when a longjmp() occurs, no matter where in the program the longjmp() happens, control resumes at the setjmp(), and the PC's original state is restored so that your program can handle the error.

The Windows programming functions, Catch() and Throw(), closely mirror C's setjmp() and longjmp() functions, and Visual C++ supports those functions' use. The Catch() function begins the exception code that handles whatever functions are

Introduction to Throwing and Catching Exceptions

thrown from `Throw()`. As with `setjmp()` and `longjmp()`, your program can `Catch()` exceptions thrown from elsewhere in the program, even if the exception is thrown from a completely different function.

Q&A

Q. What is an exception?

A. In reality, an exception is whatever you the programmer want the exception to be. Most of the time, however, an exception is an error condition that arises as the program runs.

Q. Why should I worry about handling exceptions? Won't the Visual C++ runtime system display an error message?

A. The runtime system's error message is indeed what exceptions attempt to avoid. Instead of aborting a program and possibly losing data, your exception code can gracefully handle the recovery or termination of the error condition.

Perhaps more important to your end user, the runtime error messages can be extremely cryptic. Instead of displaying the system's error message, you might want to display a more meaningful error and suggestion on how the user can restart the program and keep the error from happening again. If you work in a company with a data processing support staff, your exception's message can also tell the user which phone extension to call to get support for the error resolution.

Q. Are exceptions new to the C++ language?

A. Indeed, exceptions were designed for the C++ language. As you learned in today's chapter, however, C offers a pair of workaround functions that simulate exception handling. The `setjmp()` and `longjmp()` functions allow control in a C program to return to a preset (with `setjmp()`) point so that the program can recover or exit gracefully from the problem.

There are some problems with `setjmp()` and `longjmp()` (if there weren't, there would be no sense in designing another approach). You saw the beginnings of Visual C++ exception handling at the end of this chapter. The `catch()` and `throw()` functions mimic the `setjmp()` and `longjmp()` functions and more closely match the proposed ANSI C++ standard for exceptions. Unlike `setjmp()` and `longjmp()`, `Catch()` and `Throw()` can be used in Visual C++.

Q. Aren't Catch() and Throw() Microsoft Windows functions?

A. Yes. However, you don't have to be writing true Windows programs to use Catch() and Throw(). You can use Catch() and Throw() in your QuickWin programs as shown in Listing 19.2.

Visual C++ supplies an additional exception-handling macro mechanism that is more powerful than the simple Catch() and Throw(). You must master some of the Microsoft Foundation Classes (MFC) before learning about the exception macros.

Workshop

The Workshop offers quiz questions and exercises to hone your skills and give you feedback on today's lesson. You'll find the answers in Appendix D.

Quiz

1. What does it mean to throw an exception?
2. What does it mean to catch an exception?
3. Are the Throw() and Catch() functions part of Visual C++? Why or why not?
4. True or False: If an exception is thrown, only one kind of error at a time can handle the exception.
5. What are the two kinds of exceptions that Visual C++ supports?
6. What header file is required in order to use the Windows exception-handling functions?

Exercise

1. Write a program that asks the user for his or her first initial and throws an exception if the user enters something other than a letter of the alphabet.

DAY 20

Easy File I/O

Easy File I/O

Your training is coming to an end! Of course, that really means that your programming is just beginning. You'll never feel like an expert Visual C++ programmer until you've written your own "real world" programs.

If you think OOP isn't really that difficult to understand, you're right. However, you probably would not have believed that on Day 1! These past three weeks have taken you from an OOP recruit to an OOP pro, and the trail really hasn't been that difficult, has it? In reality, there's not much that makes OOP different from non-OOP programming, yet the small OOP knowledge base you now have will do wonders for the programs that you write. You'll now move the details of your programs into class objects, and the rest of your programs will consist of little more than high-level directors of those classes. You'll find that OOP and Visual C++ lessen the tediousness of programming.

This final day's tutorial rounds out your OOP tri-week course by teaching you how to store and retrieve disk file data. The entire book has concentrated until now on in-memory manipulation of objects because that's where true data processing occurs. Nevertheless, without the capability to store and retrieve your data, OOP would be little help indeed for long-term practical use.

If you've written disk file programs before, using C or even QBasic (the two languages offer surprisingly few differences in the methods they use for disk I/O), you'll see that Visual C++ is just as easy. Many times, Visual C++ is even easier because it does more work and removes details from your programs.

Today, you learn about the following topics:

- ☐ Sequential file I/O manipulation
- ☐ Sequential file I/O with character data
- ☐ Sequential file I/O with string data
- ☐ Sequential file I/O with class data
- ☐ Random-access file I/O manipulation
- ☐ Positioning the file pointer
- ☐ Reading and writing data in the same file

Note: You'll find a more advanced way of reading and writing data from and to files in the second Bonus chapter at the end of this book.

Sequential I/O: Read, Write, and Append

There are only three actions you can perform with a sequential file: reading data from the file, writing data to a new file, and adding data to an existing file. Think of a sequential file as being like a cassette tape: you cannot rearrange songs or change individual selections very easily. To add a song to the middle of a series of songs on a cassette, you have to create a new tape altogether. It just isn't possible to shift all the songs down to make room for the new one.

Although a disk drive offers more flexibility than a cassette, if you set up a file as a sequential file, you'll be limited to accessing the file in the three sequential ways: creating the file, reading the file, and adding to the file.

Sequential file access is actually easier than random file access. Random files give you the ability to rearrange data on the disk just as you do elements in an array. As with an array, you can access a random file in any order, not just from the first record written to the last as must be done with sequential files. However, programming for random files is a little more detailed, and some programming situations lend themselves well to sequential file access. Here are just some of the times when using sequential files makes sense:

- [ ] When storing a history file of transactions that you rarely have to access, and then only to append to the end of it. What is the most common thing done to a history file? More data is tacked onto the end as time goes by.

- [ ] When storing text files. Today's chapter shows you several programs that read and write characters and strings using Visual C++'s sequential I/O techniques.

- [ ] When storing data in a batch processing environment, such as in some accounting departments, in which data is only modified by other transactions that are batched up and run at the close of the month.

- [ ] When the data must be read by other programs not written in Visual C++. Sequentially created files are sometimes easier to access because they usually contain delimiters such as spaces, tabs, and commas that random-access files don't always need.

Whatever access method you choose, the data file to the PC is just a stream of bytes on the disk.

Easy File I/O

> **Note:** A case could be made that all the advantages of sequential file access already exist in random files because you can access a random file sequentially, from the first data value to the last. It's true that random files can be accessed sequentially, but remember that sequential file access is often easier to write, although with Visual C++ even random access is not difficult.

A major programming distinction between sequential files and random-access files appears when you consider when each is opened and closed. Before using any disk file, or before creating a disk file, you must *open* the file to prepare it for access. After you're done with a file, you must be sure to close the file properly (you'll see that opening and closing files is really easy with Visual C++'s help). The analogy to a filing cabinet should be obvious. You can open sequential files in only one access *mode* (output, input, or append) at a time. After you open a random file, you can operate on the file in more than one mode without having to close and reopen the file a second time.

Getting Ready

Data files are objects to your Visual C++ program. Each file is assumed to be an instantiation of one of the file stream classes. Each of these classes is prototyped and defined in the file FSTREAM.H, so be sure to include this header file in all Visual C++ programs that access the disk.

You'll use one or more of the following three access classes when describing your files as objects to your programs:

```
ifstream
ofstream
fstream
```

The `ifstream` class defines input member functions and related data, `ofstream` defines output member functions and related data, and `fstream` takes care of both for files you want to both read from and write to. All the common I/O member functions you're used to, such as `get()`, `put()`, and `getline()`, work for files just as easily as they do for the screen and keyboard.

Writing Character Data to a Sequential File

Perhaps the easiest place to begin understanding file I/O is a program that creates a sequential file of characters. Listing 20.1 shows such a program that uses the put member function to write character data to a file.

Listing 20.1. Writing characters to a file.

```
 1:  // Filename: CHARSEQ.CPP
 2:  // Creates a file using sequential output of characters.
 3:  #include <fstream.h>
 4:  main()
 5:  {
 6:     // First, open the file for output
 7:     ofstream outfile("DATAOUT.DAT");
 8:
 9:     // Write individual letters to the file
10:     outfile.put('T');
11:     outfile.put('h');
12:     outfile.put('i');
13:     outfile.put('s');
14:     outfile.put(' ');
15:     outfile.put('i');
16:     outfile.put('s');
17:     outfile.put(' ');
18:     outfile.put('e');
19:     outfile.put('a');
20:     outfile.put('s');
21:     outfile.put('y');
22:     outfile.put('\n');     // Becomes two characters in file, CR-LF
23:     return 0;
24:  }
```

The output for this program doesn't appear on the screen. The output appears in the file named DATAOUT.DAT. Here are the single-line contents of DATAOUT.DAT:

```
This is easy
```

The program wrote a newline character to the end of the file, but the newline character becomes a two-byte carriage return/line feed sequence at the end of the text bringing the total byte count in the file to 14. If you want to look at the file's contents, you can

Easy File I/O

go to DOS and use the TYPE command or write a program to read and display the contents of the file as shown later in today's chapter.

Line 7 defines a file object variable named outfile. The object type is the class ofstream (for *output file stream*), and the object's name is outfile. The constructor for ofstream objects opens the file and prepares it for output, so you must supply a file name string used in the constructor. The string can be stored in a character array or stored on the heap, and it can include a complete disk and pathname if you like.

Unlike C and most other programming languages, the OOP concept eliminates the need for a file handle. When you tell the outfile object to do something, such as put some data (lines 10–22), the file takes care of itself, and you don't have to refer to a file handle or file number as you do with C.

Unlike with non-OOP file output, Visual C++ automatically closes the file when the file object variable (in this case outfile) goes out of scope. Aren't destructors nice?

> **Note:** All files opened with the ofstream class are output files and considered to be newly created. If the DATOUT.DAT file already existed when line 7 opened the file, the old version would be deleted and the new data added in its place.

Listing 20.2. Writing characters from a string.

```
 1:  // Filename: CHARSTR.CPP
 2:  // Creates a file using sequential output of a string's characters.
 3:  #include <fstream.h>
 4:  #include <string.h>
 5:  main()
 6:  {
 7:    // First, open the file for output
 8:    ofstream outfile("DATAOUT.DAT");
 9:
10:    // Define the string
11:    char out[] = "This is easy\n";  // Don't forget the newline
12:
13:    // Write the string a character at a time
14:    for (unsigned int i=0; i<strlen(out); i++)
15:      { outfile.put(out[i]); }
16:    return 0;
17:  }
```

Listing 20.2 produces the same output file, named DATAOUT.DAT, as Listing 20.1 did.

Both Listings 20.1 and 20.2 wrote single characters to a new file, although Listing 20.2 wrote the characters from a character array (line 15) instead of writing individual characters.

Now that you've seen the put() function used for sequential file output of characters, forget ever using it! The FSTREAM.H overloads the << to work with characters and strings. Consider the rewritten version of Listing 20.1 shown in Listing 20.3.

Listing 20.3. Extremely easy file output.

```
 1: // Filename: CHAROVR.CPP
 2: // Creates a file using sequential output of characters.
 3: #include <fstream.h>
 4: main()
 5: {
 6:     // First, open the file for output
 7:     ofstream outfile("DATAOUT.DAT");
 8:
 9:     // Write individual letters to the file
10:     outfile << 'T';
11:     outfile << 'h';
12:     outfile << 'i';
13:     outfile << 's';
14:     outfile << ' ';
15:     outfile << 'i';
16:     outfile << 's';
17:     outfile << ' ';
18:     outfile << 'e';
19:     outfile << 'a';
20:     outfile << 's';
21:     outfile << 'y';
22:     outfile << '\n';    // Becomes two characters in file, CR-LF
23:     return 0;
24: }
```

The output from Listing 20.3 is identical to that of the preceding two program listings.

As you can see, writing data to an OOP file with Visual C++ is just as easy as writing characters to the screen. Lines 10–22 all use the insertion operator, <<,

583

to write individual characters to the file. Line 15 in Listing 20.2, which wrote characters from a character array, would also work if you rewrote it like this:

```
{ outfile << out[i]; }
```

The FSTREAM.H file also overloads << for string output as well. Listing 20.4 writes four strings to a file named STRFILE.TXT.

Listing 20.4. Writing strings.

```
 1:  // Filename: STRFOUT.CPP
 2:  // Creates a file using sequential output of strings.
 3:  #include <fstream.h>
 4:  main()
 5:  {
 6:    // First, open the file for output
 7:    ofstream outfile("STRFILE.TXT");
 8:
 9:    // Write four strings to the file, two string
10:    // constants and two from character arrays
11:    outfile << "Don't lag behind...\n";
12:    outfile << "Get in on the scoop!\n";
13:    char ara1[] = "Learn Visual C++...\n";
14:    outfile << ara1;
15:    char ara2[] = "And get ready to OOP!\n";
16:    outfile << ara2;
17:    return 0;
18:  }
```

Here are the contents of the STRFILE.TXT created from Listing 20.4:

```
Don't lag behind...
Get in on the scoop!
Learn Visual C++...
And get ready to OOP!
```

The newline character, \n, at the end of the strings being written in lines 11 through 16 are not required, but sequential files usually include newlines at the end of their lines of data. (A line of data is called a *record*, as you might already know.) The newlines help keep the file formatted properly if someone looks at the file from the DOS prompt or if another Visual C++ program that uses getline() needs to read the file.

Note: Remember that `outfile`, shown in the preceding programs, is the name of the file object you define from the `ifstream`, `ofstream`, or `fstream` classes. There is nothing special about the name `outfile`; you can call the object variable anything you like. You can also open several files, giving them each different object variable names, and write to each one separately by using their names.

Reading Character Data from a Sequential File

When you want to read characters from a file, use the `ifstream` class (for *input file stream*) rather than `ofstream`, and use the `get()` function to read the characters. Although `>>` is overloaded for file input, you cannot use `>>` to read whitespace (such as blanks or tabs) from files, so your files incorrectly read scrunched up if you use `>>` rather than the `get()` member function.

Reading data from a file requires slightly more work than writing the data because you must check for an end-of-file condition as you read the data.

The input file object variable you create contains a non-zero value as long as there is data left to read, and it becomes zero (false) when the end of file is reached, as Listing 20.5 shows.

Listing 20.5. Reading characters from an input file.

```
1:  // Filename: CHARINP.CPP
2:  // Reads the file created earlier
3:  #include <fstream.h>
4:  // No iostream.h necessary
5:  main()
6:  {
7:     // First, open the file for input
8:     ifstream inpfile("DATAOUT.DAT");
9:
10:    // Write the next character in a loop
11:    char nextChar;
12:    while (inpfile)   // True until end-of-file
13:    {
```

continues

Day 20 Easy File I/O

Listing 20.5. continued

```
14:      inpfile.get(nextChar);  // Get next character
15:      if (inpfile)  // Assuming end of file was NOT just read
16:         { cout << nextChar; }    // Display character
17:   }
18:   return 0;
19: }
```

This is easy

Although the program writes to the screen, the IOSTREAM.H header file isn't included in the entire program! FSTREAM.H derives from IOSTREAM.H, and therefore FSTREAM.H contains all the functionality of IOSTREAM.H with extended members to handle file I/O.

The program simply reads one character at a time (line 14) and displays that character (line 16) until the end of file is reached. This program mirrors the DOS TYPE command in that it displays to the screen whatever file it reads. Of course, the file should be an ASCII text file if it is to be readable on the screen.

Notice that the `while` doesn't need to compare against 0 or 1 because in Visual C++ (as in C) these two tests are equivalent, but the second is more efficient:

```
while (infile != 0)   // True until infile is equal to 0
```

and

```
while (infile)        // True until infile is equal to 0
```

If you want to read entire strings from a sequential data file, use the `getline()` member function as Listing 20.6 demonstrates.

Listing 20.6. Reading string data from an input file.

```
1:  // Filename: STRINP.CPP
2:  // Reads the file of strings created earlier
3:  #include <fstream.h>
4:  main()
5:  {
6:     // First, open the file for input
7:     ifstream inpfile("STRFILE.TXT");
8:
9:     // Loop that writes each line of text to the screen
10:    char nextStr[80];   // Assumes no record > 80 characters
11:    while (inpfile)     // True until end-of-file
```

```
12:    {
13:       inpfile.getline(nextStr, 80);   // Get next record and display it
14:       cout << nextStr << "\n";
15:    }
16:    return 0;
17: }
```

```
Don't lag behind...
Get in on the scoop!
Learn Visual C++...
And get ready to OOP!
```

Line 13 reads a record from the input file. The newline at the end of each of the file's records terminates the `getline()` member function call but is not part of the input. Therefore, the newlines are not stored in the `nextStr[]` array. When the program is printing the strings on line 14, a newline has to be inserted at the end of the output.

What If There Are Problems?

When you are reading and writing files, errors can occur that you must check for. You might attempt to read from a file that doesn't exist, a disk drive might not be available, or the disk could have mechanical difficulty. You can use any or all of the following four member functions to check for file error conditions:

```
good()
eof()
fail()
bad()
```

Notice that you can use either the end-of-file testing method from Listing 20.6's line 11 or the `eof()` member function.

These four member functions return true or false depending on the result of the previous I/O. The first function, `good()`, is true (1) if no errors occurred. `good()` returns a false value and one or more of the other member functions return true if an error occurs.

Note: The stream's `fail()` member function checks for three types of errors: hardware failures (such as a bad disk sector or a disk door open), read/write failures (so you can use it to check the status of one of your

Easy File I/O

I/O operations), and file-not-found errors (when you attempt to open a file that doesn't exist). The bad() member function checks only for major hardware and I/O problems, not for read/write errors. You can often recover from a fail() flag, but a program should not continue if the bad() flag is set to a true (nonzero) condition.

Some diligent Visual C++ programmers test for each of these functions every time they perform input or output. Listing 20.7 shows a program that attempts to open a file on drive Z:. Assuming you don't have a drive Z: (most people don't!), you'll get the error output generated.

 Listing 20.7. Attempting to use a file on a drive that doesn't exist.

```
 1:  // Filename: STRINPER.CPP
 2:  // Reads the file of strings created earlier
 3:  #include <fstream.h>
 4:  main()
 5:  {
 6:    // First, open the file for input
 7:    ifstream inpfile("Z:STRFILE.TXT");
 8:    cout << "Result of good() is " << inpfile.good() << "\n";
 9:    cout << "Result of eof() is " << inpfile.eof() << "\n";
10:    cout << "Result of fail() is " << inpfile.fail() << "\n";
11:    cout << "Result of bad() is " << inpfile.bad() << "\n";
12:    return 0;
13:  }
```

```
Result of good() is 0
Result of eof() is 0
Result of fail() is 2
Result of bad() is 0
```

 The Z: disk drive does not exist, so the fail() member function returns a true value for its error conditions.

 Tip: You can also throw an exception when a bad I/O condition appears so that you won't have to check the I/O each time you input or output data.

Appending Data to Sequential Files

When you need to add to the end of a sequential file, such as adding to an account history file, you'll have to tell Visual C++ to open the file in *append* mode. To open in append mode, you have to specifically call the open() member function instead of letting the default file object constructor do the job. The open() function is a member function of the fstream class. open() isn't needed for the ifstream class because input access is always assumed. open() isn't needed for the ofstream class because output access is always assumed.

Here's the format of the open() member function:

`objVar.open(filenameStr, modeBit(s));`

The *objVar* must be an fstream object variable name. When defining the file object variable, don't specify the filename in parentheses (such as line 7 in Listing 20.6) or Visual C++ will open the file incorrectly. *filenameStr* is the name of the file you want to open. *modeBit(s)* is one or more of the mode bits found in Table 20.1 that describe the way you want the file opened. If you include more than one mode bit, separate them with an inclusive OR operator, |.

Table 20.1. The open() member function mode bits.

Mode Bit	Description
ios::in	Open for input
ios::out	Open for output
ios::app	Open for appending
ios::ate	Erase the file before the first input or output
ios::nocreate	Returns an error if the file does not already exist
ios::noreplace	Returns an error if the file already exists and neither ios::app nor ios::ate is set

The program in Listing 20.8 demonstrates the use of open() by opening the string file created earlier and adding another stanza to the text.

Easy File I/O

Listing 20.8. Adding to the end of a text file.

```
 1: // Filename: STRAPP.CPP
 2: // Adds to the file of strings created earlier
 3: #include <fstream.h>
 4: #include <stdlib.h>
 5: main()
 6: {
 7:   // First, define the file object variable
 8:   fstream appfile;    // Notice no filename specified here
 9:
10:   // Open the file for append
11:   appfile.open("STRFILE.TXT", ios::app | ios::nocreate);
12:
13:   if (!appfile.good())    // Quit if there's a problem
14:     { cerr << "Error opening file.\n";
15:       exit(1);
16:     }
17:   appfile << "\nIn the future...\n";
18:   appfile << "I'll make some dough.\n";
19:   appfile << "Writing programs...\n";
20:   appfile << "That make computers go!\n";
21:
22:   return 0;
23: }
```

Listing 20.7 adds four lines to the STRFILE.TXT file. Here are the contents of STRFILE.TXT after appending the extra text:

```
Don't lag behind...
Get in on the scoop!
Learn Visual C++...
And get ready to OOP!

In the future...
I'll make some dough.
Writing programs...
That make computers go!
```

> **Note:** Complaint letters about the author's poetry will not be tolerated. If you write them, your computer will immediately be hexed. Neither Longfellow nor Frost could write computer programs!

Analysis: The open() member function call on line 11 opens the STRFILE.TXT file in append mode. You'll also see that the ios::nocreate mode bit is set. If the file is not found on the disk, ios::nocreate ensures that Visual C++ sets an error condition that will trigger the early program exit on line 15. Normally, a file does not have to exist to be appended to; when appending to a file that does not exist, Visual C++ creates the file automatically unless you specify ios::nocreate and check the good() member function.

After the file is open for append, you can add characters, strings, or even class data (as shown in the next section) to the end of the file.

> **Note:** A later section will use the open() function to open a file in both input and output modes at the same time.

Class Data and Disk Files

Not all data is character data. When writing data to the disk to be read later, Visual C++ programmers need a way to write class objects to the disk and also read those objects back in. The following points must be made before you see object I/O in action:

- Unlike character I/O, objects are written to files in a compressed binary format that other programs such as the DOS TYPE command cannot properly interpret.

- To see the data in class data files, you have to write programs that read the data into classes that have the same format as the class used to write the object data in the first place.

- The class used to write the data to the file must match in number and format of data members to the class used to read the data from the file. (The member functions don't have to match.)

- The write() member function writes object data to files, and the read() member function reads object data from files. Both have to be sent a character pointer to the data, so you'll have to typecast the object data using (char *) before writing objects.

Easy File I/O

The program in Listing 20.9 is a fairly comprehensive disk output program that writes inventory parts to the disk file using member functions. The Inventory class is formed by composing an Item class as a member so that Inventory can write the data to the disk using member functions. The Inventory class takes care of itself and even writes its own data to a file.

Type

Listing 20.9. Writing objects using member functions.

```
 1: // Filename: OBSTOFIL.CPP
 2: // Defines several object variables and writes them to a file
 3: #include <fstream.h>
 4: #include <string.h>
 5: class Item {          // This class will be embedded in another
 6:   char partCode[5];
 7:   char descrip[20];
 8:   int num;
 9:   float price;
10: public:
11:   Item() {partCode[0] = '\0';}   // Null part code indicates no data
12:   Item(char P[], char D[], int N, float PR) :
13:        num(N), price(PR)
14:   { strcpy(partCode, P);
15:     strcpy(descrip, D);
16:   }
17: };
18: class Inventory {     // A composed class
19:   Item parts[50];     // This class contains all the parts
20: public:
21:   static int numInInv;  // Number of items in the inventory
22:   Inventory() {}
23:   void addToInv(char [], char [], int, float);
24:   void toDisk(void);
25: };   // Class definition ends here
26: void Inventory::addToInv(char P[], char D[], int N, float PR)
27: {
28:   parts[numInInv] = Item(P, D, N, PR);   // Temporary construction
29:   numInInv++;
30: }
31: void Inventory::toDisk(void)
32: {
33:   ofstream invOut("INV.DAT");
34:   invOut.write((char *)this, sizeof(*this));   // Write the record
35: }
36: // Static member has to be initialized here
37: int Inventory::numInInv = 0;
38: ////////////////////////////////////////////////////////////////
39: main()
40: {
```

```
41:     // Construct empty inventory items
42:     Inventory parts;
43:
44:     // Create a few specific inventory items
45:     parts.addToInv("3WI", "Widgets", 14, 2.34);
46:     parts.addToInv("1BOL", "Large Bolts", 36, .45);
47:     parts.addToInv("7WN", "Wing Nuts", 109, .17);
48:     parts.addToInv("2CL", "Clamps", 31, 8.60);
49:
50:     // Now, write the data
51:     parts.toDisk();
52:     cout << Inventory::numInInv << " parts were written.";
53:     return 0;
54: }
```

Listing 20.9 creates a data file with 50 records, the first 4 of which have valid data in compressed form.

When line 42 creates a parts object, it actually creates an array of Item members defined inside the Inventory class at line 19. Therefore, 50 inventory items are contained inside the parts object. The program fills only 4 of those items, but all 50 are written to the disk. The constructor for the embedded Item member stores a null zero in the first member's character array (line 11); whenever a part's partCode is null, the program has reached the end of the value parts data.

The addToInv() function calls on lines 45–48 store data in the first four inventory parts by calling the member function in lines 26–30. The addToInv() member function stores the data in the next inventory item and increments the static numInInv integer variable so that the number of valid parts can be printed at the end of the program in line 52.

Instead of creating the inventory parts from constants on lines 45–48, the program could have prompted the user for the data.

The toDisk() member function writes the entire array, all 50 items, to a disk file named INV.DAT. The write() function call

```
invOut.write((char *)this, sizeof(*this));   // Write the record
```

writes the *this argument, which is the object containing all 50 parts, to the disk. Any data written with write() must be typecast as a character pointer because write() works with streams of character data. read() must know the number of bytes of data to write, hence the sizeof() argument.

Easy File I/O

If you look at INV.DAT from the DOS prompt using TYPE, you'll see a lot of garbage. The data written with write() is always compressed, unlike the data written using earlier sequential file I/O methods. The program in Listing 20.10 opens the INV.DAT file and prints its contents to the screen using the same Inventory class used in Listing 20.9 (except for a few member function changes).

Listing 20.10. Reading inventory objects using member functions.

```
 1: // Filename: OBSFRFIL.CPP
 2: // Reads object variables from a file
 3: #include <fstream.h>
 4: #include <iomanip.h>
 5: #include <stdlib.h>
 6: #include <string.h>
 7: class Item {          // This class will be embedded in another
 8: public:
 9:   char partCode[5];
10:   char descrip[20];
11:   int num;
12:   float price;
13:   Item() {partCode[0] = '\0';}  // Null part code indicates no data
14:   Item(char P[], char D[], int N, float PR) :
15:       num(N), price(PR)
16:   { strcpy(partCode, P);
17:     strcpy(descrip, D);
18:   }
19: };
20: class Inventory {    // A composed class
21:   Item parts[50];    // This class contains all the parts
22: public:
23:   static int numInInv;  // Number of items in the inventory
24:   Inventory() {}
25:   void prData(void);
26:   void fromDisk(void);
27: };  // Class definition ends here
28: void Inventory::prData(void)
29: {
30:   int ctr=0;
31:   cout << setprecision(2) << setiosflags(ios::showpoint);
32:   cout << setiosflags(ios::fixed);
33:   cout << "Here is the inventory:\n";
34:   while (parts[ctr].partCode[0])   // Print until empty part code
35:     { cout << "Part number: " << parts[ctr].partCode << "\n";
36:       cout << "Description: " << parts[ctr].descrip << "\n";
37:       cout << "Number in stock: " << parts[ctr].num << "\n";
38:       cout << "Price: $" << parts[ctr].price << "\n\n";
39:       ctr++;
40:     }
```

```
41: }
42: void Inventory::fromDisk(void)
43: {
44:    ifstream invIn("INV.DAT");
45:    if (!invIn)
46:       { cerr << "File doesn't exist!\n";
47:         exit(1);
48:       }
49:    invIn.read((char *)this, sizeof(*this));   // Write the record
50: }
51: // Static member has to be initialized here
52: int Inventory::numInInv = 0;      // Not used but part of class
53: /////////////////////////////////////////////////////////////////
54: main()
55: {
56:    // Construct empty inventory items
57:    Inventory parts;
58:    // Read the data from the disk
59:    parts.fromDisk();
60:    parts.prData();
61:    return 0;
62: }
```

```
Here is the inventory:
Part number: 3WI
Description: Widgets
Number in stock: 14
Price: $2.34

Part number: 1BOL
Description: Large Bolts
Number in stock: 36
Price: $0.45

Part number: 7WN
Description: Wing Nuts
Number in stock: 109
Price: $0.17

Part number: 2CL
Description: Clamps
Number in stock: 31
Price: $8.60
```

The parts object defined on line 57 contains the same format as that in the preceding listing. All 50 items are stored in the one parts object, and the program reads from a disk file into these 50 items. (Only 4 of the 50 objects in the disk file contain data, but all 50 will be read into the parts object on line 49.)

Easy File I/O

The `fromDisk()` member function on lines 42–50 reads all 50 objects from the disk using a mirror-image function to Listing 20.9's `write()` member function. The power of Visual C++ classes provides extremely complicated input of all object data from the file using only a single line of code (line 49).

The `prData()` member function on lines 28–40 prints the data on the screen. The data on the disk contains a null string for the `partCode[]` for the 46 objects that aren't yet defined in the disk file.

> **Note:** Writing and reading 50 object values when only 4 contain data is inefficient but easy to follow. The program shown in next section reads the inventory records one at a time until the end of data is reached.

DO / DON'T

DO use `put()` and `<<` to write character data to sequential text files.

DO use `get()`, `getline()`, and `>>` to read data from sequential text files.

DO use the `read()` and `write()` member functions to read and write class data.

DO use the `open()` member function to access data files when performing more than simple input or output (such as appending).

DON'T forget to check for errors when accessing files. Disk drives are mechanical, and problems can occur. If your program doesn't check for errors but an error occurs, you'll receive bad results.

Random-Access Files

You've already got most of the pieces needed to write programs that manipulate random-access files. Remember that you can read and write a random-access file from within the same program. There is nothing that physically separates a random-access file from a sequential file. The difference lies in the way you access and open the files. You can access random files in the same way you access arrays—in any order you prefer.

Use the bit modes in Table 20.1 to indicate that you want to both read and write from the file. Here is a sample `open()` member function call that prepares a file named MYFILE.DAT for both input and output:

```
rndfile.open("MYFILE.DAT", ios::in | ios::out);
```

To access a random-access file randomly (that is, in any order: forward, backward, every other record, or whatever), you must learn to manipulate the *file pointer*. File pointers are to random-access files what subscripts are to arrays. The file pointer always points to the next location in the file that you can access.

Use the `seekg()` member function to move the file pointer (which has little resemblance to regular variable pointers you use in Visual C++ source code). `seekg()` is similar to C's `fseek()` function. The `seekg()` function requires an offset and a starting position in the file. Here is the format of the `seekg()` member function:

```
seekg(offset, startFileLoc)
```

The *offset* is a signed long integer value (it can be negative) that tells how many bytes you want to access from the *startFileLoc*. The *startFileLoc* can be one of these three positions:

```
ios::beg
ios::cur
ios::end
```

The `ios::beg` references the beginning byte in a file. `ios::cur` references the current location of the file pointer (the file pointer changes during reading and writing). And `ios::end` references the ending byte in the file.

Suppose that `rndFile` were a random-access file pointer connected to a file using the `open()` member function call shown earlier. The following statements move the file pointer around the file as described by their comments:

```
rndFile.seekg(0, ios::beg);     // Move pointer to start of file
rndFile.seekg(0, ios::end);     // Move pointer to end of file
rndFile.seekg(25, ios::beg);    // Move 25 bytes past the start
rndFile.seekg(-5, ios::cur);    // Move 5 bytes before current position
rndFile.seekg(-val, ios::end);  // Move to "val" bytes from end of file
```

The program in Listing 20.11 reads the inventory file created earlier one record at a time randomly. Instead of using the `Inventory` class that holds 50 records, the program uses an individual inventory object that holds each record as it is read. The class is kept public so that encapsulation doesn't get in the way of your understanding of the `seekg()` function.

Easy File I/O

Listing 20.11. Reading different inventory items randomly.

```
 1: // Filename: RNDFILE.CPP
 2: // Reads object randomly from a file
 3: #include <fstream.h>
 4: class Item {
 5: public:    // Just to keep simple
 6:   char partCode[5];
 7:   char descrip[20];
 8:   int num;
 9:   float price;
10:   void prData(int I)
11:     { cout << "Record number " << I << ":\n";
12:       cout << "Part: " << partCode;
13:       cout << "\nDescription: " << descrip;
14:       cout << "\nNumber: " << num;
15:       cout << "\nPrice: " << price << "\n\n";
16:     }
17: };
18: //////////////////////////////////////////////////////////////////
19: main()
20: {
21:   fstream ioFile;
22:   Item invItem;
23:   ioFile.open("INV.DAT", ios::in | ios::out);
24:   ioFile.seekg(0, ios::beg);
25:   ioFile.read((char *)&invItem, sizeof(invItem));
26:   invItem.prData(1);
27:   // Put the position back to the beginning
28:   ioFile.seekg(0, ios::beg);
29:   ioFile.read((char *)&invItem, sizeof(invItem));
30:   invItem.prData(1);
31:   // Read last record
32:   ioFile.seekg(3*sizeof(invItem), ios::beg);
33:   ioFile.read((char *)&invItem, sizeof(invItem));
34:   invItem.prData(4);
35:   // Read in order
36:   ioFile.seekg(0, ios::beg);
37:   ioFile.read((char *)&invItem, sizeof(invItem));
38:   // Another seekg() isn't needed if reading in order
39:   invItem.prData(1);
40:   ioFile.read((char *)&invItem, sizeof(invItem));
41:   invItem.prData(2);
42:   ioFile.read((char *)&invItem, sizeof(invItem));
43:   invItem.prData(3);
44:   ioFile.read((char *)&invItem, sizeof(invItem));
45:   invItem.prData(4);
46:   return 0;
47: }
```

Output

```
Record number 1:
Part: 3WI
Description: Widgets
Number: 14
Price: 2.34

Record number 1:
Part: 3WI
Description: Widgets
Number: 14
Price: 2.34

Record number 4:
Part: 2CL
Description: Clamps
Number: 31
Price: 8.6

Record number 1:
Part: 3WI
Description: Widgets
Number: 14
Price: 2.34

Record number 2:
Part: 1BOL
Description: Large Bolts
Number: 36
Price: 0.45

Record number 3:
Part: 7WN
Description: Wing Nuts
Number: 109
Price: 0.17

Record number 4:
Part: 2CL
Description: Clamps
Number: 31
Price: 8.6
```

Analysis After the record object is constructed on line 22, the file is opened randomly on line 23. Throughout the rest of main(), the seekg() function moves through the file, forward and backward, printing records using the public member function prData(). The seekg() function call on line 32 positions the file pointer to the beginning of the fourth record by skipping the first three records; the size of each record is determined with sizeof().

Easy File I/O

Note: Notice that you can reread the same record when using `seekg()`. You can never reread the same record when using simple sequential I/O.

If you want to change data inside a random-access file, you can do so. After `seekg()` moves the pointer to the record you want to change, rewrite new data in its place with the `write()` member function. The second exercise at the end of this chapter requires that you change records randomly, and the answer in Appendix D shows you how to write the program if you need help.

DO	DON'T

DO open files with the `ios::in` and the `ios::out` mode bits set if you want to access the file randomly.

DO use `seekg()` to reposition the file pointer to whatever record you want.

DON'T attempt to reread the same data in sequential files unless you open the files with the `open()` member function using the `ios::in` and `ios::out` mode bits.

Summary

Today's chapter completes your schooling in Visual C++. Congratulations. After mastering today's concepts, you'll receive an A+ in C++!

Today, you learned how to write sequential data to files and read it back in. You'll want to write character data to disk files when other non–Visual C++ programs must work with the data. From DOS, you can use the TYPE command to look at the contents of sequential files.

When reading and writing sequential files, you cannot move around the file reading whatever records you prefer. However, you can read and write data extremely easily using the >> and << overloaded operators and the `put()`, `get()`, and `getline()` member functions.

You can write an entire array of objects using the `write()` member function and read an entire array of objects using a corresponding `read()` member function.

If you want to tackle the bonus section of this book, you'll find a unique approach offered by Visual C++ to write object data to files in the second bonus chapter.

Q&A

Q. Why should I learn disk I/O?

A. No computer ever has enough internal RAM memory to hold all the data needed. The disk drive not only holds more data than memory but provides long-term storage because the disk files don't get erased when you turn off the computer.

Q. What is the difference between sequential file I/O and random file I/O?

A. Sequential file access writes data to a file sequentially, with the first record following the next, and you cannot reread a record or change individual records without using random access. You can only write data, read data, and append data when using sequential files.

Random access enables you to skip around in a file, from byte to byte or record to record, reading and writing data wherever you want.

Q. Do I have to learn a lot of new functions to perform file I/O?

A. When writing character data, you can write data directly to a disk file using the familiar << overloaded operator. You can also use `get()` and `put()` for file objects just as you do for keyboard and screen data. You must also explicitly call the `open()` member function when appending sequential data.

The random-access routines require that you learn three new functions: `seekg()`, `read()`, and `write()`. These three functions are analogous to `fseek()`, `fread()`, and `fwrite()` if you've ever written C programs that performed random-access I/O. `seekg()` positions the file pointer to any location in the file so that `read()` and `write()` can access the data at that location.

Workshop

The Workshop offers quiz questions and exercises to hone your skills and give you feedback on today's lesson. You'll find some proposed answers in Appendix D.

Easy File I/O

Quiz

1. What are the three stream classes used with file I/O?
2. What are the only three things you can do to a sequential file?
3. Which is best for text files: sequential access or random access?
4. Why don't you have to include IOSTREAM.H when writing screen output in the same program in which you're performing file I/O?
5. Why must you sometimes use open() and sometimes not?
6. What mode bit must you use in the open() member function when adding data to a file?
7. Why don't you have to use open() for ifstream or ofstream class objects?
8. What physical differences are there between a sequential file and a random-access file?

Exercises

1. Combine Listings 20.9 and 20.10, adding a menu with the following selections:

   ```
   Here are your choices:

   1. Add an inventory item to the file
   2. Display items in the file
   3. Exit the program
   ```

   What do you want to do?

   So that the user can enter the data, write prompts instead of writing constant values as done in Listing 20.9.

2. Add to the end of the program in Listing 20.11 the following routines:
   A. Position the file pointer back to the beginning of the file.
   B. Zero out each record's price, and write the data back to the disk.
   C. Run your program a second time to make sure the data was zeroed in the file.

DAY 21

The Visual C++ Tools

The Visual C++ Tools

You are now at a crossroads. You have mastered virtually everything there is to master in OOP. Yet you are still new at the Visual C++ language, and you lack a lot of experience in object-oriented programming. Nothing will lock in your OOP skills better than beginning to program in OOP right away. The very next "quick and dirty" 10-line program you write should be OOP-like and not in C's old procedural style.

As you know or have probably guessed, there is a *lot* to Visual C++, and you've only now scratched the surface! Converting your thinking into an OOP programmer means that you've now opened the Visual C++ power toolbox, but there's a lot of untapped power still left in the box.

This book is coming to an end. As you've seen, there is an Extra Credit Bonus section to encourage you to take the next step at mastering Visual C++. The primary goal of this book, OOP, has been met, and you are now ready to see what else Visual C++ has to offer. Today's chapter gives you a glimpse into Visual C++'s add-on tools, including the new tools available with version 1.5.

Today, you learn about the following topics:

- ☐ What it takes to move from a novice to an expert Windows programmer
- ☐ How Visual C++ can improve your Windows programming productivity
- ☐ How to use some advanced features of the Visual Workbench editor
- ☐ How to use the interactive debugger
- ☐ The advantages of using these helpful Visual Workbench tools: AppWizard, ClassWizard, App Studio, and the browser
- ☐ The additions that version 1.5 of Visual C++ provide

The Evolution of Today's Programmer

Newcomers to programming have it tough today. The steps needed to move from novice to Visual C++ expert are many. Luckily (and because of your hard work), you've passed the most tedious stages required of programming. Whatever you learn now will strengthen your skills. You're ready to learn all about the tools available in your Visual C++ programming future.

Before looking at the tools, take a moment to think about where you've been as a programmer and where you are headed with Visual C++. Without some forethought,

Visual C++ seems like a giant and difficult programming system. Well, actually *after* some forethought, Visual C++ still seems giant and difficult! It is difficult to master every aspect of Visual C++, and although you've mastered the most important language parts already, you have some distance to go. The distance, however, is rewarding and a lot of fun.

Here are the standard stages most people go through to wear the hat of "Advanced Visual C++ Programmer":

1. Computer application user—and it's best if those applications are Microsoft Windows-based.

2. Advanced user, skilled in applications and much of the operating system commands, and a skilled Windows user.

3. Introductory programmer, learning how to write programs in a beginner's language such as QBasic or Visual Basic.

4. Learner of an advanced and more efficient language, specifically C.

5. Object-oriented programmer with C++. (You've just completed this step; you're well on your way!)

6. C-based Microsoft Windows programmer.

7. Microsoft Windows programmer using an *application framework*. An application framework speeds the development of Windows programs and cuts programming and debugging time considerably. The Microsoft Foundation Classes (MFC) supply such a framework. (More often than not, a Windows program is referred to by programmers as an *application* because of the suite of individual program files and support files that must be combined to form the final Windows product that behaves like a single program in memory.)

Note: Some people can tackle many of these steps quickly. For instance, some people (the ones with *excellent* tutorial books...) are able to learn C++ in 21 days!

The sixth step might cause you some confusion. After all, you might feel as if you're moving backward. You might be surprised to learn that even today, a lot of Windows programming is done in C, even by those proficient in C++ programming. Windows was originally designed to be programmed in C, and the Windows API

The Visual C++ Tools

(Application Programming Interface) function calls were all designed to be callable from C programs. Most Windows programmers "cut their teeth" in C-based Windows programming.

There is some argument as to the validity and need of this sixth step. It's true that a Visual C++ programmer does not have to learn the "old way" of Windows programming. C-based Windows programming is indeed more tedious and time-consuming than Visual C++–based Windows programming using the MFC classes. The MFC Windows classes are complete, and after you master them, you'll never go back to programming Windows in C.

It's the thought of this author and a lot of others in the industry that you learn to program in C-based Windows first for the same reason we learn multiplication tables and then use a spreadsheet and calculator the rest of our lives. The insight you gain by programming in the Windows API is worth the effort later. Even though you'll quickly move to MFC, you'll always know more about what's going on underneath your program. In addition, with MFC power comes some lack of freedom; that is, the MFC classes provide an added buffer between you and the lower-level API programming, but MFC also takes away a little flexibility. Even the most experienced Visual C++ MFC Windows programmer uses some of the C-based API function calls at times.

Warning: Don't be fooled into thinking that Windows programming is simple. Windows programming, whether or not you have Visual C++, is *hard*. Others might soft-sell you into this myth, but this book will not.

Visual C++ makes the "old way" of programming in Windows obsolete. Nevertheless, you will be a better Windows/Visual C++ programmer if you take some time after you've finished this book to read a good book on programming Windows in C. If you like the style of this book, you'll want to read *Teach Yourself Windows Programming in 21 Days*. It might seem like a step backward to read a C book, but Windows was originally designed to support C-based Windows programs. You won't have to master each detail in the book, but try to get a good foundation in the needs and advantages of the Windows API.

Don't fret about the C-based Windows introduction. Again, you don't have to become an expert in it. Also, there's nothing to keep you from learning both MFC-based Windows programming skills *and* the lower-level API skills at the same time.

You'll see in the bonus section at the end of this book that you can quickly grasp the MFC-based classes and write advanced Windows programs without a lot of knowledge of the underlying Windows API.

The reason the MFC classes provide such an advantage over the C-based Windows API functions is that a lot of the tedious requirements of the API are now encapsulated into C++ classes. In addition, the MFC classes offer lots of additional non-Windows-based advantages (described in the bonus section at the end of the book), such as a powerful string class, exception macros, and improved file I/O methods.

Don't Want to Program in Windows?

If you are still fighting the trend toward Windows programs, you are not alone. Lots of people still prefer to work in a DOS-based environment for many reasons. Their hardware might not yet support an efficient Windows-based system. As you've no doubt noticed, Visual C++ compiles can be slow, and adding the MFC classes to the compiles adds even more burden and time to compiling and linking. Most of the time, people just don't want to change from the way they now use and program computers. Remember that computers are the epitome of change because of the technological advancements being made. Computer speeds double every two years, and memory capacities quadruple every three.

The more powerful that computers get, the more ingenious we must be in using them. Today's multitasking, multiprocessing, and multi-user computers require more than a textual DOS-based environment. A GUI (graphical user interface) environment such as Windows will eventually improve the way everybody works with computers, although programmers in many circles still greatly resist moving toward a GUI. If you have Visual C++, you use Windows in some capacity or you couldn't run Visual C++. The more you use Windows while programming in Visual C++, hopefully, the more benefit from Windows you'll realize.

It is solely because so many products are now available for Windows and because there is a tremendous demand for Windows products that you should make the move from text-based DOS programming to Windows *as soon as possible*. The Windows-programming learning curve is steep. The sooner you tackle it, the sooner you'll be a productive and in demand Windows programmer writing the programs that will be in use in the next several years.

Day 21: The Visual C++ Tools

DO	DON'T

DO feel good about the skills you now have; you've come a long way from a novice programmer to an OOP Visual C++ programmer.

DON'T rest on your previous accomplishments! There is a long, albeit fun, way to go toward mastering the tools available in Visual C++ including the MFC classes.

Exploring the Rest of Visual C++

The rest of the chapter introduces you to the tools that come with Visual C++. It would take a book much thicker than this one to teach you all the ins and outs of the tools. Rather than a tutorial, you'll find this discussion a glimpse of things to come as you move toward mastering Visual C++.

Note: It is improbable that you can fully understand the need for a lot of the tools described here until you do begin to tackle Windows programming. Nevertheless, read through the discussion here, and you'll know what is at your disposal when you begin your foray into Windows programming.

The Visual Workbench Editor

You've already become familiar with the first tool described here. The Visual Workbench includes the powerful Windows-based editor you've used for entering all your programs in the book. This book first concentrated on achieving its goal of teaching OOP. You have to know little more than how to type, change, and save a program to learn OOP with Visual C++. There are lots of advanced editing features available within the Visual Workbench that you might want to know about now. This section describes several of those features and whets your appetite for some of the more esoteric editing characteristics of the Visual Workbench.

Before looking into the advanced capabilities of the Visual Workbench editor, keep in mind that the Visual Workbench is not just an editor. The Visual Workbench is the launchpad of the entire suite of programming tools that come with Visual C++, and it is from the Visual Workbench that you access all the other tools of Visual C++.

The Toolbar

Figure 21.1 describes the push-button tools on the toolbar at the top of the Visual Workbench screen. Not all the tools are directly related to editing programs. Some are for compiling and debugging programs. If a tool is grayed out, it is not currently available. For example, the QuickWatch tool button is available only during a debugging session.

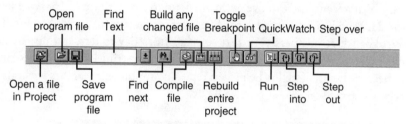

Figure 21.1. The Visual Workbench toolbar.

Tip: If you want more editing room, you can hide the toolbar from view. All the toolbar commands are available from the pull-down menus. To hide the toolbar, select View Toolbar. If you want the toolbar back, select View Toolbar again.

The first tool from the left helps you work within project files. As you might recall from Day 14's chapter, "Loose Ends: *static* and Larger Programs," a project is a collection of files that work together to build a complete application, including class headers, prototype header files, and so on. When you open a project, such as the BEV.MAK project described on Day 14, the first tool gives you convenient access to the individual files within that project.

For example, if you open a project file that contains four source files, two programs and two header files, you'll see a list of those project source and header files when you click the first button. You then can scroll and select which file you want to edit next

The Visual C++ Tools

from the list. (Only project files available for source editing will appear in the drop-down list. If your project contains precompiled object files, you won't see their names in the list.)

If you want only to open a single program without opening a project first, you can click the second tool, the Open Program File tool. This tool mimics the **F**ile **O**pen command from the menus. To save the current editor's program, click the third tool. The tool's diskette icon helps you remember that the tool saves files to the disk.

Unlike many other editors, the Visual Workbench remembers your previous text searches. You have no doubt used the **E**dit **F**ind (Alt+F3) command to search for text in your source files. Every time you search for text, the Visual Workbench adds that text to its find list. You can then click the arrow on the toolbar's Find Text box to see a list of all recent finds you've performed, up to a maximum of 16. For example, Figure 21.2 shows a find list with the five most recent text strings looked for. The Visual Workbench remembers your text searches from day to day, not just in the current editing session. Therefore, if you searched for a text string last week, the string will still appear in the list. The list helps you repeat common text searches without having to type the same search text repeatedly.

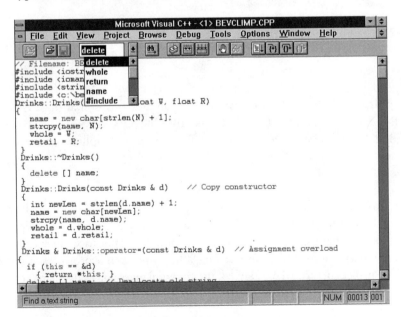

Figure 21.2. Looking at a list of previous text searches.

To find text using the drop-down list, simply follow these steps:

1. Click the down arrow next to the find list to display a list of search choices.
2. Select the text you want to find, or type in new text to find.
3. Press Enter, and the Visual Workbench finds the first occurrence of the text.

The Find Next tool repeats the last find. Therefore, if the first occurrence of the search text is not the occurrence you want, keep clicking the Find Next tool to find subsequent occurrences of the search text.

Tip: If you want to search backward in the file, hold the Shift key while performing the search.

The next three tools help you build your files. You might have been using some of these already. Day 1's chapter, "The C++ Phenomenon," briefly described the build tools. The three build tools are explained here:

> The Compile File compiles only the file you are currently editing. No linking takes place.
>
> The Build Any Changed File builds (compiles and links) only those files in your current project that have changed since the most recent build.
>
> The Rebuild Entire Project tool rebuilds all the files in your project, even those that are up-to-date and haven't changed since the most recent build.

Warning: You must have a mouse to access the tools on the toolbar. You probably have a mouse or you couldn't use Windows to its fullest extent. However, if you are still uncomfortable with the mouse, you can use the keyboard to access all the toolbar's features through the pull-down menus.

Later in this chapter, you will learn about the remaining tools on the toolbar.

The Status Bar

The status bar appears at the bottom of the screen. Figure 21.3 shows a sample status bar. The status bar details provide helpful information about the current state (the status) of your editing session.

Day 21: The Visual C++ Tools

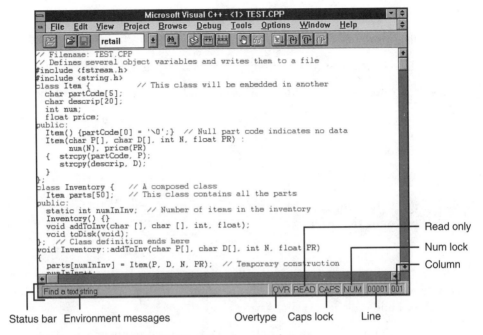

Figure 21.3. The Visual Workbench status bar.

> **Note:** Not all the status line's boxes are active at all times. At any one time, you might see only two or three of the status line boxes filled with text.

The environment messages appear throughout your editing, compiling, linking, and debugging sessions. The messages are often helpful, and sometimes Visual C++ programmers forget to look at the status line when something appears out of the ordinary. Often, Visual C++ supplies descriptive advice on the operation you are performing at the time.

Perhaps the most useful and under-utilized purpose of the environment message is to give you a quick clue as to the meaning of a tool. For example, suppose that you forget whether the tool with the diskette icon reads or saves files. If you move the mouse cursor over the diskette tool and hold down the left button (don't release it), you'll see this message appear in the environment message section of the status bar:

```
Save the active file
```

If you do indeed want to save the active file, release the left mouse button, and Visual C++ carries out the tool's purpose. If, however, you don't want to save at that time, move the mouse cursor *away* from the button before releasing it. Visual C++ then does not carry out the tool's action.

The remaining status bar items are indicators of different states of your editor, keyboard, and edited file. Here is a brief description of each of the six remaining status bar indicators:

Overtype: Shows the status of the Insert key. If OVR appears, the Visual Workbench editor is in overtype mode (typing replaces characters underneath). If OVR does not appear, the editor is in insert mode (typing pushes characters over to the right).

Read only: Describes the file attribute of the active file being viewed in the editor. If the file is a read-only file, you can look at the file but not change its contents. If you attempt to edit a file and cannot do so (the Visual Workbench keeps beeping at you as you try to type or change text), look at the status bar to see whether the file is read only. (You can turn the read-only file attribute on and off from the **E**dit Read **O**nly menu option.)

Caps lock: The Caps lock indicator tells you whether the Caps Lock key is active (all capitals will appear as you type) or not (Shift is first required before capital letters appear). The Caps Lock key toggles this status bar message on and off.

Num lock: The Num lock indicator tells whether the numeric keypad is active or whether the arrows on the keypad are active. The Num Lock key toggles this status bar message on and off.

Line: Tells the line number in the file that the text cursor (called the *caret* or *insertion point* in Windows terminology) resides on.

Column: Tells the column number that the caret resides on. If you select a nonproportional font (using **O**ptions **F**ont...), the column number indicates the character position on whatever line the caret resides on. With proportional text, not all text on all lines align with the surrounding lines because some letters such as *I* take a smaller column width than larger letters such as *M*. It is recommended that you use a nonproportional font such as Courier or Courier New so that every character in the editor consumes exactly the same column space. If you use a nonproportional font, column 13, for instance, is the same screen column for every line in the program, which makes for easier editing.

The Visual C++ Tools

Tip: As with the toolbar, you can hide the status line and get an additional line for editing. Select View Status Bar to turn the status line on or off.

Multiple Files and Windows

The Visual Workbench provides *MDI* (*Multiple Document Interface*) capabilities. MDI is a Microsoft Windows term that simply means that a Windows program allows for more than one open file at once. For example, you can open a source file named MYFILE.CPP and then open a second file named YOURFILE.CPP without first closing MYFILE.CPP. Only one of the two open files is *active* at any one time—meaning that you can edit only one at a time. But the MDI gives you lots of capabilities that would be tedious without MDI, such as easy cutting and pasting from one program to the other.

The following shortcut keys (some are also available from the **W**indows pull-down menu) help you navigate between multiple documents that you have open:

    F6: Switch to the next window.

    Ctrl+F6: Switch to the next document's window.

    Shift+Ctrl+F6: Switch to the previous document's window.

    Shift+F6: Switch to the previous window.

    Ctrl+Tab: Switch to the previously active window.

    Ctrl+F4: Close the active window.

    Alt+#: Each open window is assigned a window number. The window number is displayed within angled brackets in the title bar of each open window before the window's description or document filename (such as `<1>MYFILE.CPP` or `<5>Output`). You can activate any open window (display it so that you can view it or work within it) if you know the window's number by pressing the Alt key followed by the window number (such as Alt+1 or Alt+5).

Note: Notice the subtle difference between the F6-related keystrokes. Some keystrokes switch between document windows only (such as Ctrl+F6), and some switch to whatever the next open window is, whether that window is a document window, an editing window, a debugging window, a compilation message window, or an output window.

The navigation between MDI documents is streamlined greatly by the windowing support available in the Visual Workbench. There are several ways to arrange your open document windows, and you'll have to find the method that works best for you. Some programmers want only one editing window showing at a time, and they use Alt+# or F6 to move from window to window. Sometimes, especially when you're cutting and pasting between windows, it helps to display both windows at the same time. Here are the two ways you can display multiple open windows within the Visual Workbench:

Cascaded windows: All open windows overlap each other on-screen as shown in Figure 21.4. By cascading open windows, you can see the title bar (and therefore, the window number) of all open windows.

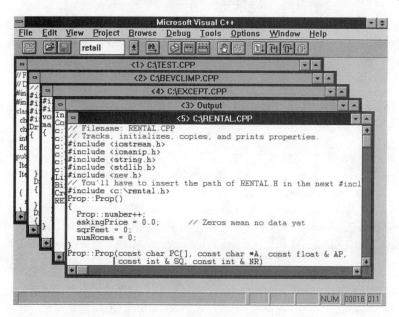

Figure 21.4. Viewing cascaded windows.

Tiled windows: Resizes all open windows so that you can see each of them without any overlap, as shown in Figure 21.5. Many Visual C++ programmers feel that tiled windows don't display enough window "real estate" at any one time to be very useful. It is true that if you open more than two or three windows at once, the tiled approach produces small windows. Hiding the toolbar and status bar gives you more window room if you can do without the toolbar and status bar—but most programmers cannot do without them.

The Visual C++ Tools

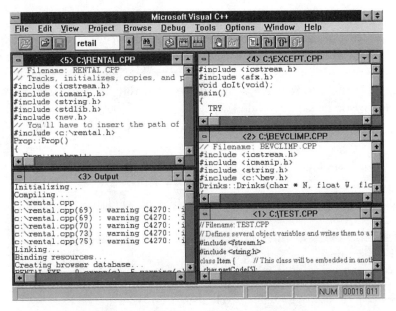

Figure 21.5. The Visual Workbench tiled windows.

> **Tip:** You can use any of the Visual Workbench tools, including the debugger and browser (described later in this chapter), within an open window. Sometimes it helps to open the output in one window, the source code in another, and the debugger in a third, and switch back and forth between them or tile them so that they appear on the screen all at once.

If you like, you can even minimize an open document's window so that it's out of the way but easily available using common Windows keystrokes. Simply click the open window's control button in the window's upper-left corner and select **M**inimize, or click the window's minimize button (the down arrow) in the window's upper-right corner. Figure 21.6 shows a Visual C++ session with three tiled windows and two minimized windows. The minimized windows are out of the way until you need them. To activate them, simply double-click the mouse cursor on one of the minimized icons.

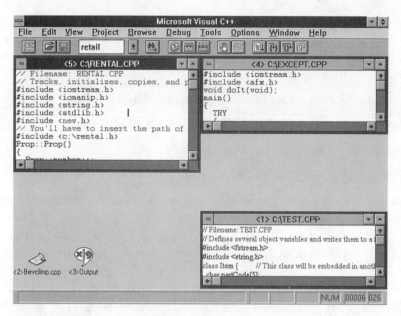

Figure 21.6. The Visual Workbench with both minimized and tiled windows.

DO / DON'T

DO learn the toolbar commands to speed your program editing.

DO display cascade and tile windows when you edit with multiple windows. They both have advantages and disadvantages; you'll want to see which kind works best with your editing sessions.

DON'T ignore the keyboard shortcut keys for the toolbar buttons. If you master the keyboard shortcut keys as well as the tools, you'll be able to select your tools from either source. If you're busy typing, you'll find that the shortcut keys are faster than the toolbar, and if your hand is on the mouse when you need a tool, you'll find that a mouse click is fastest.

A Look at Visual C++'s Debuggers

When you compile a Visual C++ program, you have the option, through the **P**roject **O**ptions menu, to compile the program with debugging information included in the compiled program. You'll want to compile with debugging information while you

The Visual C++ Tools

develop your application. To turn on the debugging information, select **O**ptions **P**roject **D**ebug. After you get the application the way you want it, rebuild the application without the debugging information included. The resulting application will be smaller and more efficient.

There are actually several ways to debug programs with Visual C++:

Debug using the menu-driven Visual Workbench debugger.

Debug using CodeView for Windows.

Debug using CodeView for DOS.

The first option is the easiest, and most newcomers to Visual C++ feel that the menu-driven debugger is superb. If you want a more conventional debugger (and one that is more difficult to master), use CodeView. This section describes how you can use the menu-driven debugger to help find problems in your C++ programs.

Warning: You must have the Professional Edition of Visual C++ to use the CodeView for Windows and DOS. If you use Visual C++ for DOS-based programs or use the *p-code compiler* option, which compiles your program into more portable but slightly less efficient code, then you must use CodeView to debug within those systems.

Stepping Through the Execution

Although there's not room here to give you an in-depth debugging tutorial, you might be surprised to see some of the power that the debugger gives you during your application's creation. Perhaps the most important feature of the debugger is its capability to enable you to step through your program's code, a line at a time, while your program executes.

The Step Into toolbar button (the third button from the right) enables you to step through your program a line at a time. The Step Into button mimics the **D**ebug Step **I**nto (F8) menu option. Step Into requests that Visual C++ run your program one line at a time. As your program runs, the Visual Workbench highlights each source code line executing at the time. As long as you continue clicking the Step Into button, Visual C++ steps through the program. Often, you'll see from the single-step execution that an `if` relational test is true when you expected it to be false, or you'll see that a certain loop executes more times than it should (or not as many times as it should). At any point during the single-stepping through the program, you can view the output window by switching to it.

Warning: Sometimes the debugger displays lines of code that you didn't type. You must remember that C++ encapsulates lots of features, including I/O classes, and when you use an I/O manipulator or perform other I/O, Visual C++ steps the execution through the internal operation's source code. Eventually, control returns to your program where you can continue single-stepping through your own code again.

If, during debugging, you reach a function call, if you continue clicking the Step Into tool (the third tool from the right), Visual C++ single-steps into the function. If you instead click the Step Over button (or select **D**ebug Step **O**ver [F10]), Visual C++ performs the function call but doesn't step through the function. Finally, click the Step Out button (the rightmost tool) if you enter a function and decide that you don't want to single-step through the rest of that function call. You can step out of internal functions that are executing as well such as I/O manipulators. The Step Out feature is also available from the **D**ebug Step Ou**t** (Shift+F7) menu option.

Although no toolbar button for this feature exists, the Debug Step to **C**ursor (F7) menu option enables you to request execution of the current program down to the line of source code where you've placed the text cursor. Even if you were single-stepping before pressing F7, the Step to **C**ursor option ceases single-step execution until the program control reaches the cursor's position. In a way, stepping to the cursor's position is similar to setting a single breakpoint, as you'll learn about in the next section.

Setting Breakpoints

Often, you will not want to single-step through your entire program. You will instead want to quickly execute down to a questionable area of code and single-step from that point, either for the remainder of the program or for at least a few lines of code. If you want control to execute normally until a specific statement in the program is reached, set a *breakpoint* at that statement. A breakpoint halts regular program execution and puts the program into single-step mode, in which you can use the toolbar buttons to continue execution as you see fit. As with all debugging features, you must ensure that you compiled the program using the debug option before you can set breakpoints.

To set a breakpoint, move the cursor to the line that you want to serve as the execution breakpoint, and click the Toggle Breakpoint button (the tool with the hand). The reason setting a breakpoint is called *toggling* the breakpoint is that you can turn the breakpoint on and off by clicking the Toggle Breakpoint tool after placing the text

The Visual C++ Tools

cursor over the line in question. The Visual Workbench highlights the source code line to indicate that the breakpoint is active at that line. You can run the program, and the Visual Workbench enters single-step mode at the breakpoint.

Tip: You can set multiple breakpoints within the same program.

Advanced Breakpoint Control

When execution reaches a breakpoint, many options are available to you. The Window pull-down menu shows a series of four kinds of windows, Watch, Locals, Output, and Registers. As you click each of these menu options, you'll see each kind of debugging aid.

In the watch window, you can look at values of variables and expressions at the point of the current execution. Switch to the watch window and type whatever variables are active (within scope) at the line about to execute. Use the watch window as a calculator or to display values of variables as your program executes.

The locals window displays all values of all local variables within the currently executing function. If the function contains aggregate variables, such as classes or structures, the local window displays ellipses (...) in place of the data.

The registers window displays the value of the computer's registers at the time of the breakpoint. The flag register bits are displayed using mnemonics. If you are unfamiliar with registers, you might want to consult an assembly language book for a review of your computer's internal architecture.

Finally, the output window's name is a little misleading. Your program's output is not shown in the window, but the build messages that appear when you compile and link a program are shown. Figure 21.7 shows a screen showing three of the debugging windows, along with the source code window. As you can see, the window can get a little busy. Instead of displaying all these windows at once, you typically display a couple of windows at a time, depending on the answer you're looking for.

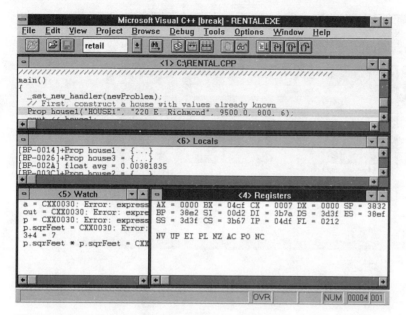

Figure 21.7. Viewing the debugging windows.

After you get comfortable with on-line breakpoint and single-step editing as described here, you'll want to explore the more advanced **D**ebug **B**reakpoints... (Ctrl+B) window. When you select the **D**ebug **B**reakpoints... menu option, you'll see a Breakpoints dialog box like the one shown in Figure 21.8.

All currently set breakpoints are listed under the Break**p**oints list box, and you can add breakpoints, or remove any already set, by clicking the appropriate command buttons on the right side of the dialog box. The Disa**b**le button disables a breakpoint but does not remove it; the **C**lear All button removes all currently set breakpoints.

You can set six types of breakpoints from the Breakpoints dialog box. The **T**ype list box displays all six kinds of breakpoints. By setting the appropriate type of breakpoint, you can control when the set breakpoint takes effect. You can set certain breakpoints that occur only if an expression is true or if an expression changes. There is also a breakpoint that stops only if specified Windows messages appear during a program's execution; you'll explore that breakpoint after you master Windows programming.

Day 21: The Visual C++ Tools

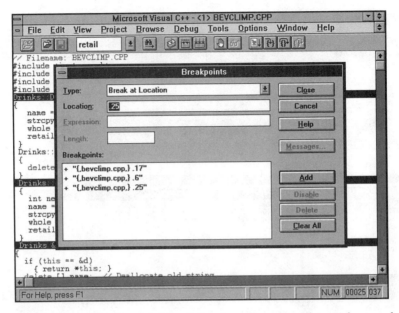

Figure 21.8. The Breakpoints dialog box gives you advanced control over breakpoints.

Tip: If you don't like the color used to indicate a source code breakpoint, you can change it by selecting from the **O**ptions Color... menu option and selecting a new color for Breakpoint Line.

Note: When you close a project or quit Visual C++, the Visual Workbench editor saves any breakpoints you have set, so the next time you open the same project, your breakpoints are still set.

Additional Control

There are two more debugging features that might aid your programming efforts. The *call stack* and *QuickWatch* options give you additional debugging information that can help you, depending on your program's needs.

The call stack contains a series of function calls that have been called but have not yet been returned from. For example, if main() calls aFun(), and aFun() calls bFun(), you can display the call stack at a breakpoint inside bFun() and see the following list of functions:

```
main()
aFun()
bFun()
```

To see the call stack during your debugging session, select **D**ebug Show Call Stac**k**... (Ctrl+K), and the Visual Workbench displays the Call Stack dialog box. If you select from the list of active functions, the Visual Workbench displays the source code for that particular function. Execution, however, remains stopped at the point of the breakpoint. If you click Step Into, the program continues on its way from the breakpoint's location.

The QuickWatch button (with the eyeglass icon) displays a dialog box similar to the **W**indow **W**atch window. You can enter variables and expressions and see their current values while executing a program.

> **Note:** If a variable in the QuickWatch window contains an aggregate data type such as a structure or class, click or press Enter while the cursor rests over the variable name, and the Virtual Workbench expands the variable into its components and shows you the individual member values.

Those of you with the professional edition of Visual C++ have an additional pair of debuggers, named CodeView for Windows and CodeView for DOS. Both versions of CodeView duplicate many of the debugging features you've seen described here. The CodeView debuggers use a command-line interface window where you can enter values and variables directly instead of pointing and clicking solely in a graphical interface.

If you have used CodeView elsewhere (several Microsoft products have included CodeView for several years now), you might be more comfortable using CodeView as well as the integrated Visual Workbench debugging system until you familiarize yourself with the integrated system.

The Visual C++ Tools

DO	DON'T

DO practice the integrated Visual Workbench debugger as soon as possible. There are far too many programmers who still insert extra `cout`s and `printf()`s throughout code trying to look at variable values during their program's execution.

DO use CodeView if you are used to it from an older Microsoft product. You'll soon find, however, that the integrated debugger is the debugger of choice in Visual C++ because its graphical nature makes many of its features more easily accessible.

DON'T forget to compile your program without debugging information after you complete your debugging sessions. The program will run faster and consume less disk space without the debugging information.

The Remaining Tools Contain the True Power

This section wraps up the chapter and the main part of the book. In a way, this section describes more topics than any other section in the book. Visual C++ is the kind of programming language that one learns in small steps. There are a lot of additional Visual C++ features that you are well on your way to mastering. Sadly, the book is coming to an end, and many of the tools you have yet to learn require more knowledge than C++ alone can provide. Many of the additional tools that come with Visual C++ require a knowledge of Windows programming, database concepts, OLE 2.0, and more.

Therefore, at this point in your learning, it is best that you are introduced to these tools, but you'll have to learn each specific tool along with the feature of Visual C++ that the tool supports. For instance, you can't fully understand the App Studio tool until you learn how Windows programs work. Nevertheless, seeing a description of the full Visual C++ toolset now gives you a glimpse into your future as a master Visual C++/Windows programmer.

The App Studio

A *resource* is just about anything you can see or move within a Microsoft Windows application. Here is a list of common Windows resources:

Menus
Dialog boxes
Icons
Bitmaps
Cursors

As you know, such resources are critical for Windows programs. The primary difference between a Windows application and a DOS-based application is the graphical user interface. The elements of that graphical interface, the resources, are vital. You must create, edit, and manipulate resources throughout your Windows programming career.

Figure 21.9 shows a sample App Studio session. If you have worked with Visual Basic, you might recognize some of the tools in the toolbar at the right of the screen. You can easily add command buttons, list boxes, and other dialog box elements to your application's dialog boxes with the App Studio tools.

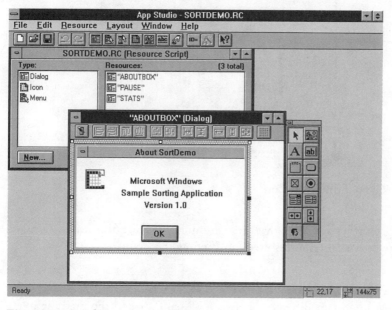

Figure 21.9. Editing an About dialog box.

The dialog box shown in Figure 21.9 illustrates an editing session of an About box. Most Windows programs contain a help menu with an **About...** option. The About box typically contains the program's version number and a short one- or two-line description of the program. Visual C++ comes with lots of sample programs, and the About box shown in Figure 21.9 is from the SORTDEMO Windows program. Although App Studio doesn't give you the tools to associate resource elements to your Windows program's code, App Studio does give you the visual editing power to create those resources.

Figure 21.10 shows you how App Studio provides icon and bitmap editing features found in many graphics programs.

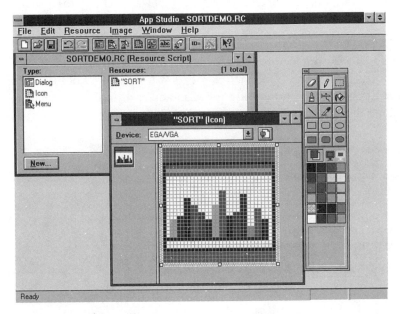

Figure 21.10. Editing an icon.

As you get further into Windows programming, you'll use App Studio more and more to create the visual resources used by Windows programs.

AppWizard: The Power Beyond

The most important difference between Visual C++ and the preceding version of Microsoft's C++ compiler is the *AppWizard*. If you have used any of Microsoft's other Windows-based products, such as Access or Publisher, you might have seen how Microsoft now includes different kinds of *Wizards*. When you request a Wizard, the program asks you a series of questions through dialog boxes and generates a database, report, worksheet, or whatever for you. There is nothing a Wizard creates that you could not do yourself through typing. The menus of the Wizard lead you by the hand and create parts of an application automatically when you finish answering the dialog prompts.

The AppWizard is a *program generator*. You run AppWizard from the Project menu option. Simply put, AppWizard creates a shell of a Windows program for you that contains the full functionality of a Windows program such as menus, a multiple-document interface (MDI), and even page preview. Through the AppWizard dialog boxes, you tell AppWizard exactly which elements of the Windows application you want created. When finished with its job, AppWizard writes all the source code needed, builds the resources, and creates the project file. All you have to do is modify the code however you want and build the final Windows application with the project file AppWizard generated for you.

The applications that AppWizard creates are generic. In other words, AppWizard cannot know how to write a Windows-based accounting system that fits the way you do business. What AppWizard does do is create a working model of a Windows program that includes all the standard Windows program features you requested when walking through the dialog boxes with AppWizard. After AppWizard generates a generic version, or shell, of the program you want, you then go in with the Visual Workbench and add all the specific features you want the program to include. In a way, you fill in the blanks left when AppWizard created the initial application.

Windows programmers need the AppWizard program generator much more than the simpler DOS-based programs. A Windows application generally comprises several files, many more than a DOS-based C++ project with a few headers and a program file. The AppWizard takes the tedium out of writing Windows applications because it does your initial detail work. After AppWizard does its job, you fill in the specifics. Of course, the code generated with AppWizard is fully documented. (Can you say the same about your own code? Most of us can't!) The comments help direct you to the areas you might want to change to suit your target application's needs.

Note: In the bonus section at the end of this book, you'll use AppWizard to create a full-featured Windows-based application.

Figure 21.11 shows a program generated with AppWizard. Notice that it looks just like any other Windows program. Nevertheless, it was created with fewer than 15 clicks of the mouse! As you can see, the application has a menu, tools on the toolbar

The Visual C++ Tools

(some are grayed out because they are unavailable until you put specific commands in the application), maximize and minimize buttons, and all the basics that any Windows application has. Of course, there is still a lot of hand-coding left to turn this generic application into one that meets your needs, but AppWizard saved a tremendous amount of work. If and when you review the concepts of Windows programming in C, you'll appreciate even more how much work AppWizard does.

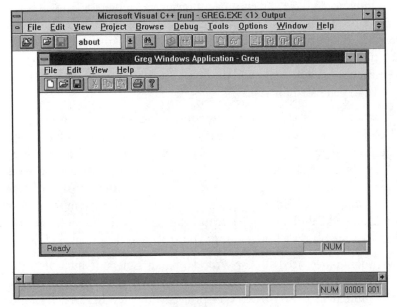

Figure 21.11. A Windows application generated with AppWizard.

Warning: Throughout this book, you have been writing QuickWin applications. However, as explained back in Day 1's chapter, "The C++ Phenomenon," a QuickWin program offers only a limited subset of the power that is available with most full-featured Windows programs. QuickWin exists solely to give DOS-based programmers an avenue to write working programs within a Microsoft Windows window, as opposed to switching first to a DOS window to run the program in text mode within Windows. Windows applications created with AppWizard can contain the full functionality of Windows programs and, perhaps most important, enable you to use the Microsoft Foundation Classes

> (MFC) within the resulting generated program. QuickWin programs are stunted compared to the Windows program you'll write when you master AppWizard and the MFC.

ClassWizard Glues Your Application

As you've seen, App Studio designs Windows resources, and AppWizard builds the shell of your application. The resources you create with App Studio must somehow be associated with the code that you add to that code generated by AppWizard. *ClassWizard* is the Visual C++ tool that associates your resources to your Windows code. ClassWizard performs other useful tasks as well that were previously tedious for the Windows programmer.

As you'll learn in the bonus chapters, a Windows program must handle many kinds of activities. If the user clicks the mouse over a menu option, you must handle that mouse click differently from the way you handle mouse clicks over dialog box command buttons. Windows passes *messages* to your Windows code telling the program what the user has just done. With ClassWizard, you can easily associate Windows messages with your program's functions so that a particular function executes when a particular message is passed from Windows to your program.

As you design resources in App Studio, you'll assign identifiers to the various components of the resources. For example, if a dialog box contains three command buttons and one list box, there would be four identifiers for the dialog box that return information to your program. ClassWizard enables you to associate those resource identifiers to appropriate code (usually functions or member functions) without your having to go to the code directly and add the associations.

Finally, ClassWizard enables you to derive new classes from existing classes. ClassWizard generates the source code that contains your derived classes and any necessary header files for the declarations of those derived classes. You'll probably want to derive classes from your own base classes and let ClassWizard derive from any MFC base classes you use.

Figure 21.12 shows a sample ClassWizard dialog box. Although understanding of the specific details can come only after you learn more about Windows programming and MFC, you can see object identifiers (the **O**bject ID list) and Windows messages (in the **M**essages box) in the top half of the screen and member functions in the Member **F**unctions list box that associate to those identifiers and messages. Again, the graphical

The Visual C++ Tools

linking provided by ClassWizard is an almost trivial task that used to provide ample tedium for Windows programmers before the Visual Workbench came along.

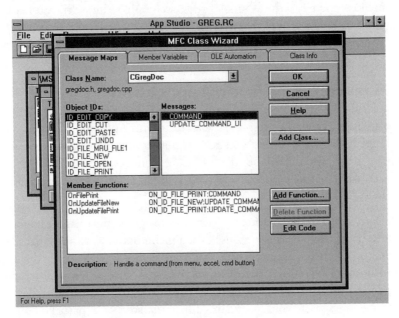

Figure 21.12. Using the ClassWizard.

Browsing Through the Application

One of the banes of Windows programming is the huge amount of data you must manage while programming. Not only do many source files make up most Windows applications, but there are resources, identifiers, messages, classes, variables, functions, and so many more elements that the programmer needs to access during the application's development. The AppWizard, App Studio, and ClassWizard tools certainly make program development easier, but when it comes time to link the parts of the application together, the programmer often must refer to several different elements scattered throughout the application. To rescue the programmer from this melee, Visual C++ offers a *browser* that quickly locates virtually any element within the currently loaded application during the development process.

Not only does the browser track and locate all the Windows application elements, but it also shows many relationships between the elements. The browser displays so much information that it might be a while before you want to locate all the information that the browser can display.

If you display the **B**rowser menu, you'll see that most of the options are grayed out. The browser features are available only after you build a *browser database.* (Browser databases contain the same name as the application with a .BSC filename extension.) When you build the database, the Visual Workbench scans your application files and builds a comprehensive cross-reference. Figure 21.13 shows the contents of a browser database. As you can see, an individual function, _ffree(), is highlighted, and the lines in the source code file are displayed on the right side of the screen. Therefore, if you questioned the behavior of one of these function calls, you could quickly go to the source code lines through the browser. Unlike simple searching within the editor, the browser database spans all files that make up the project. Notice that a reference to _ffree() (which happens to be a C memory function) is located in both MALLOC.H and SORTDEMO.C according to the figure. (The SORTDEMO program that comes as a sample application uses a lot of C code, and the figure's browser database was built from the SORTDEMO application.)

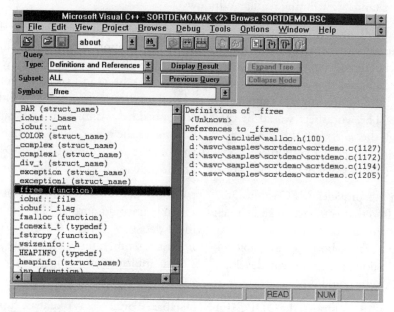

Figure 21.13. Viewing the contents of a browser database.

Day 21: The Visual C++ Tools

Features New with Visual C++ 1.5

Starting with Visual C++ Version 1.5, Microsoft included additional Visual C++ tools that prepare you for the next level of computing beyond that of DOS-based and Windows programs.

A program no longer runs in a vacuum, especially programs in environments such as Windows and Windows NT, where several tasks might be active at any one time. Programs must be able to work with other programs and data from those programs. Most of the new features of version 1.5 over the earlier version lie in its support for linking to other applications. Here is a list of the new features in Visual C++ Version 1.5:

- Support for running Visual C++ in Windows NT while creating 16-bit (DOS- and Windows-based) applications

- OLE 2.0 (Object Linking and Embedding) support

- ODBC (Open Database Connectivity) database support

There is a version of Visual C++ exclusively for NT. Version 1.5 of Visual C++, however, runs under NT and creates applications that run only in 16-bit DOS and Windows (and NT running regular Windows).

The OLE 2.0 options give you the ability to write Windows applications that share functionality with other OLE 2.0-compatible Windows applications. For example, your user could open an Excel worksheet within the application you provide. When the user indicates that he or she wants to edit the worksheet, an Excel menu opens directly inside your program's application and enables the user to edit the worksheet in place. The worksheet would be the object embedded within your application. Although the *object* in OLE is not exactly the same as the *object* in OOP, there are many similarities between them because the objects in OLE applications have properties and behaviors that are defined by their individual parent applications.

Version 1.5 provides MFC extensions, AppWizard, and ClassWizard support for OLE 2.0 so that you have to code much less than you would normally have to code without the aid of Visual C++. The individual details of OLE 2.0 are extremely complex. (Several books are available solely on OLE 2.0 programming.) As with non-OLE Windows programs, you develop OLE-compatible programs much faster than you otherwise could.

Visual C++ also supports the ODBC (Open Database Connectivity) database support with MFC, AppWizard, and ClassWizard extensions that the first version of Visual C++ did not include. Certainly not all database programs support the ODBC format, and Visual C++ 1.5 offers support only for those database programs that do support

ODBC. Nevertheless, more and more database developers are supporting the ODBC system. You can design and create your ODBC database within powerful database applications such as Microsoft Access and then access that data (by reading, changing, writing, and deleting the data) within your Visual C++ program.

> **DO** begin exploring the tools available with Visual C++. Most of the tools benefit Windows programmers more than DOS and QuickWin programmers.
>
> **DON'T** rest now that you know C++! As you've seen, there is a lot more to Visual C++ than the straight programming you have done in the past. If you want to take a break, you deserve one. (You can have a few minutes....) After the break, turn to the bonus section at the end of this book to get an introduction to Windows programming and the MFC.

Summary

This chapter differs a little from those in the rest of the book. This chapter was more descriptive than instructive, but after you've worked through 20 days' worth of C++, it is important that you see the full capabilities of Visual C++ and how the Visual C++ tools improve your life as a programmer, especially when you move to writing Windows programs.

The Visual Workbench includes lots of tools. You have already used the editor to enter and edit your programs. The editor supports multiple documents, multiple windows, and sharing data between those document windows.

The Visual Workbench integrated debugger surpasses the CodeView debugger that previous Microsoft products included. (The Professional edition of Visual C++ does include a version of CodeView for both DOS and Windows in case you are used to using CodeView and want to continue using it until you have time to master the visual debugger.) The visual interface takes the chore out of debugging your programs.

The remaining tools, AppWizard, App Studio, ClassWizard, the browser, and the additions new with version 1.5, all work together to speed your Windows program development and offer you the most powerful set of programming tools ever provided.

The Visual C++ Tools

Q&A

Q. Why would I ever want to write Windows programs?

A. Perhaps the most concrete reason is that Windows programs are in more demand than any other environment today, including DOS-based programs. Several software vendors sell Windows-only versions of their software. In addition, the more powerful that computers get, the more important it is to maintain a consistent and graphical user interface.

Some people are fighting the move to Windows, but the industry as a whole has already made the switch. As we move into 32-bit environments, such as Windows NT, there is even more need for software that can fully exploit those environments.

Q. Haven't I been writing Windows programs so far in the book?

A. No. The programs you have written here have been QuickWin programs that run within a Windows-based window. QuickWin programs, however, cannot access many of the common Windows program features such as resources and MFC classes.

One chapter cannot make you a Windows programmer. Actually, it takes a lot to become a Windows programmer, even when you're using the Visual C++ system. You'll gain good insight into writing Windows programs when you read the bonus section at the end of this book.

Q. Now that I know OOP, how can the Visual Workbench improve my productivity as I migrate to writing Windows programs?

A. The App Studio, AppWizard, and ClassWizard all offer tremendous support for writing Windows programs. As described in this chapter, a tremendous amount of effort is needed to produce a Windows application. Finally, with Visual C++, programmers can begin to eliminate the tedium from their work. The AppWizard creates the shell, or the outline of the program you want to write. The App Studio helps you design, create, and edit Windows resources. ClassWizard binds those resources to your code. After you write your program, the browser helps document the cross-references in the program and gives you almost instant access to virtually every element of the program.

Workshop

The Workshop offers quiz questions and exercises to hone your skills and give you feedback on today's lesson. You'll find some proposed answers in Appendix D.

Quiz

1. What is a GUI?
2. What is the difference between Visual C++ and the Visual Workbench?
3. What does *MDI* stand for? How does MDI improve your productivity within the Visual Workbench editor?
4. What is a Windows *resource*?
5. What is a *wizard*?
6. How does version 1.5 of Visual C++ improve your program's interactivity with other Windows programs?

Exercise

1. You deserve a holiday! You've just learned OOP with Visual C++. No exercises are appropriate for this chapter, based on the chapter's descriptive nature.

Week 3 in Review

Now that you've finished the third week, you'll find that the program in Listing WR3.1 adds a slightly different perspective to the inventory listings found in the third week's chapters.

The program maintains a simple inventory system of MAX (a global const initially defined as 75) items. All 75 items are stored on the disk. When you run the program the first time, its data file (INVENT.DAT) will not exist. After you enter a few items, the program saves those items to the disk, along with the rest of the 75 items. The program keeps track of the number of "live items" (the number of the 75 items that actually contain data). On each subsequent run, the program reads all items on disk and prints an updated listing of the inventory.

Listing WR3.1. Week three review listing.

```
1:  // Filename: INVLIVE.CPP
2:  // Maintains an on-disk inventory
3:  #include <fstream.h>
4:  #include <iomanip.h>
5:  #include <string.h>
6:  #include <ctype.h>
7:  // This global constant holds maximum number of items allowed
8:  const int MAX = 75;
9:: // An individual item class
10: class Item {
11: public:          // So composed class can access
12:    char descrip[20];
13:    float price;
14:    int quant;
15: };
16: // Composed class of all the items follows
```

continues

Week 3 in Review

Listing WR3.1. continued

```
17: class allItems {
18:    Item inventory[MAX];
19:    static int numInInv;
20: public:
21:    void saveToDisk(void);
22:    void readFromDisk(void);
23:    void addToInv(void);
24:    void prInv(void);
25:    allItems(void);
26: };
27: void allItems::saveToDisk(void)
28: {
29:    // This function ALWAYS writes all MAX inventory items to
              ➥disk
30:    ofstream diskFile;
31:    diskFile.open("INVENT.DAT");
32:    // Writes in compressed form so must use read to read it
33:    diskFile.write((char *)this, sizeof(*this));
34: }
35: void allItems::readFromDisk(void)
36: {
37:    // Always reads MAX items from disk (if the file exists) but
38:    // checks each record's descrip to count the number of real
39:    // items in the inventory (the rest are considered empty).
40:    ifstream diskFile;
41:    diskFile.open("INVENT.DAT");
42:    if(diskFile)
43:      { diskFile.read((char *)this, sizeof(*this));
44:        // Determine how many items have live data
45:        for (int ctr=0; ctr<MAX; ctr++)
46:          { if (inventory[ctr].descrip[0] == '\0') break; }
47:        numInInv = ctr;
48:      }
49: }
50: void allItems::addToInv(void)
51: {
52:    cout << "\nWhat is the Description? ";
53:    cin.getline(inventory[numInInv].descrip, 20);
54:    cout << "What is the price? ";
55:    cin >> inventory[numInInv].price;
56:    cout << "What is the quantity? ";
57:    cin >> inventory[numInInv].quant;
58:    allItems::numInInv++;    // Increase # of active items in
                                    ➥inventory
59: }
60: void allItems::prInv(void)
61: {
62:    cout << setprecision(2) << setiosflags(ios::showpoint);
```

```
63:     cout << setiosflags(ios::fixed);
64:     if (numInInv == 0)
65:     { cout << "\nThe inventory file is now empty.\n"; }
66:     else
67:     { cout << "\nHere is the inventory:\n";
68:       for (int ctr=0; ctr<numInInv; ctr++)
69:       { cout << "\n Description: " << inventory[ctr].descrip
              ↪<<"\n";
70:         cout << " Price: $" << inventory[ctr].price << "\n";
71:         cout << " Quantity: " << inventory[ctr].quant << "\n";
72:       }
73:     }
74: }
75: allItems::allItems(void)
76: {
77:     // Make all description pointers null
78:     for (int ctr=0; ctr<MAX; ctr++)
79:       { inventory[ctr].descrip[0] = '\0'; }
80: }
81: // Static must be initialized
82: int allItems::numInInv = 0;
83: /////////////////////////////////////////////////////////////////
84: main()
85: {
86:     char answer;   // To hold answer
87:     allItems inventory;
88:     cout << "Here is the inventory before you add items:\n";
89:     inventory.readFromDisk();
90:     inventory.prInv();
91:     do {
92:       inventory.addToInv();   // Get item from user
93:       cout << "Is there another item to enter? (Y or N) ";
94:       cin >> answer;
95:       cin.ignore();   // Eliminate the newline
96:     } while (toupper(answer) != 'N');
97:     // Print the inventory for the user
98:     inventory.prInv();
99:     // Now, write the items to the disk
100:    inventory.saveToDisk();
101:    return 0;
102: }
```

main() creates a single inventory object (line 87) that contains MAX individual items. The composed allItems class is designed to hold MAX occurrences of the smaller Item class (lines 10–15). By holding all the occurrences of the data, the allItems class can save and retrieve itself to and from the disk. Notice that the constructor for allItems puts a null zero in the first array element of the descrip

Week 3 in Review

member. As the user enters new items into the inventory, this null zero gets overwritten with new data (line 53).

The first job of `main()` is to print whatever data might already be in the data file. Line 89 calls the `readFromDisk()` member function to read the INVENT.DAT disk file into the `inventory` object's members. The program determines how many of the `MAX` items actually contain data in the `for` loop on lines 45 and 46 by testing for the null zero in the `descrip` member.

If `readFromDisk()` finds a file (in line 42), that file is read and the live non-null inventory items print. `main()` then regains control and begins a loop in lines 91–96 that ask the user for new inventory data to add to the file. As the user enters items, the data is *not* yet written to the disk file but instead is stored in the `inventory` array.

Only after the user signals in lines 94–96 that he or she is finished entering data does `main()` call the `saveToDisk()` member function in line 100 and exit.

Try running this program several times and enter a few new inventory items each time. As you do, you'll see that the inventory file keeps growing with new data.

If you want to break this program into several project modules, separate the class header (lines 9–26) and the class implementation (lines 27–80) so that you'll be left with a clean and simple `main()` that controls the program.

Extra Credit Bonus 1+

Introduction to Windows Programming and MFC

Extra Credit Bonus 1

The reason for this bonus chapter is simple. Visual C++ is so much more than just a C++ compiler. Yet C++ is the all-important starting point for mastering the rest of Visual C++. After you've mastered C++ with Visual C++, as you've now done, you're ready to explore the challenging and fun world of Windows programming with Visual C++. (Besides being challenging and fun, you'll also find it to be frustrating! That's the nature of Windows programs, but the fun almost always outweighs the frustration.)

The last bonus chapter in this book describes other publications you might want to explore after you've finished this text. As you can see from the list of Visual C++ reference manuals, there is a *lot* to learn about Visual C++, and most of the documentation concerns Windows-based programming topics. This bonus chapter should whet your appetite for more exploration into Windows programming and the MFC.

Tip: An advantage of the Windows programming environment is that you'll be able to use the MFC classes, which add all sorts of encapsulated power to your programs. Not all the MFC classes are solely Windows based. There is a powerful string class and time class, and you can also use more powerful exception handling than the exercise in Day 19's chapter was able to provide without the MFC.

Today, you learn about the following topics:

- How Windows programming differs from the textual DOS- and QuickWin-based programs
- How to make sense out of Visual C++'s Windows programs
- How to instruct AppWizard to create a Windows program shell
- How to interpret the classes that AppWizard generates

This bonus chapter is a little more hands-on than many of the other chapters have been. Instead of addressing each little detail along the way, this bonus chapter leads you as you watch a simple Windows application develop. Now that you've mastered the C++ tutorial, relax and follow along to see how a few mouse clicks and Visual C++ can produce comprehensive, working Windows applications.

An Overview of a Windows Program

A Windows program works differently from the programs you learned to create in other environments. Unlike many DOS-based programs, a Windows program does not proceed with the sequential timing of a DOS program. Think about your favorite Windows applications, such as Word for Windows or Excel. At any given time, there are many things you (the user) might do next. Here is a list of common tasks you might perform in any order in a Windows program:

Move the mouse
Click the mouse
Double-click the mouse
Type text
Press Alt to activate the menu
Press Ctrl+Tab to switch to another Windows application

In a sense, a Windows program interacts with its user in the same way a videocassette recorder can: at any one time, there are several things that the user can do next (play, rewind, eject, fast-forward, change the channel, or turn off the power).

DOS-based programs usually guide the user from step to step. If you want the user to enter data into a form, the program is likely to move the cursor from field to field. At best, the user has limited control in changing the order of the data entry. Perhaps the user can signal by pressing the up-arrow key that he or she wants to return to the preceding field and change the data. Generally, DOS-based programs are sequential in nature and give the user only a few options at any one time.

The user is not the only commander of a Windows program. Sometimes another Windows program triggers an event in your program. The timer might trigger an event also, as happens with Windows-based screen savers—after a certain amount of time has passed with no keyboard activity, the timer forces the execution of a Windows screen-saver program or routine. There are so many possibilities of events that might happen within a Windows program that almost everything is in control of the Windows program *except* the program itself. In a DOS-based environment, the running program controls the system, but in Windows, the running program is more like a pawn at the control of all the other events happening in the system.

Extra Credit Bonus 1

Note: The term *event* is a Windows-specific term used for all the things that can take place (mouse clicks, mouse movements, keystrokes, and so on).

As you will see when your programming power improves, your program can also trigger events of its own. You must be able to handle all the events going back and forth to and from your program. C-style Windows programs handle events by using one giant looping `switch` statement. Each event has an identifying number (defined as a named constant in a header file). Each event the program needs to handle includes an entry in the `switch` statement. If no events occur, the program continues to loop in the `switch` statement. If an event does occur, its match is found in the `switch` statement, and the appropriate `case` code executes.

The following pseudocode illustrates how a C-style Windows program operates:

```
do              /* Pseudocode to illustrate a C-like Windows program */
{
  switch (event_ID)
  {
    case ID_MOUSE_CLICK: mouseFn();
                         break;
    case ID_MOUSE_MOVE: mouseMvFn();
                         break;
    case ID_ESC_PRESSED: handleEscFn();
                         break;
    default:   break;
  }
} loop while (event_ID != ID_EXIT_PGM);
```

The C-style pseudocode actually better demonstrates how a Windows program behaves than a Visual C++ Windows program. Although many details are left out for brevity, the idea of the `switch` statement handling all the Windows events is straightforward and an easy introduction to the way Windows programs work. You have just mastered C++, however, and C++ provides object-oriented approaches to programming. The MFC classes encapsulate lots of event-handling routines, so you have to write less code. Also, rather than a switch loop handling all the events, you write specific functions that Visual C++ automatically executes if (and only if) that Windows event occurs. (The ClassWizard helps you associate Windows event identifiers with your program's event functions.) In C++, the elements on-screen become C++-like objects that your program can manipulate in the same way it manipulates variable objects.

Tip: By writing true Windows programs rather than QuickWin or DOS-based programs, you gain the following capabilities that are unavailable in QuickWin programs:

You can access the GUI API Windows functions.

You can access mouse clicks within the program's windows.

You can utilize your own Windows resources, such as menus, command buttons, and bitmaps, from within your program.

You can add customized help information to your program.

Prepare Your Environment

Before learning any more Windows programming details, you should take a few moments to set up your version of Visual C++ to handle the building of Windows programs. Earlier in the book, you set up your compiler options to build QuickWin programs. You must now tell Visual C++ that you want to build Windows-based programs that include the MFC classes. Follow these steps to set up Visual C++ for Windows:

1. Select **O**ptions **P**roject.

2. Display the Project Type list box by clicking the down arrow at the right of the box.

3. Highlight `Windows application (.EXE)`.

4. Click **U**se Microsoft Foundation Classes so that an X appears in the box. Your screen should look like the one in Figure B1.1.

Note: It doesn't really matter whether you select the project option for **D**ebug or **R**elease. If you want to use the debugger, you must select the **D**ebug option. Keep in mind that the debugging version of any built program consumes more disk space, uses more memory space, and runs more slowly than the release version.

Extra Credit Bonus 1

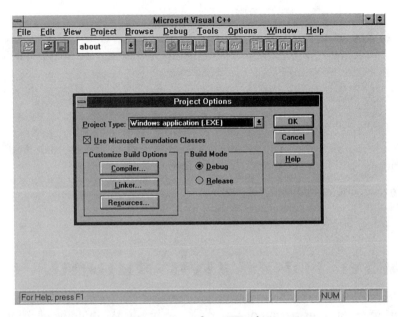

Figure B1.1. Setting the options for a Windows program.

 Tip: By stepping through the debugging version of your first few Windows programs, even those primarily generated by AppWizard, you'll learn a lot about how a Visual C++ Windows program operates. Stepping through a Windows program is time-consuming, however, so you'll want to review the single-step toolbar buttons described in Day 21's chapter, "The Visual C++ Tools."

It All Starts with AppWizard

You're about to get some insight into the true power of Visual C++. With a few simple mouse clicks and keystrokes, you'll now generate and build your first true Windows application in Visual C++. To begin building the application, close any open files and projects from within your Visual Workbench. Begin generating your Windows application with these steps:

1. Select **P**roject App**W**izard… from the menu. You'll see the MFC AppWizard dialog box shown in Figure B1.2.

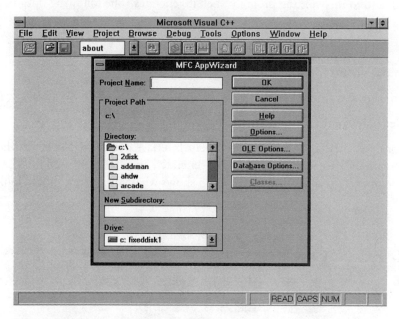

Figure B1.2. The AppWizard dialog box.

A Windows program comprises many files. It's recommended that you store each Windows program you generate in its own subdirectory. The initial AppWizard dialog box enables you to type a project name in the Project **N**ame box. As you type a name, you'll see the same letters appearing in the New **S**ubdirectory box as well. AppWizard automatically gives the target subdirectory the same name as your project. This consistency makes locating project files much easier. For now, type the name **TEACH**.

Note: AppWizard will give most of the Windows program files the name you type—in this case TEACH—followed by an appropriate extension. For example, the project make file will be named TEACH.MAK, and a Visual C++ program file will be named TEACH.CPP.

Extra Credit Bonus 1

2. After typing the project name, click the **O**ptions command button to display the AppWizard Options dialog box. You'll see all the options AppWizard can add to the working program shell it generates. The following options are set by default:

   Multiple Document Interface (MDI)

   Initial Toolbar

   Printing and Print Preview

   Generate Source Comments

   For now, click the **M**ultiple Document Interface option to deselect it (the x disappears), because the application generated here does not need multiple documents open at once. Figure B1.3 shows what your screen should look like.

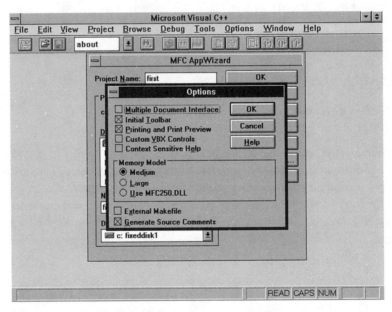

Figure B1.3. The AppWizard Options dialog box.

The VBX Controls option enables you to use customized Visual Basic controls inside your Visual C++ Windows application if you so choose. You can also request automatic context-sensitive help and an external makefile that you can control with external makefile utilities, if you have the utilities.

Leave the memory model set to Medium because there is no reason to access the large segments available in the Large memory models. The MFC250.DLL option that you'll see if you use Visual C++ 1.5 allows for smaller executable programs using dynamic link libraries rather than static libraries used by default. (Keep things simple, and stay with the medium memory model.)

3. Click the OK command button to save the options and return to the AppWizard dialog box screen.

4. Now that you've told Visual C++ what you want in the resulting Windows application, click the OK command button. Before generating the program code and make file, AppWizard displays the New Application Information screen shown in Figure B1.4.

The New Application Information screen lists the options you've requested, as well as the MFC classes that AppWizard will include in the application. After you've read through the screen's messages, select Create and sit back while Visual C++ generates your project.

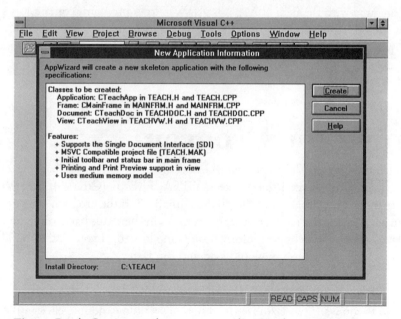

Figure B1.4. Getting ready to generate the Windows project.

Extra Credit Bonus 1

Building the Project

After AppWizard generates the source file, Visual C++ gives control back to you at the Visual Workbench. The TEACH.MAK makefile remains open so that you can build the project right away. Press Alt+F8 (or click either of the build buttons on the toolbar), and Visual C++ builds the project by compiling and linking all the necessary files.

 Warning: Be sure that you have more than 3M free before building the project. It takes a lot of room to compile and link the AppWizard files.

 Tip: You might consider going to a movie while your project builds. Seriously, even if your computer is fast, you'll find that the build process is slow because it takes a long time to build the Windows project you just generated with the help of AppWizard. Windows programs contain lots of code. Despite the sluggish speed of the build, using AppWizard cuts down your coding time by many hours. Isn't that worth a slow build time?

Running the Program

After you build the AppWizard program, click the Run tool on the toolbar (the fourth from the right), or select **P**roject **E**xecute TEACH.EXE (Ctrl+F5). The Visual Workbench runs the program, as shown in Figure B1.5. If the program takes a while to begin and you see the message Loading symbols in the status bar during the wait, the delay is due to the debugger information being loaded. If you were to build the program as a release version, it would load and run faster.

 Tip: If you want to maximize the program's window, double-click in the title area or click the maximize button.

650

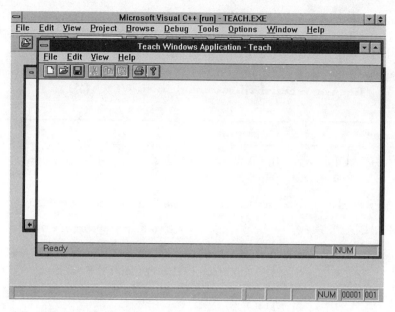

Figure B1.5. Running the generated Windows program.

The TEACH.EXE program is now a complete Windows application. You can move the window, resize the window, click the tools, and select from the menu. Go ahead and work with the window a little, and you will see that, even though all the components are there, little happens when you select from the menus or click the tools. Again, AppWizard generated a shell or a complete Windows program, but there are no specifics that can execute. Adding the specifics is *your* job as you learn more about MFC and Visual C++.

What Just Happened

AppWizard generated a lot of files. It takes a lot to create a Windows program, even a simple shell of a Windows program like the one you just created. The next two sections describe the files and classes that were needed to produce the program generated by AppWizard.

The Application's Files

When you first generated the application, AppWizard stored *19* files in the TEACH subdirectory. That's a lot of files! Three of the files—the resource files—are located

Extra Credit Bonus 1

in a new subdirectory named RES. The 19 files consist of Visual C++ source code, header files, a data file, a make file, and resource files. Table B1.1 lists these files alphabetically and gives a brief description of each.

Table B1.1. The AppWizard files stored in the TEACH subdirectory.

Filename	Description
MAINFRM.CPP	Implementation code for the primary window frame
MAINFRM.H	Header file for the primary window frame class
README.TXT	A help file generated to help you sort out the differences and meanings of the generated files
RES	The subdirectory that contains the resource files TEACH.IC2, TEACH.ICO, and TOOLBAR.BMP
RESOURCE.H	The header file for the resources
STDAFX.CPP	The MFC application frameworks implementation file
STDAFX.H	The MFC application frameworks header file
TEACH.CLW	The application's data for ClassWizard
TEACH.CPP	The primary program source-code file
TEACH.DEF	The file that holds the Windows program definitions needed by all Windows programs
TEACH.H	The primary program's header file
TEACH.ICO	The file that holds the icon image for the application (stored in the RES subdirectory)
TEACH.MAK	The project makefile that builds the application
TEACH.RC	The resource file that holds the application's menu, cursors, and so on
TEACH.RC2	The file that holds the resource information for the version information (stored in the RES subdirectory)

Filename	Description
TEACHDOC.CPP	The document handler's implementation code
TEACHDOC.H	The document handler's header file
TEACHVW.CPP	The implementation code for the window's view
TEACHVW.H	The window's view header file
TOOLBAR.BMP	The bitmap for the toolbar buttons

The files described in Table B1.1 are just the beginning. The TEACH subdirectory contains Table B1.1's files *before* you build the TEACH project. After you build the project and create its final linked application, the TEACH directory holds almost twice as many files as shown in Table B1.1! Of course, the additional files are precompiled header files, updated resource files, a browser database file, object files, and the final executable file. You don't need to keep the .SBR files, the .PCH files, the .BSC files, the .PDB files, and the .OBJ files for the application if you want to save the disk space.

Note: Just think how long it would take to figure out the order of compilation and file inclusion with all these files. AppWizard's automatically generated project makes building the project just a click away.

The Application's Classes

AppWizard creates an object-oriented, class-based application. AppWizard derives the classes for your application from the MFC classes that come with Visual C++. Although you'll need to study a lot more on Visual C++ MFC classes before you understand them fully, this section takes a moment to review the classes generated in the TEACH application.

Table B1.2 lists the classes in the TEACH application and gives a description of each.

Extra Credit Bonus 1

Table B1.2. AppWizard's generated classes.

Class Name	Description
CTeachApp	The controlling code for the TEACH application. CTeachApp initializes needed data, displays the window, and eventually helps connect the application to any document. The CTeachApp class is defined in the TEACH.H file (Listing B1.1) and the TEACH.CPP file (Listing B1.2).
CMainFrame	The *frame* window that you see on-screen when you run the application. The CMainFrame class is defined in the MAINFRM.H file (Listing B1.3) and the MAINFRM.CPP file (Listing B1.4).
CTeachDoc	The document class controls the data of the application. The CTeachDoc class is defined in the TEACHDOC.H file (Listing B1.5) and the TEACHDOC.CPP file (Listing B1.6).
CTeachView	The view class controls the way you see the document data inside the application's window. The CTeachView class is defined in the TEACHVW.H file (Listing B1.7) and the TEACHVW.CPP file (Listing B1.8).

Listing B1.1 contains the TEACH.H file that defines the application class that initiates the program.

Listing B1.1. The TEACH.H header file.

```
1:  // teach.h : main header file for the TEACH application
2:  //
3:
4:  #ifndef __AFXWIN_H__
5:    #error include 'stdafx.h' before including this file for PCH
6:  #endif
7:
8:  #include "resource.h"       // main symbols
9:
10: /////////////////////////////////////////////////////////////////
11: // CTeachApp:
12: // See teach.cpp for the implementation of this class
13: //
```

```
14:
15: class CTeachApp : public CWinApp
16: {
17: public:
18:    CTeachApp();
19:
20: // Overrides
21:    virtual BOOL InitInstance();
22:
23: // Implementation
24:
25:    //{{AFX_MSG(CTeachApp)
26:    afx_msg void OnAppAbout();
27:       // NOTE: ClassWizard will add and remove member functions here.
28:       //    DO NOT EDIT what you see in these blocks of generated code!
29:    //}}AFX_MSG
30:    DECLARE_MESSAGE_MAP()
31: };
32:
33: /////////////////////////////////////////////////////////////////////
```

Warning: Don't feel as if you must understand all the details in these long listings. AppWizard's source code is lengthy and has a lot of excess generic code that you might or might not modify later or even remove completely if it remains unneeded. The idea here is to see what goes on behind the AppWizard scenes and to gain some insight into Windows programs. The final bonus chapter lists several resources you can go to after you finish this book for a primary understanding of all the AppWizard and MFC concepts.

Listing B1.2. The TEACH.CPP implementation file.

```
1: // teach.cpp : Defines the class behaviors for the application.
2: //
3:
4: #include "stdafx.h"
5: #include "teach.h"
6:
7: #include "mainfrm.h"
8: #include "teachdoc.h"
9: #include "teachvw.h"
```

continues

Extra Credit Bonus 1

Listing B1.2. continued

```
10:
11: #ifdef _DEBUG
12: #undef THIS_FILE
13: static char BASED_CODE THIS_FILE[] = __FILE__;
14: #endif
15:
16: /////////////////////////////////////////////////////////////////////
17: // CTeachApp
18:
19: BEGIN_MESSAGE_MAP(CTeachApp, CWinApp)
20:     //{{AFX_MSG_MAP(CTeachApp)
21:     ON_COMMAND(ID_APP_ABOUT, OnAppAbout)
22:         // NOTE: ClassWizard will add and remove mapping macros here.
23:         //    DO NOT EDIT what you see in these blocks of generated code!
24:     //}}AFX_MSG_MAP
25:     // Standard file based document commands
26:     ON_COMMAND(ID_FILE_NEW, CWinApp::OnFileNew)
27:     ON_COMMAND(ID_FILE_OPEN, CWinApp::OnFileOpen)
28:     // Standard print setup command
29:     ON_COMMAND(ID_FILE_PRINT_SETUP, CWinApp::OnFilePrintSetup)
30: END_MESSAGE_MAP()
31:
32: /////////////////////////////////////////////////////////////////////
33: // CTeachApp construction
34:
35: CTeachApp::CTeachApp()
36: {
37:     // TODO: add construction code here
38:     // Place all significant initialization in InitInstance
39: }
40:
41: /////////////////////////////////////////////////////////////////////
42: // The one and only CTeachApp object
43:
44: CTeachApp NEAR theApp;
45:
46: /////////////////////////////////////////////////////////////////////
47: // CTeachApp initialization
48:
49: BOOL CTeachApp::InitInstance()
50: {
51:     // Standard initialization
52:     // If you are not using these features and want to reduce the size
53:     //  of your final executable, you should remove from the following
54:     //  the specific initialization routines you do not need.
55:
56:     SetDialogBkColor();        // Set dialog background color to gray
```

```
57:    LoadStdProfileSettings();  // Load standard INI file option
                                  ➡(including MRU)
58:
59:    // Register the application's document templates. Document
60:    // templates serve as the connection between documents, frame
          ➡windows and views.
61:
62:    CSingleDocTemplate* pDocTemplate;
63:    pDocTemplate = new CSingleDocTemplate(
64:        IDR_MAINFRAME,
65:        RUNTIME_CLASS(CTeachDoc),
66:        RUNTIME_CLASS(CMainFrame),     // main SDI frame window
67:        RUNTIME_CLASS(CTeachView));
68:    AddDocTemplate(pDocTemplate);
69:
70:    // create a new (empty) document
71:    OnFileNew();
72:
73:    if (m_lpCmdLine[0] != '\0')
74:    {
75:        // TODO: add command line processing here
76:    }
77:
78:
79:    return TRUE;
80: }
81:
82: /////////////////////////////////////////////////////////////////
83: // CAboutDlg dialog used for App About
84:
85: class CAboutDlg : public CDialog
86: {
87: public:
88:    CAboutDlg();
89:
90: // Dialog Data
91:    //{{AFX_DATA(CAboutDlg)
92:    enum { IDD = IDD_ABOUTBOX };
93:    //}}AFX_DATA
94:
95: // Implementation
96: protected:
97:    virtual void DoDataExchange(CDataExchange* pDX);    // DDX/DDV
                                                            ➡support
98:    //{{AFX_MSG(CAboutDlg)
99:        // No message handlers
100:   //}}AFX_MSG
101:   DECLARE_MESSAGE_MAP()
102: };
103:
```

continues

Extra Credit Bonus 1

Listing B1.2. continued

```
104: CAboutDlg::CAboutDlg() : CDialog(CAboutDlg::IDD)
105: {
106:   //{{AFX_DATA_INIT(CAboutDlg)
107:   //}}AFX_DATA_INIT
108: }
109:
110: void CAboutDlg::DoDataExchange(CDataExchange* pDX)
111: {
112:   CDialog::DoDataExchange(pDX);
113:   //{{AFX_DATA_MAP(CAboutDlg)
114:   //}}AFX_DATA_MAP
115: }
116:
117: BEGIN_MESSAGE_MAP(CAboutDlg, CDialog)
118:   //{{AFX_MSG_MAP(CAboutDlg)
119:       // No message handlers
120:   //}}AFX_MSG_MAP
121: END_MESSAGE_MAP()
122:
123: // App command to run the dialog
124: void CTeachApp::OnAppAbout()
125: {
126:   CAboutDlg aboutDlg;
127:   aboutDlg.DoModal();
128: }
129:
130: /////////////////////////////////////////////////////////////////////
131: // CTeachApp commands
```

Glance through the source code. You'll see several occurrences of code that looks like this:

```
//{{AFX_DATA(CAboutDlg)
    enum { IDD = IDD_ABOUTBOX };
//}}AFX_DATA
```

Don't ever add, change, or delete code inside the AFX beginning and ending braces. ClassWizard uses the AFX blocks to map Windows messages to member functions.

Listing B1.3 contains the header file for the CMainFrame class.

 Listing B1.3. The MAINFRM.H file.

```
1: // mainfrm.h : interface of the CMainFrame class
2: //
3: /////////////////////////////////////////////////////////////////////
```

```
 4:
 5: class CMainFrame : public CFrameWnd
 6: {
 7: protected: // create from serialization only
 8:     CMainFrame();
 9:     DECLARE_DYNCREATE(CMainFrame)
10:
11: // Attributes
12: public:
13:
14: // Operations
15: public:
16:
17: // Implementation
18: public:
19:     virtual ~CMainFrame();
20: #ifdef _DEBUG
21:     virtual void AssertValid() const;
22:     virtual void Dump(CDumpContext& dc) const;
23: #endif
24:
25: protected:  // control bar embedded members
26:     CStatusBar  m_wndStatusBar;
27:     CToolBar    m_wndToolBar;
28:
29: // Generated message map functions
30: protected:
31:     //{{AFX_MSG(CMainFrame)
32:     afx_msg int OnCreate(LPCREATESTRUCT lpCreateStruct);
33:         // NOTE: ClassWizard will add and remove member functions here.
34:         //    DO NOT EDIT what you see in these blocks of generated code!
35:     //}}AFX_MSG
36:     DECLARE_MESSAGE_MAP()
37:
38:
39: /////////////////////////////////////////////////////////////////////////////
```

Listing B1.4 contains the implementation code for the CMainFrame class.

Listing B1.4. The MAINFRM.CPP file.

```
1: // mainfrm.cpp : implementation of the CMainFrame class
2: //
3:
4: #include "stdafx.h"
5: #include "teach.h"
6:
```

continues

Extra Credit Bonus 1

Listing B1.4. continued

```
 7: #include "mainfrm.h"
 8:
 9: #ifdef _DEBUG
10: #undef THIS_FILE
11: static char BASED_CODE THIS_FILE[] = __FILE__;
12: #endif
13:
14: /////////////////////////////////////////////////////////////////
15: // CMainFrame
16:
17: IMPLEMENT_DYNCREATE(CMainFrame, CFrameWnd)
18:
19: BEGIN_MESSAGE_MAP(CMainFrame, CFrameWnd)
20:    //{{AFX_MSG_MAP(CMainFrame)
21:        // NOTE: ClassWizard will add and remove mapping macros here.
22:        //   DO NOT EDIT what you see in these blocks of generated code!
23:    ON_WM_CREATE()
24:    //}}AFX_MSG_MAP
25: END_MESSAGE_MAP()
26:
27: /////////////////////////////////////////////////////////////////
28: // arrays of IDs used to initialize control bars
29:
30: // toolbar buttons - IDs are command buttons
31: static UINT BASED_CODE buttons[] =
32: {
33:    // same order as in the bitmap 'toolbar.bmp'
34:    ID_FILE_NEW,
35:    ID_FILE_OPEN,
36:    ID_FILE_SAVE,
37:        ID_SEPARATOR,
38:    ID_EDIT_CUT,
39:    ID_EDIT_COPY,
40:    ID_EDIT_PASTE,
41:        ID_SEPARATOR,
42:    ID_FILE_PRINT,
43:    ID_APP_ABOUT,
44: };
45:
46: static UINT BASED_CODE indicators[] =
47: {
48:    ID_SEPARATOR,           // status line indicator
49:    ID_INDICATOR_CAPS,
50:    ID_INDICATOR_NUM,
51:    ID_INDICATOR_SCRL,
52: };
53:
54: /////////////////////////////////////////////////////////////////
55: // CMainFrame construction/destruction
```

```
56:
57: CMainFrame::CMainFrame()
58: {
59:    // TODO: add member initialization code here
60: }
61:
62: CMainFrame::~CMainFrame()
63: {
64: }
65:
66: int CMainFrame::OnCreate(LPCREATESTRUCT lpCreateStruct)
67: {
68:    if (CFrameWnd::OnCreate(lpCreateStruct) == -1)
69:         return -1;
70:
71:    if (!m_wndToolBar.Create(this) ||
72:         !m_wndToolBar.LoadBitmap(IDR_MAINFRAME) ||
73:         !m_wndToolBar.SetButtons(buttons,
74:           sizeof(buttons)/sizeof(UINT)))
75:    {
76:         TRACE("Failed to create toolbar\n");
77:         return -1;      // fail to create
78:    }
79:
80:    if (!m_wndStatusBar.Create(this) ||
81:         !m_wndStatusBar.SetIndicators(indicators,
82:           sizeof(indicators)/sizeof(UINT)))
83:    {
84:         TRACE("Failed to create status bar\n");
85:         return -1;      // fail to create
86:    }
87:
88:    return 0;
89: }
90:
91: /////////////////////////////////////////////////////////////////////
92: // CMainFrame diagnostics
93:
94: #ifdef _DEBUG
95: void CMainFrame::AssertValid() const
96: {
97:    CFrameWnd::AssertValid();
98: }
99:
100: void CMainFrame::Dump(CDumpContext& dc) const
101: {
102:    CFrameWnd::Dump(dc);
103: }
104:
105: #endif //_DEBUG
106:
```

Extra Credit Bonus 1

```
107: //////////////////////////////////////////////////////////////
108: // CMainFrame message handlers
```

Listing B1.5 contains the header file for the CTeachDoc class.

Listing B1.5. The TEACHDOC.H file.

```
 1: // teachdoc.h : interface of the CTeachDoc class
 2: //
 3: //////////////////////////////////////////////////////////////
 4:
 5: class CTeachDoc : public CDocument
 6: {
 7: protected: // create from serialization only
 8:     CTeachDoc();
 9:     DECLARE_DYNCREATE(CTeachDoc)
10:
11: // Attributes
12: public:
13: // Operations
14: public:
15:
16: // Implementation
17: public:
18:     virtual ~CTeachDoc();
19:     virtual void Serialize(CArchive& ar);    // overridden for document
                                                 ➥i/o
20: #ifdef _DEBUG
21:     virtual void AssertValid() const;
22:     virtual void Dump(CDumpContext& dc) const;
23: #endif
24:
25: protected:
26:     virtual BOOL OnNewDocument();
27:
28: // Generated message map functions
29: protected:
30:     //{{AFX_MSG(CTeachDoc)
31:         // NOTE: ClassWizard will add and remove member functions here.
32:         //    DO NOT EDIT what you see in these blocks of generated code!
33:     //}}AFX_MSG
34:     DECLARE_MESSAGE_MAP()
35: };
36:
37: //////////////////////////////////////////////////////////////
```

Tip: You'll see some TODO comments scattered throughout these program listings. AppWizard makes suggestions at places where you might want to insert specific code for your particular needs.

Listing B1.6 contains the implementation file for the CTeachDoc class.

Listing B1.6. The TEACHDOC.CPP file.

```
1:  // teachdoc.cpp : implementation of the CTeachDoc class
2:  //
3:
4:  #include "stdafx.h"
5:  #include "teach.h"
6:
7:  #include "teachdoc.h"
8:
9:  #ifdef _DEBUG
10: #undef THIS_FILE
11: static char BASED_CODE THIS_FILE[] = __FILE__;
12: #endif
13:
14: /////////////////////////////////////////////////////////////////////////////
15: // CTeachDoc
16:
17: IMPLEMENT_DYNCREATE(CTeachDoc, CDocument)
18:
19: BEGIN_MESSAGE_MAP(CTeachDoc, CDocument)
20:     //{{AFX_MSG_MAP(CTeachDoc)
21:         // NOTE: ClassWizard will add and remove mapping macros here.
22:         //   DO NOT EDIT what you see in these blocks of generated code!
23:     //}}AFX_MSG_MAP
24: END_MESSAGE_MAP()
25:
26: /////////////////////////////////////////////////////////////////////////////
27: // CTeachDoc construction/destruction
28:
29: CTeachDoc::CTeachDoc()
30: {
31:     // TODO: add one-time construction code here
32: }
33:
34: CTeachDoc::~CTeachDoc()
35: {
36: }
```

continues

Extra Credit Bonus 1

Listing B1.6. continued

```
37:
38: BOOL CTeachDoc::OnNewDocument()
39: {
40:    if (!CDocument::OnNewDocument())
41:         return FALSE;
42:
43:    // TODO: add reinitialization code here
44:    // (SDI documents will reuse this document)
45:
46:    return TRUE;
47: }
48:
49: ///////////////////////////////////////////////////////////////
50: // CTeachDoc serialization
51:
52: void CTeachDoc::Serialize(CArchive& ar)
53: {
54:    if (ar.IsStoring())
55:    {
56:         // TODO: add storing code here
57:    }
58:    else
59:    {
60:         // TODO: add loading code here
61:    }
62: }
63:
64: ///////////////////////////////////////////////////////////////
65: // CTeachDoc diagnostics
66:
67: #ifdef _DEBUG
68: void CTeachDoc::AssertValid() const
69: {
70:    CDocument::AssertValid();
71: }
72:
73: void CTeachDoc::Dump(CDumpContext& dc) const
74: {
75:    CDocument::Dump(dc);
76: }
77: #endif //_DEBUG
78:
79: ///////////////////////////////////////////////////////////////
80: // CTeachDoc commands
```

Listing B1.7 contains the class file for the CTeachView class.

Listing B1.7. The TEACHVC.H file.

```
1:  // teachvw.h : interface of the CTeachView class
2:  //
3:  /////////////////////////////////////////////////////////////////////
4:
5:  class CTeachView : public CView
6:  {
7:  protected: // create from serialization only
8:      CTeachView();
9:      DECLARE_DYNCREATE(CTeachView)
10:
11: // Attributes
12: public:
13:     CTeachDoc* GetDocument();
14:
15: // Operations
16: public:
17:
18: // Implementation
19: public:
20:     virtual ~CTeachView();
21:     virtual void OnDraw(CDC* pDC);  // overridden to draw this view
22: #ifdef _DEBUG
23:     virtual void AssertValid() const;
24:     virtual void Dump(CDumpContext& dc) const;
25: #endif
26:
27: protected:
28:
29:     // Printing support
30:     virtual BOOL OnPreparePrinting(CPrintInfo* pInfo);
31:     virtual void OnBeginPrinting(CDC* pDC, CPrintInfo* pInfo);
32:     virtual void OnEndPrinting(CDC* pDC, CPrintInfo* pInfo);
33:
34: // Generated message map functions
35: protected:
36:     //{{AFX_MSG(CTeachView)
37:         // NOTE: ClassWizard will add and remove member functions here.
38:         //    DO NOT EDIT what you see in these blocks of generated code!
39:     //}}AFX_MSG
40:     DECLARE_MESSAGE_MAP()
41: };
42:
43: #ifndef _DEBUG  // debug version in teachvw.cpp
44: inline CTeachDoc* CTeachView::GetDocument()
45:    { return (CTeachDoc*)m_pDocument; }
46: #endif
47:
48: /////////////////////////////////////////////////////////////////////
```

Extra Credit Bonus 1

Listing B1.8 contains the implementation file for the `CTeachView` class.

Listing B1.8. The TEACHVW.CPP file.

```
 1: // teachvw.cpp : implementation of the CTeachView class
 2: //
 3:
 4: #include "stdafx.h"
 5: #include "teach.h"
 6:
 7: #include "teachdoc.h"
 8: #include "teachvw.h"
 9:
10: #ifdef _DEBUG
11: #undef THIS_FILE
12: static char BASED_CODE THIS_FILE[] = __FILE__;
13: #endif
14:
15: //////////////////////////////////////////////////////////////////
16: // CTeachView
17:
18: IMPLEMENT_DYNCREATE(CTeachView, CView)
19:
20: BEGIN_MESSAGE_MAP(CTeachView, CView)
21:     //{{AFX_MSG_MAP(CTeachView)
22:         // NOTE: ClassWizard will add and remove mapping macros here.
23:         //    DO NOT EDIT what you see in these blocks of generated code!
24:     //}}AFX_MSG_MAP
25:     // Standard printing commands
26:     ON_COMMAND(ID_FILE_PRINT, CView::OnFilePrint)
27:     ON_COMMAND(ID_FILE_PRINT_PREVIEW, CView::OnFilePrintPreview)
28: END_MESSAGE_MAP()
29:
30: //////////////////////////////////////////////////////////////////
31: // CTeachView construction/destruction
32:
33: CTeachView::CTeachView()
34: {
35:     // TODO: add construction code here
36: }
37:
38: CTeachView::~CTeachView()
39: {
40: }
41:
42: //////////////////////////////////////////////////////////////////
43: // CTeachView drawing
44:
45: void CTeachView::OnDraw(CDC* pDC)
```

```
46: {
47:     CTeachDoc* pDoc = GetDocument();
48:     ASSERT_VALID(pDoc);
49:
50:     // TODO: add draw code for native data here
51: }
52:
53: /////////////////////////////////////////////////////////////////////////
54: // CTeachView printing
55:
56: BOOL CTeachView::OnPreparePrinting(CPrintInfo* pInfo)
57: {
58:     // default preparation
59:     return DoPreparePrinting(pInfo);
60: }
61:
62: void CTeachView::OnBeginPrinting(CDC* /*pDC*/, CPrintInfo* /*pInfo*/)
63: {
64:     // TODO: add extra initialization before printing
65: }
66:
67: void CTeachView::OnEndPrinting(CDC* /*pDC*/, CPrintInfo* /*pInfo*/)
68: {
69:     // TODO: add cleanup after printing
70: }
71:
72: /////////////////////////////////////////////////////////////////////////
73: // CTeachView diagnostics
74:
75: #ifdef _DEBUG
76: void CTeachView::AssertValid() const
77: {
78:     CView::AssertValid();
79: }
80:
81: void CTeachView::Dump(CDumpContext& dc) const
82: {
83:     CView::Dump(dc);
84: }
85:
86: CTeachDoc* CTeachView::GetDocument() // non-debug version is inline
87: {
88:     ASSERT(m_pDocument->IsKindOf(RUNTIME_CLASS(CTeachDoc)));
89:     return (CTeachDoc*)m_pDocument;
90: }
91: #endif //_DEBUG
92:
93: /////////////////////////////////////////////////////////////////////////
94: // CTeachView message handlers
```

Extra Credit Bonus 1

The output of listings B1.1 through B1.8 was shown back in Figure B1.5.

A line-by-line analysis of these files would be difficult and really unnecessary at this point. Visual C++ Windows application programming is best learned by first examining an overview (see the next section) and then changing the generated code to add specifics to it (as done in the next bonus chapter). In a way, an analysis of this program constitutes the remainder of the chapter, but remember that a complete line-by-line description would more confuse you than help you at this point.

Warning: You cannot use AppWizard to remove functionality after you request AppWizard's generation of the source files. In other words, if you decide you don't want print preview, it's too late to remove it via AppWizard after AppWizard generates the source files. To remove functionality from generated code (or to add new functionality that you forgot to request from AppWizard), you must edit the files by hand or generate an entire new set of files.

Describing the Classes

The application class CTeachApp (used in listings B1.1 and B1.2) defines your *application object*. An application object is nothing more than your Windows application. Each Windows application consists of one and only one application object. Therefore, each Windows program you create using Visual C++'s MFC classes defines an application object from the application class, and the name for such a class generally follows the naming convention C*Appname*App, in which *Appname* is your application's filename. The application object takes care of initializing data (through constructor calls), manages the documents and views, and takes care of cleaning up the application before its termination (through destructor calls).

Note: As long as you use AppWizard to begin your application generation, you rarely have to worry about many of the details inside the application object. However, if you want some special initialization and

> destruction to take place when your application loads and terminates, you'll need to add your own code in the files that reference the application object.

The application automatically starts and processes the message loop described earlier in this chapter. A function that is required by all Windows programs is named `WinMain()`. The MFC classes call `WinMain()` for you, and you don't have to write `WinMain()` as you would have to do without the MFC classes. Your application object initiates the needed call to `WinMain()` when your program begins.

The `WinMain()` function, although it's hidden behind the MFC scenes, sends your applications any messages that are received. Remember that a message is sent to the program any time an event such as a mouse click occurs. You can choose to respond or ignore any or all messages depending on the needs of the program. If you want to respond to a message, you must map (with the help of ClassWizard) that particular message to one of your functions. When your application object receives a message, the application object sends that message to the `CMainFrame` class.

> **Note:** The only message not sent to `CMainFrame` is the `WM_QUIT` message, which ends your program. When the user closes the application or selects **F**ile E**x**it, `WinMain()` gets the `WM_QUIT` message, and the application terminates.

The `CMainFrame` class controls the window that you see on-screen. If the application passes a message such as a window-resizing message to `CMainFrame`, it's the job of `CMainFrame` to manipulate the window you see on-screen accordingly. Figure B1.6 illustrates the process of the application sending messages to the `CMainFrame` window.

The final two classes, `CTeachDoc` and `CTeachView`, control the document and the views of the application. The `CTeachDoc` document class controls the documents your application works on. In this case, a document is not quite the same as a word-processing document. Rather, the document is the data you are working with in the application. Remember that an AppWizard application can be generated that supports MDI (a multiple document interface), even though the TEACH application does not include MDI. Also, the document you work with might or might not all fit inside the `CMainFrame` window. Therefore, the document class exists to handle the one

Extra Credit Bonus 1

or more documents your application has open and to determine which is active at any one time (that is, which document is currently being manipulated).

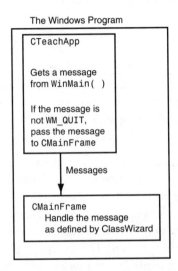

Figure B1.6. An overview of the message-handling process.

Just because your application might have more than one document open does not mean that you want both of them displayed at the same time. In addition, one or more documents can be open, and you might want *none* of them to appear in your window (such as when several files are being merged and nothing is needed on-screen but a dialog box saying `Waiting...`). Therefore, an additional class, the `CTeachView` class in your application's case, is needed to display whatever data from the document class needs to be viewed. If the document is too lengthy to fit in the `CMainFrame` window, the view class can determine exactly which portions of the document you can view at any one time. If there is more than one document, as would be the case with an MDI application, the view class controls the display of the appropriate document.

Tip: It might help to think about `CTeachDoc` and `CTeachView` in the following way: The document class is the data-handler, and the view class is the data-displayer.

DO	DON'T

DO use AppWizard to generate your application. Even though AppWizard's application is just an application shell without a lot of specifics, the application will include the classes that handle major features common to many applications, such as MDI, print preview, menu support, and a toolbar.

DO make sure that you have lots of disk space before building the AppWizard project. It's best to have more than 3M available. You can delete the object files and backup the source files after you complete the application.

DON'T forget that Visual C++ takes a long time to build Windows applications. In defense of Visual C++, there are lots of files required in any Windows program, especially Windows programs that support all the functionality that AppWizard adds.

Summary

Today's chapter offers an introductory look at Windows programming using Visual C++. You saw how a true Windows program differs from a QuickWin program. QuickWin is basically a working vehicle for your regular DOS-based programs to run in and to mimic a Windows application. However, QuickWin applications have none of the flexibility and power that come with a true Windows program.

One of the most important reasons for switching from QuickWin to full-blown Windows applications is that you can take full advantage of the MFC (Microsoft Foundation Classes) features of Visual C++. As you'll see in the next couple of bonus chapters, the MFC classes provide lots of programming power with little effort required on your part.

This chapter walks you through the creation of an AppWizard Windows application. By having you answer a few prompts and click the mouse a few times, AppWizard generates all the source code needed (all 19 files!) to build a Windows program.

The AppWizard code is little more than a shell of a program with the hooks for the major features you need, such as print preview, a menu, and a toolbar. But the consistent AppWizard coding methods make it easier to add your own code later, which will shape the generic AppWizard application into something specific for your needs.

Extra Credit Bonus 1

The AppWizard code contains four primary classes that handle the application, the screen's window, the document (data), and the view of the document.

Q&A

Q. How do Windows programs differ from DOS programs?

A. There are several differences between a Windows program and a DOS program. The most fundamental difference lies in the user interface. In a DOS program, the program guides the user through a series of choices, prompting the user along the way in a sequential manner. A Windows program must be able to handle many possible activities at one time.

At any point in a Windows program, the user might move the mouse, select from a menu, click the mouse button, or press a key. The Windows program must be able to handle these events in any order.

Q. How does a Windows program process all the events going on in the program?

A. When a Windows event occurs, whether that event was triggered by the user or another task, Windows sends a message to the user's program. The identifier of the message (all defined as named numeric constants, such as `WM_KEYDOWN` or `WM_MOVE`) tells your Windows program what just took place.

The program responds to the messages coming from the system through a Windows message loop. In C-style Windows programs, a message loop is one huge `switch` statement. In Visual C++ programs, you map messages to your program's functions, which handle those messages through ClassWizard.

Q. Do I need to understand the details of the generated source code?

A. The answer is a resounding, concrete, objective *yes and no*. The nice thing about programming with Visual C++ and the MFC is that so many details are taken care of for you. Of course, when you begin to add your own specific code to the AppWizard application shell program, you have to know where to add the code and how to integrate your code with the code that is generated by AppWizard. Therefore, you must be familiar with the generated code.

Such familiarity comes with experience, not with a lot of study. The next bonus chapter adds code to the TEACH application, and you'll see how easy it is to make the code do more than it does now. In addition, you'll see that the identifying names used by AppWizard and the comments that AppWizard places in your generated code help you determine exactly where your additions need to go.

The bottom line is that you'll eventually learn the details of the AppWizard code, but don't feel as if you must take a lot of time studying those details and memorizing the pieces of the AppWizard code.

Workshop

The Workshop offers quiz questions and exercises to hone your skills and give you feedback on today's lesson. You'll find some proposed answers in Appendix D.

Quiz

1. What is an event?
2. What is a Windows message?
3. What is a message loop?
4. What are the four primary classes that are generated by AppWizard?
5. What is the difference between the document class and the view class?

Exercise

1. Generate a new AppWizard application that includes an MDI interface, a menu, no print preview, and no toolbar. Don't store the application in the same directory as TEACH (the application created in this chapter). Store the application in a directory named EXERCISE so that you can easily remove all the files related to the application when you are finished with it. Build the application and run it a few times, trying the various menu options. Notice that there is no mention of print preview on the File menu as there was in the TEACH application. Remove the .OBJ, .H, and .CPP files in the EXERCISE directory, and rerun the program. (Don't rebuild the files when

Extra Credit Bonus 1

asked by the Visual Workbench.) You'll see that your final application doesn't need these files, so you'll be able to consolidate disk space in the future after you debug your application. (Not every Windows application you create has to consume 4M of disk space!) Finally, remove the EXERCISE directory.

Extra Credit Bonus 2+

The MFC Classes: Power You Will Gain

Extra Credit Bonus 2

This bonus chapter takes the TEACH application you created in the preceding bonus chapter and adds specific functionality to it. You'll see how the MFC classes add power to your Windows applications. The primary purpose of this chapter is to get you used to some of the things you can do after AppWizard generates your application shell. This chapter does not teach you MFC from the ground up; for that you will need a much more complete tutorial. Nevertheless, you really don't have to know all the ins and outs of MFC or of Windows programming to change the AppWizard code so that it meets some of your specific needs.

Today, you learn about the following topics:

- How to use App Studio to modify the About dialog box
- How the resource script file contains all the information about a program's resources
- The data-type prefix characters and Windows `typedefed` data types that are used in Windows programming
- How to add data-displaying functions to output text in the AppWizard application's window
- How to use the `CString` class and its helpful member functions
- How to accept and display user keystrokes in your AppWizard window

Adding Some Details

As mentioned earlier, there is no way this book can make you an MFC Windows programmer in five bonus chapters. Therefore, the remainder of this and the next chapters offers some coding suggestions that change the way the TEACH application behaves. You'll see how to change the details of the About box and how to display some text in the window frame. You'll see that you never have to understand *all* the details of the AppWizard-generated source code. You'll see that often you can simply read the source code's comments and call some common MFC functions to achieve your goals.

You can either make the changes suggested in this section or merely glance through them to gain more of an understanding of the source-code contents generated by AppWizard.

 Warning: In this chapter, you'll see how easy it is to change dialog boxes, menus, and other common resources of a Visual C++ Windows program. However, don't stray too far from the common look and feel of most Windows programs. For instance, most Windows programs have a **F**ile **O**pen command. If you change the menu to read **F**ile **R**etrieve, you might be making the application clearer to an individual more used to the term *retrieve*, but you'll lose the commonality that is so crucial to Windows programs.

The advantage of moving a user from a DOS-based environment to a Windows-based environment is in the consistency of the user interface. Maintain the common interface by keeping your menu items and descriptions as close as possible to Windows-based software (such as Excel and Word for Windows). AppWizard follows the standards found in many Windows programs. Try not to deviate too far from the ordering of AppWizard's menus and menu options.

Start Easy: The About Box

Almost all Windows programs include an About... option in the **H**elp menu that describes the program and version number. One of the many uses of the About box is to determine the version number, and the serial number if your program has one, you'll need if you call for technical assistance. The entire About box is a Windows resource because all dialog boxes are resources, changeable through the App Studio Visual C++ tool.

Run your TEACH application now, and select the **H**elp **A**bout... option. You'll notice that AppWizard created the dialog box, embedded a bitmap image in the dialog box, added an OK command button, and included the following text:

```
Teach Application Version 1.0
```

Close the About box by clicking the OK command button. Your first foray into modifying the AppWizard code is to change the message displayed in the About box and to change the About box's title, About TEACH, to some other text. There are generally two ways to change a resource:

Extra Credit Bonus 2

- [ ] Use App Studio's visual interface.
- [ ] Use a text editor, such as the one in the Visual Workbench, to change the resource *script* file (a file that describes the program's resources).

App Studio is the preferred way of changing resources. If you use a text editor to change the resource script file, you could accidentally leave out a space, add an extra comma, or make another kind of syntax error that App Studio would not make. Also, App Studio is a more intuitive way of changing resources, and with it total beginners can usually figure out how to change an application's resource without knowing much about Windows programming.

Follow these steps to change the dialog box:

1. Make sure that the TEACH project is open; if it is not, open the project with **P**roject **O**pen.

2. Select **A**pp Studio from the **T**ools menu.

3. You should see a dialog box describing the six resources in the TEACH application in the **T**ype listbox. Scroll through the items in the **T**ype list box. To the right, under **R**esources, you'll see a list of specific resources that match that type. There is one resource for the dialog **T**ype, named IDD_ABOUTBOX. The application's About dialog box resource has been assigned the resource ID defined as IDD_ABOUTBOX.

   Highlight IDD_ABOUTBOX and then select **O**pen to open the editing tool for the About dialog box. Your screen should look like the one in Figure B2.1.

4. There are five items within the dialog box that you can edit. The resource pieces that you can change are called *properties*. These are the five features of the About dialog box that you can modify:

   The entire dialog box itself: You can change the title, the size of the dialog box, and other properties of the About box.

   The command button: You can change such properties as the caption and the location of the button.

   The bitmap image: You can specify another image, a different location, a different size, and other properties.

The two text lines: Among other things, you can change the words, the font, and the location.

The way you change one of the dialog box's elements is to double-click over that element. For now, double-click the mouse cursor over the first text line that reads Teach Application Version 1.0. A new dialog box about the text opens, as shown in Figure B2.2.

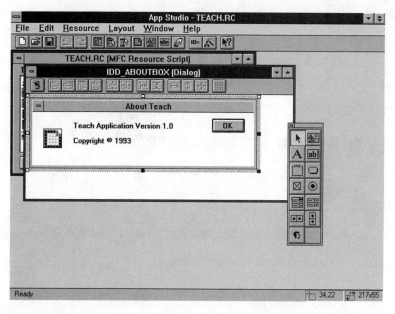

Figure B2.1. Getting ready to modify the About box resource.

5. Change the **C**aption text to read **My 1st Application**. As you delete the old text and type the new, you'll see App Studio change the text in the dialog box in the upper part of the screen. Select the second line of text (by double-clicking it), and change it to **This is easy!** Press Enter to close the property box.

6. Double-click the OK command button. Change the text (the **C**aption) to **Click Me**. Notice that the Def**a**ult option is checked. If there were more than one command button on this dialog box, only one could be marked as the default button. The default button is the selected button when the dialog

Extra Credit Bonus 2

box first appears (the button selected when the user presses Enter if the user hasn't activated another button before pressing Enter). Press Enter to close the property box.

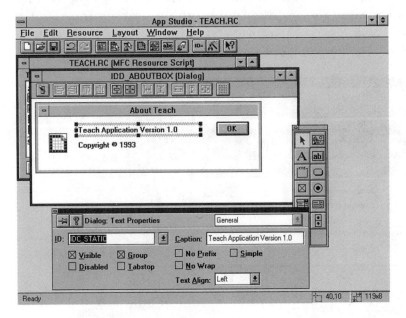

Figure B2.2. Changing the properties of the text.

7. Double-click the About box's title bar to display the dialog box's property settings. Change the **C**aption (which appears in the dialog box's title bar) to **Teach Yourself Visual C++**. Press Enter to close the property box.

8. Your screen should look like the one in Figure B2.3.

 Tip: At any point during your App Studio session, you can click the toggle switch (the leftmost tool in the IDD_ABOUTBOX window). When you click the switch, App Studio displays a prototype of the dialog box that you can look at to see whether it will appear the way you expect. Pressing Enter closes the dialog box.

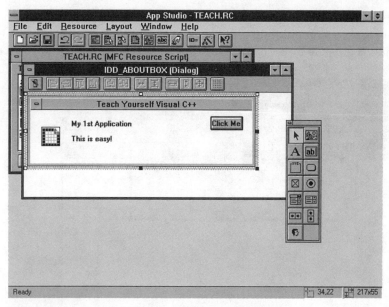

Figure B2.3. After changing the About dialog box.

9. Double-click the icon at the left of the dialog box. You'll see the Icon identifier IDD_ABOUTBOX. Remember this name, and close the property box by double-clicking its control button in the upper-left corner. Close the dialog box. Change the resource Type to Icon. You'll see a list of icon identifiers under the Resources list box. Highlight IDD_ABOUTBOX (the identifier you saw assigned to the About box icon), and select the Properties... button. You'll see the filename TEACH.ICO connected to that icon. AppWizard built the icon (which you could exchange for a different one) along with your application, and the Properties option connects the file to its icon identifier. For now, leave the icon file alone, and exit App Studio, saying Yes when asked about saving the changes you made.

10. Rebuild your project and rerun your application. Display the About box, and you'll see the dialog box shown in Figure B2.4.

Remember that App Studio is just one of two ways you can change resources. You can also change resource information by editing a text file. Listing B2.1 shows the contents of TEACH.RC, the App Studio resources (the resources that App Studio can edit). Although the file listing is lengthy, you can look through it and figure out most of it. The file contains text for the menus, menu shortcut keys, dialog box settings (the only

Extra Credit Bonus 2

dialog box in the application is the About box that you just changed), and strings that are used in the program. Keeping the strings in a resource file instead of coding them directly in the program makes converting the application to a foreign language easy.

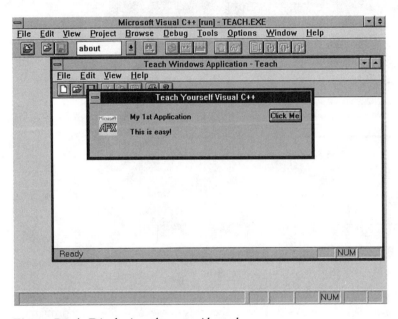

Figure B2.4. Displaying the new About box.

 Listing B2.1. The TEACH.RC resource script file.

```
 1: // Microsoft App Studio generated resource script.
 2: //
 3: #include "resource.h"
 4:
 5: #define APSTUDIO_READONLY_SYMBOLS
 6: /////////////////////////////////////////////////////////////////////
 7: //
 8: // Generated from the TEXTINCLUDE 2 resource.
 9: //
10: #include "afxres.h"
11:
12: /////////////////////////////////////////////////////////////////////
13: #undef APSTUDIO_READONLY_SYMBOLS
14:
15: #ifdef APSTUDIO_INVOKED
16: /////////////////////////////////////////////////////////////////////
17: //
18: // TEXTINCLUDE
```

```
19: //
20:
21: 1 TEXTINCLUDE DISCARDABLE
22: BEGIN
23:     "resource.h\0"
24: END
25:
26: 2 TEXTINCLUDE DISCARDABLE
27: BEGIN
28:     "#include ""afxres.h""\r\n"
29:     "\0"
30: END
31:
32: 3 TEXTINCLUDE DISCARDABLE
33: BEGIN
34:     "#include ""res\\teach.rc2""  // non-App Studio edited
     ➥resources\r\n"
35:     "\r\n"
36:     "#include ""afxres.rc""  \011// Standard components\r\n"
37:     "#include ""afxprint.rc""\011// printing/print preview
     ➥resources\r\n"
38:     "\0"
39: END
40:
41: /////////////////////////////////////////////////////////////////
42: #endif    // APSTUDIO_INVOKED
43:
44:
45: /////////////////////////////////////////////////////////////////
46: //
47: // Icon
48: //
49:
50: IDD_ABOUTBOX            ICON      DISCARDABLE
     ➥"C:\\TEACH\\RES\\TEACH.ICO"
51: IDI_ICON1               ICON      DISCARDABLE
     ➥"C:\\TEACH\\RES\\ICON1.ICO"
52:
53: /////////////////////////////////////////////////////////////////
54: //
55: // Bitmap
56: //
57:
58: IDR_MAINFRAME           BITMAP    MOVEABLE PURE   "RES\\TOOLBAR.BMP"
59: IDB_BITMAP1             BITMAP    DISCARDABLE     "RES\\BITMAP1.BMP"
60:
61: /////////////////////////////////////////////////////////////////
62: //
63: // Menu
```

continues

Extra Credit Bonus 2

Listing B2.1. continued

```
 64: //
 65:
 66: IDR_MAINFRAME MENU PRELOAD DISCARDABLE
 67: BEGIN
 68:     POPUP "&File"
 69:     BEGIN
 70:         MENUITEM "&New\tCtrl+N",                ID_FILE_NEW
 71:         MENUITEM "&Open...\tCtrl+O",            ID_FILE_OPEN
 72:         MENUITEM "&Save\tCtrl+S",               ID_FILE_SAVE
 73:         MENUITEM "Save &As...",                 ID_FILE_SAVE_AS
 74:         MENUITEM SEPARATOR
 75:         MENUITEM "&Print...\tCtrl+P",           ID_FILE_PRINT
 76:         MENUITEM "Print Pre&view",
                   ID_FILE_PRINT_PREVIEW
 77:         MENUITEM "P&rint Setup...",             ID_FILE_PRINT_SETUP
 78:         MENUITEM SEPARATOR
 79:         MENUITEM "Recent File",                 ID_FILE_MRU_FILE1,
                   GRAYED
 80:         MENUITEM SEPARATOR
 81:         MENUITEM "E&xit",                       ID_APP_EXIT
 82:     END
 83:     POPUP "&Edit"
 84:     BEGIN
 85:         MENUITEM "&Undo\tCtrl+Z",               ID_EDIT_UNDO
 86:         MENUITEM SEPARATOR
 87:         MENUITEM "Cu&t\tCtrl+X",                ID_EDIT_CUT
 88:         MENUITEM "&Copy\tCtrl+C",               ID_EDIT_COPY
 89:         MENUITEM "&Paste\tCtrl+V",              ID_EDIT_PASTE
 90:     END
100:     POPUP "&View"
101:     BEGIN
102:         MENUITEM "&Toolbar",                    ID_VIEW_TOOLBAR
103:         MENUITEM "&Status Bar",                 ID_VIEW_STATUS_BAR
104:     END
105:     POPUP "&Help"
106:     BEGIN
107:         MENUITEM "&About Teach...",             ID_APP_ABOUT
108:     END
109: END
110:
111:
112: //////////////////////////////////////////////////////////////////
113: //
114: // Accelerator
115: //
116:
117: IDR_MAINFRAME ACCELERATORS PRELOAD MOVEABLE PURE
118: BEGIN
119:     "N",            ID_FILE_NEW,            VIRTKEY,CONTROL
120:     "O",            ID_FILE_OPEN,           VIRTKEY,CONTROL
```

```
121:        "S",                ID_FILE_SAVE,           VIRTKEY,CONTROL
122:        "P",                ID_FILE_PRINT,          VIRTKEY,CONTROL
123:        "Z",                ID_EDIT_UNDO,           VIRTKEY,CONTROL
124:        "X",                ID_EDIT_CUT,            VIRTKEY,CONTROL
125:        "C",                ID_EDIT_COPY,           VIRTKEY,CONTROL
126:        "V",                ID_EDIT_PASTE,          VIRTKEY,CONTROL
127:        VK_BACK,            ID_EDIT_UNDO,           VIRTKEY,ALT
128:        VK_DELETE,          ID_EDIT_CUT,            VIRTKEY,SHIFT
129:        VK_INSERT,          ID_EDIT_COPY,           VIRTKEY,CONTROL
130:        VK_INSERT,          ID_EDIT_PASTE,          VIRTKEY,SHIFT
131:        VK_F6,              ID_NEXT_PANE,           VIRTKEY
132:        VK_F6,              ID_PREV_PANE,           VIRTKEY,SHIFT
133: END
134:
135: /////////////////////////////////////////////////////////////////////////
136: //
137: // Dialog
138: //
139:
140: IDD_ABOUTBOX DIALOG DISCARDABLE  34, 22, 217, 55
141: STYLE DS_MODALFRAME | WS_POPUP | WS_CAPTION | WS_SYSMENU
142: CAPTION "Teach Yourself Visual C++"
143: FONT 8, "MS Sans Serif"
144: BEGIN
145:     ICON            IDD_ABOUTBOX,IDC_STATIC,9,13,18,20
146:     LTEXT           "My 1st Application",IDC_STATIC,40,10,119,8
147:     LTEXT           "This is easy!",IDC_STATIC,40,25,119,8
148:     DEFPUSHBUTTON   "Click Me",IDOK,176,6,32,14,WS_GROUP
149: END
150:
151: /////////////////////////////////////////////////////////////////////////
152: //
153: // String Table
154: //
155:
156: STRINGTABLE PRELOAD DISCARDABLE
157: BEGIN
158:     IDR_MAINFRAME           "Teach Windows
         ➥Application\nTeach\nTeach
159: Document\n\n\nTeach.Document\nTeach Document"
160:
161:
162: STRINGTABLE PRELOAD DISCARDABLE
163:
164: AFX_IDS_APP_TITLE       "Teach Windows Application"
165: AFX_IDS_IDLEMESSAGE     "Ready"
166: END
167:
168: STRINGTABLE DISCARDABLE
169: BEGIN
170:     ID_INDICATOR_EXT            "EXT"
```

continues

Extra Credit Bonus 2

Listing B2.1. continued

```
171:        ID_INDICATOR_CAPS       "CAP"
172:        ID_INDICATOR_NUM        "NUM"
173:        ID_INDICATOR_SCRL       "SCRL"
174:        ID_INDICATOR_OVR        "OVR"
175:        ID_INDICATOR_REC        "REC"
176: END
177:
178: STRINGTABLE DISCARDABLE
179: BEGIN
180:        ID_FILE_NEW             "Create a new document"
181:        ID_FILE_OPEN            "Open an existing document"
182:        ID_FILE_CLOSE           "Close the active document"
183:        ID_FILE_SAVE            "Save the active document"
184:        ID_FILE_SAVE_AS         "Save the active document with a new
                                    ➥name"
185:        ID_FILE_PAGE_SETUP      "Change the printing options"
186:        ID_FILE_PRINT_SETUP     "Change the printer and printing
                                    ➥options"
187:        ID_FILE_PRINT           "Print the active document"
188:        ID_FILE_PRINT_PREVIEW   "Display full pages"
189: END
190:
191: STRINGTABLE DISCARDABLE
192: BEGIN
193:        ID_APP_ABOUT            "Display program information, version
                                    ➥number and copyright"

194:        ID_APP_EXIT             "Quit the application; prompts to save
                                    ➥documents"
195: END
196:
197: STRINGTABLE DISCARDABLE
198: BEGIN
199:        ID_FILE_MRU_FILE1       "Open this document"
200:        ID_FILE_MRU_FILE2       "Open this document"
201:        ID_FILE_MRU_FILE3       "Open this document"
202:        ID_FILE_MRU_FILE4       "Open this document"
203: END
204:
205: STRINGTABLE DISCARDABLE
206: BEGIN
207:        ID_NEXT_PANE            "Switch to the next window pane"
208:        ID_PREV_PANE            "Switch back to the previous window
                                    ➥pane"
209: END
210:
211: STRINGTABLE DISCARDABLE
212: BEGIN
213:        ID_EDIT_CLEAR           "Erase the selection"
214:        ID_EDIT_CLEAR_ALL       "Erase everything"
```

```
215:        ID_EDIT_COPY            "Copy the selection and put it on the
                                    ➥Clipboard"
216:        ID_EDIT_CUT             "Cut the selection and put it on the
                                    ➥Clipboard"
217:        ID_EDIT_FIND            "Find the specified text"
218:        ID_EDIT_PASTE           "Insert Clipboard contents"
219:        ID_EDIT_REPEAT          "Repeat the last action"
220:        ID_EDIT_REPLACE         "Replace specific text with different
                                    ➥text"
221:        ID_EDIT_SELECT_ALL      "Select the entire document"
222:        ID_EDIT_UNDO            "Undo the last action"
223:        ID_EDIT_REDO            "Redo the previously undone action"
224: END
225:
226: STRINGTABLE DISCARDABLE
227: BEGIN
228:        ID_VIEW_TOOLBAR         "Show or hide the toolbar"
229:        ID_VIEW_STATUS_BAR      "Show or hide the status bar"
230: END
231:
232: STRINGTABLE DISCARDABLE
233: BEGIN
234:        AFX_IDS_SCSIZE          "Change the window size"
235:        AFX_IDS_SCMOVE          "Change the window position"
236:        AFX_IDS_SCMINIMIZE      "Reduce the window to an icon"
237:        AFX_IDS_SCMAXIMIZE      "Enlarge the window to full size"
238:        AFX_IDS_SCNEXTWINDOW    "Switch to the next document window"
239:        AFX_IDS_SCPREVWINDOW    "Switch to the previous document
                                    ➥window"
240:        AFX_IDS_SCCLOSE         "Close the active window and prompts to
                                    ➥save the documents"
241: END
242:
243: STRINGTABLE DISCARDABLE
244: BEGIN
245:        AFX_IDS_SCRESTORE       "Restore the window to normal size"
246:        AFX_IDS_SCTASKLIST      "Activate Task List"
247: END
248:
249: #ifndef APSTUDIO_INVOKED
250: /////////////////////////////////////////////////////////////////////
251: //
252: // Generated from the TEXTINCLUDE 3 resource.
253: //
254: #include "res\teach.rc2"   // non-App Studio edited resources
255:
256: #include "afxres.rc"       // Standard components
257: #include "afxprint.rc"     // printing/print preview resources
258:
259: /////////////////////////////////////////////////////////////////////
260: #endif      // not APSTUDIO_INVOKED
```

Extra Credit Bonus 2

A line-by-line analysis of the preceding code would be a waste of your time. Look through the listing, and you'll see all the familiar elements in your application. Keep in mind that App Studio can edit this entire file. Therefore, you never *have* to understand this file's contents, although some Windows programmers still like to make manual changes from time to time. It's easier to change screen coordinate numbers than to move an icon or dialog box with the mouse in App Studio.

To get an idea of how App Studio makes changes to the file, study Listing B2.2. Listing B2.2 contains the *previous* contents of part of TEACH.RC before you made the App Studio modifications. Compare Listing B2.2 to lines 135–150 in Listing B2.1 to see how App Studio modified the dialog box from its original settings.

Listing B2.2. The original lines in TEACH.RC that were changed.

```
 1: /////////////////////////////////////////////////////////////////////////
 2: //
 3: // Dialog
 4: //
 5:
 6: IDD_ABOUTBOX DIALOG DISCARDABLE  34, 22, 217, 55
 7: CAPTION "About Teach"
 8: STYLE DS_MODALFRAME | WS_POPUP | WS_CAPTION | WS_SYSMENU
 9: FONT 8, "MS Sans Serif"
10: BEGIN
11:     ICON            IDR_MAINFRAME,IDC_STATIC,11,17,20,20
12:     LTEXT           "Teach Application Version 1.0",IDC_STATIC,40,10,
                        ➡119,8
13:     LTEXT           "Copyright \251 1993",IDC_STATIC,40,25,119,8
14:     DEFPUSHBUTTON   "OK",IDOK,176,6,32,14,WS_GROUP
15: END
```

As you can see, App Studio changed lines 7, 11, 12, 13, and 14. (See lines 142, 145, 146, 147, and 148 in Listing B2.1.) These are changes that you could have made by hand but didn't have to because App Studio took care of the edits for you.

Do you think it's hard to change other resources of the program, including menu text? It's not. AppWizard enables you to visually change or add any resource to your Windows program. You can look through the resource script file and see all the menu messages that you could change by hand, but you might as well use App Studio to keep things consistent and correct.

Try this: See whether you can find the status bar messages that AppWizard generated inside the resource script (Listing B2.1).

Adding Specifics with MFC

It's time to use MFC to add functionality to the generic application. The AppWizard application already makes many calls to MFC. The four classes described in the preceding chapter are derived from the MFC classes. This section adds some functionality, one step at a time, to the TEACH application by using MFC classes and the MFC function calls.

The most obvious need of the generic application is to display text inside the window. As it now stands, the program simply displays a blank window with nothing inside it. Therefore, you'll display a message inside the window.

Before getting to the details, it is helpful to learn something more about MFC. As you know, Windows messages are mapped to functions that execute automatically. Table B2.1 gives you a list of sample Windows messages that are typically sent to applications.

Table B2.1. Sample Windows messages.

Windows Message	Description
WM_CLOSE	The window is being closed.
WM_CREATE	The window is being created (and is probably ready for display).
WM_DESTROY	The window is closed for good.
WM_MENUSELECT	The user has just selected from a menu.
WM_MOVE	The user has moved the window.
WM_PAINT	The window must be repainted in part or in total. (Perhaps another overlapping window was closed.)
WM_QUIT	The program is terminated.
WM_SETFOCUS	The program's window has just received the focus. (This means that the window was switched to, or made active, when another window on the screen had the focus previously.)
WM_SHOWWINDOW	The window is shown (if hidden) or hidden (if shown).
WM_SIZE	The window has been resized.

Extra Credit Bonus 2

When your application receives one of these messages (or another of the approximately 150 possible messages), the MFC maps certain member functions to the messages. These member functions are sometimes called *on functions* because they have names such as `OnDraw()`, `OnButtonUp()`, `OnCancel()`, and `OnMouseMove()`. You can (and should) override and modify any of the functions your application needs to handle.

 Note: If you ignore a message or don't override an on function to handle certain messages, your application will return to the `WinMain()` procedure, and the default message action will be taken. Usually, the event that caused the message is ignored.

The `OnDraw()` member function is part of the view class. Every time your program redraws the window, the view class calls `OnDraw()` to display the window. Therefore, if you want the window to contain text, you must insert the appropriate output commands in the `OnDraw()` function.

AppWizard supplied an `OnDraw()` function, although the `OnDraw()` doesn't do much. Listing B2.3 contains the `OnDraw()` function as supplied by AppWizard (from TEACHVW.CPP).

 Listing B2.3. The `OnDraw()` member function from TEACHVW.CPP.

```
 1:  /////////////////////////////////////////////////////////////////
 2:  // CTeachView drawing
 3:
 4:  void CTeachView::OnDraw(CDC* pDC)
 5:  {
 6:    CTeachDoc* pDoc = GetDocument();
 7:    ASSERT_VALID(pDoc);
 8:
 9:    // TODO: add draw code for native data here
10:  }
```

Even though the function's contents seem cryptic, there is very little going on in Listing B2.3. When writing Windows programs, you really don't write to the screen or printer. You don't even write to a window. Instead, you write to a *device context*. The device context is an identifier that defines an output device (input devices also have device contexts).

You don't have to change the way you write to a device in Windows. For example, you might have a printer attached to your PC, or a monochrome display, or a color display. All the functions you use to send data to these output devices are the same; as long as the device context (an argument of the output functions) points to the proper device, the MFC makes sure that the correct I/O is performed for that specific device. The data type named CDC (seen in line 4 of Listing B2.2) is defining a device context. In other words, OnDraw() is always passed a device context, and the OnDraw() simply displays the view onto that device context. Unless you do some advanced coding, AppWizard passes to OnDraw() the primary screen's window as a device context argument, so OnDraw() is almost always used to draw on the mainframe window.

Line 4's argument, pDC, stands for *pointer to a device context*. There is nothing magical about the initial p. Most Windows programmers give their variable names initial prefixes that indicate what data type the variable holds. Table B2.2 lists several of these common variable prefixes. (This data type prefix notation is called *Hungarian notation* in honor of its Hungarian inventor.)

Line 7's ASSERT macro ensures that the document is valid and prints an error message if line 6 fails.

Table B2.2. Common Hungarian Notation prefixes.

Prefix	Description
a	Array
b	Boolean (true or false)
by	Byte (an unsigned character)
c	Character
cb	Count of bytes
cr	Color reference
cx, cy	Count of x coordinate, y coordinate, or length
dw	Double word
fn	Function
h	Handle
i	Integer

continues

Extra Credit Bonus 2

Table B2.2. continued

Prefix	Description
m_	Member of a class
n	Integer
np	Near pointer
p	Pointer
l	Long
lp	Long pointer
s	String (see the next section)
sz	Zero-terminated string
tm	Text metric
w	Word (unsigned integer)
x, y	x coordinate or y coordinate

Line 6 of Listing B2.2 assigns the device context pointer to the active document data. The OnDraw() function, as generated by AppWizard, does nothing with the document pointed to by pDC. If you want to open a document with **File O**pen in the application's menu, the GetDocument() will point to that file, and you can then get data and display the data from the file. However, at this time the OnDraw() function does not do anything with any data document pointed to by pDoc.

To add a message to the window, the OnDraw() function was chosen because every time your window is redrawn, for whatever reason, the OnDraw() function will be called, so your text will always remain in the window.

The view class contains a member function named TextOut() that displays data on a device context. Here is the format of TextOut():

```
TextOut(int x, int y, char sz[], int length);
```

The *x* and *y* arguments in the preceding notation determine where in the pDC's window your message will appear (in *x* and *y* coordinates). 0, 0 is the upper-left corner of the window. The larger *x* is, the farther across the screen the text appears. The larger *y* is,

the farther down the screen your text appears. The third argument in the notation is a zero-terminated string (constant, character array, or pointer to a character string). The last argument represents the number of characters in that string (not counting the zero terminating character).

Warning: There are several hundred functions in the MFC classes. How could you have known that TextOut() is the view member function to write text in the window? You couldn't with the information you've read before this section! Remember that these bonus chapters are trying to show you some of the power of MFC and the Visual C++ Windows programming tools. After you complete this book, you might want to study the classes in depth by referring to the Visual C++ manuals and other helpful books that are listed in the final bonus chapter.

It's fairly easy to guess where to add the TextOut() function calls because AppWizard *tells* you where to add your own code. The TODO comment on the ninth line lets you know that if you choose to display something in the window, you do so on or after line 9. Therefore, insert the following lines after line 9 and before line 10:

```
pDC->TextOut(0, 0, "My first words that I", 21);
pDC->TextOut(0, 20, "write to the window.", 20);
```

As you can see, you must tell the TextOut() function which device context to write to by supplying a pointer to the correct device context. You might be wondering where the *x*- and *y*-coordinate values came from. The *x*- and *y*-coordinate values must be set in screen points. The size of your font (the number of points in the font) determines how much further down the second line must be placed (on the *y* coordinate) from the first line of text. If you were using a larger font (as opposed to AppWizard's default), the *y* coordinate value would have to be much larger than 20, or the second line would infringe on the first line of text.

Figure B2.5 shows the program's output after you rebuild and run the application. As you can see, the value of 20 for the second line creates a little more spacing than was needed; there is a lot of space between the lines. A value of 20, however, is better than a value too small, which would cause the second line to overlap the bottom of the first. You can keep changing the value of the coordinate until it looks better. There is a better way, however, of spacing your text.

Extra Credit Bonus 2

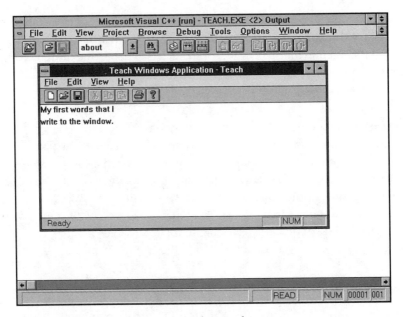

Figure B2.5. Displaying text in the window.

It's cumbersome to change coordinate values every time you or the user changes a window font. Therefore, you can more safely and easily rely on the view class's member function GetTextMetrics() to provide information about the current font being used on whatever device context for which you request the information.

GetTextMetrics() is a function that returns all the following structure information:

`int tmHeight;`	Height of the font, from highest to lowest character
`int tmAscent;`	Height of the highest nondescending characters
`int tmDescent;`	Height of the descending portion of descenders
`int tmInternalLeading;`	Height of accent mark space
`int tmExternalLeading;`	Recommended height between character rows
`int tmAveCharWidth;`	Average character width

`int tmMaxCharWidth;`	Width of widest character
`int tmWeight;`	Thickness of character, from 0 to 900 (thickest)
`BYTE tmItalic;`	1 if italic font, 0 otherwise
`BYTE tmUnderlined;`	1 if underlined font, 0 otherwise
`BYTE tmStruckOut;`	1 if strikeout font, 0 otherwise
`BYTE tmFirstChar;`	Value of the first character defined in the font
`BYTE tmLastChar;`	Value of the last character defined in the font
`BYTE tmDefaultChar;`	Substitute character if you attempt to print a character not available in the font
`BYTE tmBreakChar;`	Character used for word breaks when justifying
`BYTE tmPitchAndFamily;`	Values that specify the pitch (fixed or proportional) and family of font. The online Windows programming documentation provides description of values
`BYTE tmCharSet;`	0-ANSI, 1-default, 2-symbol, 128-SHIFTJOS, 255-OEM
`int tmOverhang;`	Extra width added to some synthesized fonts
`int tmDigitizedAspectX;`	Horizontal aspect of the font
`int tmDigitizedAspectY;`	Vertical aspect of the font

As you can see, a lot of information is available from the `GetTextMetrics()` function. For your application, you are concerned only about printing the second text line a reasonable distance from the first line. A good position for the second line would be the font's height (`tmHeight`) plus the recommended space between lines (`tmExternalLeading`). Therefore, the second line of text's *y* coordinate should be the sum of the `tmExternalLeading` plus the `tmHeight`.

Consider the replacement `OnDraw()` function shown in Listing B2.4. This function ensures that the two displayed lines of text align well, no matter what size or type of font is used for the text.

Extra Credit Bonus 2

Warning: As you can probably surmise, you should never hardcode (assign constant values to) text-positioning information in function calls for `TextOut()` and other text-displaying functions. The font size is too easily changed, and your program might scrunch the text too close together if the font is too large. By using `GetTextMetrics()`'s returned data values, you can ensure that your text always spaces apart just right.

Type

Listing B2.4. A better `OnDraw()` function in TEACHVW.CPP.

```
 1:  void CTeachView::OnDraw(CDC* pDC)
 2:  {
 3:    CTeachDoc* pDoc = GetDocument();
 4:    ASSERT_VALID(pDoc);
 5:
 6:    // TODO: add draw code for native data here
 7:    TEXTMETRIC textStruct;
 8:    pDC->GetTextMetrics(&textStruct);
 9:    int cxChar = textStruct.tmHeight + textStruct.tmExternalLeading;
10:    pDC->TextOut(0, 0, "My first words that I", 21);
11:    pDC->TextOut(0, cxChar, "write to the window.", 20);
12:  }
```

The result of using Listing B2.4 is shown in Figure B2.6.

All the non-AppWizard code follows the comment on line 6. The first thing you must do before calling `GetTextMetrics()` is define a variable of the text-metric data structure described earlier. Line 7 defines a structure variable named textStruct. Line 8 then calls the `GetTextMetrics()` function, passing the structure to the function. Notice that the textStruct structure variable is passed by address because `GetTextMetrics()` must be able to fill the structure members with data. You must call `GetTextMetrics()` via a pointer to the device context for which you want the metric information, so the pDC document device context is used for the function call.

An integer variable, cxChar (the c prefix, remember, is often used to indicate that the variable is holding a *count*) is defined on line 9. The text-metric structure's height and recommended spacing height are added together to find the starting location of the second line of text. After line 10 writes the first line of text in the window's home position (at coordinates 0, 0), line 11 places the second line of text at perfect spacing from the first line. If the font currently being used were much larger, the spacing would adjust accordingly because the metric values in the `textStruct` structure would be adjusted.

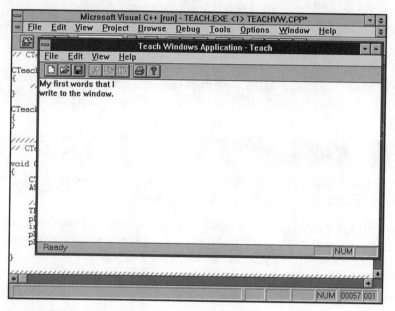

Figure B2.6. After fixing the text spacing.

What Is Meant by *BYTE*?

You'll notice that the `GetTextMetrics()` structure is made of two data types: `int` and `BYTE`. From the uppercase letters, you can probably guess that `BYTE` is typedefed elsewhere as a data type.

Often, Windows programmers use a series of more descriptive data types than the standard `int`, `long int`, and `float`, and the other regular data types provided by C++. Therefore, you'll commonly see the data types that appear in the following list for different kinds of values. (The `BYTE` values in the `GetTextMetrics()` structure are never greater than 255, so the value easily fits within an `unsigned int`.)

`BYTE` is an `unsigned int` (used for values less than 256).

`BOOL` is an `int` (usually used for true and false).

Extra Credit Bonus 2

> UINT is an unsigned int (for positive values).
>
> WORD is an unsigned int (for 2-byte positive values).
>
> LONG is a long int.
>
> DWORD is unsigned long (for *double word*).
>
> Many times more than one of the defined data types will work. The choice often depends on the context of the value being defined.

DO	DON'T

DO feel free to change the AppWizard source code all you want. That's the best way to learn how to work with the MFC classes.

DO use App Studio to change the look, size, and contents of your application's resources. You can also make the changes manually by editing the resource script file, but App Studio makes sure that no syntax errors creep into the resource script file that is used to build the final executable application.

DO use the TextOut() function to display characters on the mainframe window.

DON'T hardcode text-spacing values yourself. Use the GetTextMetrics() function to find out font size and spacing information about the current font.

The MFC String Class

Now would be a good time to study the MFC string class. Working with string constants, as displayed with TextOut() in the preceding section, is not as flexible as working with string variables. You know that C does not support string variables, and C++ does not either. However, there is nothing to keep programmers from writing their own string class, and that's just what Microsoft did.

The CString class is part of the MFC classes. CString provides string variable-like manipulation of strings. There are many member functions that support powerful string copying, searching, concatenating, and the manipulating of routines. Table B2.3 lists many of the member functions that you can use on any string object you define. Most of the functions are self-explanatory.

Table B2.3. Several `CString` member functions.

Member Function	Description
`CString()`	Constructs a string object.
`~CString()`	Destructs a string object.
`GetLength()`	Returns the string length (not including null zero).
`IsEmpty()`	Returns true if the string is null.
`Empty()`	Empties a string (sets the string to a null string with 0 length).
`GetAt()`	Returns a character given a specified position.
`operator[]`	Overloaded operator that performs GetAt() using brackets.
`SetAt()`	Changes the character at a given position.
`operator=()`	Assigns one string to another.
`operator+()`	Concatenates one string to another and returns a new string.
`operator+=()`	Concatenates a new string onto the end of an existing string.
`operator==()`	Tests whether two strings are equal.
`operator>()`	Tests whether one string is greater than another.
`operator<()`	Tests whether one string is less than another.
`CompareNoCase()`	Compares strings without regard to case.
`Mid()`	Returns the middle part of a string.
`Left()`	Returns the left portion of a string.
`Right()`	Returns the right portion of a string.

continues

Extra Credit Bonus 2

Table B2.3. continued

Member Function	Description
`MakeUpper()`	Converts a string to all uppercase letters.
`MakeLower()`	Converts a string to all lowercase letters.
`MakeReverse()`	Reverses the contents of a string.
`Find()`	Finds the position of a character or substring within another string.

Listing B2.5 shows the `OnDraw()` function with the text lines stored in a `CString` class instead of being hard-coded directly into the `TextOut()` function call. You have the added benefit of being able to use the `GetLength()` member function to pass `OutText()` the length of the strings.

Listing B2.5. Using the `CString` class in TEACHVW.CPP's `OnDraw()` function.

```
 1:  ////////////////////////////////////////////////////////////////
 2:  // CTeachView drawing
 3:
 4:  void CTeachView::OnDraw(CDC* pDC)
 5:  {
 6:    CTeachDoc* pDoc = GetDocument();
 7:    ASSERT_VALID(pDoc);
 8:
 9:    // TODO: add draw code for native data here
10:      // Moves the rest of the function's variable definitions to here
11:      TEXTMETRIC textStruct;
12:      int cxChar;
13:      CString sLine1="My first words that I";    // Notice the string
14:      CString sLine2="write to the window.";     // prefix character
15:
16:      pDC->GetTextMetrics(&textStruct);
17:      cxChar = textStruct.tmHeight + textStruct.tmExternalLeading;
18:      pDC->TextOut(0, 0, sLine1, sLine1.GetLength());
19:      pDC->TextOut(0, cxChar, sLine2, sLine2.GetLength());
20: }
```

The output for Listing B2.5 is the same as for the preceding program, as shown in Figure B2.6.

Lines 11–14 define the data, including the TEXTMETRIC structure, the x coordinate character count, and the two CString objects on lines 13 and 14. The CString class contains overloaded constructors. You can both define and *then* assign strings, as shown here:

```
CString sLine1;    // Construct a string object
sLine1="nMy first words that I";
```

You also can define and assign (a copy constructor) as shown here:

```
CString sLine1="My first words that I";   // Notice the string
```

This technique was used in lines 13 and 14. Lines 18 and 19 both use the GetLength() member function to pass the length of the two CString objects to the OutText() function.

> **Tip:** CString objects grow and shrink as needed (up to a maximum of 32,767 characters). You don't ever need to worry about dynamically allocating memory for CString objects, because the CString class takes care of memory management for you.

Getting Keyboard Input

The preceding section showed how to write to a window using TextOut(). This section gives you a glimpse into how you type keystrokes into the window. As the user types characters, Windows generates event messages. As you know, you can have multiple programs running with open windows on the screen at once. The window with the current *focus* (that is, the active window whose title bar is highlighted) is the window that accepts keystroke event messages. The text you type appears at the text cursor (known as the caret or insertion point).

There are several kinds of event messages your keyboard generates and several ways of handling the keyboard events. Following are the three messages generated by keystroke actions:

- ☐ WM_KEYDOWN: Sent when a key is pressed.
- ☐ WM_KEYUP: Sent when a key is released.
- ☐ WM_CHAR: Sent after Windows translates the keystroke into an ASCII character.

Extra Credit Bonus 2

Note: There are actually two more keyboard messages, not used here, defined as `WM_SYSKEYDOWN` and `WM_SYSKEYUP`. The two messages are sent any time the user presses a Windows system Alt keystroke such as Alt+Tab or Alt+Esc, such as happens when switching to a different window.

Although the other two messages are important elements of your application's response to the keyboard, you'll work here with the `WM_CHAR` message and send the user's keystrokes to the window as the user types those keystrokes.

You must remember that the document class holds your window's data and the view class displays that data. Therefore, you must determine a way to hold your application's data—either through strings or files. To keep things on the same keel maintained throughout these bonus pages, you'll stay simple and store the user's input in a string, and the view class will be responsible for displaying the document class's string. (You can now see that a document class doesn't always manage files, but rather data in whatever form the data happens to be in.)

The first thing to do is define the string for the typed data. In the preceding section, you saw how to define data directly inside member functions of the view class. If you want to define a string for the document class, you must open the document file and add the string definition. The string must be known throughout the document class, so it will be best to add the string's definition in the document class's header file, `TEACHDOC.H`. Therefore, follow these steps to add the string definition:

1. Select **F**ile **O**pen, and open the TEACHDOC.H header file.

2. You want the document object to hold the string data. The `// Attributes` section of TEACHDOC.H would be the perfect place for the new string data member. (In C++ terminology, an object's attribute is one of its data members.) Insert the following line directly after the `public:` line in the `// Attributes` section:

   ```
   CString sInput;      // Our newly added string
   ```

3. Save the header file with **F**ile **S**ave.

It's now time to connect a `WM_CHAR` message to a function in the view class. You want the view class to update your window every time the user presses a key. You'll use ClassWizard for the first time to connect an event message to one of your application's functions. Follow these steps to use ClassWizard:

1. Select **B**rowse... Class**W**izard... to display the ClassWizard dialog box.

2. Display the Class **N**ame list, and select `CTeachView`. The object identifiers of the `CTeachView` class will appear in the lefthand box.

3. You must change the `CTeachView` class message mapping. Therefore, highlight `CTeachView` under the Object **I**Ds listbox, and ClassWizard displays a list of messages in the lefthand list box labeled **M**essages.

4. Double-click `WM_CHAR` because that's the message you want to map to a function. Your screen should look like the one in Figure B2.7.

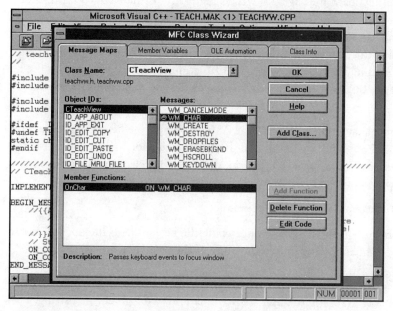

Figure B2.7. Mapping a function to a `WM_CHAR` message.

Note: If you use Visual C++ Version 1.0, your ClassWizard dialog box will differ slightly from that in Figure B2.7.

The Visual C++ name for the `WM_CHAR` message is `ON_WM_CHAR`, and you can see that ClassWizard wants to map the member function `OnChar()` to the message. `OnChar()` is a good name, so keep it.

Extra Credit Bonus 2

5. Now for one of the greatest features of ClassWizard. After you map the message to a member function, you're ready to edit that function. All you have to do is double-click the OnChar line in the Member Functions list box, and ClassWizard opens the TEACHVW.CPP file and adds the OnChar() shell function that you can modify.

    ClassWizard gives the OnChar() function a default body. You'll see the following line inside OnChar():

    ```
    CView::OnChar(nChar, nRepCnt, nFlags);
    ```

    For keyboard messages (as well as many others that ClassWizard generates for message handling), ClassWizard calls the base class's member function. You can keep the call or delete it as well as add your own code after the base class function is called. If you decide not to handle the WM_CHAR message at this time, the base class OnChar() function takes care of receiving the keystroke but does nothing with it. Go ahead and delete this line, because you won't need it for this chapter.

6. The nChar argument holds the ASCII value of the key that you just pressed. However, before you can add the key to your document, you must, as done earlier in the OnDraw() function, define a pointer to the document being worked on. Add the following line to the function body:

    ```
    CTeachDoc* pDoc = GetDocument();
    ```

7. The only thing left is to concatenate the keystroke to the document's string. Add the following line to the body of the OnChar() function:

    ```
    pDoc->sInput += nChar;
    ```

You are now grabbing the user's keystrokes and saving them in a string. However, you've done nothing yet to display that string. You're going to make those keystrokes appear after the two displayed text lines you coded earlier in OnDraw(). Therefore, you can go to the OnDraw() function to draw the keystrokes.

Drawing your keyboard string in OnDraw() poses a problem that can be overcome, but not without some effort. Before looking at the problem, add the string-displaying code to OnDraw() by inserting the following line at the end of OnDraw():

```
pDC->TextOut(0, cxChar*2, pDoc->sInput, pDoc->sInput.GetLength());
```

It appears that everything is in place. You are saving the user's keystrokes in a string and drawing that string when the window is drawn. The problem is that Windows doesn't call `OnDraw()` every time the user presses a key. The only thing Windows calls when the user presses a key is `OnChar()`. Windows calls `OnDraw()` only when you resize the window or uncover part of the window by removing another window from the program's window.

To see this problem, build the TEACH project as it now stands, and type a few keystrokes. As you type, nothing happens. Only the two text lines appear on-screen. Type 20 keystrokes and nothing happens. To see those keystrokes, minimize the window and maximize it, or resize the window by dragging one of its borders to the left or right a little. Instantly, you'll see all the keystrokes you pressed earlier!

Somehow, you've got to ensure that the window is redrawn when `OnChar()` executes. There are several ways to accomplish this task, but you'll take the quickest here. You'll *force* a Windows message, `WM_PAINT`, to be generated and sent to your program. The MFC function `SendMessage()` does just that. Whenever your program receives a `WM_PAINT` message, your view class calls `OnDraw()`. However, if you send a `WM_PAINT` message and your window hasn't changed since the preceding `OnDraw()`, Windows won't be fooled. Therefore, you must also call `Invalidate()`, which does nothing but make Windows think your window has in some way been invalidated (resized or uncovered). Therefore, add the following lines to `OnChar()`:

```
Invalidate();
SendMessage(WM_PAINT);
```

`OnChar()` now looks like this:

```
/////////////////////////////////////////////////////////////////
// CTeachView message handlers

void CTeachView::OnChar(UINT nChar, UINT nRepCnt, UINT nFlags)
{
    // TODO: Add your message handler code here and/or call default
    CTeachDoc* pDoc = GetDocument();
    pDoc->sInput += nChar;    // The overloaded += would work too
    Invalidate();
    SendMessage(WM_PAINT);
}
```

After you build the application, as you type characters, the window is redrawn and your characters appear on-screen. Calling `Invalidate()` for each keystroke is not the most efficient means of displaying the characters. Nevertheless, it is a simple approach to use for now.

Extra Credit Bonus 2

Note: What do you think—isn't Windows programming easy? OK, you're right. There is a tremendous amount of material to master before becoming a Visual C++ Windows programming expert. But you've got to admit that Windows programming is challenging and offers a lot of new skills that you can benefit from.

Tip: Take a few minutes to study the MFC class structure. You'll find a cardboard fold-out card in your Visual C++ documentation that illustrates the class hierarchy of the MFC classes. By studying the layout of the classes before studying too much more about individual examples, you'll have a better idea of what the various classes contain.

Summary

Today's bonus chapter gives you some insight into adding functionality to AppWizard applications, but no attempt is being made to make you think you're an expert. You probably have many more questions than were answered today. Nevertheless, the purpose of these bonus chapters is to show you how easy it is to modify the code that Visual C++ generates for you.

You first saw how to use App Studio to change the About dialog box. App Studio is easy to use, and its visual interface makes changing dialog boxes and other resources a snap. App Studio makes changes to the resource script file, so you don't have to make the changes manually.

The second half of today's chapter explains some of the problems you'll encounter when adding text to the window. Displaying just a couple of lines of text requires an understanding of device contexts, font information, and MFC display functions. A simple `printf()` or `cout` will not work in a Windows application (other than simple QuickWin applications).

The `CString` class helps you work with string data. With this class there's no more worry about allocating memory and increasing string length when needed. The `CString` class makes it appear that there are now string variables in Visual C++.

Q&A

Q. Why can I not edit a resource script file myself?

A. You *can* edit a resource script file. If you just want to change a word or two or make an obvious modification to your program's resources, changing the script file might be easier than starting App Studio.

You run a risk, however, of typing a syntax error or leaving out needed information. Also, it is difficult to place resource elements by using x and y coordinates. With App Studio, you can use the mouse to drag resource elements to any location you want. You'll find that App Studio offers an almost complete advantage over modifying the resource script by hand.

Q. What is a device context?

A. There are many devices available to a Windows program. Also, there could be lots of open windows, and each window could be using a different font, color, or font size. Each output window has an identifying pointer called the device context. You need to specify a device context to most of the MFC and Windows functions so that the function knows exactly where and how you want the output placed.

MFC includes several functions, such as `GetDocument()`, that help you locate the proper device context being used in your current view.

Q. Is it worth the time and effort to learn how to use the `CString` class?

A. There is no contesting the argument that the `CString` class is easier to use than coding your own string class, or worse, using C-style zero-delimited character arrays. The `CString` class contains lots of familiar and useful member functions, including control of string lengths, assignment, construction, destruction, and automatic allocation (growing and shrinking) of the string as needed.

Q. Why must I use the data type prefixes?

A. You don't have to use the data type suffixes, but most Windows programmers and Visual C++ programmers do. The suffix gives you a clue as to the kind of data the variables hold. From the prefix itself, you'll know *not* to do something like this:

```
sInitial = dAge;   // Wrong type being assigned
```

Extra Credit Bonus 2

You would not want to assign a double word to a string value. The prefixes don't always have to match in assignment statements, but you're more likely to stay aware of the data types as you assign them.

Workshop

The Workshop offers quiz questions and exercises to hone your skills and give you feedback on today's lesson. You'll find some proposed answers in Appendix D.

Quiz

1. What is a resource script?
2. What is meant by font metrics?
3. Can you use App Studio to modify resources or only create new resources?
4. Which class—the view class or the document class—contains the function code for `OnDraw()`?
5. Which keyboard message is the easiest to interpret: `WM_KEYDOWN`, `WM_KEYUP`, or `WM_CHAR`?
6. What function returns font metric information?
7. Why is the metric information so important when you're printing lines of text?
8. Why must you call `Invalidate()` before sending a `WM_PAINT` message to Windows?

Exercise

1. Write the following six-line poem in the TEACH AppWizard window:

   My hands are tired,
   My mind is numb,
   I've programmed until I'm blue.
   I hope that someday
   I'll make a mint
   Writing Visual C++ code for you.

Use `GetTextMetrics()` for the proper spacing and a `for` loop to count through the six lines. Hint: Define an array of `CString` lines. You can use the loop counter variable as part of the formula for the placement of each line.

Extra Credit Bonus 3+

Files and More MFC

Extra Credit Bonus 3

Today's bonus chapter explores more of the MFC classes by showing how easy it is to store and retrieve data to and from files. You'll begin with a simple program that stores your keystrokes in a file. There are several ways to manage files using the MFC classes, but when you use the `Serialize()` member function, one statement takes care of storing any data you want stored, and another statement retrieves any data you want retrieved.

Today's chapter also shows you how to use some exception handling to take care of file I/O errors. In Day 19's chapter, "Introduction to Throwing and Catching Exceptions," you saw how C and the Windows API support exception handling. The MFC classes take over exception handling for you (well, you do have to intervene just a bit), and the MFC makes file I/O errors and other exceptions manageable.

Today, you learn about the following topics:

- ☐ How to use printing and print preview in your application
- ☐ How to trap the Enter keystroke
- ☐ How to display line breaks in the application's window
- ☐ How to save and retrieve window data to and from the disk
- ☐ How to add safety to the application so that the user gets a warning before exiting the application if the user has not saved the window's data
- ☐ How to generate a cursor for your user
- ☐ How to implement exception handling

Adding Printing and Print Preview

In yesterday's chapter, you created an application that added the display of text and the capture of keystrokes to the AppWizard application. Things were kept simple (and therefore, the application remains primitive), but there is relatively little left for you to do after AppWizard generates your program's source code files.

Printing and print preview are capabilities that would normally require extensive coding on the programmer's part. With AppWizard, adding printing and print preview to the TEACH application requires the following steps:

1. Run the TEACH program, and select **File** **P**rint or **F**ile Print Pre**v**iew from the menu.

In other words, AppWizard took care of *all* of it for you.

Give it a try. Run the TEACH application that you created in the preceding chapter. If you happened to modify the code to fulfill yesterday's exercise requirements, your application will look slightly different from this section's figure, but you'll still be able to participate here.

At the end of yesterday's chapter, the TEACH application displayed two lines of text and displayed any characters the user typed. Rerun the program and type ABCDEFGH to put a total of three lines on-screen (the two text lines and the typed character line).

Select **F**ile P**r**eview from the menu, and you'll see a print preview of your document. Double-click the title bar to maximize the window to full screen. You'll see a preview like the one shown in Figure B3.1.

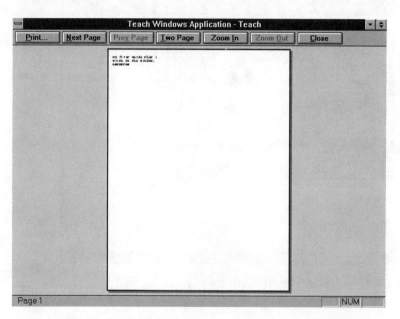

Figure B3.1. Utilizing the print preview mode of the TEACH application.

If the document spanned several pages, you could look at all the previewed pages just as you can print preview pages from within your word processor. The AppWizard print preview also contains a zooming feature. You can move the magnifying-glass cursor (the mouse cursor changes to a magnifying glass when you move the mouse cursor over the document in print preview) over any portion of the page and click the mouse to get a larger view of the document's text as it will look when you print the document. Selecting Zoom **O**ut restores the full-screen print preview.

713

Extra Credit Bonus 3

Select **C**lose to return to the document window. To print the document, select **F**ile **P**rint... (Ctrl+P), and you'll see a Print dialog box like the one shown in Figure B3.2. You should already be familiar with the Print dialog box because almost every Windows application uses a Print dialog box just like it. You can even set up your printer differently by choosing **S**etup... if you want to.

Tip: You can also print directly from within print preview by clicking the Print command button.

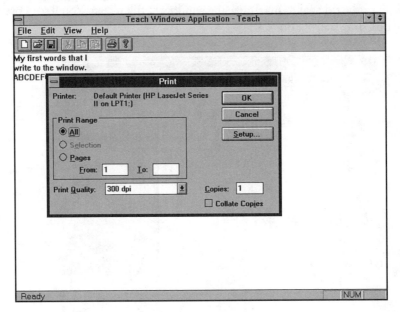

Figure B3.2. The TEACH application's Print dialog box.

If you like, you now can print the document or close the Print dialog box to cancel the printing.

Note: At the end of yesterday's chapter, you might have felt frustrated by all the hoops you had to jump through to do something as simple as putting text on-screen. Now, however, you're beginning to see some

benefits from the extra effort. Many capabilities are now available to you, such as printing and print previewing, that would require lots of tedious programming time without AppWizard and Visual C++.

DO	DON'T
DO select printing and print preview for all your AppWizard applications unless the application is one of those rare ones in which your user does not have to print. As you have seen, no extra programming effort is required on your part; after you display something in the program's window, you can print or preview the document.	**DON'T** forget to add the print options *before* you generate code with AppWizard.

Working with Files

It's now time to see how AppWizard supports file I/O. Actually, much can be said about MFC file I/O—more than will be taught here. However, you'll see here the easiest file I/O you've ever worked with, and AppWizard generates almost all the code needed to perform the file I/O of your document class.

The next section begins with a brand-new application you'll generate from AppWizard. If you're low on disk space, feel free to delete the TEACH directory and all its files, because you won't need them again. If you think you might want to work with the TEACH application some more, back up the TEACH directory before removing it. The DOS DELTREE command works great for removing directories and the files stored in the directories.

The purpose of the next section is to generate a new kind of application that accepts keystrokes differently from the way TEACH captured them. In doing so, you'll be able to add a text cursor to make it easier to follow the characters as you type them. It's easier to generate a new application and add the code (thanks to AppWizard) than to change the TEACH application so that it works as described here.

Extra Credit Bonus 3

The second section adds **F**ile **S**ave, **F**ile **O**pen, and **F**ile **N**ew menu commands to the application. Actually, this chapter virtually makes the application a text editor, although there aren't going to be a lot of bells and whistles in the program.

Generating a New Application

After you've removed the TEACH application (or if you have ample disk space for a second application, in which case you won't have to remove TEACH), restart AppWizard. Follow these now-familiar steps to produce a new application named FILES:

1. Select **P**roject **A**ppWizard... from the menu.
2. For the Project **N**ame and in the New **S**ubdirectory box, type **FILES**.
3. Select the **O**ptions... button to display the Options dialog box.
4. Click **M**ultiple Document Interface to turn off the option, and select OK.
5. When you are back at the Options dialog box, select OK again to display the application summary screen.
6. Select **C**reate and wait for AppWizard to generate your files.

If you were to build the application now, you would have just a shell. Therefore, take some time to add more functionality to the program before building it.

The first thing to do is add a keystroke handler. As you learned before, the Windows ON_CHAR message ensures that your keystrokes trigger a function call. Before doing anything else, open FILESDOC.H and define a CString variable to hold the window's text. (You performed this same step in yesterday's chapter for the TEACH application.)

Under the // Attributes and public: lines, add the following statement:

```
CString sInput;      // Our newly added string
```

Your FILESDOC.H code should now look like the code in Listing B3.1.

 Listing B3.1. FILESDOC.H after adding a CString member variable.

```
1:  // filesdoc.h : interface of the CFilesDoc class
2:  //
3:  /////////////////////////////////////////////////////////////////////
4:
5:  class CFilesDoc : public CDocument
```

```
 6: {
 7: protected: // create from serialization only
 8:     CFilesDoc();
 9:     DECLARE_DYNCREATE(CFilesDoc)
10:
11: // Attributes
12: public:
13: CString sInput;     // Our newly added string
14: // Operations
15: public:
16:
17: // Implementation
18: public:
19:     virtual ~CFilesDoc();
20:     virtual void Serialize(CArchive& ar); // overridden for document i/o
21: #ifdef _DEBUG
22:     virtual void AssertValid() const;
23:     virtual void Dump(CDumpContext& dc) const;
24: #endif
25:
26: protected:
27: virtual BOOL OnNewDocument();
28:
29: // Generated message map functions
30: protected:
31: //{{AFX_MSG(CFilesDoc)
32:     // NOTE: ClassWizard will add and remove member functions here.
33:     //    DO NOT EDIT what you see in these blocks of generated code!
34: //}}AFX_MSG
35:     DECLARE_MESSAGE_MAP()
36: };
37:
38: /////////////////////////////////////////////////////////////////////
```

Line 13 contains the line you just added.

Now you can add code to grab keystrokes using an OnChar() function in FILESVW.CPP. First, however, recall what you had to do in the preceding chapter to generate the OnChar() function. You used ClassWizard to associate the WM_CHAR message with the OnChar() function. ClassWizard even generated the skeleton OnChar() function code (header and return statement) for you. Follow along to map WM_CHAR to OnChar() here:

1. Select **B**rowse Class**W**izard... to display the ClassWizard dialog box.

2. Select CFilesView from the Class **N**ame list box if it's now already selected.

717

Extra Credit Bonus 3

3. Highlight `CFilesView` in the ObjectIDs listbox so that a list of possible Windows messages appears in the Messages listbox.

4. Select the `WM_CHAR` message, and click **A**dd Function. ClassWizard associates the `OnChar()` function with the `WM_CHAR` message.

5. Double-click the `OnChar()` function (or click **E**dit Code) to see the skeleton code that ClassWizard added to FILESVW.CPP.

Remove the one-line body of `OnChar()` (the default `WM_CHAR` message handler) that appears beneath the `// TODO:` comment. You're going to add your own code to grab keystrokes. As with the TEACH application, you'll simply store keystrokes in the `sInput` buffer you defined in FILESDOC.H. Add the keystroke code so that your `OnChar()` function looks like the function in Listing B3.2.

Listing B3.2. Adding keystroke handling to `OnChar()` in FILESVW.CPP.

```
 1:  /////////////////////////////////////////////////////////////////
 2:  // CFilesView message handlers
 3:
 4:  void CFilesView::OnChar(UINT nChar, UINT nRepCnt, UINT nFlags)
 5:  {
 6:    // TODO: Add your message handler code here and/or call default
 7:
 8:    CFilesDoc* pDoc = GetDocument();
 9:    pDoc->sInput += nChar;
10:    Invalidate();
11:    SendMessage(WM_PAINT);
12: }
```

The code you added here is identical to that in the TEACH keystroke handler. Line 8 defines a pointer to the data (in the document class), and line 9 appends each typed character to the `sInput` `CString` buffer. After the keystroke is stored, line 10 invalidates the window so that the `SendMessage()` function call on line 11 triggers a redrawing of the window and its contents.

The only thing left to do is add the text-displaying code. Here is where you'll deviate a bit from the TEACH application. Remember that the TEACH application first wrote two lines of text to the window before displaying the user's keystrokes. The FILES application will not display the lines of text, only keystrokes, so you can restructure the `OnDraw()` function a bit to make it more general purpose. As a bonus, the `OnDraw()` function will check for an Enter keystroke and break to the next line when Enter is encountered during the display of the string. (The TEACH application couldn't handle carriage returns properly, so pressing Enter did not cause a new line to occur.)

Warning: Before going any farther, you should be warned about a minor problem that will probably occur in this application. Most readers' applications will default to using a proportional Windows system font in this application. A proportional font means that all characters don't take the same amount of column width. (An *i*, for instance, takes up less space than an *M*). Therefore, the text characters entered in this application will not always be aligned properly next to each other; some will appear too close together and others too far apart.

Through the MFC classes, you can use a fixed nonproportional font, but doing so involves many details that aren't worth the effort at this point. Spacing proportional fonts correctly is tedious because you have to adjust the spacing (the x coordinate) according to the previously displayed character's width. Taking the time to code such perfect spacing would detract more from this discussion than add to it. You should still enjoy working on the Files application despite its sometimes-arbitrary character spacing.

Listing B3.3 contains the `OnDraw()` function modified to display the characters from the `sInput` array one character at a time. Take a few moments to enter the code in the body of the `OnDraw()` function in FILESVW.CPP.

Listing B3.3. Displaying characters from the string, one at a time.

```
1:  //////////////////////////////////////////////////////////////
2:  // CFilesView drawing
3:
4:  void CFilesView::OnDraw(CDC* pDC)
5:  {
6:    CFilesDoc* pDoc = GetDocument();
7:    ASSERT_VALID(pDoc);
8:
9:    // TODO: add draw code for native data here
10:   TEXTMETRIC textStruct;
11:   int cxChar=0;
```

continues

Extra Credit Bonus 3

Listing B3.3. continued

```
12:     int cyChar = 0;
13:     pDC->GetTextMetrics(&textStruct);
14:     for (int ctr=0; ctr<pDoc->sInput.GetLength(); ctr++)
15:     {
16:         if (pDoc->sInput[ctr] == '\r')
17:           { cyChar+= (textStruct.tmHeight +
                  textStruct.tmExternalLeading);
18:             cxChar=0; }
19:         else
20:           { pDC->TextOut(cxChar, cyChar, pDoc->sInput.Mid(ctr), 1);
21:             // The average character width will cause some
22:             // spacing problems, but it's OK for now
23:             cxChar += textStruct.tmAveCharWidth; }
24:     }
25: }
```

In several of these bonus chapter function listings, there is no output because you're building onto the application one function at a time. In just a moment, you'll see a figure showing the results of the completely built application.

There is a lot in Listing B3.3 that you saw in the preceding chapter. Line 13 loads the font-metrics information so that the program can space characters in the window. Notice that line 12 defines a new variable, cyChar. The FILES application will manage characters vertically as well as horizontally, because an Enter keystroke moves the insertion point to the next line as the user types.

Keep in mind that this OnDraw() function will be called after each keystroke typed by the user. As such, the entire window is redrawn every time the user presses a key (remember that the Invalidate(); and SendMessage(WM_PAINT); lines at the end of the OnChar() function trigger OnDraw() after each keystroke).

The difference between the FILES application's OnDraw() function and the one in the TEACH application is that this OnDraw() displays the characters from the string one character at a time, whereas the TextOut() function in the TEACH application displayed the entire string at once, hence the for loop starting on line 14.

The body of the for loop tests to see whether the user pressed the Enter key (which generates a \r carriage-return/escape sequence). If so, the x and y coordinates are adjusted to the start of the next line. If the character pressed is not a \r, the character is displayed and the coordinates are updated accordingly. Notice, however, that the font's average character width, tmAveCharWidth, is used in line 23 to update the x-coordinate position for the next character's display.

Build the complete FILES application and run the program. Figure B3.3 shows one sample output. Remember the earlier warning that told you about the improper spacing caused by the proportional font. The x-coordinate spacing used in the FILES program is the average character width; hence some characters are too close together, and some are too far apart. The importance of this application, however, is not in the spacing but in the ease with which you can add keystroke handlers with Enter keystroke awareness.

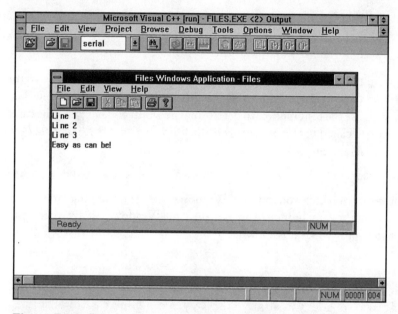

Figure B3.3. Pressing Enter sends the next characters you type to the subsequent line.

 Tip: If you type so many lines of text that the text drops off the bottom of the window, you can resize the window to a larger size to see the rest of the text. It's fairly easy to add scroll bars to your application also. You'll learn how to work with scroll bars as you learn more about the Visual C++ MFC classes.

If you ran the FILES application, you saw how an Enter keystroke helps you place the text on the lines you want. There is, however, a fairly significant problem left in the

Extra Credit Bonus 3

program. You might or might not have noticed the problem, but you probably sensed that something was wrong. Doesn't it feel strange to type characters without seeing a text cursor (the caret) precede your typed characters? The application would feel much more professional if there were a caret leading the way as you typed.

To add a caret, you must use four functions (remember that the term *cursor* is usually reserved for the mouse cursor and that a *caret* or *insertion point* is the term for the text cursor). These are the four necessary functions:

```
CreateSolidCaret()
HideCaret()
SetCaretPos()
ShowCaret()
```

The `CreateSolidCaret()` function creates a caret for your application. The arguments of `CreateSolidCaret()` determine the width and height of the caret. Usually, programmers use the font metrics to determine the width and height of the caret. For example, if you called `GetTextMetrics()`, the following `CreateSolidCaret()` would create a typical text cursor:

```
CreateSolidCaret(textStruct.tmAveCharWidth/8, textStruct.tmHeight+2);
```

After you create the caret, you must tell Windows when you want the caret shown and when you want the caret hidden. Also, you must tell Windows exactly where you want the caret to appear when it is shown.

Note: As shown in the next listing, you should hide the caret while you display text. After you display the text, you can display the caret again. You don't want the caret appearing at a point that is one or more characters behind the text on-screen, even if only for an instant.

The function in Listing B3.4 completes the `OnDraw()` display function by adding a caret to the text. The user sees the caret appear to the right of all the typed characters, and the caret also drops to the next line after an Enter keystroke.

Listing B3.4. Displaying characters from the string with a caret.

```
1:  ////////////////////////////////////////////////////////////
2:  // CFilesView drawing
3:
4:  void CFilesView::OnDraw(CDC* pDC)
```

```
 5:  {
 6:    CFilesDoc* pDoc = GetDocument();
 7:    ASSERT_VALID(pDoc);
 8:
 9:    // TODO: add draw code for native data here
10:    TEXTMETRIC textStruct;
11:    int cxChar=0;
12:    int cyChar = 0;
13:    CPoint cxyCaret;    // Needed for the caret position
14:    pDC->GetTextMetrics(&textStruct);
15:    CreateSolidCaret(textStruct.tmAveCharWidth/8,
       ➥textStruct.tmHeight+2);
16:    HideCaret();        // Temporarily hides the caret from view
17:    for (int ctr=0; ctr<pDoc->sInput.GetLength(); ctr++)
18:      {
19:        if (pDoc->sInput[ctr] == '\r')
20:           { cyChar+= (textStruct.tmHeight +
              ➥textStruct.tmExternalLeading);
21:             cxChar=0; }
22:        else
23:           { pDC->TextOut(cxChar, cyChar, pDoc->sInput.Mid(ctr), 1);
24:              // The average character width will cause some
25:              // spacing problems, but it's OK for now
26:              cxChar += textStruct.tmAveCharWidth; }
27:      }
28:    cxyCaret.x = cxChar+2;   // Update the position of the
29:    cxyCaret.y = cyChar;     // caret's location
30:    SetCaretPos(cxyCaret);
31:    ShowCaret();
32: }
```

The output in Figure B3.4 shows characters being typed with a text caret leading the way.

Line 13 provides a new Visual C++ feature that is common throughout a lot of Windows programming. CPoint is a structure defined inside the MFC classes that contains two integer coordinates, x and y. Therefore, the object named cxyCaret is a structure containing an x and y coordinate. It is with the cxyCaret object that the program locates the caret's position.

Line 15 creates the caret by specifying the caret's width and height values gotten from the font metrics. Immediately after line 15 creates the caret, line 16 hides the caret from view while the next character appears on-screen.

Extra Credit Bonus 3

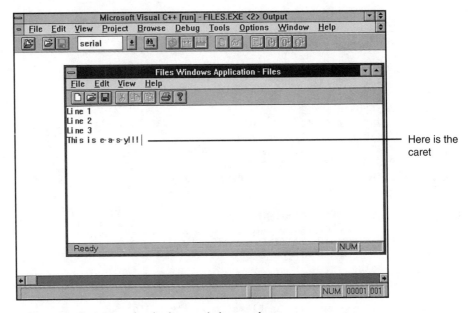

Figure B3.4. A caret leads the user's keystrokes.

 Note: Defining the caret coordinates locally inside the function, instead of defining the caret coordinates globally in a header file, takes away some efficiency but facilitates a smoother learning process for you at this point.

The caret's x coordinate always appears two points to the right of the next character's display location (see line 28), whereas the next character's y coordinate determines the vertical positioning of the caret in line 29. Line 30 sets the caret's screen position, and line 31 displays the caret until the next character must be displayed.

Adding Code for File Save, Open, and New

It's now time to save the typed text in a file. There are several ways to manipulate files and file data in Visual C++, but one of the easiest and most powerful is through *serialization*. Serialization, the process that AppWizard automatically builds into applications, requires little more than your telling the application which data to save and retrieve. AppWizard overloads the >> and << so that you can save and retrieve virtually any kind of data, class data or otherwise, without worrying about the way the data gets to the disk.

The FILES application currently saves the user's keystrokes in the sInput string. Therefore, all you have to do is locate the serialization code and input or output that string. As you might expect, the file I/O code appears in the document class's file FILESDOC.CPP. Follow these steps to hook up **File S**ave and **File O**pen:

1. Open the FILESDOC.CPP file. Find the Serialize() function. It looks like this:

```
1:  /////////////////////////////////////////////////////////
2:  // CFilesDoc serialization
3:
4:  void CFilesDoc::Serialize(CArchive& ar)
5:  {
6:  if (ar.IsStoring())
7:  {
8:       // TODO: add storing code here
9:  }
10:     else
11:     {
12:         // TODO: add loading code here
13:     }
14: }
```

The Serialize() function receives the ar argument. ar is an object of the type CArchive, a serializable class in the MFC. Notice the member function call on line 6. IsStoring() is true if a file save is being performed, and IsStoring() is false if a file open is being performed (that is, a file is to be loaded).

2. To store the sInput string, you only have to use the overloaded insertion operator as follows:

```
ar << sInput;  // For File Save
```

The ar represents whatever filename the user selects from the **File S**ave dialog box. To load the string from the disk file selected by the user, you use the extraction operator as follows:

```
ar >> sInput;  // For File Open
```

Extra Credit Bonus 3

That's all you have to do. Listing B3.5 shows the completed `Serialize()` function that you should enter into FILESDOC.CPP. Save the file and rebuild the program to see the results.

Listing B3.5. Adding the File Save and File Open code.

```
 1: /////////////////////////////////////////////////////////////////
 2: // CFilesDoc serialization
 3:
 4: void CFilesDoc::Serialize(CArchive& ar)
 5: {
 6:   if (ar.IsStoring())
 7:   {
 8:       // TODO: add storing code here
 9:       ar << sInput;  // For File Save
10:   }
11:   else
12:   {
13:       // TODO: add loading code here
14:       ar >> sInput;  // For File Open
15:   }
16: }
```

You'll probably want to try a few **F**ile **S**aves and **F**ile **O**pens to see whether the serialization code works with the two simple I/O statements you added to the program. To produce output, follow these steps after building the program:

1. Run the program.

2. Type some text into the window.

3. Select **F**ile **S**ave and type a new filename, such as FILES.DAT. (Any filename will do, but first make sure that the file doesn't exist in order to keep things simple.) Notice, as shown in Figure B3.5, that the **F**ile **S**ave produces the familiar Windows File Save dialog box.

4. Exit the program by selecting **F**ile **E**xit. (You've got to clear the window to test the **F**ile **O**pen.)

5. Start the FILES application again to display its empty window.

6. Select **F**ile **O**pen. You'll see the familiar Windows File Open dialog box. Type the filename you used in Step 3, and press Enter. The `Serialize()` function will load the `sInput` string from disk, and your `OnDraw()` function takes care of displaying the text loaded from disk as you last saved it.

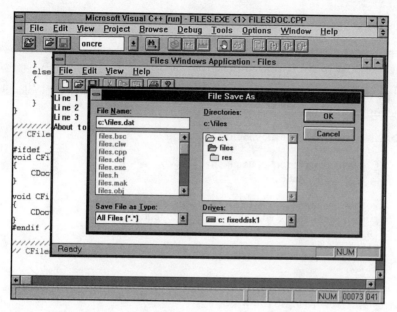

Figure B3.5. Entering a filename to save the window's text.

How about that? You did not have to write code that opens a file, tediously saves the data, and closes the file. Your only concern is using the correct operator, << or >>, in the `Serialize()` function.

Perhaps, however, you can make the application even more usable. In the preceding steps, you had to exit the application to erase the window. Yet AppWizard added a **File New** menu option. One simple line of code will activate the **File New** command.

Try to anticipate what you should do to clear the window. Where is the data stored? The window's data is in the `sInput` string. If the user selects **File New**, you only have to clear the `sInput` string. Here are two ways to clear the contents of a `CString` object such as `sInput`:

```
sInput = "";       // Store an empty string
sInput.Empty();    // Empty the string object
```

Both statements do the same thing, but the second statement retains the spirit of C++ by calling the `Empty()` CString member function (described in yesterday's bonus chapter) to empty the contents of the `CString` object. Here are the steps you follow to activate **File New**:

Extra Credit Bonus 3

1. Open the file named FILESDOC.CPP.

2. Scroll down to the OnNewDocument() function. AppWizard already mapped the **F**ile **N**ew menu option to the OnNewDocument() function.

3. Type the sInput emptying function call so that OnNewDocument() looks like the function shown here:

```
BOOL CFilesDoc::OnNewDocument()
{
    if (!CDocument::OnNewDocument())
        return FALSE;

    // TODO: add reinitialization code here
    // (SDI documents will reuse this document)
    sInput.Empty();   // Clear the window's data
    return TRUE;
}
```

4. Build the application and run it. Type some data into the window, and select **F**ile **N**ew to erase the window.

That was easy enough. There's one more feature to add. The user should be allowed to erase the window any time he or she wants. If, however, the window contains data that the user has yet to save, the application should ask whether the user wants the file saved before the **F**ile **N**ew command erases the window's data.

Visual C++ offers an MFC function called SetModifiedFlag() that you call whenever the user types a character (which, in effect, modifies the window's text). The **F**ile **N**ew option, as well as **F**ile E**x**it, checks the modified flag. It automatically displays a warning dialog box if the user activates a menu option that could destroy the window contents before the contents are saved.

Listing B3.6 shows the SetModifiedFlag() function call after it has been added to the OnChar() function. Make the correction and type data into the application. Attempt to exit the program without saving the window's contents in a file, and see what happens. (The next Output section shows the dialog box that MFC throws on the screen.)

 Listing B3.6. Making the window's text safer.

```
1:  //////////////////////////////////////////////////////////////////
2:  // CFilesView message handlers
3:
4:  void CFilesView::OnChar(UINT nChar, UINT nRepCnt, UINT nFlags)
```

```
 5: {
 6:     // TODO: Add your message handler code here and/or call default
 7:
 8:     CFilesDoc* pDoc = GetDocument();
 9:     pDoc->sInput += nChar;
10:     pDoc->SetModifiedFlag();    // The user modified the window's data
11:     Invalidate();
12:     SendMessage(WM_PAINT);
13: }
```

 Figure B3.6 shows the output the user might get.

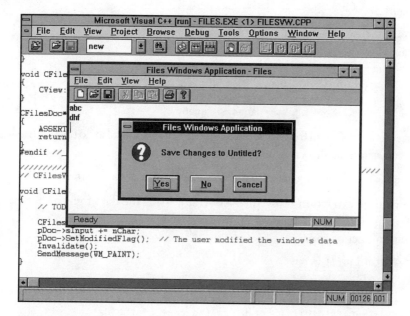

Figure B3.6. Oops! Don't forget to save before exiting the application.

Line 10 contains the only line needed to activate the warning dialog box if the user attempts to exit the program or load a new document without saving the contents of the current document. If the user answers **Y**es to the dialog box warning, the application automatically displays the **F**ile **S**ave dialog box.

Extra Credit Bonus 3

You'll see from the output in Figure B3.6 that the application calls the application UNTITLED. If you previously saved the window's data in a file, the dialog box would contain the filename under which the user last stored the file in place of UNTITLED.

Writing Other Data

The Serialize() function looks easy, and that's because it is. Nevertheless, you might be wondering just how easy Serialize() would be if you were writing more than a single string as in the FILES application.

Just about any kind of data you can define, you can also serialize. In other words, you could serialize five integer values like this:

```
ar << age1;
ar << age2;
ar << age3;
ar << age4;
ar << age5;
```

Of course, you could serialize the values all in one step, like this:

```
ar << age1 << age2 << age3 << age4 << age5;
```

If you wanted to save data from different data types, you could also do that with a single serialize insertion, as shown here:

```
ar << age << salary << name;   // Store different data types
```

A mirror-image extraction using the >> operator loads the data right back into the variables when you want them. Feel free to serialize arrays as well. Consider the following snippet of code:

```
if (ar.IsStoring())
{
  ar << numValues;   // Store the total number of array values
  for (int ctr=0; ctr<numValues; ctr++)
    { ar << myData[ctr]; }   // Store the rest of the data
}
```

The ar object is an *archive* object that represents the data file selected from the file dialog boxes.

The myData array could be an array of any data type, including complete classes and structures. The initial numValues makes sure that a subsequent read inputs the correct number of array values, as shown here:

```
ar >> numValues;   // Find out how many values were saved
for (int ctr=0; ctr<numValues; ctr++)
  { ar << myData[ctr]; }    // Read the array data
```

The `Serialize()` function places as few restrictions on you as possible. There is, however, one restriction you should know about that you'll someday need. If you are storing or retrieving class data, you must derive your class from the MFC `CObject` class. `CObject` is the base class for the entire MFC class hierarchy, and all MFC objects are derived from `CObject`.

DO / DON'T

DO watch the positioning of text in your window so that the lines break as they should (such as when the user presses Enter).

DON'T bother with opening and closing the window's document file in your application. The `Serialize()` function takes most of the work out of your hands if you want to save data.

DON'T forget to add the `SetModifiedFlag()` function to ensure that the user does not exit the program or load a new file without saving the latest changes to the current window.

Introduction to MFC Exceptions

This section introduces you to the MFC exceptions so that you can get used to the way Visual C++ supports exceptions. In the MFC, exceptions are handled by the TRY and CATCH macros. You must place the code that might generate an exception in a TRY block. The CATCH block (or blocks) handles the exception.

You can set up several CATCH blocks to handle several types of exceptions. The MFC ensures that a thrown exception lands in the appropriate CATCH block. The CATCH block receives a parameter from the exception that describes the nature of the exception thrown.

Table B3.1 lists the kinds of exceptions that the MFC handles.

Extra Credit Bonus 3

Table B3.1. The kinds of MFC exceptions.

Exception Name	Description
CArchiveException	Archive exception
CFileException	File I/O exception
CMemoryException	Memory exception
CNotSupportedException	Feature-not-supported exception
COleException	Object Linking and Embedding exception
CResourceException	Windows-resource exception
CUserException	User-generated exception
ErrnoToException	Converts an error number to an exception
OsErrorToException	Converts a DOS error to an exception

You might wonder why there is both an archive exception (`CArchiveException`) and a file I/O exception (`CFileException`). After all, you saw in the preceding section that a serialized archive performs file I/O for you. You must keep in mind, however, that the serialized object you saw in the preceding section was for the window document. You might have several files open at once, and only one of those files is to be displayed and handled by the archiving `Serialize()` function. You'll learn a little about the `CFile` class in a moment.

For some exceptions, such as `CMemoryException`, there is only one possible cause—an allocation failure. For other exceptions, there are several causes that could force the exception. It's best to start with a simple memory exception handler and then work up to an I/O exception.

Look at the code in Listing B3.7. You'll see several heap-allocation attempts using the `new` operator. If a `new` fails, the MFC generates a `CMemoryException`, and your `CATCH` exception handler, if you provide one, will take over when an error occurs. Listing B3.7 is trying to allocate too much memory. The programmer wisely put the allocation inside a `TRY` block, so the runtime module knows to look for a `CATCH` block that handles the error. Luckily, there is a `CATCH` block directly beneath the problem. (The `CATCH` block could have been elsewhere in the program.)

Note: Listing B3.7's TRY-CATCH block is shown inside the OnChar() function just to ensure that it executes in case you want to add it to the FILES application and try the exception yourself.

Listing B3.7. Trying to allocate too much memory.

```
 1: void CFilesView::OnChar(UINT nChar, UINT nRepCnt, UINT nFlags)
 2: {
 3:   // TODO: Add your message handler code here and/or call default
 4:
 5:   TRY
 6:   {
 7:     // The following would eventually lock up your system
 8:     char * pi1 = new char[32766];
 9:     char * pi2 = new char[32766];
10:     char * pi3 = new char[32766];
11:     char * pi4 = new char[32766];
12:     char * pi5 = new char[32766];
13:     char * pi6 = new char[32766];
14:     char * pi7 = new char[32766];
15:     char * pi8 = new char[32766];
16:   }
17:   CATCH(CMemoryException, e)
18:   {
19:     MessageBox("Oops a memory error!");
20:   }
21:   END_CATCH
22:
23:   CFilesDoc* pDoc = GetDocument();
24:   pDoc->sInput += nChar;
25:   pDoc->SetModifiedFlag();  // The user modified the window's data
26:   Invalidate();
27:   SendMessage(WM_PAINT);
28: }
```

The dialog box in Figure B3.7 appears on-screen if you run the FILES application with the exception handler shown in Listing B3.7.

Extra Credit Bonus 3

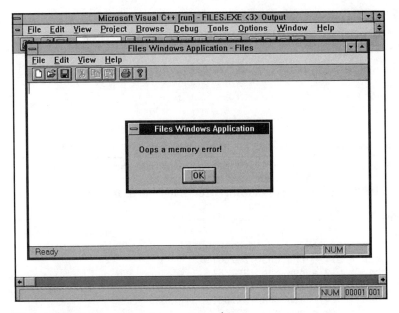

Figure B3.7. The exception was caught.

 There are several things to note about this exception-handling code. First of all, you'll see that the TRY block encloses any and all code that you want included in your exception handling. Listing B3.7's TRY block spans lines 5–16. Without the TRY, the new attempts would eventually stop the application (at best) or shut down Windows (in all probability) if left unchecked. The CATCH block, in lines 17–21, determine what happens if a memory exception occurs.

Notice the parameters in the CATCH macro in line 17. The CMemoryException parameter lets the runtime system know which exception this particular CATCH code catches. If an archive exception occurs, the CATCH block that begins in line 17 would not catch the exception. The second parameter, e, is not used for memory exceptions. The e parameter points to the cause of the exception when you are catching other kinds of exceptions, as shown in a moment.

You've not seen the MessageBox() function so far in this book. MessageBox() (line 19) displays a pop-up dialog box with the message you pass to MessageBox(). Figure B3.7 showed the dialog box that was displayed because of the memory exception. Message boxes are easy ways to display messages to the user. You might want to check the online MFC help files for more information on MessageBox(). With other parameters, you can control which icon and command buttons appear in the message box when you display it.

 Warning: Be sure to remove the exception handling from the OnDraw() function when you are ready to continue with the rest of the chapter. If you do not, the memory exception will occur and get in the way of any other exceptions you try to evoke.

You'll Want to Do More

When an exception takes place, you'll probably want to do more than display a simple message box. One of the annoyances of MFC's exception handling is that destructors are *not* called, and if you attempt several allocations of memory objects and one of them fails, you'll have to destruct the ones that were allocated by calling their destructor yourself. (The true ANSI C++ standard for exceptions helps with destructors more than the first renditions of Visual C++ do.)

Also, you might want to deallocate other memory that you allocated earlier and no longer need. If you can free some memory, you might want to attempt the allocation again. If you cannot handle the exception easily, you might have to terminate the program after displaying an appropriate reason and instructions for the user.

Many of the exception types generate an extra argument caught in the CATCH block that tells the exception handler exactly what kind of exception occurred. For example, look at Table B3.2 to see the possible causes of the CArchiveException. When an archive exception occurs, you will write different handlers depending on the cause of the exception. The e parameter you saw in the previous CATCH block will always point to the cause of the particular exception.

Table B3.2. Causes of the CArchiveException.

Cause	Description
badClass	Cannot read into the specified class.
badIndex	The file is invalid.
badSchema	The version of the object is not correct.

continues

Extra Credit Bonus 3

Table B3.2. continued

Cause	Description
endOfFile	The end of the file was reached during input.
generic	Unspecified error.
none	No error occurred.
readOnly	Output was attempted when only reading is allowed.
writeOnly	Input was attempted when only writing is allowed.

The CFileException also has several causes. You'll see the CFileException causes shown in Table B3.3. As you can see, some of the causes for a file I/O exception overlap the archive exceptions because both deal with files, and the mechanics of file I/O often trigger exceptions (disk doors are left open, filenames are incorrect, and so forth).

Table B3.3. Causes of the CFileException.

Cause	Description
accessDenied	Cannot access the file due to the file's attributes.
badPath	The specified pathname is bad.
badSeek	The file pointer cannot be set as requested.
directoryFull	The directory is full. (The root directory has a limit on the number of files it can hold.)
diskFull	The disk cannot hold more data.
endOfFile	The end of the file is reached.
fileNotFound	The specified file is not on the disk.
generic	Unspecified error.
hardIO	A hardware error occurred.
invalidFile	The file cannot be located with the information given.
lockViolation	In a networked environment, a file is in use.
none	No error occurred. (A user generated this exception.)
removeCurrentDir	The specified directory cannot be removed.

Cause	Description
sharingViolation	The file cannot be shared because SHARE.EXE was not loaded from DOS.
tooManyOpenFiles	The number of open files exceeds the CONFIG.SYS FILES= limit.

The CFile class enables you to access your own data files without manipulating the document class. For example, you might be reading archived data from the document class and read a key whose description is located in another data file. You could first open that other data file (named SAMPLE.DAT in this case) by making the data file an object of the CFile class, as shown here:

```
CFile keyFile("SAMPLE.DAT", CFile::modeRead);
  keyFile.Read(descripts; numOfDescripts);   // Read all records into
                                             //   array
keyFile.Close();
```

The Close() member function call is not even necessary because the file will be closed when the CFile object goes out of scope. However, explicitly closing the file means that the file is closed just that much sooner, and it's always a good idea to close a file when you no longer need it open.

The following code gives you an idea of how you would integrate exception handling in the CFile class code in case there's a problem. Notice that the switch statement ensures that the proper exception is taken care of. It might help to think of the CATCH locating the correct exception through the first CATCH argument while the second CATCH argument finds out the root cause of that specific exception.

```
TRY
{
  CFile keyFile("SAMPLE.DAT", CFile::modeRead);
    keyFile.Read(descripts; numOfDescripts);   // Read all records into
                                               //   array
  keyFile.Close();
}  // End of TRY block

CATCH(CFileException, e)
{
  switch (e->m_cause)    // m_cause is defined for you
  {
    case CFileException::accessDenied:
      MessageBox("Oh no...You can't access that file");
      break;
```

Extra Credit Bonus 3

```
      case CFileException::badPath:
        MessageBox("Oh no...Your pathname isn't correct");
        break;
      case CFileException::diskFull:
        MessageBox("Oh no...Your disk can't hold anything more");
        break;
      case CFileException::fileNotFound:
        MessageBox("Oh no...I couldn't find the file");
        break;
      default:
        MessageBox("Oh no...Some kind of file error just occurred");
        break;
    }
}
END_CATCH
```

In reality, you would probably do more processing to handle the errors, possibly closing all open files first and exiting the program after displaying the message box.

If you want to handle several exceptions, you can generate a multiple CATCH block using an AND_CATCH macro such as this one:

```
TRY
{
  Your code that possibly throws an exception
}
CATCH(CFileException, e)
{
  // Your CFile exception code handler goes here
}
AND_CATCH(CMemoryException, e)
{
   // Your memory exception code handler goes here
}
AND_CATCH(CArchiveException)
{
   // Your archive exception code handler goes here
}
END_CATCH        // Required to end the CATCH processing
```

Finally, if you want a catch-all exception handler, that's just what the Visual C++ MFC classes supply with the CATCH_ALL handler:

```
TRY
{
  // Code that might possibly throw any of the exceptions
}
CATCH_ALL(e)
{
```

```
    // A catch-all exception handler, possibly a destructor and
    //     program exit
}
END_CATCH
```

 Tip: You can insert a block of several CATCH and CATCH_ALL commands to handle the exceptions you expect might happen and add a final CATCH_ALL to take care of unexpected exceptions. This way, you can intercede before your user receives any cryptic error messages.

This chapter only scratched the surface of the MFC exceptions. However, we're running out of room quickly, and there's some fun graphics ahead of you in the next chapter. You now have some general insight into the MFC exception handlers. You should by now feel much more comfortable in the MFC classes than you did before you began this chapter.

Summary

Today's chapter gives you a potpourri of MFC topics, ranging from printing and print preview to exception handling. You first saw that AppWizard takes care of all printing and print previewing details for you. You don't have to add one line of code to add printing and previewing to your application. If you can get text displayed in your application's window, AppWizard ensures that you can print that text.

You then saw how to filter keystrokes, such as the Enter keystroke, and generate a new line on-screen. It would be nice if you didn't have to worry about the exact positioning of your window text, but you do have to take care of tracking the coordinates yourself.

Your user will appreciate it if you display a cursor ahead of the user's keystrokes. You learned the MFC cursor functions in this chapter that explained how to create and display the cursor at a point ahead of text. As with all other window contents, you must track the coordinates of the cursor.

Finally, you learned a little about the MFC exception handling TRY and CATCH macros. All sorts of exceptions are possible, and within most categories there are several possible causes for the exception. When an exception is thrown, the CATCH parameter determines the kind and cause of the exception that occurred.

Extra Credit Bonus 3

Q&A

Q. After I display text in the window, can the user print the text?

A. Printing and print preview are two of the easiest features you can put into your application. You can thank the Windows system for the ease of printing. AppWizard generates all the necessary code needed to print and preview the printing.

When printing, your user sees the familiar Windows print dialog box. If several printers are attached to the computer, your user can select the appropriate one and even print to a file if desired. The consistent printing interface that is available to all Windows applications makes the learning curve for your users much easier than it would be without that interface.

Q. Should my user always be allowed to exit the program or load a new file into the window?

A. Your user should be allowed to do anything he or she wants to do, within limits. If your user wants to exit the program without saving the contents of the window, that is fine. However, it is incumbent upon you to warn the user that the window's contents have not been saved.

You use the `SetModifiedFlag()` function to tell the application that the user has updated the window contents. After the user saves the window with **F**ile **S**ave, the application resets the modified flag. However, until the user saves, the application warns the user to give the user one last chance to save the file before erasing the window contents with **F**ile **N**ew or **F**ile **O**pen.

Q. How do I make sure that the caret stays ahead of my user's keystrokes?

A. Sadly, you keep track of both the caret's coordinates and the current text so that you can update the caret's position yourself. Here are the basic steps (in pseudocode form) to use a caret in your application:

```
Create the caret.
While you have text to display
{
  Hide the caret.
  Display the text.
  Update the caret's coordinates.
  Show the caret.
}
```

The hiding of the caret ensures that the caret gets out of the way while your text displays.

Q. How do the MFC classes support exception handling?

A. The TRY, CATCH, and CATCH_ALL macros control exception handling. You surround code that might trigger an exception with the TRY block. Then, a CATCH or AND_CATCH block catches the exceptions as they occur in the program. The parameters of the CATCH blocks determine which exceptions get caught and which pass by the CATCH blocks.

Workshop

The Workshop offers quiz questions and exercises to hone your skills and give you feedback on today's lesson. You'll find some proposed answers in Appendix D.

Quiz

1. What are the function names you must write to implement printing and print preview?
2. True or False: The IsModifiedFlag() function tests to see whether the user has modified the window's data since the last file save.
3. Why must you create a cursor before displaying it?
4. What should you do with the cursor before displaying the user's text?
5. Why would you use both the CFile class and the Serialize() function?
6. True or False: If you have multiple exceptions to catch, your application will have a series of CATCH blocks.
7. What macro catches any and all exceptions that have yet to be caught in the catch block?

Exercise

1. Add a Backspace handler to the Files application. To keep things simple, don't worry about backing the cursor up to the preceding line if the cursor is already in the first column on a line.

741

Extra Credit Bonus 4+

Graphics and Visual C++

Extra Credit Bonus 4

Today's bonus chapter provides a preview of what you can expect if you try to add graphics to your Visual C++ Windows programs. Several graphics functions are available in the MFC, and you'll see a few examples of implementing graphics here.

Programming graphics is a lot of fun. Not only are graphics fun to work with, but they can provide lots of appealing, attention-getting details in business programs and presentation screens. A graphics screen can show an engineer in a single glance what it takes hundreds of numeric values to convey. In today's world, a computer without graphics would be as archaic as a secretary without a word processor.

As with the preceding bonus chapters, you might feel that some things are explained here in a cursory manner. A complete graphics tutorial cannot be compressed into a single chapter. As you saw in the previous chapters, however, the Visual Workbench rescues you from a lot of details you don't really *have* to understand in order to enhance your programs.

Today, you learn about the following topics:

- ☐ How to turn on and turn off the graphics dots in your window
- ☐ How to add color to the graphics dots on your screen
- ☐ How to draw lines
- ☐ How to draw rectangles
- ☐ How to draw ellipses
- ☐ How to add color and hatching to your graphics shapes

Getting Started with Some Graphics

Clear your graphics slate by creating a new AppWizard application. Call the application PIC (for *pic*ture). You're now an old pro at using AppWizard to create the application shell, but be sure to consider the following information before you begin:

1. Make sure that you have ample disk space (more than 3 megabytes) before generating a new application. If you want, you can delete the .OBJ files from the FILES application you created in the preceding chapter. You can also remove the entire FILES subdirectory and its contents (with the DOS DELTREE command or the Windows File Manager) if you don't want it anymore.

2. Store the application in its own subdirectory, named PIC, to keep all the files together and to keep things simple.

3. Be sure to turn off the MDI option so that your application remains an SDI (*single document interface*) application, as was done in the past couple of bonus chapters. Actually, AppWizard makes MDI applications *almost* as easy to manage as SDI, but for these MFC/AppWizard introductory chapters, SDI keeps things as simple as they can possibly be.

4. Don't build the application after AppWizard generates the files. You'll be adding a few graphics commands before building the application.

Now that you've built the application, you can begin to explore the Visual C++ graphics capabilities.

Turning On and Off Points

A *pixel* (short for *picture element*) is any single graphics dot on your screen. Similar to the output of a dot-matrix printer, everything that appears on your screen is a combination of pixel dots. You reference the dots with x and y coordinates in which x represents the horizontal position and y represents the vertical position. The upper-left corner of your screen is at coordinate (0,0). Coordinate (0,0) is often called the *home* position. (Coordinates are often referred to in print as an x and y pair placed within parentheses.) Figure B4.1 shows how the x and y coordinates associate with the screen.

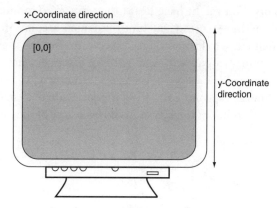

Figure B4.1. The x- and y-coordinate graphics points.

Extra Credit Bonus 4

Tip: The window coordinates are always relative to the upper-left corner of your window, whether your window is maximized to full screen or smaller. In other words, your window's home position, (0,0), is always your window's upper-left corner, no matter where the user moves your window and no matter what size the user makes your window. The coordinates are never relative to your screen, only to your window.

Note: You might remember the `CPoint` class from yesterday's bonus chapter, which defines two window x and y coordinates. You'll use the `CPoint` class quite often with the graphics functions because of the graphics functions' dependency on coordinate pairs.

The MFC `SetPixel()` member function turns pixels on and off. Here is the general format of `SetPixel()`:

`SetPixel(int x, int y, int colorValue);`

In this notation, the *x* and *y* values can range from `0` to the highest coordinate pair determined by the video adapter's resolution limits. The *colorValue* requires a little more discussion.

Each color on your computer screen has as its basis a combination of red, green, and blue colors. You might have heard the term *RGB* monitor before. The term *RGB* comes from the red, green, and blue fundamental colors that combine on your screen in different ratios to form the entire spectrum of colors available on your system. The third `SetPixel()` argument, *colorValue*, is easily generated if you call the `RGB()` macro available in the MFC. `RGB()` returns a value known as a `COLORDEF` value, recognizable to Windows as a specific color from the spectrum of available colors. In other words, `SetPixel()`'s third argument could consist of any of the following calls (among many others):

```
RGB(0, 0, 0)         // All black (lack of any color)
RGB(255, 0, 0)       // All red
RBG(0, 255, 0)       // All green
RGB(0, 0, 255)       // All blue
RGB(255, 255, 255)   // All white
RGB(128, 128, 128)   // Windows gray
RGB(50, 200, 50)     // Mostly green
```

`RGB()`'s return value is actually a 32-bit value that represents a single color as close to the red-green-blue combination as the display adapter allows. An exact color combination is often difficult to determine and sometimes requires some trial-and-error attempts before the displayed color is just right.

The following `SetPixel()` function turns on a red pixel at screen location (100,150) (100 pixels from the left of the screen and 150 pixels down from the top):

```
SetPixel(100, 150, RGB(255, 0, 0));
```

`SetPixel()` is a member of the `CView` class, which means that you must use the function within the view class. The object to which you apply the `SetPixel()` function must be a device context object that represents your screen. Therefore, you often see the `SetPixel()` function applied right after a function gets the device context, such as in this line:

```
devCon.SetPixel(100, 150, RGB(255, 0, 0));
```

The current view device is passed to most of the view class functions as the `*this` pointer. The `CClientDC()` member function finds a device context when you specify the `*this` pointer to the `CClientDC()` function. Hence, you can get the device context and set a pixel as shown here:

```
CClientDC devCon(this);    // Find the current device context
devCon.SetPixel(100, 150, RGB(255, 0, 0);
```

A simple example will help demonstrate the `SetPixel()` function. Listing B4.1 shows an `OnDraw()` function (in PICVIEW.CPP) that draws a single line diagonally down the screen. The program randomly selects colors for the line as it draws.

Type

Listing B4.1. Drawing a diagonal line.

```
1:  void CPicView::OnDraw(CDC* pDC)
2:  {
3:    CPicDoc* pDoc = GetDocument();
4:    ASSERT_VALID(pDoc);
5:
6:    // TODO: add draw code for native data here
7:    CClientDC devCon(this);
8:    CPoint cxyPoint;         // A point object
9:    // Draw a line of random colors
10:   cxyPoint.y = 0;
11:   for (cxyPoint.x=0; cxyPoint.x<150; cxyPoint.x++)
12:   {
13:     devCon.SetPixel(cxyPoint.x, cxyPoint.y, RGB(rand()%255,
14:                     rand()%255, rand()%255));
```

continues

Extra Credit Bonus 4

Listing B4.1. continued

```
15:        // Draw a second line next to the previous
16:        // one to thicken the line some
17:        devCon.SetPixel(cxyPoint.x+1, cxyPoint.y, RGB(rand()%255,
18:                        rand()%255, rand()%255));
19:        cxyPoint.y++;
20:    }
21: }
```

 Figure B4.2 shows Listing B4.1's output.

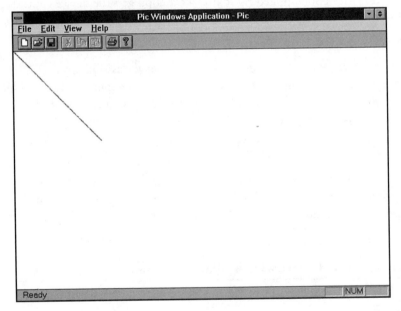

Figure B4.2. After drawing the diagonal line.

Line 8 defines a CPoint object to track the x- and y-coordinate values for the line. The for loop that begins on line 11 ensures that each x coordinate value from 0 to 150 is turned on. The y-coordinate value runs from 0, incrementing (via line 19) until all x values are drawn. You'll see that the program always draws a second point next to the first one (lines 17 and 18) to thicken the line somewhat.

Getting Smarter with Coordinates

Remember that the total number of available x and y coordinates differs among various display adapters. Windows can supply the hardware information your program needs in order to determine the display size. The MFC `GetDeviceCaps()` function returns a great deal of information about your device context.

The `GetDeviceCaps()` function accepts only a single argument, and that argument tells `GetDeviceCaps()` what kind of information you want. `GetDeviceCaps()` returns the integer value you are seeking. Table B4.1 contains several defined values you can pass to `GetDeviceCaps()`.

Table B4.1. Possible `GetDeviceCaps()` arguments.

Argument	Description
HORZSIZE	Width of the display in millimeters
VERTSIZE	Height of the display in millimeters
HORZRES	Maximum number of pixels across the display
VERTRES	Maximum number of pixels down the display
LOGPIXELSX	Number of pixels per inch of display width
LOGPIXELSY	Number of pixels per inch of display height

Unless you're writing a drawing or charting program, you will probably use `GetDeviceCaps()` to find the maximum number of pixels in either the x or the y coordinate, or in both coordinates.

Listing B4.2 contains a revised `OnDraw()` function that calls `GetDeviceCaps()`, passing the HORZRES value to ensure that the program does not exceed the maximum x coordinate. (In this program, the y coordinate actually runs out of room before the x coordinate does.)

Listing B4.2. Drawing a diagonal line with some safety added.

```
1:  void CPicView::OnDraw(CDC* pDC)
2:  {
3:      CPicDoc* pDoc = GetDocument();
4:      ASSERT_VALID(pDoc);
5:
```

continues

Extra Credit Bonus 4

Listing B4.2. continued

```
 6:      // TODO: add draw code for native data here
 7:      CClientDC devCon(this);
 8:      CPoint cxyPoint;         // A point object
 9:      // Draw a line of random colors
10:      cxyPoint.y = 0;
11:      for (cxyPoint.x=0; cxyPoint.x<devCon.GetDeviceCaps(HORZRES);
    ➥cxyPoint.x++)
12:      {
13:         devCon.SetPixel(cxyPoint.x, cxyPoint.y, RGB(rand()%255,
14:                         rand()%255, rand()%255));
15:         // Draw a second line next to the previous
16:            // one to thicken the line some
17:            devCon.SetPixel(cxyPoint.x+1, cxyPoint.y, RGB(rand()%255,
18:                         rand()%255, rand()%255));
19:         cxyPoint.y++;
20:      }
21: }
```

Figure B4.3 shows the output from Listing B4.2.

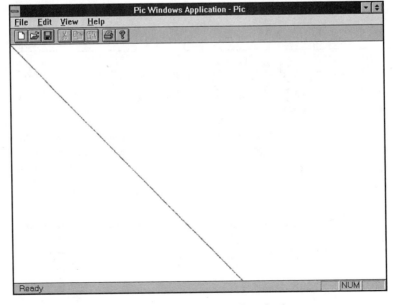

Figure B4.3. After drawing the diagonal line farther.

Line 11's for loop ensures that the maximum x-coordinate value is not exceeded in the loop. Whereas Listing B4.1 only incremented x to 150, Listing B4.2 keeps running until x reaches the maximum horizontal resolution.

Far Out

How about having some fun? Now that you know how to keep within the screen's coordinate boundaries, you can write a dot-drawing program that fills the screen with a bunch of randomly colored and randomly placed dots. The program in Listing B4.3 fills the screen with many, many pixels.

Listing B4.3. Filling the screen with dots.

```
 1: void CPicView::OnDraw(CDC* pDC)
 2: {
 3:   CPicDoc* pDoc = GetDocument();
 4:   ASSERT_VALID(pDoc);
 5:
 6:   // TODO: add draw code for native data here
 7:   CClientDC devCon(this);
 8:   CPoint cxyPoint;         // A point object
 9:     int maxX = devCon.GetDeviceCaps(HORZRES);   // Save the maximum
10:     int maxY = devCon.GetDeviceCaps(VERTRES);   // coordinates
11:     for (long int count=0; count<50000; count++)
12:     {
13:       devCon.SetPixel(rand()%maxX, rand()%maxY, RGB(rand()%255,
14:              rand()%255, rand()%255));
15:     }
16: }
```

 Figure B4.4 shows the output of Listing B4.3.

 The loop in lines 11–15 ensures that Listing B4.4 turns on 50,000 pixels randomly within the screen display's maximum coordinates. A `long int` loop value, `count`, was used because a regular `int` can hold signed values only as large as 32,767. (The Windows `WORD` type also would have worked.)

Just to wrap up the examination of the `SetPixel()` function, look over the `OnDraw()` function in Listing B4.4. The program draws three colored boxes (red, green, and blue) in the upper-left portion of the window.

Extra Credit Bonus 4

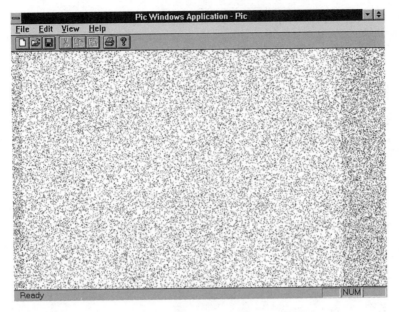

Figure B4.4. Now, get a pencil and connect the dots!

 Listing B4.4. Drawing three colored boxes.

```
1:  void CPicView::OnDraw(CDC* pDC)
2:  {
3:    CPicDoc* pDoc = GetDocument();
4:    ASSERT_VALID(pDoc);
5:
6:    // TODO: add draw code for native data here
7:    CClientDC devCon(this);
8:    CPoint cxyPoint;        // A point object
9:    // Draw red box
10:     for (cxyPoint.x=0; cxyPoint.x<150; cxyPoint.x++)
11:     {
12:       for (cxyPoint.y=0; cxyPoint.y<100; cxyPoint.y++)
13:       {
14:         devCon.SetPixel(cxyPoint.x, cxyPoint.y, RGB(255,0,0));
15:       }
16:     }
17:     // Draw green box
18:     for (cxyPoint.x=151; cxyPoint.x<300; cxyPoint.x++)
19:     {
20:       for (cxyPoint.y=0; cxyPoint.y<100; cxyPoint.y++)
21:       {
22:         devCon.SetPixel(cxyPoint.x, cxyPoint.y, RGB(0,255,0));
23:       }
```

```
24:       }
25:       // Draw blue box
26:       for (cxyPoint.x=301; cxyPoint.x<450; cxyPoint.x++)
27:       {
28:         for (cxyPoint.y=0; cxyPoint.y<100; cxyPoint.y++)
29:         {
30:           devCon.SetPixel(cxyPoint.x, cxyPoint.y, RGB(0,0,255));
31:         }
32:       }
33: }
```

Figure B4.5 shows the output from Listing B4.4. Unfortunately, this book cannot show the three colors (red, green, and blue), but the figure shows shades of gray that represent the colors.

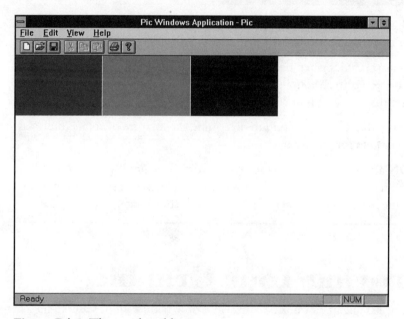

Figure B4.5. Three colored boxes.

The nested for loops in Listing B4.4 ensure that all pixels within the three boxes' boundaries are filled with the colors specified. As you can tell, drawing so many pixels takes a while. You'll see how to improve drawing speed in the next section.

Extra Credit Bonus 4

Note: You might want to add pixel drawing to your mouse movements and clicks. Use `OnButtonDown()`, `OnButtonUp()`, and `OnMouseMove()` to trigger the drawing of pixels. You must map these three functions to the `MK_LBUTTONDOWN`, `WM_LBUTTONUP`, and `WM_MOUSEMOVE` messages in ClassWizard. The last argument in all three functions is a `CPoint` value, so you can `SetPixel()` using the position of the mouse at the point of the user's mouse click. The exercise program at the end of this chapter gives you a chance to combine the mouse with `SetPixel()`.

DO	DON'T

DO add graphics to your applications. Not only are they fun to code, but your users will appreciate the eye-catching displays you add.

DO use graphics when presenting data-analysis screens. As they say, a picture is worth a thousand words, and pictures show trends in data much better than a list of numerous data values does.

DO use the RGB() function to determine the mixture of colors to display in the graphics functions.

DON'T guess at the ending screen-coordinate values if you want to fill the user's screen with a picture. DO use the GetDeviceCaps() function to find out the maximum number of pixels in each coordinate.

Improving Your Graphics

Drawing a single line or box one pixel at a time takes a lot of CPU time. There are additional graphics functions you can call that draw shapes such as lines and rectangles much more efficiently than a series of `SetPixel()` calls can. This section introduces the line-drawing function `LineTo()` and the box-drawing function `Rectangle()`, which are available in the Visual C++ MFC classes.

Before using `LineTo()`, you must learn about another function, `MoveTo()`. The `MoveTo()` function moves the *graphics pen,* a behind-the-scenes graphics pixel cursor, to a specified screen coordinate location. After you move the cursor to a coordinate

with `MoveTo()`, the `LineTo()` function draws a line from the current location to the one specified by the `LineTo()` coordinate. Here is the general format of `MoveTo()`:

```
MoveTo(int x, int y);   // Moves the graphics cursor
```

Note: Remember that `MoveTo()` does not turn on a pixel. `MoveTo()` only moves the graphics cursor so that a subsequent graphics command can draw from the `MoveTo()` location.

After you place the graphics cursor with `MoveTo()`, you can draw a line from that `MoveTo()` location with `LineTo()`. Here is the general format of `LineTo()`:

```
LineTo(int x, int y);   // Draws a line
```

Earlier, you drew a line by turning on a series of pixels with `SetPixel()`. The `OnDraw()` function in Listing B4.5 also draws a line, but it uses a `MoveTo()` and `LineTo()` combination to do so.

Listing B4.5. Drawing a diagonal line.

```
1:  void CPicView::OnDraw(CDC* pDC)
2:  {
3:    CPicDoc* pDoc = GetDocument();
4:    ASSERT_VALID(pDoc);
5:
6:    // TODO: add draw code for native data here
7:    CClientDC devCon(this);
8:    CPoint cxyPoint;        // A point object
9:      cxyPoint.x = devCon.GetDeviceCaps(HORZRES);
10:     cxyPoint.y = devCon.GetDeviceCaps(VERTRES);
11:     devCon.MoveTo(cxyPoint.x, cxyPoint.y);
12:     devCon.LineTo(0, 0);
13: }
```

Figure B4.6 shows the line drawn from Listing B4.5.

Drawing lines with `LineTo()` is actually simple. Line 11 positions the graphics cursor at the last x,y coordinate on the display (from the `GetDeviceCaps()` macro calls in lines 9 and 10). The `LineTo()` function in line 12 then draws a line from

755

Extra Credit Bonus 4

that lower-right corner to the screen's home position of (0,0). As you can see from the listing, `LineTo()` can draw in any direction on-screen.

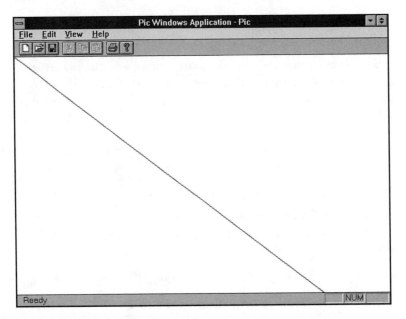

Figure B4.6. Drawing a line with `LineTo()`.

If you build the PIC application using the `OnDraw()` function shown in Listing B4.5, you'll see that the line is black and there is no way to specify a color in either the `MoveTo()` or the `LineTo()` function. You must define a *pen* before `LineDraw()` draws anything other than a thin black line. The `CreatePen()` MFC member function defines a graphics pen. After you define a graphics pen, you can determine a color for that pen and then draw lines using the particular shape and color of the pen.

Here is the general format for `CreatePen()`:

`CreatePen(int penStyle, int width, colorValue);`

You choose the value for *penStyle* from a set of defined constants, as shown in Table B4.2.

Table B4.2. Several of the possible penStyle arguments.

Argument	Description
PS_SOLID	Solid line
PS_DASH	Dashed line
PS_DOT	Dotted line
PS_DASHDOT	Line consisting of a series of dashes followed by dots
PS_DASHDOTDOT	Line consisting of a dash followed by two dots; the pattern then repeats
PS_NULL	Invisible line

Because you are creating a pen, you must define a CPen object first. There is a CPen class that you must use to define a pointer to a CPen object to be passed to CreatePen(). The following statement defines a CPen object named ballPoint:

```
CPen * ballPoint = new CPen;
```

For these examples, the CPen is the appropriate drawing object. The *width* argument specifies the width of the pen you want to draw with (in pixels), and the *colorValue* is any color value derived from the RBG() macro.

If you want to create a red pen that is three pixels wide, you can do so like this:

```
ballPoint->CreatePen(PS_SOLID, 3, RGB(255, 0, 0));
```

After you create the pen, you must then select the pen to override the default drawing pen that Visual C++ would otherwise use. The SelectObject() function selects the pen you just created. Here is the general format of SelectObject():

```
SelectObject(aPen);
```

Therefore, to activate the red ballPoint pen created earlier, you would call SelectObject() like this:

```
SelectObject(ballPoint);    // Activate the user-defined pen
```

Subsequent graphics commands that rely on the pen you created use the pen that was described with the CreatePen() function and activated with SelectObject().

Extra Credit Bonus 4

To draw with a colored pen, follow these steps:

1. Define a `CPen` object.
2. Generate the pen with `CreatePen()`.
3. Activate the pen with `SelectObject()`.
4. Use `LineTo()` and other graphics functions to draw with the pen you created.

Listing B4.6 contains an `OnDraw()` function that draws a diagonal line as in some of the listings you saw earlier. Unlike in the previous listings, the line drawn in Listing B4.6 uses a red pen.

Listing B4.6. Drawing a red diagonal line.

```
 1:  void CPicView::OnDraw(CDC* pDC)
 2:  {
 3:    CPicDoc* pDoc = GetDocument();
 4:    ASSERT_VALID(pDoc);
 5:
 6:    // TODO: add draw code for native data here
 7:    CClientDC devCon(this);
 8:    CPoint cxyPoint;          // A point object
 9:    cxyPoint.x = devCon.GetDeviceCaps(HORZRES);
10:    cxyPoint.y = devCon.GetDeviceCaps(VERTRES);
11:    CPen * ballPoint = new CPen;  // Create a new pen object
12:    // Now, define the pen's type (the style, thickness, and color)
13:    ballPoint->CreatePen(PS_SOLID, 1, RGB(255, 0, 0));
14:    devCon.SelectObject(ballPoint);           // Activate the pen
15:    devCon.MoveTo(cxyPoint.x, cxyPoint.y);    // Anchor the cursor
16:    devCon.LineTo(0, 0);                      // Draw the line
17:  }
```

The output of Listing B4.6 matches that of Figure B4.6 except that the line drawn is red and not black.

Line 11 defines a new pen object. When the pen is defined, line 13 must define its characteristics. Line 13 describes the pen as being a solid pen, one pixel wide, with a red color. The subsequent `LineTo()` on line 16 uses that red pen to draw the diagonal line from the anchor point in line 15 to the home position of (0,0).

Tip: Some newcomers to Visual C++ confuse `MoveTo()` with `LineTo()`. `MoveTo()` *moves* the graphics cursor without drawing; `LineTo()` draws as it repositions the cursor.

DO / DON'T

DO use `LineTo()` for drawing lines instead of drawing the lines one pixel at a time.

DO define your own pen and pen characteristics before using `LineTo()`, unless you want a simple black solid line.

DON'T use `LineTo()` unless you've first anchored the line with another graphics command such as `MoveTo()`.

Drawing Squares

You can draw squares and rectangles on your screen as easily as you draw lines. The `Rectangle()` function draws any size of rectangle in the window. Any rectangle can be defined by two points: the upper-left-corner coordinates and the lower-right-corner coordinates. `Rectangle()` uses whatever pen is active when you call the function. If you call `Rectangle()` without first defining your own pen, Visual C++ draws a black rectangle by default. If you define your own pen first, `Rectangle()` draws a rectangle using the pen you've selected.

Here is the general format of `Rectangle()`:

`Rectangle(int xFirst, int yFirst, int xLast, int yLast);`

The *xFirst* and *yFirst* integers define the upper-left rectangle coordinates, and the *xLast* and *yLast* integers define the lower-right coordinates.

Note: Unlike `LineTo()`, `Rectangle()` does not require a preliminary `MoveTo()` command to anchor the beginning rectangle location. You pass both required `Rectangle()` coordinates to `Rectangle()` inside `Rectangle()`'s argument list.

Extra Credit Bonus 4

Earlier, you drew three rectangles on-screen (red, green, and blue) one pixel at a time, using `SetPixel()`. The drawing was slow because plotting each point inside each rectangle takes a lot of time. To improve efficiency, use `Rectangle()`. Listing B4.7 uses `OnDraw()` to draw red, green, and blue rectangles using `Rectangle()` rather than `SetPixel()`. Three different colored pens have to be defined along the way. There is one important difference between the output of Listing B4.7 and that of the earlier listing; Listing B4.7 draws only the *outline* of the rectangle. You'll have to do one more thing to fill the rectangles with color (as you'll see in a moment).

Listing B4.7. Drawing the red, green, and blue outlines.

```
 1: void CPicView::OnDraw(CDC* pDC)
 2: {
 3:    CPicDoc* pDoc = GetDocument();
 4:    ASSERT_VALID(pDoc);
 5:
 6:    // TODO: add draw code for native data here
 7:    CClientDC devCon(this);
 8:    CPen * redPen = new CPen;    // Define 3 colored pens
 9:    CPen * greenPen = new CPen;
10:    CPen * bluePen = new CPen;
11:    // Define characteristics of the 3 pens
12:    redPen->CreatePen(PS_SOLID, 1, RGB(255, 0, 0));
13:    greenPen->CreatePen(PS_SOLID, 1, RGB(0, 255, 0));
14:    bluePen->CreatePen(PS_SOLID, 1, RGB(0, 0, 255));
15:    // Draw the 3 rectangles using each pen
16:    devCon.SelectObject(redPen);       // Red rectangle
17:    devCon.Rectangle(0, 0, 150, 100);
18:    devCon.SelectObject(greenPen);     // Green rectangle
19:    devCon.Rectangle(151, 0, 300, 100);
20:    devCon.SelectObject(bluePen);      // Blue rectangle
21:    devCon.Rectangle(301, 0, 450, 100);
22: }
```

The output from Listing B4.7 is shown in Figure B4.7.

Three pens are defined in lines 8–10. Each of these pens is colored in lines 12–14 before being used in the `SelectObject()` and `Rectangle()` functions that finish the program in lines 16–21. As you can see, drawing rectangles with `Rectangle()` is simple when you've defined the pens you want to use.

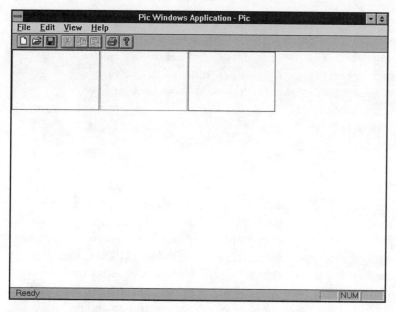

Figure B4.7. Drawing three colored rectangle outlines.

> ### You Can Save the Old Pen
>
> At times you will write a function to draw a line or other shape using a new pen, yet you will want to save the pen you were using before the function was called. Perhaps you want to draw a red line to annotate something already on-screen, but you want the annotate function to restore the original pen after drawing the red line.
>
> The SelectObject() function not only selects a new pen, but also returns a value, and that value is the old object representing the pen in use before you changed the pen to something else. Therefore, you can save the configuration of the old pen each time you call SelectObject(), and you can restore that former pen when you are through with your function.
>
> The value returned by SelectObject() is not a CPen object, but rather a *GDI* object (for *graphics device interface*). Here is a sample of code that saves the old pen and restores the pen when finished:

Extra Credit Bonus 4

```
CGdiObject * oldPen;              // Place to store old pen
CPen *newPen = new CPen;          // Define a new pen
newPen = CreatePen(PC_DASH, 2, RGB(128, 128, 128));
oldPen = devCon.SelectObject(newPen);   // Save old pen
// Your graphics functions that use new pen go here
devCon.SelectObject(oldPen);            // Restore old pen
```

Note: The graphics functions provide yet another set of examples of how Visual C++ improves the life of the Windows programmer. Many of the regular C-style Windows API functions mirror the graphics functions described here. For example, there are Windows API `Rectangle()`, `LineTo()`, and `MoveTo()` functions. Each Windows API function requires more arguments than does the MFC-equivalent function. Hence, the MFC functions take away part of your responsibility and make similar functions easier to use than if you were coding in regular C.

Filling In the Rectangle

You must use a brush to fill in your rectangle with color. Using a brush simply means using a `CBrush` object rather than a `CPen` object. (Both `CBrush` and `CPen` are members of the `GdiObject` class.) The `OnDraw()` function in Listing B4.8 shows how you would use the `Rectangle()` function with the `CBrush` object to create three rectangles, each with a different solid color.

Listing B4.8. Drawing the red, green, and blue rectangles.

```
 1:  void CPicView::OnDraw(CDC* pDC)
 2:  {
 3:    CPicDoc* pDoc = GetDocument();
 4:    ASSERT_VALID(pDoc);
 5:
 6:    // TODO: add draw code for native data here
 7:    CClientDC devCon(this);
 8:    CBrush * redBrush = new CBrush;    // Define 3 colored brushes
 9:    CBrush * greenBrush = new CBrush;
10:    CBrush * blueBrush = new CBrush;
```

```
11:     // Define characteristics of the 3 brushes
12:     redBrush->CreateSolidBrush(RGB(255, 0, 0));
13:     greenBrush->CreateSolidBrush(RGB(0, 255, 0));
14:     blueBrush->CreateSolidBrush(RGB(0, 0, 255));
15:     // Draw the 3 rectangles using each brush
16:     devCon.SelectObject(redBrush);      // Red rectangle
17:     devCon.Rectangle(0, 0, 150, 100);
18:     devCon.SelectObject(greenBrush);    // Green rectangle
19:     devCon.Rectangle(151, 0, 300, 100);
20:     devCon.SelectObject(blueBrush);     // Blue rectangle
21:     devCon.Rectangle(301, 0, 450, 100);
22: }
```

The output from Listing B4.8 is identical to that of Figure B4.5.

Lines 8–10 define three brush objects. As you can see from lines 12–14, the CreateSolidBrush() function defines the color of the brush you want to use in subsequent graphics functions, such as the Rectangle() calls in lines 17, 19, and 21.

You are not limited to using a solid brush. When you want a solid color inside a shape, the CreateSolidBrush() provides that solid color. However, there is also a CreateHatchBrush() function that produces hatching patterns inside your shapes. The CreateHatchBrush() function accepts a hatch style and an RGB() color for the hatch. The hatch style can be any of the values in Table B4.3.

Table B4.3. Possible CreateHatchBrush() arguments.

Argument	Description
HS_BDIAGONAL	Diagonal lines going up to the right
HS_CROSS	Cross-hatching
HS_DIAGCROSS	Diagonal cross-hatching
HS_FDIAGONAL	Diagonal lines going down to the right
HS_HORIZONTAL	Horizontal lines
HS_VERTICAL	Vertical lines

Figure B4.8 shows you what kind of hatching each of the CreateHatchBrush() defined constants produces.

Extra Credit Bonus 4

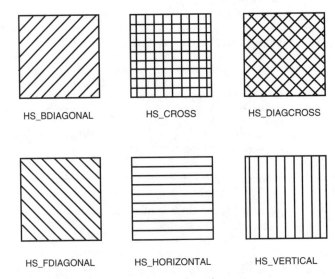

Figure B4.8. The CreateHatchBrush() hatch style patterns.

Listing B4.9 shows an OnDraw() function that creates six rectangles, each with a different hatching pattern.

 Listing B4.9. Drawing six rectangles, each with different hatching.

```
1:  void CPicView::OnDraw(CDC* pDC)
2:  {
3:      CPicDoc* pDoc = GetDocument();
4:      ASSERT_VALID(pDoc);
5:
6:      // TODO: add draw code for native data here
7:      CClientDC devCon(this);
8:      CBrush * brush1 = new CBrush;   // Define 6 colored brushes
9:      CBrush * brush2 = new CBrush;
10:     CBrush * brush3 = new CBrush;
11:     CBrush * brush4 = new CBrush;
12:     CBrush * brush5 = new CBrush;
13:     CBrush * brush6 = new CBrush;
14:     // Define characteristics of the brush hatching
15:     brush1->CreateHatchBrush(HS_BDIAGONAL, RGB(0, 0, 0));
16:     brush2->CreateHatchBrush(HS_CROSS, RGB(0, 0, 0));
17:     brush3->CreateHatchBrush(HS_DIAGCROSS, RGB(0, 0, 0));
18:     brush4->CreateHatchBrush(HS_FDIAGONAL, RGB(0, 0, 0));
19:     brush5->CreateHatchBrush(HS_HORIZONTAL, RGB(0, 0, 0));
20:     brush6->CreateHatchBrush(HS_VERTICAL, RGB(0, 0, 0));
21:       // Draw the 6 rectangles using each brush
```

```
22:     devCon.SelectObject(brush1);
23:     devCon.Rectangle(0, 0, 150, 100);
24:     devCon.SelectObject(brush2);
25:     devCon.Rectangle(151, 0, 300, 100);
26:     devCon.SelectObject(brush3);
27:     devCon.Rectangle(301, 0, 450, 100);
28:     devCon.SelectObject(brush4);
29:     devCon.Rectangle(0, 101, 150, 200);
30:     devCon.SelectObject(brush5);
31:     devCon.Rectangle(151, 101, 300, 200);
32:     devCon.SelectObject(brush6);
33:     devCon.Rectangle(301, 101, 451, 200);
34: }
```

Figure B4.9 shows Listing B4.9's six rectangles with a different hatching pattern in each.

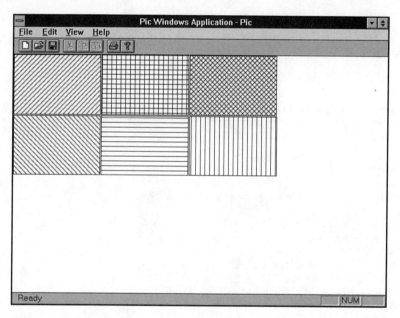

Figure B4.9. Displaying the six rectangles.

To draw the six rectangles, six brushes were defined (lines 8–13). A single brush could have been used and simply redefined with a different CreateHatchBrush() function call, but six were chosen arbitrarily for this example. Lines 15–20 define the hatching for each brush. Lines 22–33 select a different brush and draw the rectangles on-screen.

Extra Credit Bonus 4

Smooth the Path with Ellipses

An *ellipse* is a round figure, whether that figure is oval or a perfect circle. The `Ellipse()` function draws ellipses for the MFC classes. `Ellipse()` is easy because it takes the same arguments as and works almost exactly like the `Rectangle()` function.

Here is the general format of `Ellipse()`:

`Ellipse(int xFirst, int yFirst, int xLast, int yLast);`

The *xFirst* and *yFirst* integers define the upper-left ellipse coordinate, and the *xLast* and *yLast* integers define the lower-right coordinate. The ellipse fits perfectly within whatever rectangle would appear if you used those same coordinates with `Rectangle()`. In other words, if your `Ellipse()` function coordinates enclosed a perfect square, the resulting `Ellipse()` would be a perfect circle. If, however, the `Ellipse()` coordinates defined a rectangle with sides of different lengths, the resulting ellipse would be oval shaped.

The `OnDraw()` function in Listing B4.10 draws four ellipses, each a different color. As you can see, a `CBrush` object is used to define different colors for the ellipses.

 Listing B4.10. Drawing some ellipses.

```
 1:  void CPicView::OnDraw(CDC* pDC)
 2:  {
 3:    CPicDoc* pDoc = GetDocument();
 4:    ASSERT_VALID(pDoc);
 5:
 6:    // TODO: add draw code for native data here
 7:    CClientDC devCon(this);
 8:    CBrush * brush1 = new CBrush;   // Define 4 colored brushes
 9:    CBrush * brush2 = new CBrush;
10:    CBrush * brush3 = new CBrush;
11:    CBrush * brush4 = new CBrush;
12:    // Define characteristics of the brush hatching
13:    brush1->CreateSolidBrush(RGB(255, 0, 0));
14:    brush2->CreateSolidBrush(RGB(0, 255, 0));
15:    brush3->CreateSolidBrush(RGB(0, 0, 255));
16:    brush4->CreateSolidBrush(RGB(50, 150, 250));
17:    // Draw the 4 ellipses using each brush
18:    devCon.SelectObject(brush1);
19:    devCon.Ellipse(0, 0, 150, 100);
20:    devCon.SelectObject(brush2);
21:    devCon.Ellipse(100, 200, 300, 225);
22:    devCon.SelectObject(brush3);
23:    devCon.Ellipse(200, 320, 280, 380);
```

```
24:     devCon.SelectObject(brush4);
25:     devCon.Ellipse(230, 280, 290, 340);
26: }
```

Figure B4.10 contains the output, the four ellipses, drawn in Listing B4.10.

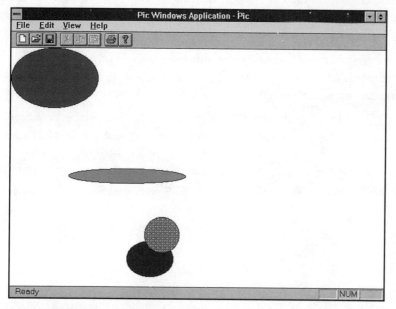

Figure B4.10. The ellipse output.

About the only thing new to note about the OnDraw() function in Listing B4.10 are the Ellipse() function calls in lines 18–25. A different brush (defined earlier to be a different color) is used to draw each ellipse.

Tip: You can use hatching in the Ellipse() functions just as you do in Rectangle() function calls if you like.

Extra Credit Bonus 4

Summary

After walking through some of the more common MFC graphics functions, you probably think graphics are easy—and they are, with the help of MFC.

If you've ever worked with graphics before in DOS-based applications, you probably used functions similar to those presented in this chapter. Pixels, lines, rectangles, and ellipses are common graphics images, and many languages support functions or commands that draw those shapes.

In this bonus chapter, you first learned how to draw individual pixels for those times when you need pinpoint accuracy. As you later learned, however, drawing with individual pixels takes a lot of CPU time. Your program speed will improve greatly if you use the shape functions instead of drawing all shapes one pixel at a time.

You use an x- and y-coordinate system to display the graphics shapes on-screen. You can also control the colors and sometimes the pattern of the shapes (such as when you draw rectangles). The pattern and color of your graphics often depends on whether you draw the shape with a pen or a brush. The pen object draws the outline of shapes, and the brush object draws shapes with solid fills and hatches.

Q&A

Q. How can I make sense of the coordinate system?

A. The x- and y-coordinate system used in Visual C++ got its roots in mathematics. Don't let that frighten you if you hated high school algebra. The coordinate system is actually very easy to understand. (If you've ever used a map to locate a town, you probably used a coordinate system to find the intersection at a letter and number coordinate, such as K8 or C3.)

The upper-left corner of the window, the *home* position, is always coordinate (0,0). When you see a coordinate pair such as (0,0) or (23,500), the first number indicates the x coordinate. The x coordinate indicates how far across the window you want to place a graphics element, starting with 0 on the far left. The second coordinate is always known as the y coordinate. It determines how far down from the top of the window you want to draw. The coordinates never relate to your screen, only to the active window.

Q. Can I turn off pixels?

A. Certainly. All you have to do is turn *on* a pixel that's the same color as the screen background. As you progress in MFC and Visual C++ Windows programming, you'll learn how to change the background color of your window. However, most Windows programs keep the window background color white.

To turn off a pixel in a graphics image located on a white background, you only have to turn *on* a white pixel. It will then appear that there is no graphics dot at the pixel's coordinate. In the same manner, you can display a white rectangle or ellipse to make the user think you erased the rectangle or ellipse.

Q. Why does the `Ellipse()` function take the same arguments as `Rectangle()`? Won't a rectangle appear on-screen rather than the ellipse?

A. The `Ellipse()` function takes the same arguments as `Rectangle()` because the `Ellipse()` arguments define a rectangle that *encloses* the ellipse. In other words, the `Ellipse()` arguments don't define an oval of any kind, but they define a rectangle that will perfectly fit over the oval that does appear as a result of the `Ellipse()` call.

Workshop

The Workshop offers quiz questions and exercises to hone your skills and give you feedback on today's lesson. You'll find some proposed answers in Appendix D.

Quiz

1. What does the term *pixel* stand for?
2. Which coordinate determines how far down the screen a graphics image should go?
3. What is the *home* position?
4. What function can you call to determine the maximum number of resolution coordinate values?
5. What function turns on pixels?

Extra Credit Bonus 4

6. What is the difference between a pen and a brush?

7. How many hatching patterns are there?

8. True or False: You must use the `Square()` function to draw squares because the `Rectangle()` draws only rectangles.

Exercise

1. Change the PIC application so that it turns on a black pixel at the mouse cursor's location when the user clicks the left mouse button. Hint: You must define an array of pixel locations so that the view class redraws all pixels on each screen update.

Extra Credit Bonus

5+

What's Next?

Extra Credit Bonus 5

You have now reached the final leg of your journey with *Teach Yourself Object-Oriented Programming with Visual C++ 1.5 in 21 Days*. When you first picked up this book, and perhaps even after making the purchase, you probably thought this book would teach you object-oriented programming. It is hoped more than you'll ever know that the OOP goal was reached, and then surpassed.

It is also hoped that you have gained some insight in these bonus chapters into what many agree is the most powerful Windows programming tool on the market: the Visual C++ MFC classes and Visual Workbench tools. As mentioned in yesterday's bonus chapter, there are several ways to write Windows programs, and even today, one of the most common methods (and the method that most people recommend that you begin with) is using straight C, calling the Windows API routines and learning Windows programming from the ground up.

You're at a crossroads. You are not a Windows programmer yet if these bonus chapters are the only study you've done so far. Nevertheless, you already have a tremendous grasp of AppWizard, the view class, the document class, and some of the windows messages that trigger the code within a Windows program. Therefore, you might find yourself drawn more and more into using Visual C++ right off the bat for your Windows application development.

Visual C++ is finally providing that OOP hook into Windows programming that Windows programmers so desperately needed for so long. OOP and C++ have now been around for over 10 years, yet until Visual C++'s first version just a little over a year ago, C++ was not considered to be the language of choice among Windows programmers. It's not that C++ was the culprit; quite the opposite because C++ and OOP offer many Windows programming advantages. The *tools*, not the languages, were missing from programmers' development libraries. Microsoft's Visual C++ finally provides those tools that fully integrate Windows programming into the C++/OOP paradigm.

Today's chapter wraps up the bonus chapters, and the book, and it provides you with some insight into your future as a Visual C++ programmer and as a C programmer.

Today, you learn about the following topics:

- ☐ Why a Windows/C background still strengthens your Windows/Visual C++ programming skills, even though you understand much of the MFC Windows classes already

- ☐ Why a Visual C++ programmer must look beyond her or his PC as a development platform

- [ ] How Visual C++ for NT compares to and contrasts with Visual C++ for Windows
- [ ] Why Visual C++ supports Visual Basic custom controls
- [ ] Where to turn now for additional help that takes you at your current skill level to that Visual C++ *Expert* status

So, Do I Still Need to Learn Windows Programming in C?

In the first bonus chapter, you read that a background in C/Windows programming would strengthen your Visual C++/Windows programming skills. Now, after four strong Visual C++/Windows chapter lessons, you might be even less inclined to accept such advice.

This author fully supports the Visual C++ implementation and the visual support tools provided by Visual C++ and the Visual Workbench tools. This author sees the two largest competing companies to Microsoft Visual C++, namely Borland and Symantec, both issuing new C++/Windows compilers that look and act more like Visual C++ than the versions of those same companies' compilers before Visual C++ made its debut. Therefore, the C++ and Windows vendors seem to be in some accord as to the approach and direction taken by Microsoft with Visual C++.

One of the reasons there is such a shift to the Visual C++ way of Windows programming is that newcomers to Windows programming, but those knowledgeable in C++, can indeed begin developing powerful and efficient Windows programs without knowing all the tedious details of the C-based Windows API.

Sadly, however, I would be performing a disservice if I steered you completely away from C/Windows programming. Learning about the Windows API from the ground up, as you have to do without a powerful tool such as Visual C++'s MFC classes, teaches you more about the structure, environment, and internals of Windows programming than backing into the same knowledge through Visual C++ and the MFC classes. Even if all you did was to glance through a single book on C-based Windows programming and write a couple or three simple C-based Windows programs, you would immediately improve your effectiveness at Visual C++/Windows programming and catapult over those who jumped into Visual C++/Windows without any background knowledge of the tedium that Visual C++ saves you.

Extra Credit Bonus 5

Tip: No matter what you decide to do with your next step, whether that step is gaining a little background into C/Windows programming or continuing with a more direct splurge straight into Visual C++/Windows programming, check out Microsoft's other award-winning product, Visual Basic.

Despite the name similarities, Visual Basic is very different from Visual C++. Visual Basic is not a true language compiler. Nevertheless, there is not another package on the market that gives you a better feel for the behavior of Windows messages and capabilities than Visual Basic. Visual Basic applications are not as flexible as Visual C++ applications, and Visual Basic applications are not nearly as efficient as Visual C++. Nevertheless, even if you were to spend an afternoon with Visual Basic, you would improve your Windows programming skills in whatever tool you ended up using in the long run. Also, as you'll see in this chapter, Visual C++ supports some features developed within the Visual Basic package, namely Visual Basic custom controls (*VBX*).

Warning: This warning might help convince you that a fundamental, even if cursory, foray into the C-based Windows programming API adds tremendous benefit to your Visual C++ future. Even though Microsoft encapsulated all the hundreds of Windows API functions into the MFC classes, there are still times when you cannot quite achieve the Windows programming flexibility you need with Visual C++ and the MFC classes by themselves. You'll find yourself, albeit rarely perhaps, in situations in which you'll settle for a programming compromise if MFC is your only background, whereas you could have resorted to a quick and tidy API function call that solved your immediate problem and enabled you get back to more productive work with the MFC. Therefore, learn a little about the C-based API or else your MFC programming might someday suffer a bit.

Other Environments

As you know, Microsoft produces Windows, MS-DOS, and the new Windows NT. In addition, Microsoft is working on a new version of Windows for PCs that helps close the gap between Windows and Windows NT. Microsoft will not comment much on the new Windows product yet because the product is still in its relatively early stages of development.

One of Microsoft's primary goals is to remain the market leader in operating environments. Although Microsoft products have virtually ruled the roost in the PC arena, Microsoft understands that computers other than PCs do exist. People use millions of PCs all over the world, but there are many minicomputers, mainframes, and supercomputers in use as well. In the past, each class of computer had its own operating environment and application programs.

In today's world, the prices and power of PCs are becoming such that more and more companies are integrating PCs into their larger system configurations. In other words, it might be many years or never before PCs replace supercomputers, but companies are finding it beneficial to combine PCs, networked and stand-alone PCs, with their larger computer strategies. The only missing link that has made the integration of these varied sizes of computers difficult was and is the operating environments each uses. The operating systems and user environments differ so much between computers of such differing sizes that it's hard to communicate between them. Hence, it's hard to share programs and data.

Beginning with Windows NT, Microsoft wants to bridge the gap, finally, between computers of different computing classes. Never before has a company chosen to write a multiplatform operating system. If Microsoft succeeds, the Visual C++ programs you write today on your PC will run on tomorrow's mainframe computer with *no* change whatsoever in code, compilation, or user interaction!

It's no secret that Microsoft isn't alone in its quest for a multi-user, multiplatform operating environment. The UNIX X/Windows system and IBM's OS/2 are still candidates for visual multiplatform installations, and either could give Microsoft a run for its money. Additionally, there might still be a multiplatform operating system answer that has yet to be developed.

Nevertheless, Microsoft seems to have made the strongest inroads, currently at least, into their multiplatform goal with Windows NT. Versions of NT are announced for several kinds of computers, and more systems, including larger mainframes and supercomputers, are in the works. In a short time, Microsoft seems to have captured

Extra Credit Bonus 5

the public's attention as a serious contender in the single-source operating environment goal. Microsoft might fail miserably in the long run, but Microsoft is turning a lot of heads currently.

Note: Users and programmers both benefit from consistent operating environments.

What does all this have to do with you, a Visual C++ programmer? No matter what you think about Windows' future, Windows NT's future, or a competitor's operating environment's future, you cannot ignore the most powerful version of Visual C++ on the market: Visual C++ for NT. In the next section, you'll see how Visual C++ for NT leapfrogs the features you like so well in Visual C++ for Windows.

As a Visual C++ programmer, you'll feel at home using Visual C++ for NT because the two systems are identical in most ways, especially in the Visual C++ language and the Visual Workbench tools such as AppWizard and ClassWizard. Nevertheless, Visual C++ for NT offers a few important additions for you, a Visual C++ programmer. This book would not be doing its job if you did not read a few words on the advantages that Visual C++ for NT brings to the table.

Note: It is rumored that Microsoft is working on a version of Visual C++ for the Apple Macintosh computer as well as the PowerPC. Rumors in the computer industry are many times just rumors, but lots of people in the industry believe that Microsoft's plans include those other microcomputers.

Visual C++ and Windows NT

The Visual C++ for NT compiler includes all the usual features you know (and love...!) in Visual C++. To prove the point, look at Figure B5.1. It's the familiar Visual C++ you've seen throughout this book, right? Not exactly. You're looking at Visual C++ for Windows NT, a completely new version of Visual C++ from the one you've learned about in this book.

Figure B5.1. Visual C++ for NT looks and acts much like the Windows version.

Regular Visual C++ for Windows is often called *16-bit Windows*. The original Windows is based on an environment of 16-bit memory register words. A register is a primary storage location inside the CPU. It takes two 16-bit words to represent the entire memory map of PCs with any extended memory. (Most standard PCs come with extended memory, which is memory over the conventional 640K limit.)

The double-word memory referencing of 16-bit Windows causes your PC to be slower than it should be. When IBM introduced the first PC in the early 1980s, it was thought that PC users would never need more than 640K of memory. With 16-bit words, programs can easily access a total of 640K. As you know, however, most stand-alone toy video games do more than a PC with only 640K is capable of doing. When users and programmers starting cramming more memory into the PC, the 16-bit memory access caused lots of problems.

To access PC memory, the program must combine two 16-bit words of memory to form an address. The first word of memory represents the *base,* which is the address of a major segment within your computer's memory. The second word of memory represents the *offset,* or *index,* from the base address. Every time your program stores or retrieves a byte of data, your PC makes a calculation using the two 16-bit words to locate the real address you're accessing. Figure B5.2 gives you an idea of how the two 16-bit words pinpoint a specific memory location.

Extra Credit Bonus 5

All the double-word memory referencing causes your computer to slow down. Starting with the 80386 CPU, MS-DOS and Windows could be rewritten to do away with the double-word memory reference. With its 32-bit registers, the 80386 CPU needs to use only one register to represent any memory address (up to a few billion bytes, more than we'll *ever* need...). In effect, 32-bit single-value memory referencing almost doubles the speed of running programs without any other change in CPU speed.

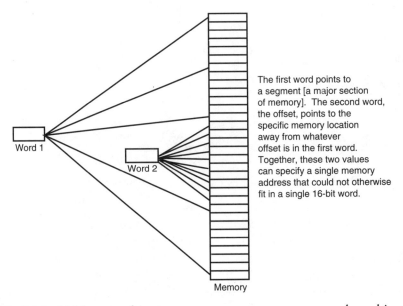

Figure B5.2. 16-bit access forces your computer to use a two-word combination to determine a single memory location's actual address.

 Note: When you run *32-bit applications,* those applications take advantage of your computer's 32-bit CPU, so they run much faster than an equivalent 16-bit application. A 32-bit application uses what is known as a *flat memory model,* meaning that the double-word memory access is no longer needed. Instead of following the stepping approach to memory access, the 32-bit locations in your CPU can hold an entire memory address. In other words, your memory address space is a *flat* straight sequential series of memory locations rather than a segment/offset memory structure.

> You might wonder why the difference in memory approaches even matters. After all, why can't an application written for 16-bit Windows run faster under 32-bit Windows NT? The answer lies in the way you compiled the program. If you used Visual C++ for Windows, your compiled program will remain segmented even when you run the program under NT, which does not require segmented memory access. To run the program as a 32-bit application, you must recompile the program using a 32-bit compiler such as Visual C++ for NT.

Starting with Visual C++ for Windows Version 1.5, you can write 32-bit Windows NT applications while working inside 16-bit Windows. You can also write 16-bit Windows applications while running Visual C++ for Windows inside a Windows window in NT. Version 1.0 of Visual C++ did not enable you to run Visual C++ under NT.

Visual C++ for NT includes extra compiler and linker options for the 32-bit environment. In addition to the compiler and linker support for 32-bit environments, you'll find Visual C++ NT containing the following features:

- A *Find in Files* multiple-file-search capability. Some programmers refer to this feature as a *grep* feature, so named after a similar UNIX command named grep. The Find in Files feature looks for a string of characters across files on your disk and returns all the filenames that contain that string. Figure B5.3 shows the Find in Files dialog box.

- A *stop* feature. By pressing Ctrl+Break or choosing **T**ools **S**top from the menu, you can stop any build process. If you've ever started a build and then changed your mind, you have not been able to stop the build until enough errors stop it or the build finishes. Being able to stop a build is nice considering how long it takes Visual C++ (even Visual C++ for NT) to compile Windows programs.

- Improved debugging features, including debugging support for multi-threading, a scheme that produces NT's superior multitasking capability.

- An integrated *profiler* that provides feedback information telling you where your application is efficient and where your application is sluggish. By using the profiler's information, you can fine-tune your applications to make them run faster and use memory and disk resources more effectively. Often, programmers develop and debug their applications without the profiler and

Extra Credit Bonus 5

then run their applications through the profiling process to remove excess inefficiency in their applications before turning the applications over to the user.

☐ Visual C++ for NT includes a CVTMAKE project converter that converts your 16-bit projects to 32-bit projects and rebuilds the projects as 32-bit applications without your needing to intervene.

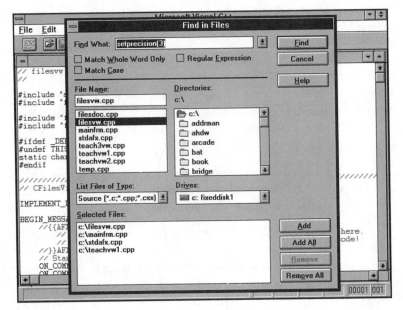

Figure B5.3. The Find in Files dialog box.

 Warning: A few slight limits are imposed on Visual C++ for NT. Most notably, you cannot use Visual Basic controls (described in the next section) in Visual C++ for NT because Visual Basic controls are 16-bit dynamic-link library routines, and 16-bit DLLs work only in 16-bit Windows.

Another limitation appears when you want to build 16-bit applications using Visual C++ for NT. You must use the command-line compiler; you cannot use the Visual Workbench to build 16-bit applications.

Several publications have written about Visual C++ for NT and tested the product thoroughly and objectively. Most reviewers agree that Visual C++ for NT is the most stable development environment they have ever used in the PC environment. It is true that Visual C++ for NT provides extreme protection from program error crashes. Sometimes, a program error forces you to reboot your PC because the memory areas of 16-bit Windows get damaged. NT, however, protects all memory areas not available to your program. At worst, a program can only crash the window you run the program within; program bugs will not crash the entire NT system.

After you've rebooted your PC a few times during the development of a Windows program, you'll really appreciate NT's superior crash-proofing.

Borrow from Visual Basic

If you aren't ready to make the leap to Windows NT, there's still so much left to learn about Visual C++ for 16-bit Windows that you'll be busy for some time. One of the more interesting features of Visual C++ is its support for Visual Basic custom controls (called the *VBX* controls). Visual Basic comes with lots of Windows controls. You have used controls such as pushbuttons, scroll bars, and list boxes in most Windows applications. Visual Basic provides several additional controls such as time meters and spreadsheet-like grid controls that you can integrate into your Visual C++ application.

Visual C++ supports all the Visual Basic version custom controls. Microsoft supplies several controls with Visual Basic, and you can also find many vendors that offer add-on VBX controls. With Visual C++, the VBX controls aren't just for Visual Basic anymore.

If you have any VBX controls, you only have to use App Studio to install those VBX controls in your application. ClassWizard ties those VBX controls to your Visual C++ code, so your final application includes the fancy VBX controls that were not possible before in C++ programs.

Warning: There are lots of companies that create and sell VBX controls. Some controls are extremely unusual, but sometimes the control's individuality is its downfall as well. If you put too many gizmos in your applications, your user will be distracted from the primary focus of the program.

Extra Credit Bonus 5

> You want your user to be interested in your program's contents, not the program's fancy controls. Don't get too carried away with exceptionally different VBX controls. You'll stray too far from the standard Windows look and feel. You'll find that the standard Windows tools that come with App Studio don't become boring; in fact, they provide a comfortable uniform environment your users will appreciate.

Stay Consistent

Before developing Windows applications, take some time to read Microsoft's publication called *The Windows Interface: An Application Design Guide,* which comes with Visual C++ compilers. The manual includes nothing about Visual C++. Rather than a Visual C++ reference, the manual is a Windows program design reference. This quick text (approximately 200 pages) tells you which features should appear in all Windows programs and describes every Windows program element that should follow the industry-accepted norms.

The Windows Interface: An Application Design Guide contains all kinds of Windows application design tips, such as menu contents, screen design, scroll-bar placement, and even keystroke standards you should follow. If you deviate too far from the standards, your application will suffer because the user will find your program more awkward to use than other, more consistent Windows programs.

Read *The Windows Interface: An Application Design Guide* before going much further in your Visual C++ education. From the start, you should understand what every common Windows program contains so that your users will accept your program faster and you'll be furthering the standards for you and others who program after you.

Improve Your Resources

You're ready to continue your Visual C++ education. More than anything, practice will improve your C++ and Windows programming techniques. As you move into Windows programming, you'll want to find other texts that you can learn from. This section offers a selection of books from Sams Publishing that you might find to be helpful now that you've mastered OOP and have been introduced to Windows programming with Visual C++.

- *Teach Yourself Windows Programming in 21 Days*

  If you like the book you now hold, you'll like the rest of the *Teach Yourself* line of books. To gain a solid foundation in the C-style Windows application programming, you'll be hard-pressed to find a better and quicker path to mastering C-style Windows programming than this book.

- *Windows Programmer's Guide to Resources*

  You'll learn all about the resources and resource script files with this excellent in-depth coverage of resources. The book describes design tips and resource efficiencies.

- *Windows Programmer's Guide to DLLs and Memory Management*

  While honing your Windows programming skills, why not hone your handling of memory as well? This book teaches you the ins and outs of dynamic-link libraries so that you'll be able to integrate your Windows applications with other Windows functions and programs. Also, you'll find out how to make the most of the memory within your Windows program.

- *Windows Programmer's Guide to Serial Communications*

  Serial communications, using your serial COM port to communicate directly or over modems to other computers and devices, require perfectly timed programs and precision coding. Although Windows adds a layer of protection between the programmer and serial ports that isn't available to DOS programmers, accessing the serial port in Windows is still more of a mystery than it should be. This book sheds some light on that mystery.

- *Windows Programmer's Guide to OLE/DDE*

  One of the most powerful reasons to switch to Windows is the ease of data-sharing that Windows makes possible through OLE (*object linking and embedding*) and DDE (*dynamic data exchange*). Your application can enable your user to run another Windows application from within your own application with OLE, and your application can use data from virtually any other Windows source with DDE.

  OLE programming, especially the new version OLE 2.0, is easy for the user to use but is difficult to program. With *Windows Programmer's Guide to OLE/DDE*, you'll find mastering OLE 2.0 a much easier task.

Extra Credit Bonus 5

☐ *Imaging and Animation for Windows*

Perhaps graphics offers the most interesting part of our future as programmers. As computers get faster, we'll see more and more animation and graphics leading our users. You learn tips, traps, and shortcuts to achieving more successful graphics Windows systems in *Imaging and Animation for Windows*.

☐ *Moving into Windows NT Programming*

If you're thinking of using Visual C++ for NT, you'll want to read this informative guide that describes what you'll encounter, enjoy, and hate about NT programming (there's really not anything you'll *hate* about NT programming—as mentioned earlier, NT provides an extremely well-integrated and solid programming environment).

Summary

Today's chapter discussed your future as a Windows developer both in Visual C++ for 16-bit Windows and Visual C++ for NT, a 32-bit Windows. You are reminded again that a quick foray into C-style Windows programming ultimately improves your Visual C++ programming as well.

Visual C++ is fun to learn and use. It's difficult to determine exactly how many hours, days, and even weeks Visual C++ saves the Windows programmer that would be spent in more tedious detail work without the Visual C++ tool. You have a fun road ahead of you as you learn more about MFC and use your OOP skills mastered in this book to catapult you into mastering Windows programming.

It is hoped also that the books mentioned at the end of this chapter present you with a toolkit of knowledge resources that you can use to improve the depth and breadth of your programming skills.

Q&A

Q. How can knowing a little about the Windows API make me a better MFC programmer?

A. The C-style Windows programming methods that access the low-level Windows API functions are certainly more tedious than using Visual C++. With that tedium, however, comes more insight and flexibility. You'll gain

insight into the workings of Windows that automatically take place when you begin to use Visual C++. Perhaps most important, you'll know when to resort to API calls even when you know of a similar but less effective method in Visual C++.

Q. Are the new features of Visual C++ for NT worth my time?

A. Certainly. NT provides superior crash protection, so your program bugs don't bomb the operating system and make a reboot necessary, as is often the case with Visual C++ for Windows.

The tools that Microsoft supplies in the NT package supersede those found in Visual C++ for Windows. You'll gain advanced profiling capabilities that fine-tune your applications. Also, you will enjoy improved debugging support and a file search feature that lessens your dependence on file names and lets Visual C++ do more work for you when you're looking for a particular piece of code.

Luckily, the look and feel of Visual C++ for NT matches that of Visual C++ for Windows, so you can migrate to Visual C++ for NT as soon as you get NT and the NT version of Visual C++.

Q. Why are 16-bit applications less efficient than 32-bit applications?

A. Sixteen-bit applications must use a segmented memory system that requires a calculation and usually two memory accesses to store or retrieve a single byte of memory. The segmentation occurs even when you run a compiled 16-bit application under NT. Therefore, if you want the fastest speed your 80386 (or later) computer offers, you will need to compile your application using Visual C++ for NT and run the application in NT's native 32-bit flat memory space.

Workshop

The Workshop offers quiz questions and exercises to hone your skills and give you feedback on today's lesson. You'll find some proposed answers in Appendix D.

Quiz

1. True or False: Learning a bit about the Windows API is a waste of time. After all, the MFC classes duplicate most of the API's functionality.

Extra Credit Bonus 5

2. Are Microsoft's C++ competitors moving toward the Visual C++–like method of application development? Why or why not?

3. True or False: You enjoyed this book tremendously. (Be careful with your answer here!)

Exercises

Due to the textual nature of this final bonus chapter, there are no exercise assignments today.

ASCII Character Chart

ASCII Character Chart

Dec X_{10}	Hex X_{16}	Binary X_2	ASCII Character
000	00	0000 0000	null
001	01	0000 0001	☺
002	02	0000 0010	☻
003	03	0000 0011	♥
004	04	0000 0100	♦
005	05	0000 0101	♣
006	06	0000 0110	♠
007	07	0000 0111	•
008	08	0000 1000	■
009	09	0000 1001	○
010	0A	0000 1010	■
011	0B	0000 1011	♂
012	0C	0000 1100	♀
013	0D	0000 1101	♪
014	0E	0000 1110	♪♪
015	0F	0000 1111	☼
016	10	0001 0000	►
017	11	0001 0001	◄
018	12	0001 0010	↕
019	13	0001 0011	‼
020	14	0001 0100	¶
021	15	0001 0101	§
022	16	0001 0110	—
023	17	0001 0111	↨
024	18	0001 1000	↑
025	19	0001 1001	↓
026	1A	0001 1010	→
027	1B	0001 1011	←
028	1C	0001 1100	FS
029	1D	0001 1101	GS
030	1E	0001 1110	RS
031	1F	0001 1111	US
032	20	0010 0000	SP
033	21	0010 0001	!

Dec X_{10}	Hex X_{16}	Binary X_2	ASCII Character
034	22	0010 0010	"
035	23	0010 0011	#
036	24	0010 0100	$
037	25	0010 0101	%
038	26	0010 0110	&
039	27	0010 0111	'
040	28	0010 1000	(
041	29	0010 1001	)
042	2A	0010 1010	*
043	2B	0010 1011	+
044	2C	0010 1100	,
045	2D	0010 1101	-
046	2E	0010 1110	.
047	2F	0010 1111	/
048	30	0011 0000	0
049	31	0011 0001	1
050	32	0011 0010	2
051	33	0011 0011	3
052	34	0011 0100	4
053	35	0011 0101	5
054	36	0011 0110	6
055	37	0011 0111	7
056	38	0011 1000	8
057	39	0011 1001	9
058	3A	0011 1010	:
059	3B	0011 1011	;
060	3C	0011 1100	<
061	3D	0011 1101	=
062	3E	0011 1110	>
063	3F	0011 1111	?
064	40	0100 0000	@
065	41	0100 0001	A

continues

ASCII Character Chart

Dec X_{10}	Hex X_{16}	Binary X_2	ASCII Character
066	42	0100 0010	B
067	43	0100 0011	C
068	44	0100 0100	D
069	45	0100 0101	E
070	46	0100 0110	F
071	47	0100 0111	G
072	48	0100 1000	H
073	49	0100 1001	I
074	4A	0100 1010	J
075	4B	0100 1011	K
076	4C	0100 1100	L
077	4D	0100 1101	M
078	4E	0100 1110	N
079	4F	0100 1111	O
080	50	0101 0000	P
081	51	0101 0001	Q
082	52	0101 0010	R
083	53	0101 0011	S
084	54	0101 0100	T
085	55	0101 0101	U
086	56	0101 0110	V
087	57	0101 0111	W
088	58	0101 1000	X
089	59	0101 1001	Y
090	5A	0101 1010	Z
091	5B	0101 1011	[
092	5C	0101 1100	\
093	5D	0101 1101	]
094	5E	0101 1110	^
095	5F	0101 1111	_
096	60	0110 0000	`
097	61	0110 0001	a

Dec X_{10}	Hex X_{16}	Binary X_2	ASCII Character
098	62	0110 0010	b
099	63	0110 0011	c
100	64	0110 0100	d
101	65	0110 0101	e
102	66	0110 0110	f
103	67	0110 0111	g
104	68	0110 1000	h
105	69	0110 1001	i
106	6A	0110 1010	j
107	6B	0110 1011	k
108	6C	0110 1100	l
109	6D	0110 1101	m
110	6E	0110 1110	n
111	6F	0110 1111	o
112	70	0111 0000	p
113	71	0111 0001	q
114	72	0111 0010	r
115	73	0111 0011	s
116	74	0111 0100	t
117	75	0111 0101	u
118	76	0111 0110	v
119	77	0111 0111	w
120	78	0111 1000	x
121	79	0111 1001	y
122	7A	0111 1010	z
123	7B	0111 1011	{
124	7C	0111 1100	¦
125	7D	0111 1101	}
126	7E	0111 1110	~
127	7F	0111 1111	DEL
128	80	1000 0000	Ç
129	81	1000 0001	ü

continues

ASCII Character Chart

Dec X_{10}	Hex X_{16}	Binary X_2	ASCII Character
130	82	1000 0010	é
131	83	1000 0011	â
132	84	1000 0100	ä
133	85	1000 0101	à
134	86	1000 0110	å
135	87	1000 0111	ç
136	88	1000 1000	ê
137	89	1000 1001	ë
138	8A	1000 1010	è
139	8B	1000 1011	ï
140	8C	1000 1100	î
141	8D	1000 1101	ì
142	8E	1000 1110	Ä
143	8F	1000 1111	Å
144	90	1001 0000	É
145	91	1001 0001	æ
146	92	1001 0010	Æ
147	93	1001 0011	ô
148	94	1001 0100	ö
149	95	1001 0101	ò
150	96	1001 0110	û
151	97	1001 0111	ù
152	98	1001 1000	ÿ
153	99	1001 1001	Ö
154	9A	1001 1010	Ü
155	9B	1001 1011	¢
156	9C	1001 1100	£
157	9D	1001 1101	¥
158	9E	1001 1110	P_t
159	9F	1001 1111	ƒ
160	A0	1010 0000	á
161	A1	1010 0001	í

Dec X_{10}	Hex X_{16}	Binary X_2	ASCII Character
162	A2	1010 0010	ó
163	A3	1010 0011	ú
164	A4	1010 0100	ñ
165	A5	1010 0101	Ñ
166	A6	1010 0110	a
167	A7	1010 0111	o
168	A8	1010 1000	¿
169	A9	1010 1001	⌐
170	AA	1010 1010	¬
171	AB	1010 1011	½
172	AC	1010 1100	¼
173	AD	1010 1101	¡
174	AE	1010 1110	«
175	AF	1010 1111	»
176	B0	1011 0000	░
177	B1	1011 0001	▒
178	B2	1011 0010	▓
179	B3	1011 0011	│
180	B4	1011 0100	┤
181	B5	1011 0101	╡
182	B6	1011 0110	╢
183	B7	1011 0111	╖
184	B8	1011 1000	╕
185	B9	1011 1001	╣
186	BA	1011 1010	║
187	BB	1011 1011	╗
188	BC	1011 1100	╝
189	BD	1011 1101	╜
190	BE	1011 1110	╛
191	BF	1011 1111	┐
192	C0	1100 0000	└
193	C1	1100 0001	┴

continues

ASCII Character Chart

Dec X_{10}	Hex X_{16}	Binary X_2	ASCII Character
194	C2	1100 0010	┬
195	C3	1100 0011	├
196	C4	1100 0100	─
197	C5	1100 0101	┼
198	C6	1100 0110	╞
199	C7	1100 0111	╟
200	C8	1100 1000	╚
201	C9	1100 1001	╔
202	CA	1100 1010	╩
203	CB	1100 1011	╦
204	CC	1100 1100	╠
205	CD	1100 1101	═
206	CE	1100 1110	╬
207	CF	1100 1111	╧
208	D0	1101 0000	╨
209	D1	1101 0001	╤
210	D2	1101 0010	╥
211	D3	1101 0011	╙
212	D4	1101 0100	╘
213	D5	1101 0101	╒
214	D6	1101 0110	╓
215	D7	1101 0111	╫
216	D8	1101 1000	╪
217	D9	1101 1001	┘
218	DA	1101 1010	┌
219	DB	1101 1011	█
220	DC	1101 1100	▄
221	DD	1101 1101	▌
222	DE	1101 1110	▐
223	DF	1101 1111	▀
224	E0	1110 0000	α
225	E1	1110 0001	β

Dec X_{10}	Hex X_{16}	Binary X_2	ASCII Character
226	E2	1110 0010	Γ
227	E3	1110 0011	π
228	E4	1110 0100	Σ
229	E5	1110 0101	σ
230	E6	1110 0110	μ
231	E7	1110 0111	τ
232	E8	1110 1000	Φ
233	E9	1110 1001	θ
234	EA	1110 1010	Ω
235	EB	1110 1011	δ
236	EC	1110 1100	∞
237	ED	1110 1101	ø
238	EE	1110 1110	∈
239	EF	1110 1111	∩
240	F0	1111 0000	≡
241	F1	1111 0001	±
242	F2	1111 0010	≥
243	F3	1111 0011	≤
244	F4	1111 0100	⌠
245	F5	1111 0101	⌡
246	F6	1111 0110	÷
247	F7	1111 0111	≈
248	F8	1111 1000	°
249	F9	1111 1001	•
250	FA	1111 1010	·
251	FB	1111 1011	√
252	FC	1111 1100	η
253	FD	1111 1101	²
254	FE	1111 1110	■
255	FF	1111 1111	

Visual C++ Keywords

Visual C++ Keywords

* __asm	enum	long	sizeof
auto	__export	__near	static
__based	extern	* new	struct
break	__far	* operator	switch
case	__fastcall	__pascal	* *template*
* catch	float	* private	* this
__cdecl	for	* protected	*throw*
char	__fortran	* public	* *try*
* class	* friend	register	typedef
const	goto	return	union
continue	__huge	__saveregs	unsigned
default	if	__self	* virtual
* delete	* __inline	__segment	void
do	int	__segname	volatile
double	__interrupt	short	while
else	__loads	signed	

Note: Those keywords marked with an asterisk, *, are new to C++ and are not found in regular C. Those words in italics are not supported in Visual C++. Some of these keywords, such as __asm, are not covered in this book due to their application-specific nature.

Operator Precedence

Operator Precedence

Visual C++ contains many operators. When you use more than one operator in the same expression, you must understand how Visual C++ interprets and orders those operators. Here is the Visual C++ operator precedence table that shows the order of operator precedence.

Table C.1. Visual C++ operator precedence.

Precedence Level	Symbol	Description	Associativity
1	`::`	C++ scope access/resolution	Left to right
2	`()`	Function call	Left to right
	`[]`	Array subscript	
	`->`	C++ indirect component selector	
	`.`	C++ direct component selector	
3 Unary	`!`	Logical negation	Right to left
	`~`	Bitwise (1's) complement	
	`+`	Unary plus	
	`-`	Unary minus	
	`&`	Addresss of	
	`*`	Indirection	
	`sizeof`	Returns size of operand in bytes.	
	`new`	Dynamically allocates C++ storage.	
	`delete`	Dynamically deallocates C++ storage.	
	`type`	Typecast	
4 Member Access	`.*`	C++ dereference	Left to right
	`->*`	C++ dereference	
	`()`	Expression parentheses	

Precedence Level	Symbol	Description	Associativity
5 Multiplicative	* / %	Multiply Divide Remainder (modulus)	Left to right
6 Additive	+ -	Binary plus Binary minus	Left to right
7 Shift	<< >>	Shift left Shift right	Left to right
8 Relational	< <= > >=	Less than Less than or equal to Greater than Greater than or equal to	Left to right
9 Equality	== !=	Equal to Not equal to	Left to right
10	&	Bitwise AND	Left to right
11	^	Bitwise XOR	Left to right
12	|	Bitwise OR	Left to right
13	&&	Logical AND	Left to right
14	||	Logical OR	Left to right
15 Ternary	?:	Conditional	Right to left

continues

Operator Precedence

Table C.1. continued

Precedence Level	Symbol	Description	Associativity
16			
Assignment	=	Simple assignment	Right to left
	*=	Assign product	
	/=	Assign quotient	
	%=	Assign remainder	
	+=	Assign sum	
	-=	Assign difference	
	&=	Assign bitwise AND	
	^=	Assign bitwise XOR	
	|=	Assign bitwise OR	
	<<=	Assign left shift	
	>>=	Assign right shift	
17			
Comma	,	Sequence point	Left to right

Note: Because of the confusion in most precedence tables, the postfix ++ and -- and the prefix ++ and -- do not appear here. Their precedence works the same in Visual C++ as it does in C. The postfix operators usually appear in level 2, and the prefix operators appear in level 3. In practice, perform prefix before all other operators except for the scope resolution operator, and perform postfix right before the statement continues to the next executable statement in the program. Visual C++ purists will cringe at this description, but it works 99.9 percent of the time, whereas "technically correct" placements of these operators simply confuse programmers 99.9 percent of the time.

Answers

Answers

This appendix lists the answers for the quiz and exercise sections at the end of each chapter. There is always more than one way to write programming statements, so if your answers vary slightly, the differences might be a matter of style.

Answers for Day 1, "The C++ Phenomenon"

Quiz

1. OOP stands for object-oriented programming.

2. A skillful C++ programmer can expect a productivity increase as much as 10 or 20 times over the current programming throughput. Such numbers obviously indicate a veteran C++ programmer, but such improvements are not uncommon for those who learn OOP.

3. Although not an ANSI-recognized standard, the AT&T standard, especially starting with version 3.0, has become the de facto standard. When ANSI finally adopts C++, you can rest easy knowing that ANSI will implement most if not all of the AT&T standard because so many vendors and programmers use AT&T's standard. Therefore, if you use an AT&T-standard compiler today (such as Visual C++), your programs should also work on tomorrow's C++ compilers.

4. Procedural programming languages.

5. The `class` keyword.

6. The .CPP filename extension.

Exercises

1. This exercise required you to enter and run the sample program in Listing 1.1, so no answer applies here.

2. This exercise required you to enter and run the sample program in Listing 1.1 after changing all the comments that begin with // (the C++ style) so that they are enclosed in /* and */.

Answers for Day 2, "C++ Is Superior!"

Quiz

1. Visual C++ comments end at the end of the line.
2. A function's signature is its prototype that describes the return data type and the number and types of arguments.
3. True. Prototypes need to know only data types, and the argument names are optional.
4. False. A function's definition line must have argument names so that the body of the function can refer to the proper variables.
5. True. In Visual C++, an empty argument list means the same as void.
6. __FILE__ and __LINE__.
7. January 1, 1994. __DATE__ supplies the date of the compile, which could differ from the run date.

Exercises

1.
```
#include <stdio.h>
main()
{
//   printf("Welcome to Visual C++.\n");    // Output
//   printf("The power is yours!\n");
   return 0;
}
```

2.
```
// Filename: FIXDEF.CPP
#include <stdio.h>
const float PI = 3.14159;

inline float cirArea(float r)
{
   return PI * (r * r);
}
```

```
main()
{
  float radius;
  printf("What is the circle's radius in inches? ");
  scanf(" %f", &radius);
  printf("The area of the circle is %.2f inches.\n",
cirArea(radius));

  return 0;
}
```

Answers for Day 3, "Simple I/O"

Quiz

1. `iostream.h`.

2. `iomanip.h`.

3. Visual C++ does not remember `setw()` settings from cout to cout.

4. All values are printed right-justified within a field's width unless you change the justification with the appropriate format flag.

5. False. The `setw()` sets the width for only the first cout, so only the first cout contains right-justified numbers in the eight-character field. The last two couts print numbers without any justification.

6. `endl` outputs a newline and flushes the output buffer. `ends` adds a terminating null zero to the end of character data, and `flush` flushes the output buffer without sending a newline.

7. `cin >>` ignores whitespace in the input stream, and `get()` reads the whitespace characters.

8. True, the second parameter of `get()` tells Visual C++ how many characters to count in the input.

Exercises

1. ```
   cout << "Hi!\n" << setprecision(2) <<
   ↪setiosflags(ios::showpoint) << amt;
   ```

2. This one's easy when you remember that `cin >>` stops reading numeric values when the first nonnumber is reached. Here is the statement:

   ```
   cin >> numVar >> charVar;
   ```

3. ```cpp
   // Filename: TOTAL.CPP
   // Prints a dollar total
   #include <iostream.h>
   #include <iomanip.h>
   main()
   {
      float price1, price2, price3;
      float total;
      cout << "What is the first price? ";
      cin >> price1;
      cout << "What is the second price? ";
      cin >> price2;
      cout << "What is the third price? ";
      cin >> price3;
      total = price1 + price2 + price3;
      // This cout spans two lines but it could be one long line
      cout << setfill('*') << setprecision(3);
      cout << setiosflags(ios::showpoint) << setw(20) << total;
      return 0;
   }
   ```

Answers for Day 4, "Powerful Pointers"

Quiz

1. False because the reference has to be initialized when you define it.

2. `ri = 67;    // Changes i`

Answers

3. A. 2.
   B. 5.
   C. 6.
   D. 7.
   E. 1.
   F. 3.
   G. 8.
   H. 4.

4. False. Although `ptr` *might* be defined as a void pointer, you cannot tell from this statement that the pointer is void. Assigning 0 to a pointer makes the pointer a *null* pointer, but assigning 0 to a pointer does not make the pointer a void pointer.

Exercises

1.
```
// Filename: MONTHPTR.CPP
// Reference an array with a constant pointer
#include <iostream.h>
main()
{
  int monthDays[] = {31, 28, 31, 30, 31, 30, 31, 31, 30, 31,
      30, 31};
  int * const mPtrConst = monthDays;
  // You could also do this:
  //   int * const mPtrConst = &monthDays[0];
  for (int m=0; m<12; m++)
    { cout << "Month " << (m+1) << " has " << *(mPtrConst+m);
      cout << " days in it.\n"; }
  return 0;
}
```

2.
```
// Filename: CHAP4VAR.CPP
// Defines, initializes, and prints various variables
#include <iostream.h>
main()
{
  int i=9;
```

```
    const int ci = 10;               // Integer constant
    int & ri = i;                    // Reference to an integer
    const int & roa = i;             // Read-only alias
    int * pi = & i;                  // Pointer to integer
    const int * pic = &i;            // Pointer to an integer constant
    int * const cpi = &i;            // Constant pointer to integer
    const int * const pcip = &i;     // Constant pointer to constant
    cout << "Integer constant: " << ci << "\n";
    cout << "Reference to an integer: " << ri << "\n";
    cout << "Read-only alias: " << roa << "\n";
    cout << "Pointer to integer: " << *pi << "\n";
    cout << "Pointer to an integer constant: " << *pic << "\n";
    cout << "Constant pointer to integer: " << *cpi << "\n";
    cout << "Constant pointer to integer constant: " << *pcip
➥<< "\n";
    return 0;
}
```

Answers for Day 5, "Memory Allocation: There When You Need It"

Quiz

1. `new` and `delete`.

2. You cannot mix `new` and `free()`.

3. True.

4. False. You cannot initialize a complete array when you allocate it.

5. C. You cannot determine how many elements are reserved until you allocate the array on the heap.

6. `_set_new_handler()`. (By the way, this name is not consistent with all other C++ compilers on the market.)

7. You cannot specify the number of elements to delete in the subscript.

Answers

Exercises

1. ```cpp
   // Filename: AGEMESGS.CPP
   // Allocates a string for each year of the user
   #include <iostream.h>
   #include <string.h>
   main()
   {
     char * mesgs[100];   // Up to 100 years old
     char words[] = "Make every year a good one!\n";
     int age;
     cout << "How old are you? ";
     cin >> age;
     for (int cnt=0; cnt<age; cnt++)
     {
       mesgs[cnt] = new char [strlen(words) + 1];
       strcpy(mesgs[cnt], words);   // Copy string to heap
     }
     // Print the strings
     for (cnt=0; cnt<age; cnt++)
     {
       cout << mesgs[cnt];
     }
     // Deallocate the strings
     // CAREFUL! Each element MUST deallocate the whole string
     for (cnt=0; cnt<age; cnt++)
       {
         delete [] mesgs[cnt];
       }
     return 0;
   }
   ```

2. ```cpp
   #include <stdlib.h>
   #include <iostream.h>
   int prMesg(size_t size);

   // The following function executes only if new fails
   main()
   {
     _set_new_handler(prMesg);
   ```

```
    // Rest of main() goes here
    // :
}

int prMesg(size_t size)
{
  cerr << "Memory Problem!\n";
  exit(1);
  return 0;   // Although exit() terminates program, the
              // return value is required in all handlers
}
```

Note: Be sure to write your error messages to the `cerr` object and not `cout`.

Answers for Day 6, "Communicating with Functions"

Quiz

1. Passing by reference is more efficient than passing by value.

2. Declaration (a prototype because of the semicolon).

3. Definition (a function's first line).

4. True. You can pass `main()` arguments through command-line arguments.

5. Yes, when you're passing by reference, if the receiving function changes a parameter, the same value changes in the sending function. (As long as you haven't specified `const`.)

6. Ellipses signify that a function is going to receive a variable-length argument.

7. The pathname and filename of the program when you ran the program.

8. Insert the `const` modifier before the received parameters.

Answers

Exercises

1.
```cpp
// Filename: DEFPRNT.CPP
// Includes a function with default arguments that prints a row
// of characters as determined by the arguments passed.
#include <iostream.h>
void doPr(char prChar='*', int prNum=10);
main()
{
  char prChar;
  int prNum;
  prChar = '!';
  prNum = 25;
  doPr(prChar, prNum);   // Override both default arguments
  doPr();                // Accept both defaults
  doPr('$');             // Accept only the last default
  return 0;
}
//////////////////////////////////////////////////////////////
// Function with two default arguments
void doPr(char prChar, int prNum)
{
  for (int i=0; i<prNum; i++)
  { cout << prChar; }
  cout << "\n";
}
```

2.
```cpp
// Filename: TOTALCMD.CPP
// Computes the product of all arguments passed
#include <iostream.h>
#include <stdlib.h>
main(int argc, char * argv[])
{
  long int total=1;
  for (int i=1; i<argc; i++)
  {
    total *= atoi(argv[i]);
  }
  cout << "The product of your values is " << total << "\n";
  return 0;
}
```

3.
```cpp
// Filename: VARAVG.CPP
// This function won't run by itself because there
// is no main() in the code.
void avgNums(int numPassed, ...)
{
   float avg=0.0;
   va_list ap;    // Points to the list of arguments
   va_start(ap, numPassed); // Tells Visual C++ where to begin
   for (int i=0; i<numPassed; i++)
   {
      avg += va_arg(ap, int);   // Add next integer
   }
   avg /= numPassed;
   va_end(ap);         // Cleanup that is always needed
   cout << "The average of the arguments is " << avg << "\n";
}
```

Answers for Day 7, "Overloaded Functions Lessen Your Load"

Quiz

1. By the argument lists that must differ in number, data types, or both.

2. True.

3. False. The first and third differ only by their return data types, and the return data type cannot differentiate overloaded functions.

4. `operator&&()`, `operator||()`, and `operator*=()`.

5. Use a language different from Visual C++! Seriously, you cannot change the way operators work on built-in data types. Some C++ programmers get fancy, however, and write structure variables that contain a single `int` member and overload the + to work on that structure. This, in a stretched way, changes the behavior of + for integers.

Answers

6. You have to return a structure, not just a regular data type. In future chapters, you'll learn more about this topic.

7. If your Visual C++ program calls C functions that you've written or purchased, you'll have to declare those functions in an `extern "C"` statement so that Visual C++ doesn't mangle the names.

8. The default arguments must be specified in the prototypes, not the function definition lines.

9. `extern "C" { char * getname(void);`
   `            float amtDoub(float x); }`

Exercises

1.
```
// Filename: AVGOVR.CPP
// Overload a function to accept two kinds of arrays
#include <iostream.h>
#include <iomanip.h>
void doAvg(int iAra[]);
void doAvg(float fAra[]);
const int araSize = 10;
main()
{
  int iAra[araSize] = {1, 4, 3, 6, 7, 5, 3, 6, 8, 9};
  float fAra[araSize] = {4.3, 2.4, 6.7, 8.6, 4.3, 2.3, 4.5,
                         6.5, 7.6, 3.1};
  cout << setprecision(1) << setiosflags(ios::fixed);
  doAvg(iAra);
  doAvg(fAra);
  return 0;
}
///////////////////////////////////////////////////////////
// Two overloaded functions that find average begin here
void doAvg(int iAra[])
{
  float avg = 0.0;
  for (int i=0; i<araSize; i++)
  { avg += float(iAra[i]); }
  avg /= araSize;
```

```cpp
    cout << "The average of the integer array is " << avg << "\n";
}
void doAvg(float fAra[])
{
  float avg = 0.0;
  for (int i=0; i<araSize; i++)
  { avg += float(fAra[i]); }
  avg /= araSize;
  cout << "The average of the floating-point array is "
  ➥<< avg << "\n";
}
```

2.
```cpp
// Filename: OVRMORE.CPP
// Demonstrates overloading of several operators
#include <iostream.h>
#include <iomanip.h>
struct People {
  int age;
  char name[25];
  int numKids;
  float salary;
};
double operator+(const People & p1, const People & p2);
int operator-(const People & p1, const People & p2);
int operator>(const People & p1, const People & p2);
void operator-=(People & p1, const People & p2);
void operator+=(People & p1, const People & p2);
main()
{
  // Define and initialize two structure variables
  People emp1 = {26, "Robert Nickles", 2, 20933.50};
  People emp2 = {41, "Don Dole", 4, 30102.32};
  double totalSal;
  int ageDiff;
  if (emp1 > emp2)
    { cout << "The first employee makes more than the
    ➥second.\n"; }
  else
```

Answers

```cpp
       { cout << "The second employee makes more than the
          ➥first.\n"; }
     totalSal = emp1 + emp2;
     ageDiff = emp2 - emp1;
     cout << setprecision(2) << setiosflags(ios::fixed);
     cout << "The total of the salaries is " << totalSal << ".\n";
     cout << "The age difference is " << ageDiff << ".\n";
     emp1 += emp2;
     cout << "\nAfter adding the second employee's salary to the
        ➥first,\n";
     cout << "the first employee's salary is now " << emp1.salary
        ➥<< "\n";
     emp2 -= emp1;
     cout << "After subtracting the first employee's age from
        ➥the ";
     cout << "second's,\nthe second employee's age is now ";
     cout << emp2.age << "\n";
     return 0;
   }
   /////////////////////////////////////////////////////////////
   // Overloaded function to add two People variables
   double operator+(const People & p1, const People & p2)
   {                     // You cannot stack these
     return (p1.salary + p2.salary);
   }
   /////////////////////////////////////////////////////////////
   // Overloaded function to subtract two People variables
   int operator-(const People & p1, const People & p2)
   {                     // You cannot stack these
     return (p1.age - p2.age);
   }
   /////////////////////////////////////////////////////////////
   // Overloaded function to compare two People variables
   int operator>(const People & p1, const People & p2)
   {                     // You cannot stack these
     if (p1.salary > p2.salary)
       { return 1; }
     else
```

```
        { return 0; }
}
/////////////////////////////////////////////////////////////////
// Overloaded function to AND-compare two People variables
void operator+=(People & p1, const People & p2)
{
  p1.salary += p2.salary;
}
/////////////////////////////////////////////////////////////////
// Overloaded function to OR-compare two People variables
void operator-=(People & p1, const People & p2)
{
  p1.age -= p2.age;
}
```

Answers for Day 8, "Add Some *class* to Your Data"

Quiz

1. Technically, an object is any variable. However, you'll often find that Visual C++ programmers reserve the use of the term *object* for `class` variables.

2. A. Two, the top pair.

   B. `computer`.

   C. Two, `PC` and `Max`.

   D. Before the first member (`RAM`).

   E. None because all class members are public by default.

3. False. Private data members cannot be accessed in *any* way outside the class, even in the parts of the program that define new class variables.

4. False because the first member of the structure is public by default.

5. True.

Answers

Exercise

1.
```cpp
// Filename: CLSREVIE.CPP
// Simple program that demonstrates abstract data type classes
#include <iostream.h>
#include <string.h>
#include <iomanip.h>
class empData {
public:                // Needed to allow access to the members
  char empCode[8];
  float wkSalary;
};
main()
{
  empData emp1;    // Regular structure variable
  empData * emp2;  // Pointer to a structure
  // Initialize the structure variable with the dot operator
  strcpy(emp1.empCode, "ACT08");
  emp1.wkSalary = 1092.43;
  // Allocate and initialize a structure on the heap
  emp2 = new empData;
  strcpy(emp2->empCode, "MKT21");
  emp2->wkSalary = 1932.23;
  // Print the data
  // Without setiosflags(ios::fixed), Visual C++ tends to print
  // floating-point data in scientific notation
  cout << setprecision(2) << setiosflags(ios::fixed);
  cout << "Employee 1:\n";
  cout << "Code:\t" << emp1.empCode << "\n";
  cout << "Salary:\t" << emp1.wkSalary << "\n\n";
  cout << "Employee 2:\n";
  cout << "Code:\t" << emp2->empCode << "\n";
  cout << "Salary:\t" << emp2->wkSalary << "\n\n";
  delete emp2;
  return 0;
}
```

Answers for Day 9, "Member Functions Activate *class* Variables"

Quiz

1. You can trigger the use of member functions just as you use data members. Call member functions using the dot operator, ., when you define non-pointer object variables, and use the structure pointer operator, ->, when you define pointers to object variables.

2. A single program can have more than one class, and each class might have overlapping member function names. For instance, two or more classes might have the member function named init(). The scope resolution operator works with a class name to tell Visual C++ which class the function definition goes with.

3. You send a message to an object when you call a member function using an object. The effect of the statement

   report.print();

   is to tell the report object to print itself by sending a print message to the object. (In reality, the object is sent to the print() function with the help of the *this pointer.)

4. False. You can use overloaded member functions as well as default argument lists.

5. main() and the rest of the program can access private members through public member functions. The member functions can access private data members, and the rest of the program can call the member functions because they are usually public.

6. True. Through the use of member functions, you can modify members but not the *this pointer itself.

Answers

Exercises

1.
```cpp
// Filename: GRADE1.CPP
// A teacher's simple class for grades
#include <iostream.h>
// Grade class declaration next
class LetterGrade {
private:
  char grade;      // Letter grade
public:
  void init(char='A');   // Initialize member from main()
  void prGrade(void);    // Displays the grade
};
void LetterGrade::init(char mainGrade)
{ grade = mainGrade;     // Assign main()'s grade
}
void LetterGrade::prGrade(void)
{ cout << "The grade is " << grade << "\n";
}
///////////////////////// Class ends here /////////////////////////
main()
{
  LetterGrade student1, student2, student3;
  student1.init();
  student2.init('B');
  student3.init('F');
  // Print the grades
  student1.prGrade();
  student2.prGrade();
  student3.prGrade();
  // By the way... If the students were defined as an array
  // like this:
  // LetterGrade students[20];
  // you could print all the grades in a loop such as this:
  // for (int i=0; i<20; i++)
  //    { students(i).prGrade(); }
  return 0;
}
```

2. ```cpp
// Filename: GRADE2.CPP
// A teacher's simple class for grades
#include <iostream.h>
#include <ctype.h>
#include <stdlib.h>
// Grade class declaration next
class LetterGrade {
private:
  char grade;   // Letter grade
  void checkGr(char & mainGrade); // Ensures accuracy
public:
  void init(char='A');   // Initialize member from main()
  void prGrade(void);   // Displays the grade
};
void LetterGrade::init(char mainGrade)
{ checkGr(mainGrade);   // Convert to upper, check for accuracy
  grade = mainGrade;   // Assign main()'s grade
}
void LetterGrade::prGrade(void)
{ cout << "The grade is " << grade << "\n";
}
void LetterGrade::checkGr(char & mainGrade) // Ensures accuracy
{
   // toupper() returns an int argument, so typecast char first
   mainGrade = char(toupper(mainGrade)); // Convert the grade
                                          // to uppercase
   if ((mainGrade < 'A') || (mainGrade > 'F'))
     { cerr << "A bad grade of " << mainGrade << " was
➥given!\n";
       exit(1);
     }
}
///////////////////// Class ends here /////////////////////
main()
{
  LetterGrade student1, student2, student3;
  student1.init();
  student2.init('b');
  student3.init('H');
```
```

Answers

```cpp
    // Print the grades
    student1.prGrade();
    student2.prGrade();
    student3.prGrade();
    // By the way... If the students were defined as an array
    // like this:
    // LetterGrade students[20];
    // you could print all the grades in a loop such as this:
    // for (int i=0; i<20; i++)
    //    { students(i).prGrade(); }
    return 0;
}
```

3.
```cpp
// Filename: LEMONCHK.CPP
// Child's lemonade sale-tracking program with checks for low
// supplies
#include <iostream.h>
#include <iomanip.h>
#include <stdlib.h>
// Lemonade class declaration next
class Lemon {
private:
   int totalLeft;         // Will start at 100
   int sugarTeasp;        // Starts at 80
   float total;           // Income for day
   void prWarn(void);     // Prints warning when supplies are low
public:
   void init(void);       // Initialize members on program start-up
   void showTot(void);    // Print the day's total income
   void buySweet(void);   // Customer buys sweetened
   void buyUnSweet(void); // Customer buys unsweetened
};
void Lemon::init(void)
{  totalLeft = 100;
   sugarTeasp = 80;
   total = 0.0;
}
void Lemon::showTot(void)
{  cout << setprecision(2) << setiosflags(ios::fixed);
```

```cpp
    cout << setiosflags(ios::showpoint); // Ensure decimal prints
    cout << "\nTotal so far today is $" << total << "\n\n";
}
void Lemon::buySweet(void)
{
  if (totalLeft == 0)
    { cerr << "Sorry, no more lemonade is left.\n\n";}
  else
    if (sugarTeasp == 0)
      { cerr << "No more sugar is left. Sorry.\n\n"; }
    else
      { prWarn();
        cout << "Enjoy your drink!\n\n";
        totalLeft--;       // One less glass left
        sugarTeasp -= 2;   // Each glass takes 2 teaspoons
        total += (float).50;
      }
}
void Lemon::buyUnSweet(void)
{
  if (totalLeft == 0)
    { cerr << "Sorry, no more lemonade is left.\n\n";}
  else
    { prWarn();
      cout << "Enjoy your drink!\n\n";
      totalLeft--;       // One less glass left
      total += (float).45;
    }
}
void Lemon::prWarn(void)
{
  if (totalLeft < 5)
    { cerr << "You are running low on lemonade.\n";}
  else if (sugarTeasp < 10)
        { cerr << "You are running low on sugar.\n"; }
}
///////////////////////// Class ends here /////////////////////////
main()
{
```

Answers

```
    Lemon drink;
    int ans;
    drink.init();   // Initialize data members to start of day
    do {
      cout << "What's happening?\n";
      cout << " 1. Sell a sweetened.\n";
      cout << " 2. Sell an unsweetened.\n";
      cout << " 3. Show total sales so far.\n";
      cout << " 4. Quit the program.\n";
      cout << "What do you want to do? ";
      cin >> ans;
      switch (ans)
        { case 1 : drink.buySweet();
                   break;
          case 2 : drink.buyUnSweet();
                   break;
          case 3 : drink.showTot();
                   break;
          case 4 : drink.showTot();   // Print total one last time
                   exit(1);
      }
    } while (ans >=1 && ans <= 4);
    return 0;
}
```

Answers for Day 10, "Friends When You Need Them"

Quiz

1. The class itself must specify its friends. A stand-alone function must gain access just with a `friend` keyword, or the data-protection barriers of classes would be destroyed.

2. False. A friend function can have access to all members.

3. Because another class might refer to that class, such as in a friend function designation, before the class definition appears in the program.

4. Friend declarations can go either place without any difference.

5. False. Friends often add to readability burdens, and if you can get by without them, do so. Despite their problems, friends become extremely helpful in operator overloading.

6. The *this pointer is not passed automatically, so the function cannot be executed like member functions can.

Exercise

1.
```cpp
// Filename: FRNDEXER.CPP
// First program that uses a friend function to access
// two different classes' private data members.
#include <iostream.h>
#include <iomanip.h>
#include <string.h>
class boysSoftball;   // Forward reference (prototype)

class girlsSoftball {
  char name[25];
  int age;
  float batAvg;
public:
  void init(char N[], int A, float B);
  friend void prData(const girlsSoftball plG,
    ➥const boysSoftball plB);
};
void girlsSoftball::init(char N[], int A, float B)
{
  strcpy(name, N);
  age = A;
  batAvg = B;
}
class boysSoftball {
  char name[25];
  int age;
  float batAvg;
public:
  void init(char N[], int A, float B);
```

Answers

```cpp
    friend void prData(const girlsSoftball plG,
 ➥const boysSoftball plB);
};
void boysSoftball::init(char N[], int A, float B)
{
  strcpy(name, N);
  age = A;
  batAvg = B;
}
/////////////////Primary Program Code Follows/////////////////
main()
{
  girlsSoftball * Gplayer[3];
  boysSoftball * Bplayer[3];
  for (int i=0; i<3;i++)
    { Gplayer[i] = new girlsSoftball;
      Bplayer[i] = new boysSoftball;
    }
  Gplayer[0]->init("Stacy", 12, .344);
  Gplayer[1]->init("Judith", 13, .326);
  Gplayer[2]->init("Leah", 12, .468);
  Bplayer[0]->init("Jim", 11, .231);
  Bplayer[1]->init("Michael", 13, .543);
  Bplayer[2]->init("Larry", 12, .345);
  for (i=0; i<3; i++)
    { prData(*Gplayer[i], *Bplayer[i]); }
  for (i=0; i<3; i++)
    { delete Gplayer[i];
      delete Bplayer[i];
    }
  return 0;
}
// Friend function's code appears next
void prData(const girlsSoftball plG, const boysSoftball plB)
{
  cout << setprecision(3);
  cout << "Player name:    " << plG.name << "\n";
  cout << "Player age:     " << plG.age << "\n";
  cout << "Player average: " << plG.batAvg << "\n\n";
```

```
    cout << "Player name:    " << plB.name << "\n";
    cout << "Player age:     " << plB.age << "\n";
    cout << "Player average: " << plB.batAvg << "\n\n";
}
```

Answers for Day 11, "Introduction to Overloading Operators"

Quiz

1. One, because the first operand is passed using the *this pointer.

2. By the function overloading mechanism inside the Visual C++ language.

3. They are both named operator++(). Their difference lies solely in the appearance of int in the postfix increment function's argument list.

4. No short-circuiting is performed with the overloaded operators.

5. int.

6. Postfix because of the int.

7. When stacking most overloaded operators (most, but not all, such as the relational operators that always return int), you'll need to return the class data type.

8. return *this;

9. It gets in your way when you want the left operand of an operator to have a built-in data type such as int while the right operand is a class data type.

10. Visual C++ issues an error that you're defining an argument but never using that argument in the function.

Exercises

1. ```
   // Filename: FLTCHANS.CPP
   // Overload a float-like class and a special alphabetic-only
   // class that accepts only uppercase or lowercase letters.
   ```
   ```

Answers

```cpp
#include <iostream.h>
#include <iomanip.h>
class Float {        // Will simulate a special floating-point
  float f;
public:
  void init(float F) {f = F;}   // Inline because it is short
  inline Float operator++(void);
  inline Float operator--(void);
  float getFloat(void) { return f; };
};
Float Float::operator++(void)    // Adds 1 to the float
{
  f += (float)1.0;
  return *this;
}
Float Float::operator--(void)    // Subtracts 1 from the float
{
  f -= (float)1.0;
  return *this;
};
// Second class next
class charAlph {
  char c;
public:
  void init(char C) {c = C;}   // Inline because it is short
  inline charAlph operator++(void);
  inline charAlph operator--(void);
  char getAlph(void) { return c; }
};
charAlph charAlph::operator++(void)
{
  if (c == 'z')
    c = 'a';
  else if (c == 'Z')
        c = 'A';
      else
        c++;        // Visual C++ adds an ASCII 1 to the character
  return *this;
}
```

```cpp
charAlph charAlph::operator--(void)
{
  if (c == 'a')
    c = 'z';
  else if (c == 'A')
        c = 'Z';
      else
        c--;      // Subtracts an ASCII 1 from the character
  return *this;
}
/////////////////////////////////////////////////////////////////
main()
{
  Float fVal;
  charAlph initial;
  fVal.init(34.5);
  cout << "Before increment, fVal is " << fVal.getFloat()
  ➥<< "\n";
  ++fVal;
  cout << "After increment, fVal is " << fVal.getFloat()
  ➥<< "\n";
  --fVal;
  cout << "After decrement, fVal is " << fVal.getFloat()
  ➥<< "\n\n";
  initial.init('Y');
  cout << "Before increment, initial is " << initial.getAlph()
  ➥<< "\n";
  ++initial;
  cout << "After increment, initial is " << initial.getAlph()
  ➥<< "\n";
  ++initial;
  cout << "Incrementing initial again produces "
  ➥<< initial.getAlph() << "\n";
  --initial;
  cout << "After decrementing, initial is "
  ➥<< initial.getAlph() << "\n";
  // Now, do the same for lowercase letters
  initial.init('y');
```

```
       cout << "Before increment, initial is " << initial.getAlph()
       ➥<< "\n";
       ++initial;
       cout << "After increment, initial is " << initial.getAlph()
       ➥<< "\n";
       ++initial;
       cout << "Incrementing initial again produces "
       ➥<< initial.getAlph() << "\n";
       --initial;
       cout << "After decrementing, initial is "
       ➥<< initial.getAlph() << "\n";
       return 0;
     }
```

2. ```
   // Filename: LOGOVER.CPP
   // Overloads and demonstrates the logical operators && and ||.
   #include <iostream.h>
   class newClass {
     int i;
     int j;
   public:
     void init(int I, int J) {i = I; j = J;}
     inline int operator||(newClass);
     inline int operator&&(newClass);
   };
   int newClass::operator||(newClass c)
   {
     if (((i != 0) && (j != 0)) || ((c.i != 0) && (c.j != 0)))
       return 1;
     else
       return 0;
   }
   int newClass::operator&&(newClass c)
   {
     // Only center operator has to change here
     if (((i != 0) && (j != 0)) && ((c.i != 0) && (c.j != 0)))
       return 1;
     else
       return 0;
   }
   ```
   ```

```
/////////////////////////////////////////////////////////////
main()
{
  newClass var1, var2;
  var1.init(1, 1);
  var2.init(0, 1);
  if (var1 || var2)
    cout << "The logical || tests true.\n";
  else
    cout << "The logical || tests false.\n";
  if (var1 && var2)
    cout << "The logical && tests true.\n";
  else
    cout << "The logical && tests false.\n";
  return 0;
}
```

Answers for Day 12, "Extending Operator Overloads"

Quiz

1. `operator<<()` and `operator>>()`.

2. So that they can work properly with the IOSTREAM.H file.

3. False. Manipulators don't use parentheses.

4. `operator[]()`.

5. True.

6. By returning a reference to the stream operator.

7. To improve efficiency at the trade-off of safety.

8. False. When overloading the subscript, you can make the subscript refer to any member of any data type inside the class.

Answers

Exercises

1.
```cpp
// Filename: DATECHK.CPP
// Inputs Date values correctly
#include <iostream.h>
char * getMonth(const int & monthNum);
class Date {
   int day;
   int month;
   int year;
public:
   friend ostream & operator<< (ostream &, Date);
   friend istream & operator>> (istream &, Date &);
};
// Overloaded output function next
ostream & operator<<(ostream & out, Date d)
{
   out << "\nHere's the date:\n";
   // It's OK to call regular functions below main() from
   // member functions
   out << getMonth(d.month) << " " << d.day << ", " << d.year
➥<< "\n";
   return out;   // Allows stacking
}
istream & operator>>(istream & in, Date & d)
{
   cout << "Please look at your calendar and enter the date as
➥follows:\n";
   do {
      cout << "What is the month (1-12)? ";
      in >> d.month;
   } while ((d.month < 0) || (d.month > 12));
   do {
      cout << "What is the day (1-31)? ";
      in >> d.day;
   } while (d.day < 1 || d.day > 31);
   do {
      cout << "What is the year (1980-2100)? ";
      in >> d.year;
```

```
      } while (d.year < 1 || d.year > 2100);
      return in;      // Allows stacking
   }
   ////////////////////////////////////////////////////////////
   main()
   {
     Date today;
     cin >> today;          // Get the date
     cout << today;         // Print it
     return 0;
   }
   char * getMonth(const int & monthNum)
   {
      static char * monthName[] = {"January", "February", "March",
               "April", "May", "June", "July", "August",
               "September", "October", "November", "December"};
      return monthName[monthNum - 1];   // Adjust for subscript
   }
```

2. ```
   // Filename: COMMAOV.CPP
   // Overload comma to do << for output
   ostream & operator,(ostream & out, int i)
   {
      out << i;
      return out;
   }
   ```

3. ```
   // Filename: MONTHDAY.CPP
   // Class that holds the days of months
   #include <iostream.h>
   class Months {
     int days[12];
   public:
     void init(void);
     int & operator[](const int sub) {return days[sub]; }
   };
   void Months::init(void)
   {
     days[0] = 31;
     days[1] = 28;   // Ignores leap years
```

Answers

```
        days[2] = 31;
        days[3] = 30;
        days[4] = 31;
        days[5] = 30;
        days[6] = 31;
        days[7] = 31;
        days[8] = 30;
        days[9] = 31;
        days[10] = 30;
        days[11] = 31;
}
main()
{
    Months year;
    year.init();
    cout << "Here are the days in each month:\n";
    for (int i=0; i<12; i++)
        { cout << "Month #" << (i+1) << ": " << year[i];
          cout << "\n"; } // Adjust for subscript
    return 0;
}
```

Answers for Day 13, "Constructing and Destructing"

Quiz

1. True as long as you overload the constructors.

2. One.

3. When you define objects without using initialization of any kind.

4. When your objects go into scope.

5. When your objects go out of scope.

6. False. Constructors and destructors determine how individual objects are created after they are defined elsewhere. If `main()` (or another function)

allocates a class object or an array of class objects on the heap, `main()` must deallocate the objects as well.

7. `operator=()`.

8. Default constructor.

9. Copy constructor.

10. When your class contains pointer members.

Exercises

1. ```
String left(const int & n)
  {
    if (strlen(st) < n) // True if user code wants to pull
      { return *this; } // more chars than exist in the string
    String leftSt = st;
    leftSt.st[n] = '\0';   // Shorten the copy of the string
    return String(leftSt);
  }
String right(const int & n)
{
  if (strlen(st) < n)   // True if user code wants to pull
    { return *this; }   // more chars than exist in the string
  String rightSt = st;
  int j = 0;   // Target string starting subscript
  for (int i=strlen(st)-n;i<strlen(st)+1;i++)   // Copy from
    { rightSt.st[j++] = st[i]; }   // left to right
  rightSt.st[j] = '\0';
  return String(rightSt);
}
```

2. ```
// Filename: BEV.CPP
// Tracks, initializes, copies, and prints beverage products.
#include <iostream.h>
#include <iomanip.h>
#include <string.h>
class Drinks {
  char * name;
  float whole;
```

```
    float retail;
public:
  Drinks(char * = "Noname", float=0.0,
  ➥float=0.0);   // Default constructor
  ~Drinks();     // Destructor
  Drinks(const Drinks &);  // Copy constructor
  Drinks & operator=(const Drinks &);  // Assignment overload
  friend ostream & operator<< (ostream &, const Drinks &);
  friend istream & operator>> (istream &, Drinks &);
};
Drinks::Drinks(char * N, float W, float R)
{
  name = new char[strlen(N) + 1];
  strcpy(name, N);
  whole = W;
  retail = R;
}
Drinks::~Drinks()
{
  delete [] name;
}
Drinks::Drinks(const Drinks & d)     // Copy constructor
{
  int newLen = strlen(d.name) + 1;
  name = new char[newLen];
  strcpy(name, d.name);
  whole = d.whole;
  retail = d.retail;
}
Drinks & Drinks::operator=(const Drinks & d)
{
  if (this == &d)
    { return *this; }
  delete [] name;  // Deallocate old string
  name = new char[strlen(d.name) + 1];
  strcpy(name, d.name);  // Copy string member
  whole = d.whole;       // Copy float members
  retail = d.retail;
  return *this;
```

```cpp
    }
    ostream & operator<< (ostream & out, const Drinks & d)
    {
       out << setprecision(2) << setiosflags(ios::showpoint);
       out << setiosflags(ios::fixed);
       out << "Name: " << d.name << "\n";
       out << "Wholesale price: " << d.whole << "\tRetail price: ";
       out << d.retail << "\n\n";
       return out;
    }
    istream & operator>> (istream & in, Drinks & d)
    {
       cout << "Please add to our line of beverage products.\n";
       cout << "What is the name of the next product? (one word
    ➥please)";
       char tempInput[80];     // Need to temporarily
       in >> tempInput;                   // store user input
       d.name = new char[strlen(tempInput) + 1];   // onto the heap
       strcpy(d.name, tempInput);
       in.ignore();  // Remove carriage return
       cout << "What is the retail price of " << d.name << "? ";
       in >> d.retail;
       cout << "What is the wholesale price of " << d.name << "? ";
       in >> d.whole;
       return in;
    }
    /////////////////////////////////////////////////////////////
    main()
    {
      Drinks * bevs = new Drinks[5];  // Array of 5 drinks on heap
      for (int i=0; i<5; i++)
        { cin >> bevs[i]; };    // Ask the user for the beverages
      cout << "\n\nHere's what you entered:\n";
      for (i=0; i<5; i++)
        { cout << bevs[i]; };   // Show the user for the beverages
      bevs[3] = bevs[4];        // Test the overloaded assignment
      Drinks newBev = bevs[1];  // Test the copy constructor
      Drinks another("Diet Peach Flavored", .23, .67);
      cout << "After some changes:\n";
```

```
        cout << bevs[3] << newBev << another << "\n";
        cout << "Mmmm... Made from the best stuff on earth!";
        delete [] bevs;
        return 0;
}
```

Answers for Day 14, "Loose Ends: *static* and Larger Programs"

Quiz

1. True.

2. False. Local variables can be either `static` or `auto`.

3. A.

4. The process of keeping global functions and global variables in other source files from clashing with the current file's global functions and global variables.

5. The process of allowing other files access to the current one's global functions and global variables.

6. That's a loaded question. They can be either, but keeping `static` data members private helps protect their values.

7. A collection of multiple source files and possibly object files that eventually compile and link into a single executable program.

8. You don't have to recompile or relink files that don't change from one build to another.

Exercises

1.  ```cpp
    // Filename: TEACHST.CPP
    // Program to track student scores
    #include <iostream.h>
    #include <iomanip.h>
    class Kids {
      char name[25];
      float grade;
    public:
      static float average;
      Kids(void);
      ~Kids() {};   // No destructor code needed
    };
    Kids::Kids(void)
    {
      cout << "What is the next kid's name? ";
      cin.getline(name, 25);
      cout << "What is the grade? ";
      cin >> grade;
      cin.ignore();   // Eliminate carriage return left on buffer
      average+=grade;
    }
    float Kids::average = 0.0;
    //////////////////////////////////////////////////////////
    main()
    {
       Kids students[5];   // Array of 5 students
       Kids::average /= (float)5.0;
       cout << setiosflags(ios::fixed)
         << setiosflags(ios::showpoint);
       cout << setprecision(2);
       cout << "\nThe class average is " << Kids::average << "\n";
       return 0;
    }
    ```

2. No answer is possible due to the interactive nature of this exercise.
    ```

D Answers

Answers for Day 15, "It's Hereditary: Inheriting Data"

Quiz

1. A is the base class.
2. B is the derived class.
3. `i` is private and therefore can never be accessed by a derived class.
4. A. Four.
   B. Protected.
   C. Public.
5. In the IOSTREAM.H header file.

Exercise

1.
```
// Filename: ACCESSFL.CPP
// The full Person class and its derivatives
class Person {
   long int interCode;    // Internal code is only private member
protected:
   char * name;           // Four protected members
   char * address;
   int areaCode;
   long int phone;
public:            // Public member functions follow
   Person();
   ~Person();
   Person inputPerson(void);
   prPerson(void);
};
class Employee : private Person { // Private receipt is default
   int dependents;
protected:
   int yrsWorked;
public:
```

```cpp
    int testYears(void);    // True if employed more than 10 years
};
class Customer : protected Person {
  char * custNum;
protected:
  float custBalance;
public:
  int prCust(void);
};
class Vendor : public Person {
  char * vendNum;
protected:
  float vendOwed;
public:
  prVend(void);
};
class Salaried : Employee {
  int numWeeksVacation;
public:
  double computeSalary(void);
};
class Hourly : Employee {
  float ratePerHour;
public:
  int testMinimumWage(void);
};
class PartTime : Hourly {      // A child of a child class
  int hoursWorked;
public:
  float computePay(void);
};
class FullTime : Hourly {      // A child of a child class
  int maxHrsAvailable;
public:
  float computePay(void);
};
```

Answers

Answers for Day 16, "Inherited Limits and Extensions"

Quiz

1. True. Most of the time, however, you cannot rely on default constructors to create a class object properly. When a default constructor is not enough to construct the object, you *must* provide your own derived constructors and parent class initialization constructor lists to create the inheritance of objects properly.

2. Constants must be initialized when they are created, not assigned values later.

3. On the constructor's definition line (separated from the constructor argument parentheses with a colon, :).

4. True.

5. The derived class B does not construct A with the proper order of arguments.

6. A.

7. B.

8. Nothing. Visual C++ properly destructs a hierarchy in the opposite direction of the construction.

Exercises

1.
```
// Filename: INHERHP.CPP
// Using the heap and deriving classes from other
// derived classes
#include <iostream.h>
#include <iomanip.h>
#include <string.h>
class Parent {
protected:            // To allow inheritance
  char * name;
  int age;
public:
```

```cpp
    Parent(char *, int);
    ~Parent() { delete [] name; }    // Needed for heap
    void display(void);
    // No overloaded output to keep program short
};
Parent::Parent(char * N, int A) : age(A) {
   name = new char[strlen(N) + 1];
   strcpy(name, N);
}
void Parent::display(void)
{
   cout << "Parent's name is " << name << "\n";
   cout << "Parent's age is " << age << "\n";
}
class Son : public Parent {
   int yrInSchool;
public:
   void display(void);
   Son(char *, int, int);
};
Son::Son(char * N, int A, int Y) : Parent(N, A), yrInSchool(Y)
{
}
void Son::display(void)
{
   cout << "Son's name is " << name << "\n";
   cout << "Son's age is " << age << "\n";
   cout << "Son's year in school is " << yrInSchool << "\n";
}

class Daughter : public Parent {
// 'protected' was removed
   int yrInSchool;
   char * friendsName;
public:
   Daughter(char *, int, int, char *);
   Daughter(char *, int);
   ~Daughter() { delete [] friendsName; }   // Needed for heap
   void display(void);
```

Answers

```cpp
};
Daughter::Daughter(char * N, int A, int Y, char * F) :
                  Parent(N, A), yrInSchool(Y)
{
  friendsName = new char[strlen(F) + 1];
  strcpy(friendsName, F);
}
Daughter::Daughter(char * N, int A) : Parent(N, A)
{  // No function body needed; initialization list does it all
}
void Daughter::display(void)
{
  cout << "Daughter's name is " << name << "\n";
  cout << "Daughter's age is " << age << "\n";
  cout << "Daughter's year in school is " << yrInSchool
   ↪<< "\n";
  cout << "Daughter's friend is " << friendsName << "\n";
};
class GrandChild : Daughter {
  float weightAtBirth;
public:
  GrandChild(char *, int, float);
  void display(void);
};
GrandChild::GrandChild(char * N, int A, float W) :
                      Daughter(N, A), weightAtBirth(W)
{  // Initialization list does it all
}
void GrandChild::display(void)
{
  cout << setprecision(1) << setiosflags(ios::fixed);
  cout << "Grandchild's name is " << name << "\n";
  cout << "Grandchild's age is " << age << "\n";
  cout << "Grandchild's weight at birth was " << weightAtBirth
   ↪<< "\n";
}
/////////////////////////////////////////////////////////////
main()
{
```

```cpp
      Parent adult("James", 61);
      Son boy("Tom", 31, 12);
      Daughter girl("Barbara", 22, 16, "Elizabeth");
      GrandChild baby("Suzie", 1, 7.5);
      adult.display();
      boy.display();
      girl.display();
      baby.display();
      return 0;
   }
```

2. ```cpp
   // Filename: INHERPET.CPP
   // Adds a Pet object to the hierarchy.
   #include <iostream.h>
   #include <iomanip.h>
   #include <string.h>
   class Parent {
   protected:              // To allow inheritance
     char * name;
     int age;
   public:
     Parent(char *, int);
     ~Parent() { delete [] name; }   // Needed for heap
     void display(void);
     // No overloaded output to keep program short
   };
   Parent::Parent(char * N, int A) : age(A) {
     name = new char[strlen(N) + 1];
     strcpy(name, N);
   }
   void Parent::display(void)
   {
     cout << "Parent's name is " << name << "\n";
     cout << "Parent's age is " << age << "\n";
   }
   //////////////////////////////////////////////////////////
   // New Pet class next
   class Pet : public Parent {
     int peopleYears;
   ```
   ```

Answers

```cpp
public:
  void display(void);
  Pet(char *, int);
};
Pet::Pet(char * N, int A) : Parent(N, A)
{
  // Must have a constructor body because of the calculation
  peopleYears = age * 7;   // Calculate people years of the pet
}
void Pet::display(void)
{
  cout << "Pet's name is " << name << "\n";
  cout << "Pet's real age is " << age << "\n";
  cout << "(That's " << peopleYears << " in people years!)\n";
}
class Son : public Parent {
  int yrInSchool;
public:
  void display(void);
  Son(char *, int, int);
};
Son::Son(char * N, int A, int Y) : Parent(N, A), yrInSchool(Y)
{
}
void Son::display(void)
{
  cout << "Son's name is " << name << "\n";
  cout << "Son's age is " << age << "\n";
  cout << "Son's year in school is " << yrInSchool << "\n";
}

class Daughter : public Parent {
// 'protected' was removed
  int yrInSchool;
  char * friendsName;
public:
  Daughter(char *, int, int, char *);
  Daughter(char *, int);
  ~Daughter() { delete [] friendsName; }   // Needed for heap
```

```cpp
    void display(void);
};
Daughter::Daughter(char * N, int A, int Y, char * F) :
                   Parent(N, A), yrInSchool(Y)
{
  friendsName = new char[strlen(F) + 1];
  strcpy(friendsName, F);
}
Daughter::Daughter(char * N, int A) : Parent(N, A)
{  // No function body needed; initialization list does it all
}
void Daughter::display(void)
{
  cout << "Daughter's name is " << name << "\n";
  cout << "Daughter's age is " << age << "\n";
  cout << "Daughter's year in school is " << yrInSchool
➥<< "\n";
  cout << "Daughter's friend is " << friendsName << "\n";
};
class GrandChild : Daughter {
  float weightAtBirth;
public:
  GrandChild(char *, int, float);
  void display(void);
};
GrandChild::GrandChild(char * N, int A, float W) :
                      Daughter(N, A), weightAtBirth(W)
{  // Initialization list does it all
}
void GrandChild::display(void)
{
  cout << setprecision(1) << setiosflags(ios::fixed);
  cout << "Grandchild's name is " << name << "\n";
  cout << "Grandchild's age is " << age << "\n";
  cout << "Grandchild's weight at birth was " << weightAtBirth
➥<< "\n";
}
////////////////////////////////////////////////////////////
main()
```

Answers

```
{
  Parent adult("James", 61);
  Pet dog("Rover", 4);
  Son boy("Tom", 31, 12);
  Daughter girl("Barbara", 22, 16, "Elizabeth");
  GrandChild baby("Suzie", 1, 7.5);
  adult.display();
  dog.display();
  boy.display();
  girl.display();
  baby.display();
  return 0;
}
```

Answers for Day 17, "Data Composition"

Quiz

1. The *is-a* and *has-a* questions.

2. A. Composition.

   B. Inheritance.

   C. Composition.

   D. Inheritance.

3. The class is attempting to assign a character value to a character pointer member.

4. Visual C++ will then perform memberwise assignment.

5. You could end up with two objects pointing to the same region in memory.

Exercises

1. ```
   class House {
       int sqFeet;
       char * address;
       float cost;
   ```
   ```

```
    int numRooms;
public:
  House(int, char *, float, int);
  ~House();
};
// Constructor initialization list added next
House::House(int S, char * A, float C, int N) :
           sqFeet(S), cost(C), numRooms(N)
{
  int newlen = strlen(A) + 1;
  address = new char[newlen];
  strcpy(address, A);
};
House::~House()
{
  delete [] address;
}
```

2. See the section "If the Heap Has a Problem" in Day 5's chapter for the _set_new_handler() function specifics. You need only one new handler for the program, not one for each class.

Answers for Day 18, "Virtual Functions: Are They Real?"

Quiz

1. No.

2. Late binding takes place when you define pointers to functions and when you use virtual functions.

3. True. It is because data does not get generated until runtime that function pointers have their late binding capabilities.

4. B.

5. B.

6. It contains at least one pure virtual function.

Answers

7. The assignment of the zero tells Visual C++ to issue a compile-time error if you attempt to instantiate an object with a pure virtual function. Without the zero, Visual C++ will not issue an error if you attempt to define an object for an abstract base class, even though you'll get runtime errors if you attempt to use the object.

8. Always specify a virtual destructor when a base class contains at least one virtual function (assuming that the class needs a destructor) so that Visual C++ calls the correct destructor when an object is deleted from the heap.

Exercises

1.
```cpp
// Filename: MENUPTR.CPP
// Demonstrates a menu without a switch or an if statement
#include <iostream.h>
#include <stdlib.h>

void funA(void);   // Prototypes needed before array of pointers
void funB(void);
void funC(void);
void quitPgm(void);

void (*menu[])(void) = {funA, funB, funC, quitPgm};

main()
{
   int ans;
   do
   {  cout << "\n\n\nDo you want to:\n\n";
      cout << "1. Run function A\n";
      cout << "2. Run function B\n";
      cout << "3. Run function C\n";
      cout << "4. Quit program\n";
      cin >> ans;

      menu[ans-1]();   // Call appropriate function w/o switch
   } while (1);   // Infinite loop that terminates by quitPgm()
   return 0;
}
```

```cpp
    void funA()
    {
       cout << "Function A called.\n";
    }

    void funB()
    {
       cout << "Function B called.\n";
    }

    void funC()
    {
       cout << "Function C called.\n";
    }

    void quitPgm()
    {
       exit(0);
    }
```

2.
```cpp
    // Filename: ABSTR.CPP
    // An abstract base class acts like a model for other classes.
    #include <iostream.h>
    #include <iomanip.h>
    #include <string.h>
    class Building {
    protected:
      int sqFt;
      char address[25];   // Don't worry about city, state, ZIP
    public:
      Building(int, char []);
      virtual void prData(void)=0;     // Makes the class abstract!
    };
    Building::Building(int S, char A[]) : sqFt(S)
    {
      strcpy(address, A);
    }
    class Shed : public Building {
```

Answers

```cpp
    char useCode;
public:
    Shed(int, char[], char);
    void prData(void);
};
Shed::Shed(int S, char A[], char U) : Building(S, A),
➥useCode(U)
{ // No body necessary due to initialization lists
}
void Shed::prData(void)   // Shed now must have its own prData()
            // because it can no longer rely on inheriting one.
            // Its base class now has no code (except for the
            // constructor), so all member functions must be
            // rewritten in all derived classes
{
    cout << "The shed has " << sqFt << " square feet.\n";
    cout << "The shed's address is " << address << ".\n\n";
}

class House : public Building {
    int numRooms;
    float cost;
public:
    House(int, char [], int, float);
    void prData(void);
};
House::House(int S, char A[], int N, float C) : Building(S, A),
            numRooms(N), cost(C)
{ // No body necessary due to initialization lists
}
void House::prData(void)
{
    cout << "The house has " << sqFt << " square feet.\n";
    cout << "The house address is " << address << ".\n";
    cout << "The house has " << numRooms << " number of
    ➥rooms.\n";
    cout << "The house cost " << cost << "\n\n";
}
class Office : public Building {
```

```cpp
    int zoneCode;
    float rent;
public:
    Office(int, char [], int, float);
    void prData(void);
};
Office::Office(int S, char A[], int Z,
➥float R) : Building(S, A),
              zoneCode(Z), rent(R)
{ // No body necessary due to initialization lists
}
void Office::prData(void)
{
    cout << "The office has " << sqFt << " square feet.\n";
    cout << "The office address is " << address << ".\n";
    cout << "The office is zoned for " << zoneCode << " code.\n";
    cout << "The office rents for " << rent << ".\n\n";
}
main()
{
    // Define pointers to class objects. Notice that the base
    // class is used to define the pointers, not any derived
    // class
    Building * properties[3];

    // Reserve heap and initialize with a constructor
    Shed aShed = Shed(78, "304 E. Tenth", 'x');
    House aHouse = House(2310, "5706 S. Carmel", 8, 121344.00);
    Office anOffice = Office(1195, "5 High Rise", 'B', 895.75);
    properties[0] = &aShed;
    properties[1] = &aHouse;
    properties[2] = &anOffice;

    // Prepare output now that objects are constructed
    cout << setprecision(2) << setiosflags(ios::showpoint);
    cout << setiosflags(ios::fixed);
    // Print the objects using a loop
    for (int ctr=0; ctr<3; ctr++)
    {
```

Answers

```
        properties[ctr]->prData();    // Hopefully, the right
                                      // prData() prints!
    }

    // Deallocate the memory
    delete properties[0];
    delete properties[1];
    delete properties[2];
    return 0;
}
```

Answers for Day 19, "Introduction to Throwing and Catching Exceptions"

Quiz

1. When your program throws an exception, control is immediately passed to the exception handling routine.

2. To catch an exception means that a thrown exception is handled.

3. Throw() and Catch() are part of the Microsoft Windows programming functions.

4. False. You can handle many kinds of exceptions with an exception handler.

5. Visual C++ supports the Microsoft Windows programming functions as well as the exception-handling macros that you'll master as you learn more about Visual C++'s supplied classes.

6. Include the WINDOWS.H header file when your program calls Catch() and Throw().

Exercise

1.
```
// Filename: ALPHEXCP.CPP
// catch() and throw() a data entry error
#include <iostream.h>
```

```cpp
#include <windows.h>
#include <stdlib.h>
#include <ctype.h>

CATCHBUF jmpBufStruct;   // You must define this global buffer
// so that Visual C++ has a place to store the system's state
// at the catch()

main()
{
  char initial;
  int badVal;   // Holds a value that determines which error
                // occurred

  badVal = Catch(jmpBufStruct);   // The system's state is saved
                                  // here in case a longjmp() happens later
  if (badVal)
  {
    cerr << "You didn't enter a letter!\n";
         exit(99);   // Stop program
  }
  cout << "What is your first initial? ";
  cin >> initial;
  if (isalpha(initial))
  {
    cout << "Thanks!\n";
  }
  else
  {
    Throw(jmpBufStruct, 1); // Throw to the catch function
  }
  return 0;
}
```

Answers

Answers for Day 20, "Easy File I/O"

Quiz

1. `ifstream`, `ofstream`, and `fstream`.

2. Read, write, and append.

3. Sequential access.

4. The FSTREAM.H classes are derived from IOSTREAM.H.

5. You must use `open()` when you need to override the default input or output opening of files.

6. `ios::app`.

7. The access mode is implied in both the `ifstream` and the `ofstream` classes.

8. There are no physical differences as far as the computer is concerned. The PC sees all files as streams of bytes. Sequential files that hold text are generally stored as ASCII text files that you can read from DOS and non-Turbo C++ programs.

Exercises

1.
```
// Filename: RANMENU.CPP
// User selects from a menu and adds data to the inventory
// file, then prints the file contents when the user selects
// that menu option.
#include <fstream.h>
#include <string.h>
#include <stdlib.h>
#include <iomanip.h>
int dispMenu(void);
void addParts(void);
void prParts(void);
// Class that defines a single instance
class inventoryItem {     // A class defining ONE inventory part
  char partCode[5];
```

```cpp
      char descrip[20];
      int num;
      float price;
   public:
      void addToInv(char P[], char D[], int N, float PR)
        { num = N;
          price = PR;
          strcpy(partCode, P);
          strcpy(descrip, D);
          this->toDisk();    // Write the data record
        }
      void toDisk(void)
      {
        ofstream invOut;
        invOut.open("INV.DAT", ios::app);
        invOut.write((char *)this, sizeof(*this));   // Write record
      }
      void getData(void); // No function with while is ever inlined
};   // Class definition ends here
void inventoryItem::getData(void)
{
   ifstream invIn("INV.DAT");
   while (invIn)
   {
     invIn.read((char *)this, sizeof(*this));   // Read record
     if (invIn.good())
     { cout << setprecision(2) << setiosflags(ios::showpoint);
       cout << setiosflags(ios::fixed);
       cout << "\nPart code: " << partCode << "\n";
       cout << "Description: " << descrip << "\n";
       cout << "Quantity: " << num << "\n";
       cout << "Price: " << price << "\n";
     }
   }
}
////////////////////////////////////////////////////////////
main()
{
   int menu;    // For menu prompt
```

Answers

```cpp
    // Construct empty inventory items
    do
      { menu = dispMenu();
        switch (menu)
        { case 1 : addParts();
                   break;
          case 2 : prParts();
                   break;
          case 3:  exit(1);
          default: cerr << "\n***Enter 1, 2, or 3***\n";
        }
      } while (menu !=3);   // The exit(1) takes care of exit
      return 0;
}
int dispMenu(void)
{
  int ans;
  cout << "\n\nHere are your choices:\n\n";
  cout << "  1. Add an inventory item to the file\n";
  cout << "  2. Display items in the file\n";
  cout << "  3. Exit the program\n\n";
  cout << "What do you want to do? ";
  cin >> ans;
  return ans;
}
void addParts(void)
{
  char pc[5];     // Define four variables to hold
  char de[20];    // input data
  int q;
  float pr;
  inventoryItem part;  // To call member function
  cin.ignore();   // Eliminate newline from menu answer's input
  cout << "Please enter a part code: ";
  cin.getline(pc, 5);
  cout << "Please enter a description: ";
  cin.getline(de, 20);
  cout << "Please enter a quantity: ";
  cin >> q;
```

```cpp
      cout << "Please enter the price: ";
      cin >> pr;
      part.addToInv(pc, de, q, pr);   // Write the data
    }
    void prParts(void)
    {
      inventoryItem part;
      part.getData();    // Trigger member function
    }
```

2. ```cpp
   // Filename: RNDCHANG.CPP
   // Changes data in a file
   #include <fstream.h>
   class Item {
   public:     // Just to keep simple
     char partCode[5];
     char descrip[20];
     int num;
     float price;
     void prData(int I)
       { cout << "Record number " << I << ":\n";
         cout << "Part: " << partCode;
         cout << "\nDescription: " << descrip;
         cout << "\nNumber: " << num;
         cout << "\nPrice: " << price << "\n\n";
       }
   };
   //////////////////////////////////////////////////////////////
   main()
   {
     fstream ioFile;
     Item invItem;
     ioFile.open("INV.DAT", ios::in | ios::out);
     ioFile.seekg(0, ios::beg);
     ioFile.read((char *)&invItem, sizeof(invItem));
     invItem.prData(1);
     // Put the position back to the beginning
     ioFile.seekg(0, ios::beg);
     ioFile.read((char *)&invItem, sizeof(invItem));
   ```
   ```

Answers

```cpp
    invItem.prData(1);
    // Read last record
    ioFile.seekg(3*sizeof(invItem), ios::beg);
    ioFile.read((char *)&invItem, sizeof(invItem));
    invItem.prData(4);
    // Read in order
    ioFile.seekg(0, ios::beg);
    ioFile.read((char *)&invItem, sizeof(invItem));
    // Another seekg() isn't needed if reading in order
    invItem.prData(1);
    ioFile.read((char *)&invItem, sizeof(invItem));
    invItem.prData(2);
    ioFile.read((char *)&invItem, sizeof(invItem));
    invItem.prData(3);
    ioFile.read((char *)&invItem, sizeof(invItem));
    invItem.prData(4);
    // New code that puts a zero in all prices begins here
    ioFile.seekg(0, ios::beg);   // Start of file
    ioFile.read((char *)&invItem, sizeof(invItem));
    ioFile.seekg(0, ios::beg); // Back up to the record just read
    invItem.price = 0.0;
    ioFile.write((char *)&invItem, sizeof(invItem));
    ioFile.read((char *)&invItem, sizeof(invItem));
    ioFile.seekg(1*sizeof(invItem), ios::beg); // Position to 2nd
    invItem.price = 0.0;
    ioFile.write((char *)&invItem, sizeof(invItem));
    ioFile.read((char *)&invItem, sizeof(invItem));
    ioFile.seekg(2*sizeof(invItem), ios::beg); // Position to 3rd
    invItem.price = 0.0;
    ioFile.write((char *)&invItem, sizeof(invItem));
    ioFile.read((char *)&invItem, sizeof(invItem));
    ioFile.seekg(3*sizeof(invItem), ios::beg); // Position to 4th
    invItem.price = 0.0;
    ioFile.write((char *)&invItem, sizeof(invItem));
    return 0;
}
```

Answers for Day 21, "The Visual C++ Tools"

Quiz

1. GUI stands for *Graphical User Interface* and describes visual operating environments and operating systems such as Microsoft Windows and Windows NT.

2. Visual C++ is the compiler and sometimes is the catch-all name for the entire programming toolset that comes with the Visual C++ programming language. The Visual Workbench is the command center from which you can access all the add-on tools that make Visual C++ programmers more productive.

3. *MDI* stands for *Multiple Document Interface*. An MDI application enables you to work with more than one open document at a time. Therefore, you can open multiple source files at once and copy, cut, and paste between them.

4. A *resource* is just about any element of a Windows program that you can click, move, display, or manipulate. Resources include icons, graphics bitmaps, dialog boxes, list boxes, menus, and command buttons.

5. A wizard is a Microsoft helper tool that enables you to create elements through a series of question-and-answer sessions instead of coding a bunch of individual instructions by hand. Visual C++ includes AppWizard and ClassWizard.

6. The OLE 2.0 and ODBC database support provided by Visual C++ 1.5 enables you to access other OLE applications from within your own program. While running your program, the user could edit an OLE worksheet directly inside your application while having access to all the worksheet's menus and commands. If you want to access a database from your Visual C++ program, you can as long as the database conforms to the ODBC standard format. ODBC is supported by many database vendors.

Answers

Exercises

Due to the nature of the chapter, no exercises were assigned for Day 21.

Answers for Bonus Chapter 1, "Introduction to Windows Programming and MFC"

Quiz

1. An event is virtually anything that happens within a Windows program due to the user's or another task's operation. Mouse clicks, mouse movements, and keystrokes are all Windows events.

2. Windows sends a message to your application whenever an event takes place while your program runs. You can choose to handle a message or ignore it.

3. The message loop is the way your program filters through incoming Windows messages and decides what to do with the messages. You don't see the true message loop when writing Visual C++ programs using MFC, but you can map those incoming messages to functions within your program.

4. The application class, the mainframe class, the document class, and the view class.

5. The document class handles the data in your program, and the view class determines how Visual C++ displays that data inside the mainframe window.

Exercise

1. Today's exercise required you to create an application with AppWizard. If the application runs and contains the features required by the exercise instruction, you've completed this exercise successfully.

Answers for Bonus Chapter 2, "The MFC Classes: Power You Will Gain"

Quiz

1. A resource script is a source file that describes your resources. Part of the build process involves compiling the resource script into resources and binding those resources into your compiled program.

2. Font metrics are the details on the size and shape of your font.

3. App Studio modifies resources and supplies the tools to create them.

4. The view class contains the OnDraw() function code.

5. WM_CHAR.

6. GetTextMetrics().

7. The font metrics contain information about the font spacing so that you don't overlap lines of output on-screen.

8. Windows knows not to send a WM_PAINT message, even if you request one with SendMessage(), unless you invalidate the window first.

Exercise

1. The file TEACHVW.CPP is the only file you need to modify. It is listed here:

```
// teachvw.cpp : implementation of the CTeachView class
//

#include "stdafx.h"
#include "teach.h"

#include "teachdoc.h"
#include "teachvw.h"

#ifdef _DEBUG
```

D Answers

```
#undef THIS_FILE
static char BASED_CODE THIS_FILE[] = __FILE__;
#endif
/////////////////////////////////////////////////////////////////
// CTeachView
IMPLEMENT_DYNCREATE(CTeachView, CView)
BEGIN_MESSAGE_MAP(CTeachView, CView)
    //{{AFX_MSG_MAP(CTeachView)
    //}}AFX_MSG_MAP
    // Standard printing commands
    ON_COMMAND(ID_FILE_PRINT, CView::OnFilePrint)
    ON_COMMAND(ID_FILE_PRINT_PREVIEW,
    ➥CView::OnFilePrintPreview)
END_MESSAGE_MAP()
/////////////////////////////////////////////////////////////////
// CTeachView construction/destruction
CTeachView::CTeachView()
{
    // TODO: add construction code here
}

CTeachView::~CTeachView()
{
}

/////////////////////////////////////////////////////////////////
// CTeachView drawing
void CTeachView::OnDraw(CDC* pDC)
{
    CTeachDoc* pDoc = GetDocument();
    ASSERT_VALID(pDoc);
// ***************************************************************
// ** Here is the modified code to display the poem
// **
    // TODO: add draw code for native data here
    // Moved the rest of the function's variable definitions
    // to here
    TEXTMETRIC textStruct;
    int cxChar;
```

```
        CString sLine[6]={"My hands are tired,","My mind is numb,",
           "I've programmed until I'm blue.",
           "I hope that someday","I'll make a mint",
           "Writing Visual C++ code for you."};
        pDC->GetTextMetrics(&textStruct);
        cxChar = textStruct.tmHeight +
        ➥textStruct.tmExternalLeading;
        for (int ctr=0; ctr<6; ctr++)
        {
           pDC->TextOut(0, cxChar*ctr, sLine[ctr],
           ➥sLine[ctr].GetLength());
        }
}
// *************************************************************
/////////////////////////////////////////////////////////////////
// CTeachView printing
BOOL CTeachView::OnPreparePrinting(CPrintInfo* pInfo)
{
    // default preparation
    return DoPreparePrinting(pInfo);
}

void CTeachView::OnBeginPrinting(CDC* /*pDC*/,
➥CPrintInfo* /*pInfo*/)
{
    // TODO: add extra initialization before printing
}

void CTeachView::OnEndPrinting(CDC* /*pDC*/,
➥CPrintInfo* /*pInfo*/)
{
    // TODO: add cleanup after printing
}
/////////////////////////////////////////////////////////////////
// CTeachView diagnostics
#ifdef _DEBUG
void CTeachView::AssertValid() const
{
    CView::AssertValid();
```

Answers

```
}

void CTeachView::Dump(CDumpContext& dc) const
{
    CView::Dump(dc);
}

CTeachDoc* CTeachView::GetDocument() // non-debug version
                                     // is inline
{
    ASSERT(m_pDocument->IsKindOf(RUNTIME_CLASS(CTeachDoc)));
    return (CTeachDoc*)m_pDocument;
}
#endif //_DEBUG

/////////////////////////////////////////////////////////////////
// CTeachView message handlers
```

Answers for Bonus Chapter 3, "Files and More MFC"

Quiz

1. You don't have to write any code to use printing and print preview.

2. False. The `SetModifiedFlag()` sets the modified flag, but there is no `IsModifiedFlag()` that you can test yourself. Luckily, if the `SetModifiedFlag()` has set the flag, you have to do nothing else; the user is warned automatically when the file contents are about to be erased.

3. You must specify the cursor's width and height so that the application knows what kind of cursor you want displayed.

4. Hide the cursor before displaying text, and show the cursor after the text display (even a single character) is finished.

5. You might use `CFile` to open data files that support your document class.

6. False. You catch only the first exception with CATCH. Subsequent exceptions are caught with AND_CATCH.
7. CATCH_ALL.

Exercise

1. The file FILESVW.CPP is the only file you need to modify. It is listed here:

```
// filesvw.cpp : implementation of the CFilesView class
//

#include "stdafx.h"
#include "files.h"

#include "filesdoc.h"
#include "filesvw.h"

#ifdef _DEBUG
#undef THIS_FILE
static char BASED_CODE THIS_FILE[] = __FILE__;
#endif

/////////////////////////////////////////////////////////////
// CFilesView

IMPLEMENT_DYNCREATE(CFilesView, CView)

BEGIN_MESSAGE_MAP(CFilesView, CView)
    //{{AFX_MSG_MAP(CFilesView)
    ON_WM_CHAR()
    //}}AFX_MSG_MAP
    // Standard printing commands
    ON_COMMAND(ID_FILE_PRINT, CView::OnFilePrint)
    ON_COMMAND(ID_FILE_PRINT_PREVIEW,
        ➥CView::OnFilePrintPreview)
END_MESSAGE_MAP()

/////////////////////////////////////////////////////////////
// CFilesView construction/destruction
```

Answers

```cpp
CFilesView::CFilesView()
{
    // TODO: add construction code here
}

CFilesView::~CFilesView()
{
}

/////////////////////////////////////////////////////////////////////////////
// CFilesView drawing

void CFilesView::OnDraw(CDC* pDC)
{
    CFilesDoc* pDoc = GetDocument();
    ASSERT_VALID(pDoc);

    // TODO: add draw code for native data here
    TEXTMETRIC textStruct;
    int cxChar=0;
    int cyChar = 0;
    CPoint cxyCaret;
    pDC->GetTextMetrics(&textStruct);
    CreateSolidCaret(textStruct.tmAveCharWidth/8,
    ➥textStruct.tmHeight+2);
    HideCaret();
    for (int ctr=0; ctr<pDoc->sInput.GetLength(); ctr++)
      {
        switch (pDoc->sInput[ctr])
          {
            case '\r' :
              { cyChar+= (textStruct.tmHeight +
                ➥textStruct.tmExternalLeading);
                cxChar=0;
                break; }
            case '\b' :
              { if (cxChar != 0)     // Back up if not at start of
                  { cxChar -= textStruct.tmAveCharWidth; // line
```

```
                        pDC->TextOut(cxChar, cyChar, "  ", 2);
                        pDoc->sInput =
                          pDoc->sInput.Left(pDoc->
                          ➥sInput.GetLength());
                                    // Removed rightmost character
                        cxyCaret.x -= cxChar; // Adjust caret posit'n
                    }
                break;
            }
            default:
                { pDC->TextOut(cxChar, cyChar,
                ➥pDoc->sInput.Mid(ctr), 1);
                // The average character width will cause some
                // spacing problems but it's OK for now
                cxChar += textStruct.tmAveCharWidth;
                break;
                }
            }
        }
    cxyCaret.x = cxChar+2;
    cxyCaret.y = cyChar;
    SetCaretPos(cxyCaret);
    ShowCaret();
}
/////////////////////////////////////////////////////////////
// CFilesView printing

BOOL CFilesView::OnPreparePrinting(CPrintInfo* pInfo)
{
    // default preparation
    return DoPreparePrinting(pInfo);
}

void CFilesView::OnBeginPrinting(CDC* /*pDC*/,
➥CPrintInfo* /*pInfo*/)
{
    // TODO: add extra initialization before printing
}
```

Answers

```
void CFilesView::OnEndPrinting(CDC* /*pDC*/,
➥CPrintInfo* /*pInfo*/)
{
    // TODO: add cleanup after printing
}

/////////////////////////////////////////////////////////////////
// CFilesView diagnostics

#ifdef _DEBUG
void CFilesView::AssertValid() const
{
    CView::AssertValid();
}

void CFilesView::Dump(CDumpContext& dc) const
{
    CView::Dump(dc);
}

CFilesDoc* CFilesView::GetDocument() // non-debug version is
                                      // inline
{
    ASSERT(m_pDocument->IsKindOf(RUNTIME_CLASS(CFilesDoc)));
    return (CFilesDoc*)m_pDocument;
}
#endif //_DEBUG

/////////////////////////////////////////////////////////////////
// CFilesView message handlers

void CFilesView::OnChar(UINT nChar, UINT nRepCnt, UINT nFlags)
{
  // TODO: Add your message handler code here and/or call
  // default
    CFilesDoc* pDoc = GetDocument();
    pDoc->sInput += nChar;
    pDoc->SetModifiedFlag();   // The user modified the
                                // window's data
```

```
        Invalidate();
        SendMessage(WM_PAINT);
}
```

Answers for Bonus Chapter 4, "Graphics and Visual C++"

Quiz

1. Picture element.

2. The y coordinate.

3. (0,0).

4. `GetDeviceCaps()`.

5. `SetPixel()`.

6. A pen draws only the outline of shapes, whereas the brush fills the inside of shapes.

7. There are six defined hatching patterns, but the MFC also supplies more advanced functions that enable you to define your own hatching patterns.

8. False. There is no `Square()` function. The `Rectangle()` draws perfect squares if you pass to `Rectangle()` the coordinates of a square.

Exercise

1. The files PICVIEW.H and PICVIEW.CPP are the only files you need to modify. Here is PICVIEW.H:

```
// picview.h : interface of the CPicView class
//
/////////////////////////////////////////////////////////////

class CPicView : public CView
{
protected: // create from serialization only
    CPicView();
```

Answers

```cpp
        DECLARE_DYNCREATE(CPicView)

// Attributes
public:
    CPicDoc* GetDocument();
    CPoint cxyMouse[1000];   // Added to track mouse
                             // coordinates for turning on pixels.
                             // You can display up to 1000 pixels
                             // clicked with the mouse
    int numPix;

// Operations
public:

// Implementation
public:
    virtual ~CPicView();
    virtual void OnDraw(CDC* pDC);  // overridden to draw
                                    // this view
#ifdef _DEBUG
    virtual void AssertValid() const;
    virtual void Dump(CDumpContext& dc) const;
#endif

protected:

    // Printing support
    virtual BOOL OnPreparePrinting(CPrintInfo* pInfo);
    virtual void OnBeginPrinting(CDC* pDC, CPrintInfo* pInfo);
    virtual void OnEndPrinting(CDC* pDC, CPrintInfo* pInfo);

// Generated message map functions
protected:
    //{{AFX_MSG(CPicView)
    afx_msg void OnLButtonDown(UINT nFlags, CPoint point);
    //}}AFX_MSG
    DECLARE_MESSAGE_MAP()
};
```

```
#ifndef _DEBUG   // debug version in picview.cpp
inline CPicDoc* CPicView::GetDocument()
   { return (CPicDoc*)m_pDocument; }
#endif
```

//

You must define an array of points or the view will display the mouse cursor's current pixel location only. Therefore, PICVIEW.H defines an array of CPoint objects and an integer member named numPix to keep track of how many pixels the user has clicked on.

PICVIEW.H first sets the numPix value to zero in the CPicView() constructor function. Then, the OnLButtonDown() function (whose skeleton was added with ClassWizard) adds the user's mouse coordinate to the pixel array each time the user clicks the mouse. The OnDraw() then redraws the array of pixel locations on each screen update. Here is the PICVIEW.CPP file listing:

```
// picview.cpp : implementation of the CPicView class
//

#include "stdafx.h"
#include "pic.h"

#include "picdoc.h"
#include "picview.h"

#ifdef _DEBUG
#undef THIS_FILE
static char BASED_CODE THIS_FILE[] = __FILE__;
#endif

/////////////////////////////////////////////////////////////////
// CPicView

IMPLEMENT_DYNCREATE(CPicView, CView)

BEGIN_MESSAGE_MAP(CPicView, CView)
    //{{AFX_MSG_MAP(CPicView)
    ON_WM_LBUTTONDOWN()
```

Answers

```
        //}}AFX_MSG_MAP
        // Standard printing commands
        ON_COMMAND(ID_FILE_PRINT, CView::OnFilePrint)
        ON_COMMAND(ID_FILE_PRINT_PREVIEW,
          ➥CView::OnFilePrintPreview)
END_MESSAGE_MAP()

/////////////////////////////////////////////////////////////////
// CPicView construction/destruction

CPicView::CPicView()
{
        // TODO: add construction code here
        numPix = 0;  // Initializes the number of pixels
}

CPicView::~CPicView()
{
}


/////////////////////////////////////////////////////////////////
// CPicView drawing
void CPicView::OnDraw(CDC* pDC)
{
        CPicDoc* pDoc = GetDocument();
        ASSERT_VALID(pDoc);

        // TODO: add draw code for native data here
        CClientDC devCon(this);
        // Turn on a pixel at the mouse click's location
        for (int ctr=0; ctr<numPix; ctr++)
        {
          devCon.SetPixel(cxyMouse[ctr].x, cxyMouse[ctr].y,
          ➥RGB(0, 0, 0));
        }
}

/////////////////////////////////////////////////////////////////
// CPicView printing
```

```
BOOL CPicView::OnPreparePrinting(CPrintInfo* pInfo)
{
    // default preparation
    return DoPreparePrinting(pInfo);
}

void CPicView::OnBeginPrinting(CDC* /*pDC*/,
➥CPrintInfo* /*pInfo*/)
{
    // TODO: add extra initialization before printing
}

void CPicView::OnEndPrinting(CDC* /*pDC*/,
➥CPrintInfo* /*pInfo*/)
{
    // TODO: add cleanup after printing
}

/////////////////////////////////////////////////////////////
// CPicView diagnostics

#ifdef _DEBUG
void CPicView::AssertValid() const
{
    CView::AssertValid();
}

void CPicView::Dump(CDumpContext& dc) const
{
    CView::Dump(dc);
}

CPicDoc* CPicView::GetDocument() // non-debug version is inline
{
    ASSERT(m_pDocument->IsKindOf(RUNTIME_CLASS(CPicDoc)));
    return (CPicDoc*)m_pDocument;
}
#endif //_DEBUG
```

Answers

```
/////////////////////////////////////////////////////////////////
// CPicView message handlers

void CPicView::OnLButtonDown(UINT nFlags, CPoint point)
{
    // TODO: Add your message handler code here and/or call
    // default

   // cxyMouse is defined in PICVW.H as a CPoint member variable
    cxyMouse[numPix].x = point.x;
    cxyMouse[numPix].y = point.y;
    numPix++;
   // You must now tell the view to redraw so the pixel is set4
    Invalidate();
    SendMessage(WM_PAINT);


}
```

Answers for Bonus Chapter 5, "What's Next?"

Quiz

1. False. Although it's true that MFC duplicates most of the API calls, the API calls are more flexible and ultimately more powerful than MFC. MFC provides advanced development support and saves you countless hours over the course of a Windows development project. Nevertheless, the API is there when you want to dive into a Windows internal that the MFC doesn't support exactly the way you prefer. All API calls are available from within your Visual C++ programs.

2. Most competitors are moving not only toward a Visual C++–like development environment but also toward an MFC-style approach to Windows classes.

3. Nothing could be truer. (Right?)

Exercises

Due to the nature of this bonus chapter, no exercises were assigned.

Review of C Concepts

Review of C Concepts

In case it's been a while since you wrote a C program, this appendix gives you a brief refresher on the C language. This by no means replaces a tutorial on C. At the end of this appendix are references for learning C from the ground up if you have never programmed in C.

Before you get started, it's important to realize that Visual C++ compiles regular DOS-based C programs as long as you first save the program file with the extension .C and select MS-DOS application (.EXE) from the **O**ptions **P**roject pull-down menu. (After you compile the DOS-based C program, you must go to a DOS prompt to execute the program by typing its filename.)

The C Difference

C was designed to be a "high low-level" language, meaning that C is more efficient than most high-level programming languages such as QBasic, but C still provides the looping, comparison, and I/O support found in most high-level languages.

C is a succinct language, second only to the older APL language in the number of operators offered. The C programming language is very small with approximately 40 keywords (QBasic has more than 200!), but its rich assortment of operators makes up for the small set of commands.

It is because of the large number of operators and few keywords that many C programs are difficult to read if you don't take the time to add indention, blanks, and extra lines here and there to make the program more readable. Future maintenance is important, and a well-written and well-documented program ensures that you'll be able to make changes later.

The Format of C Programs

Unlike programs written in QBasic, FORTRAN, COBOL, or many other programming languages, a C program is a collection of routines called *functions*. All C programs must contain at least one function named main(). Function names always end in a set of parentheses.

When a C program executes, main() is the first function executed. Although main() doesn't have to go first in the program's list of functions, it is common practice to place it first in all C programs. Usually, main() controls the rest of the program by executing other functions in the program when needed. When you list another function's name inside main(), that function will execute while main() is put on hold.

After a function's first line, which includes its name, parentheses, and optional variables called *parameters* inside the parentheses, you'll find an opening brace, {, and the statements that form the body of the function, followed by a closing brace, }. Here is an example main() function:

```
main()
{
  int i = 4;
  do
  {
    i++;
    printf("i is %d\n", i);
  } while (i<10);
  return;
}
```

As you can see, a function can contain additional sets of braces. Braces always enclose a *block*. A function body is always enclosed in a block, and that block might have additional embedded blocks of code.

If a program contains more than one function, the functions follow each other sequentially in the program listing. A function must always end with a closing brace that matches the opening brace of the function. You can never start a new function before the preceding one ends.

Note: The return statement at the end of a function is optional in most cases. When main() ends, the program ends.

The parentheses after a function name enable you to pass and receive variables between functions.

C Comments

One of the first things you'll notice about a C program is the format of the comments. All C program comments begin with a /* and end with a */. C comments can go virtually anywhere in a C program (even between keywords on the same line), but most C programmers put comments on lines by themselves or to the right of code. Listing E.1 shows a sample C program with ample comments.

Review of C Concepts

Listing E.1. A C program with C comments.

```c
/* A C program */
/* This program prints some integers inside a loop */
#include <stdio.h>
main()
{
  int i = 4;   /* Defines and initializes i */
  do {
    i++;
    printf("i is %d\n", i);   /* Print i's value */
  } while (i<10);             /* Quit looping when i reaches 10 */
  return;
}
```

Note: You cannot nest one set of comments inside another. Although some compilers, including Visual C++, support nested C comments, nesting C comments does not follow the ANSI C standard and could hamper future maintenance.

Preprocessor Directives

When you see a statement in a C program that begins with a pound sign, #, that statement is not technically a C statement but a *preprocessor directive*. A preprocessor directive instructs the C compiler to do something special before the program listing is compiled. The two most common C preprocessor directives are

`#include`

and

`#define`

The `#include` directive instructs C to merge an additional file, called a *header file*, into your program. In Listing E.1, you'll find this line:

`#include <stdio.h>`

This `#include` directive merges the file named STDIO.H from disk and replaces the `#include` line with the contents of the file. Then, the C compiler compiles the program. Although some C compilers enable you to see the expanded version of your file after the `#include` has taken place, you generally never see the results of the `#include`. After the compiler finishes compiling your program, it restores the text of your original source code.

Note: There is rarely a reason for you to look at the expanded source file that results after the `#include` takes place. Generally, you'll include built-in header files that come with the C compiler. The STDIO.H header file included in Listing E.1 helps the program produce input and output when needed.

The second preprocessor directive, `#define`, appears in many C programs. `#define` defines named constant values in C programs. `#define` is also used in some advanced C programs to write *defined macros,* or sections of code that replace other sections of code when needed. As explained in Day 2's chapter, "C++ Is Superior!," Visual C++ provides `const` and `inline` as better replacements for `#define`. Any ANSI C standard compiler (including Visual C++) offers support for `const` now that `const` has found so much success in C++. Nevertheless, `#define` is still extremely common in C programs, and some C++ programmers slip a `#define` preprocessor directive into their programs once in a while.

`#define` instructs the C compiler to replace all occurrences of one value with another. Here is a common `#define` directive:

```
#define PI 3.14159
```

PI is a mathematical value that approximately equates to 3.14159. If you were writing programs that used PI, instead of typing `3.14159` everyplace you used the value, you could insert the preceding `#define` statement at the top of the program (preprocessor directives generally appear before the first function, `main()`). Instead of using the actual value, you then could use `PI` in its place everywhere you needed the value.

Note: The advantage that `#define` gives you over using the actual value is that if you want to change the value to something else, such as rounding it down to 3.142, you have to change that value in only one place (the `#define` directive) and the C compiler will replace all occurrences of `PI` with the new value when it next compiles the program.

Review of C Concepts

C Data

Lots of different kinds of data are available in C, but the data types generally fall into those listed in Table E.1.

Table E.1. The primary C data types.

Data Type	Description
char	A single character
int	Integer values (whole numbers from –32768 to 32767)
long	Long integer values (more extreme whole numbers than regular int allows)
float	Floating-point
double	Extra-precision floating-point numbers

Note: There is no string data type in C. If you need to represent strings of data, you have to do so in arrays of characters.

The data types are often listed with the modifiers `short`, `unsigned`, and `signed`. All numeric data is automatically signed, meaning that you can store both positive and negative numbers. (`signed` variables can hold only positive numbers.)

Literal values (often called *constants*) can be characters, integers, long integers, floating-point, and double floating-point values *as well as strings*. In other words, there is not a string variable, but string literals are allowed. You must enclose all single-character literals in single quotation marks and string literals in double quotation marks. These are all character literals:

```
'A'    'a'    '&'    '['    '9'    '~'
```

These are string literals:

```
"A"    "C programs"    "Visual C++"    "576 S. Oak Street"
```

String literals can be empty, `""`. As you can see from the `"A"`, strings can also contain single characters. The difference is that strings must be enclosed in double quotation marks, whereas character literals must be enclosed in single quotation marks.

It's important to get used to the idea that all strings end in an ASCII zero. The ASCII zero value is called all sorts of things: *terminating zero, null zero,* and *binary zero.* The ASCII NULL is often represented as \0 or '\0'. The ASCII zero indicates the end of the string. You never see that terminating zero, however. When you type "Hello" in a program listing, you never type the terminating zero, but it's there. Figure E.1 shows you how "Hello" is stored in memory. There's a zero at the end so that the compiler knows when the string ends.

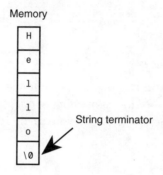

Figure E.1. All strings end in a terminating NULL. Without the NULL, a string is just a collection of individual characters.

 Note: Some languages, such as Basic, store the length of all strings in a table and constantly update the table if the strings change length. C offers more efficiency but adds a little burden to the programmer. You must always be aware of the terminating NULL and make room for the terminating NULL when you store string literals in character arrays.

By the way, if strings contain character zeros, the C compiler knows not to terminate the string at the character zeros. For example, here's a string literal that contains an address:

"1000 South Fern Ave."

The zeros in the 1000 are character zeros. They appear in the ASCII table (Appendix A provides a complete listing of an ASCII table) at location 48. The first character in the ASCII table is the *NULL* character, located at ASCII location 0. It is that NULL character that terminates all strings, thus the name *ASCII 0* for the string terminator.

Review of C Concepts

Put Variables First!

Before you do anything else in a block, you must define all variables used in the block. Unlike with C++, you can define variables only at the top of a block of code, not in the middle of a block. Use the keywords found in Table E.1 to define variables.

For example, the following first few lines of main() define three kinds of variables:

```
main()
{
  int i;
  char c;
  double x;
  /* Rest of program follows */
```

C does not automatically store zeros in automatic variables. You have no idea what is in a variable until you store something in one. If you want to put values in the three variables defined here, i, c, and x, you can do so by including statements like these:

```
i = 14;
c = 'A';
x = -12122.455437;
```

Note: All C statements end in semicolons, ;. You don't end C comments or function names with semicolons, but all executable statements, such as variable definitions, assignments, I/O, and looping statements, must terminate with a semicolon or you'll receive a compile error.

C enables you to combine variable definition and initialization into the same statements. The previous statements can be shortened like this:

```
main()
{
  int i = 14;
  char c = 'A';
  double x = -12122.455437;
  /* Rest of program follows */
```

After you define the variables, you can assign values to them using the standard math operators. Here are a few sample assignment statements:

```
x = 43.45 + 19.0 - 18.2833 * 4.3 / 5.6;
i = 5 + i + 15 - 33 / 11;
```

When you need to group several values together in an array, use brackets in C for array subscripts. An array is a list of variable values, not single variables. The following statements show you how to define and initialize arrays:

```
int iAra1[10];   /* Defines an array of 10 values */
/* The next statement defines and initializes */
int iAra2[10] = {4, 2, 6, 9, 0, 1, 3, 7, 2, 5};
/* The next statement stores characters in a character array */
char cAra1[5]  = {'T', 'P', 'U', 'L', 'A'};
/* The next statement stores a string in a character array */
char cAta[11] = "Visual C++"; /* Leaves room for null zero */
```

All array subscripts begin at zero. The following code initializes three integer array values:

```
int ara[3];   /* Define the array */
ara[0] = 20;  /* Store values in each element */
ara[1] = 30;
ara[2] = 40;
```

Input/Output

C does not contain commands for input and output (I/O). You must call built-in library functions to perform I/O. The built-in function most often used for C output is `printf()`, and the one most used for C input is `scanf()`.

Before you can print values with `printf()`, you must format using format codes like those in Table E.2. The format codes describe how C is to interpret the data you want printed. The `printf()` function cannot automatically decide what kind of data you are printing, so you must tell the compiler the printed data types with the format codes.

Table E.2. Format codes used to input and output values.

Format Code	Description
%d	Integer
%f	Floating-point
%c	Character
%s	String

Review of C Concepts

There are more format codes, but the ones in Table E.2 are the most common. A couple of example `printf()` statements will show you how the function works:

The statement

```
printf("My age is %d.", ageVar);
```

produces this output (assuming that the integer variable `ageVar` contains 18):

```
My age is 18.
```

The statement

```
printf("My name is %s and I make %f an hour.", "Sandy", 7.87);
```

produces this output (no variables are used here, just literal values):

```
My name is Sandy and I make 7.870000 an hour.
```

Oops—the floating-point literal, 7.87, comes out with too many zeros. If you want to limit the number of decimal places printed (C typically defaults to printing seven significant digits unless you override the default), insert a decimal and number between the `%` and `f` like this:

```
printf("My name is %s and I make %.2f an hour.", "Sandy", 7.87);
```

This `printf()` now produces this output:

```
My name is Sandy and I make 7.87 an hour.
```

Figure E.2 shows how each of the format codes matches the data being printed.

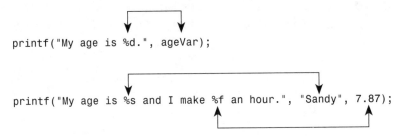

Figure E.2. The format codes tell C how to print your data.

There are a few additional output control codes called *escape sequences* that you'll often find inside `printf()` function calls. Table E.3 lists these escape sequences.

Table E.3. Escape sequences that control output.

Escape Sequence	Description
\n	Newline (carriage return and line feed)
\a	Alarm (rings the PC's bell)
\t	Tab to the next tab stop

printf() does not automatically send the cursor to the next line. These four printf()s all print on the same line:

```
printf("This ");
printf("is ");
printf("output ");
printf("to the screen.");
```

If you wanted the output to appear on different lines, you would have to add \n at where you wanted the new lines to occur. The following modified printf()s

```
printf("This\n");
printf("is\n");
printf("output\n");
printf("to the screen.");
```

produce this:

```
This
is
output
to the screen.
```

scanf() is one of the most difficult built-in functions available. C programmers are always relieved to learn about Visual C++'s cin replacement for scanf(). For a quick review, here are points to remember about scanf():

- scanf() is the mirror-image function to printf(). Both require format codes that describe variables.

- Instead of outputting data from variables as printf() does, scanf() inputs values from the keyboard and stores those values in the variables listed.

- You must precede all non-array variables inside the printf() parentheses with an ampersand, &.

Review of C Concepts

☐ Don't use floating-point decimal codes inside format codes. For example, when inputting floating-point variables, you would use %f, not %.1f.

Here is a program that uses both `printf()` and `scanf()` (notice that STDIO.H is properly included):

```c
#include <stdio.h>
main()
{
  int age = 20;
  char name[5] = "Thom";
  float weight = 166.7;
  /* Print the current values */
  printf("My name is %s.\nI am %d years old.\n", name, age);
  printf("I weigh %.1f.\n", weight);
  /* Now, ask for new values */
  printf("Enter a new age: ");
  scanf("%d", &age);     /* Get a new age from the user */
  printf("Enter a new weight: ");
  scanf("%f", &weight);
  printf("Enter a new name: ");
  scanf("%s", name);     /* Notice no & is used due to the array */
  printf("These are the values you entered:\n");
  printf("name: %s\n", name);
  printf("age: %d\n", age);
  printf("weight: %.1f\n", weight);
};
```

Here is one possible run of the program:

```
My name is Thom.
I am 20 years old.
I weigh 166.7.
Enter a new age: 40
Enter a new weight: 120.3
Enter a new name: Mary
These are the values you entered:
name: Mary
age: 40
weight: 120.3
```

The program brings up an interesting and bad side effect that can occur when you use arrays. Unlike most programming languages, C never checks for array boundaries. Therefore, the name entered must be four or fewer characters to fit in the name array. (The fifth character is the null zero that C stores when a name is entered using %s.) If you type a name longer than four characters, the data overrides other data and produces bad results because the other variables can be overwritten.

Note: Before using `printf()` and `scanf()`, you should include the STDIO.H header file that comes supplied with C compilers.

Although there is more to C I/O, that's all you need to know for this review. Visual C++'s `cin` and `cout` offer I/O mechanisms vastly superior to the built-in STDIO.H library functions.

Note: If you want to clear your screen, insert the Visual C++ ANSI-compatible STDLIB.H header file, and issue the following statement before your first `printf()`:

```
system("cls");   /* Calls DOS's erase-screen command */
```

Operators

As mentioned earlier, the C language contains lots of operators. Table E.4 contains the primary math operators.

Table E.4. C's primary math operators.

Operator	Description
+	Addition
-	Subtraction
*	Multiplication
/	Division or integer division
%	Modulus or remainder

Most of the primary operators work like their equivalents in math or other programming languages. The division operator performs integer division if integer operands appear on each side of the division operator; it produces a floating-point result if a non-integer appears on either side. Study these examples:

Review of C Concepts

```
i = 4 + 5;    /* Puts a 9 in i */
i = 5 - 4;    /* Puts a 1 in i */
i = 5 * 4;    /* Puts a 20 in i */
i = 20 / 4;   /* Puts an integer 5 in i */
i = 20 / 3;   /* Puts an integer 6 in i */
i = 20 % 3;   /* Puts a 2 in i (the integer remainder) */
x = 20.0 / 3.0; /* Puts a 6.667 in x */
```

Additional Math Operators

C attempts to help streamline your programming routine by adding operators not found in other languages. The compound, increment, and decrement operators all shortcut what you would do in other programming languages. Table E.5 lists these additional math operators.

Table E.5. Additional math operators.

Operator	Description
+=	Compound addition
-=	Compound subtraction
*=	Compound multiplication
/=	Compound division
++	Increment
--	Decrement

These operators are most useful when updating values already in variables. For example, if you want to increase a variable by 15 percent, you would normally put that variable on both sides of the equal sign like this:

```
price = price * 1.15;  /* Increase whatever's in price */
```

The compound operators keep you from having to repeat the variable name on both sides of the equal sign. The preceding statement becomes this:

```
price *= 1.15;  /* Increase whatever's in price */
```

When you want to add 1 or subtract 1 from variables, you generally do this:

```
i = i + 1;  /* Add 1 to i */
```

and

```
k = k - 1;   /* Subtract 1 from k */
```

Both of these statements are shortened using the increment and decrement operators:

```
i++;   /* Add 1 to i */
```

and

```
k--;   /* Subtract 1 from k */
```

The increment and decrement operators can appear on either side of the variable. Their placement can produce slightly different results when other values are involved in the expression. For instance, the code

```
i = 15;
j = i++ * 2;
printf("%i, %j\n", i, j);
```

produces this output:

```
16, 30
```

At first, you might wonder why i didn't get incremented before it was multiplied by 2. Because the ++ operator appeared to the right of i, C waits until the entire expression is evaluated before incrementing the i. If you list the ++ before the i, like

```
i = 15;
j = ++i * 2;
printf("%i, %j\n", i, j);
```

you get the following output:

```
16, 32
```

Notice that the i is incremented before the multiplication.

Note: Putting increment and decrement operators before variable names is called *prefix notation*. Putting increment and decrement operators after variable names is called *postfix notation*.

Be sure to follow the order of operators found in Appendix C (the order is the same for both C and Visual C++, except for the addition of extra operators to Visual C++).

Review of C Concepts

The Relational and Logical Operators

Most of C's relational operators work like their equivalents in other programming languages. Table E.6 lists the relational operators and their meanings.

Table E.6. The relational operators.

Relational Operator	Description
==	Equality
>	Greater than
<	Less than
>=	Greater than or equal to
<=	Less than or equal to
!=	Not equal to

Note: The most important relational operator to key in on at this time is the equality operator. The double equal, ==, is used only for equal comparisons, and the regular equal, =, is used only for assignment. Never attempt to test a value for equality like this:

```
if (i = 5)      /* NO! 5 is assigned to i */
```

/C also provides the logical operators shown in Table E.7 that combine one or more relational operators.

Table E.7. The logical operators.

Logical Operator	Description
&&	AND
||	OR
!	NOT

The relational and logical operators all produce true and false results. (In C, a true result can be any nonzero, and a false result is always 0.)

Testing Data

The if, while, do-while, and for statements all utilize the relational and logical operators to control their loops. Here is the format of each of these statements:

```
if (condition)
   { block of one or more C statements; }
else
   { block of one or more C statements; }
```

Note: The else portion of the if is optional and might or might not be needed by your application. You *must* enclose the condition inside parentheses. The condition must be enclosed in parentheses for all the looping statements that follow as well. if is not a loop, unlike the other three kinds of statements.

```
while (condition)
   { block of one or more C statements; }

do
   { block of one or more C statements; }
while (condition)

for (startExpression; testExpression; countExpression)
   { block of one or more C statements; }
```

Review of C Concepts

The difference between the `while` statement and the `do-while` statement is that the do-while statement always executes at least once because the conditional test appears at the bottom of the loop. The `while`'s conditional test occurs at the top of the loop and could possibly be false upon entry to the `while` loop.

Here is a program that shows the `while` loop:

```
#include <stdio.h>
main()
{
  int i = 5;
  while (i < 10)
    { printf("Ring...\a\n");  /* Rings the PC bell each iteration */
      i++;
    }
  return;
}
```

Here is the program's output (each time a line is printed, the PC's bell rings):

```
Ring...
Ring...
Ring...
Ring...
Ring...
```

Here is the same program using do-while:

```
#include <stdio.h>
main()
{
  int i = 5;
  do
     { printf("Ring...\a\n");  /* Rings the PC bell each iteration */
       i++;
     }  while (i <= 10);
  return;
}
```

Both of these programs loop five times because the loop control variable, i, begins at 5 and continues incrementing each time through the loop until it reaches 10.

The `for` loop provides a more determinate way of looping. Instead of controlling the variable values inside the loop as done with `while`, the `for` statement controls the values. Here is a `for` loop that counts up from 1 to 10. Notice that the first line in the loop initializes the loop variable ctr, tests the loop variable each time through the loop, and increments the loop variable each time through the loop.

```
for (ctr=1; ctr<=10; ctr++)
  { printf("%d\n", i); }
```

If you want to exit a loop early, use the break statement. Any time any of the loops reaches a break, the loop terminates early, and the statement following the last line of the loop takes over control.

Another related control command is the switch statement. Instead of embedding an if within an if, the switch often provides a cleaner way of testing several values. Here is the format of switch:

```
switch (expression)
  { case (expression1) : {Block of C statement(s);
                          break;}
    case (expression2) : {Block of C statement(s);
                          break;}
    case (expression3) : {Block of C statement(s);
                          break;}
    default:             {Block of C statement(s);
                          break;}
}
```

The break after each case is not required, but it almost always appears to keep execution from falling through to the next case. The switch statement is useful for testing several conditions. Here is a program that prints a department name based on the department code entered:

```
#include <stdio.h>
main()
{
  int deptCode;
  printf("What is your department code (1-5)? ");
  scanf("%d", &deptCode);
  switch (deptCode)
  { case (1) : printf("You're accounting.\n");
               break;
    case (2) : printf("You're engineering.\n");
               break;
    case (3) : printf("You're marketing.\n");
               break;
    case (4) : printf("You're data processing.\n");
               break;
    case (5) : printf("You're payroll.\n");
               break;
    default:   printf("You didn't enter a correct department code!\n");
               break;
  }
  return;
}
```

Review of C Concepts

Here's a sample run of this program:

```
What is your department code (1-5)? 2
You're engineering.
```

The `case` value that matches the `switch` value determines which set of statements executes. Without `switch`, you would have to test with several layers of `if` and `else` statements. The `default` case takes care of everything that doesn't match, as shown in this execution of the program:

```
What is your department code (1-5)? 23
You didn't enter a correct department code!
```

Pointers

A C pointer variable doesn't contain a data value, but contains the address of a data value. When defining pointers, you must use a dereferencing operator, *, like this:

```
int i = 15;   /* Regular variable */
int * ipt;    /* Pointer variable */
```

Note: C will not confuse the dereference with multiplication because of the context in which you use each one.

As with regular variables, garbage resides in pointer variables until you store something in them. The address-of operator, &, helps fill pointers with values. The following statement assigns the address of `i` to the variable `ipt`:

```
ipt = &i;
```

Figure E.3 shows how these variables logically appear in memory.

Memory Address	Memory Contents
1000	i=15
1001	
1002	
1003	ipt=1000

Figure E.3. The pointer variable contains the address of `i`.

A C array name is nothing more than a pointer variable that points to a list of items. When you work with or print an array, you are actually working with a pointer to the data.

896

Pointers are most useful when you allocate and deallocate heap memory. C uses the built-in library functions `malloc()` and `free()` to allocate and deallocate memory to and from the heap. The heap is all unused memory in your computer not currently in use by your other variables, your program, and your operating system. Instead of defining arrays of variables, you can reserve (with `malloc()`) and point to memory on the heap with pointer variables. That way, you consume memory only when you need it rather than for your entire program's run as you do with regular variables.

When you are finished with heap memory, you can throw it back to the heap's free area (for other tasks such as the operating system, for other users if you use a PC network server, or for your own program later) with `free()`.

Visual C++ offers `new` and `delete` operators that completely replace `malloc()` and `free()`. `new` and `delete` offer many additional benefits over `malloc()` and `free()`, including the best advantage to newcomers, which is their simpler notation. Therefore, as long as you have an idea of the need of the heap, you'll be better off learning `new` and `delete` and forgetting about C's `malloc()` and `free()`.

For Further Reading

If you want a more detailed introduction and tutorial on the C language, check out the following Sams titles. They walk the newcomer to C from absolute beginning status to expert, and they give anyone a solid foundation in non-OOP programming. If your C skills are rusty or nonexistent, you'll master Visual C++ easier if you tackle the groundwork presented by these titles.

Absolute Beginner's Guide to C

Written by this author, the book takes a lighthearted look at the C programming language. Helpful tips, notes, and cautions steer you along as you cover the basics of C. Fun facts, technical sections, and daily reviews make the journey easier, and your acquired knowledge is brought together with a fun blackjack program at the end of the book. (Beginning)

Teach Yourself C in 21 Days

With this best-selling book, users can achieve C success now! Each lesson can be completed in two to three hours or less. Shaded syntax boxes, Q&A sections, and "Do's and Don'ts" sections reinforce the important topics within C. (Beginning to Intermediate)

Review of C Concepts

Advanced C

Here's the next step for programmers who want to improve their C programming skills. This book gives efficiency tips as well as techniques for debugging C programs and improving their speed, memory usage, and readability. (Intermediate to Advanced)

Glossary

Glossary

Abstract Base Class A base class that contains at least one pure virtual function.

Alias Created with a reference operator (&), two or more variables that refer to the same memory location.

API Stands for Application Programming Interface. Visual C++ supplies several kinds of API libraries that enable you to call Microsoft Windows, NT, ODBC, and OLE routines. An API places a layer between you and the actual low-level code to enable you to call higher-level functions without knowing all the internals of Microsoft Windows or whatever API you are using.

App Studio A Visual C++ tool that enables you to create and bind resources to your Visual C++ program.

AppWizard The Visual C++ code generator that automatically generates a shell of a Microsoft Windows program to save you time.

Argument A constant or variable passed from one function to another.

ASCII Acronym for American Standard Code for Information Interchange. ASCII is a common PC system for collating characters.

AT&T The company that developed the first C++ compiler and whose C++ standard is still followed today by compilers such as Visual C++.

Automatic Variables The default duration for local variables indicating that the variables will lose their values when they go out of scope (when their block ends).

Base Class Sometimes called the *parent class,* a base class is the first class or top class in a hierarchy of derived classes.

Binary Zero Another name for the null terminating zero that ends strings.

Block One or more statements treated as though they are a single statement. A block is always enclosed in braces, { and }.

Browser The menu-driven browser feature of Visual C++ enables you to browse (step through) and quickly locate many aspects of your Visual C++ applications, such as functions and classes.

Byte A basic unit of data storage and manipulation. A byte is equivalent to eight bits and can contain a value ranging from 0 to 255.

Child Class Sometimes called a *derived class,* a child class is created from another class and inherits all the protected and private members of the base class.

Class A Visual C++ structure-like user-defined data type that consists of data members and member functions.

Class Variable   A variable defined from a class.

ClassWizard   A Visual C++ tool that enables you to create, browse, and edit your classes as well as those classes created for you with AppWizard.

CodeView   A Microsoft Windows, NT, and DOS-based debugger that enables you to step through code a line at a time, looking at memory, output, and variables as your program executes.

Comment   A message in a program, ignored by the computer, that tells users what the program does. A Visual C++ comment begins with two slashes, `//`.

Compile   Process of translating a program written in a programming language, such as Visual C++, into machine code that your computer understands.

Composition   Using existing classes as members inside other classes.

Constant   A value that doesn't change throughout the run of a program, defined with the `const` keyword.

Constructor Function   Describes how an object variable is to be created when an object variable first goes into scope.

Copy Constructor   Constructor function that creates and initializes new class variables from an existing class variable.

Data Hiding   The process of limiting access to private members of a class from code outside the class.

Data Member   A data component inside a class or struct.

Declaration   Declares the existence of a data object or function.

Default   A predefined action or command that the computer chooses unless you specify otherwise.

Default Argument List   A list of argument values, listed in a function's prototypes, that determines initial values of the arguments if no values are passed for those arguments.

Definition   Reserves memory for an object variable or function.

Dereference   The process of finding a value to which a pointer variable is pointing.

Derived Class   A class created through inheritance from another class.

Destructor   The function called when a class variable goes out of scope.

Glossary

Dynamic Memory Allocation   The process of allocating memory from the available memory area (called the heap) at runtime.

Early Binding   Resolving function calls at compile time. All function resolution code must be available to the compiler.

Element   An individual value in an array.

Encapsulation   Binding both class code and data into a single object variable.

Event   A mouse click, keystroke, menu selection, or other defined event that triggers Microsoft Windows and Microsoft NT routines.

Exception   A routine you write that occurs automatically when something out of the ordinary occurs. Programmers usually set up exceptions to handle error conditions such as divide-by-zero and memory problems.

Execute   To run a program.

Extraction Operator   The >> operator, which reads stream input. Usually used with the cin object.

File   A collection of data stored as a single unit on a disk.

Filename   A unique name that identifies a file.

Fixed-Length Record   A record in which each field takes the same amount of disk space, even if that field's data value does not fill the field.

Function   A stand-alone routine that performs a specific task in a program. All C++ programs must have at least one function called main(). Some functions are built-in library routines that manipulate data and perform input/output.

Global Variable   A variable that is visible to every statement in the program following the global variable's definition.

Header Files   Files that contain prototypes of Visual C++'s built-in functions.

Hierarchy of Operators   See *Order of Operators*.

Inheritance   The process of deriving classes from other classes without the programmer having to copy and maintain the code in two separate places.

Initialization List   Assigns values to object members as the object is being defined with a constructor function.

Inline Function   A function that compiles as inline code to improve efficiency and save function calling overhead.

Insertion Operator   The << operator, which sends output to a stream. Usually used with the cout object.

I/O   Acronym for Input/Output.

Instantiation   Defining a class object.

Late Binding   Resolving function calls at runtime and not at compile time.

Literal   Data that remains the same during program execution.

Link Editing   The last step the Visual C++ compiler performs to create an executable file.

Local Variable   A variable that is visible to the block in which it is defined.

Maintainability   The capability to change and update programs written in a simple style.

Manipulator   A value used by a program to inform the stream to modify one of its values.

Member   A piece of a class or structure variable that holds a specific type of data or function.

Member Function   A function defined inside a class or structure.

Message   Calling a member function using a class object.

MFC Classes   The Microsoft Foundation Classes supplied with Visual C++ that improve your productivity by offering ready-made graphics, container, and Microsoft Windows classes.

Microsoft NT   A 32-bit operating system, based on the Microsoft Windows environment, that supports modern 32-bit PC architecture.

Microsoft Windows   A graphical user interface (GUI) operating environment that enables you to operate your computer using visual clues as well as commands.

Multiple Inheritance   Deriving classes with more than one parent or base class.

Null Zero   The string-terminating character. All Visual C++ string constants and strings stored in character arrays end in null zero. The ASCII value for the null zero is 0.

Object Visual   C++ variables, usually used for class or structure variables defined in the class as having both data and member functions.

Glossary

Object Code A "halfway step" between source code and a fully compiled executable program. Object code is not directly executable by the computer. It must first be linked in order to resolve external references and address references.

Object Linking and Embedding See *OLE*.

Object-Oriented Programming A programming approach that treats data as objects capable of manipulating themselves.

ODBC Stands for Open Database Connectivity. Starting with Visual C++ Version 1.5, you can call ODBC APIs that access and manipulate data stored by any database program that supports ODBC (such as Microsoft Access).

OLE Stands for Object Linking and Embedding. In OLE terminology, an object is anything a user can manipulate within a Microsoft Windows application, including bitmaps and controls. OLE enables you to write program calls from one application that manipulate the OLE objects within another application. With OLE (now in version 2.0), your user can manipulate an object, such as a Microsoft Excel worksheet, from within your own Visual C++ program.

Operator An operator works on data and performs math calculations or changes data to other data types. Examples include the +, -, and sizeof() operators. With Visual C++, you can create operators that work on your own data types.

Order of Operators Sometimes called the *hierarchy of operators* or the *precedence of operators*. It determines exactly how Visual C++ computes formulas.

Overloading Writing more than one function with the same name. The functions must differ in their argument lists so that Visual C++ can identify which one to call.

Parameter A list of variables enclosed in parentheses that follows the name of a function or procedure. Parameters indicate the number and type of arguments that are sent to the function or procedure.

Parent Class Also called a *base class,* a parent class is a class from which you derive another class.

Passing by Address When an argument (a local variable) is passed by address, the variable's address in memory is sent to, and is assigned to, the receiving function's parameter list. (If more than one variable is passed by address, each of their addresses is sent to and assigned to the receiving function's parameters.) A change made to the parameter in the function also changes the value of the argument variable.

Passing by Copy Another name for *passing by value.*

Passing by Reference Passing an alias value by using the reference operator, &. Passing by reference replaces most needs for passing by address.

Passing by Value By default, all non-array and nonpointer Visual C++ variable arguments are passed *by value*. When the value contained in a variable is passed to the parameter list of a receiving function, changes made to the parameter in the routine do not change the value of the argument variable. Also called *passing by copy*.

Pointer A variable that holds the address of another variable.

Polymorphism Greek, meaning "many forms." Polymorphism generally refers to the process of Visual C++ objects deciding which functions to call at runtime.

Preprocessor Directive A command, preceded by a #, placed in source code that directs the compiler to modify the source code in some fashion. The two most common preprocessor directives are `#define` and `#include`.

Private Class Member A class member inaccessible except to other class members.

Project A collection of one or more header files and programs that work together to form an application.

Protected Class Member A class member inaccessible except to other class members or inherited members.

Prototype The definition of a function, including its name, return type, and parameter list.

Public Class Member A class member accessible to any function outside the class.

Pure Virtual Function A virtual function that contains no code but acts as a guide for other derived functions through inheritance.

Random-Access File Records in a file that can be accessed in any order you want.

Relational Operators Operators that compare data and tell how two variables or constants relate to each other. They tell you whether two variables are equal or not equal, or which one is less than or more than the other.

Resource A Microsoft Windows or NT element such as a menu, dialog box, picture, or cursor.

Sequential File A file that has to be accessed one record at a time, beginning with the first record.

Serialize A convenient way for you to store and retrieve objects to and from disk files.

Glossary

Single Inheritance   Deriving classes with only one parent or base class.

Source Code   The Visual C++ language instructions you write that the Visual C++ compiler translates into object code.

Standard Input Device   The target of each `cin` and input function. Normally the keyboard unless diverted by the operating system.

Standard Output Device   The target of each `cout` and output function. Normally the screen, unless diverted by the operating system.

Static Data Member   A member that exists only once no matter how many class variables you define. Static members belong to the class, not an individual object variable.

Static Member Functions   Functions that have access only to static data members of a class.

Static Variables   Variables that do not lose their values when the block in which they are defined ends.

Stream   Literally, a stream of characters, one following another, flowing among devices in your computer.

String   One or more characters terminated with a null zero.

Structure   A unit of related information containing one or more members, such as an employee number, employee name, employee address, employee pay rate, and so on. Most Visual C++ programmers use classes in place of structures.

Template   A class model from which some C++ compilers can generate other classes. Neither version 1.0 nor version 1.5 of Visual C++ supports templates.

Type Cast   Temporarily converting one object to another data type.

Variable   Data that can change as the program runs.

Variable-Length Record   A record that wastes no space on the disk. When a field's data value is saved to the file, the next field's data value is stored after it. There is usually a special separating character between the fields so that your programs know where the fields begin and end.

Variable Scope   Sometimes called the *visibility of variables,* this describes how variables are "seen" by your program. See also *Global Variable* and *Local Variable.*

Virtual Functions   Allow polymorphism by defining a function called by an object at runtime (late binding) instead of at compile time (early binding).

Index

Symbols

! (NOT) operator, 892
!= (not equal to) operator, 892-893
   overloading, 315-321
% (modulus) operator, 889-890
   overloading, 310-315
%= (compound modulus) operator,
   overloading, 321-327
& (address of) operator, defining references, 97
&& (AND) operator, 892
   overloading, 315-321
* (multiplication) operator, 889-890
   overloading, 310-315
*= (compound multiplication) operator, 890-891
   overloading, 321-327
+ (addition) operator, 889-890
   overloading, 190-191, 307-315
++ (increment) operator, 890-891
   overloading, 330-334
+= (compound addition) operator, 890-891
   overloading, 321-327
- (subtraction) operator, 889-890
   overloading, 310-315
-- (decrement) operator, 890-891
   overloading, 330-334
-= (compound subtraction) operator, 890-891
   overloading, 321-327
. (dot) operator, 283
/ (division) operator, 889-890
   overloading, 310-315
// (comment specifier), 29-30
/= (compound division) operator, 890-891
   overloading, 321-327
:: (scope resolution) operator, 40-42, 257-258
; (semicolon), 884
< (less than) operator, 892-893
   overloading, 315-321
<< (inserter) operator, 63-64, 903
   example program, 69-70
   overloading, 345-352
<= (less than or equal to) operator, 892-893
   overloading, 315-321
== (equal to) operator, 892-893
   overloading, 315-321
> (greater than) operator, 892-893
   overloading, 315-321
>= (greater than or equal to) operator, 892-893
   overloading, 315-321
>> (extractor) operator, 66-68, 902
   example program, 69-70
   overloading, 353-358
|| (OR) operator, 892
   overloading, 315-321
16-bit Windows, 777

A

About dialog box, 677-688
abstract base classes, 900
abstract data types, 210-217
   building, 211-214
   nested, 214-217
access functions, 249
access specifiers, 226-229
   base classes, 465-466
   derived classes, 464
   mixing, 229-233
   protected, 471-472
ACCESS.CPP source code, 464
ADDEMP.CPP source code, 190-191
addition (+) operator, 889-890
   overloading, 190-191, 307-315
ADDREF.CPP source code, 151-152

address of (&) operator, defining references, 97
addToInv( ) member function, 593
aggregate data types, 30
aliases, 900
    read-only, 108-109
ALLFAIL.CPP source code, 139-140
ALLINIT.CPP source code, 125
ALLINIT2.CPP source code, 128
allocating
    data members with constructors, 380-381
    dynamic memory allocation, 118-121, 732-733, 902
        exception handlers, 138-140
        fragmentation, 126-127
        initializing heap, 124-126
        matrixes, 135-137
        new operator, 116-124
        strings, 122-124
AND (&&) operator, 892
    overloading, 315-321
ANSI, 6
ANSI C++ standard, exception handling, 557-558
API functions, exception handling, 568, 900
App Studio, 624-626, 900
    resources, changing, 678-681, 688
appending data to sequential files, 589-591
applications
    displaying characters from strings, 719-720
    File Open codes, 725-726
    File Save codes, 725-726
    generating, 716
    keystroke handlers, 716-718
    PIC, creating, 744-745
    print/print preview capabilities, 712-715
    text
        displaying, 718-723
        saving, 728-729
    see also programs
AppWizard, 626-629, 646-649, 900
    adding print/print preview capabilities to applications, 712-715
    building projects, 650
    file I/O, 651, 715-731
    PIC application, creating, 744-745
    running programs, 650-651
    serialization, 724
AppWizard Options dialog box, 648
AREACOMP.CPP source code, 34-35
argc command-line argument, 164
argument lists, member functions, 253
arguments, 900
    command-line arguments, 163-167
    constructors, 381-386
    default
        argument lists, 156-159
        construct arguments, 384-386
        multiple, 159-163
        specifying, 162-163
    GetDeviceCaps( ) function, 749
    init( ) function, 253
    overloaded operator member functions, 303
    passing
        by address, 147-148, 904
        by copy, 904
        by reference, 146-154, 905
        by value, 147-148, 905
    variable-length argument lists, 167-171
ARRADD.CPP source code, 150-151
arrays
    allocating memory, 122
        matrixes, 135-137
    boundaries, 888

constant arrays, 102-103
constructing, 391-394
deallocating memory, 128-129
defining (C programming language), 885
destructing, 392-393
initializing (C programming language), 885
multidimensional, 135-137
names, 106
    C programming language, 896
passing by address, 150-151
ASCII, 900
assembly-line programming, 247-248
assignments
composed objects, 521-527
memberwise, 521
associating resources with code, 629-630
AT&T, 7, 900
atoi( ) function, 167
automatic variables, 407, 900

B

bad( ) member function, 587-588
base classes, 452-454, 900
abstract base class, 900
access specifiers, 465-466
constructing, 482-484
    from derived classes, 488-490
defining objects, 469-470
destructing objects, 483-484
base-conversion manipulators, 74-75
BASES.CPP source code, 74-75
BASESHOW.CPP source code, 80
BEV.CPP source code, 429-431
BEV.H header file, 431
BEVCLIMP.CPP source code, 432-433
BEVREST.CPP source code, 434

binary zero, 900
binding
early, 534-540
    function calls, 536
late, 534-540
    and virtual functions, 541-545
    function calls, 538-539
see also encapsulation
bitmaps, 624-626
bitwise operators, 343-344
block scope, 222-223
blocks, 900
BOOL data type, 697
boxes, drawing, 752-753
break statement, 895
Breakpoints dialog box, 621-622
breakpoints, setting, 619-622
browser, 630-631, 900
Build Any Changed File tool (Visual Workbench), 611
buySweet( ) member function, 267
buyUnSweet( ) member function, 267
BYTE data type, 697
bytes, 900

C

C programming language, 878
comments, 879-880
data types, 882-883
format of programs, 878-879
functions, calling, 184-186
I/O, 885-889
operators, 889-893
pointers, 896-897
preprocessor directives, 880-881
variables, defining, 884-885
Windows, 773-774
C++ programming language history, 6-7
call stack, 622-623

CALLC.CPP source code, 185
calling
   constructors
      explicitly, 388-390
      timing, 376-381
   destructors, 495-496
      timing, 376-381
   functions
      C language functions, 184-186
      early binding, 536
      late binding, 538-540
   static member functions, 421
capitalization, variable names, 253
Caps lock status bar indicator, 613
CArchiveException, 735-736
carets, 722-723
CARSCLSS.CPP source code, 232-233
cascaded windows, 615
CATCH blocks (MFC exceptions), 732-733, 737-739
Catch( ) function, 569-573
catching exceptions, 569-573
CATHROW.CPP source code, 571-572
CBrush object, 762
CClientDC( ) member function, 747
cerr object, 68-70
CFile class, 737
   exception handling, 737-739
CFileException, 736-737
char data type memory, 36-37
characters
   reading from files, 585-587
   writing to files, 581-585
charAlph class, 334-336
CHARINP.CPP source code, 585-586
CHAROVR.CPP source code, 583
CHARSEQ.CPP source code, 581-582
CHARSIZE.CPP source code, 37
CHARSTR.CPP source code, 582

checkData( ) member function, 265-266
child classes, *see* derived classes
cin object, 66-72
   example program, 69-70
   overloading operators, 342-345
class families, 533-534
   virtual functions, 534
class keyword, 9, 217-219
class scope, 223
class variables, 901
   defining, 219-221, 244
   friend functions, 286
   see also objects
CLASS.CPP source code, 225
classes, 900
   base classes, 452-454, 900
      abstract, 900
      access specifiers, 465-466
      constructing, 482-484, 488-490
      defining objects, 469-470
      destructing objects, 483-484
   CFile, 737-739
   characteristics, 241
   charAlph, 334-336
   child classes, 900
   cleaning up, 257-260
   component classes
      constructing, 507-509
      inheritance, 510-511
   composed classes, 504
   creating from component objects, 519-521
   declarations, inserting functions, 241
   defining pointers to, 245-246
   derived classes, 452-454, 901
      access specifiers, 464
      constructing, 484-486
      defining objects, 469-470
      inheritance, 458-459
      inherited members, 462-469
   efficiency, improving, 260-262

classes–compiling programs

Employee, 459
Float, 334-336
friend classes, 290-293
fstream, 580
grandchild classes, constructing, 490-492
ifstream, 580
instances, 221
Inventory, 478
Lemon, 267-269
MFC classes, 903
    CMainFrame, 654, 658-662, 669
    CString, 698-701
    CTeachApp, 654, 668
    CTeachDoc, 654, 662-664, 669-670
    CTeachView, 654, 665-670
    functionality, adding, 689-698
    naming, 668
ofstream, 580
Person, 451-452, 458, 461
private members, accessing, 282
protecting data, 262-267
public members, 226-229
regClass, 291-292
static data members, 416-422
Stereo, 507-509, 520-521
    class header, 513-519
String, 397-399
versus structures, 222-226
CLASSOBJ.CPP source code, 219-220
CLASSPUB.CPP source code, 227-228
ClassWizard, 629-630, 901
    connecting messages to functions, 702-704
clearing
    CString object contents, 727-728
    screen, 889
clog object, 69

Close( ) member function, 737
closing windows, 22
CLSFUN.CPP source code, 243
CLSFUN2.CPP source code, 244
CLSSCHK.CPP source code, 262-263
CLSSHEAD.CPP source code, 257-258
CLSSINL.CPP source code, 261-262
CMainFrame class, 654, 669
    header file, 658-659
    implementation code, 659-662
CMDARGS.CPP source code, 165
CMDCHK.CPP source code, 166-167
codes, composing with, 506-519
CodeView debugger, 901
    CodeView for DOS, 623
    CodeView for Windows, 623
colored boxes, drawing, 752-753
colors
    pixels, 746-747
    RGB, 746
Column status bar indicator, 613
command-line arguments, 163-167
    specifying from within Visual C++ editor, 166
comments, 13, 28-30, 901
    C programming language, 879-880
compArea( ) function, 34-35
comparing floating-point values, 320-321
COMPHEAD.CPP source code, 507-509
Compile File tool (Visual Workbench), 611
compiler directives, 880-881, 905
    #define
        alternatives, 45-53
        C programming language, 880-881
compiling programs, 16-22, 901
    date and time, determining, 54

component classes
   constructing, 507-509
   inheritance, 510-511
component objects, creating classes with, 519-521
composed objects, 504
   assigning to one another, 521-527
   constructing, 514-517
   constructor initialization lists, 514
composition, 901
   embedded structures, 513
   versus inheritance, 502-506
   with code, 506-519
compound math operators, overloading, 321-327
COMPOV.CPP source code, 322-325
CONSARG.CPP source code, 382-383
CONSARG2.CPP source code, 384-385
CONSDEST.CPP source code, 392-397
CONSHEAP.CPP source code, 380-381
CONSINIT.CPP source code, 379
CONSMESG.CPP source code, 377
CONST1.CPP source code, 43
CONST2.CPP source code, 44
constant arrays, 102-103
constant pointers, 105-107
   to constants, 107-108
constants, 101-103, 901
   C programming language, 882
   data members as, 477
   global, scope, 42-44
   pointers to, 104-105
   values, changing with pointers, 101-103
   versus #define directive, 45-48
CONSTCL2.CPP source code, 478
CONSTCL3.CPP source code, 482
CONSTLCLS.CPP source code, 477

CONSTPTR.CPP source code, 101
constructing
   base class objects, 483-484
   base classes, 482-484
      from derived classes, 488-490
   component classes, 507-509
   composed objects, 514-517
   derived classes, 484-486
   grandchild classes, 490-492
constructor initialization lists, 476-482
   composed objects, 514
constructors, 901
   adding, 478
   allocating data members, 380-381
   arguments, 381-386
      default arguments, 384-386
   arrays, constructing, 391-394
   bodies, moving, 482
   built-in, 390-391
   calling
      explicitly, 388-390
      timing, 376-381
   copy, 394-401, 901
   default, 375-376, 397-399
   defining, 371-372
   inheritance, 459
   initializing data members, 378-379
   need for, 373-376
   overloading typecasts, 386-388
   public member functions, 377
controlled access member functions, 248-250
converting source codes to object files, 426
coordinates, graphics, 745, 749-751
copy constructor, 394-401, 901
cout object, 62-66, 71-72
   combining output, 65
   example program, 69-70
   overloading operators, 342-345
COUT1ST.CPP source code, 64

COUT2ND.CPP source code–definitions

COUT2ND.CPP source code, 65
CPen objects, 757
.CPP file extension, 427
   see also source codes
CreateHatchBrush( ) function, 763
CreatePen( ) function, 756-759
CreateSolidBrush( ) function, 763
CreateSolidCaret( ) function, 722
CString class, 698-701
   clearing object contents, 727-728
CString member variable, 716-717
CTeachApp class, 654, 668
CTeachDoc class, 654, 669-670
   header file, 662
   implementation file, 663-664
CTeachView class, 654, 669-670
   header file, 665
   implementation file, 666-667
cursors, 624-626

D

data hiding, 901
data members, 241, 901
   allocating with constructors, 380-381
   and member functions, 241-242
   as constants, 477
   behavior, 246-248
   derived classes, 462-469
   initializing, 253-254
      with constructors, 378-379
   private, 241
      inheritance, 458-462
   public, inheritance, 458-460
   static, 416-422, 906
data protection, inheritance, 460-462
data types
   abstract, 210-217
      nested, 214-217
   aggregate, 30
   C programming language, 882-883
   creating, 453

declarations, 30-32
prefixes, 691-692
tags, 32
user-defined, 12
see also specific data type
DATAOUT.DAT file, 581
date, compilation date, 54
DATETIME.CPP source code, 54
deallocating memory, 126-135
   delete operator, 116-118
   for arrays, 128-129
   heap memory, 380-381
   matrixes, 136-137
debugging programs, 617-624
   breakpoints, setting, 619-622
   call stack, 622-623
   identifiers, 55-56
   QuickWatch window, 623
   stepping through code, 618-619
   windows, 620-621
dec manipulator, 73-75
declarations, 901
   data types, 30-32
   friend functions, 281
   inserting functions in classes, 241
decrement (--) operator, 890-891
   overloading, 330-334
default, 901
   argument lists, 156-159, 901
   arguments
      constructor arguments, 384-386
      multiple, 159-163
      specifying, 162-163
   constructors, 390-391, 397-399
DEFCOR1.CPP source code, 47
#define directive
   alternatives, 45-53
   C programming language, 880-881
definitions, 901
   arrays (C programming
      language), 885
   class variables, 244

definitions—dynamic memory allocation

constructors, 371-372
destructors, 372
graphics pens, 756-759
objects, 219-221
    from other objects, 394-401
    in derived classes, 469-470
    static objects, 413
pointers
    to classes, 245-246
    to integers, 93-100
references, 97-101
structures, 215-217
variables, 37-40
    as constants, 45
    C programming language, 884-885
    location of definition, 38-40
DEFPROB1.CPP source code, 46
delete operator, 116-118, 126-135, 897
dereferencing, 901
derivation, 451-452
derived classes, 452-454, 901
    access specifiers, 464
    constructing, 484-486
    constructing base classes, 488-490
    defining objects, 469-470
    inheritance, 458-459
    inherited members, 462-469
design errors, 559
destructors, 901
    arrays, destructing, 392-393
    base class objects, 483-484
    calling, 495-496
        timing, 376-381
    deallocating heap memory, 380-381
    default, 375-376
    defining, 372
    inheritance, 459
    MFC exceptions, 735
    need for, 373-376
    public member functions, 377

diagonal lines, drawing, 747-750, 755, 758
dialog boxes, 624-626
directives
    C programming language, 880-881
    #define
        alternatives, 45-53
        C programming language, 880-881
display( ) function, 494
displaying
    error messages, 68-70
    text, 718-720
        carets, 722-723
division (/) operator, 889-890
    overloading, 310-315
do-while statement, 893-896
documents
    previewing, 712-715
    printing, 712-715
doFun( ) function, 412
dot (.) operator, 283
DOUBI.CPP source code, 48
DOUBINLN.CPP source code, 50
doubling values, 48
drawing
    colored boxes, 752-753
    diagonal lines, 747-748, 755
        red lines, 758
        with coordinate values, 749-750
    ellipses, 766-767
    rectangles, 759-762
        color fills, 762-765
        hatched patterns, 764-765
    squares, 759-762
DWORD data type, 698
dynamic memory allocation, 118-121, 902
    exception handlers, 138-140
    fragmentation, 126-127
    initializing heap, 124-126
    matrixes, 135-137

new operator, 116-118
   specifying, 121-124
   strings, 122-124

E

early binding, 534-540, 902
   function calls, 536
   overriding virtual keyword, 548
editors, 16
   command-line arguments,
     specifying, 166
   see also Visual Workbench editor
elements, 902
Ellipse( ) function, 766-767
ellipses, drawing, 766-767
embedded structures, 513
Employee class, 459
encapsulation, 271, 902
   see also binding
end-of-output manipulators, 75
endl manipulator, 73-75
ends manipulator, 73-76
enum keyword, 30
enumerated constants, 30
   declaring, 30-32
environment messages, 612
eof( ) member function, 587-588
equal to (==) operator, 892-893
   overloading, 315-321
errors, 559-560
   adding error checking to member
     functions, 262-267
   displaying messages, 68-70
   sequential file errors, 587-588
   see also exception handling
events, 644, 902
**exception handling, 138-140,
   556-575, 902**
   ANSI C++ standard, 557-558
   API functions, 568
   catching exceptions, 569-573

   CFile class, 737-739
   kinds of errors, 559-560
   need for, 557-560
   QBasic, 559
   simulating exceptions, 561-568
   throwing exceptions, 569-573
   versus _set_new_handler( )
     function, 570
.EXE file extension, 427
executable files, 425
executing programs, 902
exiting loops, 895
extensibility, 334-337
extern statement, 185-186
external linkage, 44
extractor (>>) operator, 66-68, 902
   example program, 69-70
   overloading, 353-358

F

fail( ) member function, 587-588
**FANCYOUT.CPP source code,
   349-351**
file extensions, 427
file I/O, 715-731
   applications, generating, 716
   carets, 722-723
   File Open codes, 725-726
   File Save codes, 725-726
   keystroke handlers, 716-718
   Serialize( ) function, 730-731
   text
     displaying, 718-720
     saving, 728-729
File Open codes, 725-726
file pointers, positioning, 597-600
File Save codes, 725-726
file scope, 43, 222-223
_ _FILE_ _ identifier, 53-56
filenames, 902

files—functions

files, 902
   AppWizard files, 651
   DATAOUT.DAT, 581
   executable, 425-427
   header files
      BEV.H, 431
      FILESDOC.H, 716-717
      FSTREAM.H, 580, 584
      IOMANIP.H, 72
      IOSTREAM.H, 62, 456
      MAINFRM.H, 658-659
      RENTAL.H, 441-445
      TEACH.H, 654-655
      TEACHDOC.H, 662
      TEACHVC.H, 665
      WINDOWS.H, 569
   multiple, 614-617
   naming Windows files, 647
   object files, 423
   project files, 428-439
   random-access, 596-600, 905
      accessing, 596-597
      file pointers, positioning, 597
   sequential, 579-580, 905
      appending to, 589-591
      errors, 587-588
      reading from, 585-587, 594-596
      uses, 579
      writing to, 581-585, 591-593
   STRFILE.TXT, 584
FILESDOC.H header file, 716-717
FILESVW.CPP source code, 717-724
fill character, changing, 77-79
Find Next tool (Visual Workbench tool), 611
Find Text tool (Visual Workbench), 610-611
FIRST.CPP source code, 13-14
fixed-length records, 902
Float class, 334-336
floating-point pointers, 94-100
floating-point values, comparing, 320-321

FLTCHAR.CPP source code, 335-336
flush manipulator, 73-75
fonts, proportional, 719
for statement, 893-896
format flags, 72
   resetiosflags( ) manipulator, 74
   setiosflags( ) manipulator, 74
free( ) function, 392, 897
   see also delete operator
friend classes, 290-293
friend functions, 278-290
   and multiple classes, 283-290
   class variables, 286
   declaration, 281
   specifying, 280-283
friend keyword, 280-281
FRND1.CPP source code, 282
FRND2.CPP source code, 284-285
FRND3.CPP source code, 287-289
FRNDCLS.CPP source code, 291-292
fromDisk( ) member function, 596
fstream class, 580
FSTREAM.H header file, 580, 584
function pointers, late binding, 538-539
functions, 902
   API functions, exception handling, 568
   atoi( ), 167
   calling
      C language functions, 184-186
      early binding, 536
      late binding, 538-540
   Catch( ), 569-573
   compArea( ), 34-35
   CreateHatchBrush( ), 763
   CreatePen( ), 756-759
   CreateSolidBrush( ), 763
   CreateSolidCaret( ), 722
   doFun( ), 412
   Ellipse( ), 766-767
   free( ), 392, 897

functions–global variables

friend functions, 278-290
    and multiple classes, 283-290
    class variables, 286
    declaration, 281
    specifying, 280-283
GetDeviceCaps( ), 749
getUserInput( ), 567
HideCaret( ), 722
init( ), 251-253
    prototype, 272
inline functions, 48-53, 902
inserting in class declarations, 241
LineTo( ), 755
longjmp( ), 563-568
main( )
    command-line arguments, 163-165
    passing values to member functions, 250-254
    placement, 51
    returning values from member functions, 254-256
malloc( ), 392, 897
maxAra( ), 180-182
MessageBox( ), 734
minAra( ), 180-182
MoveTo( ), 754-755
OnNewDocument( ), 728
openAFile( ), 567
overloading, 178-200, 904
    calling C functions, 184-186
    name-mangling, 182-183
printf( ), 885-889
    ending, 171
prototypes, 32-36
    self-prototyping functions, 33
    void argument lists, 35-36
Rectangle( ), 759
returning objects from, 272
scanf( ), 887-889
seeVars( ), 408-409
SelectObject( ), 757

Serialize( ), 725, 730-731
_set_new_handler( ), 570
SetCaretPos( ), 722
setjmp( ), 563-568
SetModifiedFlag( ), 728
SetPixel( ), 747
ShowCaret( ), 722
signature, 32
static functions, 411-412
sTax( ), 158-159
Throw( ), 569-573
tripleIt( ), 537
virtual functions, 541-545, 906
    and late binding, 541-545
    class families, 534
    efficiency, 547-548
    pure, 549
    specifying, 545-546
WinMain( ), 669
see also member functions
FUNPTR.CPP source code, 538-539

G

generic pointers, 92-97
get( ) member function, 84-85, 585-586
GETBAD.CPP source code, 85
GetDeviceCaps( ) function, 749
getline( ) member function, 86-87, 586-587
    default arguments, 161-162
GETLINE.CPP source code, 86-87
GetTextMetrics( ) member function, 694-695
getUserInput( ) function, 567
getVals( ) member function, 251
global constants, scope, 42-44
global static objects, creating, 414-415
global variables, 409-410, 902
    static, 410-411

GLOBSCOP.CPP source code, 41-42
GLOBST.CPP source code, 409
GLOSTAOB.CPP source code, 414-415
good( ) member function, 587-588
grandchild classes, constructing, 490-492
GRANDCHLD.CPP source code, 490-492
graphics
    coordinates, 745, 749-751
    drawing
        colored boxes, 752-753
        diagonal lines, 747-750, 755, 758
        ellipses, 766-767
        rectangles, 759-765
        squares, 759-762
    filling screen with dots, 751
    improving, 754-759
    pens
        defining, 756-759
        saving, 761-762
    PIC application, 744-745
    pixels, 745-747
greater than (>) operator, 892-893
    overloading, 315-321
greater than or equal to (>=) operator, 892-893
    overloading, 315-321

H

hardware errors, 559
header files, 902
    BEV.H, 431
    FILESDOC.H, 716-717
    FSTREAM.H, 580, 584
    IOMANIP.H, 72
    IOSTREAM.H, 62
        multiple inheritance hierarchy, 456
    MAINFRM.H, 658-659
    RENTAL.H, 441-445
    TEACH.H, 654-655
    TEACHDOC.H, 662
    TEACHVC.H, 665
    WINDOWS.H, 569
heap, 118-121
    deallocating memory, 126-135, 380-381
    exception handlers, 138-140
    fragmentation, 126-127
    initializing, 124-126
    see also dynamic memory allocation
hex manipulator, 73-75
HideCaret( ) function, 722
hiding
    status line, 614
    Visual Workbench toolbar, 609
hierarchies, inheritance, 454
Hungarian notation, 691-692
hybrid OOP languages, 13

I

I/O, 903
    C programming language, 885-889
    cerr object, 68-70
    cin object, 66-72
    cout object, 62-72
    manipulators, 72-82
        creating, 358-361
    random-access files, 596-600, 905
        accessing, 596-597
        file pointers, positioning, 597
    sequential files, 579-580
        appending to, 589-591
        errors, 587-588
        reading from, 585-587, 594-596
        writing to, 581-585, 591-593
icons, 624-626
identifiers, 53-56
if statement, 893-896
ifstream class, 580

ignore() member function, 355
INCDECOV.CPP source code, 332-333
#include directive, 880-881
increment (++) operator, 890-891
inheritance, 902
    base classes, 452-454
        access specifiers, 465-466
    component classes, 510-511
    constructors, 459
    data protection, 460-462
    data types, creating, 453
    derivation, 451-452
    derived classes, 452-454, 458-459
        access specifiers, 464
        inherited members, 462-469
    destructors, 459
    hierarchies, 454
        class families, 533-534
    multiple, 455-457, 472
    private members, 458-462
    public members, 458-460
    reasons for using, 471
    single, 472, 906
    structure of, 451-457
    terms, 452-453
    versus composition, 502-506
init() function, 251
    arguments, 253
    prototype, 272
INIT2.CPP source code, 251-252
initialization lists, 902
    constructor, 476-482
initialization member functions, 250-254
initializing
    arrays, 885
    data members, 253-254
        static data members, 419
        with constructors, 378-379
    heap memory, 124-126
    references, 98
    variables, 246-247

INITRET.CPP source code, 255-256
inline functions, 48-53, 902
inline keyword, 260-262
input, 82-87
    C programming language, 885-889
    cin object, 66-72
    get() member function, 84-85, 585-586
    getline() member function, 86-87, 586-587
        default arguments, 161-162
    see also I/O
input operators, overloading, 342-358
Input/Output, *see* I/O
INPUTSIN.CPP source code, 83
inserter (<<) operator, 63-64, 903
    example program, 69-70
    overloading, 345-352
instances, 221
instantiation, 903
integer pointers, 93-100
internal linkage, 43
Inventory class, 478
IOMANIP.H header file, 72
IOSTREAM.H header file, 62
    multiple inheritance hierarchy, 456
IOTHREE.CPP source code, 70

K

keystroke handlers, 716-718
keywords, 798
    class, 9, 217-219
    enum, 30
    friend, 280-281
    inline, 260-262
    private, 226-229
    public, 226-229
    static, 407-417
    struct, 8
    union, 30
    virtual, 545-547
        overriding, 548

L

late binding, 534-540, 903
    function pointers, 538-539
    with virtual functions, 541-546
Lemon class, 267-269
LEMONS.CPP source code, 268-269
less than (<) operator, 892-893
    overloading, 315-321
less than or equal to (<=) operator, 892-893
    overloading, 315-321
Line status bar indicator, 613
__LINE__ identifier, 53-56
LINEFILE.CPP source code, 55-56
lines, drawing, 747-748, 755
    red lines, 758
    with coordinate values, 749-750
LineTo( ) function, 755
link editing, 903
listings
    1.1. C++ program, 13-14
    1.2. Sample C++ program, 19
    2.1. Declaring a `struct`, an `enum`, and a `union`, 31
    2.2. Using prototypes, 34-35
    2.3. `char` data type size, 37
    2.4. Defining variables, 37
    2.5. variable definition placement, 39
    2.6. Variable priority, 41
    2.7. Overriding scope, 41-42
    2.8. `const` values have file scope, 43
    2.9. stand-alone function that uses another function, 44
    2.10. `#define` directive problems, 46
    2.11. Correcting `#define` problems with const, 47
    2.12. Program using parameterized `#define` to double values, 48
    2.13. Using `inline` functions for efficiency, 50
    2.14. Date and time of compilation, 54
    2.15. __LINE__ and __FILE__ identifiers, 55-56
    3.1. Output with `cout`, 64
    3.2. Combining output, 65
    3.3. Input with `cin`, 67
    3.4. Base-conversion manipulators, 74-75
    3.5. Printing within different field widths, 77
    3.6. Printing left-justified within different field widths, 78-79
    3.7. Printing with base prefix characters, 80
    3.8. Printing the plus sign, 81
    3.9. Printing precisions, 81-82
    3.10. Inputting single characters, 83
    3.11. Getting strings with `get()`, 84-85
    3.12. `get()` function problems, 85
    3.13. Two `getline()` functions, 86-87
    4.1. Defining pointers, 94-100
    4.2. Changing references, 98-99
    4.3. Changing `const` values, 101
    4.4. Changing integers, but not with pointers, 105
    5.1. Allocating strings, 122-124
    5.2. Allocating and initializing heap data, 125
    5.3. Freeing heap memory, 128
    5.4. Allocating and deallocating memory, 130-133
    5.5. Allocating and deallocating matrixes, 136-137
    5.6. Forcing the allocation-failure function's execution, 139-140
    6.1. Passing by address and by value, 147-148
    6.2. Passing arrays by address, 150-151

listings

6.3. Passing by reference, 151-152
6.4. Returning references to functions, 155-156
6.5. Calling sales tax function with default argument values, 158-159
6.6. Function containing two regular arguments and a default argument, 161
6.7. Printing command-line arguments, 165
6.8. Making sure user types right number of arguments, 166-167
6.9. Finding maximum argument in a list, 169-170
6.10. Another way to find the maximum argument in a list, 170-171
7.1. Function containing two regular arguments and a default argument, 180-181
7.2. A `main()` function that calls three C functions, 185
7.3. Using `operator+()`, 190-191
7.4. Overloading several operators, 194-195
8.1. Structure variables and pointers to structure, 213-214
8.2. Using a structure to define another structure, 215-217
8.3. Defining objects from a class, 219-220
8.4. Incorrect use of a local variable, 222-223
8.5. Program with a `struct`, 224
8.6. The same program with a class seems useless, 225
8.7. Time class variables that `main()` can use, 227-228
8.8. A private `struct` is protected just like a `class`, 228-229
8.9. Using `public` members in a `class`, 232-233

9.1. Class with data members and member functions, 243
9.2. Defining two class variables, 244
9.3. Passing values to member functions, 251-252
9.4. Returning values from member function to `main()` function, 255-256
9.5. Cleaning up classes, 257-258
9.6. Improving program efficiency with `inline`, 261-262
9.7. Adding error checking to member functions, 262-263
9.8. Tracking lemonade sales, 268-269
10.1. Accessing private data with friend function, 282
10.2. Friend of two classes, 284-285
10.3. Adding more friend functions, 287-289
10.4. A friend class has full access to everything, 291-292
11.1. Simple overloaded operator program, 300
11.2. Using an overloaded member `operator+()`, 305
11.3. Overloading the addition operator, 307-308
11.4. Overloading +, -, *, /, and %, 311-313
11.5. Overloading relational operators, 318-320
11.6. Overloading compound operators, 322-325
11.7. Overloading increment and decrement operators, 332-333
11.8. Extending operation of `floats` and `chars`, 335-336
12.1. Overloading classes for easy output of objects, 346-347
12.2. Drawing boxes around output, 349-351

922

12.3. Overloading classes for easy input of objects, 354-355
12.4. Creating self-checking time classes, 355-356
12.5. Defining new manipulators, 359-360
12.6. Overloading subscripts, 362-363
12.7. Overloading smarter subscripts, 364-365
13.1. Printing messages to show constructor and destructor timing, 377
13.2. Initializing data in the constructor, 379
13.3. Allocating within constructors, 380-381
13.4. Constructing with arguments, 382-383
13.5. Constructing with default arguments, 384-385
13.6. Constructing and destructing an array of objects, 392-397
13.7. String class that overcomes string deficiencies, 397-399
14.1. static variables retain their values; auto variables are initialized, 408
14.2. The global variable named g is static, 409
14.3. static before a function name limits the use to the current source file, 411
14.4. Defining static objects, 413
14.5. Global static objects, 414-415
14.6. Using static to track the number of objects created, 418-419
14.7. Accessing static members with static member functions, 420-421
14.8. Beverage program as a single long file, 429-431
15.1. Derived class specifiers, 464
16.1. Members as constants, 477
16.2. Adding constructors, 478
16.3. Constructor bodies, moving, 482
16.4. Base class objects, constructing/destructing, 483-484
16.5. Constructing derived classes, 484-486
16.6. Constructing base classes from derived classes, 488-490
16.7. Constructing grandchild classes, 490-492
17.1. Stereo class components, 507-509
17.2. Component classes with inheritance, 510-511
17.3. `Stereo` class header, 513-519
17.4. Constructing objects that are composed of other objects, 514-517
17.5. Creating classes from component objects, 520-521
17.6. Adding overloaded `operator=()` functions, 523-527
18.1. Early binding for function calls, 536
18.2. Function pointers in late binding, 538-539
18.3. Pointer program (flawed), 542-544
19.1. Using `setjmp()` to handle two error conditions, 564-565
19.2. Using `catch()` and `throw()` to handle exceptions, 571-572
20.1. Writing characters to a file, 581-582
20.2. Writing characters from a string, 582
20.3. Easy file output, 583
20.4. Writing strings, 584

20.5. Reading characters from an input file, 585-586
20.6. Reading string data from an input file, 586-587
20.7. Using files on nonexistent drives, 588
20.8. Adding to the end of text files, 590
20.9. Writing objects using member functions, 592-593
20.10. Reading object variables from files, 594-596
20.11. Reading objects randomly, 598-599
B1.1. TEACH.H header file, 654-655
B1.2. TEACH.CPP source code, 655-658
B1.3. CMainFrame class header file, 658-659
B1.4 CMainFrame class implementation file, 659-662
B1.5. CTeachDoc class header file, 662
B1.6. CTeachDoc class implementation file, 663-664
B1.7. CTeachView class header file, 665
B1.8. CTeachView class implementation file, 666-667
B2.1. TEACH.RC resource script file, 682-687
B2.2. The original lines in TEACH.RC that were changed, 688
B2.3. OnDraw() function, 690
B2.4. OnDraw() function (improved), 696
B2.5. Using CString class in OnDraw() function, 700-701
B3.1. FILESDOC.H with CString member variable, 716-717
B3.2. Adding keystroke handling to OnChar() function, 718
B3.3. Displaying characters from a string, 719-720
B3.4. Displaying characters with carets, 722-723
B3.5. Adding File Save and File Open codes, 726
B3.6. Making window's text safer, 728-729
B3.7. Allocating too much memory, 733
B4.1. Drawing diagonal lines, 747-748
B4.2. Drawing diagonal lines with coordinate values, 749-750
B4.3. Filling the screen with dots, 751
B4.4 Drawing colored boxes, 752-753
B4.5. Drawing diagonal lines, 755
B4.6. Drawing red diagonal lines, 758
B4.7. Drawing colored rectangle outlines, 760
B4.8. Drawing red, green, and blue rectangles, 762-763
B4.9. Drawing hatched rectangles, 764-765
B4.10. Drawing ellipses, 766-767
WR1.1. Week one review listing, 201-206
WR2.1. Weeks one and two review class header listing, 441-445
WR3.1. Week three review listing, 637-640

literals, 903
 C programming language, 882
local variables, 410, 903
 and dynamic memory allocation, 118-121
LOCGLB.CPP source code, 222-223
logic errors, 559

logical operators
C programming language, 892-893
overloading, 315-321
LONG data type, 698
longjmp( ) function, 563-568
loops, exiting, 895
LOTSPTRS.CPP source code, 94-100

M

macros, parameterized, 48-50
main( ) function
command-line arguments, 163-165
passing values to member functions, 250-254
placement, 51
returning values from member functions, 254-256
MAINFRM.CPP source code, 659-662
MAINFRM.H header file, 658-659
maintainability, 903
malloc( ) function, 392, 897
see also new operator
MANIP.CPP source code, 359-360
manipulators, 72-82, 903
sticky manipulators, 76
math operators, overloading, 310-315
compound, 321-327
matrixes, 135-137
maxAra( ) function, 180-182
MAXMINAR.CPP source code, 180-181
MDI (Multiple Document Interface), 614-617
member functions, 241, 903
adding error checking, 262-267
addToInv( ), 593
and data members, 241-242
argument lists, 253
bad( ), 587-588
buySweet( ), 267

buyUnSweet( ), 267
CClientDC( ), 747
checkData( ), 265-266
Close( ), 737
constructors, *see* constructors
controlled access, 248-250
destructors, *see* destructors
eof( ), 587-588
fail( ), 587-588
fromDisk( ), 596
get( ), 84-85, 585-586
getline( ), 86-87, 161-162, 586-587
GetTextMetrics( ), 694-695
getVals( ), 251
good( ), 587-588
ignore( ), 355
initialization member functions, 250-254
MFC SetPixel( ), 746
OnChar( ), 701-706, 717-718
OnDraw( ), 690-692, 695-696, 747-748
text lines stored in CString class, 700-701
open( ), 589-591
operator...( ) functions 303
operator*( ), 389
operator+( ), 190-193, 303
operator<<( ), 345-352, 518
operator=( ) 394-401, 522
operator>( ), 195
operator>>( ), 353-358
passing values to from main( ) function, 250-254
prData( ), 281, 302, 546
private, 242
public, 242-246
put( ), 581-582
rData( ), 596
read( ), 594-596
returning values to main( ) function, 254-256

seekg( ), 597-600
showTot( ), 267
static member functions, 420-421, 906
TextOut( ), 692-693
toDisk( ), 593
write( ), 592-593
see also functions
members, 903
  private, 226-233, 905
  protected, 905
  public, 226-229, 905
    mixing with private access specifier, 229-233
memberwise assignments, 521
memory
  char data type, 36-37
  deallocating, 116-118, 126-135
    for arrays, 128-129
  dynamic memory allocation, 732-733, 902
    exception handlers, 138-140
    initializing heap, 124-126
    matrixes, 135-137
    new operator, 116-118, 121-124
    strings, 122-124
menus, 624-626
MessageBox( ) function, 734
messages, 689, 903
  connecting to functions, 702-704
MFC classes, 903
  CMainFrame, 654, 658-662, 669
  CString, 698-701
  CTeachApp, 654, 668
  CTeachDoc, 654, 662-664, 669-670
  CTeachView, 654-670
  exceptions, 731-739
    CArchiveException, 735-736
    CATCH block, 732-733, 737-739
    CFileException, 736-737
    destructors, 735
    exception handling, 737-739
    types, 732
  file I/O, 715-731
  functionality, adding, 689-698
  naming, 668
Microsoft
  multiplatform operating systems, 775-776
  Microsoft NT, 903
  see also Windows
minAra( ) function, 180-182
minimizing windows, 616
MINMAX.CPP source code, 155-156
modulus (%) operator, 889-890
  overloading, 310-315
MOSTLOC.CPP source code, 41
MoveTo( ) function, 754-755
moving constructor bodies, 482
MULTICIN.CPP source code, 67
multidimensional arrays, 135-137
multifile processing, 422-437
  class headers, 431
  compile/link review, 424-428
  implementation files, 432-433
  project files, 428-439
multiplatform operating systems, 775-776
multiple
  classes, accessing with friend functions, 283-290
  default arguments, 159-163
  files, 614-617
  inheritance, 455-457, 903
  windows, 614-617
Multiple Document Interface (MDI), 614-617
multiplication (*) operator, 889-890
  overloading, 310-315

926

N

name-mangling, 182-183
NAMENEW.CPP source code, 122-124
names
  array names, 106
    C programming language, 896
  variables, uppercase versus lowercase, 253
naming
  display functions, 494
  MFC classes, 668
  Windows program files, 647
nested abstract data types, 214-217
New Application Information screen, 649
new operator, 116-118, 897
  specifying, 121-124
NEWCOMM.CPP source code, 29
non-member functions, dot operator, 283
NOT (!) operator, 892
not equal to (!=) operator, 892-893
  overloading, 315-321
NOVIRT.CPP source code, 542-544
null pointer, 92
null zero, 92, 903
Num lock status bar indicator, 613

O

.OBJ file extension, 427
object code, 425, 904
object files, 423
  converting source codes to, 426
Object Linking and Embedding (OLE), 632, 904
object-oriented programming, *see* OOP
objects, 12, 903
  base class objects
    constructing/destructing, 483-484
    defining, 469-470
  cerr, 68-70
  cin, 66-72
    example program, 69-70
    overloading operators, 342-345
  clog, 69
  component objects, creating classes with, 519-521
  composed objects
    assigning to one another, 521-527
    constructing, 514-517
    constructor initialization lists, 514
  cout, 62-66, 71-72
    combining output, 65
    example program, 69-70
    overloading operators, 342-345
  defining, 219-221
    from other objects, 394-401
  derived class objects, defining, 469-470
  global static objects, creating, 414-415
  reading from sequential files, 594-596
  returning from functions, 272
  static, 413-416
    defining, 413
  tracking with static data members, 418-419
  writing to sequential files, 591-593
  see also class variables
OBSFRFIL.CPP source code, 594-596
OBSTOFIL.CPP source code, 592-593
oct manipulator, 73-75
ODBC (Open Database Connectivity), 632, 904
ofstream class, 580

OLE (Object Linking and Embedding)–OVCLSMP.CPP source code

OLE (Object Linking and Embedding), 904
  OLE 2.0, 632
on functions, 690
OnChar( ) member function, 701-706, 717-718
OnDraw( ) member function, 690-692, 695-696, 747-748
  text lines stored in CString class, 700-701
OnNewDocument( ) function, 728
OOP, 904
  advantages, 9-11
Open Database Connectivity (ODBC), 632
Open Program File tool (Visual Workbench), 610
open( ) member function, 589-591
openAFile( ) function, 567
opening programs, 610
operating systems, multiplatform, 775-776
operator...( ) functions
  as member functions, 303
  operator*( ), 389
  operator+( ), 190-193, 303
  operator<<( ), 345-352
  operator=( ), 394-401
  operator>( ), 195
  operator>>( ), 353-358
operators, 904
  & (address of), 97
  . (dot), 283
  :: (scope resolution), 40-42, 257-258
  << (inserter), 63-64, 69-70, 345-352, 903
  >> (extractor), 66-70, 353-358, 902
  bitwise operators, 343-344
  C programming language, 889-893
  delete, 116-118, 126-135, 897
  logical, 892-893
    overloading, 315-321

  new, 116-118, 897
    specifying, 121-124
  order of, 800-802, 904
  overloading, 186-195, 298-310
    compound math operators, 321-327
    decrement (--) operator, 330-334
    I/O manipulators, 349-351, 358-361
    increment (++) operator, 330-334
    input operators, 342-358
    logical operators, 315-321
    math operators, 310-315
    mixing class and built-in data types, 328-330
    operator...( ) functions, 189-191
    output operators, 342-358
    relational operators, 315-321
    subscript operators, 361-366
  relational, 905
    C programming language, 892-893
    overloading, 315-321
  structure pointer operator, 245
options, changing, 18-19
OR (||) operator, 892
  overloading, 315-321
order of operators, 800-802, 904
output
  C programming language, 885-889
  cerr object, 68-70
  combining, 65
  cout object, 62-66, 69-72
  field width, specifying, 76-77
  manipulators, 72-82
  overloading operators, 342-358
  precisions, setting, 81-82
  see also I/O; printing, 80
output window, 620
OVCLMEM.CPP source code, 305
OVCLSMP.CPP source code, 300

overloading
   functions, 178-200, 904
      calling C functions, 184-186
      name-mangling, 182-183
   operators, 186-195, 298-310
      compound math operators, 321-327
      decrement (--), 330-334
      I/O manipulators, 349-351, 358-361
      increment (++), 330-334
      input operators, 342-358
      logical operators, 315-321
      math, 310-315
      mixing class and built-in data types, 328-330
      operator...( ) functions, 189-191
      output operators, 342-358
      relational operators, 315-321
      subscript operators, 361-366
   typecasts, 386-388

overriding
   scope, 41-42
   virtual keyword, 548

Overtype status bar indicator, 613
OVFALL.CPP source code, 311-313
OVFULL.CPP source code, 307-308
OVRLOTS.CPP source code, 194-195

P

parameterized macros, 48-50
parameterized manipulators, 73
parameters, 904
   reference parameters, receiving, 153-154

parent classes, *see* **base classes**
PARENTCH.CPP source code, 483-484
PARENTFX.CPP source code, 488-490
PARENTSO.CPP source code, 484-486

passing arguments, 250-254
   by address, 147-148, 904
   by copy, 904
   by reference, 146-154, 905
   by value, 147-148, 905
   default argument lists, 156-159
   multiple default arguments, 159-163
   variable-length argument lists, 167-171

PAYCOMP.CPP source code, 318-320
pens, 756-759
   saving, 761-762

Person class, 451-452, 458, 461
PIC application, 744-745
pixels, 745-748
   color, 746-747
   filling screen with, 751
   turning on/off, 745-748

plus sign, printing, 81
pointers, 905
   and virtual functions, 542-545
   C programming language, 896-897
   constant pointers, 105-107
      to constants, 107-108
   constant values, changing, 101-103
   defining, 94-100
      to classes, 245-246
   floating-point pointers, 94-100
   function pointers, late binding, 538-539
   integer pointers, 94-100
   null pointer, 92
   *this, 271-272
      overloaded operators, 301
   to constants, 104-105
   to integers, 93
   typecasting, 96-97
   void pointers, 92-97
      typecasting, 96-97

polymorphism—prototypes

polymorphism, 546-549, 905
positioning file pointers, 597-600
prData( ) member function, 281, 302, 546
precedence, *see* **order of operators**
precisions, setting, 81-82
PRECNINE.CPP source code, 81-82
preprocessor directives, 905
  C programming language, 880-881
  #define, alternatives, 45-53
previewing documents, 712-715
Print dialog box, 714
printf( ) function, 885-889
  ending, 171
printing
  adding print/print preview capabilities to applications, 712-715
  command-line arguments, 165
  documents, 712-715
  field width, specifying, 77
  precisions, 81-82
  with base prefix numbers, 80
  within different field widths, 78-79
  see also output
private class members, 241, 905
  accessing with friend function, 282
  inheritance, 458-462
private keyword, 226-229
private member functions, 242
private structure members, 226-229
  mixing with public access specifier, 229-233
procedural programming, 7-9
processing, multifile, 422-437
  class headers, 431
  compile/link review, 424-428
  implementation files, 432-433
  project files, 428-439
programming
  assembly-line programming, 247-248
  procedural programming, 7-9

programmer evolution, 604-608
Windows programming, 607
  AppWizard files, 651
  building projects, 650
  functionality, adding, 689-698
  naming files, 647
  overview, 643-645
  running programs, 650-651
  setting up Visual C++, 645-646
  MFC classes, *see* MFC classes
programs
  browsing elements, 630-631
  commenting, 28-30
    C programming language, 879-880
  compiling, 16-22
    date and time, determining, 54
  debugging, 617-624
    breakpoints, setting, 619-622
    call stack, 622, 623
    identifiers, 55-56
    QuickWatch window, 623
    stepping through code, 618-619
    windows, 620-621
  efficiency, improving, 260-262
  format (C programming language), 878-879
  opening, 610
  running, 19-22
    Windows programs, 650-651
  saving, 19
project files, 428-439
projects, 905
  building, 650
proportional fonts, 719
protect access specifiers, 471-472
protected classes, 262-267, 905
prototypes, 32-35, 905
  init( ) function, 272
  overloaded operator functions, 343
  self-prototyping functions, 33
  void argument lists, 35-36

930

public class members, 226-229, 905
    inheritance, 458-460
    mixing with private access specifier, 229-233
public keyword, 226-229
public member functions, 242-246, 377
pure virtual functions, 549, 905
put( ) member function, 581-582

Q

QBasic exception handling, 559
QuickWatch tool (Visual Workbench), 623
QuickWin, 22

R

random-access files, 596-600, 905
    accessing, 596-597
    file pointers, positioning, 597
rData( ) member function, 596
Read only status bar indicator, 613
read( ) member function, 594-596
read-only aliases, 108-109
reading
    from sequential files, 585-587
        class data, 594-596
        errors, 587-588
        strings, 586-587
Rebuild Entire Project tool (Visual Workbench), 611
receiving reference parameters, 153-154
records
    fixed-length, 902
    variable-length, 906
Rectangle( ) function, 759
rectangles, drawing, 759-762
    hatched patterns, 764-765
    with color fills, 762-765

references, 97-101
    & (address of) operator, 97
    defining, 97-101
    initializing, 98
    parameters, receiving, 153-154
    read-only aliases, 108-109
    returning, 154-156
REFINTRO.CPP source code, 98-99
REFSYN.CPP source code, 100
REFSYNT.CPP source code, 153-154
REGBINDG.CPP source code, 536
regClass class, 291-292
REGCONST.CPP source code, 105
registers window, 620
relational operators, 905
    C programming language, 892-893
    overloading, 315-321
RENTAL.H header file, 441-445
resetiosflags( ) manipulator, 73-74, 78-79
resource script files, TEACH.RC, 682-687
resources, 624-626, 905
    associating with code, 629-630
    changing
        with App Studio, 678-681, 688
        with text editor, 681-687
returning
    objects from functions, 272
    references, 154-156
    values from member functions, 254-256
RGB colors, 746
RNDFILE.CPP source code, 598-599
running programs, 19-22, 650-651
runtime errors, 559-560

S

SALESMAT.CPP source code, 136-137
SAMPLE.CPP source code, 19

saving
    graphics pens, 761-762
    programs, 19
    text, 728-729
scanf( ) function, 887-889
scope, 40-42
    block scope, 222-223
    class scope, 223
    file scope, 222-223
    global constants, 42-45
    overriding, 41-42
scope resolution operator (::), 40-42, 257-258
SCOPFREE.CPP source code, 39
screen, clearing, 889
searching for text, 610-611
seekg( ) member function, 597-600
seeVars( ) function, 408-409
SelectObject( ) function, 757
self-protecting classes, 262-267
self-prototyping functions, 33
semicolon (;), 884
sequential files, 579-580, 905
    appending data, 589-591
    errors, 587-588
    reading from
        character data, 585-587
        class data, 594-596
    uses, 579
    writing to
        character data, 581-585
        class data, 591-593
serialization, 724
Serialize( ) function, 725, 730-731
serializing objects, 905
_set_new_handler( ) function, 570
SetCaretPos( ) function, 722
setfill( ) manipulator, 73, 77-79
setiosflags( ) manipulator, 73-74, 78-79
setjmp( ) function, 563-568
SETJMP.C source code, 564-565

SetModifiedFlag( ) function, 728
SetPixel( ) member function, 746-747
setprecision( ) manipulator, 73, 81-82
setw( ) manipulator, 73, 76-77
ShowCaret( ) function, 722
SHOWPOS.CPP source code, 81
showTot( ) member function, 267
signatures, 32
    name-mangling, 182-183
single inheritance, 906
    see also inheritance
SIXIN.CPP source code, 354-355
SIXOUT.CPP source code, 346-347
source code files, 906
    ACCESS.CPP, 464
    ADDEMP.CPP, 190-191
    ADDREF.CPP, 151-152
    ALLFAIL.CPP, 139-140
    ALLINIT.CPP, 125
    ALLINIT2.CPP, 128
    AREACOMP.CPP, 34-35
    ARRADD.CPP, 150-151
    BASES.CPP, 74-75
    BASESHOW.CPP, 80
    BEV.CPP, 429-431
    BEVCLIMP.CPP, 432-433
    BEVREST.CPP, 434
    CALLC.CPP, 185
    CARSCLSS.CPP, 232-233
    CATHROW.CPP, 571-572
    CHARINP.CPP, 585-586
    CHAROVR.CPP, 583
    CHARSEQ.CPP, 581-582
    CHARSIZE.CPP, 37
    CHARSTR.CPP, 582
    CLASS.CPP, 225
    CLASSOBJ.CPP, 219-220
    CLASSPUB.CPP, 227-228
    CLSFUN.CPP, 243
    CLSFUN2.CPP, 244
    CLSSCHK.CPP, 262-263
    CLSSHEAD.CPP, 257-258

source code files

CLSSINL.CPP, 261-262
CMDARGS.CPP, 165
CMDCHK.CPP, 166-167
COMPHEAD.CPP, 507-509
COMPOV.CPP, 322-325
CONSARG.CPP, 382-383
CONSARG2.CPP, 384-385
CONSDEST.CPP, 392-397
CONSHEAP.CPP, 380-381
CONSINIT.CPP, 379
CONSMESG.CPP, 377
CONST1.CPP, 43
CONST2.CPP, 44
CONSTCL2.CPP, 478
CONSTCL3.CPP, 482
CONSTLCLS.CPP, 477
CONSTPTR.CPP, 101
converting to object files, 426
COUT1ST.CPP statement, 64
COUT2ND.CPP, 65
DATETIME.CPP, 54
DEFCOR1.CPP, 47
DEFPROB1.CPP, 46
DOUBI.CPP, 48
DOUBINLN.CPP, 50
FANCYOUT.CPP, 349-351
FILESVW.CPP, 717-724
FIRST.CPP, 13-14, 14
FLTCHAR.CPP, 335-336
FRND1.CPP, 282
FRND2.CPP, 284-285
FRND3.CPP, 287-289
FRNDCLS.CPP, 291-292
FUNPTR.CPP, 538-539
GETBAD.CPP, 85
GETLINE.CPP, 86-87
GLOBSCOP.CPP, 41-42
GLOBST.CPP, 409
GLOSTAOB.CPP, 414-415
GRANDCHLD.CPP, 490-492
INCDECOV.CPP, 332-333
INIT2.CPP, 251-252
INITRET.CPP, 255-256
INPUTSIN.CPP, 83
IOTHREE.CPP, 70
LEMONS.CPP, 268-269
LINEFILE.CPP, 55-56
LOCGLB.CPP, 222-223
LOTSPTRS.CPP, 94-100
MAINFRM.CPP, 659-662
MANIP.CPP, 359-360
MAXMINAR.CPP, 180-181
MINMAX.CPP, 155-156
MOSTLOC.CPP, 41
MULTICIN.CPP, 67
multifile processing, 422-437
NAMENEW.CPP, 122-124
NEWCOMM.CPP, 29
NOVIRT.CPP, 542-544
OBSFRFIL.CPP, 594-596
OBSTOFIL.CPP, 592-593
OVCLMEM.CPP, 305
OVCLSMP.CPP, 300
OVFALL.CPP, 311-313
OVFULL.CPP, 307-308
OVRLOTS.CPP, 194-195
PARENTCH.CPP, 483-484
PARENTFX.CPP, 488-490
PARENTSO.CPP, 484-486
PAYCOMP.CPP, 318-320
PRECNINE.CPP, 81-82
REFINTRO.CPP, 98-99
REFSYN.CPP, 100
REFSYNT.CPP, 153-154
REGBINDG.CPP, 536
REGCONST.CPP, 105
RNDFILE.CPP, 598-599
SALESMAT.CPP, 136-137
SAMPLE.CPP, 19
SCOPFREE.CPP, 39
SETJMP.C, 564-565
SHOWPOS.CPP, 81
SIXIN.CPP, 354-355
SIXOUT.CPP, 346-347

source code files–STERINHE.CPP source code

STATFN.CPP, 411
STATMEM.CPP, 418-419
STATOBJ.CPP, 413
STATPRI.CPP, 420-421
STAUTO.CPP, 408
STAXDEF.CPP, 158-159
STERCOMP.CPP, 514-517
STERINHE.CPP, 510-511
STEROPEQ.CPP, 523-527
STGET.CPP, 84-85
STRAPP.CPP, 590
STRCLASS.CPP, 397-399
STREVIEW.CPP, 213-214
STRFOUT.CPP, 584
STRINP.CPP, 586-587
STRINPER.CPP, 588
STRINSTR.CPP, 215-217
STRPRIV.CPP, 228-229
STRUCT.CPP, 224
SUBOV.CPP, 362-363
SUBOV2.CPP, 364-365
TEACH.CPP, 655-658
TEACHDOC.CPP, 663-664
TEACHVW.CPP, 666-667
TIMECHK.CPP, 355-356
TRVAGNCY.CPP, 201-206
TVSHOWS.CPP, 130-133
USERDEFS.CPP, 31
VALADD.CPP, 147-148
VARARG2.CPP, 170-171
VARARGS.CPP, 169-170
VARDEF.CPP, 37
VIRT.CPP, 546
WIDTHLFT.CPP, 78-79
WIDTHS.CPP, 77
specifying
    default arguments, 162-163
    friend functions, 280-283
    virtual functions, 545-546
squares, drawing, 759-762
standard output device, 906
statements
    break, 895

do-while, 893-896
extern, 185-186
for, 893-896
if, 893-896
switch, 895-896
while, 893-896
STATFN.CPP source code, 411
static binding, 534
static data members, 416-422, 906
    initializing, 419
static functions, 411-412
static keyword, 407-417
    see also global variables
**static member functions,
    420-421, 906**
static objects, 413-416
    defining, 413
    global static objects, creating,
        414-415
static variables, 407-410, 906
    global variables, 409
**STATMEM.CPP source code,
    418-419**
STATOBJ.CPP source code, 413
STATPRI.CPP source code, 420-421
**status bar (Visual Workbench),
    611-614**
STAUTO.CPP source code, 408
sTax( ) function, 158-159
STAXDEF.CPP source code, 158-159
**Step Into tool (Visual Workbench),
    618-619**
**Step Out tool (Visual Workbench),
    619**
**Step Over tool (Visual Workbench),
    619**
stepping through code, 618-619
**STERCOMP.CPP source code,
    514-517**
Stereo class, 507-509, 520-521
    class header, 513-519
**STERINHE.CPP source code,
    510-511**

Order Your Program Disk Today!

You can save yourself hours of tedious, error-prone typing by ordering the companion disk to *Teach Yourself Object-Oriented Programming with Visual C++ 1.5 in 21 Days*. This disk contains the source code for all the programs in the book as well as the answer programs listed in Appendix D.

Samples include code for class data, overloaded operators, file I/O, virtual functions, and more, giving you almost 200 programs to help you master OOP. Each disk is only $15.00 (U.S. currency only). Foreign orders must enclose an extra $5.00 to cover additional postage and handling. (Disks are available only in low-density 3 ½-inch format.)

Just fill in the blanks below, and mail this information with your check or postal money order to:

Greg Perry
Dept. TYVC
P.O. Box 35752
Tulsa, OK 74153-0752

Please *print* the following information:

Number of disks: _____ @ $15.00 (U.S. dollars) = _____

Name: _____

Address: _____

City: _____ State: _____

ZIP: _____

On foreign orders, use a separate page if needed to give your exact mailing address in the format required by your postal service.

Make checks and postal money orders payable to *Greg Perry*. Sorry, but we cannot accept credit cards or checks drawn on a non-U.S. bank.

(This offer is made by the author, not by Sams Publishing.)

Add to Your Sams Library Today with the Best Books for Programming, Operating Systems, and New Technologies

The easiest way to order is to pick up the phone and call
1-800-428-5331
between 9:00 a.m. and 5:00 p.m. EST.
For faster service please have your credit card available.

ISBN	Quantity	Description of Item	Unit Cost	Total Cost
0-672-30344-2		Teach Yourself Windows Programming in 21 Days	$29.95	
0-672-30345-0		Wasting Time with Windows (Book/Disk)	$19.95	
0-672-30370-1		Visual C++ Developer's Guide (Book/Disk)	$49.95	
0-672-30150-4		Visual C++ Object-Oriented Programming (Book/Disk)	$39.95	
0-672-30295-0		Moving into Windows NT Programming	$39.95	
0-672-30080-X		Moving from C to C++	$29.95	
0-672-30376-0		Imaging and Animation for Windows (Book/Disk)	$34.95	
0-672-30239-X		Windows Developer's Guide to Application Design (Book/Disk)	$34.95	
0-672-30326-4		Absolute Beginner's Guide to Networking	$19.95	
0-672-30338-8		Inside Windows File Formats	$29.95	
0-672-30309-4		Programming Sound for DOS and Windows	$39.95	
0-672-30308-6		Tricks of the Graphics Gurus (Book/Disk)	$49.95	
0-672-30306-X		Memory Management for All of Us, Deluxe Edition (Book/Disk)	$39.95	
0-672-30320-5		Morphing Magic (Book/Disk)	$29.95	
0-672-30288-8		DOS Secrets Unleashed (Book/Disk)	$39.95	
0-672-30373-6		On the Cutting Edge of Technology	$22.95	
❑ 3 ½" Disk ❑ 5 ¼" Disk		Shipping and Handling: See information below.		
		TOTAL		

Shipping and Handling: $4.00 for the first book, and $1.75 for each additional book. Floppy disk: add $1.75 for shipping and handling. If you need to have it NOW, we can ship product to you in 24 hours for an additional charge of approximately $18.00, and you will receive your item overnight or in two days. Overseas shipping and handling adds $2.00 per book and $8.00 for up to three disks. Prices subject to change. Call for availability and pricing information on latest editions.

201 W. 103rd Street, Indianapolis, Indiana 46290

1-800-428-5331 — Orders   1-800-835-3202 — FAX   1-800-858-7674 — Customer Service

Book ISBN 0-672-30487-2

GO AHEAD. PLUG YOURSELF INTO
PRENTICE HALL COMPUTER PUBLISHING.

Introducing the PHCP Forum on CompuServe®

Yes, it's true. Now, you can have CompuServe access to the same professional, friendly folks who have made computers easier for years. On the PHCP Forum, you'll find additional information on the topics covered by every PHCP imprint—including Que, Sams Publishing, New Riders Publishing, Alpha Books, Brady Books, Hayden Books, and Adobe Press. In addition, you'll be able to receive technical support and disk updates for the software produced by Que Software and Paramount Interactive, a division of the Paramount Technology Group. It's a great way to supplement the best information in the business.

WHAT CAN YOU DO ON THE PHCP FORUM?

Play an important role in the publishing process—and make our books better while you make your work easier:

- Leave messages and ask questions about PHCP books and software—you're guaranteed a response within 24 hours
- Download helpful tips and software to help you get the most out of your computer
- Contact authors of your favorite PHCP books through electronic mail
- Present your own book ideas
- Keep up to date on all the latest books available from each of PHCP's exciting imprints

JOIN NOW AND GET A FREE COMPUSERVE STARTER KIT!

To receive your free CompuServe Introductory Membership, call toll-free, **1-800-848-8199** and ask for representative **#K597**. The Starter Kit Includes:

- Personal ID number and password
- $15 credit on the system
- Subscription to CompuServe Magazine

HERE'S HOW TO PLUG INTO PHCP:

Once on the CompuServe System, type any of these phrases to access the PHCP Forum:

GO PHCP **GO BRADY**
GO QUEBOOKS **GO HAYDEN**
GO SAMS **GO QUESOFT**
GO NEWRIDERS **GO PARAMOUNTINTER**
GO ALPHA

Once you're on the CompuServe Information Service, be sure to take advantage of all of CompuServe's resources. CompuServe is home to more than 1,700 products and services—plus it has over 1.5 million members worldwide. You'll find valuable online reference materials, travel and investor services, electronic mail, weather updates, leisure-time games and hassle-free shopping (no jam-packed parking lots or crowded stores).

Seek out the hundreds of other forums that populate CompuServe. Covering diverse topics such as pet care, rock music, cooking, and political issues, you're sure to find others with the same concerns as you—and expand your knowledge at the same time.

STEROPEQ.CPP source code, 523-527
STGET.CPP source code, 84-85
sticky manipulators, 76
STRAPP.CPP source code, 590
STRCLASS.CPP source code, 397-399
stream manipulators, 72
streams, 72, 906
STREVIEW.CPP source code, 213-214
STRFILE.TXT file, 584
STRFOUT.CPP source code, 584
String class, 397-399
string variables, 698-701
strings, 906
   allocating, 122-124
   C programming language, 882-883
   reading, 586-587
   writing, 584
STRINP.CPP source code, 586-587
STRINPER.CPP source code, 588
STRINSTR.CPP source code, 215-217
Stroustrup, Bjarne, 6
STRPRIV.CPP source code, 228-229
struct data type, 30
struct keyword, 8
STRUCT.CPP source code, 224
structure pointer operator, 245
structures, 30, 906
   declaring, 30-32
   defining, 215-217
   nested, 214-217
   public members, 226-229
   versus classes, 222-226
SUBOV.CPP source code, 362-363
SUBOV2.CPP source code, 364-365
subscript operators, overloading, 361-366
subtraction (-) operator, 889-890
   overloading, 310-315

switch statement, 895-896
symbolic constants, 53-56
syntax
   errors, 559
   typecasting, 40

T

tables, *see* matrixes
tags, 32
TEACH.CPP source code, 655-658
TEACH.H header file, 654-655
TEACH.RC resource script file, 682-687
TEACHDOC.CPP source code, 663-664
TEACHDOC.H header file, 662
TEACHVC.H header file, 665
TEACHVW.CPP source code, 666-667
templates, 7, 906
text
   displaying, 689-698, 718-720
      carets, 722-723
   saving, 728-729
   searches, 610-611
TextOut( ) member function, 692-693
*this pointer, 271-272
   overloaded operators, 301
Throw( ) function, 569-573
throwing exceptions, 569-573
tiled windows, 615
time, compilation time, 54
_ _TIME_ _ identifier, 53-56
TIMECHK.CPP source code, 355-356
toDisk( ) member function, 593
Toggle Breakpoint tool (Visual Workbench), 619
toggling breakpoints, 619

toolbar (Visual Workbench)–Visual C++ Version 1.5

toolbar (Visual Workbench), 17,
609-611
tripleIt( ) function, 537
TRVAGNCY.CPP source code,
201-206
TVSHOWS.CPP source code,
130-133
typecasting, 906
    overloading typecasts, 386-388
    pointers, 96-97
    syntax, 40

U

UINT data type, 698
union keyword, 30
unions, 30
    declaring, 30-32
user-defined data types, 12
    see also abstract data types
USERDEFS.CPP source code, 31

V

VALADD.CPP source code, 147-148
values
    assigning to variables, 884
    doubling, 48
    floating-point values, comparing,
        320-321
    passing from main( ) function to
        member functions, 250-254
    returning to main( ) function from
        member functions, 254-256
VARARG2.CPP source code, 170-171
VARARGS.CPP source code, 169-170
VARDEF.CPP source code, 37
variable-length argument lists,
    167-171
variable-length records, 906
variables, 8-9, 906
    as objects, 12

assigning values , 884
automatic, 407, 900
class variables, 901
    defining, 219-221, 244
    friend functions, 286
defining, 37-40
    as constants, 45
    C programming language,
        884-885
    class variables, 219-221, 244
    location of definition, 38-40
global, 409-411, 902
initializing, 246-247
local, 410, 903
    and dynamic memory allocation,
        118-121
lowercase spelling, 253
scope, 40-42, 906
static, 407-410, 906
string variables, 698-701
uppercase spelling, 253
VIRT.CPP source code, 546
virtual functions, 541-545, 906
    and late binding, 541-546
    class families, 534
    efficiency, 547-548
    pure, 549, 905
    specifying, 545-546
virtual keyword, 545-547
    overriding, 548
Visual C++, 7
    editor, 16
        command-line arguments,
            specifying, 166
    options, changing, 18-19
    suggested references, 782-784
    toolbar, 17
Visual C++ for 16-bit Windows,
    781-782
Visual C++ for Windows NT,
    776-781
Visual C++ Version 1.5, 632-633

Visual C++ workbench, 16
Visual Workbench editor, 608-617
  App Studio, 624-626
    changing resources, 678-681, 688
  AppWizard, 626-629, 646-649
    building projects, 650
    running programs, 650-651
  browser, 630-631
  ClassWizard, 629-630
  debugging programs, 617-624
  MDI (Multiple Document Interface), 614-617
  status bar, 611-614
  toolbar, 609-611
void argument lists, 35-36
void pointers, 92-97
  typecasting, 96-97

W-Z

watch window, 620
while statement, 893-896
WIDTHLFT.CPP source code, 78-79
WIDTHS.CPP source code, 77
The Windows Interface: An Application Design Guide, 782
Windows, 903
  and C programming language, 773-774
  naming files, 647
  programming, 607
    AppWizard files, 651
      building projects, 650

      functionality, adding, 689-698
    MFC classes, *see* MFC classes
    overview, 643-645
    running programs, 650-651
    setting up Visual C++, 645-646
    suggested references, 782-784
  The Windows Interface: An Application Design Guide, 782
  Visual C++ for 16-bit Windows, 781-782
  Visual C++ for Windows NT, 776-781
windows
  cascaded, 615
  closing, 22
  displaying text, 689-698
  keyboard input, 701-706
  minimizing, 616
  multiple, 614-617
  tiled, 615
WINDOWS.H header file, 569
WinMain( ) function, 669
WM_CHAR message, 701-706
WORD data type, 698
write( ) member function, 592-593
writing to sequential files, 581-585
  class data, 591-593
  errors, 587-588
  strings, 584